THE ROMANCE OF ARTHUR

NEW, EXPANDED EDITION

An Anthology of
Medieval Texts in Translation

GARLAND REFERENCE LIBRARY
OF THE HUMANITIES
VOL. 1267

Cover and Frontispiece: Galehaut Tapestry, Northern French or Flemish. (Reprinted by permission of the St. Louis Art Museum)

The
ROMANCE
of ARTHUR

NEW, EXPANDED EDITION

An Anthology of
Medieval Texts in Translation

EDITED BY

James J. Wilhelm

GARLAND PUBLISHING, INC.
New York & London • 1994

Library of Congress Cataloging-in-Publication Data

The Romance of Arthur : an anthology of medieval texts in translation
/ edited by James J. Wilhelm. — New, expanded ed.
    p.   cm. — (Garland reference library of the humanities : vol.
1267)
    Includes bibliographical references and index.
    ISBN 0–8153–0727–6 (alk. paper). — ISBN 0–8153–1511–2
(pbk. : alk. paper)
    1. Arthurian romances.   I. Wilhelm, James J. II. Series.
PN6071.A84R64   1994
808.8'0351—dc20   93–44265
                                                         CIP

Cover design by Patti Hefner

Printed on acid-free, 250-year-life paper
Manufactured in the United States of America

Contents

Preface

This volume has its roots in a smaller *Romance of Arthur* that was published in 1983. The purpose then was to offer some of the most important works of medieval Arthurian literature in fresh, new translations that would convey some sense of the development of King Arthur from Latin chronicles and Celtic mythology into the romantic king of late-medieval literature. My fellow editors decided to end the work with Sir Thomas Malory's *Morte Darthur* and to highlight such works as Chrétien de Troyes's *Lancelot, or The Knight of the Cart* and the anonymous *Sir Gawain and the Green Knight*.

This work was so enthusiastically received that we followed it with *Romance of Arthur II*, an anthology that sought to fill in some of the obvious gaps, such as adding selections from Wace and Layamon between the seminal history of Geoffrey of Monmouth and Chrétien. We also added Béroul's version of the Tristan and Isolde love tragedy, along with Thomas of Britain, and works that stressed the ever-popular Merlin.

When this work was equally well received, we followed it with *Romance of Arthur III*, which stressed lesser-known Arthurian works from Old Norse, Russian, Italian, and Spanish.

In combining the major works from these three volumes, it was often hard to select what to include and what to omit, but we feel that we have made selections that convey a broad range of development, including works written in Latin, Welsh, French, Middle English, Old Norse, Italian, and Provençal. New to this volume are poems of the Provençal troubadours, along with a few lyrics from Germany, Italy, and Spain. It was felt that we had to supply a bridge between the earlier histories and chronicles and the sudden blossoming of romantic narratives in the twelfth century, and it was the lyric writers who filled this gap.

I would like to thank the many colleagues who offered their opinions concerning what works should be included, as well as those who did the actual translating and wrote the introductions. Our Garland editor, Gary Kuris, was as helpful here as he was from the very start. I would also like to thank the now-deceased president of Garland Publishing, Gavin Borden, who supported us throughout this venture. Gavin was, as Hugh Kenner said, "the prince of publishers."

James J. Wilhelm
New York City
1993

The
ROMANCE
of ARTHUR

Chapter *I*

ARTHUR IN THE LATIN CHRONICLES

JAMES J. WILHELM

The romantic legend of King Arthur and his knights of the Round Table seems more and more to have had some foundation in history. A man named Artorius in Latin or Arthur in Welsh and English is mentioned in the Latin histories that describe the collapse of the christianized Roman Empire in Great Britain and the invasions of the Angles, Saxons, and Jutes from the lowlands of northern Germany.

After the Romans' conquest of Britain, begun in A.D. 43, they extended their advanced culture into the faraway Celtic island and later promoted the spread of Christianity there. Eventually the Roman Empire was weakened in the west by barbarian invasions. Denuded of troops, Britain passed from imperial control in 410, and the Britons were thrown back on their own resources. They still preserved something of Roman civilization, regarding themselves as Roman citizens who were superior to their insular barbaric enemies, the Irish, Scots, and the Picts from the never-Romanized northern region, and to the Germanic peoples of Holland, Germany, and Scandinavia, who were often marauding.

The first important writer to speak of these events was Gildas, a monk who around the year 547 composed his polemical treatise *On the Downfall and Conquest of Britain (De excidio et conquestu Britanniae)*. In Chapter 23 he tells how a "proud tyrant," whom we usually associate with the British chieftain Vortigern, and his counselors asked "the most ferocious Saxons of cursed name" to come over from Germany to help them fight against their insular enemies. This was a most impolitic move. Seeing that the island was relatively defenseless, the Saxons probably inflicted some losses on the British enemies, but then turned on their hosts themselves. They drove the Britons into the hills of Wales and Cornwall, where their descendants live even today, speaking the Celtic tongues of Welsh (or Cymric) and Cornish. Gildas speaks of these dispersed people in this way:

Chapter 25. And so many of the miserable survivors, who were trapped in the mountains, were slain in droves. Others, driven by hunger, stretched their hands to the enemy, offering themselves into endless servitude—if they were not cut down at once in an act that was kinder. Others ran off to overseas regions with loud wailings of grief. . . . Still others trusted their lives to the mountainous highlands, the menacing cliffs and crags, the dense forests, and the rugged sea caves, remaining, however timorously, in their homelands.

Then some time passed, and the cruel invaders retreated to their home bases. . . . The survivors collected their strength under the leadership of Ambrosius Aurelianus, a most temperate *[modestus]* man, who by chance was the only person of Roman parentage to have come through the catastrophe in which his parents, who had once worn the royal purple toga, had been killed, and whose present-day descendants have far degenerated from their former virtue. He and his men challenged their previous conquerors to battle, and by the grace of God, victory was theirs.

Chapter 26. From that time, now the native citizens and now the enemy have triumphed . . . up to the year of the siege of Mount Badon *[Badonici montis]*, when the last but certainly not the least slaughter of these lowly scoundrels occurred, which, I know, makes forty-four years and one month, and which was also the time of my birth. [Text in Chambers, *Arthur*, pp. 236–237]

Gildas seems to offer us many details, but his language is overdramatized and ambiguous, especially with reference to "forty-four years." Is that the span of time from the arrival of the Saxons or from the leadership of Ambrosius? Also, we do not know the date of Gildas's birth; his death is listed as 572 in the highly suspect *Annals of Cambria*, below. And who was Ambrosius Aurelianus? He is also mentioned by the other important chronicler, Nennius, and William of Malmesbury links him with Arthur, whom Gildas ignores. Yet despite his omissions and ambiguities, Gildas clearly establishes the milieu from which the legend springs: a downtrodden people finds salvation in a great military leader who is connected with the civilization of Rome and the Holy Church. As for the intriguing Mount Badon, it has been identified as Bath, Badbury, and Baddington, although many authorities today connect it with Liddington Castle near Swindon.

The next Latin writer, the Venerable Bede (673?–735), tends largely to repeat Gildas in his *Ecclesiastical History of the English Nation* (731):

Book 1, Chapter 15. In the year of Our Lord 449. . . . At that time the races of the Angles or the Saxons were invited by the previously mentioned king [Vortigern] to come to Britain in three long ships. . . . After the enemy had killed or dispersed the natives of the island, they went home, and the natives gradually recollected their strength and courage, and they came out of their hiding places and collectively called on heaven for help to avoid a general disaster. At that time they had as their leader Ambrosius Aurelianus, a temperate man, who by chance was the only person to have come out of the previously mentioned catastrophe in which his parents, who had a famous royal name, had been killed. With him in command the Britons gathered their strength and challenged their previous conquerors to battle. With the help of God they won the victory. And from that time, now the native citizens and now the enemy have triumphed, up to the year of the siege of Mount Badon, when the Britons inflicted great losses on their enemies, approximately forty-four years after their arrival in Britain. [Text in Chambers, pp. 237–238]

The span of forty-four years is clarified, and since the arrival time is dated the year for the battle is put at 493. This date is not totally unlikely, although Bede's indebtedness to Gildas does not inspire much confidence in his presentation.

The first Latin chronicle to mention the name "Arthur" is *The History of the Britons (Historia Brittonum)*, which is believed to have been compiled about 800 by a Welshman named Nennius. (See Chapter II for an earlier reference in Welsh.) This work was written in Latin, but many scholars feel that Nennius based his details about the Twelve Battles of Arthur upon native Welsh sources. We should remember that the modern Welsh people are the direct survivors of the ancient Britons. The passage has always led many to believe that there must be something historically real behind it, despite the sacramental nature of the number "twelve" and the shadowy geography, yet only the Caledonian Forest of Scotland and the City of the Legion (almost certainly the Welsh Caerleon) can be identified:

> *Chapter 56.* At that time the Saxons were thriving and increasing in multitudes in Britain. With [their leader] Hengist dead, his son Octha crossed over from the left side of Britain to the realm of the Kentishmen, and from him are descended the kings of Kent.
> Then Arthur fought against these people along with the kings of the Britons, and he was the leader in their battles. His first battle was at the mouth of the River Glein. The second to the fifth took place above the River Dubglas [Douglas or Dark Water], in the region of Linnuis. The sixth battle occurred at the River Bassas. The seventh was a battle in the Forest of Celidon, that is: the Battle of the Caledonian Forest. The eighth was at Castle Guinnion, in which Arthur carried an image of St. Mary, the Perpetual Virgin on his shoulders, and the pagans were put to flight on that day, and there was a great massacre of them through the power of Our Lord Jesus Christ and his mother Mary. The ninth battle was in the City of the Legion. The tenth was fought on the banks of the River Tribruit. The eleventh occurred on Mount Agned. The twelfth was the Battle of Mount Badon, in which nine hundred and sixty men fell from a single attack of Arthur, and nobody put them down except him alone, and in every one of the battles he emerged as victor. But although the others were overcome in the battles, they sent for help from Germany, and their forces were ceaselessly reinforced. The Saxons brought over leaders from Germany to rule the Britons up to the reign of Ida, Son of Eobba, the first king of Beornica. [Text in Chambers, pp. 238–239]

Later in his history, Nennius includes the following passage, which shows that the legend of Arthur was already becoming a popular myth:

> *Chapter 73.* There is another wonder in the region known as Buelt—a heap of stones piled up with the footprint of a dog upon it. While hunting the boar Troynt, Cabal, the hunting dog of Arthur the soldier, stepped on a stone, and Arthur later collected a pile beneath this and called it Carn Cabal. Men come to carry away the stone in their hands for a day and a night, yet the next day the imprinted stone is back on the pile.
> There is another wonder in the region called Ercing. It is a tomb near a brook that is called the Mound of Anir, for Anir is the man buried there. He was the son of Arthur the soldier, who killed and buried him there. Men come to measure the mound, which is sometimes six feet long, sometimes nine or twelve or fifteen. However you measure it again and again, you will never get the same figure—and I have tried this myself.

The Carn Cabal has been identified as existing in Breconshire in southern Wales, while Ercing has been placed in Herefordshire. The hunting of the boar figures prominently in the Welsh *Tale of Culhwch and Olwen* in Chapter III.

The next document is called *The Annals of Cambria*, another name for Wales, which the Welsh themselves call Cymru. It dates from the 900s, and offers these dates, which nowadays seem to be a bit late:

> 518 A.D. The Battle of Badon, in which Arthur carried the cross of Our Lord Jesus Christ for three days and three nights on his shoulders, and the Britons were victors. . . .
>
> 539 A.D. The Battle of Camlann, in which Arthur and Medraut both fell; and there was widespread death in Britain and in Ireland. . . .
>
> 572 A.D. Gildas died. . . .

This source, suspect as it is, nevertheless supplies us with a mention of a final catastrophic battle in which Arthur will go down, along with a man whose name evolves into Modred or Mordred. Although this figure will eventually become an adversary, he could here be one of Arthur's allies.

The next source is *The Legend of St. Goeznovius*, a Latin account of the life of the Breton St. Goeuznou. The work bears the date of 1019. That has been dismissed by J.S.P. Tatlock as too early, but Léon Fleuriot has since defended it as correct. In any case, an important article in *Speculum* by the Arthurian authority Geoffrey Ashe has shown that the legend must be examined closely. It is important because it establishes a continental base of operation for Arthur, which figures in the work of Geoffrey of Monmouth and later writers. It establishes, in short, a historical link between Britain and Brittany, which we know existed in literature for the transmission of such tales as those of Tristan and Parsifal. The pertinent section runs as follows:

> After the passage of time the usurping King Vortigern, in order to guarantee support for himself for the defense of the realm of insular Britain, which he was ruling unjustly, invited some warlike men from the region of Saxony and made them his allies in his kingdom. Since these were heathenish and devilish men, who from their natures lusted to make human blood flow, they called down many evils upon the British.
>
> Shortly afterward their arrogance was checked for a time by the great Arthur, King of the Britons, who forced them for the most part from the island or into servitude. But after this same Arthur had brilliantly won many victories in Britain and Gaul, he was finally called from human life, and the way once again lay open to the Saxons to return to the island to oppress the British, to overthrow churches, and to persecute saints. [Text in Chambers, p. 242]

Before this the anonymous author had described how a Briton had emigrated to Gallic Armorica and founded many colonies, thereby linking the insular and continental Britons and Bretons.

The next important chronicler is the Englishman William of Malmesbury, who wrote *The Deeds of the English Kings (De rebus gestis regum Anglorum)* in about the year 1125. In one passage from Book 1, Section 8, he verifies the earlier writings and notes that the Bretons (or Britons or both) now treat the deeds of the heroic Arthur *(bellicosi Arturis)* as if he were an Earthly Messiah:

> But with Vortimer [Guortimer, son of Vortigern] dead, the vigor of the Britons flagged, and their hopes diminished and flowed away, and indeed would have vanished entirely if Ambrosius, the lone survivor of the Romans who ruled after Vortigern, had not checked the unruly barbarians with the exemplary assistance of the heroic Arthur. This is that Arthur who is raved about even today in the trifles of the Bretons (Britons)—a man who is surely worthy of being described in true histories rather than dreamed about in fallacious myths—for he truly sustained his sinking homeland for a long time and aroused the drooping spirits of his fellow citizens to battle. Finally at the siege of Mt. Badon, relying on the image of the Lord's mother, which he had sewn on his armor, looming up alone, he dashed down nine hundred of the enemy in an incredible massacre. [Text in Chambers pp. 249–250]

Then in Book 3, Section 287, William adds more of the kind of information that tends toward the creation of a myth linking a hero to the land around him:

> At that time [1066–87] in the province of Wales known as Ros was found the tomb of Walwen [Gawain], who was the by no means degenerate nephew of Arthur through his sister. He ruled in that part of Britain which is still called Walweitha and was a warrior most famous for his courage; but he was driven from his rule by the brother and the nephew of Hengist, though he made them pay dearly for his exile. He shared deservedly in his uncle's praise, because for several years he postponed the collapse of his tottering homeland.
>
> However, the tomb of Arthur is nowhere to be found—that man whose second coming has been hymned in the dirges of old. Yet the sepulcher of Walwen . . . is fourteen feet long. It is said by some that Walwen's body was cast up from a shipwreck after he had been wounded by his enemies, while others say that he was murdered by his fellow citizens at a public feast. And so the truth lies in doubt, though neither story would lessen the assertion of his fame. [Text in Chambers, p. 250]

The passage also marks the entry of the name Walwen (Gawain) into Latin literature, showing that the future paragon of courtly excellence had already developed a legend of his own by 1125.

The next important writer is Geoffrey of Monmouth, whose *History of the Kings of Britain* combines history with legend in a highly imaginative form. The Arthurian segment of his work is given at length in Chapter IV. This section will close with a writer later than Geoffrey, the Norman-Welsh Giraldus Cambrensis, who lived from about 1146 to 1223 and was patronized by King Henry II of England. In his *On the Instruction of Princes (De instructione principum)*, written in the 1190s, Giraldus gives a fascinating description of Arthur's grave and also mentions Queen Guinevere and the magician Morgan the Fay, who plays an important role in *Sir Gawain and the Green Knight:*

> Then Arthur's body, which legends have fancifully treated as being phantom-like at its end and carried away by spirits to a faroff place where it is immune to death, was discovered in these days of ours, buried deep in the earth in a hollowed-out oaktree located between two stone pyramids that had been set up a long time ago in a holy burial ground at Glastonbury. The body was revealed by strange and almost miraculous signs and was transported to a church with great honor and fittingly housed in a marble tomb that bore a lead

cross with a stone placed under it. . . . I myself have seen this, and I have traced the letters engraved on the cross, which do not project forward but rather inwardly toward the stone: "Here lies buried the famous King Arthur with Guinevere [Wenneveria] his second wife on the Island of Avalon."

There are several things to note here, for he did indeed have two wives, of whom the last was buried with him, and her bones were found at the same time with her husband's, but set apart in this way: two-thirds of the tomb toward the head contained the bones of the man, while the other third held the woman's remains. A golden handful of woman's hair was found there, retaining its fresh wholeness and radiance, but when a certain monk greedily reached out and grabbed it the hair dissolved into dust.

Now although there had been certain indications in writings that the body would be found there . . . and visions and revelations were made to many virtuous and holy men, King Henry II of England revealed everything to the monks, just as he had heard it recited to him by a Welsh bard who sang of ancient deeds: that they would find the body sixteen feet deep in the earth in a hollow oak, not in a marble tomb. It had been buried this deeply so that the Saxons, who took over the island after Arthur's death, and whom he had vigorously beaten back while alive and had almost totally destroyed, could not find it; and that is why the inscription was turned inwardly toward the stone. . . .

The burial place is now known as Glastonbury, and in ancient times it was called the Island of Avalon. It is indeed almost an island, being surrounded by marshes; and so in the British language it was called Inis Avallon or Apple Island, since apples grow there in abundance. Then too Morgan, the noble matron and lady-ruler of those parts, who was closely related by blood to King Arthur, transported Arthur after the Battle of Kemelen [Camlan] to this island, now called Glaston, to heal his wounds. In the British language it was once called Inis Gutrin (that is, Glass Island), and for that reason the Saxons dubbed it Glastonbury since *Glas* means "glass" in their tongue, and *bury* is "city" or "camp."

You should also know that Arthur's bones were huge. . . . His shinbone, when placed on the ground by a monk next to that of the tallest man there, reached three fingers beyond the man's knee. And his skull was so broad and long as to be a wonder or marvel, and the space between his brows and eyes was the breadth of a full palm. There appeared on him also ten wounds or more, largely scarred over, except for one, which was larger than the rest and showed a big cut, which seemed to have been lethal. [Text in Chambers, pp. 269–271]

These are the most important Latin writings for the question of Arthur's actual existence. Work done in the 1980s by Geoffrey Ashe and others has shown that behind the puzzling traditions we may glimpse the figure of a known British leader who took an army to Gaul in the final confusion surrounding the collapse of the Western Roman Empire. This man is documented overseas as "Riothamus," a name that latinizes a Celtic title meaning "Supreme King"; and it could have been used as the official epithet of a chieftain whose actual name was something else—Arthur, for instance. Hints in *The Legend of St. Goeznovius* do in fact suggest that its author is referring to the same person when he indicates that Arthur went over to Gaul, and several other medieval writers give Arthur much the same dating as this "Supreme King." If the identification or semi-identification is correct there is an even broader base for assuming Arthur's true historical presence.

Similarly, work has been done to try to identify Camelot and other places of Arthurian interest. Leslie Alcock has made a good case for placing the otherwise mythical Camelot in Cadbury. There are also possible or probable locations for numerous other sites. Tintagel Castle has long been known to have existed in Cornwall, while Mt. Badon has been identified most convincingly as Liddington Castle near Swindon, and the Isle of Avalon probably was, as the chronicles themselves say, Glastonbury.

But for many readers of Arthurian tales the historical side, while fascinating, is the least important part of a broad vehicle of legend and myth that has replenished the European imagination for centuries, from Chrétien de Troyes to T.H. White. The true father of this mythic material is the pseudo-historian Geoffrey of Monmouth, whose work appears in Chapter IV. Meanwhile, aside from the chronicles, which were written by men of the church who were often Germanic rather than Celtic in their sympathies, the myth of Arthur grew where he properly belonged: among the common people who had been displaced in Wales and Cornwall and who were looking desperately for a messianic figure of salvation. Their literature appears in Chapters II and III.

Bibliographic note. All historical citations are taken from E.K. Chambers's *Arthur of Britain*, which, although published in 1927 (reprinted by Barnes and Noble in 1964), remains a standard source. For Tatlock's discussion of *Goeznovius* see *Speculum*, *14* (1939), 361–365; for Fleuriot's see *Les Origines de la Bretagne* (1980), p. 277. Ashe's consideration of "Riothamus" appears in *Speculum*, 56 (1981), 301–323. See also Some General Books for Further Reading at the end of this work.

The Roman amphitheater at Caerleon in Wales, one of the last of the ruins of this once mighty fortress on the River Usk. (Courtesy of the British Tourist Authority)

Chapter *II*

ARTHUR IN THE EARLY WELSH TRADITION

JOHN K. BOLLARD

The texts in this chapter include most of the Welsh references to Arthur that are earlier than Geoffrey of Monmouth's *History of the Kings of Britain,* and they give evidence that stories of Arthur and his men were well integrated into the body of Welsh tradition before the twelfth century. These tales and poems do not portray an abstract and elegant world where Arthur is surrounded by his knights and where questions of courtly conduct predominate. The poetry here gives us a glimpse of a society in which the realities of war were ever present. The most persistent images are those of blood, death, and grief. Surely these poems, whether evoking figures of history or of legend, served in some measure to help both poet and audience to understand and to cope with those same fierce images as they occurred and reoccurred in their own war-torn lives.

Medieval Welsh verse is not narrative, and it tends to be more allusive than informative. It does, however, make frequent references to characters, events, and stories that the original audience must have recognized. Some of these references are familiar to us today because the names or tales have survived in some other source. But because narrative traditions develop and change over a period of time, we can rarely be absolutely certain that the tale known to us is the same one that was intended in the earlier poetry. The very words of a language also undergo changes over time, and, especially when dealing with the earliest records of a culture quite different from our own, we cannot always be sure that a word had the same range of meaning in some past century that it has for us today. Faced with a similar problem, thirteenth- and fourteenth-century scribes may have imperfectly understood the older manuscripts they were copying, thus generating new errors that are left for us to puzzle over. For all of these reasons there is much that is tentative in these translations of early Welsh texts. Even though there are many obscurities, however, it seems preferable to give a single version of each, rather than to intersperse the translations with alternative readings or append lengthy discussions.

Sometime around the year 600 Mynyddog the Wealthy, a ruler of the Goddin,* in what is now southern Scotland, assembled a company of warriors from all over Britain. For a year they feasted at his expense before attacking and suffering a disastrous defeat from a much larger English force at Catraeth, which is probably the modern Catterick in Yorkshire. All but one of the three hundred warriors were killed. The survivor may have been the poet Aneirin, who is mentioned, as Neirin, in Chapter 62 of the chronicle attributed to Nennius. Whether or not he was actually present at the battle the poet was contemporary with the fallen heroes, and he composed a long series of elegiac stanzas eulogizing them. From the surviving thirteenth-century copy of this poem, called *The Gododdin*, we can piece together the outline of the events of this expedition. The poem was undoubtedly passed on orally for many years; its language changed with the development of Welsh, and additional stanzas and references were added to the original composition. The extant poem, therefore, presents a complex puzzle that we cannot completely solve. The standard edition of the poem is *Canu Aneirin*, edited with Welsh notes and introduction by Ifor Williams (University of Wales, 1938); it has been edited, translated and discussed in some detail by A.O.H. Jarman in *Aneirin: Y Gododdin* (Llandysul: Gomer Press, 1988).

In the following stanza praising a certain Gwawrddur there is nothing that would exclude it from being part of the original composition of Aneirin. The reference to Arthur, therefore, may well be the earliest surviving mention of him, and the poet himself may have been born during Arthur's lifetime. Within a generation or two after his death Arthur has become an ideal warrior to whom others are compared, and we can see here the beginnings of the long-lasting tradition by which other heroes were glorified and their tales enhanced simply by coupling them with the name of Arthur:

> He pierced over three hundred of the finest.
> He struck at both the center and the flank.
> He was worthy in the front of a most generous army.
> He gave out gifts from his drove of steeds in the winter.
> He fed black ravens [killed many of the enemy] on the wall of the
>   fortress, though he was not Arthur.
> He gave support in battle.
> In the van, an alder shield-wall was Gwawrddur.

---

*Note on the pronunciation of Welsh names: Pronounce *a* as in f*a*ther, *ai*, *au*, and *ei* as in *ai*sle, *aw* as in n*ow*, *c* as in *c*at, *ch* as in Scottish lo*ch*, *dd* as in *th*en, *e* as in b*e*d, *f* as in o*f*, *ff* as in e*ff*ect, *g* as in *g*o, *i* as in b*i*d, *th* as in *th*ink, *u* as in b*u*sy or b*ea*d, *w* as in *w*ith or as the vowel in t*oo*th, *y* as in m*y*th or c*i*ty in a single or final syllable and as in *a*live or glov*e* in other syllables. Pronounce *ll* with the tongue in the same position as for *l* by gently blowing air, without voice, past the side of the tongue (the *l* in English c*l*ean is very similar). The stressed syllable in Welsh is almost always the next-to-last syllable.

Curiously enough, the name of Gwawrddur is again coupled with that of Arthur in a fragmentary and obscure poem in the late thirteenth-century manuscript known as *The Book of Taliesin* (edited by J.G. Evans, Llanbedrog, 1910). This poem, which is manifestly some centuries older than the manuscript, praises the horses of traditional heroes. The names in the following two lines were chosen partly on the basis of rhyme, and the poet may have even taken the name of Gwawrddur from his knowledge of *The Gododdin*:

> And the horse of Gwythur and the horse of Gwawrddur
> and the horse of Arthur, fearless in causing pain.

The following poem is included in this collection because it is a contemporary elegy written in praise of Owain, a sixth-century lord of Rheged in northern Britain, who was drawn into and achieved some prominence in the Arthurian cycle. Owain son of Urien appears frequently in later Arthurian tales, especially as the hero of a romance that gained widespread popularity in Europe. He is the hero of *Yvain*, by Chrétien de Troyes, and appears in the Middle English *Ywain and Gawain*.

The present poem is found in *The Book of Taliesin* and has been edited by Ifor Williams and J.E. Caerwyn Williams in *The Poems of Taliesin* (Dublin Institute for Advanced Studies, 1968). It was composed by the sixth-century poet Taliesin, who is mentioned in the Nennian chronicle. Taliesin's elegy reveals the poet's personal sense of the loss of his lord, patron, and friend:

Elegy for Owain son of Urien

> The soul of Owain son of Urien,
> may the Lord consider its need.
> The lord of Rheged whom the heavy greensward covers,
> it was not shallow to praise him.
> The grave of a man renowned in song, of great fame.
> His whetted spears were like the dawn's rays,
> since no equal is found
> to the resplendent lord of Llwyfenydd,
> reaper of enemies, captor,
> with the nature of his father and his forebears.
> When Owain killed Fflamddwyn,
> it was no harder than sleeping.
> The broad host of Lloegr sleep
> with the light in their eyes.
> And those who did not retreat
> were bolder than necessary.
> Owain punished them severely,
> like a pack of wolves attacking sheep.
> A worthy man above his many-colored arms,
> who gave horses to suitors;
> though he hoarded them as a miser,
> they were shared for the sake of his soul.
> The soul of Owain son of Urien,
> may the Lord consider its need.

As the Anglo-Saxons gained sway over what is now England, many of the displaced British traditions were relocated in Wales. Considerable evidence for this can be seen in a series of seventy-five stanzas known as "The Stanzas of the Graves," composed during the ninth or tenth century. These verses list the traditional Welsh gravesites of legendary heroes, a number of whom are known to have been rulers or warriors from other parts of Britain. The earliest version of this poem is found in the thirteenth-century manuscript known as *The Black Book of Carmarthen* and it has been edited, annotated, and translated in full by Thomas Jones in *Proceedings of the British Academy* (1967).

A few of the names in "The Stanzas of the Graves" figure in Arthurian tradition. Gwalchmai is the Welsh name of the character better known to us in English as Gawain; Bedwyr, whose name is frequently coupled with that of Cei (Sir Kay) in early Welsh Arthurian tradition, appears in French and English as Bedivere; March is the King Mark of the Tristan legend. However, most important for Arthurian studies is a much-debated line naming Arthur: *anoeth bit bet y Arthur*. The troublesome word in this line is *anoeth*; it has been variously interpreted, but other instances of the word suggest that a likely sense in this context is "thing difficult to find or obtain; a wonder." A tradition that Arthur's grave was unknown may reflect (or may even have given rise to) a belief that Arthur was not dead and that he would return as a deliverer. Such a belief was certainly current among the Bretons by the early twelfth century. William of Malmesbury's comments, quoted in Chapter I, on the grave of Walwen and on the unknown site of Arthur's grave strongly suggest that William had a knowledge of Welsh traditions about the graves of heroes similar to what is found in this poem:

> From *"The Stanzas of the Graves"*
>
> The grave of Gwalchmai in Peryddon
> as a reproach to men;
> in Llanbadarn the grave of Cynon.
>
> The grave of the son of Osfran at Camlan
> after many a slaughter;
> the grave of Bedwyr on Tryfan hill.
>
> The grave of Owain son of Urien in a square grave
> under the earth of Llanforfael;
> in Abererch, Rhydderch the Generous.
>
> A grave for March, a grave for Gwythur,
> a grave for Gwgawn Red-sword;
> hard to find in the world, a grave for Arthur.

Another character originally independent of any connection with Arthur is Geraint son of Erbin. Like Owain, he too became the hero of a widely known Arthurian romance, though in the French version by Chrétien de Troyes, *Erec and Enide*, the hero is given a Breton name, Erec. Early genealogical evidence points to a late sixth-century date for Geraint, and his name is frequently connected with southwestern Britain and south Wales. Geraint son of Erbin may possibly be the Geraint referred to in *The Gododdin* in the line "Geraint before the South, the battle-cry was given," a line that seems to be faintly echoed in the poem given below.

This tenth- or eleventh-century poem in praise of Geraint is found in several manuscripts, though only the verses found in the earliest version from *The Black Book of Carmarthen* are translated here. It has been edited in Welsh by Brynley F. Roberts in *Astudiaethau ar yr Hengerdd: Studies in Early Welsh Poetry* (University of Wales, 1978) and by A.O.H. Jarman in his edition of the entire manuscript, *Llyfr Du Caerfyrddin* (University of Wales, 1983). This poem is a series of three-line stanzas or *englynion* (singular *englyn*), and its effect is achieved through the use of repetition with some variation in each *englyn*. One stanza mentions Arthur as taking some part in the battle of Llongborth, perhaps the modern Langport in Somerset. This is a significant reference for two reasons. It shows that at a fairly early date Geraint, a hero from the southwest of Britain, was being brought into the penumbra of Arthur's fame, as were other heroes from the north. This is also the first known instance of the title "emperor" being applied to Arthur, a title that is regularly used in later Arthurian tales and romances in Welsh. Thus this poem provides further evidence of the early growth of Arthurian legend, and it illustrates a step in the gradual transfiguration of early historical leaders into the traditional knights of Arthur's court:

> *Geraint filius Erbin*
>
> Before Geraint, afflictor of the enemy,
> I saw white steeds with fetlocks bloodstained,
> and after the battle-cry—grievous death.
>
> Before Geraint, disinheritor of the enemy,
> I saw steeds with fetlocks bloodstained from battle,
> and after the battle-cry—grievous reflection.
>
> Before Geraint, oppressor of the enemy,
> I saw steeds, white their skin,
> and after the battle-cry—grievous silence.
>
> At Llongborth I saw wrath
> and biers more than many
> and men blood-red before the rush of Geraint.
>
> At Llongborth I saw hewing,
> men in battle with heads bloodied
> before great Geraint, son of his father.
>
> At Llongborth I saw spurs
> and men who would not retreat before spears
> and drinking wine from bright glass.
>
> At Llongborth I saw the weapons
> of men and blood flowing,
> and after the battle-cry—grievous burial.
>
> At Llongborth I saw Arthur
> (brave men hewed with iron),
> emperor, ruler of battle-toil.

At Llongborth were killed Geraint's
brave men from the Devon lowlands,
but before they were killed, they killed.

Swiftly there ran under Geraint's thigh
long-legged horses, fed on wheat,
red, with the rush of speckled eagles.

Swiftly there ran under Geraint's thigh
long-legged horses, grain was theirs,
red, with the rush of black eagles.

Swiftly there ran under Geraint's thigh
long-legged horses, grain scattering,
red, with the rush of red eagles.

Swiftly there ran under Geraint's thigh
long-legged horses, grain-consuming,
red, with the rush of white eagles.

Swiftly there ran under Geraint's thigh
long-legged horses, with the leap of a stag,
with the roar of a blaze on a mountain waste.

Swiftly there ran under Geraint's thigh
long-legged horses, grain-greedy,
grey-tipped their hair like silver.

Swiftly there ran under Geraint's thigh
long-legged horses, deserving grain,
red, with the rush of blue eagles.

Swiftly there ran under Geraint's thigh
long-legged horses, grain their food,
red, with the rush of grey eagles.

When Geraint was born, open were
the gates of Heaven; Christ gave what was asked—
a noble form, Britain's glory.

One of the most interesting, if perplexing and tantalizing, early Arthurian sources is a tenth- or eleventh-century poem also in *The Black Book of Carmarthen* and edited by Roberts and Jarman in the volumes noted above. It begins as a dialogue between Arthur himself and the porter Glewlwyd Mighty-grip and is largely a catalog of names in which Arthur praises his warriors. The place-name "Tryfrwyd" of line 48 is undoubtedly a reference to the battle listed in the Nennian chronicle, with its earlier orthography, as having been "fought on the banks of the River Tribruit."

However, in this poem we have moved away from the more or less historical milieu of the earlier poetry into the realm of legend, mythology, and folktale. Some of the names in the poem come not from early historical tradition but from Celtic mythology. Mabon son of Modron and Manawydan son of Llŷr, for instance, are names that can be traced back to the names of early Celtic deities. An important place in this poem is given to Cei. In later tradition he becomes the obstreperous Sir Kay, but here he is, or has become, more than simply a renowned warrior; he appears in this poem as a slayer of witches and monsters. Unfortunately the manuscript is defective, and the poem breaks off at the end of a page before we learn how Cei fared against the Clawing Cat (Welsh *cath palug*):

[Arthur:]   What man is the porter?

[Glewlwyd:]   Glewlwyd Mighty-grip.
                Who asks it?

[Arthur:]   Arthur and Cei the Fair.

[Glewlwyd:]   Who comes with you?

[Arthur:]   The best men in the world.

[Glewlwyd:]:   To my house you will not come
                unless you deliver them.

[Arthur:]   I shall deliver them
                and you will see them.
                Wythnaint, Elei,
                and Sywyon, these three;
                Mabon son of Modron,
                servant of Uther Pendragon,
                Cystaint son of Banon,
                and Gwyn Godybrion;
                harsh were my servants
                in defending their rights.
                Manawydan son of Llŷr,
                profound was his counsel.
                Manawyd carried off
                shields pierced and battle-stained.
                And Mabon son of Mellt
                stained the grass with blood.
                And Anwas the Winged
                and Lluch of the Striking Hand,
                they were defending
                on the borders of Eidyn.
                A lord would protect them;
                my nephew would give them recompense.
                Cei would entreat them
                as he struck them by threes.
                When the grove was lost
                cruelty was suffered.
                Cei would entreat them
                while he cut them down.

[Cei (?):]   Though Arthur was but playing,
                blood was flowing
                in the hall of Afarnach
                fighting with a hag.
                He pierced the cudgel-head
                in the halls of Dissethach.
                On the mount of Eidyn
                they fought with Dog-heads;
                by the hundred they fell.

[Arthur:]   They fell by the hundred
              before Bedwyr the Fine-sinewed
              on the strand of Tryfrwyd.
              Fighting with Garwlwyd,
              fierce was his nature
              with sword and shield.
              Vain was an army
               compared to Cei in battle.
              He was a sword in battle;
              he pledged with his hand.
              He was a resolute chieftain
              of a host for the country's good.
              Bedwyr and Bridlaw,
              nine hundred to listen,
              six hundred to disperse
              would his attack be worth.
              The servants that I had,
              it was better when they were alive.
              Before the lords of Emrys
              I saw Cei in haste;
              prince of plunder,
              the tall man was hostile.
              His revenge was heavy;
              his anger was sharp.
              When he drank from the buffalo horn
              he would drink for four;
              when he came into battle
              he would strike like a hundred.
              Unless it were God who did it,
              Cei's death could not be achieved.
              Cei the Fair and Llachau,
              they made slaughter
              before the pain of the blue-tipped spears.
              In the uplands of Ystafngwn
              Cei pierced nine witches.
              Cei the Fair went to Anglesey
              to destroy lions;
              his shield was small
              against the Clawing Cat.
              When people ask
              who pierced the Clawing Cat
              (nine score warriors would fall for its food,
              nine score champions
              and. . . .

The name of Llachau, which is coupled with that of Cei above, also occurs in another tenth- or eleventh-century poem from *The Black Book of Carmarthen* in a series of englynion lamenting the deaths of traditional Welsh heroes.

Though little is known about Llachau, he was clearly a figure of some importance in early Arthurian tradition, for in addition to these early references his name is invoked no less than eight times by the twelfth- and thirteenth-century Welsh bards. The englyn in which he is named below is of particular interest because it names Arthur as his father:

> I have been where Llachau was slain,
> son of Arthur, marvelous in songs,
> when ravens croaked over blood.

Firmly ensconced in mythological tradition is an important Arthurian poem in *The Book of Taliesin*, to which a later hand has added the title *Preiddeu Annwfn*, "The Spoils of Annwn." The historical poet Taliesin had gradually become a figure of legend and folklore himself, and various poems with mythological content were attributed to him. "The Spoils of Annwn" is obscure both in its language and in its allusions, and no satisfactorily complete edition or translation has been published, though R.S. Loomis edited and translated parts of it in *Wales and the Arthurian Legend* (University of Wales, 1956). The following translation is speculative, and ellipses have been used where the text defies translation.

The general outline is clear. Annwn is the Celtic otherworld. At times it would appear that Annwn is coextensive with the world in which we live, though it may not be discernible. In some sources, such as this poem, it seems to be an island. In the first part of the medieval Welsh prose masterpiece known as *The Four Branches of the Mabinogi* the story is related how Pwyll, a ruler of Dyfed in southwest Wales, repaid a debt of honor to Arawn, the king of Annwn, by remaining for a year in Annwn in Arawn's form and by defeating one of Arawn's enemies in single combat. Upon his return to his own land Pwyll became known as Pwyll, Head of Annwn. The latter half of the story tells of the strange circumstances surrounding the birth and rearing of Pwyll's son, Pryderi. The second branch of *The Mabinogi* tells, among other things, of a magical cauldron that could restore the dead to life. In a battle in Ireland in which this cauldron was eventually destroyed the entire population of Ireland was killed except for five pregnant women, and all of the Welsh army was slain except for seven survivors, among whom were Pryderi and Taliesin.

It is clear that "The Spoils of Annwn" reflects much of this same mythological material in an Arthurian context. The poem alludes to a journey to Annwn in Arthur's ship Prydwen. The purpose of this journey was apparently to rescue Gwair, known elsewhere as a renowned prisoner and perhaps to bring back among the spoils of war the cauldron of the Head of Annwn. This magical cauldron also bears some affinity to that of Diwrnach the Giant in the story of *Culhwch and Olwen*.

The latter part of the poem remains obscure, though the poet seems to be discontented with the lowly men and cowardly monks around him, in contrast to the warriors whom he accompanied on Arthur's disastrous expedition to Annwn. Thus, like much early Welsh verse, "The Spoils of Annwn" is an expression of loss and grief, reflected most poignantly in the refrain "except for seven, none returned":

The Spoils of Annwn

I will praise the Lord, the Sovereign, the King of the land,
who has extended his rule over the strand of the world.
Well equipped was the prison of Gwair in Caer Siddi [Fairy Fortress],
according to the story of Pwyll and Pryderi.
None before him went to it,
to the heavy blue chain; it was a faithful servant whom it
        restrained,
and before the spoils of Annwn sadly he sang.
And until Judgment Day our bardic song will last.
Three shiploads of Prydwen we went to it;
except for seven, none returned from Caer Siddi.

I am honored in praise, song is heard.
In Caer Pedryfan [Four-cornered (?) Fort], four-sided,
my eulogy, from the cauldron it was spoken.
By the breath of nine maidens it was kindled.
The cauldron of the Head of Annwn, what is its custom,
dark about its edge with pearl?
It does not boil a coward's food; it had not been so destined.
The sword of Lluch Lleawg was raised to it,
and in the hand of Lleminawg it was left.
And before the door of the gate of hell, lanterns burned.
And when we went with Arthur, renowned conflict
except for seven, none returned from Caer Feddwid [Fort of
        Carousal].

I am honored in praise, song will be heard.
In Caer Pedryfan, island of the strong door,
noon and jet-black are mixed.
Bright wine their drink before their warband.
Three shiploads of Prydwen we went on the sea;
except for seven, none returned from Caer Rigor.

I, lord of learning, do not deserve lowly men.
Beyond Caer Wydr [Glass Fort] they had not seen Arthur's valor.
Three score hundred men stood on the wall;
it was difficult to speak with their watchman.
Three shiploads of Prydwen we went with Arthur;
except for seven, none returned from Caer Goludd.

I do not deserve lowly men, slack their defense.
They do not know what day. . . ,
what hour of the midday God was born,
who. . . .
They do not know the Speckled Ox, thick his headring,
seven score links in his collar.
And when we went with Arthur, disastrous visit,
except for seven, none returned from Caer Fanddwy.

I do not deserve lowly men, slack their attack.
They do not know what day. . . ,
what hour of the midday the lord was born,
what animal they keep, silver its head.
When we went with Arthur, disastrous strife,
except for seven, none returned from Caer Ochren.

Monks crowd together like a choir of whelps
from the battle of lords who will be known.
Is the wind of one path? Is the sea of one water?
Is fire, irresistible tumult, of one spark?

Monks crowd together like a pack of wolves
from the battle of lords who will be known.
They do not know when darkness and dawn separate
or the wind, what is its path, is its onrush,
what does it destroy, what land does it strike?
How many lost saints and how many others?

I will praise the Lord, the Great Prince.
May I not be sad; Christ will endow me.

From the earliest times the Celtic peoples have used triple groupings as a means of classifying, remembering, and passing on a wide range of information and lore. Laws, genealogical and geographical information, rules of poetic composition, and much else besides have come down to us arranged in triplets. One such body of lore has survived in various collections known as *The Triads of the Isle of Britain*, which preserve the names of the traditional heroes of Welsh legend, along with summaries of or references to stories about many of them. Poets and storytellers who memorized or copied them down could then draw upon these lists for names, details, and stories as they needed them. The earliest and most important versions of these triads are found in thirteenth-, fourteenth-, and fifteenth-century manuscripts, but the information they contain is demonstrably much older. The standard edition and discussion is *Trioedd Ynys Prydein: The Welsh Triads*, edited by Rachel Bromwich (University of Wales, 1961; rev. 1978)—itself an invaluable store of information about the development of Arthurian legend. The number of each triad in Bromwich's edition is given below in brackets.

Of the ninety-six triads in this collection those translated below mention Arthur or other characters well known in Arthurian literature, thus giving us a glimpse of the scope of Arthurian lore in Wales before the publication of Geoffrey of Monmouth's *History of the Kings of Britain*. It should perhaps be made explicit here that the triads are written in prose, not verse, with the exception of the englyn recited by Arthur himself in Triad 18W. Other verse, such as the englyn he recites in *Culhwch and Olwen*, has also been attributed to Arthur, and these poems account for his inclusion among the three Frivolous Bards of Triad 12. Many of the names in these triads have been encountered in the poetry above; other names are readily recognizable. A few names are better known in their French or English forms. Bishop Bidwini (Triad 1) also turns up in the catalog in *Culhwch and Olwen* and he is probably the original of the Bishop Bawdewyn (Baudwin or Baldwin) who sits next to Ywain son of Urien in line 112 of *Sir Gawain and the Green Knight*. Medrawd (54) is the Medraut of *The Annals of Cambria* and the Modred or Mordred of Malory and others. Gwenhwyfar (54, 56, 80, 84) is Guinevere.

From *The Triads of the Isle of Britain*

Three Tribal Thrones of the Isle of Britain: Arthur as Chief
Ruler in Mynyw, and David as Chief Bishop, and
Maelgwn Gwynedd as Chief Elder; Arthur as Chief Ruler
in Celli Wig in Cornwall, and Bishop Bidwini as Chief
Bishop, and Caradog Strong-arm as Chief Elder; Arthur
as Chief Ruler in Pen Rhionydd in the North, and
Gerthmwl Wledig as Chief Elder, and Cyndeyrn
Garthwys as Chief Bishop. [1]

Three Men of Substance of the Isle of Britain: Gwalchmai son of
Gwyar, and Llachau son of Arthur, and Rhiwallawn
Broom-hair. [4]

Three Chieftains of Arthur's Court: Gobrwy son of Echel
Mighty-thigh, Cadriaith son of Porthawr Gadw, and
Ffleudur Fflam. [9]

Three Frivolous Bards of the Isle of Britain: Arthur, and
Cadwallawn son of Cadfan, and Rahawd son of Morgant.
[12]

Three Favorites of Arthur's Court, and Three Battle-horsemen;
and they never sought a captain over them. And Arthur
composed an englyn:
These are my Three Battle-horsemen:
Menedd, and Lludd of the Breastplate,
and the Pillar of the Welsh, Caradog. [18W]

Three Red-reapers of the Isle of Britain: Rhun son of Beli, and
Lleu Skillful-hand, and Morgant the Wealthy. But one
was more of a Red-reaper than the three; Arthur was his
name. For a year neither grass nor plants would come up
where one of the three walked, but for seven years none
would come up where Arthur walked. [20W]

Three Diademed Men of the Isle of Britain: Drystan son of
Tallwch, and Hueil son of Caw, and Cei son of Cenyr the
Fine-bearded. But one was diademed above the three of
them; that was Bedwyr son of Bedrawg. [21]

Three Unbridled Ravagings of the Isle of Britain: The first of
them, when Medrawd came to Arthur's court in Celli Wig
in Cornwall; he left neither food nor drink in the court he
did not consume, and he also pulled Gwenhwyfar out of
her chair of state, and then he struck a blow upon her.
And the second Unbridled Ravaging, when Arthur came
to Medrawd's court; he left neither food nor drink in
either the court or the cantref [district]. And the third
Unbridled Ravaging, when Aeddan the Treacherous came
as far as Dumbarton to the court of Rhydderch the
Generous, and he left neither food nor drink nor animal
alive. [54]

Three Great Queens of Arthur: Gwenhwyfar daughter of
Cywryd Gwent, and Gwenhwyfar daughter of Gwythyr
son of Greidiawl, and Gwenhwyfar daughter of Gogfran
the Giant. [56]

And these were his three Mistresses: Indeg daughter of Garwy
the Tall, and Garwen daughter of Henin the Old, and
Gŵyl daughter of Gendawd. [57]

Three Unfortunate Counsels of the Isle of Britain: Giving to
Julius Caesar and the men of Rome a place for the forefeet
of their horses on the land, in payment for the horse
Meinlas. And the second, allowing Horsa and Hengist and
Ronnwen into this isle. And the third, Arthur dividing his
men thrice with Medrawd at Camlan. [59]

Three Men of the Isle of Britain most courteous to guests and
strangers: Gwalchmai son of Gwyar, and Cadwy son of
Geraint, and Cadriaith son of Saidi. [75]

Three Faithless Wives of the Isle of Britain: three daughters of
Culfanwyd of Britain: Essyllt [Isolde] Fair-hair, mistress of
Trystan, and Penarwan, wife of Owain son of Urien, and
Bun, wife of Fflamddwyn; and one was more faithless than
those three: Gwenhwyfar, wife of Arthur, since she
shamed a better man than any of them. [80]

Three Futile Battles of the Isle of Britain: One of them was the
Battle of Goddau; it was brought about because of a bitch
together with a roebuck and a lapwing. The second was
the Battle of Arfderydd, which was brought about because
of a lark's nest. And the third was the worst; that was
Camlan. And that was brought about by the quarrel
between Gwenhwyfar and Gwenhwyfach. This is the
reason those were called Futile: because they were
brought about by such a fruitless cause as that. [84]

King Arthur's round Table

Preserved as a curious piece of Antiquity in the Castle of Winchester.

The Round Table in the Great Hall of Winchester Castle. Once believed to be the work of Joseph of Arimathea, it has since been dated to the mid-13th century. In 1486, King Henry VII painted it white and green and set a Tudor rose in the middle. The solar significance is obvious, with Arthur placed at Christmas or the winter solstice. (Courtesy of the British Tourist Authority)

Chapter III

CULHWCH AND OLWEN

Richard M. Loomis

The oldest Arthurian tale, *Culhwch and Olwen*, survives in two Welsh manuscripts of the fourteenth century, but evidence of language and allusion support the conclusion that the work was given substantially its present form toward the end of the eleventh century. Its language also suggests that it was composed in regions of South Wales where the great boar, Twrch Trwyth, is hunted in the tale's climax. Topographical references indicate that the narrator is tracking the beast through places familiar to him and his audience. The storytelling calls for an audience responsive to a variety of styles, including burlesque and parody, familiar with numerous persons and topics cited, and ready to follow narrative lines marked by abrupt turns, stalls, large symmetries, small connective threads, and startling disparities.

The story tells how a young nobleman, Culhwch, wins Olwen, daughter of Ysbaddaden Chief Giant, by fulfilling the giant's demands for the wedding. In meeting these demands, Culhwch is aided by companions commissioned by his cousin, King Arthur. This is an Arthurian shaping of the international folktale motif, "Six go through the whole world" (Aarne and Thompson 513A). The giant opposes the marriage because he will die when his daughter marries. His demands are meant to be impossible obstacles, and the hero needs prodigiously endowed helpers. Their tasks turn into an attack on the giant himself, the original deadly obstacle, as revealed in their initial encounter with him. Of the forty tasks set by the giant, eighteen are not subsequently mentioned; the giant's death resolves the issue. Arthur and his warriors embrace the challenge of seeking the *anoethau*, the "wonders," or rare and difficult things required for the wedding, and these quests usually culminate in a fight. Thus the tale has more battling than courtship, like the parallel Irish tale of Cuchulainn's wooing of Emer. The pursuit of Twrch Trwyth, costing many lives, has the goal of seizing the grooming implements (comb, scissors, and an added razor) lodged between the boar's ears, with which to trim the giant for the wedding-feast. In the upshot, the giant is not groomed but hacked and beheaded.

The story's modes include spare chronicling, vivid rhythmic description, dialogue, and lists alive with wordplay, miniature portraits, and story-fragments. The opening lines tell of a marriage subject to the demands and constraints of tribal life in ancient Britain. A chieftain seeks a wife as wellborn as he, and after he finds one, the people pray for an heir. A son is born, but in calamitous circumstances. The mother's pregnancy has caused her to go mad, and she doesn't recover her right mind until a herd of pigs so frighten her that she gives birth. The boy is named "Culhwch" at his baptism; the name means *pigsty*. Since he's of noble parentage, he is placed in the care of foster parents, a custom of the Celtic aristocracy. Culhwch's birth is enhanced by the circumstance that he is a first cousin to Arthur. Arthur's name signals that the world of the story is heroic.

Culhwch's father Cilydd is a lord, *gwledig*. The term is one of many archaic elements in the tale, for it is a title used in the earliest Welsh texts to designate leaders of the warrior aristocracy of ancient Britain. The people would pray for an heir because a warrior lord is expected to be his people's guardian and an heir is their promise of stable rule. Every resource, including those pigs, is needed to achieve a fruitful marriage. The tale proceeds to make an international drama of the transactions involved in Culhwch's own marriage, involving giants, otherworldly figures, and boar-hunting, coordinated by Arthur, who is styled chief of the princes of the island. It ends with the dry observation, that's how Culhwch won Olwen.

The warriors contend for honor, women, and land in ways that are so unapologetically self-assertive and violent that the tale seems amoral. In fact, their warrior ways are exposed to critical perspectives. On her deathbed, Culhwch's mother, Goleuddydd (the name means "Bright Day"), realizes that her husband will want another wife. Knowing that women bestow gifts, that is, manage a household's treasures, and not wanting her son to be deprived by a stepmother, Goleuddydd gets her husband to promise not to remarry until he sees a two-headed briar growing on her grave. Then she commissions a counselor of hers to keep the grave stripped so that nothing will grow there. After her death, as she had expected, her husband is obsessed with taking a second wife; he has the grave inspected every day. Seven years pass; the counselor forgets to strip the grave; Cilydd sees the longed-for briar and looks for another wife. An advisor recommends the wife of King Doged: "They agreed to go seek her. And they killed the king and carried his wife home with them, and an only daughter she had with her. And they conquered that king's land."

Not only has Cilydd taken a second wife as soon as the letter of his promise permits him, but he has abducted another man's wife, slaying the king and seizing his land while he's at it. The woman obviously has more than the usual motives of a second wife for making the most of the marriage imposed upon her. She finds no children in the household, for Culhwch is in fosterage. Is her husband incapable of fathering a child? She gets an answer from a town hag, another knowing woman, who first equivocates and then reveals that there is a son. Presumably to secure her own interests, the stepmother attempts to arrange a marriage between her daughter and the boy. When Culhwch declines to commit himself as being too young, she pronounces the destiny upon him that he shall marry only a giant's daughter. The stepmother is sentencing Culhwch to death.

Culhwch's response is not prudent anxiety but heroic sexual excitement, instantly recognized and appreciated by his father, who doesn't steer him away from the danger but tells him how to manage it: Get Arthur to trim your hair and ask him for Olwen as a gift. The hair-cutting is symbolic recognition of consanguinity; once the blood-tie is acknowledged, Culhwch can tap the generosity that flows in a kinsman's veins. The narrator's way of recounting the hair-cutting heightens its apparent absurdity as a strategy for going against a giant; farcical discontinuity hanging by a thread of sense is a frequent comic turn in the tale. Arthur proves to be not only a good relative but a noble prince who welcomes boon-seekers because they're a means of enhancing his honor.

The tale moves from narration to lists, like those in the traditional lore of Wales that a *cyfarwydd* (knowledgeable guide, storyteller) was expected to command. Here they are burlesqued into hyperboles for Arthur's glory or for the intransigence of the Giant Ysbaddaden. Culhwch calls upon Arthur's followers as sureties for Arthur's pledge to help in winning Olwen. The ensuing flock of names is a display of the storyteller's learning and wit, for some 260 persons are named, beginning with Kei and Bedwyr (the Kay and Bedivere of later romance) and ending with Guinevere and other beautiful women of Britain.

Besides names from Welsh tradition, there are punning inventions, nonsense, a sprinkling of Irish heroes, and possible allusions to eleventh-century contemporaries of the storyteller. Sulien, a learned Bishop of St. David's, may be the source for "Sulyen mab Iaen" ["Sunday-born son of Ice"], and the "Guilenhin King of France" who is recruited for and dies during the tale's climactic boar-hunt may allude to William the Conqueror. William died in 1087, having visited St. David's in 1081, on one of those political journeys by which he sought to consolidate Norman authority. 1081 was also the year of a famous battle in that part of Wales. Rhys ap Tewdwr, King of Deheubarth (a region of southwestern Wales) and Gruffudd ap Cynan of North Wales, who had been in exile in Ireland and had brought Irish allies to fight with him, were leagued there against rival Welsh forces.

One of the notable clusters of invented names in Culhwch's list of sureties is that of a family emblematic of war, among whose offspring are Plague, Want, and Need. The horrors of war were not a remote experience for an eleventh-century storyteller. As the Normans extended their power into Wales, Welsh lords jockeyed for survival and eminence, and their contentions were for women as well as land. Nest, the daughter of Rhys ap Tewdwr, became known as the Helen of Wales because of her many liaisons. The list of sureties advertises the storyteller's repertoire and reminds an audience that Culhwch's courtship is no private matter but unfolds in an arena crowded with warriors, wonders, and beauties.

After Arthur's messengers vainly search for Olwen for a year, he commissions six men to accompany Culhwch on a quest for the giant's castle— Kei, Bedwyr, Cynddylig the Guide, Gwrhyr the Interpreter of Languages, Gwalchmai (the Welsh Gawain), and Menw the Magician. They come to a great fort before which they meet the shepherd Custennin, who tells them that Ysbaddaden ("Hawthorn" or "Whitethorn") Chief Giant, who holds the fort, is his brother. The giant has oppressed Custennin on account of Custennin's wife and has slain all but one of her twenty-four sons. At the end of the tale, the remaining son, Goreu, kills the giant and takes possession of the fort and territory. Goreu's mother, like Arthur, recognizes Culhwch as kin; his mother, Goleuddydd, is her sister. She counsels Culhwch how to approach Olwen, and Olwen herself readily gives him her love and warns him not to waver when negotiating with her father.

Once Culhwch has presented to the giant his bid to marry Olwen and has agreed with characteristic brio to accomplish everything the giant demands as preparation for the wedding, Culhwch does no more than return at last and marry Olwen. The rare and difficult things are obtained by the six original companions and a host of men and animals who help out. They start with the last and deadliest wonder, Wrnach's sword (not used to kill the boar but that which Goreu will use to behead Ysbaddaden). They do battle with the forces of Ireland for a cauldron, and when Arthur returns to hunt Twrch Trwyth there, he is treated as an overlord by the Irish. The intimidating effect of military power is casually noted, an ironic echo of early Welsh saints' lives that depicted Arthur as a tyrant needing reproof. Arthur and his men have made off with a cauldron full of the treasure of Ireland, and their return campaign causes fear and trembling there, but the saints ask his protection, while the men give him food. Thereupon Irish forces leagued with Arthur fight Twrch Trwyth at great cost: "one-fifth of Ireland was laid waste." The disparity between hunting a boar and devastating a nation is presented flatly. When the hunt ends in Cornwall, many men have died, but Twrch Trwyth is driven beyond pursuit into the sea.

Ethical subtlety cannot be ascribed to a tale in which King Arthur whacks a witch into two tubs of blood, or in which Caw of Pictland gives Ysbaddaden his shave right to the bone, whisking off his ears too. "Have you been shaved, man?" asks Culhwch. The bloody skull replies, "I have." The difference between the favored protagonists and their opponents is cultural. When Arthur's warriors show up at Ysbaddaden's court, they wear combs in their hair.

Culhwch is himself described as a triumph of art over nature; even the clods his horse kicks into the air fly like choreographed swallows. And Olwen, whose name means "White Track," leaves white trefoils growing where she steps.

Ysbaddaden, on the other hand, is sluggish (his eyelids need propping up) and grossly rude. He hurls stone spears at his guests. Arthur's men, evidently blessed with a magical version of the iron technology of the Celts, catch the spears and hurl them back with what the giant describes as iron points. These make the giant's eyes water and his limbs ache, but he is not easily quelled. "If I had my way," he tells Culhwch at the end, "you would never win her."

Among the tasks the heroes must accomplish is the freeing of Mabon son of Modron, and the counsel of the oldest animals is needed to find him. The name "Mabon" is derived from the Romano-British deity Apollo Maponos, and "Modron" comes from the Celtic goddess Matrona. The name translates as "Youth God, son of the Mother Goddess." Whatever this might have meant to an eleventh-century audience no longer believing in pagan deities, Mabon is given a history in the tale. Ysbaddaden tells that he was taken from his mother as an infant and is held prisoner somewhere; no one knows where or knows even whether he is alive or dead. Once freed with the help of a mighty salmon, Mabon joins Arthur, who from his court at Celliwig in Cornwall directs the several expeditions. Mabon's release is an instance of the freeings that occur (more happily than devastations) as Arthur's soldiers range for treasure, culminating in the defeat of Ysbaddaden that frees Goreu as well as Culhwch and Olwen.

Courtship is shown as also engaging the otherworldly character Gwyn ap Nudd ("Gwyn son of Nudd"—in this translation all the Welsh patronymics are translated). In Welsh tradition, he is the leader of the *tylwyth teg*, a band of spirits from the Otherworld. Here he is said to have been filled with demons to spare the world (like the swine of Gadarene), yet he is listed as one of Arthur's own band of companions. He is also one of those whom Ysbaddaden tells Culhwch he'll need but won't get for the hunting of Twrch Trwyth, and Culhwch's "Easy!" has more than bravado to support it in this and similar instances, since Gwyn has already been invoked by Culhwch as a follower of Arthur's. Later we learn that Gwyn has abducted the bride of Gwythyr ap Greidawl before they could sleep together, provoking a war that requires Arthur to mediate a truce. The girl is to remain in her father's house, while Gwyn ap Nudd and Gwythyr ap Greidawl fight for her every May Day till Doomsday. Their endless competition for a wife, linked to summer's recurring emergence and retreat, echoes other courtship battles in the tale. Gwyn gives counsel and assistance to Arthur in trying to subdue the witch whose blood is needed as shaving cream for Ysbaddaden. Arthur's own strength prevails, but his exercising leadership over Gwyn ap Nudd gives him an otherworldly cast, too, like Irish heroes who freely mingle with the *sidhe*.

Pieces of the tragic drama of the fall of Arthur and his court are discernible in *Culhwch and Olwen*. They are allusions only, like the references to Camlan, scene of Arthur's last battle, but evidently ones the audience could catch. An instance is the depiction of Kei, whose own murder is mentioned. Kei objects to admitting the obstreperous Culhwch to Arthur's court and has to be reminded by Arthur that they are noble only so long as they are sought after. To win glory, they have to be generous. Kei has prodigious traits, such as being as tall as he wishes or generating heat that can ignite a campfire to warm his companions. But his father Cynyr has said that if his son resembles him, he will be cold of heart, cold of hand, and stubborn. These qualities are shown later in the tale. Kei brings to Arthur a leash made from the beard of the giant Dillus, whom Kei has subdued by trickery and killed after plucking his beard. Arthur, noted in the Welsh *Triads* as a "frivolous bard," a lord capable of composing playful verses, responds with an epigram that if Dillus were well, he'd kill Kei. The court list had earlier noted that Arthur would be the avenger of the murder of Kei. Now, after hearing Arthur's epigram, Kei sulks, while Arthur prepares to go questing for another rare and difficult thing. The storyteller comments that from that time on, even when Arthur lacked resources and his men were slain, Kei would not go with him. The tale edges its comedy with shadows.

Bibliographic note: A critical edition is now available: *Culhwch and Olwen: An Edition and Study of the Oldest Arthurian Tale*, edited by Rachel Bromwich and D. Simon Evans (Univ. of Wales Press, 1992). This is an expansion of the editors' Welsh edition of 1988, which was built on work that Sir Idris Foster left unfinished at his death. The 1992 edition has a full critical apparatus and commentary in English. The editors have also assembled a complete glossary, published separately as *Glossary to Culhwch ac Olwen*, compiled by Rachel Bromwich and D. Simon Evans, Welsh Studies Volume 7 (Edwin Mellen Press, 1992).

The tale has been translated by Lady Charlotte Guest (first published in 1849) in *The Mabinogion* (Everyman's Library, 1906), 95–135; Gwyn Jones and Thomas Jones, *The Mabinogion* (Everyman's Library, 1949), 95–136; Jeffrey Gantz, *The Mabinogion* (Penguin, 1976), 134–76; Patrick K. Ford, *The Mabinogi and Other Medieval Welsh Tales* (Univ. of California, 1977), 119–57. For commentary on traditional characters and motifs of early Welsh literature, see Rachel Bromwich, *Trioedd Ynys Prydein: The Welsh Triads* (Univ. of Wales, 1961; 2nd edition, 1978); on the international folktale, Antti Aarne and Stith Thompson, *The Types of the Folktale: A Classification and Bibliography* (New York: Burt Franklin, 1928; 1971), and Kenneth Jackson, *The International Popular Tale and Early Welsh Tradition* (Univ. of Wales Press, 1961), 71–81. On literary relationships and Irish affinities, see Idris Foster in R.S. Loomis, ed., *Arthurian Literature in the Middle Ages* (Oxford, 1959), 31–9. On saints' lives, see Elissa R. Henken, *Traditions of the Welsh Saints* (D.S. Brewer, 1987).

Critical studies include Proinsias Mac Cana, *The Mabinogi* (Univ. of Wales Press, 1977; 1992); Doris Edel, "The Arthur of *Culhwch ac Olwen* as a Figure of Epic Heroic Tradition," *Reading Medieval Studies* 9 (1983), 3–15; Joan N. Radner, "Interpreting Irony in Medieval Celtic Narrative: The Case of *Culhwch ac Olwen,*" *Cambridge Medieval Celtic Studies* 16 (1988), 41–59. Brynley F. Roberts discusses the tale in chapter 3 of *The Arthur of the Welsh*, edited by Rachel Bromwich, A.O. Jarman, and Brynley F. Roberts (Univ. of Wales Press, 1991), 73–95. See also Roberts' earlier study of the tale in the reissued *A Guide to Welsh Literature*, edited by A.O.H. Jarman and G.R. Hughes, vol. I (Univ. of Wales Press, 1976; 1992), 214–20; and his "From Traditional Tale to Literary Story: Middle Welsh Prose Narratives," ch. 7 in L.A. Arrathoon, ed., *The Craft of Fiction: Essays in Medieval Poetics* (Solaris, 1984), 211–30. For an analysis of the tale as a document of political ideology, see Stephen Knight, ch. 1 in *Arthurian Literature and Society* (London: Macmillan, 1983; 1985), 12–37.

Culhwch and Olwen

Cilydd son of Lord Celyddon wanted a wife as noble as himself. The wife he chose was Goleuddydd daughter of Lord Anlawdd.* After he lodged with her, the country went to prayers that they might have an heir. And through the prayers of the country, they had a son. And from the hour that she became pregnant, she went mad and would not approach any dwelling-place. When her time came, her right mind came to her. It came in a place where a swineherd was keeping a herd of pigs. And from fear of the pigs the queen gave birth. And the swineherd took the boy and came to the court. And the boy was baptized, and the name Culhwch was given him because he was born in a pig-run. But the boy was noble; he was a first cousin to Arthur; and he was entrusted to the care of foster parents.

And after that the boy's mother, Goleuddydd daughter of Lord Anlawdd, became sick. She called her husband to her and said, "I shall die of this sickness, and you will want another wife. Nowadays wives are the bestowers of gifts. But it is bad for you to deprive your son. So I beg you not to choose a wife until you see a briar with two heads upon my grave."

He promised her that. She summoned her counselor to her and asked him to strip the grave every year so that nothing would grow on it. The queen died. Then the king sent a servant every morning to see whether anything was growing on the grave. After seven years the counselor forgot to do what he had promised the queen. One day while hunting the king came to the cemetery; he wanted to see the grave that might permit him to marry. And he saw the briar.

When he saw it, the king went to be advised where he could find a wife. One of his advisers said, "I know a woman well suited for you to marry. She is the wife of King Doged." They agreed to go seek her. And they killed the king and carried his wife home with them, and an only daughter she had with her. And they conquered that king's land.

One day the good woman went out for a walk and came to the house of an old hag in the town who had no teeth in her head. The queen said, "Old

---

*See the note on Welsh pronunciation in the introduction to Chapter II.

woman, tell me what I shall ask you, for God's sake. Where are the children of the man who took possession of me by violence?" The hag answered, "He has no children." The queen said, "A sad thing for me, to come to a childless man." The hag said, "There is no need to be sad. It is prophesied he will have an heir, and by you, since he has not had one by another woman. Besides, do not be sorrowful, he has one son."

The good woman went home happy. And she asked her husband, "What reason did you have to hide your children from me?" The king said, "I will not hide him." They sent messengers for the boy, and he came to the court. His stepmother said to him, "It would be good for you to marry, son, and I have a daughter fit for any nobleman in the world." The boy responded, "I am not yet old enough to marry." She said, "I shall lay a destiny on you: that your side will not strike a woman until you win Olwen daughter of Ysbaddaden Chief Giant."

The boy blushed, and love of the girl entered all his limbs, though he had not yet seen her. His father said to him, "Ho, my son, why are you reddening? What's the matter with you?"

"My stepmother has sworn that I shall not have a wife until I take Olwen daughter of Ysbaddaden Chief Giant."

"It's easy for you to do that, son," said his father to him. "Arthur is your first cousin. Go to Arthur so that he can trim your hair, and ask that of him as a gift for you."

The boy went off on a steed with a dapple-grey head. It was four winters old, firm-jointed and shell-hoofed, with a bridle of tubular gold in its mouth. A costly gold saddle was under the boy, and two sharpened silver spears in his hand. A battle-ax was in his hand, from ridge to edge as long as a grown man's forearm. It would draw blood from the wind; it would be swifter than the swiftest dew from the stalk to the ground, when the dew is heaviest in June. A sword with a golden hilt was on his thigh, and its blade was gold. And on him a shield of braided gold having the color of the lightning of heaven in it and an ivory boss. And two greyhounds white of breast dappled, were in front of him, with a collar of red gold about the neck of each one, from the swell of the shoulder to the ear. The one that was on the left side would be on the right, and the one that was on the right side would be on the left, like two sea-swallows playing around him. The four hooves of the steed cut four divots, like four swallows in the air over him, now above him, now under him. A four-cornered purple mantle was on him, with an apple of red gold at each corner; each apple was worth a hundred cattle. There was precious gold worth three hundred cattle in his footgear of shoes and stirrups, from the top of his thigh to the end of his toe. Not a strand of hair on him out of place, so light was the steed's pace under him, heading for the gate of Arthur's court.

The youth said, "Is there a gatekeeper?"

"There is. And you, you may lose your head because you ask. I am gatekeeper for Arthur every first day of January. But my deputies for the rest of the year are none other than Huandaw and Gogigwr and Llaesgymyn and Penpingion, who goes on his head to spare his feet, neither heavenward nor earthward, but like a rolling stone on the floor of the court."

"Open the gate."

"I will not."

"Why won't you open it?"

"Knife has gone into meat and drink into the drinking horn, and there is a thronging in Arthur's hall. No one may enter but the son of a king of legitimate rule or a craftsman who brings his craft. There is mash for your dogs and grain for your horse and hot hearty chops for you, with wine overflowing and delightful songs before you. Food for fifty men awaits you in the guest house; men from afar eat there, and the sons of foreign lands who offer no craft in Arthur's court. It will not be worse for you there than with Arthur in his court. A woman to sleep with you and delightful songs before your two knees. Tomorrow at midmorning, when the gate is opened for the throng that came here today, the gate will be opened for you first, and you will sit in Arthur's hall wherever you choose, from its upper to its lower end."

The youth said, "I will do none of that. If you open the door, it is well. If you do not open it, I will bring shame on your lord and slander on you. And I shall raise three shouts at the door of this gate that will be as loud at the top of Pengwaedd in Cornwall as in the depths of Dinsol in the North and in Esgeir Oerfel in Ireland. And every pregnant woman in this court will miscarry, and for those who are not pregnant, their wombs will become an affliction so that they will never be pregnant from this day on."

Glewlwyd Mighty-grip answered, "Whatever you may shout regarding the laws of Arthur's court, you will not be let in till I go speak to Arthur first."

And Glewlwyd came into the hall. Arthur said to him, "Have you news from the gate?"

"I do. Two-thirds of my life are past, and two-thirds of yours. I was once in Fort Se and Asse, in Sach and Salach, in Lotor and Ffotor. I was once in India the Great and India the Less. I was once in the battle of the two Ynyrs, when the twelve hostages were brought from Llychlyn. And I was once in Europe. I was in Africa, and in the islands of Corsica, and Fort Brythwch and Brythach and Nerthach. I was there when you slew the band of Gleis son of Merin, when you slew Black Mil son of Dugum. I was there when you conquered Greece in the East. I was once in Fort Oeth and Anoeth and Fort Nefenhyr. Nine fair generous rulers we saw there. But I never saw a man so handsome as the one who is now at the door of the gate."

Arthur said, "If you came in walking, go out running. And whoever looks at the light and shuts his eyes, an injunction on him. Let some serve with golden drinking horns and some with hot hearty chops, till there be enough food and drink for him. It's a disgrace to leave in wind and rain such a man as you speak of."

Kei [Cei, Kay] said, "By the hand of my friend, if my counsel were taken, the laws of the court would not be broken for him."

"Not so, good Kei. We are noblemen so long as we are sought after. The greater the reward we give, the greater will be our nobility and our praise and our glory."

And Glewlwyd came to the gate and opened the gate to Culhwch. And Culhwch did not dismount at the gate on the mounting block, as everyone did, but came inside on his steed. Culhwch said, "Hail, chief prince of this island! Greetings to the lower end of this house no less than to the upper! Greetings equally to your lords and your men and your warriors. May none be without a share of the greeting I give you. May your grace be as full as my greeting, and your faith, and your glory in this island!"

"By God's truth, so be it, chieftain! Greetings to you as well! Sit between two of the warriors, with delightful song before you, and the privilege of an heir upon you, a successor to a kingdom, as long as you are here. And when I distribute my goods to guests and men from afar, it shall be with your hand that I shall begin in this court."

The youth said, "I did not come here to seek food and drink. But if I get my gift, I shall give recompense for it and praise it. If I do not get it, I shall deprive you of your renown as far as your fame has reached to the four quarters of the world."

Arthur said, "Though you do not dwell here, chieftain, you shall have the gift your mouth and tongue may name, as far as the wind dries, as far as the rain wets, as far as the sun runs, as far as the sea spreads, as far as there is earth—except for my ship and my mantle, and Caledfwlch [Hard Breach] my sword, and Rhongomyniad [Lance Hewer] my spear, and Wynebgwrthucher [Face of Evening] my shield, and Carnwennan [Bright Hilt] my knife, and Gwenhwyfar [Guinevere] my wife."

"God's truth on that?"

"You shall have it gladly. Name what you will."

"I will. I want my hair trimmed."

"You shall have that." Arthur took a golden comb and scissors with silver handles, and he combed his hair. And he asked who he was; Arthur said, "My heart grows tender towards you. I know you come of my blood. Say who you are."

"I shall: Culhwch son of Cilydd son of Lord Celyddon, by Goleuddydd daughter of Lord Anlawdd, my mother."

Arthur said, "It is true: you are a first cousin to me. Name what you will and you shall have it, whatever your mouth and tongue may name."

"God's truth to me on that? And the truth of your kingdom?"

"You shall have it gladly."

"I ask you to get me Olwen daughter of Ysbaddaden Chief Giant. And I call upon your warriors to confirm this."

The Catalog of Arthur's Companions

To confirm that gift from Arthur he called upon Kei, and Bedwyr [Bedivere], and Greidawl Gallddofydd, and Gwythyr son of Greidawl, and Greid son of Eri, and Cynddyllg the Guide, and Tathal Open-deceit, and Maelwys son of Baeddan, and Cnychwr son of Nes [Conchobar mac Nesa], and Cubert son of Daere, and Fercos son of Poch [Fergus mac Róich], and Lluber Beutach, and Corfil Berfach [Conall Cernach], and Gwyn son of Esni, and Gwyn son of Nwyfre [Firmament], and Gwyn son of Nudd, and Edern son of Nudd, and Cadwy son of Geraint, and Fflewdwr the Flamelord, and Rhuawn the Strong son of Dorath, and Bradwen son of Prince Moren, and Prince Moren himself, and Dalldaf son of Cimin Cof, and the son of Alun of Dyfed, and the son of Saidi, and the son of Gwryon, and Uchdryd Protector in Battle, and Cynwas Cwryfagyl, and Gwrhyr Rich-in-Cattle, and Isberyr Cat-claw, and Gallgoid Gofynynad, and Duach and Brathach and Nerthach, sons of Gwawrddur Cyrfach [Steel-king the Hunchback]—from the uplands of Hell did these men come. And Cilydd Hundred-holds, and Hundred-holds Hundred-hands, and Bog Hundred-claws, and Esgeir Gulhwch the Reed-cutter, and Drust Iron-fist, and Glewlwyd Mighty-grip, and Llwch Stormy-hand, and Restless the Winged, and Sinnoch son of Seventh, and Wadu son of Seventh, and Naw son of Seventh, and Gwenwynwyn son of Naw son of Seventh, and Bedyw son of Seventh, and Gobrwy son of Echel Mighty-thigh, and Echel Mighty-thigh himself. And Prince son of Roycol, and Dadweir the Blind-headed, and Garwyli son of Gwythawg Gwyr, and Gwythawg Gwyr himself. And Excess son of Ricca, and Menw son of Teirgwaedd [Little Son of Three Cries], and Enough son of Too-much, and Selyf [Solomon] son of Sinoid, and Gwsg son of Lineage, and Strength son of Strong, and Brave-lad son of Tryffin, and Boar son of Perif, and Boar son of Restless, and Iona, King of France, and Watch son of Watch-dog. And Teregud son of Iaen, and Sulien son of Iaen, and Bradwen son of Iaen, and Moren son of Iaen, and Siawn son of Iaen, and Cradawg son of Iaen—men of Fort Dathal, kin of Arthur's on their father's side.

Scorn son of Caw, and Iustig son of Caw, and Honor son of Caw, and Angawdd son of Caw, and Smith son of Caw, and Holly son of Caw, and Stalk son of Caw, and Patron-saint son of Caw, and Gwyngad son of Caw, and Path son of Caw, and Red son of Caw, and Meilyg son of Caw, and Cynwal son of Caw, and Protector son of Caw, and Striker son of Caw, and Someone son of Caw, and Gildas son of Caw, and Calcas son of Caw, and Huail son of Caw—he never begged at a lord's hand.

And Samson Dry-lip, and Taliesin Chief of Bards, and Manawydan son of Llŷr, and Llary son of Lord Casnar, and Sberin son of Fflergant king of Brittany, and Saranhon son of Glythwr, and champion son of Acre, and Anynnawg son of Menw son of Teirgwaedd, and Gwyn son of Nwyfre [Firmament], and Flame son of Firmament, and Geraint son of Erbin, and Ermid son of Erbin, and Dywel son of Erbin, and Gwyn son of Ermid, and Cyndrwyn son of Ermid, and Hyfeidd One-cloak, and Eiddon the Magnanimous, and Rheiddwn Arwy, and Excess son of Ricca—a brother to Arthur on his mother's side, his father being the chief elder of Cornwall. And Llawnrodded the Bearded, and Nodawl Cut-beard, and Berth son of Cado, and Rheiddwn son of Beli, and Isgofan the Generous, and Isgawyn son of Banon. And Morfran son of Tegid; no man put his weapon into him at Camlan, he was so ugly; everyone supposed he was a devil assisting; he had hair on him like a stag's hair. And Sandde Angel-face; no man put his spear in him at Camlan, he was so fair; everyone supposed he was an angel assisting. And Saint Cynwyl, one of the three men who escaped from Camlan; he parted last from Arthur, on his horse Hengroen [Old-skin].

And Uchdryd son of Erim, and Eus son of Erim. And Winged Henwas [Old Servant] son of Erim, and Henbeddestyr [Old Walker] son of Erim, and Sgilti Lightfoot son of Erim. Three features had these three men: Henbeddestyr never found a man who ran as fast as he did, on horseback or on foot; Henwas the Winged, no four-footed creature could ever travel alongside him the length of an acre, let alone a distance farther than that; Sgilti Lightfoot, when the impulse was on him to go on his lord's errand, he never took a road, provided he knew where he was going, but if there were trees, he would go on the tops of the trees, and if there was a mountain, he would go on the tips of the reeds, and all his life, not a stalk bent under his feet, much less broke, he was so light.

Teithi Hen [Old Right] son of Gwynnan, whose land the sea overran and who himself just barely escaped and came to Arthur; his knife had this feature, that from the time he came here, the hilt never stayed on it, and because of that, a sickness developed in him and a weakness as long as he lived, and he died of that. And Carneddwr son of Gofynion the Old, and Gwenwynwyn son of Naf, Arthur's first warrior, and Llygadrudd Emys [Red-eye the Stallion], and Gwrfoddw the Old (they were Arthur's uncles, his mother's brothers). Culfanawyd son of Gwryon, and Llenlleawg the Irishman from the headland of Gamon, and Dyfnwal the Bald, and Dunarth the King of the North. Terynon Twryf Liant, and Tegfan the Lame, and Tegyr Talgellawg. Gwrddywal son of Efrei, and Morgant the Generous. Gwystyl son of Nwython, and Rhun son of Nwython, and Llwydeu son of Nwython, and Gwydre son of Llwydeu by Gwenabwy daughter of Caw, his mother (Huail his uncle stabbed him, and for that there was hatred between Arthur and Huail, because of the wound).

Drem son of Dremidydd [Sight son of Seer] who saw from Celliwig in Cornwall as far as Pen Blathaon in Scotland when a fly would rise in the morning with the sun. And Eidoel son of Nêr, and Glwyddyn the Builder, who built Ehangwen [Spacious-fair], Arthur's hall. Cynyr Fair-beard; Kei was said to be son to him, who said to his wife, "If there is something of me in your son, girl, his heart will always be cold, and there will be no warmth in his hands; another feature will he have if he is my son, he will be stubborn; another feature will he have, when he carries a load, great or small, it will never be seen either from in front or from behind; another feature will he have, no one will stand water and fire as well as he, another feature will he have, there will not be a servant or officer like him."

Henwas [Old Lad] and Hen Wyneb [Old Face] and Hen Gedymddeith [Old Companion]. Gallgoig, another one; whatever town he came to, though there were three hundred homesteads there, if he needed anything, he never allowed sleep on a man's eye while he was there. Berwyn son of Cyrenyr, and Paris, King of France (for whom the citadel is called Paris). Osla Big-knife, who carried Bronllafn Ferllydan [Sloping Blade, Short and Wide]; when Arthur and his armies came to the edge of a river, a narrow place was found on the water, and his knife in its sheath was placed across the river, and it would be enough of a bridge for the armies of the Three Realms of Britain and its Three Adjacent Islands and their booty.

Gwyddawg son of Menestyr, who killed Kei (and Arthur killed him and his brothers to avenge Kei). Garanwyn son of Kei, and Amren son of Bedwyr [Bedivere]. And Eli, and Myr, and Rheu Rhwydd Dyrys [Rheu the Generous and Wild], and Rhun Rhuddwern [Red-alder], and Eli, and Trachmyr, Arthur's chief huntsman. And Llwydeu son of Cel Coed, and Huabwy son of Gwryon, and Gwyn Godyfron, and Gweir Dathar the Attendant, and Gweir son of Cadellin the Pay-master. And Gweir Treacherous-valor, and Gweir Bright-shaft (uncles of Arthur, his mother's brothers).

The sons of Llwch Stormy-hand from beyond the Tyrrhenian Sea. Llenlleawg the Irishman, and Ardderchawg [the Excellent One] of Britain. Cas [Enmity] son of Saidi, Gwrfan Rough-hair, Gwilenhin the King of France, Gwitard son of Aedd the King of Ireland, Garselid the Irishman, Panawr the Chief of the Host, Atlendor son of Naf, Gwyn Hywar the overseer of Cornwall and Devon, one of the nine who plotted the battle of Camlan. Celi, and Cuel, and Gilla Stag-leg (he would leap three hundred acres in one bound, the chief leaper of Ireland).

Sol, and Gwadyn Osol, and Gwadyn Oddeith [Blazing Sole]. Sol could stand all day on one foot. If Gwadyn Osol stood on top of the greatest mountain in the world, it would become a level plain under his foot. When something hard met Gwadyn Oddeith, the bright fire of his soles was like the hot metal when it is drawn from the forge; he cleared the way for Arthur in battle.

Tall Erwm and Tall Atrwm. The day they came to a feast, they would seize three districts for themselves, feasting till noon and drinking till night. When they went to sleep, they would consume the heads of insects from hunger, as if they had not eaten food before. When they went to a feast, they left neither fat nor lean, neither hot nor cold, neither sour nor sweet, neither fresh nor salt, neither boiled nor raw.

Huarwar son of Halwn, who, as his reward, asked Arthur for his fill. He was one of the three great plagues of Cornwall and Devon when they got him his fill. Not a faint smile was found on him except when he was full.

Gwarae Golden-hair. The two whelps of the bitch Rhymhi. Gwyddrud and Gwydden the Obscure. Sugyn son of Sugnedydd [Suck son of Sucker], who would suck up the sea on which there were three hundred ships till there was nothing but dry beach; he had red breast-fever. Cacamwri, Arthur's servant; let him be shown a barn, though the harvest of thirty plows were in it, he would strike it with an iron flail till it was no better for the planks and the cross-beams and the side-beams than for the small oats in the bin on the floor of the barn.

Llwng [Damp], and Dygyflwng, and Anoeth the Bold. And Tall Eiddyl and Tall Amren (they were two servants of Arthur). And Gwefyl son of Gwastad [Lip son of Constant]; the day he was sad, he would let one of his lips down to his navel and the other would be a hood upon his head.

Uchdryd Cross-beard, who would cast his projecting red beard across fifty rafters in Arthur's hall. Elidyr the Guide. Ysgyrdaf and Ysgudydd; they were servants of Gwenhwyfar [Guinevere]; on their errand, their feet were as swift as their thoughts. Brys son of Brysethach, from the Hill of the Black Fernbrake in Britain. And Gruddlwyn Gor [Cheek-bush the Dwarf].

Bwlch [Breach] and Cyfwlch [Perfect] and Sefwlch, sons of Cleddyf Cyfwlch [Perfect Sword], grandsons of Cleddyf Difwlch [Unbroken Sword]. Their three shields were three brilliant gleams; their three spears were three pointed thrusts; their three swords were three sharp carvers. Glas [Blue], Glesig, Gleisad, their three dogs. Call [Prudent], Cuall [Sudden], Cafall [Steed], their three horses. Hwyrddyddwg [Late-bearer] and Drwgddyddwg [Ill-bearer] and Llwyrddyddwg [Full-bearer], their three wives. Och [Oh] and Garym [Cry] and Diasbad [Shriek], their three grandchildren. Lluched [Plague] and Neued [Want] and Eisywed [Need], their three daughters. Drwg [Bad] and Gwaeth [Worse] and Gwaethaf Oll [Worst of All], their three maidservants.

Eheubryd son of Cyfwlch, Gorasgwrn son of Nerth [Bigbone son of Strength], Gwaeddan son of Cynfelyn Ceudod, Pwyll Half-man.

Dwn the High-spirited Chieftain. Eiladar son of Pen Llarcan, Cynedyr the Wild son of Hetwn Silver Brow, Sawyl High Head, Gwalchmai [Gawain] son of Gwyar, Gwalhafed son of Gwyar. Gwrhyr the Interpreter of Languages, who knew all languages. And Cethtrwm the Priest.

Clust son of Clustfeinad [Ear son of Hearer], if he were buried seven fathoms in the earth, he would hear an ant fifty miles away when it rose from its couch in the morning. Medyr son of Medredydd [Skill son of Hitter], who from Celliwig would hit a wren on Esgeir Oerfel in Ireland precisely through its two legs. Gwiawn Cat-eye, who would cut a corner [of a lid] on the eye of a gnat without harm to the eye. Ôl son of Olwydd [Track son of Tracker]; seven years before he was born, his father's pigs were stolen, and when he grew to be a man, he tracked the pigs and came home with them in seven herds. Bidwini [Baudwin] the Bishop, who blessed Arthur's food and drink.

The gentle, gold-torqued maidens of this island. Besides Gwenhwyfar [Guinevere], the first lady of this island, and her sister, Gwenhwyach, and Rathtyen, the only daughter of Clememyl, Celemon daughter of Kei, and Tangwen daughter of Gweir Dathar, the Attendant. Gwen Alarch [White Swan] daughter of Cynwal Hundred-pigs, Eurneid daughter of Clydno Eidin, Eneuawg daughter of Bedwyr [Bedivere]. Enrhydreg daughter of Tuduathar, Gwenwledyr daughter of Gwaredur the Hunchback, Erdudfyl daughter of Tryffin, Eurolwyn daughter of Gwyddolwyn the Dwarf. Teleri daughter of Peul, Indeg daughter of Garwy the Tall. Morfudd daughter of Urien of Rheged. Beautiful Gwenlliant the Great-hearted Maiden. Creiddylad daughter of Lludd Silver-hand, the girl of most grandeur who ever lived in the three realms of Britain and its three adjacent islands, and for her Gwythyr son of Greidawl and Gwyn son of Nudd fight every May Day till Doomsday. Ellylw daughter of Neol Cyncrog (she lived for three generations). Essyllt [Isolde] Fair-neck and Essyllt Slender-neck.

In the name of all these did Culhwch son of Cilydd implore his gift.

The Quest for Olwen

Arthur said, "Ah, chieftain, I have never heard of the maiden you speak of, nor of her parents. I shall gladly send messengers to find her. Give me time to find her." The youth said, "Gladly. From this night till the same night next year."

And then Arthur sent messengers to every land in his domain to find the maiden. From that night till the same night a year later the messengers went wandering. By the end of the year Arthur's messengers had found nothing. And then Culhwch said, "Everyone has received his gift, but I am still without one. I shall leave and take your honor with me."

Kei said, "Ah, chieftain, you scorn Arthur too much. Come with us; till you say she is nowhere in the world or till we find her, we shall not part from you." Then Kei stood up. Kei had this feature, that for nine nights and nine days he would hold his breath under water. For nine nights and nine days he would go without sleep. A sword stroke of Kei's no physician could heal. Well endowed was Kei: he would be as tall as the highest tree in the wood when it pleased him. Another feature he had: his natural heat was so great that when it rained hardest, whatever was in his hand would be dry a handsbreadth above and below his hand. And when it was coldest for his companions, that heat would be kindling for them to light a fire.

Arthur called on Bedwyr [Bedivere], who never feared a quest on which Kei would go. It was true of Bedwyr that no one in this island was as handsome as he, except Arthur and Drych son of Cibddar [Mirror son of Cuplord]. And this too, that though he were one-handed, three warriors would not draw blood faster than he in the same field with him. Another feature he had, that there would be one thrust of his spear to nine counterthrusts.

Arthur called on Cynddylig the Guide, "Go on this quest for me with the chieftain." He was no less able a guide in a land he had never seen than in his own land. He called Gwrhyr, Interpreter of Languages, who knew all languages. He called Gwalchmai [Gawain] the son of Gwyar, because he never came home without the quest he had gone seeking. He was the best on foot and the best on horseback. He was Arthur's nephew, his sister's son, and his first cousin. Arthur called on Menw son of Teirgwaedd, because if they came to a heathen land, he could cast a spell on them so that no one would see them, but they would see everybody.

They went off till they came to a great open plain. There they saw a fort that was the greatest fort in the world. They walked that day. When they thought they were near to the fort, they were no nearer than before. And the second and the third day they walked. And they barely came there. But when they came to the same field as the fort, they saw a great flock of sheep there without limit or end to it, and a shepherd on top of a mound tending the sheep. He had a cloak of skins on him and at his side a furry mastiff larger than a stallion of nine winters. It was his custom that he never lost a lamb, much less a grown animal. No company had ever gone past him that he had not done them injury or death. His breath would burn every dead tree and bush on the field right to the ground.

Kei said, "Gwrhyr, Interpreter of Languages, go talk to that man there."

"Kei, I promised to go only as far as you would go too."

"Let us go together."

Menw the son of Teirgwaedd said, "Do not be afraid to go there. I will cast a spell on the dog so that he will not hurt anyone."

They came to where the shepherd was. And they said to him, "You are well off, shepherd."

"May it never be better for you than for me."

"By God, yes, for you are a chief!"

"There is no harm can damage me but for my wife."

"Whose are the sheep you are tending, and who owns the fort there?"

"Slow-witted men that you are. It is known throughout the world that it is the fort of Ysbaddaden Chief Giant."

"And you, who are you?"

"Custennin son of Mynwyedig am I. And because of my wife, my brother Ysbaddaden Chief Giant did me damage. And you, who are you?"

"Messengers of Arthur are here, seeking Olwen."

"Ah, men! God help you! For all the world, do not do it! No one has come seeking that who went away with his life."

The shepherd stood up; and as he got up, Culhwch gave him a golden ring. The shepherd tried to wear the ring, but it would not go on him. And he put it on the finger of his glove and went home and gave the glove to his wife.

She took the ring from the glove. "From where did this ring come to you, husband?" she said. "It is not often that you have treasure."

"I went to the sea to find sea-food, and look! I saw a dead body coming in with the waves. I never saw a dead body as beautiful as that. And on its finger I found this ring."

"Alas, husband, the sea does not leave the dead in it beautiful. Show me that body."

"Wife, he whose body it is you will soon see here!"

"Who is he?" said his wife.

"Culhwch son of Cilydd son of Lord Celyddon, by Goleuddydd daughter of Lord Anlawdd, his mother; he has come to seek Olwen."

Two feelings were hers: joy that her nephew, her sister's son, was coming to her; and sorrow because she had never seen anyone go away with his life who had come on that quest.

They came to the gate of the court of the shepherd Custennin. She heard the sound of their coming. She ran to meet them joyfully. Kei took a log from the woodpile. And she came to meet them, to try to put her hands around their necks. Kei put the stake between her two hands. She squeezed the stake till it became a twisted twig. Kei said, "Woman, if you had squeezed me like that, no one else would ever need to love me. That's a bad love!"

They came to the house, and they were attended. After a while, when they all went thronging, the woman opened a stone chest that was in front of the chimney, and a lad with curly yellow hair rose from it. Gwrhyr said, "It would be a pity to hide a lad like this. I know it is for no fault of his that he is punished."

The woman said, "He is the remnant. Ysbaddaden Chief Giant has slain twenty-three of my sons, and I have no more hope of this one than of the others."

Kei said, "Let him keep company with me, and we shall not be slain except together."

They ate. The woman said, "What have you come here for?"

"We come to seek Olwen."

"For God's sake, since no one from the fort has seen you yet, turn back!"

"God knows we shall not turn back till we see the girl. Will she come where she may be seen?"

"She comes here every Saturday to wash her head. And in the basin where she washes, she leaves all her rings, and neither she nor her messenger ever comes for them."

"Will she come here if she is sent for?"

"God knows I will not kill my own dear soul! I will not trap one who trusts me. But if you pledge to do her no injury, I will send for her."

"We give our word," they said.

She was sent for. And she came, with a robe of flame-red silk about her and a torque of red gold around the girl's neck, and precious pearls on it and red gems. Her hair was yellower than the flowers of the broom. Her flesh was whiter than the foam of the wave. Her palms and her fingers were whiter than buds of sweet clover amid the fine gravel of a welling spring. Not the eye of the mewed hawk, not the eye of the thrice-mewed falcon, not any eye was lovelier than hers was. Her two breasts were whiter than the breast of the white swan; redder were her two cheeks than the reddest foxgloves. Whoever saw her would be filled with love for her. Four white clovers would grow up behind her wherever she went. And because of that, she was called Olwen [White-track].

She entered the house and sat beside Culhwch on the front bench, and as soon as he saw her, he recognized her. Culhwch said to her, "Ah, girl, it is you that I have loved. Come with me."

"I cannot do that, for sin would be charged to you and to me. My father has asked me to pledge not to leave without his counsel, because there is life for him only until I go off with a husband. But I'll give you advice, if you will take it. Go ask my father for me. And however much he may ask of you, promise to get it. And you shall win me. But if he doubts a thing, you will not win me, and it will be well for you if you escape with your life."

"I promise all that, and I shall get it."

She went to her chamber. They got up to follow her to the fort. And they killed nine gatekeepers who were at nine gates, without a man crying out, and nine mastiffs without one of them squealing. And they went on to the hall. They said, "Greetings to you, Ysbaddaden Chief Giant, from God and man!"

"And you, where are you going?"

"We come to seek your daughter Olwen for Culhwch son of Cilydd."

"Where are my worthless servants and my louts?" he said. "Raise the forks under my two eyelids so that I can see my intended son-in-law." That was done. "Come here tomorrow. I will give you some answer."

They arose, and Ysbaddaden Chief Giant seized one of the three poisoned stone spears that were at his hand and threw it after them. And Bedwyr caught it and threw it back and pierced Ysbaddaden Chief Giant squarely through the kneecap. Said the giant, "Cursed savage son-in-law! I shall walk the worse on a slope. The poisoned iron has hurt me like a gadfly's sting. Cursed be the smith who made it and the anvil he made it on, it is so sore!"

They lodged that night in the house of Custennin. On the next day they came to the hall with majesty and with fine combs fixed in their hair. They said, "Ysbaddaden Chief Giant, give us your daughter in exchange for her dowry and her marriage fee to you and her two kinswomen. And unless you give her, you will meet your death because of her."

"She and her four great-grandmothers and her four great-grandfathers are still alive. I have to confer with them."

"You will do that," they said. "Let us go to our food." As they got up, he took the second stone spear that was at his hand and threw it after them. And

Menw the son of Teirgwaedd caught it and threw it back and pierced him in the middle of the breast, so that it came out in the small of the back.

"Cursed savage son-in-law! The hard iron has hurt me like the bite of a many-mouthed leech. Cursed be the forge where it was heated. When I go up a hill, there will be tightness in the chest for me and stomach ache and frequent queasiness."

They went to their food. And on the third day they came to the court. They said, "Ysbaddaden Chief Giant, do not shoot at us any more. Do not seek harm for yourself and mortal injury and death."

"Where are my servants? Raise the forks—my eyelids have fallen over the balls of my eyes—so that I can look at my intended son-in-law."

They got up. And as they got up, he took the third poisoned stone spear and threw it after them. And Culhwch caught it. And he threw it back just as he wanted to and pierced him through the eyeball so that it came out at the nape of the neck.

"Cursed savage son-in-law! So long as I am left alive, the sight of my eyes will be the worse. When I go against the wind, they will water. There will be headache and dizziness for me at every new moon. Cursed be the forge where it was heated! The poisoned iron has pierced me like the bite of a mad dog."

They went to their food. The next day they came to the court. They said, "Do not shoot at us, nor seek the deadly injury and harm and martyrdom that are upon you—and what might be worse, if you keep after it. Give us your daughter."

"Where is he who is said to be seeking my daughter?"

"It is I who seek her, Culhwch son of Cilydd."

"Come here where I may see you." A chair was placed under him, facing him. Ysbaddaden Chief Giant said, "Is it you who seek my daughter?"

"It is I who seek her."

"I want your pledge that you will not do me less than justice."

"You have my pledge."

"When I have got what I shall name to you, you will get my daughter."

"Name what you will."

"I will. Do you see that great brushwood there?"

"I do."

"I want it uprooted from the earth and burnt on the ground so that the char and its ashes will be fertilizer for it. And I want it plowed and sown so that by morning when the dew dries, it will be ripe, and from it, food and drink may be made for your wedding guests and the girl's. And I want all this done in one day."

"It's easy for me to manage that, though you think it's not easy."

"Though you manage that, there's something you won't get: a farmer to farm that land. And no one can do it but Amaethon son of Dôn. He won't come with you freely, and you can't force him."

"It's easy for me to manage that, though you think it's not easy."

"Though you manage that, there's something you won't get: Gofannon son of Dôn to come to the top of the field to tend the iron blades. He won't work freely except for a legitimate king; you can't force him."

"It's easy for me to manage that, though you think it's not easy."

"Though you manage that, there's something you won't get: the two oxen of Gwlwlydd Wineu, yoked together to plow that hard land well. He won't give them freely, and you can't force him."

"It's easy for me to manage that, though you think it's not easy."

"Though you manage that, there's something you won't get: I want the Yellow-white and the Speckled Ox yoked together."

"It's easy for me to manage that, though you think it's not easy."

"Though you manage that, there's something you won't get: the two horned oxen, one from the farther side of Mynydd Bannawg [the Horned Mountain], and the other from this side; and to drive them together after the same plow. They are Nyniaw and Peibiaw, whom God turned into oxen for their sins."

"It's easy for me to manage that, though you think it's not easy."

"Though you manage that, there's something you won't get: do you see that red tilled ground there?"

"Yes."

"When I first met the girl's mother, nine hestors [eighteen bushels] of flaxseed were sown there; neither black nor white has come from it yet. And I still have that measure. I want it sown in the new ground, so that it may become a white linen veil for my daughter's head at your wedding-feast."

"It's easy for me to manage that, though you think it's not easy."

"Though you manage that, there's something you won't get: honey nine times sweeter than the honey of the first swarm, without drone or bees, to make bragget for the feast."

"It's easy for me to manage that, though you think it's not easy."

"Though you manage that, there's something you won't get: the cup of Llwyr son of Llwyrion, that has the best drinks in it. For there's no vessel in the world except it that can hold that strong drink. You won't get it from him freely, and you can't force him."

"It's easy for me to manage that, though you think it's not easy."

"Though you manage that, there's something you won't get: the basket of Gwyddneu Garanhir. If the world, three times nine men at a time, came around it, everyone would get from it the food he wanted, as he liked it. I'd like to eat from it the night my daughter sleeps with you. He won't give it freely to anyone, and you can't force him."

"It's easy for me to manage that, though you think it's not easy."

"Though you manage that, there's something you won't get: the drinking horn of Gwlgawd Gododdin, for pouring for us that night. He won't give it freely, and you can't force him."

"It's easy for me to manage that, though you think it's not easy."

"Though you manage that, there's something you won't get: the harp of Teirtu to entertain me that night. When a man pleases, it plays itself; when wished, it is silent. He will not give it freely, and you can't force him."

"It's easy for me to manage that, though you think it's not easy."

"Though you manage that, there's something you won't get: the birds of Rhiannon, that waken the dead and put the living to sleep; these I would have entertain me that night."

"It's easy for me to manage that, though you think it's not easy."

"Though you manage that, there's something you won't get: the cauldron of Diwrnach the Irishman, the Steward of Odgar son of Aedd, King of Ireland, to boil the meat for your wedding guests."

"It's easy for me to manage that, though you think it's not easy."

"Though you manage that, there's something you won't get: I have to wash my head and shave my beard. I want the tusk of Ysgithyrwyn Chief Boar for shaving me. It won't do me any good unless it's pulled from his head alive."

"It's easy for me to manage that, though you think it's not easy."

"Though you manage that, there's something you won't get: no one in the world can pull it from his head but Odgar son of Aedd, King of Ireland."

"It's easy for me to manage that, though you think it's not easy."

"Though you manage that, there's something you won't get: I don't trust anyone to keep the tusk but Cadw [Caw] of Pictland. The sixty districts of Pictland are subject to him. He won't come freely from his kingdom, and he can't be forced."

"It's easy for me to manage that, though you think it's not easy."

"Though you manage that, there's something you won't get: I have to stretch out my hairs to shave myself. I'll never stretch them out unless we get the blood of the Dark Black Witch, daughter of the Pale White Witch, from the head of the Valley of Sorrow in the uplands of Hell."

"It's easy for me to manage that, though you think it's not easy."

"Though you manage that, there's something you won't get: I can't benefit from the blood unless we get it warm. There's no vessel in the world that keeps the warmth of a liquid put inside it except the bottles of Gwyddolwyn the Dwarf that keep the warmth in them from when liquid is put inside them in the east till they are carried to the west. He won't give them freely, and you can't force him."

"It's easy for me to manage that, though you think it's not easy."

"Though you manage that, there's something you won't get: some may desire milk. There's no way to get milk for everybody till we get the bottles of Rhynnon Rough-beard. No liquid ever goes sour in them. He won't give them freely to anyone, and he can't be forced."

"It's easy for me to manage that, though you think it's not easy."

"Though you manage that, there's something you won't get: no comb and scissors are in the world by which to dress my hair, it's so rough, except the comb and scissors that are between the two ears of the boar Twrch Trwyth son of Lord Taredd. He won't give them freely, and he can't be forced."

"It's easy for me to manage that, though you think it's not easy."

"Though you manage that, there's something you won't get: Twrch Trwyth can't be hunted till you catch Drudwyn the young dog of Greid son of Eri."

"It's easy for me to manage that, though you think it's not easy."

"Though you manage that, there's something you won't get: there's no leash in the world that will hold him except the leash of Bog Hundred-claws."

"It's easy for me to manage that, though you think it's not easy."

"Though you manage that, there's something you won't get: there's no collar in the world that will hold the leash except the collar of Hundred-holds Hundred-hands."

"It's easy for me to manage that, though you think it's not easy."

"Though you manage that, there's something you won't get: the chain of Cilydd Hundred-holds to hold the collar and the leash together."

"It's easy for me to manage that, though you think it's not easy."

"Though you manage that, there's something you won't get: no hunts-man in the world is capable of hunting with that dog except Mabon son of Modron, who was taken from his mother when he was three nights old. It's not known where he is, nor in what condition, whether alive or dead."

"It's easy for me to manage that, though you think it's not easy."

"Though you manage that, there's something you won't get: White Dun-mane, the horse of Gweddw, swift as a wave is he, to be under Mabon for hunting Twrch Trwyth. He won't give him freely, and you can't force him."

"It's easy for me to manage that, though you think it's not easy."

"Though you manage that, there's something you won't get: Mabon will never be found nor will it be known where he is until you find Eidoel son of Aer, his foremost kinsman, for he will be unrelenting in searching for him. He is his first cousin."

"It's easy for me to manage that, though you think it's not easy."

"Though you manage that, there's something you won't get: Garselid the Irishman. He is the chief huntsman of Ireland. Twrch Trwyth will never be hunted without him."

"It's easy for me to manage that, though you think it's not easy."

"Though you manage that, there's something you won't get: a leash from the beard of Dillus the Bearded, because there's nothing else that can hold those two young dogs [the two whelps of the bitch Rhymhi; an omitted request?]. And you can't use it unless it's pulled from his beard while he's alive and plucked with wooden tweezers. He won't let anyone do that to him while he's alive, and it's useless dead, because it'll be brittle."

"It's easy for me to manage that, though you think it's not easy."

"Though you manage that, there's something you won't get: no huntsman in the world can hold those two young dogs except Cynedyr the Wild, son of Hetwn the Leper. He's nine times wilder than the wildest wild animal on the mountain. You'll never get him, and you'll never get my daughter."

"It's easy for me to manage that, though you think it's not easy."

"Though you manage that, there's something you won't get: you won't hunt Twrch Trwyth until you get Gwyn son of Nudd, in whom God has put the spirit of the demons of Annwn [the Welsh Otherworld], lest this world be ruined. They won't get along without him there."

"It's easy for me to manage that, though you think it's not easy."

"Though you manage that, there's something you won't get: no horse will be of use to Gwyn to hunt Twrch Trwyth except Black, the horse of Moro Oerfeddawg."

"It's easy for me to manage that, though you think it's not easy."

"Though you manage that, there's something you won't get: until Gwilenhin, the King of France, comes, Twrch Trwyth will not be hunted without him. It displeases him to leave his kingdom, and he will never come here."

"It's easy for me to manage that, though you think it's not easy."

"Though you manage that, there's something you won't get: Twrch Trwyth will never be hunted without getting the son of Alun of Dyfed. He's a good one for unleashing the dogs."

"It's easy for me to manage that, though you think it's not easy."

"Though you manage that, there's something you won't get: Twrch Trwyth will never be hunted till you get Aned and Aethlem. They would be swift as a gust of wind. They were never unleashed on a beast that they did not kill."

"It's easy for me to manage that, though you think it's not easy."

"Though you manage that, there's something you won't get: Arthur and his huntsmen to hunt Twrch Trwyth. He is a powerful man, but he will not come with you. The reason is that he is subject to my authority."

"It's easy for me to manage that, though you think it's not easy."

"Though you manage that, there's something you won't get: Twrch Trwyth can never be hunted until you get Bwlch and Cyfwlch and Sefwlch, sons of Cilydd Cyfwlch, grandsons of Cleddyf Difwlch. Their three shields are three brilliant gleams. Their three spears are three pointed thrusts. Their three swords are three sharp carvers. Their three dogs are Glas, Glesig, and Gleisad. Their three horses are Call, Cuall, and Cafall. Their three wives are Hwyrddyddwg and Drwgddyddwg and Llwyrddyddwg. Their three witches are Oh and Cry and Shriek. Their three daughters are Plague and Want and Need. Their three maidservants are Bad and Worse and Worst of All. The three men will sound their battle-horns, and all the others will come to make battle-cry, until no one would be concerned if the sky fell to the earth."

"It's easy for me to manage that, though you think it's not easy."

"Though you manage that, there's something you won't get: the sword of Wrnach the Giant. Twrch Trwyth can never be slain except with that. He will not give it to anyone, neither for a price nor as a favor, and you can't force him."

"It's easy for me to manage that, though you think it's not easy."

"Though you manage that, there's something you won't get. You will get sleeplessness at night seeking these things. But you will not get them, and you will not get my daughter."

"I shall have horses and horsemen, and my lord and kinsman Arthur shall get me all those things. And I shall win your daughter. And you will lose your life."

"Go now. You are not responsible for food or clothing for my daughter. Seek those things, and when they are won, you shall win my daughter too."

The Expeditions of Arthur's Men: Wrnach's Sword

That day they went forth until evening, till there appeared a fort of stone and mortar, the greatest fort in the world. With amazement they saw a dark man coming from the fort who was larger than three of this world's men. They said to him, "Where is it you come from, man?"

"From the fort that you see there."

"Who owns the fort?"

"Slow-witted men that you are, there's no one in the world who doesn't know who owns this fort. Wrnach the Giant owns it."

"What courtesy is there for a guest and a man from afar stopping at this?"

"Ah, chieftain, God help you! No guest has ever come out of there with his life. No one gets in there except one who brings his craft."

They went to the gate. Gwrhyr, the Interpreter of Languages, said, "Is there a gatekeeper?"

"There is. And you, you may lose your head because you ask."

"Open the gate."

"I will not."

"Why won't you open it?"

"Knife has gone into meat and drink into the drinking horn, and there is a thronging in Wrnach's hall. Except for a craftsman who brings his craft, the gate is not opened."

Kei said, "Gatekeeper, I have a craft."

"What craft do you have?"

"I am the best burnisher of swords in the world."

"I will go tell that to Wrnach the Giant and bring an answer to you."

The gatekeeper came inside. Wrnach the Giant said, "Have you news from the gate?"

"I do. There is a company at the door of the gate who want to come in."

"And have you asked whether they have a craft?"

"Yes. And one of them said that he can burnish swords."

"That one I have needed. For some time I've been looking for someone to polish my sword, and I haven't found him. Let that one in, since he has a craft."

The gatekeeper came and opened the gate, and Kei came inside alone. And he greeted Wrnach the Giant. A chair was set under him. Wrnach the Giant said, "Is it true what is said of you, that you can burnish swords?"

"I can." The sword was brought to him. Kei took a mottled whetstone from under his arm. "Which do you prefer on it, a white hilt or a dark hilt?"

"Whatever you would prefer if it were your own that you were working on."

He polished one half of the blade for him and put it in his hand. "Does that suit you?"

"More than anything in my land, I wish all of it were like this. It's unfortunate that a man as good as you has no companion."

"Very well, sir, I have a companion, though he doesn't follow this craft."

"Who is he?"

"Let the gatekeeper go out, and I'll tell his special features. The head of his spear will leave its shaft and draw blood from the wind and come down again on the shaft." The gate was opened, and Bedwyr came in. Kei said, "Bedwyr is proficient, though he can't practice this craft."

And there was great talk among the men outside, of Kei and Bedwyr coming inside. And a young lad came inside with them, the only son of Custennin the Shepherd. What he and his companions with him did, as if it were nothing for them, was to go across the three courtyards till they came inside the fort. His companions said to the son of Custennin, "You did it! You're the best man!" From then on, he was called Goreu [Best] son of Custennin. They went separately to their lodgings, to manage to kill their lodgekeepers without the giant knowing.

The polishing of the sword was finished, and Kei put it in the hand of Wrnach the Giant, as if to inspect whether the work satisfied him. The giant said, "The work is good, and I am satisfied." Kei said, "Your sheath has spoiled your sword. Give it to me to remove the wooden side-pieces from it, and I can make new ones for it." And he took the sheath, with the sword in his other hand. He came above the giant as if to put the sword in its sheath. He drove it into the giant's head, and the blow cut his head off. They laid waste to the fort and made off with what treasures they wanted. On that very day a year later they came to Arthur's court, with the sword of Wrnach the Giant.

The Oldest Animals and the Freeing of Mabon

They told Arthur what had happened to them. Arthur said, "What's best of those rare and difficult things for us to seek first?"

They said, "It's best to search for Mabon son of Modron, but we can't find him till we first find Eidoel son of Aer, his kinsman."

Arthur rose up, and the warriors of the Island of Britain with him, to go to seek Eidoel. And they came to the outer fortress of Glivi, where Eidoel was in prison. Glivi stood on the rampart of the fort and said, "Arthur, what do you want of me, that you do not leave me alone on this rocky hill? I have no wealth here and nothing pleasant, neither wheat nor oats do I have, even if you were not trying to do me damage."

Arthur said, "I have not come here to harm you, but to seek a prisoner of yours."

"I shall give you the prisoner, though I hadn't planned to give him to anyone. And with that, you shall have my strength and my support."

The men said to Arthur, "Lord, go home. You cannot go with your army to seek things as slight as these."

Arthur said, "Gwrhyr, Interpreter of Languages, it is right for you to go on this quest. You have all languages, and you share language with some of the birds and animals. Eidoel, it is right for you to go searching with my men; he is your first cousin. Kei and Bedwyr, I hope you will achieve the quest on which you go. Go on this quest for me."

They went till they came to the Blackbird of Cilgwri. Gwrhyr asked her, "In God's name, do you know anything of Mabon son of Modron, who was taken when three nights old from between his mother and the wall?"

The Blackbird said, "When I first came here, a smith's anvil was here, and I was a young bird. No work has been done on it except when my beak was at it every evening. Today there is no more of it than the size of a nut that is not worn away. God's revenge on me if I have heard anything about the man you ask for. But what is right and fitting for me to do for Arthur's messengers, I shall do. There is a species of animal that God made before me; I shall go as your guide there."

They came to where the Stag of Rhedynfre was. "Stag of Rhedynfre, we have come to you here as Arthur's messengers, because we know no animal older than you. Tell us whatever you may know about Mabon son of Modron, who was taken from his mother when three nights old."

The Stag said, "When I came here first, there was only one antler on either side of my head, and there were no trees here except one oak sapling. And that grew into an oak with a hundred branches, and afterward the oak fell, and today there is nothing but a red stump of it. From then till today I have been here, and I have heard nothing of the person you ask for. But since you are Arthur's messengers, I will be your guide to where there is an animal God made before me."

They came to where the Owl of Cwm Cawlwyd was. "Owl of Cwm Cawlwyd, here are messengers of Arthur. Do you know anything about Mabon son of Modron, who was taken from his mother when three nights old?"

"If I knew anything, I'd tell it. When I first came here, the great valley you see was a wooded glen. And a race of men came to it, and it was laid waste, and a second wood grew there. And this is the third wood. And as for me, my wings are mere stumps. From then till today I haven't heard anything about the man you ask for. But I will be a guide for Arthur's messengers, till you come to where there is the oldest animal in this world and the most traveled, the Eagle of Gwernabwy."

Gwrhyr said, "Eagle of Gwernabwy, we have come as messengers of Arthur to you, to ask you whether you know anything about Mabon son of Modron, who was taken from his mother when three nights old."

The Eagle said, "I came here a long time ago, and when I first came here I had a stone, and from its top I could peck at the stars every night. Now it is only a fist high. From then till today I have been here, and I have not heard anything about the man you ask for. But on one expedition I went looking for my food to Llyn Llyw. And when I came there, I dug my claws into a salmon, supposing he would be my food for a long time. And he pulled me into the depths till it was hard for me to get free of him. What I and all my family did was to go and attack him, and try to destroy him. He sent messengers to come to terms with me. And he himself came to me, to have fifty harpoons removed from his back. Unless he knows something of what you are after, I know of none who may. But I will be your guide to where he is."

They came to where he was. The Eagle said, "Salmon of Llyn Llyw, I have come to you with Arthur's messengers, to ask whether you know anything about Mabon son of Modron, who was taken from his mother when three nights old."

"I'll tell as much as I know. With every tide I go up along the river till I come beside the wall of Caer Loyw [Gloucester]. And there I found such grief as I never found before. In order that you may believe it, one of you should come on my two shoulders here."

And it was Kei and Gwrhyr, Interpreter of Languages, who went on the two shoulders of the Salmon. And they advanced till they came to the wall where the prisoner was. There was wailing and grieving that they could hear on the other side of the wall. Gwrhyr said, "What man mourns in this stone house?"

"Ah, man, there is cause for the one here to be sad. Mabon son of Modron is here in prison. And no man was so painfully imprisoned in such a prison as I, not the prison of Lludd Silver-hand nor that of Greid son of Eri."

"Have you hope of getting free, either for gold or silver or worldly wealth, or by battle or by fighting?"

"Whatever is had of me will be won by fighting."

They returned from there and came to where Arthur was. They told where Mabon son of Modron was in prison. Arthur summoned the warriors of this island and went to Caer Loyw, where Mabon was in prison. Kei and Bedwyr went on the two shoulders of the fish. While Arthur's warriors attacked the fort, Kei broke open the wall and took the prisoner on his back, fighting on with the men as before. And Arthur came home and Mabon came with him, free.

Dillus the Bearded and Other Quests

Arthur said, "Now what's best of the rare and difficult things for us to seek first?"

"The best is to seek the two young dogs of the Bitch of Rhymhi."

Arthur said, "Is it known where she is?"

One said, "She is at Aber Deu Gleddyf [the estuary at Milford Haven]."

Arthur came to the house of Tringad at Aber Cleddyf, and he asked "Have you heard of her here? What does she look like?"

He said, "She looks like a she-wolf. And she goes about with her two young dogs. She has often killed my livestock. And she's down in Aber Cleddyf in a cave."

Arthur put to sea in his ship Prydwen, and the others went on land to hunt the bitch, and so they surrounded her and her two young dogs. And for Arthur's sake, God transformed them back to their own shape. Arthur's army dispersed one by one, two by two.

And while Gwythyr son of Greidawl was walking one day over a mountain, he heard crying and sad groaning, and it was a fearful sound to hear. And he hurried in that direction. And when he came there, he drew his sword and cut down an anthill to the ground and thus saved the ants from fire. And they said to him, "Take God's blessing and ours with you. What no man can ever recover, we will come to recover for you." Afterward they came with the eighteen bushels of flaxseed that Ysbaddaden Chief Giant had named to Culhwch, in full measure, without anything missing from it, except one flaxseed. And the lame ant brought that one before night.

When Kei and Bedwyr were sitting atop Mount Pumlumon, on Carn Gwylathyr, in the greatest wind in the world, they looked around them and saw a great smoke to the south, far away from them, not crossing over with the wind. And then Kei said, "By the hand of my friend, look there, the fire of a hero!" They hurried toward the smoke and came near and watched from a distance as Dillus the Bearded singed a wild boar. Yet he was the greatest hero who ever kept free of Arthur. Bedwyr said to Kei, "Do you know him?"

"I know him," said Kei. " That's Dillus the Bearded. There's no leash in the world that can hold Drudwyn, the young dog of Greid son of Eri, except a leash from the beard of the fellow you see there. And it's no good unless it's pulled live from his beard with wooden tweezers, because it will be brittle if it's dead."

"What's our plan for that?" said Bedwyr.

Kei said, "We'll let him eat his fill of meat, and after that, he'll go to sleep." While Dillus did that, they made wooden tweezers. When Kei knew for sure that he was alseep, he dug beneath his feet the biggest pit in the world. He hit him a blow too big to measure and forced him down into the pit till they completely plucked out his beard with the wooden tweezers. And after that they killed him altogether.

And from there the two of them went to Celliwig in Cornwall with a leash from the beard of Dillus the Bearded, and Kei put it in Arthur's hand. And then Arthur sang this *englyn* [traditional Welsh stanza]:

> Kei made a leash
> From the beard of Dillus son of Eurei.
> If he were well, he'd be your death!

And because of that, Kei sulked, so that the warriors of this island barely made peace between Kei and Arthur. And still, neither when Arthur lacked resources nor his men were slaughtered would Kei go with him in his need from that time on.

And then Arthur said, "Which is best of the rare and difficult things to seek now?"

"It is best to seek Drudwyn, the young dog of Greid son of Eri."

A little before this Creiddylad daughter of Lludd Silver-hand went with Gwythyr son of Greidawl. And before he slept with her Gwyn son of Nudd came and took her away by force. Gwythyr son of Greidawl gathered an army and came to fight with Gwyn son of Nudd. And Gwyn was the victor, and he imprisoned Greid son of Eri, and Glinneu son of Taran, and Gwrgwst the Half-naked, and Dyfnarth his son. And he imprisoned Oben son of Nethawg and Nwython and Cyledyr the Wild, his son. And he killed Nwython and took out his heart. And he forced Cyledyr to eat his father's heart, and for that reason Cyledyr went mad. Arthur heard of this and came to the north and summoned Gwyn son of Nudd to him, and released his noblemen from Gwyn's prison. And he made peace between Gwyn son of Nudd and Gwythyr son of Greidawl. This is the peace that was made: to keep the maiden in her father's house, undisturbed by either side. And every May Day from that day till Doomsday, there should be fighting between Gwyn and Gwythyr. And whichever of them won on Doomsday would take the girl. And when these noblemen were reconciled thus, Arthur got Dun-mane the horse of Gweddw, and the leash of Bog Hundred-claws.

After that Arthur went to Brittany, with Mabon son of Mellt and Gware Golden-hair, to seek the two dogs of Glythfyr the Breton. And after getting them, Arthur went to the west of Ireland for Gwrgi Seferi and also Odgar son of Aedd, King of Ireland. From there Arthur went to the north and captured Cyledyr the Wild. Then he went after Ysgithyrwyn Chief Boar. And Mabon son of Mellt went with the two dogs of Glythfyr the Breton in his hand, and Drudwyn, the young dog of Greid son of Eri. And Arthur himself went on the hunt, with his dog Cafall in his hand. And Caw of Pictland mounted Llamrei, Arthur's mare, and joined the encounter. He took a hatchet as weapon and fiercely and brilliantly went after the boar and split its head in two and took the tusk. It was not the dogs that Ysbaddaden had named to Culhwch that killed the boar, but Cafall, Arthur's own dog.

The Hunting of Twrch Trwyth

And after the slaying of Ysgithyrwyn Chief Boar, Arthur and his followers went to Celliwig in Cornwall. From there he sent Menw son of Teirgwaedd to see whether the treasures were between the two ears of Twrch Trwyth. For it would be base to go fight with him if he did not have the treasures. But *he* was there, certainly; he had already devastated a third of Ireland. Menw went seeking the treasures, and the place where he saw them was at Esgeir Oerfel in Ireland. Menw changed himself into a bird and alighted above Twrch's lair. He tried to pluck one of the treasures from him. But he didn't get a thing except one of his bristles. The boar got up very fiercely and shook himself so that some of his poison got onto him; from then on, Menw was never without a sore.

After that Arthur sent a messenger to Odgar son of Aedd, King of Ireland, to ask for the cauldron of Diwrnach of Ireland, his Steward. Odgar asked him for it. Diwrnach said, "God knows, though he should be better for getting one glimpse of it, he won't have it." And Arthur's messenger came back from Ireland with a "no." Arthur set out with a light force with him and boarded Prydwen his ship and went to Ireland. They went to the house of Diwrnach the Irishman. The troops of Odgar saw their number. After they ate and drank their portion, Arthur asked for the cauldron. Diwrnach answered that if he were to give it to anyone, he would give it at the word of Odgar, King of Ireland. After he said no to them, Bedwyr got up and took hold of the cauldron and put it on the back of Hygwydd, Arthur's servant. He was brother by the same mother to Cacamwri, Arthur's servant, and his regular function was to carry Arthur's cauldron and to start a fire under it.

Llenlleawg the Irishman seized Caledfwlch [Arthur's sword] and swung it in a circle and killed Diwrnach the Irishman and all his band. The hosts of Ireland came and fought with them. And when the hosts fled utterly, Arthur and his men went in their presence into his ship, and with them was the cauldron full of the treasure of Ireland. And they disembarked at the house of Llwydeu son of Cel Coed at Porth Cerddin in Dyfed. And [a place called] "Cauldron's Measure" is there.

And then Arthur assembled the soldiers to be found in the Three Realms of Britain and its Three Adjacent Islands, and those in France and Brittany and the Land of Summer; and the available choice hounds and celebrated horses. And he went with all these forces to Ireland. And there was great fear and trembling in Ireland because of him. And after Arthur landed, the saints of Ireland came to him to ask his protection. And he gave them protection, and they in turn gave him their blessing. The men of Ireland came to Arthur and gave him a tribute of food.

Arthur came to Esgeir Oerfel in Ireland, to the place where Twrch Trwyth was, and his seven young pigs with him. Dogs were unleashed at him on every side. That day till evening, the Irish fought with Twrch Trwyth. Despite that, one-fifth of Ireland was laid waste.

The next day Arthur's warband fought with Twrch Trwyth; apart from what they got of evil from him, they got nothing good. The third day Arthur himself fought with him—for nine nights and nine days. He killed only one youngling of his pigs. The men asked Arthur what was the explanation for that pig [Twrch Trwyth]. He answered, "He was a king, and for his sins God turned him into a pig."

Arthur sent Gwrhyr, Interpreter of Languages, to try to talk to him. Gwrhyr went in the form of a bird and alighted above the lair of him and his seven young pigs. And Gwrhyr, the Interpreter of Languages, asked him, "For His sake who made you in this shape? If you can speak, I implore one of you to come and talk with Arthur."

Grugyn Silver-bristle gave a response. Like wings of silver were all his bristles; the path he took through wood and meadow could be seen by how his bristles shone. This is the answer Grugyn gave: "By Him who made us in this shape, we will not do it, and we will say nothing to Arthur. It was enough evil that God did to us, who made us in this shape, without you, too, coming to fight with us."

"I tell you that Arthur will fight for the comb and the razor and the scissors that are between the two ears of Twrch Trwyth."

Grugyn said, "Until his life is first taken, those treasures will not be taken. And tomorrow morning we shall set out from here and go to Arthur's land and do the greatest damage there that we can."

They set out by sea for Wales. And Arthur came with his armies and his horses and his dogs aboard Prydwen. And a sharp eye they kept on them. Twrch Trwyth landed at Porth Clais in Dyfed [to the south of St. David's]. That night Arthur came as far as Mynyw [St. David's]. The next day Arthur was told they had gone by. And he overtook Twrch Trwyth killing the cattle of Cynwas Cwryfagyl, after killing the men and beasts that were in Deu Gleddyf [the region about the estuary at Milford Haven] before Arthur's coming.

From the time Arthur came Twrch Trwyth headed from there toward Presseleu [the Preseli mountain range in north Pembrokeshire]. Arthur came there with the world's armies. He sent his men to the hunt: Eli and Trachmyr and Drudwyn, the young dog of Greid son of Eri, in his own hand; and Gwarthegydd son of Caw on another flank, with the two dogs of Glythfyr the Breton in his hand; and Bedwyr with Cafall, Arthur's dog, in his hand. And he grouped all the soldiers on either side of the Nyfer [a stream in north

Pembrokeshire]. The three sons of Cleddyf Difwlch came, men who had won great fame at the killing of Ysgithyrwyn Chief Boar.

And then Twrch Trwyth set out from Glyn Nyfer and came to Cwm Cerwyn, and there he stood at bay. And he killed four of Arthur's champions: Gwarthegydd son of Caw, and Tarawg of Allt Clwyd, and Rheiddwn son of Eli Adfer, and Isgofan the Generous. After killing these men he again stood at bay against them. And he killed Gwydre son of Arthur, and Garselid the Irishman, and Glew son of Ysgawd, and Isgawyn son of Banon. And then he himself was wounded.

The next morning at break of day some of the men overtook him. And he killed Huandaw, Gogigwr, and Penpingion, three servants of Glewlwyd Mighty-grip, so that God knows there was no servant of his in the world but Llaesgymyn, a man who improved no one's situation. And along with these he killed many men of the land, and Gwylddyn the Builder, Arthur's Chief Builder. And then Arthur overtook him at Pelumiawg, and he slew Madawg son of Teithion, Gwyn son of Tringad son of Nefedd, and Eiriawn Penlloran. From there he went to Abertywi and made a stand against them. He killed Cynlas son of Cynan and Gwilenhin, King of France. He went from there to Glyn Ystu, and then the men and dogs lost him.

Arthur summoned Gwyn son of Nudd to him, and asked him if he knew anything of Twrch Trwyth. He said that he did not. Thereupon all the huntsmen went hunting the pig, to the Vale of Llychwr. And Grugyn Silver-hair and Llwydawg the Suitor descended upon them and slew the huntsmen so that none of them escaped alive except one man. In response Arthur came with his armies to where Grugyn and Llwydawg were and unleashed against them all the appointed dogs. And as soon as Grugyn and Llwydawg stood at bay, Twrch Trwyth came to protect them. Since they crossed the Irish Sea, he had not seen them till then. The men and dogs fell upon him. He broke into flight to Mount Amanw. Then one of his young pigs was slain, and they went at it life for life. Twrch Llawin was killed and another of his pigs named Gwys. They moved on to Amanw Vale, and there Banw and Benwig were killed. From that place, none of his pigs accompanied him alive except Grugyn Silver-hair and Llwydawg the Suitor.

They proceeded to Lake Ewin, where Arthur overtook him. Twrch made a stand and killed Echel Mighty-thigh and Arwyli son of Gwyddawg Gwyr and many other men and dogs. From there he went to Lake Tawy. Then Grugyn Silver-bristle separated from them and went to Fort Tywi and on to Ceredigion. After him went Eli and Trachmyr and a great throng. He came as far as Garth Grugyn, and there he was killed.

Llwydawg the Suitor was in the vicinity and killed Rhuddfyw Rhys and many besides. Then Llwydawg went as far as Ystrad Yw. There the men of Brittany encountered him. He killed Tall Peisawg, the King of Brittany, and Red-eye the Stallion, and Gwrfoddw, Arthur's uncles, his mother's brothers. Then Llwydawg himself was slain.

Twrch Trwyth then made his way between the Tawy and Ewyas [a region in southeastern Wales]. Arthur summoned the men of Cornwall and Devon to stop him at the mouth of the Severn. Arthur said to the warriors of the island: "Twrch Trwyth has slain many of my subjects. By men's valor, so long as I live, he shall not go to Cornwall! I will not chase after him any more, but will go at him life for life! You do what you will."

What happened is that by his counsel an army of knights, and dogs of the island with them, was sent to Ewyas; from there they came back to the Severn and ambushed Twrch Trwyth with whatever tested fighters were in the island. They drove him battling into the Severn. And Mabon son of Modron went with him into the Severn River on White Dun-mane, Gweddw's steed, and Goreu son of Custennin, and Menw son of Teirgwaedd, between Llyn Lliwan and the estuary of the River Wye. And Arthur fell on him, and the champions of Britain with him. Osla Big-knife closed in, and Manawydan son of Llŷr, and Cacamwri, Arthur's servant, and Gwyngelli surrounded him. First they grabbed him by the feet and dunked him in the Severn till it flooded over him. On one side Mabon son of Modron spurred his horse and got the razor from him; and on the other side, Cyledyr the Wild on another horse plunged with him into the Severn and took the scissors from him. Before they could remove the comb, Twrch found land with his feet, and from the time he reached land, no dog nor man nor horse could keep up with him till he got to Cornwall.

Whatever trouble they had had trying to get those treasures, they had worse trouble trying to rescue the two men from drowning. As Cacamwri was pulled up, two millstones pulled him back to the depths. As Osla Bigknife was running after Twrch, his knife fell from its sheath, and he lost it; then his sheath got filled with water, and when he was pulled up his sheath dragged him down to the depths.

Arthur went on with his armies till he reached Twrch Trwyth in Cornwall. Whatever trouble he had had before was play compared with what he now had seeking the comb. Yet through trouble upon trouble the comb was won from him. Then Twrch Trwyth was harried out of Cornwall and driven straight into the sea. Afterward it was never known where he went and Aned and Aethlem [two pursuing hounds] with him. And Arthur went from there to Celliwig in Cornwall to bathe and cast off his weariness.

The Witch's Blood

Arthur said, "Are there now any of the rare and difficult things that we do not have?"

One of the men said, "There is. The blood of the Dark Black Witch, daughter of the Pale White Witch, from the head of the Valley of Sorrow in the uplands of Hell."

Arthur set out for the north and came to where the hag's cave was. And it was the advice of Gwyn son of Nudd and Gwythyr son of Greidawl to send Cacamwri and his brother Hygwydd to fight the witch. But when they came inside the cave, the witch attacked them and seized Hygwydd by the hair of his head and threw him to the ground under her. And Cacamwri grabbed her by the hair of her head and pulled her off Hygwydd to the ground. But she turned on Cacamwri and beat them both down and disarmed them and drove them out whooping and howling.

Arthur was infuriated to see his two servants almost killed, and he attempted an assault on the cave. And then Gwyn and Gwythyr said to him, "It's not decent or pleasing for us to see you wrestling with a witch. Send Tall Amren and Tall Eiddil into the cave."

And they went in. And if there was a bad time for the first two, there was a worse time for these two, till God knows whether any of the four of them could have got out of the place if they hadn't all four been placed on Arthur's mare, Llamrei.

Then Arthur occupied the entrance to the cave and overcame the hag with his knife Carnwennan and cut her in half, so that she became two tubs of blood. Caw of Pictland took the witch's blood and kept it with him.

The Winning of Olwen

And then Culhwch set out, and with him Goreu the son of Custennin and those who wished ill to Ysbaddaden Chief Giant, taking the rare and difficult things with them and heading for his court. And Caw of Pictland came and shaved the giant's beard—the flesh and skin to the bone, and the two ears completely. And Culhwch said, "Have you been shaved, man?"

"I have," he said.

"And is your daughter mine now?"

"She is," he said, "but you don't have to thank me for that. Instead thank Arthur, the man who made it happen for you. If I had my way, you would never win her. But it is past the time to take away my life."

And then Goreu son of Custennin seized him by the hair of his head and dragged him after him to the refuse mound and cut off his head and put it on the post of the castle yard. And he took possession of the fort and his territory.

And that night Culhwch slept with Olwen. And she was his only wife as long as he lived. And the armies of Arthur dispersed, each to his own country.

And thus did Culhwch win Olwen daughter of Ysbaddaden Chief Giant.

Chapter *IV*

ARTHUR IN GEOFFREY OF MONMOUTH

RICHARD M. LOOMIS

In the early twelfth century Geoffrey of Monmouth wrote a Latin history of Britain that made Arthur known to Europe. The work was completed about 1138; a year later the English historian Henry of Huntingdon was shown a copy at the monastery of Le Bec in Normandy. What is astonishing about Geoffrey's *Historia Regum Britannie (History of the Kings of Britain)* is that it narrates matters of which historians such as Henry had failed to find any record. These include the history of Britain before the Roman conquest and the full career of Arthur. In his dedication, Geoffrey reports that when he was once puzzling over these gaps in the historical record, Walter, Archdeacon of Oxford, presented him with just the source that he was looking for: an ancient book in the British language that told in orderly fashion the deeds of all the kings of Britain. In his plain and modest style, Geoffrey says, he has translated this ancient book into Latin.

Other historians of his own century and since have dismissed Geoffrey's claim as an imposture. No such consecutive account of the kings of Britain in the British language (that is, Welsh or Breton) has ever come to light. Archdeacon Walter could have given Geoffrey a volume containing genealogies and legends that served as a source for Geoffrey's history. But even if he made use of written Welsh or Breton traditions, the *Historia* is not just a translation. It is an artfully contrived literary composition that weaves the author's own inventions together with gleanings from various sources, including earlier Latin historians such as Gildas and Bede as well as Celtic lore. Following the *Historia Brittonum* ascribed to "Nennius," Geoffrey traces the origin of the Britons to Brutus, great-grandson of Aeneas, Prince of Troy, on the model of the mythic origin of Rome presented in Virgil's *Aeneid*. Geoffrey's account climaxes in a portrayal of Arthur as the mightiest and noblest of the kings of Britain, one who staves off the Saxon advance and subdues much of

Europe. Arthur's reign is followed by the gradual collapse of British power, the last independent British king being Cadwallader, who dies a pilgrim in Rome in 689, realizing that God has driven his people from rule as a punishment for their sins. Meanwhile, the disciplined and united Saxons consolidate their hold on the island. With this narrative, Geoffrey bestows upon Britain an antiquity matching that of Rome and delineates in King Arthur a national hero as formidable as Charlemagne. The Normans, who were Geoffrey's patrons, readers, and first translators, were fascinated by this portrait of the nation.

Britain had been conquered by the Saxons, who were in turn conquered by the Normans. Geoffrey's vision is of a vanished world, but the shadows of defeat and time give range to his intellect and imagination. What made Britain great? Why did it fall? What endures? He freely endows Arthurian Britain with styles and institutions of his own age, so that the work is charged with contemporary relevance. At its center, he presents the prophecies of Merlin that point obscurely to a restoration of British rule; centuries later, these prophecies would help launch the Tudor dynasty. More potently for the Normans, Geoffrey celebrates an imperial Britain, one that, like Norman England, is expansionist, centralized, and authoritarian, a model of manners and mastery for the world.

While ordered as history, Geoffrey's work dramatizes folklore and legend. Some leading elements of Arthurian fiction are introduced by him. He shows Arthur to be a figure of destiny, his reign foretold in the stars. Yet he is subject to the fluctuations of fortune that can turn triumph into ruin through forces beyond a hero's control, especially the machinations of envious and ambitious foes. Arthur is born from the adulterous union of Uther Pendragon and the beautiful wife of Count Gorlois of Cornwall. Uther's treatment of Gorlois is shown to be as ruthless as Cilydd's treatment of King Doged in *Culhwch and Olwen*; it is made even more interesting by the cunning deceptions wrought by Merlin that enable Uther to sleep with Igerna by being disguised as her husband. Geoffrey shapes Merlin by building into his story the warrior, poet, and prophet Myrddin of Welsh tradition, changing the name to Merlin (perhaps to avoid the Latin form, *Merdinus*, that French readers would associate with *merde*).

Following Arthur's birth, Merlin disappears from the scene, and Arthur later becomes king not by magic but by demonstrating at the age of fifteen that he has the valor and command needed in a king. He enjoys the support of the church and recruits knights to serve him by making them gifts and promising them plunder. As a warrior, he is severe, yet amenable to the beseechings of threatened victims. The Celtic motif of king as giant-killer appears as an episode of one of his continental campaigns. A giant from Spain has abducted the niece of Arthur's ally and nephew, Hoel of Brittany, and taken her to the summit of Mont St. Michel; she kills herself before the giant can rape her. Arthur kills the giant and has him decapitated for this brutal assault. The giant's unrestrained savagery is a challenge to sexual decency, shown here as Arthur's responsibility to defend.

But in the setting of Arthur's brilliant court at Caerleon, Geoffrey introduces the new topic of noble love or *fin' amors*, the sophisticated version of sexual love then being explored in the poetry of the troubadours. The knights are motivated to compete for the love of the women who observe their tournaments, where glances feed and reward their valor. Arthur's own generosity is feudal. Before the assembled court, he rewards those who have served him by giving them secular and ecclesiastical possessions—cities, castles, episcopacies—exactly as the Normans endowed their followers.

After his victories on the continent, Arthur bestows Normandy upon Bedivere and Anjou upon Kay, the homelands of Norman and Angevin leaders who were contending for control of England in Geoffrey's lifetime. When Arthur is about to move against Rome, to establish the principle that Britain is not obliged to pay tribute to the emperor, word comes to him that he has been betrayed, primal bonds of feudal loyalty having been broken: his nephew Modred has joined Guinevere in adulterous love and has usurped Arthur's crown. Arthur returns to Britain to engage in a civil war that culminates in his being mortally wounded. He is carried to the Isle of Avalon for healing. That ambiguous ending leaves open the possibility of Arthur's return.

Geoffrey of Monmouth is presumed to have been born in the town of Monmouth by which he names himself; the town is located in eastern Wales. Between 1129 and 1151, his name appears on charters relating to religious houses in the vicinity of Oxford, and he probably lived in Oxford during that period. In 1152 he was consecrated Bishop of St. Asaph's in north Wales, though he seems not to have gone there. The Welsh *Chronicle of the Princes* (*Brut y Tywysogion*) records that he died in 1155. His patrons included Robert, Earl of Gloucester, the "noble duke" to whom he will not confide the scandalous details of the adultery of Modred and Guinevere; and Alexander, Bishop of Lincoln, whose large diocese, created by the Normans, included Oxford and was an intellectual capital of the age.

Geoffrey is sometimes named "Geoffrey Arthur," the Arthur being either his father's name or a second name of his own. He locates some principal events of Arthur's life in his own region of southern Britain: Arthur's birth and death in Cornwall, his cosmopolitan court at Caerleon, his victory over the Saxons on a hill in Bath (Geoffrey's identification of the Mount Badon named by Gildas as the site of a British victory over the Saxons). Arthur's battles take him from one end of Britain to another and include rapid conquests of Ireland, Iceland, and Scandinavia, but his major campaigns are in France. The prominence that Geoffrey gives to Brittany in these campaigns may derive from his being of Breton ancestry. A grandson of Henry II, Arthur of Brittany, was later named for Geoffrey's hero, as would be the firstborn son of Henry VII. While his account of Arthur is Geoffrey's greatest contribution to literature, his *History* (in passages not included here) is also the source for other celebrated figures such as Lear, Cordelia, and Sabrina.

Bibliographic note: Neil Wright has edited a twelfth-century manuscript as the first volume of a new series devoted to Geoffrey's work: Neil Wright, ed., Geoffrey of Monmouth, *Historia Regum Britannie: Bern, Burgerbibliothek, MS. 568* (Brewer, 1985). The introduction to this edition discusses Geoffrey's life and work and the grounds for beginning the series with the Bern manuscript. Over 200 manuscript copies of Geoffrey's *Historia* exist, and their relationships are too complex and obscure to attempt a critical edition at present. The 1929 editions by Acton Griscom and Edmund Faral were based on a limited number of manuscripts and cannot be regarded as definitive.

The present translation is based on Griscom's edition (Longmans, Green, 1929), which Wright characterizes as careful though eccentric in method; it is a diplomatic edition of Cambridge University Library MS. Ii.1.14 (1706), with variants from Bern 568 and a National Library of Wales manuscript, MS. Porkington 17.

The Renaissance edition of Commelin (1587) divided the work into twelve books, a feature not found in the early manuscripts. Faral (1929) instead divided the text into 208 chapters. Wright employs Faral's chapter numbers in his edition and provides a conversion table for the Commelin book numbers and Faral's chapter numbers. The present translation is of all the passages from Geoffrey's *Historia* relating to Arthur, identified by the traditional book and chapter divisions, with Faral's chapter numbers added in parentheses. In his introduction to his edition of Bern 568, Wright points out (p. lix) that the Bern manuscript has variants suggesting it is the work of a scribe concerned to exonerate the English in their take-over of the island. After Arthur is carried to Avalon, the Bern scribe adds, "Anima eius in pace quiescat"—"May his soul rest in peace"—a tag that lays to rest both Arthur and the hope that he would return! Wright has also edited, as volume 2 of this series, *The First Variant Version: A Critical Edition* (D.S. Brewer, 1988).

There are translations by J.A. Giles (1848); Sebastian Evans, revised by Charles W. Dunn (Dutton, 1958); and Lewis Thorpe (Penguin, 1966). The myriad names and sometimes inconsistent specifics of Geoffrey's work are treated by Thorpe, who gives an index correlating all the names. J.S.P. Tatlock presents findings on Geoffrey's names, sources, subjects, and techniques in *The Legendary History of Britain* (Univ. of California, 1950). For critical assessments and interpretations of Geoffrey's work, see John Jay Parry and Robert A. Caldwell, chapter 8 of *Arthurian Literature in the Middle Ages*, ed. R.S. Loomis (Oxford, 1959); Robert W. Hanning, *The Vision of History in Early Britain from Gildas to Geoffrey of Monmouth* (Columbia, 1966); Antonia Gransden, *Historical Writing in England c. 550 to c. 1307* (Cornell, 1974); Christopher Brooke, "Geoffrey of Monmouth as a Historian," in *Church and Government in the Middle Ages*, ed. Christopher Brooke, et al. (Cambridge, 1976); Nancy F. Partner, *Serious Entertainments: The Writing of History in Twelfth-century England* (Univ. of Chicago, 1977); V.I.J. Flint, "The *Historia Regum Britanniae* of Geoffrey of Monmouth: Parody and Its Purpose: A Suggestion," *Speculum* 54 (1979) 447–68; S.M. Schwartz, "The Founding and Self-betrayal of Britain: An Augustinian Approach to Geoffrey of Monmouth's *Historia Regum Britanniae*," *Medievalia et Humanistica* 10 (1981) 33–53; R. William Leckie, Jr., *The Passage of Dominion: Geoffrey of Monmouth and the Periodization of Insular History in the Twelfth Century* (Toronto, 1981); Geoffrey Ashe, "A Certain Very Ancient

Book," *Speculum* 56 (1981), 301–23; Stephen Knight, chapter 2 of *Arthurian
Literature and Society* (London: Macmillan, 1983; 1985); Brynley F. Roberts,
chapter 4 of *The Arthur of the Welsh: The Arthurian Legend in Medieval Welsh
Literature*, ed. Rachel Bromwich, A.O.H. Jarman, Brynley F. Roberts (Univ. of
Wales Press, 1991). An earlier essay by Brynley Roberts, "Geoffrey of
Monmouth and Welsh Historical Tradition," originally published as
Nottingham Medieval Studies 20 (1976) 29–40, has been reissued as chapter 2 of
Studies on Middle Welsh Literature, Welsh Studies 5 (Edwin Mellen, 1992).

The History of the Kings of Britain

[Geoffrey's account of Arthur is preceded by his treatment of the reign of the
virtuous Aurelius Ambrosius—a figure from history eulogized by Gildas—
who struggled to preserve British civilization only to be treacherously poisoned at the instigation of one of his own countrymen, Paschent, in league
with the Saxon enemy—a treachery that anticipates Modred's. It is the death
of this king at Winchester that occasions the first portent of the coming reign
of Arthur.]

Book 8, the conclusion of chapter 14 through chapter 17 (Faral 133–135):

While this was happening at Winchester, a star appeared of amazing size and
brightness, having a single ray. This ray ended in a fiery ball spread out in the
shape of a dragon, and from its mouth there issued two beams, one of which
seemed to reach beyond the area of Gaul, while the other bent toward the
Irish Sea, in seven smaller rays.

When this star appeared three times, all who saw it were overcome with
fear and astonishment. The king's brother, Uther, who was pursuing the
enemy in Wales, was no less overcome with dread, and he summoned wise
men to tell him what the star meant. Among others he ordered Merlin called,
who had accompanied the army so that the fighting might be managed with
his counsel. Standing before the commander, he was told to explain the meaning of the star. He burst into tears, invoked his prophetic spirit, and said: "O
irreparable loss! O bereaved people of Britain! O the passing of a most noble
king! The glorious king of the Britons is dead, Aurelius Ambrosius, by whose
death we shall all die, unless God brings help. Hurry, noble commander!
Hurry, Uther, and do not put off fighting the enemy! Victory will be yours,
and you shall be king of all Britain. For that star signifies you, as does the fiery
dragon under the star. But the beam that is extended to the region of Gaul is
the sign of a future son of yours who will be supremely powerful and whose
might will control all the kingdoms that this beam covers. The other beam
represents a daughter whose sons and grandsons in succession will have the
kingship of Britain."

Although wondering whether Merlin had proclaimed the truth, Uther nonetheless advanced against the enemy as before. He had come so near St. David's that a half-day's march remained. When his approach was reported to Gillomanius and Paschent and the Saxons who were there, they went out against him to engage in battle. Once these caught sight of each other, they drew up their battle lines on either side, advanced face to face, and fought. In the fighting soldiers died on both sides, as happens in such encounters. When much of the day had passed, Uther finally prevailed and with the slaying of Gillomanius and Paschent, achieved victory. The barbarians retreated therefore and sped to their ships but were cut down in flight by native citizens, who pursued them. Through Christ's favor victory fell to the commander, who after that great effort, made his way to Winchester as quickly as possible. For messengers had come who reported the king's death and that he was to be buried by the bishops of the land near the monastery of Ambrius, inside the Giant's Circle, which Aurelius, when alive, had ordered to be made. At the word of his death the bishops and abbots and all the clergy of the province assembled in Winchester, and they arranged for a funeral that was fitting for so great a king. Since he had decreed while alive that he should be buried in the cemetery he had made, they carried him there and laid him in the earth with royal rites.

His brother, Uther, took possession of the crown of the island after a convocation of the clergy and the people of the kingdom, and with the consent of all he was elevated to be king. Remembering the interpretation Merlin had given to the previously mentioned star, he ordered that two dragons be made of gold, like the dragon he had seen at the end of the star's ray. When these were completed with wonderful craftsmanship, he presented one to the cathedral church of Winchester and kept the other for himself, to carry into battle. From that time, therefore, he was called Uther *Pendragon*, which means in the British tongue "dragon's head."

Book 8, most of chapter 19 through chapter 20 (Faral 137–138):

The following Easter Uther commanded the lords of the realm to meet in London so that he might wear the crown and celebrate so great a day with ceremony. They all made their preparations accordingly and from their various cities came together at the time of the feast. The king celebrated the occasion as he had planned and with his lords enjoyed himself. They were all happy, because he had welcomed them with a glad heart. So many nobles had gathered, with their wives and daughters, as were worthy of the joyful banquet. Among them was Gorlois, the Duke of Cornwall, with his wife, Igerna, whose beauty surpassed that of all the other women in Britain. When the king noticed her amid the rest, he grew warm with sudden love for her, so that, neglecting the others, he gave all his attention to her. To her alone he continually sent dishes; to her he sent wine-cups of gold by his personal messengers. He smiled at her several times and exchanged playful words. When her husband perceived this, he was immediately outraged and left the court without permission. No one there was able to summon him back because he dreaded the loss of the one thing he loved most.

Angry at this, Uther ordered him to return to the court, to get satisfaction from him for the offense. When Gorlois failed to obey him, the king was enraged and swore to lay waste to his territory unless he promptly made satisfaction. Without delay, since the bitterness between them persisted, the king collected a great army, advanced on Cornwall and set fire to the towns and fortified settlements. But Gorlois, since his troops were fewer, dared not confront him and consequently chose to fortify his castles until he could win help from Ireland. Since he was more troubled about his wife than himself, he placed her in the castle of Tintagel, beside the sea, which he regarded as a more secure retreat. He himself withdrew to the citadel of Dimilioc, lest they both be in danger together if misfortune overtook them. When that was made known to the king, he went to the fort where Gorlois was and besieged it and closed off every approach to it.

Finally, after a week had passed, being mindful of his love for Igerna, the king summoned Ulfin of Ridcaradoch, a friend and soldier of his, and told him what he felt in these words: "I burn with love for Igerna, and I do not think I can avoid danger to my health unless I win her. Tell me how I can satisfy my desire, or I shall die from torment." Ulfin answered: "And who can tell you what to do, when no power exists by which we might get to her in the castle of Tintagel? For it stands on the sea and is enclosed by the sea on all sides, and there is no other access to it than that which a narrow causeway of rock affords. Three armed soldiers can block the way, even if you were to make a stand there with the whole kingdom of Britain. But if Merlin the prophet were to give help, I think you could get what you want by his direction." The king put faith in this and had Merlin summoned since he had also come to the siege.

Called at once, Merlin, when he stood in the king's presence, was ordered to propose how the king might satisfy his longing for Igerna. Upon discovering the anguish the king was suffering because of her, Merlin marveled at his great love and said, "To gain what you wish, you must use new arts unheard of in your day. I know by my drugs how to give you the appearance of Gorlois, so that you will resemble him in everything. If you follow my instructions, I will make you look exactly like him, and I will make Ulfin like Jordan of Tintagel, his servant. I shall be the third, disguised as yet another, and you will be able to go to the castle for Igerna and gain admittance."

The king approved and paid close heed. After having entrusted the siege to his subordinates, he submitted to Merlin's drugs and was transformed into the likeness of Gorlois. Ulfin was also changed into Jordan, and Merlin into Britaelis, so that it was evident to no one what their appearance had been before. Then they set out for Tintagel and came to the castle at dusk. After they hurriedly told the gatekeeper that the duke had arrived, the doors were opened and the men were admitted. For who could suspect anything since Gorlois himself was thought to be present? The king then spent the night with Igerna and satisfied himself with the lovemaking he had longed for, for he had deceived her by the disguise he had assumed. He had deceived her, too, with false words that he artfully contrived. He said he had come in secret from the besieged fort so that he might take care of the one he so loved and of his castle. Believing him, therefore, she denied nothing that he asked. This night also she conceived that most renowned of men, Arthur, who afterward won fame by his extraordinary valor.

In the meantime, when it was learned at the siege that the king was not there, the army, acting on its own, tried to assault the walls and to provoke the besieged duke to battle. He, behaving as rashly as they, came forth with his soldiers, thinking that with his little band he might resist so many men in arms. As they fought on all sides, Gorlois was among the first to be slain, and his followers were scattered. The besieged fort was captured, and the riches stored there were divided in unequal portions. For as luck and boldness served them, each one snatched with an open claw.

When the savagery of this action was at last finished, messengers came to Igerna reporting both the death of the duke and the end of the siege. But when they saw the king sitting beside her in the likeness of the duke, they blushed and marveled that he whom they had left for dead at the siege should have arrived thus before them unharmed. For they were ignorant of the drugs Merlin had compounded. So the king laughed at such reports and embraced the duchess, saying, "I am certainly not dead, but as you see yourself, I am alive. Yet I mourn the destruction of my fortress and the slaughter of my comrades. Now we have to fear lest the king show up and take us captive in this castle. I will therefore go first to meet him and be reconciled with him, so that nothing worse will befall us." He went out and sought his army and, after the appearance of Gorlois was removed, he reappeared as Uther Pendragon. When he learned all that had happened, he mourned the death of Gorlois but rejoiced that Igerna was freed from the bond of marriage. Therefore he went back to Tintagel Castle, took it, and took Igerna, and had his wish. They dwelt together thereafter as equals, bound by a great love, and had a son and a daughter. The son's name was Arthur and the daughter's, Anna.

Books 9, 10, and the first two chapters of Book 11 (Faral 143–178):

After the death of Uther Pendragon the leaders of the Britons assembled from the various provinces in the city of Silchester and proposed to Dubricius, Archbishop of Caerleon, that he consecrate the king's son, Arthur, as king. Necessity drove them, for the Saxons, upon hearing of the death of King Uther, had invited their countrymen from Germany and under the leadership of Colgrin were trying to exterminate the Britons. Already they had subdued all that portion of the island that extends from the Humber to the Sea of Caithness. Distressed for the plight of his country and joined by the bishops, Dubricius therefore invested Arthur with the crown of the kingdom. Arthur was a youth of fifteen years, of remarkable valor and generosity, whose natural goodness displayed such grace that he was loved by virtually all the people. After receiving the royal insignia, he observed the custom of generously bestowing gifts to all. So many soldiers thronged to him that he ran out of resources for giving. But while a naturally generous and spirited man may thus temporarily lack means, he will not remain poor. Arthur, accordingly, in whom courage was combined with generosity, decided to harry the Saxons, so that he could bestow their wealth on the retainers who served him. Justice recommended this course as well, since Arthur had a hereditary claim to the kingship of the entire island. He gathered the youths subject to him and set out for York.

As soon as this was revealed to Colgrin, he assembled Saxons, Scots, and Picts, and came to meet Arthur with a great multitude near the River Douglas. When they joined battle there, the greater part of both armies was in mortal danger. But Arthur prevailed. He chased the fleeing Colgrin and laid siege to him at York, where he had gone. When Baldulf heard of his brother's flight, he advanced to the siege with six thousand men to set Colgrin free. At the time when his brother had been fighting Arthur, Baldulf was on the coast awaiting the arrival of Duke Cheldric, who was expected to bring them help from Germany. When he was ten miles from the city, Baldulf decided to travel by night and make a clandestine attack. Once Arthur learned of this, he ordered Duke Cador of Cornwall to meet Baldulf that night with six hundred knights and three thousand foot-soldiers. Cador discovered the route the enemy was taking, made a surprise attack, and, after rending and killing the Saxons, forced the survivors to flee.

Baldulf was greatly distressed that he could not bring help to his brother and debated how he might manage to confer with him. For he thought he could work out some rescue by joint counsel, if he could get to him. Since he could not approach in any other way, he shaved off his hair and beard and took on the guise of a harp-player. Strolling outside the British camp, he performed like a harper with melodies that he composed on the instrument. Because no one suspected him, he gradually drew near the city walls, maintaining his disguise. As soon as those inside the city recognized him, he was hoisted up by ropes to the other side of the wall and brought to his brother. Upon seeing his own brother, he was revived by wished-for kisses and embraces, as if he had been raised from death. They conferred at great length. Finally, just when they had given up hope of escaping, envoys returned from Germany. Led by Duke Cheldric, they had gathered six hundred ships filled with brave soldiers.

At this news Arthur's advisers persuaded him not to maintain the siege any longer, to avoid committing themselves to hazardous conflict if so many enemy troops should arrive. Arthur took the counsel of his attendants and withdrew to London. There he convened the clergy and sought the advice of the leaders of his whole domain as to what would be the best or safest way to resist the pagans' invasion. At length a consensus was reached, and envoys were sent to Brittany to King Hoel to report to him the crisis in Britain. Hoel was the son of Arthur's sister, his father being Budicius, the King of the Armoricans. When he heard of the distress being inflicted upon his uncle, Hoel ordered his fleet readied. After assembling fifteen thousand armed men, he took the next fair wind and landed at Southampton. Arthur received him with due honor and they embraced again and again. A few days later they made for Kaerluideoit, which was under siege by the pagans I have spoken of. This city is in the province of Lindsey, located on a hill between two rivers, and is also called Lincoln. When they arrived there with all their forces to do battle with the Saxons they inflicted unheard-of slaughter. That day, six thousand Saxons fell, some of whom died by drowning in the rivers, some by the sword. The rest abandoned the siege in terror and fled.   *Nenius*

Arthur pursued them without pause till they came to the <u>Wood of Caledon</u>. There from all sides the Saxons converged in their flight and tried to resist Arthur. Defending themselves vigorously, they massacred the Britons. For they managed to avoid the weapons of the British by availing themselves of the protection of the trees. When he saw this, Arthur commanded the trees in that part of the forest to be cut down and the trunks set in a ring so that escape would be denied the Saxons. He was determined to besiege them, shut in thus, for so long that they would die of hunger. After enclosing them, he ordered his squadrons to surround the forest, and he remained there three days. When the Saxons ran out of food, they petitioned for release, for fear they might die of sudden starvation. It was agreed that in exchange for leaving behind all their gold and silver, they would be permitted to return to Germany with only their ships. They promised in addition that they would give Arthur tribute from Germany and would send hostages from there. After conferring with his advisers, Arthur granted their petition. He retained their treasure and hostages for the tribute to be paid and only allowed them to depart.

On their return home, as they put to sea, the Saxons regretted their agreement and turned their sails about, headed for Britain, and came ashore at Totnes. They seized the land and depopulated the country as far as the Severn Sea, assailing the inhabitants with mortal wounds. Then they made a march toward the district of Bath and laid siege to the town. When this was reported to the king, he was outraged at their betrayal and ordered that justice be done to their hostages, who were to be hanged at once. Postponing the campaign he had launched against the Scots and Picts, he sped to relieve the <u>siege of Bath</u>, though troubled by the greatest of anxieties, since he was leaving in the city of Alclud his nephew Hoel, who was seriously ill. After he entered the province of Somerset and neared the siege, he spoke these words:

Battle of Baden

"Because the Saxons, who are known for being ungodly and hateful, have scorned to keep faith with me, I, who remain faithful to my God, will strive to be avenged on them today for the blood of my countrymen. Arm yourselves, men! Arm, and manfully attack those we shall surely conquer, with the help of Christ!"

While Arthur was saying this, holy Dubricius, Archbishop of Caerleon, climbed to the top of a hill and cried out in a loud voice: "Men marked with Christian faith, let your devotion to your countrymen and your country be constant. If your countrymen are slain by the treachery of the pagans, it will be a lasting reproach to you, unless you press on to defend them. Fight for your country, and if death comes, suffer death willingly for your country. For that is a victory and health for the soul. Whoever undergoes death for his brothers gives himself a living sacrifice to God and swerves not from following Christ, who consented to lay down His life for His brothers. Should then any of you suffer death in this war, may that death be a penance and purification for him, if he does not shrink from accepting it thus."

Gladdened by the holy man's benediction, each of them soon hurried to arm and obey his precepts. Arthur himself, dressed in a leather corselet appropriate for so great a king, placed on his head a helmet of gold engraved with the figure of a dragon. A circular shield on his shoulders, called Pridwen, on which was painted the image of holy Mary, the Mother of God, kept him always mindful of her. He was girded with the best of swords, Caliburn, which had been made on the Isle of Avalon. And a spear called Ron graced his right hand. This was a hard, broad spear apt for giving wounds.

After the companies were drawn up, Arthur boldly invaded the Saxon lines, which were drawn up in their usual wedge formations. The Saxons fought back courageously all day, repelling the Britons everywhere. As the sun set, the Saxons took a nearby hill, planning to hold it as their camp. Trusting in the great number of their comrades, the mountain alone seemed to be all they needed. But when the next sun restored the day, Arthur climbed to the top with his army, even though in the ascent he lost many of his men. For the Saxons rushing forward from the summit struck blows more easily, since men marching downward could wound with more speed than those marching upward. But the Britons, who had taken the summit with great force, grappled arm to arm with the enemy. Fronting them with their breasts, the Saxons strained every muscle to resist. When most of the day passed in this fashion, Arthur was indignant that the Saxons were succeeding and that victory was not yet his. Consequently he drew his sword Caliburn, proclaimed the name of St. Mary, and cast himself with a swift rush into the dense lines of the enemy. Invoking God's name, he slew with a single blow every man he struck. Nor did he cease his assault until he killed four hundred and seventy men with only his sword Caliburn. At sight of this the Britons came after him in close-packed squadrons, killing on all sides. Colgrin fell in that place and

Baldulf his brother, and many thousands of others. Cheldric however, seeing the peril of his allies, at once turned to flee with the survivors.

The king, having therefore achieved victory, ordered Cador, the Duke of Cornwall, to pursue the enemy, while Arthur himself hastened toward Albany [Scotland]. For he had been informed that the Scots and the Picts had besieged his nephew Hoel in the town of Alclud, where Arthur, as I said before, had left him seriously ill. For this reason Arthur hurried to his aid lest he be captured by the barbarians. The Duke of Cornwall, accompanied by ten thousand men, decided not to chase the fleeing Saxons yet, but instead advanced toward their ships to prevent their boarding them. As soon as he gained possession of these, he fortified them with superior soldiers who were to deny entrance to the pagans if they ran toward them. Then he hastened after the enemy, ready to execute the command of Arthur to massacre pitilessly all those whom he found. The Saxons, who just before had thundered with instinctive savagery, now fled with quaking heart; some sought the recesses of the woods; some, the mountains and the mountain caves, to win some chance for life. Since nothing afforded them protection, they afterward came to the island of Thanet with their battle-line in pieces. The Duke of Cornwall followed them there, slaughtering as he was accustomed to do. He did not rest till, after Cheldric was captured, he forced them all to surrender, and hostages were taken.

Once peace was established, he went on to Alclud, which Arthur had already liberated from the pagans' control. Then he led his army to Moray, where the Scots and Picts were under siege, fighting for the third time against the king and his nephew. Having been overcome by Arthur, they had retreated to that region, and, when they came to Loch Lomond, they occupied the islands there, in search of a secure refuge. This lake has forty islands and is fed by sixty streams, and only one river flows from it to the sea. Sixty cliffs are visible in the islands, supporting the same number of eagles' nests; the eagles gather each year and, with a high-pitched cry that they give in unison, proclaim anything extraordinary that is about to happen in the kingdom. The enemy I spoke of fled to these islands to use the lake as a defense, but it was little help to them. For Arthur assembled a fleet and made a circuit of the rivers and by besieging the enemy for fifteen days crushed them with such famine that they died by the thousands.

While Arthur was subduing them thus, Gillmaurus, the King of Ireland, joined by an enormous number of barbarians, arrived with his fleet to bring help to those under siege. Arthur broke off the siege, began to turn on the Irish, and forced them, assailed without pity, to return home. Having won immediate victory, he was again free to destroy the race of the Scots and Picts, which he did with inflexible severity. Since he spared none of them the moment each was taken, all the bishops of that poor land, with all the clergy under their authority, advanced together barefoot, carrying relics of the saints and holy treasures of the church, to implore the king's mercy for the deliverance of their people. As soon as they were admitted to his presence they begged him on their knees to have pity on a nation broken in spirit. He had brought peril enough and had no need to exterminate to the last one the handful who survived. He should grant a small portion of the land to them, who were consenting to bear forever the yoke of subjection. Since they appealed to the king in this way, pity moved him to tears, and, yielding to the prayers of the holy men, he granted them mercy.

After this Hoel explored the site of the lake I have mentioned and marveled that there should be so many streams, islands, cliffs, and eagles' nests, and all in the same number. Since that impressed him, Arthur approached and told him there was another pool in the same district even more remarkable. It was not far from there and had a width of twenty feet and the same length, and a depth of five feet. Whether it had been made square by human art or by nature, it breeds four kinds of fish in its four corners, and the fish of one part are not found in another. He added that there was another lake in Wales near the Severn, which the natives call Llyn Lliawn. When the tide flows into it, the sea is received as by a whirlpool, and while the pool sucks in the surge, it never gets so filled that seawater tops its banks. And when the sea ebbs, the lake spews out the swallowed waters as high as a mountain and eventually covers and splashes its banks. Meanwhile, if the people of all that area stand nearby facing the lake and their clothes get sprinkled with the waves, they can scarcely, or not at all, avoid being sucked into the lake. But if their backs are turned, they need not fear being sprinkled, even when they stand on the shore.

Having granted mercy to the Scots, the king made for York, to celebrate the feast of the approaching Nativity of the Lord. When he entered the city, he mourned to see the desolation of the sacred churches. For after blessed Archbishop Samson was expelled with other men of devout faith, the half-burned temples ceased to be used for the worship of God—so thorough had been the effect of the pagans' rage. Arthur convened the clergy and people and appointed his chaplain, Piramus, to the metropolitan see. He restored the churches that had been leveled to the ground and endowed them with religious communities of men and women. He restored to their hereditary privileges the nobles who had been driven away by the disruption of the Saxons.

There were three brothers in that place descended from the royal line: namely, Loth, Urian, and Auguselus, who had exercised command in those parts before the Saxons came to power. Wishing therefore to bestow their native right upon them as he had done for the other nobles, Arthur gave back to Auguselus the royal power of the Scots, and to his brother Urian, the scepter of Moray. Loth he restored to the dukedom of Lothian. In the time of Aurelius Ambrosius Loth had married Arthur's sister, who bore him Gawain and Modred. When he had finally brought the state of the whole country to its original dignity, Arthur married a woman named Guinevere, who was descended from a noble family of Romans and reared in the household of Duke Cador. She was the loveliest woman in all the island.

At the start of the following summer he readied his fleet and went to the island of Ireland, which he wished to subject to himself. At his landing King Gillmaurus, whom I have already spoken of, came to fight against him with a throng beyond counting. When battle broke out, Gillmaurus's naked and unarmed people were pitifully cut down on the spot and ran to wherever some place of refuge lay open to them. Gillmaurus was captured immediately and forced to surrender. The other princes of the land surrendered in consequence, stunned at what had happened to the king.

With all of Ireland conquered Arthur directed his fleet toward Iceland and took possession of it after defeating the inhabitants. When word spread through the other islands that no nation could resist him, Doldavius, the King of Gotland, and Gunhpuar, the King of the Orkneys, came on their own, pledged tribute, and made their submission. When winter had passed, Arthur returned to Britain, settled the realm in secure peace, and remained there for twelve years.

Then he summoned all who were most distinguished from kingdoms far and wide and began to enlarge his household and to have such elegance in his court that he stirred emulation in people living far away. The result was that whoever had a noble spirit counted himself nothing unless in dress or arms he bore himself like Arthur's knights. As his magnanimity and valor became celebrated throughout the world, extreme dread filled the rulers of kingdoms overseas that, if they were crushed by an invasion of Arthur's, they might lose the nations they governed. Troubled with gnawing concern, then, they rebuilt their towns and the ramparts of their cities and constructed fortifications in strategic places, so that if Arthur should be provoked to move against them, they would have a refuge in case of need. And when this was told to Arthur, he felt exalted that he was a source of dread to everyone, and he longed to win all of Europe for himself.

Arthur had ships prepared and went first to Norway, in order to honor his sister's husband, Loth, with that country's crown. But Loth was the nephew of Sichelm, the King of the Norwegians, who had just then died and willed his kingdom to Loth. The Norwegians were opposed to accepting Loth and promoted a certain Riculf to the royal power. They fortified their cities and thought themselves able to resist Arthur. Loth had a son, Gawain, who was twelve years old at the time; he had been entrusted by his uncle to the service of Pope Sulpicius, who had knighted him. When therefore, as I started to say, Arthur landed on the coast of Norway, King Riculf met him with all the people of the country and began to fight. Ater much blood had been shed on both sides, the Britons finally won and with an assault killed Riculf and many others. After this victory mounting flames swept the cities. The natives were scattered, and the Britons did not refrain from violence until they subdued to Arthur's rule all of Norway and Denmark as well.

Upon the surrender of these lands, after promoting Loth to be king of Norway, Arthur sailed to Gaul. He organized divisions and began to ravage the country on every side. Gaul was then a province of Rome, charged to the Tribune Frollo, who governed it on behalf of Emperor Leo. When Frollo learned of Arthur's approach, he led all the armed soldiery obedient to his power to do battle with Arthur, but he could not stand against him. For the youth of the islands that he had just conquered joined Arthur, so that he was known to have such a powerful army that it was hard for any other to over-power it. The better members of the armed forces of Gaul, indebted to Arthur by his largess, also entered his service. When he saw that he was heading toward the worst of the battle, Frollo forsook his camp at once and raced to Paris with a few companions. There he regrouped his scattered people, garrisoned the city, and once more ventured to fight Arthur. But just as Frollo was negotiating to strengthen his army with help from his neigh-bors, Arthur unexpectedly arrived and laid siege to him in the city. After a month passed, Frollo grieved that his people were dying of hunger, and he proposed to Arthur that they two alone should enter upon a duel, and the one to whom victory fell would gain the other's kingdom; for Frollo was great in stature and daring and courage. These qualities made him excessively sure of himself, and he offered this proposal so that he might by this means have a chance for deliverance. When it was communicated to Arthur, Frollo's pro-posal pleased him enormously, and he sent word back that he would be ready to abide by these terms. A pledge was therefore given on both sides, and the two met on an island outside the city, while the people awaited what was to come of their encounter.

They were both appropriately armed and mounted on horses of wonder-ful speed, and it was not obvious who might win. Standing on opposite sides with lances raised, they suddenly spurred their horses and struck at one an-other with mighty blows. But by managing his lance more surely Arthur hit Frollo in the upper chest and, keeping clear of Frollo's weapon, with all his strength knocked him to the ground. Arthur unsheathed his sword, too, and was hurrying to kill him, when Frollo stood up quickly and, with his lance held straight before him, ran at Arthur. He sank a mortal wound into the breast of Arthur's horse and forced them both to fall. When the Britons saw the king prostrate, they feared that he was slain. Scarcely could they be kept from violating their pledge and attacking the Gauls as one body. But just as they were considering breaching the pact, Arthur swiftly got to his feet, holding his shield in front of him, and with a rapid dash attacked the mena-cing Frollo. Now face to face they redoubled their matching blows, each intent on the death of the other. Frollo finally found an opening and hit Arthur on the brow. If he had not blunted his sword's edge by striking Arthur's helmet, Frollo might have dealt a mortal wound. Blood was flowing, and when Arthur saw that his corselet and shield were red, he was inflamed with a more burning anger. Using all his strength, he hoisted Caliburn and drove it through the helmet and into the head of Frollo, dividing it in two. With this wound Frollo fell, his heels beating the earth, and he loosed his spirit to the winds. As soon as that became known to the army, the inhabitants of the city ran in a body, opened the gates, and handed the city over to Arthur.

This victory achieved, he divided his army in two. One part he entrusted to Duke Hoel and commanded him to go fight Guitard, Duke of the men of Poitou. With the other part of the army Arthur would devote himself to subduing the remaining provinces that resisted him. Hoel entered Aquitaine, invaded the cities of that land, and forced Guitard, harried by much fighting, to surrender; and he depopulated Gascony with sword and flame and subjugated their princes. When nine years had passed and Arthur had brought all of Gaul under his control, he returned to Paris. There he held court, convened the clergy and people, and established the affairs of the kingdom in peace and law. Then he granted Neustria, which is now called Normandy, to his Cupbearer, Bedivere. To his Seneschal, Kay, he granted the province of Anjou. And he bestowed many other provinces on noblemen who had been in his service. When all the cities and peoples were at peace, he went back to Britain at the beginning of the spring.

When the feast of Pentecost drew near, Arthur, whose heart was full of happiness after such a triumph, desired to hold his court then. He would place the crown of the kingdom on his head and call to the feast the kings and dukes subject to him, so that he might celebrate the feast with reverence and renew lasting peace among his princes. Having told his attendants what he desired, he accepted their advice that he carry out his plan in Caerleon. For it was located in a delightful spot in Glamorgan, on the River Usk, not far from the Severn Sea. Abounding in wealth more than other cities, it was suited for such a ceremony. For the noble river I have named flows along it on one side, upon which the kings and princes who would be coming from overseas could be carried by ship. But on the other side, protected by meadows and woods, it was remarkable for royal palaces, so that it imitated Rome in the golden roofs of its buildings. It was distinguished by two churches, one of which, built in honor of the martyr Julius, was beautifully graced with a virgin choir of nuns dedicated to God. The other was founded in the name of blessed Aaron, the friend of Julius, with an attached convent of canons, and was the third metropolitan see of Britain. Moreover, the city had a college of two hundred philosophers, learned in astronomy and other arts, who diligently observed the courses of the stars and with sound interpretations foretold to King Arthur wonders to come in that time. Famous for so many pleasant features, Caerleon was made ready for the announced feast.

Messengers were sent to various kingdoms, and those who deserved to attend the court were invited, from the parts of Gaul as well as from the neighboring islands of the ocean. Consequently there came Auguselus, the King of Albany, now called Scotland; Urian, the King of the men of Moray; Cadwallo Long-Arm, the King of the Venedotians, who are now called the

North Welsh; Stater, the King of the Demetians, that is, the South Welsh; Cador, the King of Cornwall; the archbishops of the three metropolitan sees, that is, London and York, as well as Dubricius of Caerleon. Dubricius was the Primate of Britain and Legate of the Apostolic See, so renowned for religion that by his prayers he could cure anyone who was gravely ill.

Noble lords of noble cities came: Morvid, Earl of Gloucester; Mauron of Worcester; Anarauth of Salisbury; Artgualchar of Guerensis, now called Warwick; Jugein from Leicester; Cursalem from Caistor; Kynniarc, Duke of Durobernia; Urbgennius from Bath; Jonathal of Dorchester; and Boso of Rydychen, that is, Oxford. In addition to these lords heroes of equal honor came: Donaut map Papo, Cheneus map Coil, Peredur map Eridur, Grifud map Nogord, Regin map Claut, Eddelivi map Oledauc, Kynar map Bangan, Kynmaroc, Gorbonian map Goit, Worloit, Run map Neton, Kymbelin, Edelnauth map Trunat, Cathleus map Kathel, Kynlit map Tieton, and many others whose names it is tiring to enumerate. From the neighboring islands came Gillmaurus, King of Ireland; Malvasius, King of Iceland; Doldavius, King of Gotland; Gunvasius, King of the Orkneys; Loth, King of Norway; Aschil, King of the Danes. From nations overseas came Holdin, Duke of Flanders; Leodegarius, Earl of Boulogne; Bedivere the Cupbearer, Duke of Normandy; Borellus of Maine; Kay the Seneschal, Duke of Anjou; Guitard of Poitou; the Twelve Peers of the parts of Gaul, led by Gerin of Chartres; Hoel, Duke of the Armorican Britons, with the nobles subject to him. They marched with such an array of trappings, mules, and horses that it is difficult to record. Besides these there remained no prince of any worth on this side of Spain who did not come at that call. No wonder—Arthur's generosity, famous throughout the world, had attracted everyone by his love.

When they had finally all gathered in the city, the feast being now at hand, the archbishops were led to the palace to crown the king with the royal diadem. Since the court was convening in his diocese, Dubricius, vested for mass, undertook responsibility for the ceremony. After the king was crowned, he was led in procession to the church of the metropolitan see. The two archbishops, one on the right and one on the left, escorted him. But four kings, that is, of Albany and Cornwall, Demetia and Venedotia, whose privilege it was, went before him bearing four golden swords. A choir of many religious orders performed with marvelous melodies. From another quarter the archbishops and bishops led the queen, crowned with her regalia, to the church of the nuns. Four queens of the kings named above carried four white doves in front of her, as was the custom. All the women followed her there with great joy. Afterward, when the procession was completed, so many organs were played, so many songs performed in each church, that from the surpassing sweetness the knights in attendance did not know which church they should visit first. Hence they rushed in crowds now to this one, now to that one, and if the whole day had been given to this celebration, it would not have wearied them.

After the masses were sung in both churches, the king and queen laid aside their crowns and put on lighter adornments. He went to dine at his palace with the men, she to another palace with the women, for the Britons kept the ancient custom of Troy by which the men celebrated feasts separately with men, the women with women. When they had been seated as the dignity of each demanded, Kay the Seneschal, decked in ermine, was accompanied by a thousand nobles, all wearing ermine, who served the dishes with him. On the other side just as many diversely gowned followed Bedivere the Cupbearer, who was wearing miniver, and with him distributed many different kinds of drinks. In the palace of the queen, also, countless servants decked in various ornaments presented their service according to custom. If I should describe all of them, I would make too prolix an account. For Britain was then restored to such a state of distinction that it excelled other kingdoms in the burgeoning of wealth, the lavishness of ornaments, the elegance of its inhabitants. Every knight in Britain who was noted for valor had clothing and arms identical in color, and the women had exquisitely matching garments. They deigned to love no man till he was three times proven in military combat. Thus the women were made more chaste, and the knights more valiant because of their love of them.

Having feasted, they all went to fields outside the city, different ones to play different games. Soon knights who had knowledge of tournaments arranged a mock-battle. Women looking on from stations on the walls playfully roused them to mad flames of love. After the tournament they passed the remaining time in contests, some with bows and arrows, some with spears, some by hurling heavy rocks, some with stones, some with dice, and in a variety of other pleasant games. Whoever achieved victory in his game was rewarded by Arthur with generous gifts. The first three days were spent thus, and when the fourth day came, all were summoned who had done him service, to receive recognition, and each was endowed with possessions, that is, cities and castles, archbishoprics, episcopacies, and other rewards.

Then blessed Dubricius, desiring to live as a hermit, resigned from the archiepiscopal see. In his place was consecrated David, the king's uncle, whose life was a model of all goodness for those whom he had taught. To succeed the Archbishop of York, Saint Samson of Dol, Tebaus was chosen a well-known priest of Llandaff, endorsed by Hoel, King of the Armorican Britons, who was impressed by the man's life and virtue. The see of Silchester went to Maugannius, and Winchester to Diuvanius. Eledenius was chosen bishop of Alclud.

While Arthur was distributing these honors among them, unexpectedly there entered, with measured steps, twelve men of mature age and dignified countenance, carrying olive branches in their right hands as the sign of a diplomatic mission. After saluting the king, they presented a letter to him on behalf of Lucius Hiberius, which read: "Lucius, Procurator of the Republic to Arthur, King of Britain, the greetings he has deserved. With great amazement I marvel at the insolence of your tyranny. I marvel, I say, remembering the injury you have done to Rome, and I am outraged that you have transgressed and avoid acknowledging the fact. Nor are you in haste to recognize what it is to have offended criminally the Senate, which you know the entire world should obey. For the tribute of Britain, which the Senate commanded you to pay—since Gaius Julius Caesar and other men of Roman rank received it many times—you have presumed to withhold, neglecting the command of so great an authority. You have also seized Gaul from Rome, you have taken the province of Burgundy, you have seized all the islands of the ocean, whose kings, while Roman power held sway there, paid tax to my ancestors. Since, therefore, the Senate has voted to have redress for your accumulated offenses, I order you to come to Rome by mid-August of the coming year, so that, giving satisfaction to your masters, you may accept the sentence that their justice will pronounce. Otherwise I myself will go to your lands, and whatever your madness has wrested from the Republic, I will venture to restore to Rome by the sword."

Once those words were spoken before the kings and lords, Arthur accompanied them to a gigantic tower that was at the gatehouse, to debate what should be done to counter these commands. But as they started to climb the steps, Duke Cador of Cornwall, who had a jovial disposition, broke into a laugh with these words in the king's presence: "Till now, I have feared that the quiet rest the Britons have known through a long peace might make them cowardly and deprive them of fame for warfare, in which they are thought to excel other races. Indeed, where there is no practice of arms but the enticements of dice and women and other amusements, it is no wonder that cowardice should stain what once there was of virtue, honor, courage, and fame. For it has been almost five years since we have indulged in those pleasures and have not been exercised in war. It is to free us from this sloth that God has stirred the Romans to such a mood, that they might restore our valor to its original state." These and like remarks he made to the others as they went to the benches.

Once they had all gathered there, Arthur spoke: "Comrades in good fortune and bad," he said, "whose valiant spirits I have before now tested both in giving counsel and in waging war, now put your minds together and prudently decide what you think we should do about these commands. For whatever is carefully foreseen by a wise man is more easily borne when it comes time for realization. We shall more easily bear the assault of Lucius if with common zeal we plan in advance how we can withstand it. I do not think that we should fear him greatly, since he demands on unreasonable grounds the tribute he wants from Britain. For he says that it should be given to him because it was paid to Julius Caesar and his successors, who were induced by civil dissension among our ancestors to make an armed attack on them and subdue them to Roman power by force and violence, as our country was then reeling from domestic troubles. Since they conquered the land thus, they taxed it unjustly. For nothing acquired by force and violence is justly possessed by anyone. Because the Romans used violence, he makes an unreasonable claim, thinking us to be tributaries to him by right. And since he presumes to exact from us what is not due him, let us by parallel reasoning seek from him the tribute of Rome, and whoever emerges the stronger, let him make off with what he wishes to possess! For if he concludes that a tax should be paid him because Julius Caesar and other Roman leaders once conquered Britain, I believe on the same grounds that Rome ought to pay you tribute, since my ancestors conquered it in ancient times. For Belinus, the most fortunate King of the Britons, with the help of his brother, Brennius, Duke of Burgundy, after hanging twenty of the higher-ranking Romans in the middle of the Forum, took the city and, after taking it, held it for a long time. And Constantine, the son of Helena, and Maximian, each of them a blood relative of mine, who succeeded one another in wearing the crown of Britain, gained the throne of Roman rule. Do you not therefore think that a tax should be sought from the Romans? As to Gaul, however, or the nearby islands of the sea, no answer is to be given, since Rome avoided defending them when we were subduing them to our power."

After Arthur spoke thus, Hoel, the King of the Armorican Britons, who was ordered to speak before the others, responded with these words: "Even if we could each summon to mind and profoundly review all things, I do not think that anyone could find advice better than what the good sense of your keen foresight yields. For your deliberation, touched with Ciceronian eloquence, has met our need. Therefore we should staunchly praise the plan of a constant man like you, the act of a wise soul, and the performance of superior counsel. For if by the argument just expressed, you choose to go to Rome, I do not doubt that we shall have the victory while we defend our liberty, while we justly exact from our enemies what they tried to take from us. For whoever tries to steal another's possessions deserves to lose his own possessions to the very one whom he attacks. Since, then, the Romans want to take our possessions from us, we should surely take theirs from them, if we have an opportunity to do battle. This is a battle deeply desired by all the Britons! Consider the Sibylline prophecies, which testify in verses that three times there will be one born of British stock who will obtain the rule of Rome! Two times the oracles have already been fulfilled, since it is clear, as you have said, that the famous princes Belinus and Constantine have worn the regalia of the Roman Empire. But now we have you as the third to whom the summit of this great honor is promised. Hasten, therefore, to take what God wishes to grant! Hasten to subdue that which itself wishes to be subdued! Hasten to exalt us all! We will not flee from being wounded or losing life so that you may be raised on high. In order that you may accomplish this, I shall join you with ten thousand armed men!"

When Hoel had finished speaking, Auguselus, the King of Albany, offered to make known what he felt about it: "From realizing that my lord desires the things he has spoken of, a joy has fallen on my soul that I cannot express before him. It seems that we have accomplished nothing in the conquests we have inflicted on so many and such great kings, so long as the Romans and the Germans remain unhurt, and we do not manfully avenge on them the injuries that they once did to our countrymen. Now, since liberty to do battle is promised us, I rejoice exceedingly, and I burn with desire for the day we shall meet. I thirst for their blood as I would for a spring if for three days I had been kept from drinking. Ah, shall I ever see that day? How sweet will be the wounds I shall receive or give, when we engage hand to hand! And that death will be sweet which I face in avenging our fathers, in defending our liberty, in exalting our king. Let us advance on those half-men, and in our advance let us be steadfast, so that once they are defeated, we may possess their honors with a happy victory. I shall augment our army with two thousand armed knights, and infantry as well."

After the others had said what yet remained to be said, each of them promised Arthur as many men as they owed in their feudal service, so that in addition to those the Duke of Armorica had pledged, there were added from the island of Britain alone sixty thousand armed men. But the kings of the other islands, since they were not accustomed to have cavalry, pledged infantry as each one was obliged, so that from the six islands—Ireland, Iceland, Gotland, the Orkneys, Norway, and Denmark—one hundred and twenty thousand were enrolled. From the duchies of Gaul—Flanders, Ponthieu, Normandy, Maine, Anjou, Poitou—eighty thousand. From the twelve districts of those who went with Gerin of Chartres, twelve hundred. The total number of the army was therefore one hundred and eighty-three thousand, three hundred, besides foot soldiers, who were not easily counted.

King Arthur received them all, ready and united, into his service, and he ordered them to go home again quickly and organize the promised army, and at the beginning of August to speed to the port of Barfleur, so that with him, on the border of the territory of Burgundy, they might confront the Romans. He instructed the emperors through their envoys that he was by no means going to pay them tribute, nor would he go to Rome to submit to their sentence regarding that. Instead he wanted from them that which they had decreed by judicial sentence as a claim from him. The envoys therefore departed, the kings departed, the chieftains departed, and they did not put off executing what they had been commanded to do.

Once the import of this reply was known, at the command of the Senate Lucius Hiberius issued a proclamation to the Kings of the East to raise an army to go with him to conquer Britain. Swiftly there assembled Epistrofus, the King of the Greeks; Mustensar, the King of the Africans; Ali Fatima, the King of Spain; Hirtacius, the King of the Parthians; Boccus of the Medes; Sertorius of Libya; Serses, the King of the Itureans; Pandrasus, the King of Egypt; Micipsa, the King of Babylon; Politetes, the Duke of Bithynia; Teucer, the Duke of Phrygia; Evander of Syria; Echion of Boeotia; Hippolytus of

Crete, with dukes and nobles subject to him. And from the Senate, in order, came Lucius Catellus, Marius Lepidus, Gaius Metellus Cocta, Quintus Milvius Catullus, Quintus Carucius, and more, to a total count of four hundred thousand, one hundred and sixty. All things necessary being arranged, they made for Britain at the start of August.

When Arthur learned of their approach, he entrusted the security of Britain to his nephew Modred and Queen Guinevere. He led his army to the port of Southampton, where he put to sea with a strong wind blowing. But as with joy he divided the deep sea, surrounded by countless ships on a prosperous course, a profound sleep overtook him about midnight. In his sleep he saw in a dream a bear flying through the sky, at whose roar all the coasts trembled. And a terrible dragon flew from the west, which lit up the land with the splendor of its eyes. They met and engaged in an awesome fight. With fiery breath the dragon burned the bear as it rushed forward again and again and hurled it burnt to the earth. Awakened by that, Arthur told those standing near what he had dreamed. They interpreted it, saying that the dragon represented him, but the bear represented some giant he was going to encounter. Their fight was the sign of a battle that would be between them, and the dragon's victory was the victory that would come to Arthur. But Arthur interpreted it otherwise, believing that the vision was rather about himself and the emperor. After night passed and dawn reddened at last, they landed at the port of Barfleur. Promptly they set up their tents and then waited for the kings of the islands and the dukes of the adjoining provinces to arrive. While they waited, Arthur was told that a giant of extraordinary size had come from Spain and had seized Helena, the niece of Duke Hoel, from her guardians and fled with her to the summit of the mountain now called Mont St. Michel. The soldiers of that land went in pursuit but could do nothing against the giant. Whether they attacked him by sea or by land, he either sank their ships with huge stones or killed them with many kinds of spears. And he caught several of them and devoured them half-alive.

The next night, therefore, at two in the morning, taking Kay the Seneschal and Bedivere the Cupbearer, Arthur left his tent, unknown to the rest, and made his way to the mountain. Endowed as he was with great strength, he scorned to lead an army against such monsters, and he hoped to give inspiration to his men by showing that he alone was enough to destroy them. As they neared the mountain, they saw a fire burning atop it. Another fire was on a smaller mountain, toward which, on the king's orders, Bedivere the Cupbearer sailed. He could not reach it otherwise, since it stood in the sea. Just as he had begun his ascent to the top, Bedivere heard a woman's wail. His first response was to shudder, not knowing whether the monster was there. Quickly recovering courage, he drew his sword, but when he got to the top, he found only the fire he had seen and a newly made grave, and beside it an old woman sobbing and wailing. When she caught sight of him, she checked her tears at once and broke out: "Unhappy man, what calamity brings you here? Unspeakable are the pains of death you are about to suffer! I pity you, since a loathsome monster will consume the flower of your youth tonight. For there will come a depraved giant of hated name, who carried to this mountain the duke's niece, whom I have just buried here, and me, her nurse. By a kind of death never heard of—and swiftly—the giant will do away with you! Ah, how sad your fate, bright child. . . . With fear in her tender breast while that abomination embraced her, she ended her life which was worthy of a longer duration. Because he burned with hateful lust and could not disfigure her with his shameful intercourse—she was another soul for me, another life, another sweetness in joy—he used force and violence on me, unwilling, I swear to God and by all my years! Flee, my friend! Flee, lest he come (for it is his habit) to have intercourse with me and so find you and tear you to pieces in pitiful slaughter!"

Moved as much as human nature can be, Bedivere calmed her with friendly words. He promised the comfort of quick relief and returned to Arthur to tell him all that he had discovered. Arthur mourned the girl's death and told them he would permit only himself to attack the giant, but if necessity demanded, they should come to help and advance like men to his side. So they directed their steps from there to the greater mountain, left their horses with the squires, and, with Arthur leading, climbed the mountain.

The beast was there at the fire, his lips stained with the gore of half-eaten swine. He had consumed some and was roasting others impaled on spits, with live coals underneath. As soon as he saw them, having expected nothing of the sort, he hurried to grab his club, which two young men could hardly lift off the ground. In response the king drew his sword and, with shield extended, lunged as fast as he could to reach him before he got his club. But the giant, accustomed to evil calculation, had already seized it. He struck the king upon the raised shield, with such force as to fill the entire coast with the sound of the blow and deafen Arthur's ears. But Arthur, who burned with bitter anger, hoisted his sword and gave such a wound to the giant's brow that, though not mortal, the blood flowing from it over his face and eyes blinded them from clear seeing. The giant had deflected the blow with his club and so spared his forehead a deadly wound. Yet, blinded by the flowing blood, he got up more enraged and, like a wild boar passing the spear of a hunter, he rushed past the sword toward the king. Grabbing Arthur around the waist, he forced him to bend his knees to the ground. Arthur soon summoned his strength and got free. With speed—now here, now there—he thrashed the beast with his sword and did not rest till a death-wound was struck. He drove the whole blade against the skull-cover that protected the brain. Then the detestable one cried out and, like an oak uprooted by the force of winds, collapsed with a great crash.

The king burst into a laugh. He ordered Bedivere to cut off the giant's head and give it to one of the squires to carry to the camp, to be a spectacle for gazers. Arthur declared that he had never found another of equal strength since the time he had killed huge Retho of Mount Arvaius, who had invited him to fight. From the beards of kings that he had slain, Retho had made a cloak for himself; he ordered Arthur to cut his beard neatly and send the detached part to him. As Arthur surpassed the other kings, so, in his honor, Retho would fasten his beard above the other beards. If he would not oblige, Retho pressed him to fight. The one who emerged stronger would carry off the cloak as well as the loser's beard. Thus the contest began. Arthur was the victor, and he got Retho's beard and his cloak. Afterward he used to say he had never met anyone as strong as Retho.

Having gained the victory, as I said, when the ensuing night gave place to dawn, they returned to their tents with the head. Crowds ran to marvel at it giving praise to him who had freed the country from such voraciousness. Hoel, however, grief-stricken for the death of his niece, had a church built on her grave, upon the mount where she lay. Taking its name from the girl's grave, it is called to this day "Helena's Tomb."

When all those whom Arthur had been awaiting finally assembled, he advanced from there to Autun, where he believed the emperor was. But as soon as he reached the River Aube, he was informed that the emperor had pitched his camp not far from there and was marching forward with an army so great that, they said, Arthur could not oppose it. Not in the least frightened on that account, Arthur chose not to give up what he had started, but pitched his own camp on the bank of the river, from where he would be free to lead his army out, and where, in case of need, he could retreat. He dispatched two leaders, Boso of Oxford and Gerin of Chartres, together with his nephew Gawain, to Lucius Hiberius, to tell him that he should withdraw from Gallic territory or the next day come to test which of them had the greater right to Gaul. The youths of the court were consequently moved to great high spirits and began urging Gawain to start something in the emperor's camp, to give them an occasion to engage with the Romans.

The envoys went to Lucius accordingly and ordered him to leave Gaul, or the next day to come to fight. When Lucius answered them that he had an obligation not to withdraw but rather to move ahead and take command of Gaul, his nephew Gaius Quintillianus was present and said that the Britons excelled more in boasting and threats than they did in bravery or valor. Gawain was immediately infuriated. He unsheathed the sword that he was wearing and lunged at Gaius, cut off his head, and then started back to the horses with his comrades. The Romans followed in pursuit, some on foot, some on horseback, straining to avenge their fellow citizen upon the rapidly fleeing envoys. But Gerin of Chartres, when one of the Romans began to strike at him, turned around without warning, aimed his lance, and with all his strength threw the man to the ground, pierced straight through his armor and mid-body. Boso of Oxford envied the man of Chartres for showing such courage, and, turning his own horse about, thrust his lance into the throat of the first man he met, forcing him to fall mortally wounded from the horse on which he had been chasing him. Meanwhile Marcellus Mutius, longing with all his heart to avenge Quintillianus, was already threatening Gawain from behind and was just on the point of capturing him when Gawain turned around suddenly and, with the sword he was carrying, hacked through his helmet and head clear to the chest. He commanded him to report in Hell to Quintillianus—whom Gawain had slain in the Roman camp—that this was the way the Britons excelled in threats and boasting. He rejoined his comrades then and urged each to return blow for blow and strive to put down his opponent. They agreed and went back to the fight, and each of them unhorsed his man. The Romans pursuing them could not, whether they struck with swords or lances, capture them or unhorse them.

But it is said that, as they pursued near a certain wood, some six thousand Britons suddenly marched out. Upon learning of the flight of their leaders, they had hidden there to give them aid. As they emerged, they spurred their horses and, filling the air with shouts and holding their shields before their breasts, they attacked the Romans without warning and put them to instant flight. Chasing them as one man, they knocked some from their horses with their lances, took some captive, and some they killed. When news of that came to the Senator Petreius, he made haste to join his fellow soldiers with a company of ten thousand men, and he forced the Britons to race back to the wood from which they had sallied—not without loss for the Romans. For as they fled, the Britons circled back in the narrow pathways and inflicted a massacre on the pursuers. While they were withdrawing in this manner, Hyder, the son of Nu, hurried with five thousand men to help them. That encouraged the Britons to resist, and they strove like men to hit powerful blows on those whom they had a little before shown their backs to, now opposing them with their chests. The Romans fought back, and as often as they leveled the Britons, they were also leveled by them. The Britons wanted military action with all their heart, but they gave little thought to the result of an action when they began it. The Romans, however, acted more wisely, for Petreius Cocta, in the style of a good commander, prudently instructed them now to attack, now to retreat, and thereby threatened the Britons with great loss.

When Boso realized this, he separated from the others several men whom he knew to be more valiant, and addressed them in this way: "Since we began this battle without Arthur's knowledge, we must take care not to end up the worse for our attempt. For if we suffer that reversal, we will incur great loss among our soldiers and move our king to curse us. Regain your courage and follow me through the Roman host, so that if fortune favors us we may kill or capture Petreius." So they spurred their horses, and, penetrating the wedge formations of the enemy with matching force, they came to where Petreius was admonishing his troops. Boso burst in there, seized Petreius by the neck, and, as he had planned, fell to the ground with him. The Romans closed in to tear Petreius away from his adversaries. But the Britons ran together to give

Boso help. There was great killing among them with shouts and clamor, while one side sought to free their leader and the other to hold on to him. Men were wounded on both sides, throwing opponents down and being thrown down. There one could see who would prevail with the spear, who with the sword, who with the knife. At last the Britons moving in close formation and bearing up under the attack of the Romans, retired with Petreius to the security of their battle-line. And they made an unexpected attack on the Romans, who, bereft of their general, were now mostly weakened, scattered, and showing their backs to them. As the Romans rushed off, the Britons hit them from behind, felled those who were hit, stripped those who were felled, and slew those they had stripped, as they went after the others. They also took many prisoners to present to the king. When they had terrorized enough, the Britons returned to their camp with their spoils and prisoners.

Reporting what had happened to them, they handed over to Arthur Petreius Cocta and their other prisoners, in the gladness of victory. He congratulated them and promised them honors and promotions, since they had performed so valiantly in his absence. But desiring to lead the captives to confinement, he called aside those who might conduct them to Paris the next day and deliver them to the city guards, to keep them till he gave other orders regarding them. He commanded Duke Cador and Bedivere the Cupbearer and two of his military leaders, Borellus and Richerius, with their retinue, to guide them until they came where there was no fear of a rescue by the Romans. But the Romans happened to discover that plan and on the orders of the emperor selected fifteen thousand of their men to move ahead of the British march that night. Once they met the Britons, they were told to hold their ground, in order to free the captives. They assigned as leaders Vulteius Catellus and Quintus Carucius, who were Senators, and Evandrus, the King of Syria, and Sertorius, the King of Lybia. With the soldiers already mentioned they took the commanded journey that night and, having reached a site with suitable hiding places, lay concealed where they thought the Britons would pass.

When morning came, the Britons got underway with their captives, and soon they drew near that spot, not aware what traps the shrewd enemy had set. But when they had begun to pass by, the Romans appeared without warning and fell upon them, who were anticipating nothing of the sort, and penetrated their ranks. But the Britons, though they had been unexpectedly attacked and finally scattered, regrouped and fought back like men. They stationed some of their men around the prisoners, while they dispatched others into the throng to engage the enemy. Richerius and Bedivere they put in command of the force assigned to guard the prisoners. Cador, Duke of Cornwall, and Borellus were put in charge of the others. But the entire Roman force burst forward in confusion; without bothering to group their men by squadrons, but succeeding with all their might, they slaughtered the Britons as they were trying to organize their troops and defend themselves. Much weakened as a result, the Britons would shamefully have lost those they were escorting if fortune had not sped to bring them welcome aid.

For Guitard, the Duke of Poitou, as soon as the entrapment was known, came up with three thousand men. Confident in their help, the Britons prevailed at last and gave back to the heartless waylayers a counter-massacre. Yet they lost many of their own men in the first engagement. They lost that distinguished leader of Maine, Borellus, who, while confronting Evandrus, the King of Syria, spewed out his life with his blood with the Syrian's lance fixed in his throat. They lost, too, four noble lords: Hirelgas of Periron, Maurice Cador of Cahors, Aliduc of Tintagel, and Her, the son of Hider—men not to be easily matched in bravery. But they did not slacken in courage or show despair, but pressed forward with every effort, trying both to keep the prisoners and to overthrow the enemy. At length, the Romans, being unable to bear the contest with them, sped from the field and headed for their camp. Yet the Britons kept in pursuit and inflicted great slaughter. They seized very many, and did not rest until, after Vulteius Catellus and Evandrus, the King of Syria, were slain, they utterly routed the remnant. Victory being theirs, they sent the prisoners whom they were convoying on to Paris and returned to their king with the ones they had just taken. They assured the king of supreme victory, since, though they were but a few, they had gained a triumph over an enormous attacking enemy.

Lucius Hiberius suffered these reverses with bitterness. He turned his mind—stung with mixed torments—now here, now there—debating whether to engage in the fighting already begun with Arthur or, having withdrawn to Autun, to await the assistance of the Emperor Leo. At length he yielded to fear, and the next night, heading for Autun, he entered Langres with his army. When Arthur learned of this, wanting to get ahead of the Roman march that night, he bypassed the city on his left and entered a valley called Saussy, which Lucius was about to cross. Desiring to organize his soldiers by troops, he ordered one legion under the command of Morvid to be in reserve so that, if necessary, he would know where he could retreat and, after regrouping his squadrons, again do battle with the enemy. He distributed the others into seven divisions, assigning to each division five thousand, five hundred and fifty-five men fully equipped with arms. A part of these divisions was organized as cavalry, the other part as infantry. The order was given them that, while an infantry group was attempting an attack, cavalry were to attack in the same place, obliquely and in close formation, to scatter the enemy. The infantry were drawn up in the British manner, in a square, with a right and a left wing. Placed in command of the first of these divisions were Auguselus, the King of Albany, and Cador, the Duke of Cornwall, the first for the right wing and the second for the left. For the second division Arthur named two other outstanding generals, Gerin of Chartres and Boso of Rydychen (which is called Oxford in the Saxon tongue). For the third he named King Aschil of Denmark and King Loth of Norway; for the fourth

Duke Hoel of the Armoricans and Gawain, his own nephew. Four divisions were stationed behind as support. In charge of the first Arthur appointed Kay the Seneschal and Bedivere the Cupbearer; of the second Duke Holdin of Flanders and Duke Guitard of Poitou, of the third Iugenis of Leicester, Jonathal of Dorchester, and Cursalem of Caistor, of the fourth Urbgennius of Bath. Following these the king chose for himself a legion that he wanted to be available to him, placed at a location where he raised up his golden dragon as a standard to which the wounded and battle-weary might in necessity flee, as to a fort. In that legion of his there were six thousand, six hundred and sixty-six men.

When all was in order, he addressed his troops in these words: "My countrymen, who have made Britain the mistress of thirty kingdoms, I pay tribute to your valor, which I judge to be not failing but rather flourishing more and more. You were unexercised in battle for five years, when you were given to the sweets of idleness rather than to the practice of arms, yet you have not degenerated from inborn worth but persevered, and you have put the Romans to flight. Provoked by their own pride, they wanted to deprive you of liberty; advancing with a greater number, they began to wage battle; unable to withstand an engagement with you, they have shamefully retreated to this city. You can meet them as they now leave this city and head for Autun through this valley and fall upon them like unsuspecting sheep. Surely they were thinking that the sloth of Eastern races is in you, when they desired to make your country a tributary and to make slaves of you. Could they be ignorant of the wars you waged with the Danes and the Norwegians and the leaders of the Gauls, whom you have subdued to my power and liberated from their shameful rule? We who prevailed in harder conflict shall surely prevail in this easier fight, if with equal passion we labor to crush those half-men. What great honors each of you will possess if as faithful soldiers you obey my will and my orders! For once we have beaten them we will aim straight for Rome and will capture the city we have aimed for and will take possession of what we have captured. You shall therefore have the gold, the silver, the palaces, the towers, the forts, the cities, and the other riches of the conquered." Even as he was speaking, they all gave their assent with one shout, ready as long as Arthur lived to accept death first rather than abandon the field by flight.

But Lucius Hiberius, learning about the stratagems being prepared against him, chose not to flee, as he had wanted to do, but having recovered courage, proposed to confront them in that valley. He called his generals and spoke to them in these words: "Venerable fathers, to whose command the kings of East and West ought to be subject, be mindful of our ancestors, who, in order to vanquish the enemies of the Republic, did not shrink from shedding their blood, but, leaving an example of valor and arms to their descendants, fought as if God had destined them not to die in battle. Thus they triumphed most often and, by triumphing, escaped death, since for none was any other death destined than that which came by the providence of God. So the Republic grew, their valor grew, and whatever decency, honor, and generosity are usually found in the noble flourished longer in them and promoted them and their descendants to lordship over the whole world. Desiring then to rouse the same spirit in you, I urge you to revive the gallant courage of your ancestors and, persevering in that, seek out your enemy in the valley where they lie in wait for you and fight to win from them what is yours. Do not suppose I have retreated to this city because I shrink from them or from a contest with them. I think rather that they are attacking foolishly and that we should surprise the attackers and, with great devastation, attack them as they rush forward in uncoordinated ranks. Since they have now done something other than we had thought, let us also do something unexpected. Let us go after them and attack them audaciously. Or if they should regain themselves, let us fight back with one heart and withstand the first attack, and so we shall surely triumph. For in many battles, whoever could stand in the first engagement has most often made off with the victory."

When he finished speaking these and many other words, all showed approval with one assent, holding up both faces and hands in an oath, and they hastened to arm. Once armed, they left Langres and approached the valley where Arthur had stationed his troops. They too formed twelve wedge-shaped divisions, and all infantry. These, drawn up as wedges in the Roman style, each contained six thousand, six hundred and sixty-six soldiers. They appointed their own commanders to each of them, so that by their command the divisions might both attack and repulse attacks. Of the first, therefore, they put in charge Lucius Catellus and Ali Fatima, the King of Spain; of the second Hirtacius, the King of the Parthians, and Marius Lepidus, Senator; of the third Boccus, the King of the Medes, and Gaius Metellus, Senator; of the fourth Sertorius, the King of Libya, and Quintus Milvius, Senator. These four columns were stationed in the front line. After these another four followed, of which they made Serses, the King of the Itureans, commander of the first; of the second Pandrasus, the King of Egypt; of the third Politetes, the Duke of Bithynia; of the fourth Teucer, the Duke of Phrygia. Behind these were yet another four divisions, and to the command of the first of these, they appointed Quintus Carucius, Senator; of the second Lelius Hostiensis; of the third Sulpicius Subuculus, of the fourth Mauricius Silvanus. Lucius Hiberius, moreover, moved among them here and there, reminding and instructing them how they should conduct themselves. In their midst he ordered a golden eagle, which he carried as a standard, to be securely placed, and he counseled that anyone whom misfortune might isolate should try to return to it.

Finally they stood on opposite sides—here the Britons, there the Romans—with weapons raised. When the sound of the battle-trumpets was heard, at once the division led by the King of Spain and Lucius Catellus boldly plunged into the division led by the King of Scotland and the Duke of

Cornwall, but could by no means separate that closely joined body of men. The division led by Gerin and Boso raced up to the Roman division that was attacking fiercely, and, while the other British division was resisting, as I have said, they made an attack on the Romans with a sudden cavalry charge. Having broken that line, they encountered the division which the King of the Parthians was leading against the division of Aschil, King of the Danes. Immediately troops engaged everywhere and, penetrating one another's ranks, waged a mighty combat. Terrible slaughter took place among them in the midst of loud cries; and, beating the earth with head and heels, everywhere they coughed out their life with their blood.

First a loss was inflicted on the Britons, because Bedivere the Cupbearer was slain and Kay the Seneschal mortally wounded. For while Bedivere was fighting Boccus, King of the Medes, he was pierced by that one's lance among the enemy troops and collapsed, slain. When Kay the Seneschal tried to avenge him, he was surrounded by the troops of the Medes and received his death wound. Yet like a good soldier, with a flank that he was leading, he opened a way through slain and routed Medes and would have retreated to his own lines with his division still intact, if he had not encountered the division of the King of Libya, whose assault wholly dispersed the men whom Kay was leading. But he withdrew with a few men and fled to the golden dragon with Bedivere's body. How great the lamentations of the men of Normandy when they saw the body of their Duke Bedivere torn to pieces with so many wounds! How great the cries of anguish of the men of Anjou as by many means they dressed the wounds of Kay, their leader! But there was no call for mourning, since everywhere the battle-lines bloodily rushing at one another gave them no chance to groan, but forced them to defend themselves.

Therefore Hirelgas, the nephew of Bedivere, greatly moved by his death, gathered three hundred of his men around himself and, like a boar in a pack of dogs, making a sudden cavalry dash through the enemy ranks, sought the place where he had seen the standard of the King of the Medes, little thinking what might befall him while he avenged his uncle. When he reached that place, he killed that king and carried his corpse back to his fellow warriors. When this body was brought next to the body of the Cupbearer, Hirelgas tore it apart. Then with a tremendous shout he urged the troops of his fellow citizens to rush against the enemy, to attack with repeated attacks while courage burned freshly in them and while the breast trembled in those fearful ones, and, while menacing them face to face, they were organized in their division more wisely than the others and could more cruelly and more often inflict a loss.

Stirred by his exhortation, the Britons attacked the enemy at every point, and so great slaughter came to both sides. For on the side of the Romans, not counting many others, there fell King Ali Fatima, Micipsa of Babylon, and Senators Quintus Milvius and Marius Lepidus. There fell, on the side of the

Britons, Duke Holdin of Flanders and Leodegarius of Boulogne, and three lords of Britain: Cursalem of Caistor, Guallauc of Salisbury, and Urbgennius of Bath. Then the troops they were leading fell back much weakened, till they reached the line of the Armorican Britons, which Hoel and Gawain were leading. This line, like a burning flame, made an assault on the enemy. Those who had retreated were renewed, and the Armorican line forced the enemy, who shortly before were in pursuit, to flee. Always pursuing, the Armorican line now unhorsed those in flight, now slew them, now kept on slaughtering until it came to the Roman commander's division. When Lucius saw the distress of his allies, he hastened to give them assistance. At the start of that engagement the Britons lost strength. Chinmarchocus, the lord of Tréguier, fell, and with him went two thousand men. There also fell three notable chieftains: Riddomarcus, Bloctonius, and Iaginvius of Bodloan, whose valor was so great that, had they been princes of kingdoms, ages to come would celebrate their fame. For while they made that attack with Hoel and Gawain, the enemy they threatened did not escape, but they ripped life from them by sword or lance. Yet after reaching the line commanded by Lucius, being everywhere surrounded by Romans, they fell with the lord and soldiers I have named.

Hoel and Gawain—past ages have given birth to no better men—heard of the massacre of their troops and pressed on more strongly, now here, now there, one on this side, the other on that; charging through, they attacked the Roman commander's wedge formation. Gawain, always fiery in courage, sought the opportunity of engaging with Lucius. As he made the attempt, like an audacious soldier, he rushed forward, and as he rushed forward, he unhorsed the enemy, and as he unhorsed them, he slew them. Hoel, no less a man, thundered on the other side. He exhorted his comrades, struck at the enemy, took their blows unafraid, and did not fail at any hour, but repeatedly was hit and hit back. It could not easily be said which of the two outdid the other.

Gawain, however, by hewing down troops, as has been told, found at last the opportunity he wanted and attacked the Roman commander and engaged with him directly. But Lucius, vigorous with youth, had much bravery, much energy, much valor, and he desired nothing more than to encounter a soldier who forced him to test what he could do in arms. Confronting Gawain therefore, he was glad to enter combat with him, and he gloried, for he had heard so much of Gawain's great fame. As the battle was long waged between them, they dealt powerful blows, extending their shields against the attacks, and each labored to bring on the death of the other. While they fought very ferociously in this way, suddenly the Romans recovered and made an attack on the Armoricans. Supporting their commander by killing, they hurled back Hoel and Gawain and their troops, until they came unexpectedly before Arthur and his division. He had heard of the massacre just done to the Britons and had rushed forward with his own legion. He drew out his excellent sword

Caliburn and in a loud voice inspired his soldiers with these words, saying: "What are you doing, men? Why do you let these womanish creatures go off uninjured? Do not let one of them escape! Remember your right arms, exercised in so many battles, that have subdued thirty kingdoms to my power! Remember your ancestors, whom the Romans, while they were stronger, made vassals! Remember your liberty, which those half-men, mere weaklings compared with you, desire to steal! Don't let one get away alive, not one! What are you doing?"

Shouting these and many other taunts, Arthur attacked the enemy. He overthrew, he killed, and whomever he met, he slew either him or his horse with one blow. They fled from him as from a ferocious beast, a lion provoked by savage hunger to devour whatever chance offers. Their arms did not prevent Caliburn, wielded in the right hand of so able a king, from making them spit out their souls with their blood. Bad luck led two kings, Sertorius of Libya and Politetes of Bithynia, to meet Arthur, and he cut off their heads and sent them to Hell. When they saw their king fight in this way, the Britons gained greater courage, attacked the Romans with a single spirit, and assaulted with close-packed squadrons. As the infantry attacked on one side, the cavalry on the other side tried to unhorse and penetrate the enemy ranks. Still the Romans fought back strongly, and under the command of Lucius they labored to give the Britons retaliation for the slaughter done by their renowned king. As a result they fought with as great force on each side as if they had just begun to fight.

On this side Arthur was again and again, as I have said, thrusting at the enemy and urging the Britons to stand their ground. But on the other side Lucius Hiberius both admonished his Romans and led them many times into brilliant deeds of valor. And he himself did not cease to wield his sword, but as he circled through his troops, he killed with lance or sword any enemy that chance presented to him. Appalling slaughter occurred on each side, for now the Britons, now the Romans, in turn prevailed. Then, as this fight was being waged, Morvid, the Earl of Gloucester, dashed forward with the legion that, as I noted above, was in the hills, and from the rear he rushed upon the unwitting enemy. Rushing he entered their lines and scattered them, causing great ruin. Then many thousands of Romans fell. And finally the commander, Lucius, was caught among the troops and killed, pierced by some unknown soldier's lance. Though with great labor, the unrelenting Britons pressed on and got the victory.

The Romans were dispersed: some of them, impelled by fear, chose secret byways and woods; some, towns and forts; and all fled to whatever might be the safest places. The Britons strained on after and crushed them with pitiful carnage, capturing and stripping them, as most of the Romans held their hands out like women to be bound, hoping to get a little more life. This outcome was ordained by the providence of God, since the Roman ancestors in ancient times had harassed the Britons' ancestors with hostile oppressions and now the Britons were trying to defend the liberty the Romans wanted to take from them and were denying the tribute unjustly demanded of them.

In victory Arthur ordered that the bodies of his lords be separated from the bodies of the enemy and, having been separated, that they be prepared royally and carried thus to abbeys nearby, to be honorably buried there. But Bedivère the Cupbearer was carried by the men of Normandy with great lamenting to his own city of Bayeux, which Bedivere the First, his grandfather, had built. There in a certain cemetery that was in the western part of the city, next to the wall, he was honorably laid to rest. Kay was carried to Chinon—a town that he himself had built—gravely wounded, and a little after he died of that wound. As became the Duke of Anjou, he was buried in a wood belonging to a monastic community there, not far from the main town. And Holdin, the Duke of Flanders, was taken to Flanders and buried in his city of Thérouanne. But other lords and chieftains, as Arthur had ordered, were borne to nearby abbeys. Merciful also to his enemies, he ordered the natives to bury them, and the body of Lucius to be conveyed to the Senate, with the message that nothing else was to be paid from Britain. Until the following winter he stayed on in that region and was free to subdue the cities of the Burgundians.

Then as summer approached, when he wanted to go to Rome and had just begun to cross the mountains, it was announced to him that his nephew Modred, to whose guardianship he had entrusted Britain, was wearing its crown in tyranny and treachery, and that Queen Guinevere, having broken the oath of her prior nuptials, had been joined to him in unconscionable lust. Geoffrey of Monmouth will not speak about this, my noble duke. But since he finds it told in the British work previously mentioned, and since he heard it from Walter of Oxford, a man well schooled in many histories, he will make public, though in an ordinary style and briefly, what battles that illustrious king engaged in with his nephew when he returned to Britain after his victory over the Romans.

When the infamy of this notorious crime reached his ears, Arthur postponed the invasion he had wanted to make against Emperor Leo, and having sent Duke Hoel of the Armoricans with an army of Gauls to pacify those districts, he immediately returned to Britain with only the kings of the islands and their armies. But that criminal traitor Modred sent Chelric, the Duke of the Saxons, to Germany, so that there he might league with himself those he could and might quickly return with any allies he could muster. For by agreement Modred had promised that he would give Chelric that part of the island which extends from the River Humber to Scotland, and whatever Hengist and Horsa had possessed in Kent in the time of Vortigern. Chelric had carried out his command and had already landed with eight hundred ships full of armed pagans. He had given a pledge to the traitor and was obeying him as his king. Modred had also allied with himself the Scots, the Picts, the Irish, and anyone who he knew from experience hated his uncle. They were about eight hundred thousand in all, both pagans and Christians.

Relying on their help and on the multitude of his own army, Modred met Arthur landing in the port of Richborough. Battle having been engaged, he devastated those coming ashore. King Auguselus of Albany and Gawain, the nephew of the King, with countless others, fell that day. But Ywain, the son of Urian, succeeded Auguselus in the kingdom and afterward in those battles distinguished himself by many acts of valor. Finally, though they got to the shore with great difficulty and killing on both sides, Arthur's men put Modred and his army to flight. Practiced through rigorous conquests, they had ordered their troops wisely, partly as cavalry to fight, so that when an infantry division intended to attack or resist, the cavalry would rush in there from an angle and try to penetrate the enemy ranks and so put them to flight. That perjurer, having regrouped his troops from all quarters, entered Winchester the next night. When this was made known to Queen Guinevere, she instantly despaired, fled from York to Caerleon, and among the nuns in the church of the Martyr Julius embraced their way of life and vowed to live in chastity.

But Arthur raged with tougher anger, since he had lost so many hundreds of his fellow soldiers, and on the third day, having buried the slain, he approached the city of Winchester and besieged the scoundrel who was sheltered inside. That one was unwilling to desist from what he had begun, but animating in every way those who followed him, he came with his troops and arranged to fight his uncle. Once the contest had begun, there was much slaughter on both sides, but finally more was borne by Modred's side, which forced him with humiliation to abandon the field. Taking little care about what burial might be given to his slain, he quickly fled, conveyed by boat, on his way toward Cornwall. Arthur suffered torment that Modred had so often escaped, and at once went after him into that country, to the River Camblan, where Modred awaited his approach.

Supremely audacious and always swift to attack, Modred immediately divided his soldiers into squadrons, wishing rather to conquer or die than flee any longer as he had done before. Sixty thousand of his allies still remained loyal to him, from which he made six divisions, and in each one he placed six thousand, six hundred and sixty-six armed men. Moreover, he made one division from the remaining soldiers, and, after generals were appointed for each of the other divisions, he took this one under his own command. Having organized these divisions, he encouraged each of them, promising them the possessions of their enemies if they held on to victory. Arthur also positioned his army on the opposite side, and he divided it into nine divisions of infantry, with a right and left wing, square-shaped, and with leaders assigned to each. He urged them to kill the perjurers and thieves who, at the command of his betrayer, had been drawn from distant regions to this island and wanted to take their honors from them. He also said that Modred's allies were mongrel barbarians from many kingdoms, unwarlike and ignorant in the practice of war, who could not at all resist Arthur's forces, who were powerful men practiced in many conquests—provided Arthur's men chose to attack boldly and fight manfully.

After Arthur and Modred had urged their troops on in this way, the two lines rushed together in a sudden burst. They joined in battle, striving to give blow after blow. At that place there occurred on both sides such killing, such groans of the dying, such furies of the attackers that it is tragic to describe. For everywhere they wounded or they were wounded, they killed or they were killed. After they had spent much of the day in this manner, Arthur finally rushed with his one division, in which he had put six thousand, six hundred and sixty-six men, into that squadron where he knew Modred to be. By opening a way with swords, he entered it and caused frightening bloodshed. Then that abominable traitor fell and many thousands with him. And yet the rest did not flee because of his death, but joining from every field, they tried to resist with as much bravery as was theirs. The hardest of fighting was waged between them, in which almost all the leaders present on both sides fell with their troops. On Modred's side there fell Chelric, Elaf, Egbrict, and Bruning, who were Saxons; Gillapatric, Gillamor, Gillasel, Gillarvus, who were Irish; Scots also and Picts, with almost all whom they commanded. On Arthur's side Odbrict, the King of Norway, fell; Aschil, the King of Denmark; Cador Limenich; Cassibellaunus; with many thousands of their men, who were Britons or from other races they had led with them. Furthermore, the glorious King Arthur was mortally wounded, and was carried from there to the Isle of Avalon, so that his wounds might be healed. To Constantine, his cousin, who was the son of Duke Cador of Cornwall, he granted the crown of Britain, in the year of Our Lord 542.

[handwritten annotation:] Life of Merlin — prophesy - King Arthur will come again.

Stonehenge. According to legend, Merlin transferred these monolithic stones from Ireland to this location in Wiltshire. (Courtesy of the British Tourist Authority)

Chapter *V*

WACE: *ROMAN DE BRUT*

(Merlin Episodes and "The Birth and Rise of Arthur")

James J. Wilhelm

Wace's *Roman de Brut* is the first full account of the Arthurian story in a vernacular language: Old North French. Other versions may have existed before Wace but none has survived. The little we know about Wace's life comes from his last work, the *Roman de Rou*, a verse history of the dukes of Normandy. He wrote this book for King Henry II of England, beginning it in 1160 but being supplanted in the undertaking by one Master Beneeit, apparently at the king's insistence. Five years before he began his Norman compilation, he undertook the massive task of rendering into French Geoffrey of Monmouth's *History of the Kings of Britain*, which had been written in Latin. This was dedicated to Henry's queen, the famous Eleanor of Aquitaine, and it was presented to the queen in 1155. Before this, Wace also translated some saints' lives from Latin into French.

Wace was born on the Norman-controlled island of Jersey at some point in the early twelfth century, possibly around 1110. He was educated at Caen in Normandy (which he calls the city of Kay) and then near Paris, but he spent most of his later life in his beloved Normandy. Although he was himself of Germanic stock, in his *Roman de Brut* his sympathies are always with the British Celts. Following Geoffrey he tells their early history, beginning with a legendary progenitor named Brutus, who is of Trojan-Roman stock. Brut, as he is called, is a descendant of the great Roman hero Aeneas, celebrated in Vergil's *Aeneid*. He frees some enslaved Trojans in Greece and takes them to the island of Albion, which was then renamed "Britain" in honor of him. Needless to say, none of this is historically proven. Geoffrey (and Wace and Layamon, who followed him) then recounts British history in a highly imaginative and undocumented way, although several of his kings and other characters can be found in Welsh myth and legend. Wace is noted for his lively narration and his ability to create scenes and characters with a few strokes of the brush. He excels in dramatic episodes, such as King Uther's wooing of Igerna, and in comic scenes, such as Merlin's being questioned about his father and family history. He is weakest in scenes of violence and valor, just where Layamon is strongest. We have thus selected the Merlin episodes and the early periods of Arthur's life from Wace's work and left the dramatic and violent end of the Arthurian story for Layamon in the chapter that follows. Arthur's battles in the middle portion of his life can be found in Geoffrey of Monmouth's work.

Wace is the first author to mention the Round Table. He also refers directly to Breton storytellers, who served as the link between Celtic Britain and Celtic Brittany, showing that they existed around 1150. These minstrels and narrators would be necessary for the transmission of remote Celtic materials on the British islands to the mainland, where they could then enter the main course of European literature. Wace also mentions the so-called "Breton Hope" that became attached to Arthur's ending. According to this messianic wish, Arthur never fully died, and he will return to free the Celts from their Saxon dominators. This ending to his work is added to the earlier selections here.

Bibliographic note: The 14,800-odd octosyllabic lines in rhymed couplets are not readily translatable into modern English poetry. My prose version is quite free, using compressions and clarifications wherever deemed necessary. I consulted but did not rely on the antiquated translation by S. Evans (Everyman, 1911); the thesis translation by D.A. Light (New York University, 1970) did afford some help with certain problems.

I have used as my base Ivor Arnold's critical edition of *Le Roman de Brut* in two volumes (SATF, 1938–40) and have also consulted the two-volume edition by Le Roux de Lincy (Rouen, 1838), which is antiquated but interesting for its notes. Lincy includes some lines and words rejected by Arnold, and I have adopted a few of these because of the color they add.

The criticism on Wace is extensive. Further reading can be found in the bibliography accompanying extracts from the *Roman* in the edition of Arnold and M.M. Pelan (Klincksieck, 1962): *La Partie arthurienne du "Roman de Brut."* See also the entry "Wace," by William W. Kibler, in *The Arthurian Encyclopedia,* edited by Norris J. Lacy et al. (Garland, 1991).

Roman de Brut

[*After the departure of the Romans from Britain the treacherous Vortigern kills King Constant and forces his two younger brothers, Aurelius Ambrosius and Uther, to flee to Brittany. King Vortigern then calls upon the Saxons of Germany under the leadership of Horsa and Hengist to protect him against the Picts. After this victory Vortigern marries Rowena, the daughter of Hengist, who becomes the ruler of Kent; but Hengist soon lusts for the kingship and forces Vortigern to flee to the Gloucester area, where Vortigern wants to enclose himself in a tower. He tries to build one on Mount Snowdon, but every night the day's construction tumbles to the ground. He consults some wise men, who tell him that he has to speak with a man who has no earthly father. Vortigern tries to find such a man, but cannot, until his messengers stumble on two men in Carmarthen, Wales, who are speaking together as follows.]*

[*Line 7373*] "Hold your tongue, Merlin!" said Dinabus. "Be still. I am from a much nobler line than you. Don't you know who you are, you evil thing? You shouldn't argue with me or degrade my lineage! I was born of kings and counts; and if *you* tried to account for your parents, you couldn't name your father even, because you don't know who he is, and you never will. You don't know his name because you never had one!"

On hearing this quarrel, the messengers, who were looking for such a man, went over to some neighbors to ask who this creature was who did not have a father. The neighbors replied that, indeed, this fellow had never had a father, and his mother had no idea at all who had engendered the boy. But although Merlin knew nothing about his father, he did have a mother who was known. She was the daughter of the king of Demetia, which is a part of Wales. Now a nun in an abbey in the town, she was a woman of great integrity. The messengers then went to the provost, demanding in the name of the king that this fatherless Merlin and his mother be brought before the king. Unable to refuse, the provost had them summoned before Vortigern.

The king received them kindly and spoke to them warmly. "Lady," he said, "tell me the truth. Without your help I can never learn who fathered your son, Merlin."

The nun stood with head bowed. After she had considered for a moment, she said: "God help me, I never knew or saw the man who fathered this fellow on me. I never heard and I certainly can't tell for sure if it even was a man by whom I had him, but I do know this for certain and I'll swear to its truth: after I had grown up, a certain creature—I don't know if it was a phantom even— used to come to me and kiss me hotly. He used to speak to me like a man and he felt like one, for many times he spoke with me, but he never really revealed himself. He came to me again and again, and he kissed me and slept with me so often that I finally grew pregnant, but I never knew any man but him. This man here—this is the child I had. More than that I do not know, and more I cannot tell."

The king had Magant, a clerk whom he considered very wise, summoned, and he asked if what the lady had said could be true. Magant replied: "We have found it written that between the moon and the earth there is a certain kind of peculiar spirit. If you want to know what they're like—they're partly human and partly celestial. These spirits are known as incubi. Their territory is the air, but their home is the earth. They are not capable of great evil, and they can't hurt us, except to tease and annoy us. But they can easily assume our human shape and nature. They have deceived many a young girl and tricked her by this disguise. This is the way that Merlin was probably fathered and probably born."

"King!" interrupted Merlin. "You summoned me here. What do you want of me? Why did you bring me here?"

"Merlin," said the king, "that you will learn. Listen well, and you'll hear it. I started to build a tower, and put stone to mortar, but whatever I built during the day tumbled down at night. I don't know if you've heard about this, but the day can do nothing that the night can't undo—and much of my wealth has been squandered. My sages tell me that I'll never get my tower if your blood isn't mixed with the mortar, since you've been born without a father."

"I hope to God," cried Merlin, "that my blood won't make your tower stand! I'll call them liars openly if you summon the men who prescribed my blood, for they are liars indeed!"

The king had the men summoned, and he put them in front of Merlin. When Merlin had looked them over, he said: "My lords who prophesy, tell me why this building won't stand up. If you can't tell me why this tower crumbles to the ground, how can you predict that my blood is needed to make it stand up? Tell us why the foundation gives way so often, and what it lacks and what it needs. If you can't tell us what makes the work fall down, how can you be believed when you say that my blood will make it stand? Tell the king the problem and the solution."

All of the wise men were silent, not knowing how to reply. And when Merlin saw this he immediately said to the king: "Your Majesty, listen! Under the foundation of your tower lies a pool that is broad and deep and that makes your tower crumble. If you want to believe me, then dig down and you'll see!"

The king ordered men to dig, and the pool that Merlin mentioned was found. "Masters," said Merlin, "hear me! You who tried to mix my blood with your mortar, tell me what's in this pool."

They all stood mute and dumbfounded, not wanting to add a word. Turning to the king so that his men could hear, Merlin ordered: "Empty this pool by draining the water off. Down at the bottom are two sleeping dragons lying on two large stones. One of these dragons is white, while the other is as crimson as blood."

When the water was drained into the fields, two dragons rose from the depths and faced each other glaringly. With great ferocity they leaped at each other before the barons. You could truly see them foaming, with flames shooting out of their mouths. The king sat down at the edge of the pool and begged Merlin to tell him the significance of the dragons, which were clashing with such rage. And so Merlin recited his prophecies, which you have heard, I suppose, about the kings to come who would control the earth. I do not want to translate his book since I do not know how to interpret it. I do not want to say anything that is not all true.

The king praised Merlin very highly and considered him a marvelous prophet. He asked when he would die and how, because he was terrified about his end. "Be careful," said Merlin; "be very careful of the sons of Constantine [Aurelius and Uther], because through them you will come to your end. They've already left Brittany and are coming boldly over the sea. I can tell you this for certain: they will arrive at Totnes tomorrow. You did wrong to them, and they'll do wrong to you to avenge your crime. You evilly betrayed their brother [Constant] and made yourself king in an evil manner, and you viciously lured pagans and Saxons into this realm. You face danger on two sides, and I don't know which is worse. On one side the Saxons want to make war on you and destroy you; on the other are the heirs who want to regain their kingdom. They want to wrench Britain away from you and avenge their brother. If you can run, go now, because these two brothers are on the way! Aurelius will be king first, but he will also die first, from poison. Uther Pendragon, his brother, will rule the realm after him, but he will quickly become sick and be poisoned by your heirs. Arthur, his son from Cornwall, who is as fierce as a boar in battle, will devour the traitors against him and will destroy your kinsmen. He will be valiant and fine and will wipe out all of his enemies." Merlin finished this speech, and Vortigern turned away from there.

[*True to Merlin's word, the two brothers reenter Britain and burn Vortigern to death in his tower; the throne falls to Aurelius. The new king wants to build a monument at Ambresbury in honor of his faithful men who had fallen at the hands of the Saxon Hengist.*]

[*Line 8003*] Tremorius, a wise man who was the Archbishop of Caerleon, told Aurelius to send for Merlin and to build according to his advice. No one else could advise him better, since Merlin had no equal when it came to creating and divining. The king wanted to see Merlin and evaluate his wisdom firsthand. At Labenes [Galabes] far away in Wales (a place I do not know, since I have never been there) the king sent for him. Merlin answered the summons and was well received by Aurelius, who welcomed him with great honor, offering him good cheer and companionship and begging him solicitously to teach him about the future, for he eagerly wanted to hear this from him.

"Sir," said Merlin, "I can't do this. I won't open my mouth unless I'm forced to, and this is because of humility. If I spoke braggingly or jestingly or proudly, my guardian spirit, who teaches me all that I know, would leave my lips and take all of my knowledge away. My mouth would not be any more valuable than anyone else's. Let such secrets lie. Think about what you have to do now. If you want to create a lasting work that's beautiful and fitting and will be talked about for all time to come, then bring over here the circle that the giants built in Ireland—a wonderful, huge, round work with stone set on stone—so strong and heavy that no strength of men now alive can ever lift them."

"Merlin," said the king, laughing, "since these stones weigh so much that nobody can budge them, who could possibly bring them over here? Don't we have stones enough in our kingdom already?"

"King," said Merlin, "don't you realize that brains are better than brawn? Strength is fine, but cunning is much better, since it often succeeds where muscles fail. Intelligence and cunning can accomplish much that brute strength would never dare. Cunning can move those rocks and bring them over here to you. After all, they were carried from Africa, where they were first sculpted. Giants transported them from there to Ireland. These stones are beneficial and healthful for the sick. People used to pour water over these rocks and then heat the water as baths for the sick and the infirm. After they bathed, they were cured. They never needed any other kind of medicine for their illness."

When the king and the British heard that those stones had this magic power, they were eager to import the circle that Merlin had described. They chose Uther, who accepted, to lead 15,000 armed men across to Ireland to fight for the stones if they were defended, along with Merlin, who would engineer their transport. When Uther had collected his men, he made the crossing to Ireland, where King Guillomer assembled his own forces to threaten the Britons and drive them out of his land. When the Irish learned that the Britons were searching for these stones, they were full of mockery, saying that it was crazy to come looking for rocks over land and sea. The Britons would not get a single one to carry away. But it is easier to mock someone than to outdo him. The Irish kept ridiculing and threatening and tracking the Britons down until the two forces finally met and were locked in battle. But the Irish were neither so well armed nor so used to fighting, and as a result the once-vilified Britons emerged as the victors. King Guillomer fled madly from town to town.

When the Britons disarmed themselves to rest, Merlin, who was in their company, led them up to a mountain where the eagerly sought circle had been built. The hill was called Killomar, where the circle loomed on top. The Britons gazed at all those rocks, and as they walked around them they told one another that they had never seen such a marvelous feat. "How had all those stones been erected there, and how could they possibly be carried away?"

"My lords," said Merlin, "see if you have the strength to move these rocks and carry them off." The men approached the rocks on every side, front and back. They pushed and they pulled and they heaved and they tugged, but they could not move one of them an inch. "Move away," shouted Merlin, "for your strength won't do a thing. Now see what craft and cunning can accomplish that bodily strength cannot." Then he walked forward and stood gazing around. He moved his lips like a man uttering a prayer; I do not know if he prayed or not. Then he shouted again to the Britons: "Come over here! Come on! Now you can pick up these rocks and carry them down to the ships."

Just as Merlin directed, and exactly the way he prescribed and commanded, the Britons took the stones down to the ships and put them inside. They transported the stones to Britain, putting them on the plain at Ambresbury. The king went there at Pentecost, having ordered his bishops, abbots, and barons to assemble, along with many others; and they held a feast for his coronation. It lasted for three days, and on the fourth he dutifully bestowed croziers on St. Dubris of Caerleon and St. Samson of York, both of whom were great clergymen who led lives of great saintliness. And then Merlin arranged the rocks in order, side by side. The Britons [Welsh] call this the Giants' Carol in their tongue; in English the name of the place is Stonehenge; in French it is "Hanging Rocks."

[*Paschent, a son of Vortigern, flees to Germany and then to Ireland, where he joins forces with the Irish king and attacks Wales. Aurelius rushes to meet him but falls sick and is poisoned by a false doctor in the pay of Paschent.*]

[*Line 8274*] After the king was inflamed and his body was permeated by the poison, O God, what grief! He had to die. When Aurelius was aware of his oncoming death, he made his retainers swear to carry his body to Stonehenge and to inter him there. And then he ended his days, and the traitorous poisoner fled.

Uther had entered Wales and found the Irish in Menevia. Then a star appeared to the view of many, called the Comet according to the clergy. This signified a change of kings. It was marvelously clear as it shot forth its single ray. The fire from this ray assumed the shape of a dragon, and two further beams issued from its jaws. One ray spread over France all the way to Mount St. Bernard [in the Alps]. The other extended toward Ireland and divided into seven other lights. Each of these seven beams shone clearly over the land and the sea. The people were all shaken as they saw this sign. Uther wondered deeply about it and was greatly disturbed. He begged Merlin to tell him what it meant. Merlin also was much troubled, with misgivings in his heart, and he did not answer a word at first. When his spirits returned, he sighed deeply and said sorrowfully: "O God, what great unhappiness, what great loss, what trouble have now descended over our Britain! We have lost our great captain! Our king is dead, that fine champion who delivered our country from grief and evil, wrenching it from the hands of the heathens!"

When Uther heard that the end had come for his brother, that fine lord, he was filled with sadness and dismay. But Merlin comforted him, saying "Uther, don't be depressed. Nobody escapes from death. Carry out what you started. Fight your enemy. The triumph tomorrow will be yours over Ireland and Paschent. You will win that engagement tomorrow and will become the king of Britain. The sign of the dragon refers to you, who are brave and hardy. The ray to the east is a son you will have who will be very powerful and who will conquer lands beyond France. The other ray to the west with its seven offshoots signifies a daughter who will marry the king of Scotland. Many fine heirs will be born from her who will conquer lands and seas."

When Uther heard what Merlin told him in consolation, he had his men rest that night and arm themselves in the morning. He wanted to attack the city, but when the Irish saw him coming they took up their armor and gear and rushed out to fight. The battle was fierce, and many men were overcome. When the Britons had killed both Paschent and the Irish king, those who left the field alive fled away to their ships. Uther pursued them, harassing them to the bitter end. There were some who escaped by boarding their ships and speeding across the sea so that Uther could not catch them.

On finishing this business, Uther made his way to Winchester with the flower of his knighthood. On the road he met a messenger who told him in all truth that the king had died and how this had happened. The bishops, with great care and ceremony, had arranged his burial inside the Giants' Carol, as Aurelius had asked his sergeants and barons while he was still alive. When Uther heard this, he rushed to Winchester. The people there ran out crying and shouting in a loud voice: "Uther, my lord! For the sake of God, the man who once looked after us and gave us many favors is now gone! Protect us! Take the crown that is yours by due right and heritage. We all beg you, good sir, since we desire nothing but your profit and honor."

Uther saw that his profit was there, and he could do no better than to seize it. He was happy at what he heard and immediately did as they requested. He took the crown, became king, loved honor, and maintained the people well. In token and memory of the dragon's reference to a bold man who would be king and would have many conquering heirs, upon the advice of his barons he had two golden dragons created. One he always carried into battle; the other he granted to Winchester, to the bishop's church. For this reason he was always thereafter called Uther Pendragon. The British word "Pendragon" means "Dragonhead" [Chief Dragon] in French.

[*Uther is a good king, but he is challenged by the Saxon leader Octa, the son of Hengist, and his cousin Ossa. With the help of Gorlois, the count of Cornwall, Uther captures them in York and takes them back to London to prison.*]

[*Line 8551*] When Uther had finished his affairs in the north, he returned directly to London, and on Easter Day he planned to be crowned. Dukes and counts and knights from far and wide and all his other lieges he summoned by letter and proclamation to come with their wives and retainers to London for the festival, which he wanted to be lavish. They all came as he had requested, bringing wives if they were with them. The festival was celebrated with grandeur, and when the mass had been sung the king sat down for dinner at the head of the table on a dais. The barons sat around him, each according to his rank. Facing Uther was the lord of Cornwall, and beside him was Igerna, his wife, the most beautiful woman in the whole kingdom. She was courteous, elegant, and wise and came from excellent lineage. The king had heard a great deal about her, and it was all praise. Even before he showed it and before he set eyes on her figure, he loved and coveted her because of this extravagant praise.

Uther kept staring at her during dinner, turning his whole attention her way. If he ate or drank or talked or sat silent, he was always thinking about her and glancing her way; and as he looked, he smiled, showing her signs of love. He honored her by having his private pages attend her with little favors. He joked with her, winked at her, and showed her every sign of affection. Igerna controlled herself, neither granting him anything nor denying it.

Her husband noticed these jibes and jests and endearments and compliments and courtesies, and he soon realized that the king was in love with his wife. Never would he show faith to a lord who so blatantly wooed his wife! He leaped up from the table, grabbed his wife by the hand, and darted out of the chamber. Calling his companions, he ran out to mount his horse. The king quickly sent word to Gorlois that it would cast disgrace and shame on him if he left the court without begging His Majesty's leave. Gorlois should act correctly, not discourteously! And if he failed to do this, the king warned him, wherever Gorlois might go he could not trust what would happen. But Gorlois had no desire to return. He left the court without asking the king's permission. The king had threatened him sternly, but the count dismissed this, not guessing the outcome.

Gorlois returned to Cornwall and prepared two of his castles for invasion. He put his wife in Tintagel, which had long been his ancestral holding. Tintagel was easily defensible—hard to take by any craft since it was perched on a steep cliff and largely surrounded by the sea. If one held only the main gate, he had no fear of entry from any other quarter. Gorlois enclosed Igerna there, since no other place could guarantee her from being seized and carried away. Then he took his men-at-arms and the larger part of his knights to another castle that guarded most of his fief.

The king learned that Gorlois had stocked his castles in defense against him. In order to attack the count and draw near his wife, Uther assembled his forces and crossed the River Tamar. He arrived at the castle where the count was enclosed and wanted to storm it, but it held firm. Then he set siege to it, and he stayed there for a week, but he could not capture it. The count would not give up because he was waiting for help to come from the king of Ireland. The British king was angered by this delay, which only caused him anguish, since his love for Igerna, which exceeded everything else, was constantly urging him forward. He called in one of his closest barons and said: "Ulfin, give me your advice. I put all my faith in you. My love for Igerna has overwhelmed me, beaten me down, vanquished me totally. I can't go or come, wake or sleep, rise or lie down, drink or eat without thinking about her. But I don't know how I can win her. I'll die if you can't advise me well."

Ulfin replied: "O what marvels I hear! You've harassed the count with war and cut off his land and enclosed him in his castle. Now do you really think that his wife approves of this? You love his wife and you make war on him—I don't know what counsel you're looking for or what I can give you. But call for Merlin, who's imbued with all the arts and is among our entourage. If he doesn't know how to advise you, nobody can."

Acting on Ulfin's advice, the king sent for Merlin and soon declared all of his needs. He cried and begged him in his mercy to lend some advice, because he would certainly die in a cruel way if he did not win the favors of Igerna: "Please try to do all you can! I'll give you anything you want, since I'm suffering such evil sorrow now."

"Sir," said Merlin, "you shall have her. You won't die for Igerna's sake. I'll give you all you want and you won't have to repay me a thing. But Igerna is closely guarded, locked up in Tintagel, which can't be taken by any force because it's impregnable. Her coming and her going are carefully watched by two loyal guards. But I can get you in there through my powerful enchantments. I know how to change the shape of a man and how to transform one human being into another. I can make one person resemble another, and vice versa. Without any doubt I can give you the body, face, manner, speech, and habits of the count of Cornwall. Why make this talk too long? I'll turn you into the count, and I'll go along with you, taking on the appearance of Bretel, and Ulfin, who'll accompany us, will look like Jordan. The count has these two very dear counselors with him. This way you can enter the castle and get whatever you want. You will never be perceived or mistrusted by anyone there."

The king believed Merlin completely and considered his advice excellent. He privately gave control of his men to one of his barons. Merlin effected his enchantments: he changed their faces and clothing, and so they entered Tintagel that very night. Those who thought they knew the three received and welcomed them and served them with joy. The king lay that night with Igerna, who conceived the good, strong, and certain monarch whom you all know as King Arthur.

The king's men soon realized that the king was not in their midst. There was not a baron whom they respected or for whom they would do a thing. Because of the delay they anticipated, they took up their arms and put them on. Without proper formations or equipment they rushed the castle in disarray, assailing it on every side. The count defended himself bravely, but he was killed and the castle was quickly captured. Some men got away, and they dashed to report at Tintagel how things had gone badly for their lord and how many people they had lost.

On hearing this report about the death of their leader being sorrowfully recounted, the king got up quickly and sprang forward, shouting: "Keep still!

It's not at all like that! I'm completely alive and well, thanks to God, as you can plainly see. This news is not true! Don't believe it or disbelieve it. I can tell you why my men so fear for me. I left that other place without saying a word of good-bye to any of them. I never said that I was going and was coming back here to you because I was afraid of treachery. Now they're all afraid that I'm dead because nobody saw me since the king entered the castle. Of course we have to grieve for the men killed and the castle that's fallen, but it still bodes well that I'm alive. I'll still stand up against that king! I'll ask him for peace, promising an accord before he besieges this castle and brings us worse mischief. For if he surprises us here, we'll have to plead more humbly."

Igerna praised this plan, since she was always afraid of the king. And then the king embraced her and kissed her at his departure. And so he left the castle, having enjoyed all his desire.

When the king and Ulfin and Merlin were safely out on the road, everyone changed his shape and once again became the man that he ought to be. Then they arrived quickly back with the main army. The king wanted to know how the castle had fallen so fast, and if the count had been truly slain. He was told the truth on both accounts. Uther said that he was very disturbed by the count's death, since he had not wanted that. He mourned and regretted this deed, acting very angry toward the lieges who had done it. He clearly assumed the appearance of a mourner, but very few of his men believed him.

Then he returned to Tintagel. He called up to the householders, asking them why they defended the place, since the other castle had been taken and their count was dead. They could not expect any aid inside their own country or from abroad. They all realized that the king was telling the truth, and they had no hope whatever of being rescued. And so they opened the gates of the stronghold and handed the fortress over to him. Since the king was so deeply in love with Igerna, he married her without any delay. The night before, she had conceived a son, and after the proper time she gave birth to him. Arthur was his name. Many words have been voiced about his goodness. After him Anna was born, a daughter who was given to the fine and upstanding lord of Lothian, who had the name of Lot.

[*Ossa and Octa, freed from prison, wage war against Uther and Lot; they are slain, but they pass on the torch of rebellion to their cousin Colgrin. When Uther falls sick, he is given a cup from a poisoned well.*]

[*Line 8993*] When the king wanted to drink, and then did drink, he was poisoned and had to die. After downing the water, he swelled up, looking dark and discolored, and soon he passed away. Everyone else who partook of that well also died, so that the treacherous deed was apparent and known to all. The leaders of the city assembled and sealed up the well, filling it with enough earth to create a mound.

After King Uther had met his end, he was carried to Stonehenge and there interred by the side of his brother. The bishops then got together, convening with the barons. They sent for Arthur, Uther's son, and crowned him at Silchester.

Arthur was a young man of fifteen, tall and strong for his years. I shall describe all his qualities, not falsifying anything. He was a very worthy knight, one of great valor and glory. He was arrogant toward the arrogant, and sweet and humble toward the lowly. He was strong and hardy and domineering, but also a gracious and generous giver. If anybody in need asked him for something, he would give it to that person if he could. He loved praise and glory very much, and he wanted all of his good deeds to be remembered. He maintained an elegant court and conducted himself there very nobly. As long as he lived and ruled, he surpassed all other princes in courtesy and nobility and valor and generosity.

[*Arthur attempts to drive the Saxons, especially Colgrin, out of the land, fighting battles from the Caledonian Forest in Scotland to Badon, which Wace interprets as Bath.*]

[*Line 9267*] With all his forces Arthur went to Bath as fast as he could. He wanted to break the Saxon siege and rescue the citizens trapped inside. In a neighboring wood on a great plain Arthur armed his troops. He divided his forces and put them in ranks and then armed himself. He put on his thigh-pieces, which were beautiful and well made, and he donned his fine and handsome hauberk, which was worthy of such a king. He strapped on his sword, Excalibur, which was very long and broad. It had been forged on the island of Avalon, and it always assisted the man who held it. Arthur wore a bright and shiny helmet on his head; its nose-piece was made of gold, and circlets of gold ran around the sides. On its crest a dragon was portrayed. This helmet, which sparkled with many jewels, had belonged to Uther, his father. Arthur rode on a very fine stallion that was strong and fast and lithe; Pridwen, his shield, dangled from his neck. In no way would you take him for a coward or a fool. On his shield was masterfully portrayed an image of Our Lady St. Mary, for her honor and remembrance. He also carried a stiff lance called Ron, which was very sharp at its point and long and sturdy, and was very much feared in time of action.

[*Arthur wins the Battle of Bath with the help of Cador of Cornwall. He then rescues Hoel of Brittany in Scotland.*]

[*Line 9597*] Arthur returned to York and stayed there until Christmas. He celebrated the day of Christ's nativity there. He saw that the city was extremely impoverished, weakened, and degraded. He saw the churches deserted and the houses ruined and fallen. He appointed Pyramus, a wise chaplain, who had always served him well, as the archbishop to maintain the churches and restore the monasteries that had been devastated by the pagans. He then proclaimed peace everywhere and told the farmers to return to the fields. All of the honorable men who had been disinherited he summoned to him and restored their heritages, giving them back their fiefs and increasing their incomes.

There were three brothers of fine, even royal, lineage: Lot, Aguisel, and Urien. Their ancestors had held the land north of the River Humber, as they would during the following peace, most justly and without harming anyone. Arthur gave them back their fiefs and inheritances. To Urien, the eldest of the family, he restored Moray without his having to pay rents or fees, proclaiming him the ruler there; he became the lord of the province of Moray. To Aguisel he gave Scotland, which had been claimed as his fief. To Lot, who had married his sister and had stood by him for a long time, he gave all of Lothian and many other fiefs besides. Gawain, Lot's son, was still just a handsome young courtier at this time.

When Arthur had settled his realm and established justice everywhere and restored the whole kingdom to its ancient dignity, he took for his queen Guinevere, a charming and fresh young maiden. She was lovely, well mannered, and gracious and had noble Roman relatives. Cador had reared her richly in Cornwall for a long time as his near cousin, since his mother was also Roman. Guinevere was a young lady of great charm and noble bearing. She spoke beautifully and acted generously. Arthur adored her and cherished her completely, but the two of them never had an heir; no, she never gave birth to a child.

[*Arthur then subdued the Irish and on returning to Britain established a legendary twelve years of peace; then:*]

[*Line 9751*] Arthur created the Round Table, about which the Britons tell many a tale. There sat his vassals, all in royalty and equality; yes, they sat at his table in equal rank and were served equally; neither one nor another could brag that he sat higher than a peer. They were all gathered closely around the king; nobody was relegated to a corner. No man was considered courtly—not a Scot or Breton or Frank or Norman or Angevin or Fleming or Burgundian or man of Lorraine, wherever he maintained his land from the West to Mount St. Bernard—who did not come and stay for a while with Arthur in equality, and who did not have the clothing, the trappings, and the armor of the sort that those who served at Arthur's court had. People came from many lands seeking praise and honor, some to hear his courteous speech, or to see his elegant court, or to get to know his barons, or to receive rich gifts. He was much adored by the poor and much honored by the rich. Foreign kings envied him because they feared and trembled that he would conquer the whole world and take their possessions away from them.

I do not know if you have heard of the great wonders that occurred during this long period of peace, both out of love of his generosity and out of fear of his prowess, or if you have heard some of the adventures told about Arthur that have turned into fables—some of them lying, some of them true, some of them showing wisdom and some foolishness. The storytellers have narrated and the fable-makers have told tales in order to embellish their plots, and they have made everything seem unreal.

[*From this point Arthur engages in actions on the Continent, eventually warring against the Roman emperor Lucius Hiberius, who is finally slain. This part of the story is continued in Chapter VI, as narrated by the Englishman Layamon in his* Brut, *along with the episode of Mordred's betrayal and the king's death. Wace's final words about those cataclysmic events are memorable.*]

[*Line 13,276*] If the chronicle does not lie, Arthur was mortally wounded in his body. He had himself carried to Avalon to heal his wounds. He is still there, and the Britons are still awaiting him. As they always say and firmly believe: he will come back from Avalon; yes, he will live again. Master Wace, who made this book, does not wish to discuss this ending any further than the prophet Merlin did. Merlin said of Arthur (and he spoke rightly) that his death would be a thing of doubt. Yes, the prophet spoke the truth. For all time men have wondered—and indeed they will always wonder—if he is dead or alive. In truth, he was carried to Avalon five hundred and forty-two years after the birth of Christ. It is a pity that he had no heir. He gave his kingdom to his cousin Constantine of Cornwall, son of Cador, telling him to rule until the day when Arthur himself would return.

Chapter *VI*

LAYAMON: *BRUT*

("The Death of Arthur")

JAMES J. WILHELM

Layamon's *Brut* is the first full account of the Arthurian story in the English language. It is the second major poetic adaptation of Geoffrey of Monmouth's *History of the Kings of Britain*, taking as its immediate model Wace's *Roman de Brut*. Layamon's poem is extremely long, consisting of over 32,000 half-lines, which cover British history from the time of the mythic Brutus to the retreat of Cadwallader before the Saxons in A.D. 689.

In his prologue Layamon tells us that he was a priest who was living at a noble church at King's Areley in Worcestershire. He says that he used as his primary sources for his poem the *Ecclesiastical History* of the Venerable Bede and, more importantly, Wace, who had presented his work to Queen Eleanor, the wife of King Henry II. Layamon probably composed his own poem after the death of Henry in 1189 and before that of Eleanor in 1204.

Layamon's *Brut* survives in only two manuscripts, both in the British Library: Cotton Caligula A.ix and Cotton Otho C.xiii, both of which were probably copied in the middle of the thirteenth century or not long thereafter. The Caligula manuscript, which is translated here, is both more complete in its composition and more archaic in its language than the often-fragmentary Otho. Layamon (or Lawman, as we believe his name was probably pronounced) clearly tried to be very English in his language, avoiding borrowing any French phrases or locutions from Wace. He was also willfully old-fashioned, writing an alliterative verse that attempted to recall the grandeurs of the Anglo-Saxon epic past. Yet Layamon's alliterations often break down, and sometimes his half-lines are linked by end-rhyme. His poetry is often criticized for being rough and ill hewn; it seems to have descended from popular rather than "classical" Old English verse.

The value of Layamon's work lies precisely in its vigor. Unlike Wace, Layamon is not primarily interested in nuances of character or affairs of love. He is at his best in describing scenes of action and violence. It is for this reason that the "Death of Arthur" segment of his poem has been selected to represent his work. Layamon tells this story dramatically, creating a vivid sense of a massive tragedy stemming from lust, duplicity, and recklessness. His King Arthur acts far more like a primitive British chieftain than a Norman monarch, especially in his brutal handling of the rebels of Winchester. The work's sympathy toward Arthur's crushing of a refractory Britain may reflect Layamon's own sympathy toward the conquering Normans of his own time; but in the work itself, the author is always fiercely on the side of the Celts rather than the Saxons or the French.

Layamon also relates the death and disappearance of Arthur in a way that is mystically suggestive. He has the king go off with Argante (confused in some way with Morgan the Fay) to Avalon, the island of the elves, and elsewhere in the work he mentions these trappings from Celtic mythology. It is obvious that he had access to various kinds of folklore and local legend that a Frenchman like Wace did not have.

The selection chosen here begins at the point where Arthur is finishing his French campaign against the Roman emperor Lucius Hiberius. This occurs at line 13,897 of the Caligula manuscript, and it runs to line 14,297.

> *Bibliographic note:* The text is taken from the 1978 Oxford University Press edition by G.L. Brook and R.F. Leslie, Volume 2. I have also consulted the outmoded translation and edition by Frederic Madden, issued by the Society of Antiquaries in 1847. On Layamon's style see E.G. Stanley, "Layamon's Antiquarian Sentiments," *Medium Aevum*, 38 (1969), 23–37; also the article "Layamon," by E.D. Kennedy, in *The Arthurian Encyclopedia* (Garland, 1991). My thanks to Valerie Krishna for her suggestions for improving the following translation.

Brut

Tidings came to Arthur, who was in his tent,
That the emperor was dead, deprived of his days.
Amid a broad meadow Arthur made a pavilion,
And there he commanded Lucius to be carried,   13,900
And he ordered him covered with golden clothes
And kept under watch for three whole days.
And all this while he had a rich work made:
A chest that was long and overlaid with gold.
Inside this bier he put Lucius's body,
A most lordly man while his lifetime lasted.
Then Arthur did more, that marvelous Briton;

He made a collection of all of the corpses
Of the noblest kings and earls and knights
Who had fallen in battle, had fled from life.   13,910
He had them buried with brilliant pomp.
Three kings he commanded to carry Lucius
In a casket that was grand and exceedingly costly.
And soon afterward he ordered them sent to Rome
And told them to taunt the Roman people
By saying that he sent them the tribute they sought,
And he was prepared to send plenty more
If they still were so callous as to crave Arthur's gold.
Furthermore, he'd be happy to hurry to Rome
To carry the tidings of the British king,   13,920
And to fix up the walls that had long ago fallen:
"Yes, I will rule the unruly men of Rome!"
But these vaunts were in vain; events went elsewhere;
Fate befell otherwise for the folk left behind—
All because of Mordred, that most wicked of men!
      In the oncoming fight Arthur lost many knights:
Five and twenty thousand slain on the sod,
The boldest of the Britons bereft of their lives.
Kay was grievously wounded in the worst of ways;
He was borne to Kinun [Chinon] and there breathed his last.   13,930
He was buried there by the castle's side
Among the many hermits, that most worthy man.
Yes, Kay he was called and his castle Kinun;
Arthur gave him that town where he's now entombed,
And he ordered a new name as a mark of honor:
Kain [Caen] it was called in memory of Kay;
This now and after will live on as the name.
After Bedivere was laid low, giving up his life-days,
Arthur had him borne to the castle of Bayeux,
And there he was buried inside the burg;   13,940
They laid him in a grave by the southern gate.
Howeldin's body was floated north to Flanders
And his noblest knights were also ferried north
Into the counties from which they had come.
In the turf of Terouane they lie totally true;
Lear, the great baron, they bore to Boulogne.
      Arthur then set up his own settlement
In Burgundy, in a place that he thought the best.
He held sway of the land and took over some castles,   13,950
And he said he would handle that land by himself.
Then he threatened that in the summer he'd travel

All the way to Rome to take over that realm
And become the ruler where Lucius had reigned.
Many of the citizens of Rome wished this were so,
For they desperately stood in dread of their deaths.
Many had absconded, abandoning their ownings,
And many sent messages to Arthur the mighty;
Yes, many spoke to him suing for his peace,
While others wanted to fiercely fend off the invader,   13,960
Supporting their city against this new Caesar;
Yet foolishly, for they all were afraid for themselves,
Never claiming any good counsel from Christ.
And so what Merlin had prophesied came to pass:
That the ramparts of Rome would crumble before great Arthur.
This proved true once Emperor Lucius had perished
And fifty thousand Romans fell in the fight—
All those grand Roman legions laid low on the ground!
Then Arthur truly hoped to gain all of Rome
While he lived in Burgundy, the lordliest of lords.   13,970
            But suddenly a single man rode in on saddle,
Carrying new tidings to Arthur the king
From Mordred, his nephew; the man was well met
Since Arthur was guessing that his news was good.
Arthur spent the whole night in talk with the newcomer,
Who was afraid to unfold how affairs had fared,
But when the sun rose and the people were roused,
Arthur bolted up and stretched his arms broadly;
He got up; then he sat as if suddenly sick
Till the newcomer asked: "How fared you last night?"   13,980
Arthur then answered with an uneasy mind:
"Last night in my sleep while I nestled in bed,
I suffered a dream that has filled me with dread:
I dreamed I was raised up high on the roof
Of a hall that I strode as if on saddle,
Where I could survey the land of which I'm lord.
Walwain [Gawain] sat before me, with my sword in my hand,
And Mordred hove up there with numberless hosts.
In his hand he brandished a strong battle-ax,
With which he made swipes very sharp and swift,
Hewing down the posts that propped up the hall.   13,990
I also saw Wenhaver [Guinevere], the dearest of women;
With her fingers she was ripping the roof off the hall.
The building started foundering; I fell to the ground.
My right arm was shattered. Mordred shouted: 'Take that!'
Down fell the whole hall; even Walwain was falling,

Landing on the bottom with both arms broken.
I grabbed my fine sword with my one good hand
And sliced Mordred's head, sending it to the sod.
Then the queen I dismembered with my dearly loved sword,   14,000
Pitching her deep down into a dark pit;
Then all of my fine people began to flee from me.
I can't recall, by Christ! what became of them!
Then all by myself I was alone in a copse;
I started to meander widely on the moors;
Suddenly I spied griffins and grisly birds;
Then a golden lioness glided over the downs,
The crassest of beasts that our Creator makes.
The lioness ran up and lunged for my loins,
Bearing me away to a beach by the sea;   14,010
And I noticed the waves washing over the water,
While the lioness bore me straight into the brine.
As she stepped into the sea, we were sundered by water,
But a fish came by and ferried me back to land.
I felt soaked and weary from sorrow, and sick.
Then I shot up and started to tremble and shake;
I began to quiver as if kindled inside.
For the whole night I was haunted by horrid thoughts,
Since I knew now for certain: my bliss would be gone,
And all my life long I must languish in sorrow.   14,020
Woe is me that I didn't bring my Wenhaver here!"
        The knight replied: "My lord, that's not right!
You should never interpret a dream so dolefully.
You're the richest of men who rule this earth
And the wisest of humans hale under the heavens.
If it so happened—and pray Heaven that it won't—
That your sister's offspring has filched your queen
And grabbed your royal ground as his own right
That you trusted to him as you traveled to Rome,
And if he has done such deeds with deadly fraud   14,030
Still you could avenge all this with an active hand
And retake your land and rule again your people,
And strike down the wicked who have worked this woe,
Slaying them cleanly, so that none will survive!"
Arthur, the ablest of kings, then answered:
"Never in my entire life did I ever envision
That Mordred, my nephew, the man whom I most love,
Would betray me so totally for the treasure I own,
Or that Wenhaver my queen would waver in her mind;
She shall not accomplish this—not for any man on earth!"   14,040

Finally the knight spoke these forthright words:
"Since I'm your subject, sir, I shall speak what is so:
Mordred is guilty—he has grabbed your queen,
And your lovely lands now lie in his hands.
He is king, she is queen; they have cast you aside,
Since they're sure that you'll never return from the south.
I'm a tried and true subject; I witnessed this treason,
And I've traveled here to tell you all this myself.
I lay my head in pledge that I haven't lied,
But have spoken the truth of your once-loved spouse,   14,050
And of your sister's son, who has stolen your Britain!"
Then everyone sat very still in King Arthur's hall.
They all felt great sorrow for their fondest king;
All of his British underlings looked most unhappy.
Then, after a little while, some voices were lifted;
Far and wide you could hear all the Britons humming
As they started to tell in their different talks
How they would doom that most damnable pair
And would slay any masses who merged with Mordred.
Then Arthur, the almightiest, gave the final address: 14,060
"Sit down, my fond knights; sit silent in my hall,
For I shall plan out a plot that is stark and strange.
Tomorrow when day dawns, as God shall deem it,
I shall bolt at once toward our birthplace, Britain.
There I'll kill cunning Mordred and torch the queen
And destroy all those who are tied to this treason.
Here I shall leave my most loyal, loving friend,
Howell, most praised of men and prized of our kin.
Half of my army I'll ask to hang back in this land
To cover this kingdom that I now control.   14,070
And when all is restored, I shall rush back to Rome,
Leaving my homeland in the hands of my Walwain;
And I'll answer all my pledges, I quite assure you:
All of my damnable foes shall face down their fates!"
        Then our Walwain arose, the kinsman of Arthur,
And uttered these words in a most unhappy way:
"Almighty God, the dispenser of dooms,
Ruler of all under Heaven, why has it happened
That my brother Mordred did this baleful deed?
Right now I forsake him before all this force;   14,080
I shall destroy him through the destiny of God!
I shall string him up, that most sinful scoundrel,
And I'll pull the queen to pieces with my horses!
For I'll never know bliss as long as they draw breath

Until my beloved uncle's avenged with the best!"
Then the other Britons broke out with bold voices:
"All of our weapons are ready; tomorrow we return!"
          In the morning, as the sun was sent out by the Savior,
Arthur led out the loyalest of his lieges,
Taking about half and leaving half behind him.   14,090
He wended through the land till he came to Whitsand;
Soon he had ships both sundry and well stocked,
But for a full fortnight the army had to stand firm
As they waited for a while for the winds to lift.
There was a vile follower in Arthur's fold
Who, when he heard Mordred's murder widely spoken,
Sent one of his lackeys straight over to Britain
To inform Queen Wenhaver what lay in store:
How Arthur would arrive shortly with his army
And what he planned to breach and how he would behave.   14,100
The queen ran to Mordred, now her dearest consort,
And told him about the coming of Arthur the king,
And how he planned to act and what he was plotting.
Mordred immediately sent someone to Saxony
To confer with Childerich, that most powerful king.
He bade the Saxon come and snatch up some bargains;
Mordred asked Childerich, that mightiest chieftain,
To send out messengers over all of Saxony,
To invite any warriors whom he could win to the cause
To come over with haste to help out the Britons,   14,110
And he would give half of his holdings to Childerich:
Everything north of the Humber was his for his help
If he became Mordred's ally against Arthur.
Childerich charged at once to the British kingdom.
When Mordred had finally gathered his mighty force,
There were sixty thousand soldiers in the sum
Who were hardy, hostile warriors of heathen stock,
All of whom had come over here to harass King Arthur
And to lend aid to Mordred, that most miserable of men!
When his army was pulled together from all the people,   14,120
There were a good hundred thousand in that throng
Of heathens and Christians who claimed Mordred as king.
          Arthur lay two weeks at Whitsand (it was indeed too long!),
While Mordred was fully aware of what Arthur wanted.
Every day a courier came over from Arthur's court.
Then finally it befell—the rains began to fall,
And a wind began to whip up toward the west.
Arthur hurried into his ships with all of his host,

Ordering his mariners to rush him over to Romney,
Where he planned to set foot again on his native sod.   14,130
When he got to the harbor, Mordred was there to greet him.
As the daylight flared, the men fell at once to fighting
For the whole day; and many a man was massacred.
Some struggled on the high ground and some by the shore;
Some shot sharp spears from out of the ships.
Walwain advanced, clearing out the approaches,
And he undid the lives of eleven underlings.
He felled Childerich's son, who had come with his father.
The sun sank westward, with woe to all men!
Walwain was lopped down, loosed from his days,   14,140
By a Saxon baron—cursed be his soul!
Arthur was now wounded deeply within his heart;
This mightiest of Britons sighed these sad words:
"Now I've surrendered the lives of my loyal swains.
I knew from my dream that I was doomed to sorrow!
Dead is King Angel, one of the dearest of men,
And Walwain my nephew—I wish I had never been born!
Come off those ships quickly, my courageous men!"
          With these words some sixty thousand warriors,
Fiercest of men, now rushed into the fray,   14,150
Attacking Mordred's ranks and almost taking him.
Mordred started to run, and his men rushed after him,
Dashing like fiends while all the fields were quaking,
And amid the stones you saw streamings of blood.
The fight would have ended, but nighttime fell;
The enemy would have perished, but it was now pitch-dark.
Darkness split fighters as it spread over dale and dune.
Mordred lunged away madly; he was soon in London.
All the good burghers knew that things had gone badly;
They refused him entry with his entourage;   14,160
So Mordred went with haste westward toward Winchester
And quickly took over the town with his many troops.
Meanwhile Arthur followed with his powerful forces
Till he arrived at Winchester with his awesome army,
Besieging that citadel where Mordred lurked inside.
When Mordred realized that Arthur was around him,
He pondered deeply about what plan to adopt.
That very night he ordered his men to go outside,
To issue forth from the walls, bearing their weapons,
And he told them that there they would have to take a stand.   14,170
He promised the townsfolk their legal privileges
If they would only help him in his hour of need.

When dawn was breaking, the burghers were eager to fight,
And Arthur was outraged when he saw that they were rebels.
He had trumpets blown, warriors readied for battle.
He ordered all of his nobles, his finest knights,
To get ready for the onslaught, to overthrow their foes,
To raise havoc on the town, hang the treacherous townsfolk.
His men moved in masses and hacked with mighty rage.
Mordred was very worried about what he might do.   14,180
And he acted at this time just as he acted elsewhere:
He was utterly wicked, as he was always so.
He betrayed all the burghers there before Winchester.
He cozened up to the closest courtiers he had
And the fondest friends he had among his folk,
And sneaked away from the fray—may the Great Fiend seize him!
He left people who were loyal there to perish.
All the day they labored, thinking their lord among them,
Believing that he stood by them in their hour of need.
But he was galloping on the road that goes to Hampton;   14,190
That perversest of persons was heading for the port.
He annexed all the ships that were active and able,
Told the sailors that he needed to sail them away.
Then he sped off to Cornwall—that crassest of men!
Arthur quickly won over the castle of Winchester,
Slaying all of their citizens, the sorrow was great!
The young and the elderly—he undid them all.
When he killed all the townsfolk, he torched the town,
And he broke the ramparts into little bits.
So it came to pass what Merlin had prophesied: 14,200
"Woe to you, Winchester; the earth shall swallow you up!"
These words Merlin uttered, the wisest of wizards.
            Wenhaver was in York, she was never so worried—
Yes, Wenhaver the queen, most wretched of women.
She had heard all of these most unhappy reports:
How Mordred had fled and how Arthur had followed.
Her life was now loathsome as long as she was living.
In nighttime she slipped out of the shire of York,
Heading for Caerleon as quickly as she could.
There under cover she called for two of her courtiers   14,210
To hallow her head with a holy veil.
She became now a nun—that unhappiest of women.
No man knew then what became of the queen,
And for years thereafter nothing was known,
Whether she was alive or lying in her grave,
Or if she had sunk into some flowing stream.

Meanwhile in Cornwall Mordred summoned many men.
Swiftly to Ireland he sent over a message
And then to Saxony he also sent some words,
And finally to Scotland he quickly dealt some dispatches.   14,220
He told them all to come if they coveted land
Or silver or gold, some chattel or some goods;
Thus in every which way he watched out for himself,
As does a cunning creature who is cornered by fate.
But Arthur, now angriest of kings, heard this all:
How Mordred in Cornwall cowered with his company
And was waiting for the time that he would approach.
Arthur sent out an order over all his kingdom,
Calling forth all those who were living in his land
Who were ready for war, to come with weapons in hand;   14,230
And if anyone berated what the king now begged,
Arthur would see that he was seared at the stake.
Then countless people came to join in that crowd,
Walking and riding while the rain fell down!
Arthur tramped into Cornwall with a huge train.
Mordred heard this mumbled and hurried out to meet him
With unnumbered warriors—many dooms were weighed.
Near the banks of the Tamar they banded together,
At a place known as Camelford, a name of great fame.
Yes, at Camelford there gathered some sixty thousand,   14,240
With thousands besides who hailed Mordred as their lord.
       Then to that place appeared Arthur the powerful
With legions of forces whose lives were all fated.
On the banks of the Tamar they tangled together;
They lifted their standards and lunged to attack,
Drawing out their long swords, slashing at helmets,
While sparks flinted out and spears flew in two.
Shields started to crumble while shafts were cracking.
Countless men were now clashing together there,
And the River Tamar was now rife with blood.   14,250
Nobody could fathom who fared well in that fighting:
Who did better or worse; the warring was mixed.
They were all slaying outright—whether squire or knight.
Then Mordred was cut down, cut short from his days,
And all of his followers were felled on that field.
Many of the mighty were massacred in that place
Of Arthur's loyal lieges, the high and the low,
And all of the Britons who were attached to his board,
Along with the fosterlings from lands far and wide,
While Arthur was shafted badly by a broad spear;   14,260

In fact he received fifteen fatal gashes.
In the greatest of these you could thrust two gloves!
          Finally not a single person stood on that plain.
Two hundred thousand were hacked down to the ground,
Except for noble Arthur and two of his knights.
Arthur had been sorely wounded in a serious way.
Then up to him crept a youngster of his kin:
He was the son of Cador, the earl of Cornwall.
His name was Constantine; he was cousinly to the king.
Arthur gazed up at him as he groveled on the ground,   14,270
Whispering these words that betokened a woeful heart:
"Dear Constantine, son of Cador, please now hear me.
I bestow upon you now my entire British kingdom.
Please protect my British people for all of your life
And defend the laws that have lasted through my days,
And all of the useful laws that stood under our Uther.
I shall go forth to Avalon to the fairest of maidens,
To Argante [Morgan] the queen, the comeliest of fays,
And she shall heal my wounds and make me healthy
And sound, by preparing for me health-giving potions.   14,280
And then I shall come again into my own kingdom,
And I shall abide with my Britons in joyous bliss."
A light little boat came lilting over the waters
Even as he spoke, gliding in there from the sea,
And two women were in it of wonderful appearance.
They raised Arthur up and rapidly took him away;
They laid him softly down, and outwardly they sailed.
          And so once again there occurred what Merlin had uttered:
Countless cares would be felt when Arthur was faring forth.
The Britons still hold that he is alive in health,   14,290
That he lingers on Avalon with the loveliest of fays,
And they are always awaiting the time when Arthur returns.
There never was a man who was born of a blessed lady
Who can tell you any more about Arthur's true fate.
But once there was a magus whose name was Merlin
And he proclaimed these words, his prophecies were true:
An Arthur will return who will redeem the Britons!

Chapter VII

CHRÉTIEN DE TROYES: *LANCELOT,* OR *THE KNIGHT OF THE CART*

WILLIAM W. KIBLER

Although nearly all of what Geoffrey of Monmouth wrote concerning Arthur is believed to be unsubstantiated and fictional, his contemporaries (and perhaps Geoffrey himself) believed that he was writing history. Chrétien de Troyes was the first writer who consciously used the myth of Arthur as the basis for long fictional narratives. *Lancelot,* like most of Chrétien's works, had its roots in the soil of the British Isles. In particular, it seems related to a Celtic abduction tale, the *aithed,* in which a mysterious stranger claims a married woman, makes off with her through a ruse or by force, and carries her off to his otherworldly home. Her husband pursues the abductor and, after overcoming seemingly impossible odds, penetrates the mysterious kingdom and rescues his wife. However, this material is only distantly related to the *Lancelot* as we have it—the role of Lancelot himself, for example, is nowhere to be found—and the precise manner by which the Celtic materials reached the French-speaking world is unclear.

In the prologue to his first romance, *Erec and Enide,* Chrétien tells us that he *"tret d'un conte d'aventure/une molt bele conjointure"* (creates from an adventure tale a very beautiful arrangement). In the opening lines of *Lancelot* he writes that the Countess Marie of Champagne, his principal literary patroness, gave him the *matiere* (material) and *san* (sense) for his romance. Critics generally agree that the *matiere* referred to Chrétien's source story, perhaps given him orally and in a loosely connected manner by the Countess, and that the *san* was the interpretation or meaning to be given to this matter. Both statements give proof of a conscious literary artistry on the part of Chrétien; and the fact that he signed all his works, in a period when many literary productions remained anonymous, is another indication of the pride of accomplishment of a great writer. In a deliberate fashion, and with often unappreciated artistry, Chrétien gathered together the threads of a tradition to weave his beautiful fabric. From Geoffrey and the Norman-French poet Wace before him, as from oral tradition, he could have taken little more than the names of characters, perhaps some rudiments of story lines or characterizations, and a general tone. It was his genius alone to assemble these various fictions into a coherent form that would guarantee them their immense and lasting success.

What little we know of Chrétien's biography must be drawn from allusions found in his work, or what can be surmised from a careful study of them. His name does not appear in any official records, and neither his life nor his works can be dated with certainty. In the prologue to *Erec and Enide* our author refers to himself as *Chrestiens de Troies* (line 9), from which we can assume that he was born or at least spent the better part of his formative years in Troyes, one of the leading cities in the region of Champagne. At Troyes he was most assuredly associated with the court of the Countess Marie of Champagne, to whom he dedicated his *Lancelot*. This Marie, a daughter of Eleanor of Aquitaine by her first marriage, to Louis VII of France, was married in 1159 to Henry the Liberal, Count of Champagne. Sometime after Count Henry's death in 1181 Chrétien shifted patrons and began his never-to-be-completed romance *Perceval* for Philip of Flanders. The *Perceval* was no doubt begun before Philip's departure for the Third Crusade in September of 1190.

Chrétien's literary career probably began no earlier than the mid-1150s and ended around 1190. In the prologue to his second major romance he tells us that he had previously composed some adaptations of Ovidian materials as well as a poem treating the Tristan legend, which he enigmatically refers to as being "about King Mark and Isolde the Blonde." All of this early material, with the exception of an adaptation of the Philomela story (*Metamorphoses*, Book 6), has been lost. After honing his technique on the adaptations, he created his first masterpiece when he turned from Rome to the Celtic world for his inspiration and wrote *Erec and Enide*. This fine psychological story of a knight and his new bride is the first extant literary work to incorporate the Arthurian material. Its success was followed by *Cligès*, which, though set in part at Arthur's court, is principally an adventure romance based on Greco-Byzantine material.

After *Erec* and *Cligès* Chrétien composed two of his greatest romances, *Lancelot* and *Yvain*. Then finally, toward the end of his career, he wrote his most enigmatic work, *Perceval*, or the *Conte du Graal* (Story of the Grail). *Perceval* was left unfinished, just as *Lancelot* was turned over to Godefroy of Lagny to complete.

A romance such as *Lancelot* may at first appear ill composed and loosely structured to a reader who is raised on the realistic novel. The plot is based on the motif of the quest, and the various adventures are all related to the expiation of Lancelot's great sin against the courtly code: his two-step hesitation before mounting the cart of infamy. Thus each of his adventures demands

that he serve women unhesitatingly, for having shown the slightest preference for knightly honor over amorous duty. The *Lancelot* is not "unified" in
the modern sense but shows rather a cohesiveness based on the principle of
analogy. Scenes that may have no direct bearing on the development of the
central intrigue nonetheless serve the meaning of the story as analogues of
other actions. The complex interrelationship of the individual episodes, in
which a later scene may serve to clarify an earlier one, demands a greater
effort on the part of readers, requiring them to reread or reflect upon earlier
episodes in the light of later ones before the sense can manifest itself clearly.
For those with patience and an openness to an unfamiliar esthetic, the reading will prove most rewarding.

Bibliographic note: A detailed bibliography up to the mid-1970s can be found in
Douglas Kelly, *Chrétien de Troyes, An Analytic Bibliography* (Grant & Cutler,
1976). A good general introduction to Chrétien can be found in Jean Frappier,
Chrétien de Troyes, the Man and His Work (English translation by Raymond J.
Cormier, Ohio University, 1982), and U.T. Holmes, *Chrétien de Troyes*
(Twayne, 1970). Important recent studies in English include Douglas Kelly,
Sens and Conjointure in the "Chevalier de la Charrette" (Mouton, 1966); Norris
Lacy, *The Craft of Chrétien de Troyes: An Essay on Narrative Art* (Brill, 1980); and
L.T. Topsfield, *Chrétien de Troyes: A Study of the Arthurian Romances* (Cam-
bridge University, 1981). A perceptive recent study is by Matilda T. Bruckner,
"Le Chevalier de la Charrette (Lancelot)" in *Romances of Chrétien de Troyes,* ed.
Douglas Kelly (Kentucky, 1985), 132-181. This translation is based on my new
edition of the Guiot manuscript, B.N. 794 (Garland, 1981); line numbers from
that text are indicated periodically throughout the translation in brackets.

Lancelot, or *The Knight of the Cart*

Since my lady of Champagne wishes me to begin a romance, I shall do so
most willingly, like one who is entirely at her service in anything he can
undertake in this world. I say this without flattery, though another might
begin his story with the desire to flatter her; he might say (and I would agree)
that she is the lady who surpasses all women who are alive, just as the foehn
that blows in May or April surpasses the other winds. Certainly I am not one
intent upon flattering his lady. Will I say, "As the polished gem eclipses the
pearl and the sard, the countess eclipses queens"? Indeed not; I'll not say
anything of the sort, though it be true in spite of me. I will say, however, that
her command has more importance in this work than any thought or effort I
might put into it.

Chrétien begins his book about the Knight of the Cart; the subject matter and meaning are furnished and given him by the countess, and he strives
carefully to add nothing but his effort and careful attention. Now he begins
his story.

1st ref. to Camelot

On a certain Ascension Day King Arthur was in the region near Caerleon and held his court at Camelot, splendidly and luxuriantly as befitted a king. After the meal the king did not stir from among his companions. There were many barons present in the hall, and the queen was among them, as were, I believe, a great number of beautiful courtly ladies, skillful at conversing in French. And Kay, who had overseen the feast, was eating with those who had served. While Kay was still at table, there appeared before them a knight, who had come to court splendidly equipped and fully armed for battle. The knight came forward in his splendid armor to where the king was seated among his barons. Instead of the customary greeting he declared, "King Arthur, I hold imprisoned knights, ladies, and maidens from your land and household. I do not bring you news of them because I intend to return them to you; rather, I want to inform you that you have neither wealth nor power enough to ensure their release. And know you well that you will die before you are able to come to their aid."

The king replied that he must accept this, since he could not change it for the better, but that it grieved him deeply.

Then the knight made as if to leave: he turned and strode from the king until he reached the door of the great hall. But before descending the stairs, he stopped and proffered this challenge: "Sir, if at your court there is even one knight in whom you have faith enough to dare entrust the queen to accompany her into these woods where I am going, I give my oath that I will await him there and will deliver all the prisoners who are captive in my land if he is able to win the queen from me and bring her back to you."

Many there in the palace heard this, and all the court was in turmoil. Kay, who was eating with the servants, also heard this challenge. He left his meal, came directly to the king, and spoke to him in indignation: "My king, I have served you well, in good faith and loyally. But now I take my leave; I shall go away and serve you no more; I've neither the will nor desire to serve you any longer."

The king was saddened by what he heard; but when he was able to reply he said to him at once: "Is this in truth or jest?"

"Fair king," replied Kay, "I have no need to jest—I take my leave in truth. I ask no further wages or recompense for my service; I have firmly resolved to depart without delay."

"Is it out of anger or spite that you wish to leave?" asked the king. "Sir seneschal, remain at court as you have in the past, and be assured that there's nothing I have in all this world that I'd not give you at once to keep you here."

"Sir," he replied, "no need for that. For each day's stay I wouldn't take a measure of purest gold."

In desperation King Arthur went to his queen and asked, "My lady, have you no idea what the seneschal wants from me? He has asked for leave and says that he will quit my court. I don't know why. But what he wouldn't do for me, he'll do at once if you beg him. Go to him, my dear lady; though he deign not stay for my sake, pray him to stay for yours and fall at his feet if necessary, for I would never again be happy if I were to lose his company."

The king sent his queen to the seneschal. She went and found him with the other barons; when she had approached him, she said, "Sir Kay, I'm most upset at what I've heard said of you—I'll tell you straight out. I've been informed, and it saddens me, that you wish to leave the king's service. What gave you this idea? What feelings compel you? I no longer see in you the wise and courtly knight that once I knew. I want to urge you to remain: Kay, I beg of you—stay!"

"My lady," he said, "and it please you, but I could never stay."

The queen once again implored him, as did all the knights around her. Kay replied that she was wasting her efforts asking for what would not be granted. Then the queen, in all her majesty, fell down at his feet. Kay begged her to rise, but she replied that she would not do so: she would never again rise until he had granted her wish. Thereupon Kay promised her that he would remain, but only if the king and the queen herself would grant in advance what he was about to request. "Kay," said she, "no matter what it may be, both he and I will grant it. Now come and we shall tell him that on this condition you will remain."

Kay accompanied the queen, and together they approached the king. "My lord," said the queen, "with great pains I have retained Kay. But I bring him to you with the assurance that you will do whatever he is about to ask."

The king was overwhelmed with joy and promised to grant Kay's request, no matter what he might demand. "My lord," said Kay, "know then what I want and the nature of the gift that you have promised me; I consider myself most fortunate to obtain it with your blessing: you have agreed to entrust to me the queen whom I see here before me, and we shall go after the knight who is awaiting us in the forest."

Though it saddened the king, he entrusted her to Kay, for never was he known to break his word; but his anger and pain were written clearly upon his face. The queen was also very upset, and all those in the household insisted that Kay's request was proud, rash, and mad. Arthur took his queen by the hand and said to her: "My lady, there is no way to prevent your going with Kay."

"Now trust her to me," Kay insisted, "and don't be afraid of anything, for I'll bring her back quite safe and sound."   [196]

The king handed her over to Kay, who led her away. The members of the court followed after the two of them; not a soul remained unmoved. You must know that the seneschal was soon fully armed. His horse was brought to the middle of the palace yard; beside it was a palfrey, as befitted a queen: it was neither restive nor high-spirited. Weak, sad, and sighing, the queen approached the palfrey; she mounted, then said beneath her breath so as not to be heard: "Ah! My friend, if you knew, I don't believe you'd ever let Kay lead me even a single step away." (She thought she had spoken in a whisper, yet she was overheard by Count Guinable, who was near her as she mounted.)

As she was led away by Kay, every man and woman who was present at court and saw this lamented as if she were already lying dead in her bier; no one thought she would ever return alive. In his rashness the seneschal led her toward where the knight was waiting; yet no one was troubled enough to attempt to follow him until my lord Gawain said loudly to his uncle the king: "My lord, it surprises me that you have done such a foolish thing. However, if you will accept my advice, you and I, with any others who might wish to come, should hurry after them while they are yet near. I cannot refrain myself from setting out at once in pursuit. It would be unseemly if we didn't follow them at least until we know what will become of the queen and how well Kay will acquit himself."

"Let us be off, fair nephew," said the king. "Your words are nobly spoken. Since you have proposed this course, order our horses to be brought forth, bridled and saddled and ready to mount."

The horses were led out immediately, saddled and fully equipped. The king mounted first, my lord Gawain after him, then the others as quickly as they could. Everyone wanted to be among the party, and each went as it pleased him: some with armor, and many unarmed. My lord Gawain was armed for battle and had ordered two squires to accompany him, leading in hand two war horses. As they were nearing the forest, they recognized Kay's horse coming out and saw that both reins were broken from the bit. The horse was riderless, its stirrup-leathers stained with blood; the rear part of its saddle was broken and in pieces. Everyone was upset by this; they nudged one another and exchanged comprehending glances. My lord Gawain was riding well in advance of the others; it was not long before he saw a knight approaching slowly on a horse that was sore and tired, breathing hard and lathered in sweat. The knight greeted my lord Gawain first, and my lord Gawain then returned his greeting. The knight, who recognized my lord Gawain, stopped and said, "My lord, do you not see how my horse is bathed in sweat and in such state that he is no longer of use to me? And I believe these two war-horses are yours. Now I beg you, with the promise to return you the service and favor, to let me have one or the other at your choice, either as a loan or gift."

Gawain replied, "Choose whichever of the two you prefer."

But the unknown knight, who was in desperate need, did not take the time to choose the better, or the more handsome, or the larger; rather, he leapt upon the one that was nearest him, and rode off with full speed. And the horse he had been riding fell dead, for that day it had been overridden and hardspent, and had suffered much. The knight galloped straightway back into the forest, and my lord Gawain followed after him in hot pursuit until he reached the bottom of a hill.

After he had ridden a great distance, Gawain came upon the war-horse that he had given the knight. It was now dead. Gawain saw that the ground had been much trampled by many horses and was strewn with the fragments of many shields and lances. It clearly appeared that a pitched battle had been waged there between many knights; Gawain was bitterly disappointed not to have been present. He did not tarry long, but passed quickly beyond until by chance he again caught sight of that same knight, now alone and on foot, although still fully armed—with helmet laced, shield strung from his neck, and sword girded. He had overtaken a cart.   [320]

In those days carts were used as are pillories now; where each large town now has three thousand or more carts, in those times they had but one. Like our pillories, that cart was for all criminals alike, for all traitors and murderers, for all those who had lost trials by combat, and for all those who had stolen another's possessions by larceny or snatched them by force on the highways. The guilty person was taken and made to mount in the cart and was led through every street; he had lost all his feudal rights and was never again heard at court, nor invited or honored there. Since in those days carts were so dreadful, the saying first arose, "Whenever you see a cart and cross its path, make the sign of the cross and remember God, so that evil will not befall you."

The knight, on foot and without his lance, hurried after the cart and saw, sitting on its shaft, a dwarf who held a driver's long switch in his hand. The knight said to the dwarf, "Dwarf, in the name of God, tell me if you have seen my lady the queen pass by this way?"

The vile, low-born dwarf would give him no information; instead he said, "If you want to get into this cart I'm driving, by tomorrow you'll know what has become of the queen."

At that, the dwarf continued on his way without slowing down even an instant for the knight, who hesitated but two steps before climbing in. He would regret this moment of hesitation and be accursed and shamed for it; he would come to consider himself ill-used. But Reason, who does not follow Love's command, told him to beware of getting in, warned and counseled him not to do anything for which he might incur disgrace or reproach. Reason, who dared tell him this, spoke from the lips, not from the heart; but Love, who held sway within his heart, urged and commanded him to climb into the cart at once. Because Love ordered and wished it, he jumped in; since Love ruled his action, the disgrace did not matter.

My lord Gawain quickly spurred on after the cart and was astonished to find the knight seated in it. Then he said, "Dwarf, if you know anything about the queen, tell me."

The dwarf answered, "If you think as little of yourself as this knight sitting here, then get in beside him and I'll drive you along with him."

When my lord Gawain heard this, he thought it was madness and said that he would not get in, for it would be a poor bargain to trade a horse for a cart. "But go wherever you will and I will follow after."   [394]

So they set off on their way—the one on horseback, the two others riding in the cart, and all on the same path. About nightfall they came to a fortified town that, I want you to know, was very elegant and beautiful. All three entered through a gate. The people marveled at the knight who was being transported in the dwarf's cart. They did not hide their feelings, but all—rich and poor, young and old—mocked him loudly as he was borne through the streets; the knight heard many a vile and scornful word at his expense. Everyone asked, "How will this knight be put to death? Will he be flayed or hanged, drowned or burned upon a fire of thorns? Say, dwarf—you're driving him—tell us what he's guilty of? Is he convicted of theft? Is he a murderer? Did he lose a trial by combat?"

The dwarf held his silence and answered not a one of them. Followed constantly by Gawain, the dwarf took the knight to his lodgings: a tower keep that was on the opposite side of town and level with it. Meadows stretched out beyond where the keep stood on a high granite cliff that fell sharply off into the valley. Gawain, on horseback, followed the cart into the keep. In the great hall they met an attractively attired girl, the fairest in all the land. They saw that she was accompanied by two comely and beautiful maidens. As soon as the maidens saw my lord Gawain, they greeted him warmly and inquired about the other knight: "Dwarf, what ill has this knight done whom you drive around like a cripple?"

Instead of answering he had the knight get down from the cart, then left; no one knew where he went. My lord Gawain dismounted; then several valets came forward to relieve both knights of their armor. The girl had two miniver-lined cloaks brought forward for them to wear. When the supper hour came, the food was splendidly prepared. The girl sat at table beside my lord Gawain. Nothing would have made them wish to change their lodging to seek better, for the girl did them great honor and provided them fair and pleasant company all through the evening.

After they had eaten their fill, two long, high beds were set up in the hall. Alongside these was a third bed, more resplendent and finer than the others, for, as the tale affirms, it had every splendor one could wish for in a bed. When it came time to retire for the night, the girl took both of the guests to whom she had offered lodging and showed them the two spacious and comfortable beds, saying, "These two beds over here are made up for you; but only the one who has earned the privilege may sleep in this third bed nearest us. It was not prepared for you."

The knight who had arrived in the cart answered that he held her injunction in perfect contempt. "Tell me," he said, "why we are forbidden to lie in this bed?"

The girl, having anticipated this question, replied without hesitation: "It is not for you to ask or inquire. A knight who has ridden in a cart is shamed throughout the land; he has no right to be concerned with what you have asked about the beds, and he certainly has no right to lie in it, for he might soon regret it. Nor did I have it arrayed so splendidly for you to lie upon; you would pay dearly for even thinking of doing so."

"You will see about that in due time," he said.

"Will I?"

"Yes."

"Then let's see!"

"By my head," said the knight, "I don't know who will pay dearly for this, but I do know that I intend to lie down in this bed and rest as long as I like, whether you like it or not."

As soon as he had removed his armor, he got into the bed, which was half an ell longer and higher than the other two. He lay down beneath a gold-starred coverlet of yellow samite; the fur that lined it was not skinned squirrel, but sable. The coverlet over him was suited for a king; the mattress was not thatch, nor straw, nor old matting.

Just at midnight a lance like a bolt of lightning came hurtling at him point first and nearly pinned the knight through his flanks to the coverlet, to the white sheets, and to the bed in which he was lying. On the lance was a pennon that was all ablaze; it set fire to the coverlet, the sheets, and the entire bed. The iron tip of the lance grazed the knight's side; it removed a little skin, but he was not actually wounded. The knight sat up, put out the flame, then grabbed the lance and hurled it to the middle of the hall. Yet in spite of all this he did not get out of the bed; instead he lay back down and slept just as soundly as he had before.   [534]

The next morning at daybreak the girl of the keep had preparations made for mass, then awoke the knights and bade them rise. When mass had been celebrated for them, the knight who had been seated in the cart came to the window that overlooked the meadow and gazed worriedly out across the fields below. The girl had come to the window nearby, where my lord Gawain spoke with her awhile in private. (I assure you that I don't know what words they exchanged.) But as they were leaning on the window ledge, they saw down in the meadows below a bier being carried along the riverbank; a knight was lying in it, and beside it three girls were weeping bitterly. Behind the bier they saw a crowd coming, at the head of which rode a tall knight escorting a beautiful lady, who was riding to his left. The knight at the other window recognized that it was the queen; as long as she was in view he gazed attentively and with pleasure at her. When he could no longer see her, he wanted to throw himself from the window and shatter his body on the ground below; he was already half out the window when my lord Gawain saw him and, after dragging him back inside, said to him, "For pity's sake, sir, calm down! For the love of God, never think of doing such a foolish thing again; you're wrong to hate your life!"

"No, it is right he should," countered the girl, "for won't the news of his disgrace in the cart be known to all? He certainly should want to be killed for he's better off dead than living. Henceforth his life is shamed, scorned and wretched."

Thereupon the knights requested their armor, which they donned. Then the girl had a special touch of courtesy and generosity: since she had mocked and ridiculed the knight sufficiently, she now gave him a horse and lance as token of her esteem and sympathy.

The knights took leave of the girl with proper courtesy. Having thanked her, they then set off in the direction they had seen the crowd taking and were able to pass through the castle yard without anyone speaking to them. They rode as quickly as possible to where they had seen the queen, but they were unable to overtake the crowd, since it was moving at a rapid pace. Beyond the meadows they entered into an enclosed area and found a beaten path. They rode along in the forest until mid-morning, when they encountered a girl at a crossroads.   [607]

They both greeted her, imploring and praying her to tell them, if she knew, where the queen had been taken. She replied courteously, saying, "If you promise me enough, I can show you the right road and direction and can name for you the land where she is going and the knight who is taking her. But whoever would enter into that land must undergo great tribulations; he will suffer much before getting there."

My lord Gawain said to her, "So help me God, my lady, I pledge my word that if it should please you I will put all my might into your service, if only you will tell me the truth."

The knight who had ridden in the cart did not say that he pledged her all his might, but rather swore (as one whom Love has made strong and bold for any endeavor) to do anything she might wish without hesitation or fear, and to be entirely at her command in everything.

"Then I shall tell you," said she. And she spoke to them as follows: "By my faith, lords, Meleagant, a huge and mighty knight and the son of the King of Gorre, has carried her off into the kingdom from which no foreigner returns. In that land he must remain in exile and servitude."

Then the knight asked further, "Dear lady, where is this land? Where can we find the way that leads there?"

"You will be told," she replied, "but you must know that you will encounter difficulties and treacherous passes, for it is no easy matter to enter there without the permission of the king, whose name is Bademagu. Nonetheless, it is possible to enter by two extremely perilous ways, two exceptionally treacherous passes. One is named 'The Underwater Bridge,' because the bridge is below the water, with as much running above it as beneath—neither more nor less, since the bridge is precisely in the middle; and it is but a foot and a half in width and of equal thickness. This choice is certainly to be shunned, yet it is the less dangerous. And it has many more perils about which I say nothing. The other bridge is more difficult and so much more dangerous that it has never been crossed by man, for it is like a trenchant sword; therefore everyone calls it 'The Sword Bridge.' I have told you the truth as far as I can give it to you."

Then he asked her further, "Miss, would you deign to show us these two ways?"

And the girl replied, "This is the right way to the Underwater Bridge, and that way goes straight to the Sword Bridge."

Thereupon the knight who had been driven in the cart said, "Sir, I willingly share with you: choose one of these two ways and leave me the other; take whichever you prefer."

"In faith," said my lord Gawain, "both passages are exceedingly perilous and difficult. I cannot choose wisely and hardly know which to take, yet it is not right for me to delay when you have given me the choice: I take the Underwater Bridge."

"Then it is right that I go to the Sword Bridge without complaint," said the other, "which I agree to do."

The three then parted, commending one another gently to God's care. When the girl saw them riding off, she said, "Each of you must grant me a favor at my choosing, whenever I ask it. Take care not to forget that."

"In truth, we'll not forget, fair friend," the two knights replied. Then they went their separate ways.   [710]

The Knight of the Cart was lost in thought, a man with no strength or defense against love, which torments him. His pensiveness was so deep that he forgot who he was; he was uncertain whether or not he truly existed; he was unable to recall his own name; he did not know if he were armed or not, nor where he was going nor whence he came. He remembered nothing at all save one creature, for whom he forgot all others; he was so intent upon her alone that he did not hear, see, or pay attention to anything. His horse carried him swiftly along, following not the crooked way, but taking the better and more direct path. Thus unguided it bore him onto a heath. In this heath was a ford, and across the ford was an armed knight who guarded it; with him was a girl who had come on a palfrey. Though by this time it was nearing nones, our knight had not grown weary of his unceasing meditations. His horse, by now quite thirsty, saw the good clear water and galloped toward the ford. From the other side the guardian cried out, "Knight, I guard the ford and I forbid you to cross it!"

Our knight did not hear or pay attention to this, for he was still lost in his thoughts; all the while his horse kept galloping toward the water. The guard cried out loudly enough to be heard: "You would be wise not to take the ford, for that is not the way to cross!" And he swore by the heart within his breast to slay him if he entered the ford.

Yet the knight heard him not, and so the guard shouted to him a third time: "Knight, do not enter the ford against my order, or by my head I'll strike you the moment I see you in it!"

The knight, still wrapped in his thoughts, heard nothing. His horse leapt quickly into the water, freed himself from the bit, and began to drink thirstily. The guardian swore that the knight would pay for this and that neither his shield nor the hauberk on his back would ever save him. He urged his horse to a gallop, and from the gallop to a run; he struck our knight from his steed flat into the ford that he had forbidden him to cross. The knight's lance fell into the stream and his shield flew from round his neck. The cold water awakened him with a shock; he leapt startled to his feet, like a dreamer from sleep. He regained his sight and hearing and wondered who could have struck him. Then he saw the guard and shouted to him, "Varlet, tell me why you struck me when I didn't know you were before me and had done you no wrong?"

"In faith, you have indeed wronged me," he answered. "Did you not show me no respect when I shouted to you three times as loudly as I could not to cross the ford? You certainly must have heard at least two of my warnings, yet you entered in spite of me, and I said that I would strike you as soon as I saw you in the water."

To that the knight replied, "May I be damned if ever I heard you or if I ever saw you before! It's quite possible you did warn me not to cross the ford—but I was lost in my thoughts. Rest assured that you'll regret this if I ever get even one hand on your reins!"

The guardian of the ford replied, "What good would that do you? Go ahead and grab my reins if you dare. I don't give a fistful of ashes for your haughty threats!"

"I'd like nothing better than to seize hold of you right now," he retorted, "no matter what might come of it!"

Thereupon the guardian advanced to the middle of the ford. The unknown knight grabbed the reins with his left hand and a leg with the right. He pulled and tugged and squeezed his leg so hard that the guard cried out, for it felt as if his leg was being yanked from his body. He implored him to stop: "Knight, if it pleases you to fight me on equal terms, then remount your horse and take your lance and shield and come joust with me."

"Upon my word, I won't do it. I think you'll try to run away as soon as you're free from my grasp."

When the other heard this, he was greatly shamed, and answered, "Sir knight, mount your horse and have no fear, for I give you my solemn oath that I'll not flee. You have cast shame upon me and I am offended."

The unknown knight replied, "First you will pledge me your word: I want you to swear to me that you will not flinch or flee, and that you will not touch or approach me until you see me remounted. I shall have been very generous indeed to set you free, when now I have you."

The guardian of the ford had no choice but to give his oath. When the knight heard his pledge, he went after his lance and shield, which had been floating in the ford, going along with the current, and were by now a good distance downstream. Then he returned to get his horse; when he had over-taken it and remounted, he took the shield by the straps and braced the lance against the saddletree.

Then the two spurred toward each other as fast as their steeds could carry them. The knight whose duty it was to guard the ford reached the other knight first and struck him so hard that he completely shattered his lance at once. The other dealt him a blow that sent him tumbling flat beneath the water, which closed completely over him. Then the Knight of the Cart with-drew and dismounted, confident that he could drive away a hundred such before him. He drew his steel-bladed sword from his scabbard, and the other knight sprang up and drew his fine, flashing blade. Again they engaged in hand-to-hand struggle, protected behind their shields, which gleamed with gold.

Their swords flashed repeatedly; they struck such mighty blows and the battle was so lengthy that the Knight of the Cart felt shame in his heart and said that he would be unable to meet the trials of the way he had undertaken, since he needed so long to defeat a single knight. Had he met a hundred such in a valley yesterday, he felt certain they would have had no defense against him, so he was exceedingly distressed and angry to be so weak today that his blows were wasted and his day spent. Thereat he rushed the guardian of the ford until he was forced to give way and flee, though loath to do so; he left the ford's passage free. Our knight pursued him until he fell forward onto his hands; then the rider of the cart came up to him and swore by all he could see that he would rue having knocked him into the ford and having disturbed his meditations.

Upon hearing these threats, the girl whom the knight of the ford had brought with him was most fearful and begged our knight for her sake not to kill the other. But he said that in truth he must; he could not show the mercy she asked since the other had shamed him so. Then he came up to him, with sword drawn. Frightened, the guardian said, "For God's sake and mine, show me the mercy I ask of you!"

"As God is my witness," replied the Knight of the Cart, "no person has ever treated me so vilely that, when he begs me for mercy in God's name, I would not show him mercy at once for God's sake, as is right. Since I would do wrong to refuse what you have asked in His name, I will show you mercy; but first you will swear to become my prisoner wherever and whenever I summon you."

With heavy heart he swore this to the knight, whereupon the girl said, "Sir knight, since in your goodness you have granted him the mercy he requested, if ever you have released a captive, release this one now to me. If you free him for me, I swear to repay you in due course whatever you would be pleased to request that is within my power to grant."

And then the knight understood by the words she spoke who she was, and he released his prisoner to her. She was troubled and upset, for she feared he had recognized her, which she did not want him to do. But he was eager to be off, so the girl and her knight commended him to God and asked his leave, which he granted.   [930]

Then he continued on his way until near nightfall, when he beheld a most comely and attractive girl approaching. She was splendidly attired and greeted him properly and graciously. He replied, "May God keep you well and happy."

"Sir," she then said, "my lodging nearby is set to welcome you if you are willing to accept my hospitality. But you may lodge there only if you agree to sleep with me—I make my offer on this condition." Many would have thanked her five hundred times for such an offer, but he became quite downcast and answered her very differently: "I thank you most sincerely for your kind offer of hospitality; but, if you please, I would prefer not to sleep with you."

"By my eyes," said the girl, "on no other condition will I lodge you."

The knight, when he saw he had no choice, granted her what she wished, though it pained his heart to do so. Yet if it wounded him now, how much more it would do so at bedtime! The girl who accompanied him would likewise suffer disappointment and sorrow; perhaps she would love him so much that she would not want to let him go. After he had granted her her wish, she led him to the finest bailey from there to Thessaly. It was enclosed round about by high walls and a deep moat. There was no one within, save him whom she had been awaiting.

For her residence she had had a number of fine rooms outfitted, as well as a large and spacious hall. They reached the lodging by riding along a riverbank, and a drawbridge was lowered to let them pass. They crossed over the bridge and found the tile-roofed hall open before them. They entered through the opened door and saw a table covered with a long, wide cloth; upon it a meal was set out. There were lighted candles in candelabra and gilded silver goblets, and two pots, one filled with red wine and the other with a heady white wine. Beside the table, on the end of a bench, they found two basins brimming with hot water for washing their hands. On the other end they saw a finely embroidered white towel to dry them. They neither saw nor found valet, servant, or squire therein. The knight lifted the shield from round his neck and hung it on a hook; he took his lance and laid it upon a rack. Then he jumped down from his horse, as did the girl from hers. The knight was pleased that she did not want to await his help to dismount.

As soon as she was dismounted, she hastened to a room from which she brought forth a short mantle of scarlet that she placed upon his shoulders. Though the stars were already shining, the hall was not at all dark: a great light from the many large, twisted-wax candles banished all darkness from the room. Having placed the mantle over her guest's shoulders, the girl said, "My friend, here are the water and the towel; no one else offers them to you, for you see that there is no one here except me. Wash your hands and be seated when it pleases you; the hour and food require it, as you can see. So wash now, then take your place."

"Most willingly."

Then he sat down and she took her place beside him, which pleased him greatly. They ate and drank together until it was time to leave the table. When they had risen from eating, the girl said to the knight, "Sir, go outside and amuse yourself, if you don't mind; but if you please, only stay out until you think I'm in bed. Don't let this upset or displease you, for then you may come in to me at once, if you intend to keep the promise you made me."

He replied, "I will keep my promise to you and will return when I believe the time has come."

Then he went out and tarried a long while in the courtyard, until he was obliged to return, for he could not break his promise. He came back into the hall, but he could not find his would-be lover, who was no longer there. When he saw she had disappeared, he said, "Wherever she may be, I'll look until I find her."

He started at once to look for her on account of the promise he had given her. As he entered a room, he heard a girl scream out loudly; it was that very girl with whom he was supposed to sleep. Then he saw before him the opened door of another room; he went in that direction and right before his eyes he saw that a knight had attacked her and was holding her nearly naked across the bed. The girl, who was sure he would help her, screamed, "Help! sir knight—you are my guest—if you don't pull this knight off me, I'll never find anyone to pull him away! And if you don't help me at once, he'll shame me before your very eyes! You are the one who is to share my bed, as you've already sworn to me. Will this man force his will upon me in your sight? Gentle knight, gather your strength and help me at once!"

He saw that the other held the girl uncovered to the waist, and he was troubled and embarrassed to see that naked body touching hers. Yet this sight evoked no lust in our knight, nor did he feel the least touch of jealousy. Moreover, two well-armed knights guarded the entrance with drawn swords; behind them were four men-at-arms, each holding an ax—the kind that could split a cow's backbone as easily as a root of the juniper or broom.   [1095]

The knight hesitated at the doorway and said, "My God, what can I do? I have set off in pursuit of nothing less than the queen, Guinevere. I must not have a hare's heart if I am in quest of her. If Cowardice lends me his heart and I follow his command, I'll never attain what I pursue. I am disgraced if I don't go in to her. Indeed I am greatly shamed even to have considered holding back—my heart is black with grief. I am so shamed and filled with despair that I feel I should die for having delayed here so long. May God never have mercy on me if there's a word of pride in anything I say, and if I would not rather die honorably than live shamed. If the way to her were free and those fiends were to let me cross to her unchallenged, what honor would there be in it? To be sure, the lowliest man alive could save her then! And still I hear this poor girl constantly begging me for help, reminding me of my promise and reproaching me most bitterly!"

He approached the doorway at once and thrust his head and neck through; as he looked up toward the gable, he saw swords flashing toward him and drew back swiftly. The knights were unable to check their strokes and both swords shattered as they struck the ground. With the swords shattered, he was less afraid of the axes. He leapt in among the knights, jabbing one man down with his elbows and another after him. He struck the two nearest him with his elbows and forearms and beat them both to the ground. The third swung at him and missed, but the fourth struck him a blow that ripped his mantle and chemise and tore open the white flesh of his shoulder. Though blood was pouring from his wound, our knight took no respite, and without complaining of his wound he redoubled his efforts until he managed to grab the head of the knight who was trying to rape his hostess. (Before he leaves he will be able to keep his promise to her.) He forced him up, in spite of the other's resistance; but meanwhile the knight who had missed his blow rushed upon our knight as fast as he could with his ax raised to strike—he meant to hack the knight's skull through to the teeth. But our knight skillfully maneuvered the rapist between himself and the other, and the axman's blow struck him where the shoulder joins the neck, splitting the two asunder. Our knight seized the ax and wrested it free; he dropped the man he'd been holding to look once more to his own defense, for the two knights were fast upon him and the three remaining axmen were again most cruelly assailing him. He leapt to safety between the bed and the wall and challenged them: "Come on, all of you! As long as I'm in this position, you'll find your match, even if there were twenty-seven of you! You'll never manage to wear me out."

As she watched him, the girl said, "By my eyes, you needn't worry from now on, since I am with you." She dismissed the knights and men-at-arms at once, and they immediately left her presence without question. Then the girl continued, "You have defended me well, sir, against my entire household. Now come along with me." They entered the hall hand in hand; yet he was not pleased, for he would gladly have been free of her.

A bed had been prepared in the middle of the hall, with smooth, full, white sheets. The bedding was not of cut straw or rough quilted padding. A covering of two silk cloths of floral design was spread over the mattress. The girl lay down upon the bed, but without removing her chemise. The knight was at great pains to remove his leggings and take off his clothes. He was sweating from his efforts; yet in the midst of his sufferings his promise overpowered him and urged him on. Is this duress? As good as such, for because of it he had to go sleep with the girl. His promise urged him on. He lay down with great reluctance; like her, he did not remove his chemise. He carefully kept from touching her, moving away and turning his back to her. Nor did he say any more than a lay is forbidden to speak when lying in bed. Not once did he look toward her or anywhere but straight before him. He could show her no favor. But why? Because his heart, which was focused on another, felt nothing for her; not everyone desires or is pleased by what is beautiful and fair. The knight had but one heart, and it no longer belonged to him; rather, it was promised to another, so he could not bestow it elsewhere. His heart was kept fixed on a single object by Love, who rules all hearts. All hearts? Not really, only those she esteems. And whomever Love deigns to rule should esteem himself the more. Love esteemed this knight's heart and ruled it above all others and gave it such sovereign pride that I would not wish to find fault with him here for rejecting what Love forbids him to have and for setting his purpose by Love's commands.

The girl saw clearly that he disliked her company and would gladly be rid of her, and that he would never seek her favors, for he had no desire to touch her. "If it does not displease you, sir," she said, "I will leave you and go to bed in my own room so you can be more at ease. I don't believe that the comfort of my presence is pleasing to you. Do not consider me ill bred for telling you what I believe. Now rest well this night, for you have kept your promise so fully that I have no right to ask even the least thing more of you. I'm leaving now and I wish to commend you to God."

With these words she arose. This did not displease the knight; on the contrary, he was glad to have her go, for his heart was devoted fully to another. The girl perceived this clearly; she went into her own room, disrobed completely, and lay in her bed saying to herself: "Of all the knights I have ever known this is the only one I would value the third part of a penny, for I believe he is intent upon a quest more dangerous and difficult than any ever undertaken by a knight. May God grant him success in it!"   [1278]

Thereupon she fell asleep and lay abed until the light of day appeared. As dawn broke, she rose quickly from her bed. The knight awoke, arose, then dressed and armed himself without waiting for anyone. The girl arrived in time to find him fully dressed.

"I hope a good day has dawned for you," she said when she saw him.

"The same to you, dear lady," replied the knight. And he added that he was in a hurry to have his horse brought forth.

The girl had it led to him and said, "Sir, if you dare to escort me according to the customs and usages that have been observed in the Kingdom of Logres since long before our days, I will accompany you some distance along this way." The customs and practices at this time were such that if a knight encountered a girl alone—be she lady or maidservant—he would as soon cut his own throat as treat her dishonorably, if he prized his good name. And should he assault her, he would be forever disgraced at every court. But if she were being escorted by another, and the knight chose to do battle with her defender and defeated him at arms, then he might do with her as he pleased without incurring dishonor or disgrace. This was why the girl told him that she would accompany him if he dared to escort her according to the terms of this custom and to protect her from those who might try to do her ill. "I assure you," he replied, "that no one will ever harm you unless he has first defeated me."

"Then," she said, "I wish to accompany you."

No sooner had she ordered her palfrey to be saddled than it was done; then it was brought forth along with the knight's horse. Both mounted without waiting for a squire's help and rode off rapidly. She spoke to him but he paid no heed to what she said and refused to speak himself; to reflect was pleasing, to speak was torment. Love frequently reopened the wound she had dealt him; yet he never wrapped it to let it heal or recover, for he had no wish to find a doctor or to bandage it, unless the wound grew deeper. Yet gladly he sought that certain one. . . .

They kept to the tracks and paths of the main road without deviating until they came to a spring in the middle of a meadow. Beside the spring was a flat rock on which someone (I don't know who) had left a comb of gilded ivory. Not since the time of the giant Ysoré had anyone—wise man or fool—seen such a fine comb. In its teeth fully half a handful of hair had been left by her who had used it.

When the girl noticed the spring and the flat rock, she took a different path, since she did not want the knight to see them. And he, delighting in and savoring his pleasant meditations, did not immediately notice that she had led him from the main path. But when he did notice, he was afraid of being tricked, believing she had turned aside to avert some danger. "Stop!" he said to her. "You've gone astray; come back here! I don't think anyone ever found the right way by leaving this road."

"Sir," the girl said, "I'm certain we'll do better to go this way."

And he replied, "I don't know what you're thinking, miss, but you can plainly see that this is the beaten path. Since I have started along this road, I'll take no other! So if it pleases you, come with me, for I plan to continue along this way." They rode on together until they neared the stone and saw the comb. "Never in all my life," said the knight, "have I seen a finer comb than this!"

"Give it to me," the girl requested.

"Gladly, miss," he answered. Then he bent down and picked it up. As he held it, he gazed steadfastly at the hair until the girl began to laugh. When he noticed her laughing, he asked her to tell him why, and she replied, "Don't be so curious; I'll tell you nothing for the moment."

"Why?" he asked.

"Because I don't want to."

Upon hearing this reply, he begged her as one who feels that lovers should never betray one another in any way: "If you love anyone in your heart, miss, in his name I beg and urge you not to hide your thoughts from me."

"Your appeal is too powerful," she said. "I'll tell you and hide nothing from you: I'm as sure as I have ever been that this comb belonged to the queen—I know it. Believe me when I assure you that the bright, beautiful, shining hair you see entangled in its teeth has come from the queen's own head. They never grew in any other meadow."

The knight replied, "In faith, there are many kings and queens; which one do you mean?"

"Upon my word, sir, the wife of King Arthur."

On hearing this, the knight did not have strength enough to keep from falling forward and was obliged to catch himself upon the saddle-bow. When the girl saw this, she was amazed and terrified, fearful he might fall. Do not reproach her for this fear, because she thought he had fainted. Indeed he had come quite near fainting, for the pain he felt in his heart had driven away his speech and the color from his face. The girl dismounted and ran as quickly as she could to aid and support him, because she would not have him fall for anything. When he saw her, he was ashamed and said to her, "Why have you come here before me?"

Do not suppose that the girl would reveal the true reason. He would be ashamed and troubled, and it would cause him pain and anguish were she to reveal the truth. Therefore she hid the truth and said with utmost tact, "Sir, I came to get this comb. That's why I dismounted. I wanted it so much I couldn't wait any longer."

He was willing for her to have the comb, but first he removed the hair, being careful not to break a single strand. Never will the eye of man see anything so highly honored as those strands, which he began to adore, touching them a hundred thousand times to his eyes, his mouth, his forehead, and his cheeks. He expressed his joy in every way imaginable and felt himself most happy and rewarded. He placed the strands on his breast near his heart, between his chemise and his skin. He would not have traded them for a cart loaded with emeralds and carbuncles; nor did he fear that ulcers or any other disease could afflict him; he had no use for magic potions mixed with pearls, nor for drugs against pleurisy, nor for theriaca, nor even for prayers to St. Martin and St. James! He placed so much faith in these strands of hair that he felt no need for any other aid.

But what were these strands like? I'd be taken for a fool and liar were I to describe them faithfully: when the Lendi fair is at its height and all the finest goods are gathered there, this knight would not accept them all—it's the absolute truth—should it prevent his finding this hair. And if you still demand the truth, I'd say that if you took gold that had been refined a hundred thousand times and melted down as many, and if you put it beside these strands of hair, the gold would appear, to one who saw them together, as dull as the darkest night compared to the brightest summer day of all this year. But why should I lengthen my story?   [1495]

The girl remounted at once, still holding the comb; and the knight rejoiced and delighted in the strands that he held to his breast. Beyond the plain they entered a forest and took a sidetrack that eventually narrowed to where they were obliged to continue one behind the other, since it was impossible to ride two horses abreast. The girl preceded her escort along the path.

At the very narrowest place along the trail they saw a knight coming toward them. The girl recognized him the moment she saw him and said to her escort, "Sir knight, do you see that man coming toward us fully armed and ready for battle? He fully intends to carry me off with him without meeting any resistance. I know he thinks this, because he loves me (though in vain) and has implored me for a long while, both in person and by messenger. But my love is not for him; there is no way I could love him. God help me, I'd rather die than ever love him at all! I know he's as happy at this moment as if he'd already won me. But now I'll see what you can do! I'll see if you are bold and if your escort can bring me safely through. If you can protect me, then I shall be able to say without lying that you are a bold and worthy knight."

He answered only, "Go on, go on," which was as much as to say, "I'm not worried by anything you've told me. You've no cause to be afraid."

As they went along conversing thus, the single knight was rapidly approaching them at full gallop. He hastened so because he was confident of success and considered himself very fortunate to see the one he most loved. As soon as he drew near her, he greeted her with words of his heart on his tongue, saying, "May the girl whom I most desire, who gives me the least joy and the greatest pain, be well come from wherever she is coming."

It was fitting that she not be so stingy with her words as to refuse to return his greeting—from her tongue, if not from her heart. The knight was elated to hear the girl respond, though it cost her little effort and was not allowed to stain her lips. And had he fought brilliantly that moment at a tournament he would not have esteemed himself so highly nor felt that he had won as much honor or renown. Out of pride and vanity he reached for her bridle rein. "Now I shall lead you away with me!" he said. "Today's fine sailing has brought my ship to a good port. Now my troubles are ended: after shipwreck I've reached port; after trial, happiness; after pain, health. At this moment all my wishes are fulfilled, since I have found you under escort and will be able to take you away with me now without incurring dishonor."

"Don't be too confident," she said, "for I'm being escorted by this knight."

"Then you have poor protection indeed!" said he. "I intend to take you at once. This knight would sooner eat a whole hogshead of salt, I believe, than dare to try to wrest you from me. I don't think I've ever met a man I couldn't defeat to get you. Since now I have you here so opportunely, I intend to lead you away before his very eyes, in spite of anything he may do to try to stop me."

Our knight did not become angered by all the arrogant words he had heard; rather, without boasting or mockery, he began to challenge him, saying, "Sir, don't be too hasty and don't waste your words. Speak more reason-ably. Your rights will not be denied you once you win them. But just remem-ber that this girl has come here under my safekeeping. Now let her be; you've detained her much too long and she has no reason to fear you."

The other granted that he would rather be burned alive than fail to carry her off in spite of her knight. He said, "It would not be good if I were to allow you to take her from me. Consider it settled: I must fight. But if we wish to do combat properly, we cannot by any means do it here on this path. Let us go rather to a main road, or to a meadow or heath."

The other replied that this suited him perfectly: "Indeed I grant your request, for you are quite right that this path is too narrow—my horse would be so hampered here that I'm afraid he'd break his leg before I could turn him about." Then with very great effort and attentive not to injure his steed, he managed to wheel him about. "I'm very angered indeed that we've not met in an open place where other men could witness which of us fights better. But come along, let's go look; we'll find a wide clearing nearby."

They rode until they reached a meadow in which there were knights, ladies, and ladies-in-waiting playing at many games, for the place was de-lightfully pleasant. Not all were occupied in idle sport; some were playing backgammon and chess, while others were occupied in various games of dice. Most were engaged in these diversions, though some others were playing at childhood games—rounds and dances and reels, singing, tumbling, and leap-ing. A few were struggling in wrestling matches.   [1648]

Across the meadow from the others was an elderly knight mounted on a Spanish sorrel. His saddle and trappings were of gold, and his armor was of grey mesh. One hand was placed smartly on one of his hips as he watched the games and dances. Because of the warm weather, he was clad in his chemise, with a scarlet mantle trimmed in vair thrown over his shoulders. Opposite him, beside a path, were more than twenty armed knights seated on good Irish steeds. As soon as the three riders neared them, they abandoned their pursuit of joy, and their shouts could be heard throughout the meadows: "Look at that knight, just look! It's the one who was driven in the cart. Let no one continue his play while he's among us. Damned be anyone who seeks to amuse himself or dares to play as long as he is here!"

While they were speaking in this manner, the old knight's son (the one who loved the girl and already considered her his) approached his father and said: "Sir, I'm bursting with joy! Let anyone who wishes to hear this harken to it: God has granted me the one thing I have always most desired. He could not have rewarded me more if he had made me a crowned king, nor would I have been as grateful, nor would I have gained as much, for what I have been granted is fair and good."

"I'm not sure it's been granted you yet," said the old knight to his son.

"You're not sure!" snapped his son. "Can't you see, then? By God, sir, how can you have any doubts when you see me holding her fast? I met her just now as she was riding along in this forest from which I've just come. I believe God was bringing her to me, so I took her as my own."

"I'm not yet sure that that knight I see following you will agree to this. I think he's coming to challenge you for her." While these words were being exchanged, the others abandoned their dancing; they stopped their games and sport out of spite and hatred for the knight they saw approaching. And this knight unhesitatingly followed swiftly on the heels of the girl. "Knight," he said, "give up this girl, for you've no right to her. If you dare fight me, I'll defend her against you here and now."

Then the old knight said: "Was I not right? My son, don't keep the girl any longer; let her go."

The son was not at all pleased and swore that he would never give her up: "May God never again grant me joy if I give her up to him. I have her and intend to keep her as my own. Before I abandon her to him I'll break my shield strap and all its armlets; I'll have lost all faith in my strength and weapons, in my sword and lance!"

"I'll not let you fight," retorted his father, "no matter what you say. You place too much faith in your own prowess. Now do as I order."

The son answered proudly, "Am I a child to be cowed? Of this I boast: though there are many knights in this wide world, there's not one for as far as the sea stretches who is so mighty that I'd abandon her to him without a fight. I'm sure I can bring any knight to quick submission."

"I have no doubt, fair son," said his father, "that you believe this, so greatly do you trust in your own strength. But I do not consent and will not consent this day to have you test yourself against this knight."

"Were I to do as you say, I would be shamed," said the son. "May anyone who'd take your advice and abandon the field without fighting bravely be damned! It's true when they say it's bad business to deal with friends: it is better to trade elsewhere since you intend to cheat me. I can see that I could better test my courage in some far-off place, where no one would know me and attempt to dissuade me from my intention, as you do who seek to bring me low. I am all the more upset because you have found fault with me, for as you well know, when anyone reproaches a person's intent, this sparks and inflames him all the more. May God never again grant me joy if I should hesitate because of you. No, in spite of your wishes, I intend to fight!"

"By the faith I owe the holy apostle Peter," said his father, "I can clearly see that pleading is to no avail. I'm wasting my time chastising you. But before long I'll come up with a way to force you to do my will, whether you want to or not, for I'll get the best of you." Thereupon he called all his knights. When they came to him, he ordered them to seize his son, who would pay no attention to him: "I'll have him bound before I'll let him fight. You are all my liegemen and owe me esteem and loyalty. By whatever you hold from me, respect my order and my wish. My son has acted rashly, it seems to me, and with unbridled pride in opposing my desires."

They answered that they would seize him and that he would never want to fight as long as they held him; and they said that they would force him to release the girl in spite of his wishes. Then they all seized him by grabbing him by the arms and around the neck.

"Now don't you feel like a fool?" asked his father. "Admit the truth: you no longer have the power to fight or joust, and no matter how much you might be upset, your feelings will do you no good now. Give in to what I want; you'll do well to follow my advice. And do you know what I am thinking? In order to lessen your disappointment, you and I, if you want, will follow this knight today and tomorrow, through the forest and across the plain, each of us on ambling steed. We might soon find him to be of such character and bearing that I would permit you to fight him as you desire."

Then the son agreed against his will, for he had no choice. The other knight, seeing no other solution, reluctantly accepted this proposal, provided they both would follow him.   [1814]

When the people who were gathered in the meadow saw this, they all said, "Did you see that? The knight who was in the cart has won such honor this day that he is leading away my lord's son's lady, and my lord permits it. We may truthfully say that he believes there is some merit in the man to let him lead her off. A hundred curses on anyone who stops his play on his account! Let's return to our games!" Then they resumed their games and returned to their rounds and dances.

The knight turned and rode out of the meadow at once. He took the girl with him and both set off with dispatch. The son and father followed at a distance. Through a mowed field they rode until the hour of nones, when in a most picturesque setting they found a church with a walled cemetery alongside the chancel. Being neither a boor nor fool, the knight entered the church on foot to pray to God; the girl looked after his horse until his return. When he had said his prayer and was returning, he saw an elderly monk coming directly toward him. As they met, the knight asked him politely to explain what was within these walls. The monk answered that there was a cemetery.

"As God is your help, please take me there."

"Gladly, sir." Then he led him into the cemetery, among the most beautiful tombs that could be found from there to Dombes, or even to Pamplona. Upon each were carved letters forming the names of those who were to be buried in the tombs. The knight himself began to read through the list of names and discovered: "Here will lie Gawain, here Lionel, and here Yvain." After these three there were many resting places bearing the names of many fine knights, the most esteemed and greatest of this or any other land. Among the tombs he found one of marble, which seemed to be more finely worked than all the others. The knight called to the monk and asked: "What is the purpose of all these tombs here?"

"You have seen the letters," he replied. "If you have comprehended them well, then you know what they say and the meaning of the tombs."

"Tell me what that largest one is for?"

The hermit replied, "I'll tell you all there is to know: this sarcophagus surpasses all others that have ever been made. Never has anyone seen a more elaborate or finely carved tomb; it is beautiful without and even more so within. But do not be concerned about that, for it can never do you any good and you will never see inside, because if anyone were to wish to open the tomb, he would need seven large and very strong men to open it, since it is covered by a heavy stone slab. You can be sure that to lift it would take seven men stronger than you or I. On it are carved letters that say: 'He who will lift this slab by his unaided strength will free all the men and women who are imprisoned in the land from which no one returns: since first they came here, no cleric or nobleman has been freed. Foreigners are kept prisoners, while those of this land may come and go as they please.'"

The knight went at once and seized hold of the slab and lifted it without the least difficulty, more easily than ten men could have done by putting their combined strength to the task. The monk was so astounded that he nearly fainted when he saw this marvel, for he never thought to see the like of it in all his life. "Sir," he said, "now I am most eager to know your name. Will you tell me?"

"Upon my word, I will not," answered the knight.

"Indeed, this weighs heavily upon me," said the other. "But to tell me would be a worthy action, and you could be rewarded well. Who are you? Where are you from?"

"I am a knight, as you see, born in the kingdom of Logres—I think that is enough. Now, if you please, it is your turn to tell me who will lie in this tomb."

"Sir, he who will free all those who are trapped in the kingdom from which none escape."

When the monk had told him all there was to know, the knight commended him to God and to all His saints, then returned to the girl as quickly as he could. The elderly, grey-haired monk accompanied him from the church till they reached the road. As the girl was remounting, the monk told her all that the knight had done while inside and begged her to tell him his name, if she knew it. She assured him that she did not know it, but one thing was certain: there was not a living knight his equal as far as the four winds blow.

[1954]

The girl left the monk and hurried after the knight. The two who had been following them arrived then and found the monk alone before the church. The old knight said: "Sir, tell us if you have seen a knight escorting a girl."

The monk answered, "It will be no trouble to tell you all I know, for they have just this moment left here. While the knight was inside he did a most marvelous thing by lifting the stone slab from the huge marble tomb alone and with no effort at all. He is going to rescue the queen. There is no doubt that he will rescue her and all the other people with her. You who have often read the letters inscribed on the stone slab know well that this is so. Truly no mortal knight who ever sat in a saddle was as worthy as he."

Then the father said to his son, "My son, what do you think? Is he not exceedingly bold to have performed such a deed? Now you can clearly tell whether it was you or I who was in the wrong. For all the wealth in Amiens I'd not have wanted you to fight with him. Yet you resisted mightily before you could be swayed from your purpose. Now we can return, for it would be madness to follow them beyond this spot."

"I agree with that," replied his son; "we are wasting our time following him. Let us return as soon as you are ready." He acted very wisely in turning back.

The girl rode on beside the knight; she was eager to get him to pay attention to her and learn from him his name. She asked him to tell her; time and time again she begged him until in his annoyance he said to her: "Did I not tell you that I am from the Kingdom of Arthur? I swear by God and His might that you'll not learn my name." Then she asked him for leave to turn back, which he gladly granted her. Thereupon the girl left and the knight rode on alone until it was very late.

After vespers, about compline, as he was riding along he saw a knight coming out of the woods after hunting. He had his helmet strapped on and the venison God had permitted him to take was tied over the back of his iron-grey hunter. This vavasor rode swiftly up to the knight and prayed him to accept lodging. "Sir," said he, "it will soon be night and is already past the time when it is reasonable to think of lodging. I have a manorhouse nearby where I will take you. I will do my best to lodge you better than you've ever been lodged before. I'll be happy if you'll accept."

"For my part, I am very happy to accept," said the knight.

The vavasor immediately sent his son ahead to make ready the house and hasten the supper preparations; and the youth loyally and willingly did as he was bid, riding off rapidly. The others, in no hurry, continued their easy pace until they reached the house. This vavasor had married a very accomplished lady and was blessed with five beloved sons (three mere youths and two already knighted) as well as two beautiful and charming daughters, who were still unmarried. They were not natives of this land, but were held captive there, having been imprisoned for a long while away from their homeland of Logres.

As the vavasor led the knight into his courtyard, his wife ran forward to meet him, and his sons and daughters all hastened out and vied with one another to serve him. They greeted the knight and helped him dismount. The sisters and five brothers almost ignored their father, for they knew that he would want it so. They made the stranger welcome and honored him. When they had relieved him of his armor, one of his host's two daughters took her own mantle from off her shoulders and placed it about his neck. I do not intend to give you any details about the fine dinner he was served; but after the meal they showed no reluctance to converse about many topics. First, the vavasor began to ask his guest who he was and from what land, but did not ask him his name. Our knight answered at once, "I am from the Kingdom of Logres and have never before been in this land."

When the vavasor heard this, he and his wife and all his children were most astonished. They were all very upset and began to say to him: "Woe that you were ever here, fair sir, for you will suffer for it: like us you will be reduced to servitude and exile."

"And where then are you from?" the knight asked.

"Sir, we are from your land. Many good men from your land are held in servitude in this country. Cursed be the custom, and those who promote it, that dictates that all foreigners who enter here must stay, prisoners in this land. Anyone who wishes may come in, but once here he must remain. Even for you there is no hope: I don't think you'll ever leave."

"Indeed I will," said he, "if I am able."

The vavasor said, "What! Do you believe you can escape?"

"Yes, if God is willing. And I'll do everything within my power."

"Then all the others would be able to leave without fear, for when one person can escape this imprisonment without trickery, all the others, I assure you, will be able to leave unchallenged." The vavasor then remembered that he had been told that a knight of great goodness was coming boldly into the land to seek the queen, who was being held by Meleagant, the king's son. He thought, "Indeed, I am quite convinced that this is he; I shall tell him so." Then he spoke: "Sir, do not hide your purpose from me. For my part I swear to give you the best counsel that I know. I myself stand to gain by any success you might have. For your good and mine tell me the truth. I am convinced that you came into this land to seek the queen among this heathen people, who are worse than Saracens."

"I came for no other purpose," replied the knight. "I do not know where my lady is imprisoned, but I am intent upon rescuing her and am thus in great need of counsel. Advise me if you can."

"Sir," said the vavasor "you have chosen a most difficult path. The one on which you are presently engaged will lead directly to the Sword Bridge. You must heed my advice. If you will trust me, I'll have you led to the Sword Bridge by a safer route."

Eager to take the shortest route, he inquired, "Is that path as direct as the one before me?"

"No," said his host, "it is longer, but safer."

"Then I have no use for it. Tell me about this path, for I am set to take it."

"Indeed, sir, it will never profit you. If you take this path I advise you against, you will come tomorrow to a pass where you might easily be harmed. It is called the Stone Passage. Do you want me to give you some idea of how bad a pass it is? Only one horse can go through there at a time; two men could not go abreast through it, and the pass is well defended. Do not expect them to surrender it to you when first you get there; you'll have to endure many a sword's blow and return full measure before you can pass through."

When he had told him all this, one of the knighted sons of the vavasor came forward and said, "Sir, I will go with this knight, if it is not displeasing to you." Thereupon one of the young boys rose and said: "And I'll go too!" Their father willingly gave leave to both. Now the knight would not have to travel alone; and he thanked them, being most happy for the company. [2186]

Then they broke off their conversation and showed the knight to his bed so that he might sleep, if he wished. As soon as he could see the day he arose, and those who were to accompany him noticed this and immediately got up. The knights donned their armor, took their leave, and rode off with the young boy before them. They traveled on together until they came to the Stone Passage right at the hour of prime. In the middle of the pass was a brattice in which a man always stood guard. While they were yet a good distance away, the man in the brattice saw them and shouted loudly, "Enemy approaching! Enemy approaching!"

Then immediately a mounted knight appeared upon the brattice, armed in unspotted armor and surrounded by men-at-arms carrying sharp battle-axes. As our knight was nearing the pass, the mounted knight reproached him bitterly for having ridden in the cart: "Vassal! You acted boldly, yet like a naive fool, in coming into this land. A man who has ridden in a cart should never enter here. And may God never reward you for it!"

Thereupon the two spurred toward each other as fast as their horses would carry them. The knight whose duty it was to guard the pass split his lance with the first blow and let both pieces fall. The other took aim at his throat just above the upper edge of his shield and tossed him backwards flat upon the stones. The men-at-arms leapt to their axes, yet they deliberately avoided striking him, for they had no desire to injure either him or his horse. The knight saw clearly that they did not wish to wound him in any way and harbored no desire to harm him, so without drawing his sword he passed beyond them unchallenged, with his companions after him.

"Never have I seen such a good knight," the younger son said to his brother, "and never was there anyone to equal him. Has he not performed an amazing feat by forcing passage through here?"

"Good brother," the older son replied, "for God's sake, hurry now to our father and tell him of this adventure!" The younger son swore that he would never go tell him and would never leave this knight's company until he had been dubbed and knighted by him. Let his brother deliver the message if he was so eager to do so!

The three then rode on together until about the hour of nones, when they encountered a man who asked them who they were. They answered, "We are knights going about our business."

And the man said to the knight who seemed to him to be lord and master of the others, "Sir, I would like to offer lodgings to you and to your companions as well."

"It is impossible for me to accept lodging at this hour," replied our knight. "Only cowardice permits one to tarry or relax when he has undertaken such a task as I have; and I am engaged in such a task that I will not take lodging for a long while yet."

Upon hearing this, the man replied, "My house is not at all nearby, but rather a long distance ahead. I promise that you will be able to lodge there at a suitable hour, for it will be late when you reach it."

"In that case I will go there," said the stranger. The man who was their guide then set off before them, and the others followed after. When they had been riding for some while, they encountered a squire galloping full speed toward them on a nag that was as fat and round as an apple. The squire called out to the man, "Sir, sir, come quickly! The men of Logres have raised an army against the people of this land and the skirmishes and fighting have already begun. They say that a knight who has fought in many places has invaded this land, and they cannot keep him from going wherever he wishes, whether they like it or not. All the people in this land say that he will soon free them and defeat our people. Now take my advice and hurry!"

The man quickened his pace to a gallop. The others, who had likewise heard this, were filled with joy and eager to help their countrymen. "Sir," said the vavasor's son, "listen to what this servant has said! Let's go to the aid of our people who are fighting their enemies!"

Their guide hurried off without waiting for them and made his way to a fortress that stood mightily on a hill. He rode until he reached the entrance, with the others spurring after him. The bailey was surrounded by a high wall and moat. As soon as they had entered, a gate was lowered upon their heels so they could not get out again. "Let's go! Let's go!" they shouted. "Let's not stop here!" They hastened after the man until they reached a passage that was not closed to them; but as soon as the man they were pursuing had gone through, a gate slammed shut behind him. They were most distressed to find themselves trapped within and thought they must be bewitched. But the knight about whom I have the most to say had a ring upon his finger whose stone had the power to break any spell, once he gazed upon it. He placed the ring before his eyes, looked at the stone, and said: "Lady, lady! By the grace of God I greatly need you to come now to my aid." This lady was a fairy who had given him the ring and had cared for him in his infancy, so he was certain that she would come to succour him wherever he might be. But he could see from his appeal and from the stone in the ring that no spell had been cast here; and he realized perfectly well that they were trapped and locked in.

They came now to the barred door of a low and narrow postern gate. All three drew their swords and struck so many blows that they hacked through the bar. Once out of the tower they saw the fierce battle raging in the meadows below, with a full thousand knights at least on either side, not counting the mass of peasants. When they came down into the meadows, the vavasor's son spoke with wise and measured words: "Sir, before entering the fray we would do well, I believe, to have one of us go learn which side is made up of our countrymen. I'm not sure which side they are on, but I'll go ask if you want."

"I wish you would go quickly," he said, "and return just as quickly." He went quickly and returned quickly. "It has turned out well for us," he said. "I've seen for certain that our men are on the near side."

Then the knight rode straight into the melee. He jousted with a knight he encountered coming at him and hit him such a blow in the eye that he struck him dead. The vavasor's younger son dismounted, took the dead knight's horse and armor, and outfitted himself properly and skillfully. When he was armed, he remounted at once and took up the shield and the long, straight, and colorfully painted lance; at his side he hung the sharp, bright sword. Into battle he followed his brother and their lord, who had been defending himself fiercely throughout the melee—breaking, cleaving, and splitting shields, helmets, and hauberks. Neither wood nor iron was any defense for those he attacked, as he knocked them dead or wounded from their horses. With unaided prowess he routed all he met, and those who had come with him did their share as well. The men of Logres marveled at the deeds of this unknown knight and asked the vavasor's son about him. They persisted in their questioning until they were told, "My lords, this is he who will lead us out of exile and free us from the great misery we have been in for so long. We owe him great honor because, to free us, he has already traversed many a treacherous pass and will cross many more to come. Though he has done much already, he has much yet to do."

When the news had spread throughout the crowd, everyone was filled with joy; all heard, and all understood. From the elation they felt sprang the strength that enabled them to slay many of their enemies. Yet it seems to me that the enemy was defeated more by the efforts of a single knight than by those of all the others combined. Were it not already so near nightfall the enemy would have been fully routed; but the night grew so dark that the armies were obliged to separate.   [2436]

As the armies separated, all the prisoners from Logres pressed excitedly about the knight, grabbing his reins from every side and saying, "Good sir, you are welcome indeed!" And everyone added, "Sir, in faith, you'll be sure to take your lodging with me! Sir, by God and His Holy Name, don't stay anywhere but with me!" What one said, they all said, because young and old alike wanted him to stay with them. "You will be better provided for at my house than anywhere else," they all said. Everyone crowded about him there was saying this and trying to pull him away from the others, because each wanted to host him; they nearly came to blows.

He told them all that it was foolish to quarrel so. "Stop this bickering," he said, "for it won't help me or you. Rather than quarrel among ourselves, we should aid one another. You should not argue over who will lodge me, but should be intent upon lodging me somewhere that will bring honor to everyone and will help me along my way."

Yet each kept repeating: "At my house—no, at mine!"

"You're still talking foolishly," said the knight. "In my opinion the wisest of you is a fool for arguing this way. You should be helping me along, but all you want to do is turn me aside. By all the saints invoked in Rome, I'm as grateful now for your good intentions as I would have been if all of you, one after another, had provided me as much honor and service as one can give a man. As surely as God gives me health and happiness, your good intentions please me as much as if each of you had already shown me great honor and kindness. So may the intentions be counted for the deed!"

In this manner he persuaded and appeased them all. They brought him to the house of a very well-to-do knight that was situated along the road he was to take, and everyone took pains to serve him. They all honored and served him and showed how happy they were for his presence; because of their great respect for him, they entertained him until bedtime.   [2496]

In the morning, when it was time to depart, everyone wanted to accompany him and all offered him their services. But it was not his pleasure or will to have anyone accompany him except the two he had brought there with him. He took these two and no others. They rode that day from early morning until dusk without encountering adventure. Late in the evening as they were riding rapidly out of a forest, they saw the manorhouse of a knight. His wife, who seemed a gentle lady, was seated in the doorway. As soon as she caught sight of them, she rose up to meet them. With a broad and happy smile she greeted them: "Welcome! I want you to accept lodgings in my house. Dismount, for you have found a place to stay."

"My lady, since you command it, by your leave we'll dismount and stay this night at your house."

When they had dismounted, the lady had their horses cared for by the members of her fine household. She called her sons and daughters, who came at once: young boys, who were courteous and proper knights, and comely daughters. Some she asked to unsaddle and groom the horses, which they willingly did without a word of protest. At her request the girls hastened to help the knights remove their armor; when they were disarmed, they were each given a short mantle to wear. Then they were led straightway into the magnificent house. The lord of the manor was not there, for he was out in the woods hunting with his two sons. But he soon returned, and his household, showing proper manners, hastened to welcome him at the gate. They untied and unloaded the venison he was carrying and said as they reached him, "Sir, you don't know it yet, but you are entertaining three knights."

"May God be praised!" he replied.

The knight and his two sons were delighted to have this company, and even the least member of the household did his best to do what had to be done. Some hastened to prepare the meal, others to light the tapers; still others fetched the towels and basins and brought generous amounts of water for washing their hands. They all washed and took their places. Nothing to be found therein was unpleasant or objectionable.

While they were partaking of the first course, there appeared before them at the outside door a knight who was prouder than the proudest bull. He was armed from head to foot and sat upon his charger, with one foot fixed in the stirrup but the other, for style, thrown jauntily over his steed's flowing mane. No one noticed him until he was right before them and said, "I want to know which one of you was so proud and foolish and so empty-headed as to come into this land, believing he can cross the Sword Bridge? He's wasting his strength; he's wasting his steps."

Unruffled, our knight answered confidently, "I am he who wishes to cross the Sword Bridge."

"You! You? What ever gave you that idea? Before undertaking such a thing you should have thought how you might end up, and you should have recalled the cart you climbed into. I don't know whether you feel shamed for having ridden in it, but no one with good sense would have undertaken such a great task if he were open to blame on this account."

To these insults our knight did not deign to reply a single word; but the lord of the manor and all those with him were rightly astounded beyond measure at this. "Oh God! What a misfortune!" thought each to himself. "Damned be the hour when a cart was first conceived of and built, for it is a vile and despicable thing. Oh God! What was he accused of? Why was he driven in the cart? For what sin? For what crime? He will be reproached forever for it. Were he innocent of this reproach, no knight in all the world could match him in boldness; and if all the world's knights were assembled in a single place, you'd not see a more fair or noble one, if the truth be told." Concerning this, everyone agreed.

The intruder continued his haughty words, saying, "Knight, hear this, you who are going to the Sword Bridge: if you wish, you can cross over the water quite safely and easily. I will have you taken swiftly across in a boat. However, if I decide to exact the toll once I have you on the other side, then I'll have your head if I want it; or, if not, it will be at my mercy."

Our knight answered that he was not seeking trouble: he would never risk his head in this manner, no matter what the consequences. Whereupon the intruder continued, "Since you refuse my aid, you must come outside here to face me in single combat, which will be to the shame and grief of one of us."

"If I could refuse, I'd gladly pass it up," said our knight to taunt him, "but indeed, I'd rather fight than have something worse befall me."

Before rising from where he was seated at table, he told the youths who were serving him to saddle his horse at once and to fetch his armor and bring it to him. They hurried to do as he commanded. Some took pains to arm him; others brought forward his horse. And you can rest assured that, as he was riding off fully armed upon his horse and holding his shield by the armstraps, he could only be counted among the fair and the good. The horse suited him so well that it seemed it could only be his own—as did the shield he held by the armstraps. The helmet he had laced upon his head fit him so perfectly that you'd never have imagined he'd borrowed it or wore it on credit; rather, you'd have said—so pleasing was the sight of him—that he had been born and raised to it. All this I'd have you believe on my word.

Beyond the gate, on a heath where the battle was to be held, the challenger waited. As soon as the one saw the other, they spurred full speed to the attack and met with a clash, striking such mighty thrusts with their lances that they bent like bows before flying into splinters. With their swords they dented their shields, helmets, and hauberks; they split the wood and broke the chainmail, and each was wounded several times. Every blow was in payment for another, as if in their fury they were settling a debt. Their sword blows often struck through to their horse's croups; they were so drunk in their blood-thirst that their strokes fell even on the horses' flanks, and both were slain. When their steeds had fallen, they pursued one another on foot. In truth they could not have struck more mightily with their swords had they hated one another with a mortal passion. Their payments fell more swiftly than the coins of the gambler who doubles the wager with each toss of the dice. But this game was quite different: there were no dice cast, only blows and fearful strokes, vicious and savage.

Everyone—the lord, his lady, their daughters and sons—had come forth from the house and assembled to watch the battle on the broad heath. When he saw his host there watching him, the Knight of the Cart blamed himself for faintheartedness; then, as he saw the others assembled there observing him, his whole body shook with anger, for he was convinced he should have defeated his adversary long since. With his sword he struck him a blow near the head, then stormed him, pushing him relentlessly backward until he had driven him from his position. He forced him to retract and pursued him until the intruder had almost lost his breath and was nearly defenseless.

Then our knight recalled that the other had reproached him most basely for having ridden in the cart; he pummeled and assailed him until no strap or lacing remained unbroken around his neckband. He knocked the helmet from his head and the ventail flew off. He pressed and beleaguered him so that he was compelled to beg for mercy. Like the lark, which is unable to find cover and is powerless before the merlin that flies more swiftly and attacks it from above, the intruder to his great shame was forced to plead for mercy, since he could not better his adversary. When the victor heard his foe pleading for mercy, he did not strike or touch him, but said, "Do you want me to spare you?"

"That's a smart question," he retorted, "such as a fool would ask! I've never wanted anything as much as I now want mercy."

"Then you shall have to ride in a cart. Say anything you wish, but nothing will move me unless you mount the cart for having reproached me so basely with your foolish tongue."

But the proud knight answered him, "May it never please God that I ride in a cart!"

"No?" said the other. "Then you shall die!"

"Sir, my life is in your hands. But in God's name I beg your mercy, only don't make me climb into a cart! There is nothing I wouldn't do except this, no matter how painful or difficult. But I know I'd rather be dead than be so disgraced. No matter what else you could ask of me, however difficult, I'd do it to obtain your mercy and pardon."   [2778]

Just as he was asking for mercy, a girl came riding across the heath on a tawny mule, with her mantle unpinned and hair disheveled. She was striking her mule repeatedly with a whip, and no horse at full gallop, to tell the truth, could have run faster than that mule was going. The girl addressed the Knight of the Cart: "May God fill your heart with perfect happiness and grant you every wish."

Delighted to hear this greeting, he replied, "May God bless you and grant you happiness and health!"

Then she announced her purpose: "Sir knight, I have come from far off in great distress to ask a favor of you, for which you will earn the greatest reward I can offer. And I believe that a time will come when you will need my assistance."

"Tell me what you wish," he answered, "and if I have it, you will receive it at once, so long as it is not impossible."

"I demand the head of this knight you have just defeated. To be sure, you have never encountered a more base and faithless knight. You will be committing no sin but rather will be doing a good and charitable act, for he is the most faithless being who ever was or ever might be."

When the defeated knight heard that she wanted him killed, he said to his conqueror, "Don't believe a word she says, because she hates me. I pray you to show mercy to me in the name of the God who is both Father and Son, and who caused His daughter and handmaiden to become His mother."

"Ah, knight!" said the girl. "Don't believe this traitor. May God give you as much joy and honor as you desire, and may He give you success in the quest you have undertaken!"

Now the victorious knight hesitated and reflected upon his decision: should he give the head to this girl who has asked him to cut it off, or should he be touched by pity for the defeated knight? He wishes to content them both: Generosity and Compassion demand that he satisfy them both, for he is equally generous and merciful. Yet if the girl carries off the head, Compassion will have been vanquished and put to death; and if she must leave without it, Generosity will have been routed. Compassion and Generosity hold him doubly imprisoned, with each in turn spurring him on and causing him anguish. One wants him to give the head to the girl who asked for it; the other urges Pity and Kindness. But since the knight has begged for mercy, will he not have it? Indeed he must, for no matter how much our knight hates another, he has never refused to grant mercy once—except for once—when that knight has been defeated and forced to plead with him for his life. So he will not refuse mercy to this knight who now begs and implores him, since this is his custom. Yet will she who desires the head not have it? She will, if possible.

"Knight," he said, "you must fight with me again if you wish to save your head. I will have mercy enough on you to let you take up your helmet and arm yourself anew as best you are able. But know that you will die if I defeat you again."

"I could wish no better and ask no other mercy," replied the knight.

"I shall give you this advantage," added the Knight of the Cart, "that I will fight you without moving from this spot I have claimed."

The other knight made ready, and they soon returned hotly to the fight but he was defeated now with more ease than he had been the first time.

The girl immediately shouted, "Don't spare him, sir knight, no matter what he says, for he would certainly never have spared you even the first time! If you listen to his pleas, you know he'll deceive you again. Cut off the head of this most faithless man in the whole kingdom and give it to me, fair knight. It is right that you give it to me, because that day will yet come when I shall reward you for it. If he could, he would deceive you again with his false promises."

The knight, seeing that his death was at hand, cried out loudly for mercy, but his cries and all the arguments he could muster were of no avail to him. Our knight grabbed him by the helmet, ripping off all the fastenings; the ventail and the white coif he struck from his head. The knight struggled till he could no more: "Mercy, for the love of God! Mercy, noble vassal!"

"Having once set you free, I'll never again show mercy, even if it were to ensure my eternal salvation."

"Ah!" said he. "It would be a sin to believe my enemy and slay me thus!"

All the while the girl, eager for him to die, was urging the knight to behead him quickly and not to believe his words. His blow fell swiftly: the head flew out onto the heath, the body crumpled. The girl was pleased and satisfied. The knight grasped the head by the hair and presented it to her. She was overjoyed and said, "May your heart find great joy in whatever it most desires, as my heart has now in what I most hated. I had only one sorrow in life: that he lived so long. I have a recompense awaiting you, which will come when you most need it. Rest assured that you will be greatly rewarded for this

service you have done me. I am going now, but I commend you to God, that
He might protect you from harm." Thereupon the girl took her leave, and
each commended the other to God.   [2941]

A very great joy spread through all those who had seen the battle in the
heath. They all happily removed the knight's armor and honored him as best
they knew how. Then they washed their hands once again, for they were
eager to return to their meal. Now they were much happier than ever, and
the meal passed amid high spirits.

After they had been eating for some time, the vavasor remarked to his
guest, who was seated beside him: "Sir, we came here long ago from the
Kingdom of Logres, where we were born. We want you to find great honor,
fortune, and happiness in this land, for we ourselves and many others as well
stand to profit greatly if honor and fortune were to come to you in this land
and in this undertaking."

"May God hear your prayers," he replied.

When the vavasor had finished speaking, one of his sons continued,
saying, "We should put all our resources in your service and offer you more
than promises. If you have need of our help, we should not wait to give it until
you ask for it. Sir, do not worry that your horse is dead, for there are many
more strong horses here. I want you to have whatever you need that we might
give you: since you need it, you will ride off on our best horse to replace your
own."

"I gladly accept," replied the knight.

With that they had the beds prepared and went to sleep. They arose
early the next morning, outfitted themselves, and were soon ready to be off.
As they left, the knight did not forget any politeness: he took leave of the lady
and the lord, then of all the others. But I must tell you one thing so that
nothing will be omitted: our knight did not wish to mount upon the borrowed horse that had been presented him at the gate. Instead (I would have
you know) he had one of the two knights who had accompanied him mount
it, and he mounted that knight's horse, since thus it pleased and suited him.
When each was seated on his horse, the three of them rode off with the
blessings of their host, who had served and honored them as best he could.

They rode straight on until night started to fall, reaching the Sword
Bridge after nones, about vespers. At the foot of that very dangerous bridge
they dismounted their horses and saw the treacherous water, black and roaring, swift, dark and thick, as horrifying and frightening as if it were the
Devil's stream, and so perilous and deep that there's nothing in the whole
world that, if it were to fall into it, would not be lost as surely as if it had fallen
into the frozen sea. The bridge across was unlike any other: there never was
nor ever will be another like it. Were you to ask me for the truth, I'd say that
never has there been such a treacherous bridge and unstable crossing. The
bridge across the cold waters was a sharp and gleaming sword—but the sword
was strong and stiff and as long as two lances. On either side were large

stumps into which the sword was fixed. No one need fear falling because of the sword's breaking or bending, for it was forged well enough to support a heavy weight.

What caused the two knights who accompanied the third to be most discomfited, however, was that they thought there were two lions or two leopards tethered to a large rock at the other end of the bridge. The water and the bridge and the lions put them in such a state that they were trembling in fear. "Sir," they said, "be forewarned by what you see before you! This bridge is vilely constructed and joined together, and vilely built. If you don't turn back now, it will be too late to repent. There are many things that should only be undertaken with great foresight. Suppose you should get across—but that could never happen, no more than you could contain the winds or forbid them to blow, or prevent the birds from singing their songs; no more than a man could reenter his mother's womb and be born again; all this could not be, any more than one could drain the oceans—if you should get across, could you be sure that those two wild lions that are chained over there would not kill you and suck the blood from your veins, eat your flesh, and then gnaw upon your bones? It takes all my courage just to look at them! If you are not careful, I assure you they'll kill you: they'll break and tear the limbs from your body and show no mercy. So take pity on yourself and stay here with us. It is wrong to put yourself knowingly in such certain danger of death."

He reassured them with a laugh: "My lords, receive my thanks for being so concerned about me. It is sincere and springs from love. I know that you would never wish me to fall into any misfortune, but my faith in God is so strong that He will protect me always. I have no more fear of this bridge and this water than I do of this solid earth, and I intend to prepare myself to undertake a crossing. I would rather die than turn back!"

They did not know what more to say to him; both sighed deeply and wept with compassion. The knight prepared himself as best he could to cross the chasm, and he did a most unusual thing in removing the armor from his hands and feet—he certainly wouldn't be whole and uninjured when he reached the other side! Yet he could get a better grip on the sword, which was sharper than a scythe, with his bare hands and feet, so he left nothing on his feet—not shoes, mail leggings, nor socklets. It mattered not to him if he should injure his hands and feet: he'd rather maim himself than fall from the bridge into the water from which there was no escape.

He crossed in great pain and distress, wounding his hands, knees, and feet. But Love, who guided him, comforted and healed him at once and turned his suffering to pleasure. He advanced to the other side on hands, feet, and knees. Then he remembered the two lions that he thought he had seen while he was still on the other side. He looked, but there was not so much as a lizard to do him harm. He raised his hand before his face, gazed at his ring, then looked again. (Since he had found neither of the lions that he thought he'd seen, he believed there must be some sort of enchantment, yet there was no living thing there.)

The two knights on the other shore rejoiced to see that he had crossed, as well they should; but they were unaware of his injuries. The knight considered himself most fortunate not to have been more seriously wounded; he was able to staunch the flow of blood from his wounds by wrapping them with his chemise.   [3137]

Now he saw before him a tower more mighty than any he had ever seen before; there was no way it could have been finer. Leaning on a window ledge was King Bademagu, who was most scrupulous and keen in every matter of honor and right and who esteemed and practiced loyalty above all other virtues. And resting there beside him was his son, who strove constantly to do the opposite, since disloyalty pleased him, and he never tired of baseness, treason, and felony. From their vantage point they had watched the knight cross the bridge amid great pain and hardship. Meleagant's face reddened with anger and wrath; he knew well that he would be challenged now for the queen. But he was such a knight that he feared no man, no matter how strong or mighty. Had he not been treasonous and disloyal, one could not have found a finer knight; but his wooden heart was utterly devoid of kindness and compassion.

Yet what caused Meleagant to suffer so made his father the king pleased and happy. The king knew with certainty that he who had crossed the bridge was far better than any other knight, for no one would dare cross who harbored within himself Cowardice, which shames those who have it more than Nobility brings them honor. Nobility cannot do as much as Cowardice and Sloth, for it's the truth—and never doubt it—that more evil can be done than good.

I could tell you many things about these qualities if we could linger here, but I must return to my matter and turn toward something else, and you will hear how the king addressed and instructed his son. "Son," said he, "it was by chance that you and I came here to lean upon this window ledge, and we have been repaid by witnessing with our own eyes the very boldest deed that has ever been conceived. Now tell me if you don't esteem the knight who performed such a wondrous feat? Go make peace with him and surrender the queen. You will gain nothing by fighting with him, and are likely to suffer great hurt for it. So let yourself be known as wise and noble, and send him the queen before he comes to you. Honor him in your land by giving him what he came to seek before he asks it of you—for you know quite well that he is seeking Queen Guinevere. Don't let anyone find you obstinate or foolish or proud. Since he has entered alone into your land, you must offer him hospitality, for a gentleman must welcome, honor, and praise another gentleman and never snub him. He who does honor is honored by it. Know you well that honor will be yours if you honor and serve him who without any doubt is the best knight in the world."

"May I be damned if there is not another as good or even better than he!" retorted his son. (The king had unwisely overlooked Meleagant, who thought himself not a bit inferior to the other.) "Perhaps you want me to kneel before him with hands joined and become his liegeman and hold my lands from him? So help me God, I'd rather be his liege than return Guinevere to him! She'll certainly never be handed over by me without a fight, and I'll defend her against all who are fool enough to come seeking her!"

Then the king answered him at once, "Son, you would do well not to be so stubborn. I urge and advise you to hold your peace. You know that it would cast shame upon this knight not to win the queen from you in battle; there can be no doubt that he would rather regain her through battle than generosity, for it would enhance his fame. In my opinion he's not sought after her in order to have her given peaceably to him but because he wants to win her in battle. So you would do well to keep him from having the battle. It hurts me to see you play the fool: but if you ignore my advice, I won't care if he gets the better of you. You stand to suffer greatly for your obstinacy, since this knight need fear no one here but yourself. I offer him peace and protection on behalf of myself and all my men. I have never acted disloyally or practiced treason or felony, and I will no more do so for your sake than for that of a total stranger. I don't want to give you any false hopes: I intend to assure the knight that everything he needs in the way of armor and horses will be provided him, since he has shown such courage in coming this far. He need fear for his safety from no man but you alone; and I want you to know that, if he can defend himself against you, he need fear no other."

"For the moment I am content to listen and say nothing," replied Meleagant. "You may say what you will, but I'm not bothered by anything you've said. I don't have the cowardly heart of a monk or do-gooder or almsgiver, nor do I care to have any honor that requires me to give him what I most love. This task won't be so easily and quickly accomplished and will turn out quite differently than you and he think. Even if you aid him against me, we'll not make our peace with you. If you and all your men offer him safe-conduct, what do I care? None of this causes me to lose heart. In fact it pleases me greatly, so help me God, that he has no one to fear but myself. Nor do I ask you to do a thing for me that might be interpreted as disloyalty or treason. Be a gentleman as long as you please, but let me be cruel!"

"What, will you not change your mind?"

"Never!" he replied.

"Then I've nothing more to say. Do your best. I shall leave you and go speak with the knight. I want to offer him my aid and counsel in every matter, for I am entirely in his camp."   [3302]

Then the king went down and ordered his horse saddled. A huge warhorse was brought to him, which he mounted by the stirrup. He ordered three knights and two men-at-arms, no more, to accompany him. They rode down from the castle heights until they neared the bridge and saw the knight, who was tending his wounds and wiping the blood from them. The king presumed that he would have him as a guest for a long while as his wounds were healing, but he might as well have expected to drain the sea.

King Bademagu dismounted at once, and the knight, though he was seriously wounded and did not know him, rose to greet him. He showed no sign of the pain he felt in his feet and hands. The king observed his self-control and hastened to return his greeting, saying, "Sir, I am astounded that you have fought your way into this land among us. But be welcome here for no one will undertake this feat again. Never has it happened and never will it happen that anyone but you will have the courage to face such danger. Know that I esteem you the more for having done this deed that no one before you dared even conceive. You will find that I am most agreeable, loyal, and friendly toward you; I am the king of this land and freely offer you my counsel and aid. I'm quite certain that I know what you are seeking here: you have come to seek the queen, I presume?"

"Sir," replied the wounded knight, "you presume correctly—no other duty brings me here."

"My friend, you will have to suffer before you win her," said the king, "and you are already grievously hurt, to judge by the wounds and blood I see. You won't find the knight who brought her here generous enough to return her without battle, so you must rest and have your wounds treated until they are fully healed. I shall provide you the ointment of the Three Marys—and better, if such be found—for I am most anxious about your comfort and recovery. The queen is securely confined, safe from the lusts of men, even from that of my son (much to his chagrin), who brought her here with him. I've never known anyone so crazed and mad as he! My heart goes out to you and, so help me God, I will gladly provide you everything you need. Though he'll be angry with me for it, he'll never have such fine arms that I'll not give you some equally good, and a horse that suits your needs. I shall protect you against everyone, no matter whom it might displease; you need fear no one except him alone who brought the queen here. No one has ever threatened another as I threatened him, and I was so angry at his refusal to return her to you that I all but chased him from my land. Though he is my son, you needn't worry, for unless he can defeat you in battle he can never, against my will, do you the least harm."

"Sir," he answered, "I thank you! But I'm wasting too much time here—time I don't want to waste or lose. I'm not hurt at all, and none of my wounds are causing me pain. Take me to where I can find him, for I'm ready to do battle with him now in such armor as I'm wearing."

"My friend, it would be better for you to wait two or three weeks for your wounds to heal; a delay of at least a fortnight would do you good. And I would never permit and could never countenance your fighting in my presence with such arms and equipment."

"If it pleases you," he replied, "I would have no arms but these, and gladly would I do battle in them. Nor do I seek even the slightest respite, postponement, or delay. However, to please you I will wait until tomorrow; but no matter what anyone may say, I'll not wait any longer!" Thereupon the king confirmed that all would be as the knight wished. He had him shown to his lodging and prayed and commanded those who were escorting the knight to do everything to serve him; and they saw to his every need.

The king, who would gladly arrange peace if he could, went meanwhile to his son and spoke to him in accordance with his desire for peace and harmony. "Fair son," he told him, "reconcile yourself to this knight without a fight. He has not come into this land to amuse himself or to participate in the hunt, but rather has come to seek his honor and to increase his renown. I have seen that he is in great need of rest. Had he taken my advice, he would have put off for several months at least the battle he is already eager to have. Are you afraid of incurring dishonor by returning the queen to him? Have no fear of this, for no blame can come to you from it; on the contrary, it is a sin to keep something to which one has no right. He would willingly have done battle here without delay, even though his hands and feet are gashed and wounded."

"You are a fool to be concerned," said Meleagant to his father. "By the faith I owe St. Peter, I'll not listen to your advice in this affair. Indeed I'd deserve to be torn apart by horses if I did as you suggest. If he is seeking his honor, so do I seek mine; if he is seeking his renown, so do I seek mine; if he is eager for battle, I am a hundred times more so!"

"I plainly see that you have your mind set on madness," said the king, "and you will find it. You shall try your strength against the knight tomorrow, since you will have it so."

"May no greater trial than this ever come to me!" said Meleagant. "I would much rather it were for today than tomorrow. See how I am acting more downcast than usual: my eyes are troubled and my face is very pale. Until I do battle I won't feel happy or at ease, nor will anything pleasing happen to me."   [3474]

The king recognized that no amount of advice or pleading would avail, so reluctantly he left his son. He selected a strapping fine horse and good weapons, which he sent to the one who needed them. In that land there lived an aged man and excellent Christian: no more loyal man could be found in all the world—and he was better at healing wounds than all the doctors of Montpellier. That night he summoned all his knowledge to care for the knight, since such was the king's command.

Already the news had spread to the knights and maidens, to the ladies and barons from the whole land round about. Both friend and stranger rode swiftly through the night until dawn, coming from every direction as far away as a long day's ride. By daybreak there were so many crowded before the tower that there wasn't room to move. The king arose that morning worried about the battle; he came directly to his son, who had already laced his Poitevin helmet upon his head. He could arrange no further delay and was unable to establish peace; though the king did all in his power to make peace, he was unable to achieve anything. So the king ordered that the battle was to take place in the square before the keep, where all the people were gathered.

The king sent at once for the foreign knight, who was led into the square, filled with people from the Kingdom of Logres. Just as people are wont to go to hear the organs at churches on the great feasts of Pentecost and Christmas, so in like manner they had all assembled here. The foreign maidens from the kingdom of King Arthur had all fasted three days and gone barefoot in hairshirts so that God might give strength and courage to their knight, who was to do battle against his enemy on behalf of the captives. In like manner the natives of this land prayed that God might give honor and victory in the battle to their lord.

Early in the morning, before the bells of prime had rung, the two champions were led fully armed to the center of the square on two iron-clad horses. Meleagant was handsome and bold: his arms, legs, and feet rippled with muscles, and his helmet and shield complemented him perfectly. But no one could take his eyes from the other—not even those who wished to see him shamed—and all agreed that Meleagant was nothing in comparison with him.

As soon as both had reached the center of the square, the king approached and did his best to postpone the battle and establish peace, but again he was unable to dissuade his son. So he said to them, "Rein in your horses at least until I have taken my place in the tower. It will not be too much to delay that long for my sake."

Downcast, he left them and went straight to where he knew he'd find the queen, for she had begged him the night before to be placed somewhere where she might have a clear view of the battle. He had granted her request and went now to find and escort her, for he strove constantly to do her honor and service. He placed her before a window while he reclined at another, beside and to the right of her. Together with the two of them were many knights, courtly ladies, and maidens of this land. There were also many captive maidens, who were intent upon their prayers and petitions, and many prisoners, both men and women, who were all praying for their lord, because to him and to God they had entrusted their help and deliverance.

Then at once the two combatants had the people fall back. They seized their shields from their sides and thrust their arms through the straps; they spurred forward until their lances pierced fully two arm's lengths through their opponent's shield, which broke and splintered like flying sparks. Quickly their horses squared off head to head and met breast to breast. Shields and helmets clashed together and rang round about like mighty claps of thunder. Not a breast-strap, girth, stirrup, rein, or flap could support the shock; even the sturdy saddle-bows split. Nor did they feel any shame in falling to the ground when all this gave way beneath them.

They leapt at once to their feet and without wasting words rushed together more fiercely than two wild boars. What good were challenges? Like hated enemies they struck mighty blows with their steel-edged swords; savagely they slashed helmets and gleaming hauberks, as blood rushed out from beneath the gashed metal. The battle was a mighty one as they stunned and wounded one another with powerful and treacherous blows. They withstood many fierce, hard, long assaults with equal valor, such that it was never possible to determine who was in the right. Yet it was inevitable that the knight who had crossed the bridge would begin to lose strength in his wounded hands. Those who sided with him grew most concerned, for they saw his blows weakening and feared he would be defeated; they were certain now that he was getting the worst of it, and Meleagant the better. A murmur ran through the crowd.   [3633]

But looking from the windows of the tower was a clever maiden, who recognized within her heart that the knight had not undertaken the battle for her sake, nor for that of the common people assembled in the square: he would never have agreed to it had it not been for the queen. She felt that if he realized that the queen herself was at the window watching him, it would give him renewed strength and courage. If only she could learn his name, she would willingly shout out for him to look about himself a little. So she came to the queen and said, "For God's sake and your own, my lady, as well as for ours, I beg you to tell me the name of this knight, if you know it—because it may be of some help to him."

"In what you have requested, young lady," replied the queen, "I perceive no wicked or evil intention, only good. I believe the knight is called Lancelot of the Lake."

"Praise God! You've made me so happy; my heart is full of joy!" exclaimed the girl. Then she rushed forward and shouted to him, in a voice that everyone could hear: "Lancelot! Turn around to see who is watching you."

When Lancelot heard his name, he turned at once and saw above him, seated in one of the tower loges, that person whom he desired to see more than anyone else in the whole world. From the moment he beheld her, he began to defend himself from behind so he would not have to turn or divert his face or eyes from her. Meleagant pursued him with renewed eagerness, elated to think that now he had him defenseless. The men of that kingdom were likewise elated, but the foreign prisoners were so distraught that many of them could no longer stand, and sank to their knees or fell prostrate upon the ground. Thus were felt both joy and sorrow in full measure.

Then the girl shouted again from the window: "Ah! Lancelot! What could make you behave so foolishly? Once you were the incarnation of all goodness and prowess, and I don't believe that God ever made a knight who could compare with you in valor and worthiness! Yet now we see you so distracted that you're striking blows behind you and fighting with your back turned. Turn around and come over here where you can keep the tower in sight, for seeing it will bring you strength and help."

Lancelot was shamed and vexed and despised himself because he well knew that for a long while now he'd been getting the worst of the fight—and everyone present knew it too! He maneuvered around behind his enemy, forcing Meleagant to fight between himself and the tower. Meleagant struggled mightily to regain his position, but Lancelot carried the fight to him, shoving him so powerfully with his full weight behind his shield when he tried to get to the other side, that he caused him to stagger twice or more in spite of himself. Lancelot's strength and courage grew because Love aided him, and because he had never before hated anything as much as this adversary. Love and mortal Hatred, the greatest ever conceived, made him so bold and courageous that Meleagant realized that this was deadly serious and began to fear him exceedingly, for Meleagant had never before faced such a bold knight, nor had any knight ever before injured him as this one had. He withdrew willingly and kept his distance, dodging and avoiding his hated blows.

Lancelot did not waste threats upon him, but drove him steadily with his sword toward the tower where the queen was seated—he often served and did homage to her—until he had driven him in so close that he had to desist for he would have been unable to see her, had he advanced a step farther. Thus Lancelot constantly drove him back and forth at will, stopping each time before his lady the queen, who had so inflamed his heart that he gazed upon her continually. And this flame so stirred him against Meleagant that he could drive and pursue him anywhere he pleased: he was driven mercilessly, like a man blinded or lame.

The king, seeing his son so pressed that he could no longer defend himself, took pity on him. He intended to intervene if possible; but to proceed properly he must first ask the queen. "My lady," he began by saying, "I have always loved, served, and honored you while you have been in my care, and I have always been prompt to do anything that I felt would be to your honor. Now I wish to be repaid. But I want to ask you a favor that you should only grant me through true affection: I clearly see that my son is getting the worst of this battle; I don't come to you because I am sorry to see him defeated, but so that Lancelot, who has the power to do so, will not kill him. Nor should you want him slain—though it is true that he deserves death for having so wronged both you and Lancelot! But for my sake I beg you in your mercy to tell Lancelot to refrain from slaying him. Thus you might repay my services, if you see fit."

"Fair sir, because you request it, I wish it so," replied the queen. "Even if I felt a mortal hatred for your son, whom I do not love, yet you have served me well, and because it pleases you, I wish Lancelot to restrain himself."

These words, which had not been spoken in a whisper, were overheard by Lancelot and Meleagant. One who loves totally is ever obedient and willingly and completely does whatever might please his love. Thus Lancelot, who loved more than Pyramus (if ever a man could love more deeply), must do her bidding. No sooner had the last word flowed from her mouth—no sooner had she said, "Because it pleases you, I wish Lancelot to restrain himself"—than nothing could have made Lancelot touch Meleagant or make any move to defend himself, even had the latter attempted to kill him. He did not move or touch him; but Meleagant, shamed and out of his mind with rage at hearing he had sunk so low that his father had had to intervene, struck Lancelot repeatedly.

The king hurried down from the tower to reproach him; he stepped into the fray and shouted to his son at once: "What! Is it right for you to strike him when he doesn't touch you? You are unspeakably cruel and savage, and your rashness condemns you! Everyone here knows for certain that he has vanquished you."

Beside himself with shame, Meleagant then said to the king, "You must be blind! I don't think you can see a thing! Anyone's blind who doubts that I've defeated him!"

"Then find someone who believes you!" said the king. "All these people know full well whether you're lying or speaking the truth. We know the truth." Then the king ordered his barons to restrain his son. They immediately did his bidding and pulled Meleagant away. But no great force was necessary to restrain Lancelot, for Meleagant could have done him serious harm before he would ever have touched him. Then the king said to his son, "So help me God, now you must make peace and hand over the queen! You must call an end to this whole dispute."

"Now you're talking like an old fool! I hear nothing but nonsense. Go on! Get out of our way and let us fight!"

And the king replied that he would intervene indeed, for he was certain that Lancelot would kill his son if he were to let them continue fighting.

"Him, kill me? Hardly! I'd kill him at once and win this battle if you'd let us fight and not interrupt us!"

"By God," said the king, "nothing you say will have any effect on me!"

"Why?" he challenged.

"Because I don't wish it! I refuse to lend credence to your folly and pride, which would only kill you. It takes a real fool to seek his own death, as you do, without realizing it. I am well aware that you detest me for wanting to protect you. I don't believe that God will ever let me witness or consent to your death, because it would break my heart."

He reasoned with his son and reproached him until a truce was established. This accord affirmed that Meleagant would hand over the queen on the condition that Lancelot would agree to fight him again one year and no more from that day on which he would be challenged. Lancelot readily consented to this condition. With the truce, all the people hastened around and decided that the battle would take place at the court of King Arthur, who held

Britain and Cornwall; there they decided it would be. And the queen was obliged to grant, and Lancelot to promise, that if Meleagant were to defeat him there, no one would prevent her return with him. The queen confirmed this, and Lancelot consented. So upon these conditions the knights were reconciled, separated, and disarmed.   [3898]

It was the custom of this land that when one person left, all the others could leave. They all blessed Lancelot, and you can be sure that great joy was felt then, as well it should be. All those who had been held captive came together, greatly praising Lancelot and saying, so that he might hear, "Sir, in truth, we were very elated as soon as we heard your name, for we were quite certain that soon we would all be freed."

There were a great many people celebrating there, and everyone was striving to find some way to touch Lancelot. Those who were able to get nearest were happy beyond words. There was great joy, but sadness too: those who had been freed were given over to happiness; but Meleagant and his followers shared none of their joy; rather, they were sorrowful, downcast, and dejected. The king turned away from the square, leading Lancelot, who begged to be taken to the queen, away with him.

"I am not reluctant to take you there," said the king, "for it seems to me to be a proper thing to do. If you wish, I'll show you the seneschal Kay as well."

Lancelot was so overjoyed that he nearly cast himself at the king's feet. Bademagu led him at once into the hall where the queen had gone to await him. When the queen saw the king leading Lancelot by the hand, she stood up before the king and acted as if she were angered. She lowered her head and said not a word.

"My lady," said the king, "this is Lancelot, who has come to see you."

"Me? Sir, he cannot please me. I have no interest in seeing him."

"My word, lady," exclaimed the king, who was very noble and courtly. "What makes you feel this way? Indeed you are much too disdainful of one who has served you well, who has often risked his life for you on this journey, and who rescued you and defended you against my son, Meleagant, who was most reluctant to give you up."

"Sir, in truth he has wasted his efforts. I shall always deny that I feel any gratitude toward him."

You could see Lancelot's confusion, yet he answered her politely and like a perfect lover: "My lady, indeed this grieves me, yet I dare not ask your reasons."

Lancelot would have poured out his woe if the queen had listened, but to pain and embarrass him further she refused to answer him a single word and passed instead into a bedchamber. Lancelot's eyes and heart accompanied her to the entrance; his eyes' journey was short, for the room was near at hand, yet they would gladly have entered in after her, had that been possible. His heart, its own lord and master, and more powerful by far, was able to follow after her, while his eyes, full of tears, remained outside with his body.

The king whispered to him: "Lancelot, I am amazed that this has happened. What can this mean when the queen refuses to see you and is so unwilling to speak with you? If ever she was pleased to speak with you, she should not now be reticent or refuse to listen to you, after all you have done for her. Now tell me, if you know, what reason she has to treat you this way."

"Sir, I never expected this sort of welcome. But clearly she does not care to see me or listen to what I have to say, and this disturbs me greatly."

"Of course," said the king, "she is wrong, for you have risked death for her. So come now, my fair friend, and go speak with the seneschal Kay."

"I am very eager to do so," replied Lancelot.

The two of them went to the seneschal. When Lancelot came before him, the seneschal addressed him first, saying: "How you have shamed me!"

"How could I have?" answered Lancelot. "Tell me what shame I've caused you."

"An enormous shame, because you have completed what I was unable to complete and have done what I was unable to do."

At that the king left the two of them and went out of the room alone. Lancelot asked the seneschal if he had suffered greatly.

"Yes," he answered, "and I am still suffering. I have never been worse off than I am now, and I would have been dead long ago had it not been for the king who just now left us, who in his compassion has shown me such kindness and friendship. Whenever he was aware I needed anything, he never failed to arrange to have it prepared for me, as soon as he knew of my need. But each time he tried to help me, his son Meleagant, who is full of evil designs, deceitfully sent for his own physicians and ordered them to dress my wounds with ointments that would kill me. Thus I've had both a loving father and a wicked stepfather: for whenever the king, who did everything he could to see that I would be quickly healed, had good medicine put on my wounds, his son, in his treachery and desire to kill me, had it removed straightway and some harmful ointment substituted. I am absolutely certain that the king did not know this, for he would in no way countenance such base treachery.

"And you aren't aware of how kindly he has treated my lady: never since Noah built his ark has a tower in the march been as carefully guarded as he has had her kept. Though it upsets his son, he has not let even Meleagant see her except in his own presence or with a company of people. The good king in his kindness has always treated her as properly as she could require. No one but the queen has overseen her confinement; she arranged it so, and the king esteemed her the more because he recognized her loyalty. But is it true, as I've been told, that she is so angry with you that she has publicly refused to speak to you?"

"You have been told the truth," replied Lancelot, "the whole truth. But for God's sake, can you tell me why she hates me?"

Kay replied that he did not know and was extremely amazed by her behavior.

"Then let it be as she orders," said Lancelot, who could not do otherwise. "I must take my leave and go seek my lord Gawain, who has come into this land having sworn to me to go directly to the Underwater Bridge."

Lancelot left the room at once, came before the king, and asked his leave to depart. The king willingly consented; but those whom Lancelot had delivered from imprisonment asked what was to become of them. Lancelot replied, "With me will come all those who wish to seek Gawain, and those who wish to stay with the queen should remain. They need not feel compelled to come with me."

All who so wished accompanied him, happier than they'd ever been before. There remained with the queen many maidens, ladies, and knights, who were likewise filled with joy. Yet all of those remaining would have preferred to return to their own country rather than stay in this land. The queen only retained them because of the imminent arrival of my lord Gawain, saying that she would not leave until she had heard from him.

Word spread everywhere that the queen was freed, that all the captives were released, and that they would be able to leave without question whenever it might please them. When people came together, they all asked one another about the truth of this matter and spoke of nothing else. They were not at all upset that the treacherous passes had been destroyed. Now people could come and go at will—this was not as it had been!

When the local people who had not been at the battle learned how Lancelot had fared, they all went to where they knew he was to pass, for they thought that the king would be pleased if they captured and returned Lancelot to him. Lancelot's men had all removed their armor and were quite bewildered to see these armed men approaching. It is no wonder that they succeeded in taking Lancelot, who was unarmed, and returned with him captive, his feet tied beneath his horse. "Lords, you do us wrong," said the men of Logres, "for we are traveling under the king's safe-conduct. We are all under his protection."

"We know nothing of this," replied the others. "But captive as you are, you must come to court."

Swift-flying rumor reached the king, saying that his people had captured and killed Lancelot. On hearing this, Bademagu was greatly upset and swore by more than his head that those who had killed him would die for it. He said that they would never be able to justify themselves, and if he could catch them, he'd have them hanged, burned, or drowned at once. And should they try to deny their deed, he would never believe them, for they had brought him such grief and had caused him such shame that he himself would bear the blame for it unless he took vengeance—and without a doubt he would.

The rumor spread everywhere. It was even told to the queen, who was seated at dinner. She nearly killed herself when she heard the lying rumor of

Lancelot's death. She thought it was true and was so greatly perturbed that she was scarcely able to speak. Because of those present, she spoke openly: "Indeed, his death pains me, and I am not wrong to let it, for he came into this land on my account, and therefore I should be grieved." Then she said to herself in a low voice, so she would not be overheard, that it would not be right to ask her to drink or eat again, if it were true that he for whom she lived were dead. She arose at once from the table, and was able to give vent to her grief without being noticed or overheard. She was so crazed with the thought of killing herself that she repeatedly grabbed at her throat. Yet afterward she confessed in conscience, repented, and asked God's pardon; she accused herself of having sinned against the one she knew had always been hers, and who would still be, were he alive. Anguish brought on by her own lack of compassion destroyed much of her beauty. Her lack of compassion, the betrayal of her love, combined with ceaseless vigils and fasting, caused her to lose her color.

She counted all of her unkindnesses and called them each to mind; she noted every one, and repeated often: "Oh misery! What was I thinking, when my lover came before me and I did not deign to welcome him, nor even care to listen! Was I not a fool to refuse to speak or even look at him? A fool? No, so help me God, I was cruel and deceitful! I intended it as a joke, but he didn't realize this and never forgave me for it. I believe that it was I alone who struck him the mortal blow. When he came happily before me and expected me to receive him joyfully, and I shunned him and would never even look at him—was this not a mortal blow? At that moment when I refused to speak, I believe I severed both his heart and his life. Those two blows killed him, I think, and not any highway brigands.

"Ah God! Will I be forgiven this murder, this sin? Never! All the rivers and the sea will dry up first! Oh misery! How it would have brought me comfort and healing if once, before he died, I had held him in my arms. How? Yes, quite naked next to him, in order to enjoy him fully. Since he is dead, I am wicked not to kill myself. Can my life bring me anything but sorrow if I live on after his death, since I take pleasure in nothing except the woe I bear on his account? The sole pleasure of my life after his death—this suffering I now court—would please him, were he alive. A woman who would prefer to die rather than to endure pain for her love is unworthy of it. So I am happy indeed to mourn him unceasingly. I prefer to live and suffer life's blows than to die and be at rest."   [4244]

The queen mourned thus for two days, without eating or drinking, until it was thought she was dead. Many there are who would prefer to carry bad news than good, and so the rumor reached Lancelot that his lady and love had succumbed. You need not doubt that he was overcome with grief, and everyone can understand that he was sorrowful and depressed. He was so saddened (if you care to hear and know the truth) that he disdained his very life: he intended to kill himself at once, but not before he'd unburdened his soul. He tied a sliding loop in one end of the belt he wore around his waist, and said to himself, weeping, "Ah death! How you have sought me out and overcome me in the prime of life! I am saddened, but the only pain I feel is the grief in my heart—an evil, fatal grief. I want it to be fatal so that, if it please God, I shall die of it. And if it doesn't please God that I should die of grief, could I not die in another way? Indeed I shall, if he lets me loop this cord about my neck! In this manner I am sure that I can force Lady Death to take me, even against her will. Though Death, who seeks out only those who don't want her, does not want to come to me, my belt will bring her within my power, and when I control her she will do my bidding. Yet she will be too slow to come because of my eagerness to have her!"

Then, without waiting, he put the loop over his head until it was taut about his neck; and to be sure of death, he tied the other end of the belt tightly to his saddle horn, without attracting anyone's attention. Then he let himself slip toward the ground, wishing to be dragged by his horse until dead. He did not care to live another hour. When those who were riding with him saw him fallen to the ground, they thought he had fainted, for no one noticed the loop that he had tied around his neck. They lifted him up at once, and when they had him in their arms, they discovered the noose, which had made him his own enemy when he had placed it around his neck. They cut it immediately, but it had been pulled so tight around his throat that he could not speak for a long while. The veins of his neck and throat were nearly severed. Even had he wanted, he could no longer harm himself.

He was so distraught at being stopped that he was aflame with anger and would have killed himself had he not been watched. Since he could no longer harm himself physically, he said, "Ah! vile, whoring Death! Why didn't you have the strength and power to slay me before my lady's death? I suppose it was because you wouldn't deign to do a good turn to anyone. You did this out of treachery, and you will never be anything but a traitor. Ah! What kindness! What goodness! How wonderful you've been with me! But may I be damned if I ever welcome this kindness or thank you for it!"

"I don't know which hates me more: Life, who wants me, or Death, who refuses to take me! Thus they both destroy me: but it serves me right, by God, to be alive despite myself, for I should have killed myself as soon as my lady the queen showed me her displeasure. She did not do so without reason—there was certainly a good cause, though I do not know what it was. Yet had I known, I would have reconciled myself to her in any way she wished, so that before her soul went to God she might have forgiven me. My God! What could this crime have been? I think that perhaps she knew that I had mounted into the cart. I don't know what else she could have held against me. This alone was my undoing.

"But if she hated me for this crime—oh God! how could this have damned me? One who would hold this against me never truly knew Love; for there is nothing known that, if prompted by Love, should be contemptible; rather, anything that one can do for his lady-love should be considered an act of love and courtliness. Yet I did not do it for my lady-love. Ah me! I don't know what to call her. I don't know whether I dare name her my 'lady-love.' But I think that I know this much of love: if she had loved me, she would not have esteemed me the less for this act, but would have called me her true love, since it seemed to me honorable to do anything for her that love required, even to mounting into the cart. She should have ascribed this to love, its true source. Thus does Love test her own, and thus does she know her own. But by the manner of her welcome I knew that this service did not please my lady. Yet it was for her alone that her lover performed this deed for which he has often been shamed, reproached, and falsely blamed. I have indeed done that for which I am blamed, and from sweetness I grow bitter, in faith, because she has behaved like those who know nothing of Love and who dip honor into shame; yet those who dampen honor with shame do not wash it, but soil it. Those who condemn lovers know nothing of Love, and those who do not fear her commands esteem themselves above Love. There is no doubt that he who obeys Love's command is uplifted, and all should be forgiven him. He who dares not follow Love's command errs greatly.   [4396]

Thus Lancelot lamented, and those beside him who watched over and protected him were saddened. Meanwhile word reached them that the queen was not dead. Lancelot took comfort immediately and, if earlier he had wept bitterly over her death, now his joy in her being alive was a hundred thousand times greater.

When they came within six or seven leagues of the castle where King Bademagu was staying, news that was pleasing came to him about Lancelot—news that he was glad to hear: that Lancelot was alive and was returning hale and hearty. He behaved most properly in going to inform the queen. "Fair sir," she told him, "I believe it, since you have told me. But were he dead, I assure you that I could never again be happy. If Death were to claim a knight in my service, my joy would leave me altogether."

Thereupon the king left her. The queen was most eager for the arrival of her joy, her lover. She had no further desire to quarrel with him about anything. Rumor, which never rests but runs unceasingly all the while, soon returned to the queen with news that Lancelot would have killed himself for her, had he not been restrained. She welcomed this news and believed it with all her heart, yet never would she have wished him ill, for it would have been too much to bear.

Meanwhile Lancelot came riding swiftly up. As soon as the king saw him, he ran to kiss and embrace him; his joy so lightened him that he felt as if he had wings. But those who had taken and bound Lancelot cut short his joy. The king cursed the hour in which they had come and wished them all dead and damned. They answered only that they thought he would have wanted Lancelot.

"Though you may think that," replied the king, "nonetheless it displeases me. Worry not for Lancelot—you have brought him no shame. No! But I, who promised him safe-conduct, am dishonored. In all events the shame is mine, and you will find it no light matter if you try to escape me."

When Lancelot perceived his anger, he did his very best to make peace and was finally able to do so. Then the king led him to see the queen. This time the queen did not let her eyes lower toward the ground but went happily up to him and had him sit beside her, honoring him with her kindest attentions. Then they spoke at length of everything that came into their minds; they never lacked for subject matter, which Love supplied them in abundance. When Lancelot saw how well he was received, and that anything he said pleased the queen, he asked her in confidence: "My lady, I wonder why you acted as you did when you saw me the other day and would not say a single word to me. You nearly caused my death, yet at that moment I didn't have enough confidence to dare to ask you, as now I am asking you. My lady, if you would tell me what sin has caused me such distress, I am prepared to atone for it at once."

The queen replied, "What? Were you not shamed by and frightened of the cart? By delaying for two steps you showed your great unwillingness to mount. That, to tell the truth, is why I didn't wish to see you or speak with you."

"In the future may God preserve me from such a sin," said Lancelot, "and may He have no mercy upon me if you are not completely right. My lady, for God's sake, accept my penance at once; and if ever you could pardon me, for God's sake tell me so!"

"Dear friend, may you be completely forgiven," said the queen. "I absolve you most willingly."

"My lady," said he, "I thank you. But I cannot tell you in this place all that I would like to. If it were possible, I'd gladly speak with you at greater leisure."

The queen indicated a window to him with a glance, not by pointing. "Tonight when everyone within is asleep, you can come speak with me at this window. Make your way first through the orchard. You cannot come inside or be with me: I shall be inside and you without. It is impossible for you to get inside, and I shall be unable to come to you, except by words or by extending my hand. But for love of you I will stay by the window until the morrow, if it pleases you. We cannot come together because Kay the seneschal, suffering from the wounds that cover him, sleeps opposite me in my room. Moreover, the door is always locked and guarded. When you come, be careful lest some informer see you."

"My lady," said Lancelot, "I will do everything possible so that no one will observe my coming who might consider it evil or speak badly of us." Having set their tryst, they separated joyfully.   [4532]

On leaving the room, Lancelot was so full of bliss that he did not recall a single one of his many cares. But night was slow in coming, and this day seemed longer to him, for all his anticipation, than a hundred others or even a whole year. He ached to be at the tryst, if only night would come. At last dark and somber night conquered day's light, wrapped it in her covering, and hid it beneath her cloak. When Lancelot saw the day darkened, he feigned fatigue and weariness, saying that he had been awake a long while and needed repose. You who have behaved in like manner will be able to understand that he pretended to be tired and went to bed because there were others in the house; but his bed had no attraction for him, and nothing would have made him sleep. He couldn't have slept, nor had he the courage, nor would he have wanted to dare fall asleep.

He crept out of bed as soon as possible. It bothered him not at all that there was no moon or star shining outside, nor any candle, lamp, or lantern burning within the house. He moved slowly, careful not to disturb anyone; everyone thought he had slept the whole night in his bed. Alone and unobserved, he went straight to the orchard. He had the good fortune to discover that a part of the orchard wall had recently fallen. Through this breach he quickly passed and continued until he reached the window, where he stood absolutely silent, careful not to cough or sneeze, until the queen approached in a spotless white chemise. She had no dress or coat over it, only a short mantle of scarlet and marmot fur.

When Lancelot saw the queen leaning upon the window ledge behind the thick iron bars, he greeted her softly. She returned his greeting promptly, since she had great desire for him, as did he for her. They did not waste their time speaking of base or tiresome matters. They drew near to one another and held each other's hand. They were troubled beyond measure at being unable to come together, and they cursed the iron bars. But Lancelot boasted that, if the queen wished it, he could come in to her—the iron bars would never keep him out. The queen responded, "Can't you see that these bars are too rigid to bend and too strong to break? You could never wrench or pull or bend them enough to loosen them."

"My lady," he said, "don't worry! I don't believe that iron could ever stop me—nothing but you yourself could keep me from coming in to you. If you grant me your permission, the way will soon be free; but if you are unwilling, then the obstacle is so great that I will never be able to pass."

"Of course I want you with me," she replied. "My wishes will never keep you back. But you must wait until I am lying in my bed, so that you will not be endangered by any noise, for we would be in real trouble if the seneschal sleeping here were to be awakened by us. So I must go now, for if he saw me standing here he'd find no good in it."

"My lady," said Lancelot, "go then, but don't worry about my making any sound. I plan to separate the bars so smoothly and effortlessly that no one will be aroused."

Thereupon the queen turned away, and Lancelot prepared and readied himself to unbar the window. He grasped the iron bars, strained, and pulled until he had bent them all and was able to free them from their fittings. But the iron was so sharp that he cut the end of his little finger to the quick and severed the whole first joint of the next finger; yet his mind was so intent on other matters that he felt neither the wounds nor the blood flowing from them.

Although the window was quite high up, Lancelot passed quickly and easily through it. He found Kay still asleep in his bed. He came next to that of the queen; Lancelot bowed low and adored her, for he did not place such faith in any holy relic. The queen stretched out her arms toward him, embraced him, clasped him to her breast, and drew him into the bed beside her, looking at him as tenderly as she could, prompted by Love and her heart. She welcomed him for the sake of Love; but if her love for him was strong, he felt a hundred thousand times more for her. Love in other hearts was as nothing compared with the love he felt in his. Love took root in his heart, and was so entirely there that little was left for other hearts.

Now Lancelot had his every wish: the queen willingly sought his company and affection, as he held her in his arms, and she held him in hers. Her loveplay seemed so gentle and good to him, both her kisses and caresses, that in truth the two of them felt a joy and wonder, the equal of which has never been heard or known. But I shall let it remain a secret forever, since it should not be written of: the most delightful and choicest pleasure is that which is hinted, but never told.

Lancelot had great joy and pleasure all that night, but the day's coming sorrowed him deeply, since he had to leave his love's side. So deep was the pain of parting that rising was a true martyrdom, and he suffered a martyr's agony: his heart repeatedly turned back to the queen where she remained behind. Nor was he able to take it with him, for it so loved the queen that it had no desire to quit her. His body left, but his heart stayed. Lancelot went straight to the window, but he left enough of his body behind to stain and spot the sheets with the blood that dripped from his fingers. As Lancelot departed he was distraught, full of sighs and full of tears. It grieved him that no second tryst had been arranged, but such was impossible. Regretfully he went out the window through which he had entered most willingly. His fingers were badly cut. He straightened the bars and replaced them in their fittings so that, from no matter what angle one looked, it did not seem as if any of the bars had been bent or removed. On parting, Lancelot bowed low before the bedchamber, as if he were before an altar. Then in great anguish he left.   [4719]

On the way back to his lodging he did not encounter anyone who might recognize him. He lay down naked in his bed without awakening anyone. And then for the first time, to his surprise, he noticed his wounded fingers; but he was not the least upset, for he knew without doubt that he had cut himself pulling the iron bars from the window casing. Therefore he did not grow angry with himself, since he would rather have had his two arms pulled from his body than not to have entered through the window. Yet, if he had so seriously injured himself in any other manner, he would have been most upset and distressed.

In the morning the queen was gently sleeping in her curtained room. She did not notice that her sheets were stained with blood, but thought them still to be pure white, fair, and proper. As soon as he was dressed, Meleagant came into the room where the queen had been sleeping. He found her awake and saw the sheets stained with fresh drops of blood. He nudged his men and, as if suspecting some evil, looked toward the seneschal Kay's bed. There, too, he saw bloodstained sheets—because, you can surmise, his wounds had reopened during the night. "My lady," said Meleagant, "now I've found the proof I've been seeking! It's certainly true that a man is a fool to take pains to watch over a woman—all his efforts are wasted. And the man who makes the greater effort loses his woman more quickly than he who doesn't bother. My father did a fine job of protecting you from me! He has guarded you carefully from me, but in spite of his efforts the seneschal Kay has looked closely upon you this night and has done all he pleased with you. This will be easily proven!"

"How?" she asked.

"I have found blood on your sheets—clear proof, since you must be told. This is how I know, and this is my proof: that on your sheets and his I have found blood that dripped from his wounds. This evidence is irrefutable!"

Then, for the first time, the queen noticed the bloody sheets on both beds. She was dumbfounded, shamed, and red-faced. "As the Lord Almighty is my protector," she said, "this blood you see on my sheets never came from Kay. . . my nose bled last night—it must have come from my nose." She felt as if she were telling the truth.

"By my head," replied Meleagant, "all your words are worth nothing! There is no need for lies, for you are proved guilty and the truth will soon be known." Then he spoke to the guards who were there: "Lords, don't move. See that the sheets are not removed from the bed before my return. I want the king to acknowledge my rights when he sees this for himself."

Meleagant sought out his father, the king, then let himself fall at his feet saying, "Sir, come and see something that you would never have expected. Come and see the queen, and you will be astounded at what I have found and proved. But before you go there, I beg you not to fail me in justice and righteousness. You are well aware of the dangers to which I have exposed myself for the queen; yet you oppose me in this and have her carefully guarded for fear of me. This morning I went to look at her in her bed, and I saw enough to recognize that Kay lies with her every night. By God, sir, don't be disturbed if this angers me and I complain, for it is most humiliating to me that she hates and despises me, yet lies every night with Kay."

"Silence!" said the king. "I don't believe it!"

"Sir, then just come and see what Kay has done to the sheets. If you don't believe my word and think that I am lying to you, the sheets and spread, covered with Kay's blood, will prove it to you."

"Let us go then," said the king. "I want to see this for myself: my eyes will teach me the truth." The king went at once into the room, where he found the queen just getting up. He saw the bloody sheets on her bed and those on Kay's bed as well. "Lady," he said, "you are in a terrible plight if what my son says is true."

"So help me God," she answered, "not even about a dream has such an awful lie been spread! I believe the seneschal Kay is so courteous and loyal that it would be wrong to mistrust him, and I have never offered my body for sale or given it away. Kay is certainly not a man to insult me like this—and I have never had the desire to do such a thing and never will!"

"Sir, I shall be most grateful to you," said Meleagant to his father, "if Kay is made to pay for his offense in such a manner that shame is cast upon the queen as well. It is for you to dispense the justice that I seek. Kay has betrayed King Arthur, his lord, who had faith enough in him that he entrusted to him what he most loved in this world."

"Sir, now permit me to reply," said Kay, "and I shall acquit myself. May God never absolve my soul after I leave this world if ever I lay with my lady. Indeed I would much rather be dead than to have committed such a base and blameworthy act against my lord. May God never give me healing for these wounds I bear, but may Death take me at once, if I ever even contemplated such an act! I know that my wounds bled profusely this night and soaked my sheets. This is why your son suspects me, but he certainly has no right to."

Meleagant answered him, "So help me God, the demons and the living devils have betrayed you! You became too excited last night, and no doubt because you overtaxed yourself your wounds were reopened. No lies can help you now. The blood in both beds is proof—is there for all to see. One must by right pay for a sin in which he has been openly caught. Never has a knight of your stature committed such an impropriety, and you are disgraced by it."

"Sir, sir," Kay pleaded with the king, "I will defend my lady and myself against your son's accusations. He causes me grief and torment but is clearly in the wrong."

"You are in too much pain to do battle," replied the king.

"Sir, with your permission, I am ready to fight him in spite of my injuries to prove that I am innocent of that shame of which he accuses me."   [4900]

Meanwhile the queen had sent secretly for Lancelot. She told the king that she would provide a knight to defend the seneschal against Meleagant in this matter, if his son would dare accept the challenge. Meleagant replied without hesitation, "I am not afraid to do battle to the finish with any knight you might select, even if he were a giant!"

At this moment Lancelot entered the hall. There was such a mass of knights that the room was filled to overflowing. As soon as he arrived, the queen explained the situation so that all, young and old, could hear: "Lancelot," she said, "Meleagant has accused me of a disgraceful act. I am considered guilty by all who have heard this accusation, unless you force him to retract it. He asserts that Kay slept with me this night, because he has seen my sheets and Kay's stained with blood. He says that the seneschal will be proved guilty unless he can defend himself in single combat, or find another to undertake the battle on his behalf."

"You have no need to beg for help as long as I am near," said Lancelot. "May it never please God that anyone should doubt either you or Kay in such a matter. If I am worth anything as a knight, I am prepared to do battle to prove that Kay never so much as conceived of such a deed. I will undertake the battle on his behalf and defend him as best I can."

Meleagant sprang forward and declared: "As God is my Savior, I'm quite satisfied with this arrangement. Let no one ever think otherwise!"

"My lord king," spoke Lancelot, "I am knowledgeable in trials, laws, suits, and verdicts. When a man's word is doubted, an oath is required before the battle begins."

Sure of himself, Meleagant replied immediately, "I'm fully prepared to swear my oath. Bring forward the holy relics, for I know that I'm in the right."

"No one who knows the seneschal Kay," countered Lancelot, "could ever mistrust him on such a point."

They called for their armor at once and ordered their horses to be fetched. They donned their armor when it was brought them, and their valets armed their horses. Next the holy relics were brought out. Meleagant stepped forward with Lancelot beside him. They both knelt, and Meleagant stretched forth his hand toward the relics and swore his oath in a powerful voice: "As God and the saints are my witnesses, the seneschal Kay slept this night with the queen in her bed and took his full pleasure with her."

"And I swear that you lie," said Lancelot, "and I further swear that he never slept with her or touched her. And if it please God, may He show His righteousness by taking vengeance on whichever of us has lied. And I will take yet another oath and will swear that, if on this day God should grant me the better of Meleagant, may He and these relics here give me the strength not to show him any mercy, no matter whom it may grieve or hurt!" King Bademagu could find no cause for joy when he heard this oath.

After the oaths had been sworn, the horses, fair and good in every respect, were led forward, and each knight mounted his steed. Then they charged headlong toward one another as fast as their horses could carry them. As their steeds rushed full speed, the two vassals struck each other two such mighty blows that each was left holding only the half of his lance. They thrust each other to the ground, but neither remained there defeated. They both rose up at once with drawn swords to strike with all the might of their naked blades. Burning sparks flew from their helmets toward the heavens. So enraged were they in their assaults with unsheathed blades that, as they thrust and parried and struck one another, there was no desire to rest nor even to catch their breath. The king, gravely concerned, summoned the queen, who had gone up into the tower loge to observe the battle. He asked her in the name of God the Creator to let them be separated.

"Whatever suits and pleases you," replied the queen. "In faith, you would be doing nothing that would displease me."

As soon as Lancelot heard what the queen had replied to King Bademagu's request, he had no further desire for combat and abandoned the fight altogether. But Meleagant struck and slashed at him unceasingly, until the king forced his way between them and restrained his son, who swore that he had no intention of making peace: "Peace be damned! I want to fight!"

"You will be wise to keep silent and do as I say," the king answered him. "Certainly no shame or harm will come to you for taking my advice. So do what is right. Don't you remember that you have arranged to do battle with Lancelot in the court of King Arthur? And can you doubt that it would be a far greater honor to defeat him there than anywhere else?" The king said this in an attempt to appease his son, and eventually he was able to calm him and separate them.

Lancelot, who was very eager to find my lord Gawain, then asked leave of the king, and next of the queen. With their permission he rode off rapidly toward the Underwater Bridge. He was followed by a large company of knights, but he would have been happier if many of those with him had remained behind.   [5053]

They rode for several full days until they were about a league from the Underwater Bridge. But before they could get near enough to see the bridge, a dwarf came forth to meet them. He was riding on a huge hunter and brandishing a whip to encourage and incite his steed. Promptly he inquired, as he had been ordered, "Which one of you is Lancelot? Don't hide him from me, I am one of your party. You must tell me in perfect confidence, because it is for your profit that I ask."

Lancelot spoke for himself, saying, "I am he whom you are seeking."

"Ah, Lancelot! Brave knight! Quit these men and place your faith in me. Come along with me alone, for I wish to take you to a very wonderful place. Let no one watch which way you go. Have them wait at this spot, for we shall return shortly."

Suspecting no deceit, Lancelot ordered his companions to remain behind, and he himself followed the dwarf, who was betraying him. His men who are awaiting him there could wait forever, because those who have captured him and hold him prisoner have no intention of returning him. His men were so distressed at his failure to return that they did not know what to do. They all agreed that the dwarf had deceived them, and they were very upset, but felt it would be folly to seek after him. They approached the search with heavy hearts, because they did not know where they might find him or in which direction to look. They discussed their predicament among themselves: the wisest and most reasonable men agreed that they should proceed first to the Underwater Bridge, which was nearby, then seek Lancelot afterward with the aid of my lord Gawain, should they succeed in finding him.

They proceeded toward the Underwater Bridge and, upon reaching it, saw my lord Gawain, who had slipped and fallen into the deep water. He was bobbing up and down, in and out of sight. They approached and reached out to him with branches, poles, and crooked sticks. Gawain had only his hauberk on his back, and on his head his helmet, which was worth ten of any others. He wore chainmail greaves rusted with sweat, for he had been sorely tried and had endured and overcome many perils and challenges. His lance, his shield, and his horse were on the far bank. Those who dragged him from the water feared for his life, since he had swallowed a lot of water, and they heard no word from him until he had heaved it up. But when he had cleared his chest and throat and had regained his voice enough to make himself understood he began to speak. His first question to those before him was whether they had any news of the queen. Those who answered him said that she never left the presence of King Bademagu, who served and honored her well.

"Has anyone come recently into this land to seek her?" inquired my lord Gawain.

"Yes," they replied, "Lancelot of the Lake, who crossed the Sword Bridge. He rescued her and freed her and all of us along with her. But a humpbacked, sneering dwarf tricked us—with insidious cleverness he has kidnapped Lancelot, and we don't know what he's done with him."

"When was this?" my lord Gawain asked.

"Sir, today, quite near this spot, as we were coming with Lancelot to find you."

"And what has Lancelot done since coming into this land?"

They began to tell him, giving every detail and not omitting a single word. And they told Gawain that the queen was awaiting him and had sworn that nothing would make her leave this land until she had seen him. My lord Gawain inquired of them, "When we leave this bridge, will we go to seek Lancelot?"

They all thought it best to go first to the queen: Bademagu would make provisions for seeking Lancelot. They believed that his son Meleagant, who hated him profoundly, had had him taken prisoner. If the king knew his whereabouts, he would have him freed no matter where he was; therefore they could delay their search. They all concurred in this suggestion, and so they rode on together until they neared the court, where they found King Bademagu and the queen. Together with them was the seneschal Kay, along with that traitor, overflowing with deceit, who had villainously caused all of those who were approaching to be anxious about Lancelot. These knights felt deceived and defeated, and could not hide their grief.

The news of this misfortune was not pleasing to the queen, yet she tried to act as cordially as she could. For the sake of my lord Gawain she managed to appear cheerful. However, her sorrow was not so well hidden that a little didn't appear. She had to express both joy and sorrow, since her heart was empty because of Lancelot, yet toward my lord Gawain she felt great happiness. Everyone who heard of the disappearance of Lancelot was overcome with grief and sorrow. The king would have been cheered by the arrival of my lord Gawain and by the pleasure of his acquaintance had he not felt such grief and pain and been so overwhelmed by sorrow at the betrayal of Lancelot. The queen urged King Bademagu to have him sought throughout his land, both high and low, without a moment's delay. My lord Gawain, Sir Kay, and everyone else without exception likewise urged him to do this. "Leave this to me," said the king, "and say no more about it, for I am long since persuaded. You need beg me no further to have this search begun."

Every knight bowed low before him. The king straightway sent wise and prudent men-at-arms as messengers throughout his land to ask news of Lancelot wherever they went. Though they sought everywhere for information, they were unable to learn a thing. When they found no trace of him, they returned to where the other knights were staying—Gawain, Kay, and all the others, who said they would set off to seek him themselves, fully armed and with lances ready. They would send no one else in their stead.

One day, after eating, they were all assembled in the hall arming themselves (they had by now reached the moment set for their departure) when a squire entered there. He passed among them until he stood before the queen. She had lost the rosy tint in her cheeks, and all her color had faded because of her deep sorrow for Lancelot, of whom she had heard no news. The squire greeted her and the king who was near her, and afterwards he greeted all the others, including Sir Kay and my lord Gawain. In his hand he held a letter that he extended toward the king, who took it. To avoid any misunderstanding, the king had it read aloud so everyone could hear. The reader well knew how to communicate everything he found written on the parchment, and said, "Lancelot sends greetings to the king as his noble lord, and like one who is willingly and completely at his command he thanks him for the honor and services he has rendered him. And he wishes you to know that he is strong and in good health, and that he is with King Arthur, and that he bids the queen to come there—this he orders—with my lord Gawain and Sir Kay." The letter bore such seals as to cause them all to believe that the message was true. They were happy and full of joy. The whole court resounded with gaiety, and their departure was set for the next day at dawn.   [5275]

When morning came, they outfitted themselves and made ready. They arose, mounted, and set forth. The king escorted them amid great joy and exultation a good bit of the way. When he had accompanied them beyond the frontiers of his land, he took leave first of the queen, then of the others as a group. On bidding him farewell, the queen very graciously thanked him for his many services. She embraced him and offered him her service and that of her husband—she could make no finer promise. My lord Gawain likewise pledged to serve him as his lord and friend, as did Sir Kay. Having promised this, they all set off at once on their way. King Bademagu commended the queen and the two knights to God; after these three he bid farewell to all the others, then returned home.

The queen and the crowd accompanying her did not delay a single day, but rode on until the welcome news reached King Arthur of the imminent arrival of his queen. News of his nephew Gawain kindled great joy and happiness in his heart, for he thought that the queen, Sir Kay, and all the common people were returning because of his daring. But the truth was quite other than they assumed. The whole town emptied to greet them; everyone went forth to meet them and each one, knight and commoner alike, said: "Welcome to my lord Gawain, who has brought back the queen and many another captive lady, and who has returned many a prisoner to us!"

"My lords, I am due no praise," Gawain said to them. "Your praise must stop at once, because none of this is of my doing. I am ashamed to be honored so, for I did not get there soon enough and failed because of my delay. But Lancelot was there in time and to him fell greater honor than any knight has ever received."

"Where is he then, fair sir, since we do not see him here with you?"

"Where?" replied my lord Gawain then. "Why, at the court of King Arthur—isn't he here?"

"In faith, he is not, nor is he anywhere in this land. We have heard no news of him since my lady was led away."

Then for the first time my lord Gawain realized that the message that had betrayed and deceived them was forged. They had been tricked by the message and were once again plunged into sadness. They arrived at court full of sorrow, and the king immediately asked what had happened. There were many who were able to give him an account of all that Lancelot had accomplished, how the queen and all the captives had been rescued by him, and how through deceit the dwarf had stolen him away from them. This news vexed the king, overwhelming him with grief and anguish. But his heart was so elated at the queen's return that his grief soon gave way to joy; now that he had what he most desired, he gave little thought to the rest.

It was while the queen was out of the country, I believe, that the ladies and the maidens who lacked the comfort of a husband came together and decided that they wished to be married soon. In the course of their discussions they decided to organize a splendid tournament, in which the Lady of Pomelegoi would be challenged by the Lady of Noauz. The women would refuse to speak to those who fared poorly, but to those who did well they promised to grant their love. They announced the tourney and had it cried throughout all the lands nearby, and those distant as well. They had the date of the tournament heralded well in advance so that there might be more participants.

The queen returned while preparations for the tournament were still being made. As soon as they learned of the queen's return, most of the ladies and maidens hastened to court to urge the king to grant them a favor and do their bidding. Even before learning what they wanted, he promised to grant them anything they might desire. Then they told him that they wished him to permit the queen to come to observe their tournament. Being unable to refuse anything, the king said that if the queen wished to attend, it would please him. Overjoyed at this, the ladies went before the queen and stated at once: "Our lady, do not refuse us what the king has already granted."

"What is it? Don't hide it from me."

"If you are willing to come to our tournament," they replied, "he will not try to stop you or refuse you his permission." So the queen promised to attend, since Arthur had given his permission.

The ladies immediately sent word throughout the realm that the queen would be in attendance on the day set for the tournament. The news spread far and wide and everywhere; it spread so far that it reached the kingdom from which no man had been able to return (though now whoever wished could enter or leave and never be challenged). The news spread through this kingdom and was repeated so often that it reached a seneschal of the faithless Meleagant—may hellfires burn the traitor! This seneschal was guarding Lancelot, imprisoned at his castle by his enemy Meleagant, who hated him with a mortal hatred.   [5431]

Lancelot learned of the date and hour of the tourney, and immediately his eyes filled with tears and all joy left his heart. The lady of the manor saw how sad and pensive he was and questioned him privately: "Sir, for the love of God and your soul, tell me truthfully why you have changed so. You no longer eat or drink, nor do I see you happy or laughing. You can confide your thoughts and what is troubling you in me."

"Ah, my lady! If I am saddened, for God's sake don't be surprised. Indeed I am greatly troubled because I am unable to be there where everything that is good in this world will be: at that tourney where everyone, I am sure, is gathering. However, if God has granted you the kindness to let me go there, you can be assured that I shall feel compelled to return afterward to my imprisonment here."

"Indeed," she answered, "I would willingly do this if I did not feel that it would cost me my life. I am so afraid of the might of my lord, the despicable Meleagant, that I dare not do it, for he would utterly destroy my husband. It is no wonder that I dread him so, for as you well know he is a most wicked man."

"My lady, if you are afraid that I will not return at once to your keeping after the tourney, I shall take an oath that I will never break and shall swear that nothing will ever keep me from returning to imprisonment here as soon as the tournament has ended."

"In faith," she said, "I will do it on one condition."

"My lady, what is that?"

"Sir," she answered, "that you will swear to return and will, moreover, assure me that I shall have your love."

"My lady, upon my return I will certainly give you all that I have."

The lady responded with a laugh, "It seems to me that you have assigned and given to another this love I have asked of you. Nevertheless, I shall not disdain to receive whatever I can have. I'll hold to what I can and will accept your oath that you will honor me by returning to imprisonment here."

In accordance with her wishes Lancelot swore by Holy Church that he would not fail to return. Thereupon the lady gave him her husband's red armor and his marvelously strong, brave, and handsome steed. Armed in his magnificent new armor, Lancelot mounted and rode forth until he reached Noauz. He selected this camp for the tournament and took his lodging just outside the town. Never had such a noble knight chosen such lowly lodgings, but he did so because he did not wish to stay anywhere he might be recognized. Many fine and worthy knights had assembled within the castle walls, yet there were even more outside. Indeed, so many had come when they learned that the queen would attend that not one in five was able to find lodging within: for every one who might ordinarily have come, there were seven who attended only because of the queen. The many barons were housed in tents, shelters, and pavilions stretching for five leagues round about. And so many ladies and maidens were present that it was a marvel to behold.

Lancelot had placed his shield before the door of his lodging place and, in order to relax, had removed his armor and was stretched out on an uncomfortably narrow bed, with thin matting covered by a coarse hemp cloth. While he was lying in this hovel, a barefooted young fellow clad only in his chemise came running up. He was a herald-at-arms who had lost his cloak and shoes gambling in the tavern, and who was now barefoot and exposed to the cool air. He noticed the shield before the door and began to examine it, but there was no way for him to recognize it or to know who bore it. Seeing the open door, he entered and found Lancelot lying on the bed. As soon as he saw him, he recognized him and crossed himself. But Lancelot warned him not to tell a soul about this; if he mentioned having seen him, the boy would rather have his eyes put out or neck broken than receive the punishment Lancelot would give him.

"Sir," replied the herald, "I have always esteemed you highly and still do. As long as I live, no amount of money will ever make me do anything that might cause you to be unhappy with me." He hurried out of the house and ran off shouting: "The one is come who will take their measure! The one is come who will take their measure!" The youth shouted this everywhere he went, and people hastened up from every side to ask him what this meant. He was not so rash as to tell them, but continued shouting as before. This is when the expression was coined: "The one is come who will take their measure." The herald who taught us this is our master, for he was the first to say it.

Already the crowds had assembled on every side: the queen with all her ladies and the knights with their many men-at-arms. The most magnificent, the largest, and the most splendid viewing stands that had ever been seen had been built there on the tournament field, since the queen and her ladies were to be in attendance. All the ladies followed the queen onto the platform for they were eager to see who would do well or poorly in the combat. The knights arrived by tens, by twenties, by thirties—here eighty and there ninety, a hundred or more here, two hundred there. So great was the crowd gathered before and about the stands that the combat was begun.

Knights clashed whether or not they were already fully armed. There seemed to be a forest of lances there, for those who had come for the pleasure of the tourney had brought so many that everywhere one turned one saw only lances, banners, and standards. Those who were to joust moved down the lists, where they encountered a great many companions of like mind. Others, meanwhile, made ready to perform other knightly feats. The meadows, fields, and clearings were so packed with knights that it was impossible to guess how many there were. Lancelot did not participate in this first encounter; but when he did cross the meadow and the herald saw him coming onto the field, he could not refrain from shouting: "Behold the one who will take their measure! Behold the one who will take their measure!"

"Who is he?" they all asked. But the herald refused to answer.

When Lancelot entered the fray, he alone proved the match of twenty of the best. He began to do so well that no one could take his eyes from him, wherever he might go. A bold and valiant knight was fighting for Pomelegoi, and his steed was spirited and swifter than a wild stag. He was the son of the king of Ireland, and he fought nobly and well, but the unknown knight pleased the onlookers four times as much. They all troubled themselves over the question, "Who is this knight who fights so well?"

The queen summoned a clever, pretty girl to her and whispered, "Miss you must take a message, quickly and without wasting words. Hurry down from these stands and go at once to that knight bearing the red shield; tell him in secret that I bid him to 'do his worst.'"

The girl swiftly and discreetly did as the queen asked. She pursued the knight until she was near enough to tell him in a voice that no one could overhear, "Sir, my lady Queen Guinevere asks me to tell you to 'do your worst.'"   [5654]

The moment he heard her, Lancelot said that he would gladly do so, as one who wishes only to please the queen. Then he set out against a knight as fast as his horse would carry him, but when he should have struck him, he missed. From this moment until dark he did the worst he could, because it was the queen's pleasure. The other knight, attacking him in turn, did not miss, but struck Lancelot such a powerful blow that Lancelot wheeled and fled and did not turn his horse against any knight the rest of that day. He would rather die than do anything unless he were sure that it would bring him shame, disgrace, and dishonor, and he pretended to be afraid of all those who approached him. The knights who had praised him before now laughed and joked at his expense. And the herald, who used to say, "This one will beat them all, one after another!" was very dissipirited and embarrassed on becoming the butt of the knights' jibes. "Hold your peace now, friend," they said mockingly. "He won't be taking our measure any more. He's measured so much that he's broken that measuring stick you bragged so much about!"

"What is this?" many asked. "He was so brave just a while ago; and now he's so cowardly that he doesn't dare face another knight. Perhaps he did so well at first because he'd never jousted before. He just flailed about like a madman and struck so wildly that no knight, however expert, could stand up to him. But now he's learned enough about fighting that he'll never want to bear arms again as long as he lives! His heart can no longer take it, for there's no bigger coward in the world!"

The queen was not upset by anything she heard. On the contrary, she was pleased and delighted, for now she knew for certain (though she kept it hidden) that this knight was truly Lancelot. Thus throughout the day until dark he let himself be taken for a coward. When darkness brought an end to the fighting, there was a lengthy discussion over who had fought best that day. The son of the king of Ireland felt that beyond any doubt he himself deserved the esteem and renown; but he was terribly mistaken, for many there were equal to him. Even the Red Knight pleased the fairest and most beautiful of the ladies and maidens, for they had not kept their eyes on anyone that day as much as on him. They had seen how he had done at first, how brave and courageous he had been. But then he had become so cowardly that he dared not face another knight, and even the worst of them, had he wanted, could have defeated and captured him. So the ladies and knights all agreed that they would return to the lists the following day, and that the young girls would marry those who won honor then.

Once this was settled, they all returned to their lodgings, where they gathered in little groups and began to ask: "Where is the worst, the lowliest, and the most despicable of knights? Where has he gone? Where has he hidden himself? Where might we find him? Where should we seek him? Cowardice has probably chased him away, and we'll never see him again. He's carried Cowardice off with himself, so that there cannot be another man in the world so lowly! And he's not wrong, for a coward is a hundred thousand times better off than a valorous, fighting knight. Cowardice is a facile thing, and that's why he's given her the kiss of peace and taken from her everything he has. To be sure, Courage never lowered herself enough to try to find lodging in him. Cowardice owns him completely. She has found a host who loves and serves her so faithfully that he has lost all his honor for her sake." All night long those given to slander gossiped in this manner. Though the one who speaks ill of another is often far worse than the one he slanders and despises, this did not keep them from having their say.

When day broke, all the knights donned their armor once more and returned to the fighting. The queen, with her ladies and maidens, came back to the stands, and together with them were many knights without armor who had either been captured on the first day or had taken the cross, and who were now explaining to them the heraldry of the knights they most admired.

"Do you see the knight with the gold band across a red shield?" they inquired. "That's Governal of Roberdic. And do you see the one behind him who has fixed a dragon and an eagle side by side on his shield? That's the son of the king of Aragon, who has come into this land to win honor and renown. And do you see the one beside him who rides and jousts so well? One half of his shield is green with a leopard upon it, and the other half is azure. That's Ignaures the Covetous, a handsome man who pleases the ladies. And the one with the pheasants painted beak to beak upon his shield? That is Coguillant of Mautirec. And do you see those two knights beside him on dappled horses, with dark lions on gilded shields? One is called Semiramis, the other is his companion—they have painted their shields to match. And do you see the one whose shield has a gate painted upon it, through which a stag seems to be passing? In faith, that is King Yder."

Such was the talk in the stands: "That shield was made in Limoges and was brought by Pilades, who is always eager for a good fight. That shield, with matching harness and stirrups, was made in Toulouse and brought here by Sir Kay of Estral. That one comes from Lyons on the Rhone—there's none so fine under heaven!—and was awarded to Sir Taulas of the Desert for a great service. He bears it well and uses it skillfully. And that other shield there, on which you see two swallows about to take flight, yet which stay fast to take many a blow of Poitevin steel, is an English model, made in London. It is carried by Sir Thomas the Young."

In this manner they pointed out and described the arms of those they recognized; but they saw no sign of that knight whom they held in such low esteem. So they assumed that he had stolen off in the night, since he did not return that day to the combat. When the queen, too, did not see him, she determined to have him sought through the lists until he was found. She knew of no one she could trust more to find him than that girl she had sent the day before with her message. So she summoned her at once and said to her, "Go, miss, and mount your palfrey. I am sending you to that knight you spoke to yesterday. You must seek until you find him. Make no delay! Then tell him once again to 'do his worst.' And when you have so instructed him, listen carefully to his reply."

The girl set off without hesitation, for the evening before she had carefully taken note of the direction he went, knowing without a doubt that she would once again be sent to him. She rode through the lists until she saw the knight, then went at once to advise him to continue "doing his worst" if he wished to have the love and favor of the queen, for such was her command.

"Since she so bids me," he replied, "I send her my thanks."

The girl left him at once. As he entered the field, the young men, the squires, and the men-at-arms began jeering: "What a surprise! The knight with the red armor has returned! But what can he want? There's no one in the world so lowly, so despicable, and so base. Cowardice has him so firmly in her grip that he can do nothing to escape her."

The girl returned to the queen, who would not let her go until she had heard that reply which filled her heart with joy, for now she knew beyond a doubt that that knight was the one to whom she belonged completely, and she knew, too, that he was fully hers. She told the girl to return at once and tell him that she now ordered and urged him to "do the best" that he could. The girl replied that she would go at once, without delay. She descended from the stands to where her serving-boy was waiting for her, tending her palfrey. She mounted and rode until she found the knight, and she told him immediately, "Sir, my lady now orders you to 'do the best' you can."

"Tell her that it would never displease me to do anything that might please her, for I am intent upon doing whatever she may desire."   [5893]

The girl hurried back as quickly as she could with her message, for she was certain that it would please the queen. As she approached the viewing stands, eager to deliver her message, the queen stood up and moved forward to meet her. But in order not to betray her own eagerness, the queen did not go down to her, but waited at the head of the steps. The girl started up the steps, and as she neared the queen she said, "My lady, I have never seen a more agreeable knight, for he is perfectly willing to do whatever you command of him. And, if you ask me the truth, he accepts the good and the bad with equal pleasure."

"In faith," she replied, "that well may be."

Then the queen returned to the window to observe the knights. Without a moment's hesitation Lancelot thrust his arm through the shield straps, for he was inflamed with a burning desire to show all his prowess. He neckreined his horse and let it run between two ranks. Soon all those deluded, mocking men, who had spent much of the past night and day ridiculing him, would be astounded—they had laughed, sported, and had their fun long enough!

With his arm thrust through the straps of his shield, the son of the king of Ireland came charging headlong across the field at Lancelot. They met with such violence that the son of the king of Ireland wished to joust no more, for his lance was splintered and broken, having struck not moss but firm dry shield-boards. Lancelot taught him a lesson in this joust, striking his shield from his arm, pinning his arm to his side, then knocking him off his horse to the ground. Knights from both camps rushed forward at once, some to help the fallen knight and others to worsen his plight. Some, thinking to help their lords, knocked many knights from their saddles in the melee. But Gawain, who was there with the others, never entered the fray all that day, for he was content to observe the prowess of the knight with the red shield, whose deeds seemed to make everything the other knights did pale by comparison. The herald, too, found new cause for happiness and cried out for all to hear: "The one is come who will take their measure! Today you will witness his deeds; today you will see his might!"

At this moment Lancelot wheeled his horse and charged toward a magnificent knight, striking him a blow that carried him to the ground a hundred feet or more from his steed. Lancelot performed such deeds with both his lance and sword that all the spectators marveled at what they saw. Even many of the knights participating in the jousts watched him with admiration and delight, for it was a pleasure to see how he caused both men and steeds to stumble and fall. There was scarcely a knight he challenged who was able to remain in the saddle, and he gave the horses he won to any who wanted them. Those who had been mocking him now said, "We are ashamed and mortified. We made a great mistake to slander and disdain him. Truly he is worth a thousand of the likes of those on this field, since he has vanquished and surpassed all the knights in the world, so that there now remains no one to oppose him."

The young women who were watching him in amazement all said that he was destroying their chances for marriage. They felt that their beauty, their wealth, their positions, and their noble births would bring them little advantage, for surely a knight this valiant would never deign to marry any one of them for beauty or wealth alone. Yet many of them swore that if they did not marry this knight, they would not take any other lord or husband in this year. The queen, overhearing their boastful vows, laughed to herself. She knew that the knight they all desired would never choose the most beautiful, nor the fairest among them, even if one were to offer him all the gold of Arabia. Yet the young women had but one thing in mind: they all wanted to have that knight. And they were already as jealous of one another as if they had married him, because they believed him to be so skilled in arms that they could not conceive of any other knight, no matter how pleasing, who could have done what he had done.

Indeed he had fought so well that when it came time for the two camps to separate, those on both sides agreed that there had never been an equal to the knight who bore the red shield. It was said by all, and it was true. But as the tournament was breaking up, our knight let his shield, lance, and trappings fall where the press was thickest and hastened away. His departure was so furtive that no one in all that great crowd noticed it. He rode on swiftly and purposefully in order to keep his pledge to return directly to that place from where he had come.   [6039]

On their way from the tournament everyone inquired after him, but they found no trace, for he had left so as not to be recognized. The knights, who would have been overjoyed to have had him there, were filled instead with great sorrow and distress. But if the knights were saddened that he had left in this fashion, the young women, when they learned of it, were far more upset and swore by St. John that they would refuse to marry in this year: if they could not have the one they wanted, they would take no other. Thus the tournament ended without any one of them having taken a husband.

Lancelot returned to his prison without delay. The seneschal into whose charge he had been entrusted reached home some two or three days before Lancelot's return and inquired after his whereabouts. The lady who had outfitted Lancelot with her husband's magnificent red armor, his trappings, and his horse, told her husband truthfully how she had sent their prisoner to take part in the jousting at the tournament of Noauz.

"My lady," said the seneschal, "truly you could have done nothing worse! Great misfortune will surely befall me because of this, for I know that my lord Meleagant will treat me worse than a fierce giant would if I were shipwrecked on his lonely island. I shall be destroyed and ruined as soon as he hears of this. He will never show me pity!"

"Dear husband, do not be distraught," replied the lady. "There is no need to be so fearful. He will not fail to return, for he swore to me by the saints above that he would be back as quickly as possible."

The seneschal mounted his horse and rode at once to his lord, to whom he related the whole of this adventure. Meleagant was reassured when the seneschal told him how Lancelot had sworn to his wife to return to prison.

"He will never break his oath," said Meleagant. "This I know. Nonetheless I am greatly troubled by what your wife has done, for there was no way that I wanted him to be at the tournament. But go back now and see to it that when he returns he is guarded so securely that he will never be able to escape from prison or have any freedom of movement. Send me word as soon as this is done."

"It shall be as you command," said the seneschal. When he reached his castle, he found Lancelot returned, a prisoner once more at his court. The seneschal sent a messenger straight to Meleagant to inform him that Lancelot had returned.

Upon hearing this, Meleagant engaged masons and carpenters who did as he ordered, whether willingly or by constraint. He summoned the best in the land and told them to work diligently until they had built him a tower. Meleagant knew an island set within an inlet on one shore of the land of Gorre, where there was a broad, deep arm of the sea. There he ordered that the stone and wood for constructing the tower be brought. The stone was shipped in by sea, and the tower was completed in less than two months. It was thick-walled and solid, broad and tall. When it was ready, Meleagant had Lancelot brought there and placed within the tower. Then he ordered that the doorways be walled up, and he forced all the masons to swear that they would never speak of this tower to anyone. He had it sealed so that there remained no door or opening, save only a small window, through which

Lancelot was given niggardly portions of poor fare to eat at fixed hours. Now Meleagant had everything he wished, and all was done just as the traitorous felon had ordered.   [6146]

Meleagant next went directly to Arthur's court. As soon as he arrived, he came before the king and, filled with arrogance and perfidy, addressed him in these words: "My king, I have agreed to single combat against Sir Lancelot at your court and in your presence, but I do not see him anywhere! However, to fulfill my promises, I hereby offer him my challenge before your assembled court. If Lancelot is present, let him come forward and swear to meet me here in your court one year from this day. I do not know whether anyone here has told you under what circumstances this combat was arranged, but I see knights here who were at our pledging and who can tell you everything if they are willing to acknowledge the truth. And if Lancelot should attempt to deny this, I'll not hire any second to defend me but oppose him myself."

The queen, who was seated at court beside the king, leaned toward him and said, "Sir, do you know who this is? He is Meleagant, who captured me while I was in the protection of the seneschal Kay, and who thereby caused him great shame and suffering."

"My lady," the king replied, "I have clearly understood that this is the man who held my people prisoner."

The queen spoke no further. The king now turned to Meleagant and said "My friend, so help me God, we've had no news of Lancelot, which grieves us deeply."

"My lord king," said Meleagant, "Lancelot assured me that I would not fail to find him here, and I am pledged not to undertake this combat except at your court. I want all of the barons here present to bear witness that I now summon him to be present here one year from this day, in accord with the pledges we gave when we first agreed to this combat."

On hearing these words my lord Gawain arose, for he was deeply troubled by what had been said. "Sir," he spoke, "Lancelot is nowhere to be found in this land; but we shall have him sought and, if it please God, he will be found before the year is out—unless he is imprisoned or dead. But should he fail to appear, let me assume the combat, for I am willing. I will take up my arms for Lancelot at the appointed day, if he is not here before then."

"By heavens!" said Meleagant. "In the name of God, King Arthur, grant Gawain this battle. He wants it and I urge it, for I know of no knight in the world against whom I'd rather test myself, unless it is Lancelot himself. But know for certain that if I cannot fight against one of these two, I'll not accept any substitute or fight against anyone else."

And the king said that he would grant the challenge to Gawain if Lancelot failed to return in time.   [6225]

Having received this promise, Meleagant left King Arthur's court and rode until he reached that of his father, King Bademagu. In order to appear noble and distinguished before him, he haughtily assumed an air of importance. This day the king was hosting a festive celebration in his capital city of Bath. The court was assembled in all its splendor to celebrate his birthday. People of every sort came there to be with him, and the palace was overflowing with knights and maidens. There was one among them (she was Meleagant's sister) about whom I'll gladly tell you more later; I do not wish to speak further of her now, however, since it is not part of my story to tell of her at this point, and I do not want to inflate or confuse or alter my story but develop it in a proper and straightforward manner. So now I shall tell you that upon his arrival Meleagant addressed his father in a loud voice, which commoner and noble alike could hear: "Father, as God is your salvation, please tell me truthfully whether one who has made his prowess feared at King Arthur's court is to be considered worthy and whether he should be filled with great joy."

Without waiting to hear more, his father answered these questions: "My son, all good men should honor and serve one who has shown himself worthy in this fashion, and keep his company." Then his father cajoled him and urged him to say why he had asked this, what he was seeking, and from where he had come.

"Sir, I don't know whether you recall the terms of the agreement that was established when you made peace between Lancelot and myself. But you must remember, I'm sure, that we were both told before many witnesses to be ready in one year's time to meet again in King Arthur's court. I went there at the appointed time, armed and equipped for battle. All that was required of me I did: I sought Lancelot and inquired after him, but I was unable to find any trace of him. He had turned and fled! So I arranged to have Gawain pledge his word that there would be no further delays. Even if Lancelot is no longer alive and fails to return within the fixed term, Gawain himself has promised to fight me in his stead. Arthur has no knight more praiseworthy than Gawain, as is well known. But before the elderberries blossom, I will see when we fight whether his deeds match his fame. The sooner we fight the better!"

"Son, said his father, "now indeed you have shown yourself a fool to everyone here. Those who did not know it before have learned it now by your own words. True it is that a great heart is humble, but the fool and the braggart will never be rid of their folly. Son, I'm telling you this for your own good: you are so hard and dry of character that there is no trace of gentility or friendship in you. You are filled with folly and your heart lacks all mercy. This is why I find fault with you; this will bring you down. If one is of noble heart, many will bear witness to it at the appropriate time; a gentleman need not praise his courage to magnify his act, for the act is its own best praise. Self-flattery does not enhance your renown at all; rather, it makes me esteem you the less. Son, I chastise you, but to what avail? It is of little use to advise a fool, and he who tries to rid a fool of his folly wastes his efforts. The

goodness that one preaches, if it is not transformed into works, is wasted—
wasted, lost, and gone forever."

Meleagant was beside himself with fury and rage. I can assure you truthfully that no man alive was ever as full of wrath as he was; and in his anger the
last bond between father and son was broken, for he did not mince words
with his father, but raged. "Are you dreaming or deluded to say that I'm crazy
to have told you of my triumph? I thought I'd come to you as to my lord, as
to my father; but that doesn't seem to be the case, and I feel you've treated me
more odiously than I deserve. Nor can you give me any reason for having
done so."

"Indeed I can."

"What then?"

"That I see nothing in you but lunacy and madness. I know only too well
that heart of yours, which will yet bring you to great harm. Damned be
anyone who could ever believe that Lancelot, this perfect knight who is esteemed by all but yourself, would ever flee out of fear of you! Perhaps he's
been buried in some underground cell or locked up in a prison, whose gate is
so tightly kept that he cannot leave without permission. I assure you I'd be
sorely angered if he were injured or dead. It would be a great loss indeed if a
person so skilled, so handsome, so valiant, and so just were to perish before
his time. May it please God that this not be so!"   [6373]

With these words Bademagu grew silent; but all that he had said had
been heard and carefully noted by one of his daughters—the one I mentioned
earlier in my story—and she was not at all pleased to hear such news of
Lancelot. It was evident that he was being kept locked up, since no one had
heard anything from him. "May God never have mercy upon me," she swore,
"if ever I rest before I know for certain what has become of him."

She stole noiselessly away and ran immediately to mount her comely and
smooth-gaited mule. For my part I can assure you that she had no idea which
way to turn upon leaving the court. Yet instead of inquiring, she took the first
path she found. She rode swiftly along, uncertain of her destination, guided
by chance, without servant or knightly escort. She sought far and wide in her
eagerness to reach her goal, but her search was not destined to be brief. Yet
she could not stop long in any one place if she wished to accomplish properly
what she had set out to do: release Lancelot from prison if she could find him
and manage it. And I believe that she will have traversed many a country
before hearing anything of him. But what good is it for me to tell of her
nightly lodgings and daily wanderings? She traveled so many roads over mountains, through valleys, high and low, that a month or more passed without her
having been able to learn more than she already knew—which was less than
nothing.

One day as she was riding sad and pensive through a field, she saw in the
distance beside the shore near an inlet—a tower! But for a league on any side
there was not any house, or cabin, or hut. Meleagant had had it built in order

to keep Lancelot, but his sister knew nothing of that. As soon as she saw it, she fixed her sights upon it and never turned away; and her heart promised her that this was what she had sought for so long. Now her search was ended; after many tribulations Fortune had guided her to the right path.

The girl rode straight up to the tower, then circled it, listening carefully to see whether she might hear something that would bring her joy. She examined the tower from bottom to top and saw that it was tall and wide. But she was amazed to find no opening in it, except for a small and narrow window. Nor was there any stair or ladder to enter this high tower. She reasoned that this was deliberate and that therefore Lancelot was within, and she was determined to find out for sure or never eat again. She was going to call out his name and was about to say "Lancelot!" when she heard a weak voice from within the tower that caused her to hold her tongue.

The voice was filled with deepest doom and was calling for death. Lamenting piteously, it longed for death; in its suffering it asked only to die; life and its own body no longer held any value for it. Feebly, in a low and trembling voice, it lamented: "Ah, Fortune, how cruelly your wheel has now turned for me! Once I was on the top, but now I've been thrown down to the bottom; once I had everything, now I have nothing; once you wept to see me, now you laugh at me. Poor Lancelot, why did you trust in Fortune when she abandoned you so quickly? In no time at all she has cast me down from high to low. By mocking me, Fortune, you behave despicably—but what do you care? All has come to naught, no matter what. Ah! Holy Cross, Holy Spirit! I am lost! I am damned! How totally destroyed I am!

"Ah, most worthy Gawain, unequaled in goodness, how I marvel that you've not come to rescue me! Certainly you are unchivalrous to have delayed so long. You should come to the aid of one you once loved so dearly. Indeed I can say with certainty that there's no hideaway or secluded place on either side of the sea that I'd not have spent seven years or even ten to seek out had I known you to be imprisoned there. But why am I bothering with this? You are not brave enough to expose yourself to hardships on my account. Peasants are right to say that it's hard to find a good friend any more: in times of trial it is easy to test one's friends. Alas! I've been a prisoner for over a year now, and you are a faithless friend indeed, Gawain, to have left me to linger here so long.

"Yet if you don't know that I'm imprisoned here, then it's unfair of me to accuse you so. Indeed that must be the case—I'm sure of it now! And I was wrong and unreasonable to have such thoughts, for I know that you and your men would have searched to the ends of the earth to release me from this evil confinement, had you but known the truth. And you would do it out of the love and friendship you bear me—yes, this is what I truly believe. But I'm wasting my breath. It can never happen! May Meleagant, who has brought me to this shame, be damned by God and St. Sylvester! Out of envy he has done me all the evil he could conceive—he's surely the most wicked man alive!"   [6529]

With these words he took comfort and grew silent, as grief gnawed away at his life. The girl stood staring at the ground as she listened to everything he said. Knowing that her search was ended, she hesitated no more. She shouted "Lancelot!" with all her strength and more. "Fair knight in the tower there, speak to a friend who loves you."

But the one within was too weak to hear her. She shouted louder, and louder still, until Lancelot with his last bit of strength heard her and wondered who could be calling him. Though he knew he was being called, still he did not recognize the voice—he thought perhaps it was some ghost. He looked all about him, but saw only himself and the tower walls. "My God" he wondered, "what am I hearing? I hear words but I see nothing. This is truly amazing! Yet I'm awake and not asleep. If it were a dream, I would probably think it was a lie; but I am awake, and therefore it troubles me."

Then with great effort Lancelot arose and moved slowly, step by step, toward the tiny crevice. When he reached the opening, he wedged his body in, from top to bottom and on each side. He looked out in every direction and finally saw the girl who had called to him. Though he saw her now, he did not recognize her. She, however, knew him at once and spoke: "Lancelot, I have come from afar seeking you. Now, thank God, my search is ended, for I have found you. I am the one who asked a favor of you as you were going to the Sword Bridge. You granted it to me willingly when I requested it: I asked for the head of the defeated knight, because I bore him no love. For that boon and that service I have exposed myself to these hardships; because of them I will get you out of here!"

"My thanks to you," said the prisoner upon hearing her words. "The service I did you will be well repaid if I am freed from this place. If you are able to free me, I swear to you that with the aid of the Apostle Paul I will be yours from this day forth. As God is my witness, the day will never come on which I fail to do everything that you may be pleased to request from me. Whatever you ask from me you shall have immediately, if I am able to do it."

"Have no doubt, my friend, that you will be set free this very day. I would not leave, not even for a thousand pounds, without seeing you released before daybreak. Afterward I will put you at ease, in great comfort and repose: whatever I have that is pleasing, if you want it, will be given to you. Don't be worried: I must leave you for a short while to find something to use to enlarge this window enough so that you can escape through it."

"May God help you find it," he said in heartfelt agreement. "Here inside I have plenty of rope, which the soldiers gave me to haul up my food—stale barley bread and stagnant water that have ruined my health!"

Then the daughter of King Bademagu found a solid pickax, as strong as it was sharp. She brought it to Lancelot, who in spite of his weakened body hammered and pounded and struck and dug until he was able to crawl easily through the crevice. How very relieved and happy he was—you can be sure— to be out of that prison and able to leave that place where he had been confined for so long! At last he was free and at large, and even if all the gold in the world were gathered together and piled mountain high and offered to him, he would never choose to go back in.   [6636]

Now Lancelot was free, but he was still so weak that he staggered on his feeble limbs. Gently, so as not to cause him injury, the girl helped him mount her mule ahead of her, and they set off in great haste. She kept off the main roads deliberately, so that they would not be seen. They rode on cautiously, fearful that if they traveled openly someone might recognize them and do them harm, and this she was anxious to prevent. Therefore she avoided narrow passes, and they finally reached a retreat where, because of its beauty and charm, she had often stayed. The castle and its occupants were all in her service; the place was well-equipped, secure, and very private. There Lancelot would be safe. As soon as he had arrived, she had him undressed and gently stretched out upon a beautiful, thickly cushioned couch. She then bathed and cared for him so well that I could not tell you half of all the good she did. She handled and treated him as gently as she would her own father, completely reviving and healing him and giving him new life. No longer was he starved and weak. Soon he was strong and fair, no less handsome than an angel, and able to rise.

When he arose, the girl found him the most beautiful robe she had and dressed him in it. Lancelot slipped it on with more joy and grace than a bird in flight. He kissed and embraced the girl, then said to her fondly: "My dear friend, to God and to you alone, I give thanks for being healed and healthy. Because you have made possible my escape, I give you my heart, my body, my aid, and my possessions to take and keep whenever you wish. For all that you have done, I am yours. Yet I have been absent now for a great while from the court of King Arthur, who has honored me greatly, and I have much still to do there. Therefore, my sweet noble friend, I must beg your leave with love. If it is pleasing to you, I am most eager to go there."

"Beloved Lancelot, fair gentle friend," replied the girl, "I grant your request, for I seek only what is for your honor and good, both now and forever."

She gave him the most marvelous horse that anyone had ever seen, and he leapt swiftly into the saddle without even touching the stirrups. When he had mounted, they heartily commended one another to the ever truthful God. Lancelot set off on his way, so overjoyed that, I swear, nothing I could ever say would convey to you how happy he was to have escaped from that place where he had been imprisoned. He repeated over and over to himself that that despicable traitor who had held him prisoner was about to become the victim of his own deceits and be damned by his own doing.

"I am free in spite of him!" exclaimed Lancelot. Then he swore by the heart and body of the Creator of this world that Meleagant would never

escape with his life if ever he succeeded in overpowering and capturing him—
no, not for all the riches from Babylon to Ghent. He had been too deeply
shamed.   [6725]

And it would come to pass that Lancelot would avenge himself, for this
very Meleagant, whom he had been threatening and he was eager to encounter, had reached the court this same day without having been summoned.
Upon his arrival he sought out and found my lord Gawain. Then the evil
proven traitor inquired whether Lancelot had been found or seen—as if he
himself knew nothing of him! (And he did not, in fact, although he thought
that he did.) Gawain replied that he had not seen him, nor had he come to
court since Meleagant had been there last.

"Since it is you whom I have found here," said Meleagant, "come forward and keep your promise to me. I will wait for you no longer."

"If it is pleasing to God, in whom I place my trust," answered Gawain, "I
shall shortly keep my promise to you. I am confident that I shall acquit myself
well. It is like casting dice; and with God and St. Foy on my side, I shall cast
more points than you, and before it's over I shall pocket all the wagers."

Then Gawain ordered a carpet to be spread out before him. His squires
quickly did as he commanded, carrying out his bidding without complaint or
question. After they had taken the carpet and placed it where he had ordered,
Gawain stepped upon it at once and summoned three valets in his suite, still
unarmed themselves, to bring him his armor. These young men were his
cousins or nephews, I'm not sure which, and were truly brave and well bred.
The three youths armed him so fittingly that no one in the world could have
found fault with anything they did. After arming him, one among them went
to fetch a Spanish warhorse, which could run more swiftly through open field
and woodland, over hill and dale, than could the fine Bucephalus. The renowned and worthy Gawain, the most skilled knight ever to be blessed by the
sign of the cross, mounted his magnificent steed. He was about to grasp his
shield when he beheld Lancelot dismounting before him. He had never expected to see him here!

Lancelot had appeared so suddenly that Gawain stared in wonder at him,
and I do not exaggerate when I tell you that he was as astonished as if Lancelot
had just fallen at his feet from a cloud. When he saw that it was indeed
Lancelot, no other duty could have kept Gawain, too, from dismounting and
going forth to welcome him with outstretched arms. Gawain greeted him,
then embraced and kissed him; he was filled with joy and relieved at having
found his companion. You must never doubt me when I assure you that
Gawain would not have wanted to have been chosen a king if it meant losing
Lancelot.

Soon King Arthur and everyone at court knew that Lancelot, whom they
had been seeking for so long, had returned healthy and safe—to the great
displeasure of one among them. The court, which had long been anxious
about him, came together in full assembly to celebrate his return. Young and

old alike rejoiced in his presence. Joy dissipated and obliterated the grief that had reigned there; grief fled and joy appeared, eagerly beckoning again to all. And was the queen not there to share in this joy? Indeed she was, and among the first. Heavens, and where else would she be? Never had she experienced greater joy than that she now felt at his return; how could she have stayed away? To tell the truth, she was so near him that she could scarcely restrain her body (and nearly didn't!) from following her heart to him. Where then was her heart? Welcoming Lancelot with kisses. Why then was the body reticent? Was her joy not complete? Was it laced with anger or hatred? No indeed, not in the least; rather, she hesitated because the others present—the king and his entourage, who could see everything—would immediately perceive her love if, before their very eyes, she were to do all that her heart desired. And if Reason did not subdue these foolish thoughts and this love-madness, everyone present would understand her feelings. O, height of folly! In this way Reason encompassed and bound her foolish heart and thoughts and brought her to her senses, postponing the full display of her affections until she could find a better and more private place, where they might reach a safer harbor than they would have now.

The king gave Lancelot every honor, and, when he had welcomed him properly, said, "My friend, I've not heard in many a year such welcome news of anyone as that of you today. But I have no idea what land you've been in for so long. All winter and all summer I have had you sought high and low, yet you were nowhere to be found."

"Indeed, fair sir," answered Lancelot, "in but a few words I can tell you everything just as it happened to me. Meleagant, the wicked traitor, has kept me imprisoned since the day the prisoners were released from his land. He has forced me to live shamefully in a tower by the sea. He had me captured and walled in there, and there I would still be suffering, were it not for a friend of mine, a girl for whom I had once done a small favor. For that tiny favor she has given me a huge reward; she has done me great honor and great good. Now, however, without further delay, I wish to repay him for whom I have no love. He has long sought and pursued me, and has treated me with shame and cruelty. He has come here to court to seek his payment, and he shall have it! He need wait no longer for it, because it's ready. I myself am prepared for battle, as is he—and may God never again give him cause for boasting!"

Then Gawain said to Lancelot, "My friend, it would cost me little to repay your creditor for you. I am already equipped and mounted, as you can see. Fair gentle friend, do not refuse me this favor I eagerly beg of you."

Lancelot replied that he would rather have both his eyes gouged from his head than to be so persuaded. He swore never to let Gawain fight for him. He had given his own pledge to fight Meleagant, and he himself would repay what he owed. Gawain saw that nothing he might say would be to any avail, so he loosed his hauberk and lifted it from his shoulders, then disarmed himself completely. Lancelot immediately donned these same arms, so eager was he for his debt to be repaid and canceled. He was determined not to rest until he had repaid the traitor.   [6914]

Meleagant, meanwhile, was stunned beyond belief at everything he had just witnessed with his own eyes. He felt his heart sink within and nearly lost his mind. "Indeed," he said to himself, "what a fool I was not to check before coming here to be certain that Lancelot was still secure within my prison tower. Now he has gotten the better of me. Ah, God, but why should I have gone there? There was never any reason to suspect that he could have escaped. Was the wall not solidly constructed and the tower tall and strong? There was no flaw or crack through which he could slip without help from outside. Perhaps someone gave away my secret? But even granted that the walls cracked before their time and crumbled and fell, would he not have been buried under them and killed, his body crushed and dismembered? Yes, by God, if they had fallen he would surely have died within. Yet I am positive that those mighty walls would not crack before the last drop of water in the oceans had dried up and the mountains been leveled unless they were destroyed by force. All this is impossible. There must be another answer: he had help in escaping; otherwise he'd not be free. I have no doubt that I've been betrayed. So I must accept the fact that he is out. If only I had taken more precautions, it would never have happened, and he would never again have come to court! But now it is too late to feel sorry for myself. The peasant, who doesn't like to lie, spoke the truth in his proverb: it is too late to lock the barn door after the horse has been stolen. I know that I shall be brought to shame and greatly vilified unless I endure great trials and sufferings. What trials and sufferings? So help me God, in whom I place my trust, I'll fight my best for as long as I am able against the knight I have challenged."

Thus he gathered his courage and now asked only that they be brought together on the field of battle. I don't believe there'll be a long delay, for Lancelot is eager to meet him, anticipating a quick victory. But before either charged the other, the king asked that they go down below the tower onto the heath, the fairest from there to Ireland. They did as he ordered, going there without delay. The king, accompanied by milling crowds of knights and ladies, followed. No one remained behind; and the queen with her fair and beautiful ladies and maidens crowded the windows to watch Lancelot.

On the heath was the finest sycamore that ever grew, spreading wide its branches. About it, like a woven carpet, was a beautiful field of fresh grass that never lost its green. From beneath the beautiful sycamore gushed a sparkling spring of rapid-running water over a bed of beautiful stones that shone like silver. The water flowed off through a pipe of purest, rarefied gold and ran down across the heath into a valley between two woods. Here it suited the king to take his place, for he found nothing that displeased him.

After King Arthur ordered his people to keep their distance, Lancelot rode angrily toward Meleagant like a man bursting with hatred. But before striking a blow, he shouted in a loud, bold voice: "Come forward, I challenge you! And be assured that I will not spare you!"

Then he spurred his horse hotly, pulling back to a spot about a bowshot's distance. Now they charged toward one another as swiftly as their horses could run; each knight struck the other's sturdy shield so forcefully with his lance that it was pierced through. Yet neither knight was wounded. They rode past, then wheeled about and returned full gallop to strike more mighty blows on their strong, good shields. Each was a courageous, bold, and valiant knight, and each rode a swift and powerful steed. Their mighty thrusts hammered the shields they bore at their sides, piercing them through with lances that forced their way right to the bare flesh, without breaking or splitting. With powerful blows they drove one another to the ground. Breast-straps, girths, stirrups—nothing could keep them from being tumbled backward from their saddles onto the bare earth. Their frightened horses reared and plunged, bucking and biting: they too wished to kill each other!

The fallen knights leapt up as quickly as they could. They drew their swords, with their mottoes engraved upon them. Protecting their faces with their shields, they sought how best to injure one another with their sharp steel blades. Lancelot was unafraid, for he was twice as skilled at fencing as Meleagant, having practiced it since his youth. Both struck such powerful blows to the shields and gold-plated helmets that they split and broke. But Lancelot relentlessly pursued Meleagant and gave him a mighty blow that severed the steel-covered right arm, so that his enemy could no longer shield himself. When Meleagant felt the loss of his right arm, he determined to sell his life dearly. If he could grasp the opportunity, he would avenge himself, for he was nearly insane with anger, spite, and pain. His situation was hopeless if he could not find some evil trick to destroy Lancelot. He rushed toward him, thinking to take him by surprise, but Lancelot was on his guard and with his trenchant sword opened Meleagant's belly so wide that he would not be healed for months. A second blow slashed his helmet, knocking the nasal into his mouth and breaking three teeth.

Meleagant was so enraged that he couldn't speak a word, not even to ask for mercy, because his foolish heart, which bound him and held him prisoner, has so besotted him. Lancelot approached, unlaced Meleagant's helmet, and cut off his head. Never again would Meleagant deceive him: he had fallen in death, finished. But I assure you now that no one who was there and witnessed this deed felt any pity whatsoever. The king and all the others there rejoiced greatly over it. Then the happiest among them helped Lancelot remove his armor and led him away amid great joy.

My lords, if I were to tell any more, I would be going beyond my matter. Therefore I draw to a close: the romance is completely finished at this point. The clerk Godefroy of Lagny has put the final touches on *The Knight of the Cart;* let no one blame him for completing the work of Chrétien, since he did it with the approval of Chrétien, who began it. He worked on the story from the point at which Lancelot was walled into the tower until the end. This much only has he done. He wishes to add nothing further, nor to omit anything, for this would harm the story.   [7112]

Here ends the romance of *Lancelot of the Cart.*

A page from a typical troubadour songbook showing words and music. This is a song by Arnaut Daniel. (Courtesy of the Biblioteca Ambrosia Milano)

Chapter *VIII*

SELECTED LYRICS

James J. Wilhelm

Although it has long been posited that there is a connection between the love lyrics of the Middles Ages and medieval romances, it is difficult to prove the point. The famous French scholar Joseph Anglade searched for mentions of Arthurian personae in the troubadour poems of southern France, which were written in the Provençal language, and could find preciously few: twenty-four mentions of Arthur and only one of Guinevere, while there were fifty-nine mentions of Tristan and Isolde. Still Rita Lejeune, in her article in Roger Sherman Loomis's *Arthurian Literature of the Middle Ages* (393 ff.), tried to insist that the computations were misleading because they did not account for the richness of the oral tradition.

One has to agree to some part with Lejeune. It seems only natural that the cult of love exhibited in such romances as Chrétien's *Lancelot* has to bear some relationship to the great outburst of lyric love poetry emanating from southern France in that same twelfth century. The first troubadour, Duke William IX of Aquitaine (d. 1126), was the grandfather of the famous patroness Eleanor of Aquitaine, the wife of King Henry II of England. She alone can serve as a link between the lyrics of southern France and the Arthurian narratives of northern Europe, which Henry promoted. Chrétien himself was patronized by her daughter from Louis VII of France, the Countess Marie of Champagne, as he acknowledges in the opening of his *Lancelot*. The minstrels or *conteurs* of Brittany, who plied their skills between the British Isles and the Continent, also supply a missing link.

Generically speaking, it is not natural for a writer of lyrics to rely on ponderous narratives to give him sustenance; all one can expect are random allusions. On the other hand, it is quite natural for a writer of romances to deal in lyrical love dialectic, as is evident in the monologues and dialogues of *Lancelot*, *The Romance of Tristan*, and other works.

The selections here show a variety of allusions in four cultures: first, the cradle of lyric expression in southern France, as shown in two poems by Bernart de Ventadorn, who flourished from 1140 to 1180 and who is usually considered the master troubadour. Both poems show the mystical rapture that Lancelot expresses in Chrétien's romance. In the second poem, known as the Lark Poem (which is available in many recordings), the name "Tristan" is merely a secret name for the beloved (curiously the troubadours often referred to their female lovers by masculine names, which were usually abstract).

A poem by the Minnesinger Heinrich von Veldeke, who flourished from about 1170 to 1210, shows that the Germans were not unaware of the lyric tradition, although their greatest performances occur in narratives like Gottfried von Strassburg's *Tristan* or Wolfram von Eschenbach's *Parzival*.

Although the Italian lyric poets seldom mention Arthurian motifs, their greatest poet, Dante Alighieri (1265–1321), nevertheless wrote a memorable invitation to his friend Guido Cavalcanti to ride with him in a magic ship propelled by a "good enchanter" who almost everyone agrees is Merlin. Besides Guido and his lady, Giovanna (Vanna), Dante invites the poet Lapo Gianni and his lady, Lagia.

Finally I include two Spanish poems, fifteenth-century *romances* or ballads, which show a connection with the northern tradition. The first perpetuates the notion developed in popular culture that a plant with magic powers grew on the site where Tristan and Isolde died. The second poem tells how Lancelot overcame a curse put on him by Lady Quintañona, who in other poems is a friendly old go-between for him and Guinevere. This poem also mentions three strange transformations of the King's sons into beasts, a kindly hermit, and a mysterious white-footed stag.

> *Bibliographic note:* The Spanish poems are newly translated by me. For originals, see C. Colin Smith's *Spanish Ballads* (Oxford, 1964); also the article by Harvey L. Sharrer in Norris J. Lacy's *Arthurian Encyclopedia*, 516–21. The other translations are taken from my *Lyrics of the Middle Ages* (Garland, 1990), 69–72, 207, and 149, respectively.

Provençal

Bernart de Ventadorn:

Tant ai mo cor ple de joya

1. I have a heart so filled with joy
    Everything changes its nature:
   Flowers white, crimson, and gold
    Seems the frost,

For with the wind and the rain
  My fortune keeps on growing;   5
Ah yes, my worth keeps mounting,
  My song's improving too.
I have a heart so full of love
  And joy and sweetness,   10
That the ice appears to me a flower,
  And the snow lies green.

2. I can go out without my clothes,
  Naked in my shirt,
For fine, true love will keep me safe   15
  From wintry blasts.
But a man's a fool to lose measure
  And not to toe the line,
And so I've taken special care
  Ever since I fixed on   20
The most pretty love who ever lived,
  From whom I expect great honor.
For in place of the wealth of her
  I'd not take Pisa.

3. She can cut me off from her friendship,   25
  But I rest secure in my faith
That at least I've carried away
  The beautiful image of her.
And I have for my own devices
  Such a store of happiness   30
That until the day when I see her,
  I'll feel no anxiousness.
My heart lies close to Love and
  My spirit runs there too,
Though my body's anchored here, alas!   35
  Far from her, in France.

4. Still I have steady hope from her
  (Which does me little good),
For she holds me as if in a balance
  Like a ship upon the waves,   40
And I don't know where to hide myself
  From woes besetting my senses.
All night long I toss and I turn
  Heaving upon my mattress:
I suffer greater torment in love   45
  Than that archlover Tristan,

Who underwent so many pains
    To gain Isolde the Blonde.

5. O God! Why am I not a swallow
    Winging through the air,   50
Coming through the depths of night
    There inside her chamber?
My good, joy-bearing lady,
    Your lover here's expiring.
I'm afraid my heart may melt   55
    If things go on like this.
Lady, because of your love
    I join my hands and adore:
Beautiful body with healthy hues,
    You make me suffer great woe.   60

6. There isn't any affair of the world
    That can occupy me more
Than the mere mentioning of her;
    Then my heart leaps high
And light suffuses my face, and   65
    Whatever you hear me say of it,
It will always appear to you
    That I really want to laugh.
I love that woman with such good love   70
    That many a time I cry,
And to me my sighs contain
    A far better savor.

7. Messenger, go on the run:
    Tell to my pretty one   75
The pain, O yes the grief
    I bear—and torment.

Can vei la lauzeta mover

1. When I see the lark moving
    His wings with joy toward the light,
Then forget and let himself fall
    From the sweetness that enters his heart,
O! what great envy I feel   5
    Toward whomever I see who's glad!
I wonder why my heart
    Doesn't melt right away from desire.

2. Alas! how much I thought I knew
    About love, and how little I know!   10

For I can't keep myself from loving
   Her who'll give me nothing in return.
She's stolen my heart and all of me
   And all herself and all the world;
And after she robbed me, left me nothing   15
   Except desire and a longing heart.

3. Yes, I lost all power over myself,
   I wasn't mine from that moment on
When she let me look into her eyes,
   Into a mirror I like so well.   20
Mirror, since I first saw myself in you,
   Deep sighs have murdered me,
And I lost myself the way
   Handsome Narcissus lost himself in the pool.

4. About women I feel great despair.   25
   Never again will I trust them.
And although I used to protect them,
   From now on, I'm defecting,
Since I see not a one will help me
   Against her who destroys and upsets me.   30
I despair of them all, distrust them all,
   For I know very well that they're all like that!

5. And so My Lady's acting like a "woman"
   (And I blame her for it!),
For she doesn't want what a man ought to want   35
   And whatever a man forbids, she does.
I've fallen into very foul grace.
   I've carried on like the fool on the bridge,
And I don't know why it's happened:
   Did I climb too high on the hill?   40

6. All grace is lost—it's true—
   (And I never even tasted it!)
Since she who ought to have it most
   Has none; where will I find it?
O! how bad it seems (if you see her)   45
   That she who owns this longing slave
Who'll never have anything good without her
   Lets me die, won't lend me her aid.

7. Since prayers, thanks, and the rights I own
   Can't help me gain Milordess,   50
And she doesn't care a bit
   That I love her, I'll never tell her of it.

No, I'll leave her. I'll give her up.
    She's murdered me. As a corpse I speak.
I'm going away since she won't retain me   55
    Downcast, to exile, I don't know where.

8. Tristan, you'll get nothing more from me.
    I'm going away, downcast, I don't know where.
I'm through with songs, I'm giving them up.   60
    I'm hiding myself from love and joy.

German

Heinrich von Veldeke:

Tristrant muose sunder danc

Tristan stood, without giving thanks,
Among Isolde's loyal ranks,
For the magic philter could impel
Stronger even than love's spell.
My Lady then should give me thanks   5
Because that brew I never drank;
And yet my love fares valiantly,
Better than his, if that can be.
    O Lady fair,
    Of falseness bare,   10
    I'll belong to you
    If you will love me true.

Italian

Dante Alighieri:

Guido, i' vorrei che tu e Lapo ed io

Guido, I wish that you and Lapo and I,
Spirited on the wings of a magic spell,
Could drift in a ship where every rising swell
Would sweep us at our will across the skies;
Then tempest never, or any weather dire   5
Could ever make our blissful living cease;
No, but abiding in a steady, blesséd peace
Together we'd share the increase of desire.

And Lady Vanna and Lady Lagia then

And she who looms above the thirty best 10
Would join us at the good enchanter's behest;
And there we'd talk of Love without an end
To make those ladies happy in the sky—
With Lapo enchanted too, and you and I.

Spanish

Anonymous:

Herido está Don Tristán

Sir Tristan has been wounded / by the wicked blow of a lance;
His uncle the King gave it to him / with a poisoned lance;
He wielded it from a tower / since he didn't dare come nearer.
Tristan holds the point inside him / while the shaft trembles outside.
Queen Iseo goes to see him, / his beautiful belovéd, 5
Wearing a dress of black, / which is called the cloth of mourning.
Seeing him so badly off, / the distraught lady addresses him thus:
"Whoever has wounded you, Sir Tristan, / may he suffer pangs of woe,
Since there exists no surgeon / who is capable of curing you."
They joined together mouth to mouth / like domestic turtle-doves. 10
One was weeping, the other crying, / bathing the bed with tears.
Then there was born a bush / that is called the white lily.
Any woman who eats of it / suddenly finds herself pregnant.
I, poor girl, did just this—to my own evil fate!

Anonymous:

Tres hijuelos había el Rey

Three little sons had the King, / three little sons and no more.
Out of ill will that he felt for them, / he cursed them all.
One was turned into a deer, / and another into a dog,
And the third became a Moor / and crossed over the sea.
Lancelot came on the scene, / playing games with some ladies. 5
One cried out in a loud voice: / "Sir knight, stay for a while!
If it was my fate, / my destiny would be fulfilled
If I should marry you, / and you willingly agreed,
And if you would give me as gift / the white-footed deer!"
"I'd give it to you, my lady, / willingly with all my heart 10
If I only knew in what country / that deer came to life."
Then Sir Lancelot rode along, / he rode and went away,
And ahead of him his hunting-dogs / he guides upon a leash.

He came upon a hermit's cell, / where a hermit dwelled:
"God save you, my good man!" / "And a welcome to you!   15
You look to me like a hunter / from the hounds you lead."
"Tell me please, my hermit, / you who lead a holy life,
That deer with the white foot— / where does it dwell?"
"Rest with me here, my son, / until the dawn shall come,
And I shall tell you all I've seen / and all that I have known.   20
A day ago it passed by here / two hours before the dawn,
In company with seven lions / and a lioness with young.
Seven counts then died / and many a once-bold knight.
May God forever guard you, son, / wherever you may fare!
For whoever it was who sent you here / did not hold your life dear! 25
Ay, Lady Quintañones, / may you burn in the fires of Hell,
Since so many fine caballeros / have lost their lives for you!"

Chapter IX

THE SAGA OF THE MANTLE

Marianne E. Kalinke

Mǫttuls saga (The Saga of the Mantle) is an anonymous Old Norse translation of the French *Lai du cort mantel* (Tale of the Short Mantle), also known as *Le Mantel mautaillié* (The Ill-cut Mantle), which was presumably composed toward the end of the twelfth or the beginning of the thirteenth century. The preface to *Mǫttuls saga* informs us that it is the account of a curious and amusing incident that took place at the court of King Arthur and that the translation was undertaken at the behest of King Hákon Hákonarson, who ruled Norway from 1217 to 1263. *Mǫttuls saga* is part of a group of Arthurian narratives that were translated for King Hákon from the French bestsellers of the day. In 1226 a certain Brother Robert translated Thomas of Britain's *Tristan (Tristrams saga ok Ísǫndar)* and this was followed by anonymous translations of Chrétien de Troyes's *Yvain (Ívens saga)* and a collection of Breton *lais* entitled in Old Norse *Strengleikar* (Stringed Instruments).

Among the Arthurian narratives *The Saga of the Mantle* is in a class by itself because of its irreverent portrayal of courtly society. The saga, like *Le Lai du cort mantel*, is a ribald tale of a chastity test conducted by means of a magic mantle at King Arthur's court. With one exception, all the ladies at court, starting with Guinevere, are ignominiously exposed as unfaithful wives and lovers.

The chastity-testing mantle is central to a number of medieval and modern Arthurian narratives. It is celebrated in French, German, English, and Icelandic literature. The mantle-test narratives constitute only a small group, however, within a larger—mostly non-Arthurian—corpus of tales, medieval as well as modern, devoted to chastity tests by means of such objects as shirts, gloves, girdles, rings, and roses. Antedating the *Lai du cort mantel*, Robert Biket wrote the *Lai du cor* (Lay of the Horn), in which cuckolded knights—and not their unfaithful ladies—are incapable of drinking from a horn without spilling its contents. The mantle-test compositions are nevertheless distinguished from other chastity-testing tales in that the trial by mantle always takes place at a social gathering; during a public event the infidelity of a woman becomes known not only to her lover or husband but also to society at large.

Like all the other Old Norse translations of foreign (primarily French) literature, *Mǫttuls saga* is written in prose, and like the other translations commissioned by King Hákon Hákonarson, the saga is characterized by amplification as an explicatory, emphatic, or anticipatory device. Although the translator adhered carefully to the content of his French source, he nonetheless augmented the narrative by employing alliteration and other collocations, both synonymous and antithetical, for emphasis and to achieve semantic, syntactic, and rhythmical euphony. Thus, despite its accuracy in transmitting the French matter, the saga may also be considered an interpretation.

Although *Mǫttuls saga* is translated into Old Norse, it is preserved only in Icelandic copies of the original Norwegian translation. There are two redactions: A, which is extant in one leaf, dated 1300 to 1350 (AM 598 Iβ 4to; the oldest manuscript containing an Arthurian text in Scandinavia) and B (represented by the fragments AM 598 1α 4to and Stockholm 6 4to) from around 1400. The latter redaction was transcribed in Iceland in the seventeenth century when the manuscript was still complete. The present translation is based on a copy made by Jón Erlendsson, which is preserved in the manuscript AM 179 fol.

The Old Norse-Icelandic translations of continental literature are characterized by a paratactic style, like indigenous Icelandic prose, with frequent repetition of "and," "now," and "then," by changes in tense, and by ellipsis. Whenever these stylistic devices have been deemed too disturbing to the flow of narrative, they have been silently emended.

> *Bibliographic note:* The text translated here is based on my edition: *Mǫttuls saga*, Editiones Arnamagnæanæ, Series B, Vol. 30 (Reitzel, 1988), which also contains an edition of *Le Lai du cort mantel* by Philip E. Bennett and my translation of the saga into English. Although I have based the following translation on this edition, the text presented here is a freer version. For a history of the Mantle-Tale in Europe consult the Introduction to this edition. See also Marianne E. Kalinke, *King Arthur, North-by Northwest. The matière de Bretagne in Old Norse-Icelandic Romance*, Bibliotheca Arnamagnæana, Vol. 37 (Reitzel, 1981).

The Saga of the Mantle

Chapter I

King Arthur was the most renowned ruler with regard to every aspect of valor and all kinds of manliness and chivalry, combined with perfect compassion and most appealing mildness, so that in every respect there was no ruler more renowned or blessed with friends in his day in the world. He was the most valiant man at arms, the most generous with gifts, the gentlest in words, the cleverest in his designs, the most benevolent in mercy, the most polished in good manners, the noblest in all kingly craft, godfearing in his undertakings, gentle to the good, harsh to the wicked, merciful to the needy, hospitable to the companionable, so perfect in his entire authority that neither ill will nor malice was found in him, and no one could adequately laud the splendid magnificence and honor of his realm. This is attested by truthful accounts about him and much dependable intelligence recorded by worthy clerks about his many deeds—sometimes about various illustrious events that occurred in diverse ways at his court as well as throughout his realm, sometimes about valiant deeds of chivalry, sometimes about other curious matters.

This book tells about a curious and amusing incident that took place at the court of the illustrious and renowned King Arthur, who held all England and Brittany under his sway. And this true account, which came to me in French, I have translated into Norwegian as entertainment and diversion for you, the listeners, since the worthy King Hákon, son of King Hákon, asked me, ignorant though I be, to provide some entertainment through the following story.

Chapter II

During that festive period which the Holy Church calls Pentecost but the Norse call *Pikkisdagar*, there came to King Arthur illustrious chieftains and kings of many lands, together with dukes and other honorable men, as is attested by this saga, as well as many others that were composed about him. King Arthur was the most inquisitive of men and wanted to be apprised of all news of events that took place within his realm as well as in other lands, wherever he might learn of them. And therefore he let it be trumpeted about, in woods, on roads and crossroads, that everyone who was traveling about should come to his court and his celebration. The king's summons went on to say that any man's ladylove might accompany him, and the king would make her equally welcome. As a result there came so many that the gathering was too large to be counted. For this reason the wisest of men found it difficult to choose the most courtly woman in such a large gathering.

The queen rejoiced at their coming and allowed the maidens to stay in her chambers. The queen, who was the most beautiful of women, conversed with them and engaged in all manner of diversion and amusements in courtly fashion. She herself had costly garments and she gave each of the women splendid clothing of all kinds of colors and qualities, even the poorest of which was made of costly stuff and lined with grey and white fur. Whoever had occasion to look at the clothing carefully had much to talk about. But I do not want to detain you, and thus I will say but little about much: that no better garments existed in the world than those given away, and no merchant could have sold them or purchased them for what they were worth. The queen was laudable because of her exceedingly noble deportment and most blessed with friends because of her renowned munificence. She let precious brooches and rich belts be brought out, as well as rings with all kinds of precious stones. No man had ever seen such rare or excellent treasures as the queen bestowed of her abundant good will, for each of them was allowed to take whatever she wanted to have.

But now we must speak about King Arthur, that renowned man, who let rich garments and trusty weapons, magnificent apparel, and the best of weapons be given to his court and to the assembled chieftains and knights, and in addition, horses that had been sent to him from the West, from Spain, Lombardy, and Alemannia. There had come no knight, no matter how poor, who did not receive rich garments and trusty weapons, magnificent apparel, and a good horse, for there was no lack of things that one might want. And at no king's court were such rich gifts received and bestowed with such abundance as were given there. Moreover, the king was worthy of great praise because he never regretted giving, and therefore he was so free with them, as if all that he gave away cost nothing.

The Saturday before Pentecost the great court had assembled, and it was so well outfitted with horses and weapons and good clothing that nowhere in the world was there another court like this. Much diversion and all kinds of entertainments with abundant pastimes were provided for the many well-bred persons who had assembled there. When they had spent the whole day in such pastimes and evening came, all went to their lodgings, and the shield-bearers made the beds, and then all the people went to sleep.

Chapter III

When day came and it began to grow light, they all got dressed and all the people went to the king's palace and accompanied the king to the cathedral of the town. The queen with her maidens also came to attend the divine service, and one could see there many a courtly man and beautiful woman very well attired because the handsomest people in the world were assembled there. When the divine service was finished, all the court went to the king's palace, and the queen led her group of women into the chambers with her. The stewards in the king's palace and the servants had a most abundant supply of good provisions and the best beverages to be found in the world to provide for the king's tables in every way. They first covered the tables with the whitest of tablecloths and placed on them silver spoons and gold spoons, highly ornamented knives, and silver dishes with salt. Then the food was ready for the king and all his court. But it was King Arthur's custom not to go to table or to be truly content on any day until he had first received news about some event or other that had happened near or far and from which he might derive enjoyment and pleasure. The queen summoned Sir Valven

[Walwen, Gawain], the chief of all the king's stewards, and asked how it came about that the king did not go to table, now that the food was prepared and all his court assembled and it was already mid-afternoon. He went at once to the king and spoke to him thus: "Lord, what is the reason that you are not eating, even though the tables have been set for a long time?"

The king looked at him and answered: "Steward, when have you seen me hold court at a feast when I did not receive news of some event before I went to table?"

Just as the king was saying this, a young man came up quickly on a galloping horse and headed toward the king's palace; he was riding so fast that the horse was all in a sweat under him, for he was hastening exceedingly.

Sir Valven saw him first and spoke to the courtiers: "If God wills it," he said, "we shall quickly dine, for I see a young man galloping vigorously on his horse in this direction, and he will surely bring us some news."

Thereupon the young man came to the doors of the king's hall and dismounted, and the servants led off his horse. The young man was most courtly; he immediately removed his outer garments and threw his mantle over the horse's neck. And when he was without his outer garments, he seemed most handsome. His hair was flaxen; his shoulders were broad and powerful; his arms were both long and sturdy; his hands were white and strong; by nature he was well built, as handsome as one might desire with respect to physical strength and prowess, so that no one could wish him otherwise than as God had created him. He did not lack for words, and chose them cleverly.

Chapter IV

When he had come into the king's hall, where the court was, he spoke to them with courteous words: "May that almighty God," he said, "Who created us all, help and preserve your assembly and fellowship!"

"Friend," they said, "may God bless you!"

Then Kay the steward spoke up: "Your horse is in a sweat. Tell us some news about your journey."

"No, sire," he said, "you shall first tell me where the good King Arthur is. And I swear, by my troth, I shall give the king such news that won't please all of you; nonetheless, some will derive pleasure from it."

All thought it took a long time to find out what it was that he wanted to say. Then a knight spoke to the young man: "Look, friend, there he is, sitting on the throne."

He went there immediately, while all those who were in his path made room for him. And when he came before the king, he greeted him with these words: "May God, Who created heaven and earth and all those creatures who are in the world, bless and preserve you, the crowned king who is highest among all those who have been and who ever will be." And then he said.

"Now I'm pleased to have found you, for I have long sought you. A most beautiful maiden," he said, "far from your land, sent me here to find you, and she asks that you, as is your duty, grant her a boon, but if you refuse to do so, then she will not ask again. You are not to know, however, what she is asking or who she herself is before granting the boon. She is exceedingly beautiful and illustrious, so that there is no one like her in all the world. But I want you to know, since I am to ask this favor on her behalf, that I ask for nothing that will disgrace your honor or damage your kingdom."

The king granted what the young man asked for, and he thanked the king profusely. Thereupon he took out of a small, gold-embroidered pouch a mantle of silk that was so beautiful that mortal eye had never seen one that resembled it or was its equal. An elf-woman had fashioned it with such great and inconceivable skill that in that whole assembly of skillful and intelligent men gathered there, there was no one who could perceive in what manner the garment had been made. It was shot through with gold in a pattern of such beautifully embroidered leaves that never the like was seen, for no one could find either the beginning or the end. What was strangest, moreover, was that those who scrutinized it most closely could least discover how that wondrous piece of workmanship was put together. But I do not want to draw things out, for the mantle was even stranger than one might imagine: the elf-woman had woven a charm into the mantle so that the misdeed of every maiden who had been intimate with her beloved would be revealed at once when she dressed in it: it would become very long or very short in a flagrant manner so as to reveal how she had sinned. Thus it would expose all false women and maidens, so that nothing could be hidden when it was put on. Before the entire court and that great gathering of chieftains who were assembled there, the young man announced clearly and boldly in what manner the mantle was woven and what power it had to put women to the test.

Thereupon he spoke to the king. "Lord," he said, "I bid you now to have the ladies and the maidens of the court try on the mantle at once, for far from here I heard what illustrious women and maidens are assembled here; but do this speedily now so that they are not first apprised of this intelligence. This is the reason I have come: to ask this favor of you rather than any other, and for no other purpose."

The entire court and all the chieftains who had come there wondered and were curious about the mantle. Then Valven said that this favor was worth granting just as the boon was worth accepting.

Chapter V

The king now sent Sir Valven and Kay the steward and Meon the page for the queen. He bade them tell the queen to come to him at once, together with all those maidens and women who were with her, and to come one and all so that no one stayed behind, "because I certainly intend to keep the promise I made to the young man." They went now and found the queen in her chambers, ready to go to table, for she was hungry, since she had fasted for so long.

Sir Valven conveyed the king's message. "Lady," he said, "the king bids you not to delay to come at once to him, because a very handsome young man has come to him and brought him such a precious mantle that no mortal eye has ever seen another like it. The cloth is red and is a treasure the likes of which we have never yet seen, fashioned with such wondrous and extraordinary skill that it is uncertain whether another like it exists or can be found in all the world. And know for certain that the king has promised the mantle to the one whom it fits and best suits. Try your luck now, milady; do not delay, and bring along all the women who have come here, for the king wants to see their appearance and beauty. It is not known to me, however, on whom this praiseworthy gift will be bestowed."

Chapter VI

The queen went at once to the king, accompanied by the entire large group of beautiful women and illustrious maidens, so that never before had the eye of man seen in one spot so great an assemblage of beautiful women and beautiful maidens, and there had never been better garments in the world than those with which they were adorned. For this reason every man looked at them, and many a man was captivated by them as well. Immediately the entire court went into the hall, wondering who it would be who would possess the mantle. Thereupon the king took the mantle and spread it out, showing it to the queen and saying that he would give it to her or to anyone whom it might fit. But not a whit more did he tell them about it, for if they had known what else pertained to the mantle, none of them would have dressed in it, not for all the gold in Araby, and it would have been as repulsive to them as a maggot or a serpent.

Now, however, the time had come for the mantle to tell how faithfully each had conducted herself toward her husband or how faithful she had been to her beloved. The queen took the mantle first and put it on, and it became so short on her that it did not reach her heels. As much as she wanted to own the mantle, she would never even have let it touch her body had she known what spell had been woven into it. She immediately blushed with shame and then immediately paled from anger and rage when the mantle did not fit.

Meon the page stood beside her and saw her face changing color, and so he spoke to her at once:

"Milady," he said, "it does not seem to me that the mantle is too long for you; instead, it is a good ell too short and in no way does it fit you. This maiden, however, who is standing here beside you and who is nearly the same size as you, neither taller nor shorter, she is the beloved of Aristes, son of King Artus; give her the mantle and then you will see how it fits her though it was too short for you."

Thereupon the queen took the mantle and handed it to the maiden beside her, who gladly took it and immediately put it on, but on her it was much shorter than on the queen. Then Meon the page spoke: "The mantle has now shrunk much in a short time and yet it has not been worn long."

The queen asked the nobles and all the chieftains: "Tell me, lords, was the mantle not longer than this?"

"Milady," said Valven, "it seems to me that you are somewhat more faithful than she is, and yet you are quite alike, but there is less falsehood in you than in her."

Then the queen spoke to Kay the steward. "Tell me," she said, "what is this faithfulness that you are speaking about and what power is inherent in this mantle?" And Kay told her from the beginning to the end just what the young man had said. The queen thought that if she got angry or became enraged about this in any way, that she would earn shame and disgrace for having been unfaithful to such a ruler, and thus she turned everything into entertainment and diversion, into laughter, jest, and ridicule. "Now," she said, "all maidens and women will surely try on the mantle since I put it on first."

"Milady," said Kay the steward, "today the faithfulness of all of you shall be made manifest, as well as the steadfastness of your love, which husbands or trueloves expect, when you claim that you have long preserved a firm faithfulness; because of the love that the knights have for your virginity, they hazard mortal danger and take many risks for your sakes. In the past you have all pretended to be so pure and faithful that if somebody asked any of you, or if a brave man wished to win one of you, you would immediately swear that you have never had anything to do with a man."

When they fully understood with what cunning the mantle had been woven and what power the elf-woman had embroidered and sewn into the leaves on the mantle, there was not a single woman in that large assemblage who would not have preferred to stay at home with honor rather than come there, for there was not a single one in that entire gathering who dared to put on the mantle or dress in it or hold it in her hands or come near it.

Chapter VII

When all drew back from the mantle and no one dared to put it on, the king spoke: "Now we shall return the mantle to the young man, for he cannot stay here with us on account of the maidens in our charge."

But the young man answered: "That is not right, sire, nor honorable, nor in keeping with your station; by no means do I intend to take back the mantle before I see that all the women and maidens have tried it on, for whatever a king grants and promises must never be rescinded or revoked because of anyone's demanding or inciting words."

"My young man," said the king, "you speak wisely; what you said is true and just, and no one shall prevent me from keeping to what has been spoken and giving what I have promised you. Now every single lady shall try on the mantle."

While all stood in silence, Kay the steward, in the presence of all the knights and men of the realm, called to his beloved with these words: "Beloved," he said, "come forward; you may take the mantle unafraid and fearless. There is no one your equal here in true faithfulness and other fitting, womanly accomplishments. With honor and distinction we two shall carry off the victory today."

But the maiden answered: "If it be your will, then I would like someone else to take the mantle, for I want to see how she fares; I see here more than a hundred of those who dare not come near it, and no one wants to put it on."

"Ho, ho!" said Kay; "it seems to me that you are somewhat fearful, and I don't know what that means."

"That is not so, sir," she said. "Much more excellent and prominent women than I am have already taken the mantle, and it is not that I am afraid of it; rather it is," she said, "that there is here such a gathering of prominent women who are good and faithful and from the finest families, and it will be ill received if I run forward ahead of them; I might suffer hatred and ridicule as a result."

"You must not," said Kay, "fear their anger, because no one desires to put on the mantle. Nonetheless, I know that you are safe and that it will be to your honor if you get the mantle but to your shame if you fail."

Then the maiden put on the mantle before all the assembled nobles and many other lords, and the mantle became so short for her in back that it hardly reached the hollow of her knees; in front, however, it did not even reach the knee.

Then all the nobles derided her and said: "Kay, our steward, can rejoice much in your love and practice great deeds of chivalry for your sake, for now your fidelity has been manifested, so that we may all know that no one like you can be found in the realm of the king of England."

When Kay saw how his beloved had fallen, he would have preferred that she had never come there rather than to receive such shame and disgrace. Ideus then spoke to Kay. "It is good," he said, "that derision and disgrace turn on you, since you deride everyone. What do you say? Doesn't the mantle fit your beloved well, whose faithfulness you praised so highly?"

The maiden was greatly distressed, since she could not defend herself against their words, for the whole court had seen how the mantle had fit her.

Then Kay spoke to the other knights. "Don't be too hasty," he said; "we shall see how beautifully the mantle fits your ladyloves."

Kay's beloved threw the mantle down, however, and went to her seat in shame and disgrace.

Chapter VIII

Now when the entire group of women saw how poorly this maiden had fared, they all cursed the young man who had brought the mantle there, for now that they were truly informed about it, there was no use objecting to putting on the mantle, even though they might come up with a satisfactory excuse for refusing. Then the courteous page Bodendr spoke to the king. "My lord," he said, "it seems to me that we are not following the proper order in trying on the mantle. The beloved of Sir Valven is so pleasingly beautiful that she should have tried on the mantle after the queen."

But Valven the steward was not pleased that she should try on the mantle because he suspected that she would not receive any more honor than those who had tried it on before. The king then said that Bodendr, the courteous page, should call her. She stood up at once because she dared not do otherwise. The king had the mantle brought to her and she tried it on at once as the king had asked. But as soon as she had it on, it was so long for her in back that she dragged it behind her for four and a half ells, but in front it shrank up to her knees and on the left side it rose as high up as her back. Kay the steward was glad when he saw that the mantle was so short for her, because people thought that she was probably more faithful than all other maidens and women who were at the king's court.

"By my troth," said Kay the steward, "praised be God! I shall not be the only one to be disgraced today because of my beloved, for I now deduce something from the mantle and I can easily interpret what that means: this beautiful maiden," said Kay, "has raised up her right leg but the left leg she let lie quietly while she allowed the man she liked to do what she wished him to do."

Sir Valven was annoyed that the wrongdoing of his beloved was so openly manifested, but he made no comment about it.

Then Kay spoke to her. "Come here, my lovely," he said. "I shall lead you to a seat beside my beloved because there are no women more alike than you two are."

Then the king took by the hand the daughter of King Urien, who was a most lovely maiden. The king, her father, was a powerful man who often went hunting with dogs and hawks.

"My lovely," said the gracious King Arthur, "the test will rightly award you this mantle, because no one finds fault in you."

"Lord," said Geres the Little, "do not speak at length about this before you have really seen how the mantle fits her."

Now the maiden knew right away that it was no use objecting to what the king had ordered, and therefore she took the mantle at once. But as soon as she was dressed in it, it became so long for her on the right side that one and one half ells dragged on the ground, while on the left side it rose over her knee.

"Lord," said Geres the Little, "foolish is he who trusts any woman because all deceive their beloveds and not a single one is trustworthy; moreover, the least faithful are they who act and speak most virtuously, and betrayal comes from those from whom one least expects it. No woman comes off well when she is tested. All deceive their husbands and want a man who is new as soon as they have tired of the old one. They have such a desire for novelty that no one can trust their actions. And now I want to say what I think is obvious about the conduct of this maiden: the mantle is long for her on the right side to show us that she more willingly let herself fall on that side, but the left side—where the mantle is raised—shows us that she is not annoyed if someone should lift up her dress there."

Then the maiden was so overcome by anger that at first she was speechless; she took hold of the ties on the mantle and cast it far from her and cursed repeatedly the one who had brought it to the court.

Kay the steward then said. "Don't get angry, lovely maiden; you too will sit beside my beloved. The three of you are equal in this respect and none of you can blame the others."

Chapter IX

Thereupon the king ordered that the beloved of Paternas should come forward, and he spoke to her with gentle words. "You, my lovely," said the king, "will undoubtedly get the mantle because you have a true and loyal love for your beloved."

Then Gerflet, the king's fool, could not keep quiet. "Milord," he said, "for the sake of God, do not settle the matter so quickly with words before you see how things turn out, for the day is to be praised at evening, and many a thing can turn out otherwise than one expects."

The maiden took the mantle at once because she knew that it was no use objecting. But when she was about to put it on, the mantle's ties broke off and right away they fell to the ground, with the mantle following so readily that it didn't stay in place anywhere. The maiden immediately trembled all over and did not know what she should do because she was surrounded by a large group of illustrious women and handsome shield-bearers and many other powerful men. They all cursed the mantle and the one who had made it, as well as the one who had brought it to the court. They all asserted that no one would be found in that great assemblage of court-ladies whom the mantle would fit; it would rightfully fit neither wife nor maiden, and there probably was no one created, no matter how fair or beautiful, who had a figure to which the mantle would conform, no matter how much she wept or grieved. Despite all this, everyone still wanted to own the mantle.

Valven then went to his beloved and spoke: "I bring this beautiful maiden to you here so that she might join your company." There was no one among them who thanked her for her coming. But Valven made light of it and then turned back laughing. Thereupon the young man picked the mantle very quickly up from the ground and took ties out of his pouch and attached the ties at once, since he did not want his mission to fail. The king then took the mantle and spoke in great anger: "We are fasting too long," he said. "What is the matter with these women? Why do we delay in having them put on the mantle?"

But Gerflet, the king's fool, spoke: "Milord, for God's sake, you might as well acquit those who are left, or do you want to bring even greater disgrace on them? Now that they see the mantle, they all admit here to their husbands and their lords and trueloves that they have gone somewhat astray." Once more the fool spoke to him: "What else do you want to demand from all of them?"

The king wanted to leave matters as they stood. Then the young man hastened before the king and spoke so that all the court heard him: "Lord," he said, "keep your word to me and the favor that you promised me. These knights do not know what they should say concerning their ladyloves, if it should turn out that some are tested but some are not and are let off free."

Then Ideus spoke up and called to his beloved: "You, my lovely," he said, "earlier today I thought that there was no one more faithful than you at this court, and Kay the steward answered me when I reproached his beloved; but I was rash in saying that I had such great confidence in your faithfulness, and that I was quite fearless about you. Now I regret this greatly, since I see that you are afraid. Take this mantle now and put it on."

The king had the mantle taken to her at once, and she took it right away and put it on. And when she had put it on, it fit perfectly in front, so that all thought nothing but good might be revealed about her. In the back, however, it was so short that it did not reach down to her loins, so that it hardly covered her belt. Gerflet the fool, who saw this first, spoke at once with a loud voice. "Noble maiden," he said, "the mantle is too short for you in the back, and it will never become so long in front that it will fit you well."

Then Kay could not keep silent any longer because Ideus had derided his beloved, and he quickly addressed Ideus with mockery and derision: "Look, Ideus, how do you think matters are going? Has your beloved not gone somewhat astray? This is what I think about her affairs, since you can deride all of us and yet we, in truth, can all see that your beloved is not properly clothed where her loins are bare. Now I will tell all of you who are listening that she is accustomed to let herself be taken shamelessly from behind, as the mantle openly manifests."

Ideus did not know what to say; he could only snatch the mantle in anger and rage and cast it at the feet of the king. Kay then took his beloved by the hand and led her where those were sitting who had tried the mantle on before, and said: "I know for certain that there will soon be a large and fine gathering here."

Chapter X

Now there was no longer anything else to do but for all those who had come there, both wives and maidens, old and young, to put on the mantle as quickly as possible, one after the other, while the beloved of each was watching. And it fit not a single one. Kay took each one of them by the hand and led her to a seat in that large circle that they made on the floor of the hall. There was no one in that large gathering of chieftains and knights who were there who did not have a beloved, and everyone who saw their faces could right away discover distress and sorrow in them. It was a consolation that no one could mock another without himself being implicated.

Then Kay the steward spoke: "Good lords," he said, "do not become enraged or angry on account of this, for we are all in the same position. Our ladyloves have been honored and exalted over and above all other court-ladies near and far, wherever they may be, and today they have earned for themselves a certain renown; their only consolation may be that not one can blame another."

Then Sir Valven responded thus: "It does not seem to me that you are considering this case correctly, because it would be improper and in every way abominable if I took consolation in their disgrace; we shall never admit that a good, valiant man is reprehensible because his beloved besmirches herself with another man; rather, she herself is as evil because of her deeds and vices as is he who consented to her follies."

At this moment the young man hastened before the king and said: "I suspect, my lord, that I shall have to take the mantle back, even though I cannot understand how in such a large group it can be that there is not a single woman who can wear it. Have your chambers searched now, wherever the ladies are accustomed to sleep or sit, to make sure that no one is hidden or concealed there. The members of your court have fame and renown above all other people in the world, but if, as matters stand, I must leave, less news will come from now on to you than before if I have to depart with my mission unaccomplished."

"By my troth," said Sir Valven, "the young man speaks the truth; have the chambers searched as quickly as possible to ascertain that no one is hiding there."

The king then ordered all the upper chambers to be searched, and when he had said this, Gerflet the fool ran very quickly into the chambers and found a noble maiden right away. She had not hidden herself, however; instead, she was not feeling well and was lying in bed. Gerflet the fool then spoke to her right away: "Noble maiden," he said, "no one has ever seen a fairer adventure than the one now taking place in the king's hall, and you will have to take part in it as all the others have already done."

"I shall gladly go there," said the maiden, "but you must wait until I am dressed suitably."

Now the maiden got up and dressed in keeping with her station, in the finest clothes that she had; these were very costly because she came from a noble family. Then she went into the hall. Although her beloved was cheerful and in good spirits before she came in, he became distressed and angry when he saw her coming because he did not want her ever to try on the mantle. He loved her so much that even though he were to find out for certain about any misdeed of hers, he did not care; on account of the great love that he had for her, he never wanted to leave her.

The young man then brought her the mantle and told her with what artifice it had been woven. But Karadin, her beloved, called out with a loud voice while all were listening: "You, sweet beloved," he said, "if you have gone astray in any way, then don't ever go near the mantle. I love you so profoundly that I certainly don't want to lose your love—not for all the gold in the world, even though I were to be aware of any misdeed of yours."

But Kay the steward responded: "Why do you speak in such a way? Anyone who loses an unfaithful beloved should be joyful and delighted."

Then the maiden answered with gentle mien: "Sir," she said, "it may in truth cause a good man lasting distress if his beloved is proven to be unfaithful to him; still, if my beloved does not take it amiss, then I will put on the mantle."

"By my troth," said the knight, "there is no way you can avoid the test or refuse to take the mantle, since all the others have tried it on."

But she still did not want to try it on before her beloved allowed her to do so. As soon as he permitted it, she took the mantle and put it on before the entire court, and it fit her so well that it was neither too short nor too long; instead, it reached the ground evenly on all sides.

Then the young man spoke: "By my troth, this maiden may fittingly and boldly ask to keep the mantle, and I think, noble maiden, that your beloved has reason to be happier than the others who are here. But now you are to know the truth: I have taken this mantle to many courts where there are many people, where more than a thousand of those considered to be maidens have been exposed by this mantle. Never before has it shown your like in the purity of your maidenhood. And now I bestow on you this precious mantle, which is so excellent that there is none like it in all the world. No man can estimate its true value, and you alone may rightfully keep it, wear it, possess it, and leave it to your heirs." Thus the young man concluded his speech. Then the king spoke and said that she alone might rightfully have the mantle since she alone was worthy of owning it.

Chapter XI

Although all the women who sat about were envious because all of them wanted to own the mantle themselves, still none of them had been able to obtain it, and no one dared to object. Then Sir Valven spoke: "You, noble maiden," he said, "I take it upon myself on your behalf to proclaim that you are not indebted to anyone for the mantle except to yourself, to the purity of your maidenhood. For that reason all men and women who see your goodness now grant it to you, although they would gladly object if they could find true grounds for reproaching you. But now the situation has undergone a change for the better, as their envy and grief become your joy, their sorrow your consolation, their disgrace your honor, and their misdeeds your praise, which will swell in every land."

Thereupon the young man took leave of the king. By no means did he want to stay there any longer and eat the food; instead, he wanted to hurry back to his lady and report to her about his mission. The king sat down at table, however, as did all his court, and it can be said in truth that many a good knight sat there distressed on account of his beloved. But King Arthur let his court be entertained at such great cost that never had there been such entertainment either offered or enjoyed.

When the court had eaten its fill, Karadin went before the king and asked permission to depart; cheerfully and in good spirits he left with his beloved. They placed the mantle in a monastery, however, for safekeeping.

Recently inquiries have been made about it, and he who has it says that he will have it taken everywhere in order to test lovely maidens and beautiful women. We expect that few will be found who will be able to own it, and thus it will remain new for a long time. He who has the mantle intends to send it to all the courts, so that all the court-ladies and court-maidens will have to try it on. I would rather not be the messenger accompanying the mantle, so as not to be ill-treated by those powerful men who are confronted by such a gift.

Now let no one say anything but good about women, because it is more fitting to conceal than to reveal something, even though one may know the true state of affairs. No matter who puts it on, the mantle will show what the one trying it on is truly like. Therefore let us praise good women according to their merits, because they have earned renown and happiness.

Now the *Saga of the Mantle* ends here; may you live happily for many years to come. Amen.

Tintagel Castle in Cornwall, the birthplace of King Arthur and home of King Mark. The ruins look out from a steep cliff over the Atlantic Ocean. (Courtesy of the British Tourist Authority)

Chapter *X*

BÉROUL: *THE ROMANCE OF TRISTAN*

Norris J. Lacy

The love story of Tristan and Isolde is one of the most famous in literature. It tells of a passionate and illicit love born of a potion that the two drank by mistake. Because Isolde was pledged to marry Tristan's uncle, King Mark of Cornwall, their love could bring the young couple no happiness; instead it condemned them to suffering, guilt, exile, and a tragic end. This tragedy, throughout the centuries, has inspired countless authors, as well as painters, sculptors, and composers. Two of the greatest retellings of the Tristan and Isolde legend are among the earliest, dating from the second half of the twelfth century; they are the French texts of Béroul (translated here) and of Thomas of Britain in Chapter XII.

In the medieval tradition the Tristan texts can be divided into two groups, known as the courtly and the primitive (or common) versions. The former, strongly influenced by court culture and by the spirit of courtly love, is a "refined" version, which gives a good deal of attention to the analysis of emotional and psychological states. The so-called primitive tradition includes texts that are less introspective and analytical and often more violent than the courtly version. Thomas's work is a representative of the courtly group, while Béroul's poem belongs to the primitive version. Béroul's work is known to us only in a single long fragment of nearly 4,500 lines of octosyllabic verse, preserved in one manuscript.

The term "primitive" should not be taken as an indication either of date (since Thomas may well predate Béroul) or of quality. Béroul's romance is in fact a highly effective work, composed by a poet of considerable talent. It offers a lively and engaging text. The many problematical or awkward passages (and internal contradictions, as when one of Tristan's enemies is killed, only to reappear later in the text) are no doubt due, not to authorial ineptitude, but to errors or changes introduced when the manuscript was copied—and perhaps, as some would contend, to dual authorship.

The narration is cyclical in form, as King Mark repeatedly becomes suspicious of the lovers and acts on those suspicions by threatening or punishing Tristan and Isolde, only to be somehow persuaded that his wife and nephew are guiltless; he then pardons them, and the cycle begins anew. A number of such cyclical episodes lead up to the long and remarkable scene at Mal Pas, where Isolde swears the equivocal oath that establishes her innocence in all eyes except ours. Béroul prepares that scene elaborately and with careful attention to its dramatic effect: King Arthur and his knights are summoned to witness the trial; Tristan disguises himself as a leper and deceives everyone who passes, taking childlike pleasure in his trickery and even bantering with Mark about the remarkable resemblance Isolde bears to the leper's own lady; and Isolde is depicted almost as a saint—but as a saint who has time for some suggestive asides to her lover. The entire scene is played out in a festive spirit of rollicking fun and mock-seriousness, rather than in the atmosphere of suspense and foreboding that we might expect when Isolde's reputation and life are at stake. The explanation, of course, is that they are *not* at stake. Isolde's vindication has been ensured by four allies: Tristan, Béroul, God, and herself. If we should doubt that God is on the side of the lovers and against their enemies, Béroul intervenes directly and frequently, either to reassure us explicitly of that fact or to comment in his own voice on the events of the story.

Throughout the text Tristan and Isolde remain (for most readers) thoroughly sympathetic and likable characters, despite the fact that, technically, they are both traitors and unabashed sinners. But if they are sinners, they have an excuse: they drank a love potion and cannot escape its power for three years. However, even after the potion's power wanes, they feel regret rather than repentance—regret, not for having loved each other, but for the poverty and isolation to which their love has reduced them. Their concerns are far more material than moral. Eventually the hateful dwarf and other enemies of the lovers are punished, and Tristan and Isolde (at least temporarily) are free to see each other. Unfortunately the text breaks off in mid-sentence, leaving us to guess the ending from related texts.

The Béroul who composed this version of the legend identifies himself twice, in the third person, but we know nothing at all about him. Some have suggested in fact that the poem was the work of two authors, the second of whom took up the writing at the point where Tristan returns Isolde to King Mark, or perhaps when Isolde agrees to defend herself by oath. That conclusion, although rejected by a good many scholars, is based on considerations of style and versification and on the fact that the narrative content of the first part closely parallels a related German version of the story (the *Tristrant* of Eilhart von Oberge), while the second division diverges significantly from the German text. Yet, despite undeniable differences between the earlier and later portions of the text, the questions of Béroul's identity and of dual authorship remain unsettled.

Béroul—whoever he or they may have been—wrote during the last quarter of the twelfth century. While we cannot conclusively situate the text much more precisely than that, the mention of the *mal d'Acre* (*dagres* in the manuscript) has often been taken as a reference to an epidemic that struck the Crusaders at Acre in 1190 or 1191; if that interpretation is correct, Béroul's *Tristan* dates from the final decade of that century. Recently, that explanation of the passage has been challenged and a date in the 1170's suggested, but the proposed alternatives to *mal dagres* have not been entirely persuasive. We can thus safely assign the composition of the *Tristan* only to the late twelfth century. The single manuscript that preserves the text (Paris, Bibliothèque Nationale, fr. 2171) dates from the middle or end of the following century.

Bibliographic note: The present translation is based on Muret's fourth edition of *Le Roman de Tristan* (Champion, 1947). Since first preparing this translation, I have published a new critical edition of the text with facing line-by-line translation (*The Romance of Tristan*, Garland,1989), and I have used that edition as a basis for restoring some manuscript readings that Muret, perhaps needlessly emended. I have been guided in the interpretation of numerous passages by two textual commentaries: A. Ewert, *The Romance of Tristan by Béroul*, Vol. II: Introduction, Commentary (Blackwell, 1970); and T.B.W. Reid, *The "Tristan" of Béroul: A Textual Commentary* (Blackwell, 1972). In addition I occasionally consulted two translations in Modern French, the line-for-line translation (*Le Roman de Tristan*) by Herman Braet (Gand, 1974) and the freer prose rendering by J.C. Payen: *Tristan et Yseut* (Garnier, 1974).

My translation follows the manuscript closely but not slavishly. I have made minor interpolations (rarely more than a few words) where transitions were needed for clarity. In only one case—a passage containing obviously and frequently corrupt readings—have I significantly altered the order of lines. I have retained the poet's addresses to his readers (although without his frequent *seigneurs*, "lords"). Lacunae in the original are indicated by [. . .]; when I have, infrequently, provided a hypothetical reading to remedy a textual difficulty, I have enclosed my suggestions within brackets; the bracketed material at the beginning of the text summarizes from other sources the events leading up to the opening of Béroul's fragment. Throughout the translation I have periodically inserted line numbers to facilitate comparison with the Old French edition of Muret.

The Romance of Tristan

[*The young Tristan, trained by his tutor and squire Governal on the Continent, had distinguished himself at Mark's court in Cornwall by defeating the Irish giant Morholt, who had demanded that Cornish youths be delivered to him as tribute. A fragment of Tristan's sword remained embedded in Morholt's skull and was found by the giant's niece Isolde. Later, when Tristan was sent to find a wife for King Mark, he came to Ireland, where he killed a dragon but was overcome by its poison. Isolde took care of him until, discovering the notch in his sword, she realized that he had*

killed Morholt. She spared his life only to avoid marriage to a dishonest seneschal,
and she agreed to marry Mark. On the trip back to Cornwall she and Tristan
unintentionally drank a love potion and fell hopelessly in love with each other. To
conceal the loss of Isolde's virginity, her servant Brangain sacrificed her own by
taking Isolde's place in the nuptial bed. Following the marriage Tristan and Isolde
saw each other often, and Mark periodically became suspicious (often at the urging of
barons who were jealous of Tristan). Béroul's text begins as Mark, warned by the
dwarf that Tristan and Isolde intended to meet, had hidden in a tree in order to
entrap them. The lovers saw his reflection in a fountain; Isolde, unsure whether
Tristan had seen the king, spoke first, while taking care . . .]

. . . not to give any indication that she was aware of Mark's presence. She
approached her friend. Listen how she warned him: "Tristan, for God's sake,
it is wrong of you to send for me at this hour!" Now she pretended to weep.
[. . .] "In the name of God, the Creator of the heavens and the sea, never
send for me again. I warn you, Tristan, I will not come. The king thinks I
have slept with you, Tristan; but I affirm my fidelity before God, and may He
punish me if anyone ever made love to me except the man who took my
virginity. Yet the slanderous barons of this land, for whose sake you fought
and killed Morholt, apparently make him believe the worst about us. Sir, I
know you have no such desire; nor, in God's name, is there a shameful passion in my heart. I would rather be burned alive and have my ashes scattered
in the wind than live a single day in love with anyone but my lord. Oh, God,
he does not believe me! How far I have fallen! Sir, Solomon told the truth:
whoever saves thieves from the gallows earns their hatred. If the traitors of
this land [. . .] they should hide. You suffered greatly from the wound you
received in your battle with my uncle. I cured you, and it is hardly astonishing
that you became my friend as a result! And they have made the king believe
that you love me sinfully. If they were to come before God for judgment, they
would be damned! Wherever you may be, Tristan, do not send for me again
for any reason. I would not be so daring as to come to you. In fact I'm staying
here too long. If the king even suspected that I were here, he would kill me
without hesitation, and it would be such a terrible injustice! I'm sure that he
would kill me. Surely, Tristan, the king does not realize that he himself is the
reason I have affection for you: I loved you because you were his relative. I
recall that my mother loved my father's family a great deal, and she told me
that a wife does not love her husband much if she does not also love his
relatives. I know she was telling the truth. Sir, I loved you for his sake, and I
thereby lost his favor." [. . .]

"Surely he is not entirely at fault," replied Tristan. "So his men made
him believe something false about us."

"Can you doubt that, Tristan? The king, my husband, is honorable. He
would never have suspected us of his own accord. But a man can be misled

and made to do wrong. That is what they have done to my husband. Tristan, I am leaving now; I have stayed too long."

"My lady, for God's sake, have mercy on me. I sent for you; now you are here. Listen to my request. I have held you in such high esteem!"

When he heard his mistress speak, he knew that she was aware of the king's presence. He gave thanks to God and knew they would escape without harm: "Oh, Isolde, noble and honorable daughter of a king, several times have I sent for you in good faith. Since I am not permitted in your chamber, this is the only way I can speak with you. Lady, I now implore your mercy, and ask that you not forget this unhappy man who suffers pain and sorrow; and the fact that the king ever thought badly of us saddens me so much that there is nothing left for me to do but die. [. . . If only he] had been so wise as not to believe the liars who urged him to send me away! The traitors from Cornwall laugh and joke about it. Now I understand: they would not want anyone of his lineage around him. His marriage has caused me a great deal of pain. God! why is the king so foolish? I would let myself be hanged by the neck from a tree before I would be your lover! He does not even permit me to defend myself. Those traitors make him angry with me. He is wrong to believe them: they have deceived him, and he doesn't see that! When Morholt came here, I noticed that they never opened their mouths; nor was there a single one of them who dared take up arms. My uncle was very worried then. He would rather have been dead than alive. But I armed myself in order to defend his honor, I did battle, and I won. My uncle should not have believed what his informers say. I am enraged by it! Does he think himself guiltless in this? Surely he cannot fail to see it. Lady, in the name of God, the son of the Virgin Mary, tell him to have a fire made, and I will enter it; if even a single hair is singed on the hair-shirt I will be wearing, then let him have me burned to death; for I know that there is no one at court who will dare do battle with me. Lady, in your generosity, will you not take pity on me? Lady, I implore your mercy. Intercede for me with the king. When I came here to him from across the sea, [I came as a nobleman, and] I want to go back as a nobleman."

"Sir, it is wrong of you to ask me to speak to him about you and to urge him to pardon you. I am not ready to die! He suspects you of being my lover, and you expect me to speak on your behalf? That would be far too rash! I will not do it, Tristan, and you should not ask me to. I am all alone in this land. Because of me he has denied you admission to his chambers. It would be foolish of me to speak to him now about you. Indeed I will not say a word about it; but I will tell you this: I want you to know that if he did pardon you, I would be very happy. But if he knew of this meeting, Tristan, there is no way I could escape death. I am leaving, but I will not rest easy. I am afraid someone may have seen you come here. If the king heard that we met here, it would surprise no one if he had me burned alive. I must leave because I am afraid; I have stayed here too long."

Isolde turned away, and he called her back: "Lady, in the name of God, who to save the world took human form in the Virgin, have compassion and advise me! I know that you don't dare stay longer, but I have no one to turn to except you. I know the king hates me. My equipment has been confiscated. Have it returned to me, and I will flee, for I don't dare stay. I know my worth, and I know that there is no court in the world where I would not be welcomed. And I swear, Isolde, that before the year is up, my uncle will dearly regret having suspected that I ever had anything that belonged to him. I am telling you the truth. Isolde, in God's name, think of me and settle my debt to my host."

"Tristan, I am astonished at what you are asking! You are trying to ruin me. Those are not the words of a loyal friend. You know my husband's suspicions, however unjustified they may be. In the name of God, who created heaven and earth and us, too, if Mark heard that I had settled your debt, he would take that as proof of our guilt. I don't dare do that! And you can be assured that I am not refusing out of avarice."

Then Isolde turned and left, and Tristan, weeping, gave a gesture of farewell. Leaning against a stone, Tristan lamented all alone: "Oh, God! By St. Ebrulfus, I never thought I would suffer such a loss and have to flee in such poverty. I will not even have arms or a horse, nor any companions except Governal. O, God, no one respects a poor man! When I am in another country, if I hear a knight speak of war, I will have to hold my tongue: an unarmed man has no right to speak of battle. I will have to tolerate what fate has brought me, and it has done me an injustice. Good uncle, whoever suspected my conduct with your wife did not know me well! I had no desire to commit such folly."

[. . .] The king, who was up in the tree, had witnessed the meeting and heard the conversation. He was so overcome by pity that nothing could keep him from crying. His sorrow was great, and he hated the dwarf of Tintagel. "Alas," cried the king, "now I see that the dwarf deceived me! He has made me climb this tree and has shamed me completely. He made me believe a lie about my nephew, and for what he did I will have him hanged! He stirred up my anger and made me hate my own wife. I was a fool to believe him. He will pay for it. If I get my hands on him, I will have him burned to death! He will meet a worse fate at my hands than that inflicted on Segoncin, whom Constantine had castrated when he found him with his wife. He had crowned her in Rome, and she was served by many. He loved and honored her, but later he mistreated her and eventually regretted it."

Tristan had left earlier. The king came down from the tree. He told himself that he now believed his wife and doubted the barons, for they had made him believe something he knew to be untrue, something now proved false. With his sword he would give the dwarf what he deserved. Never again would he speak evil words! And never again would Mark suspect Tristan's intentions concerning Isolde. They could meet at will in the chamber. "Now

I know the truth. If the rumors were true, this meeting would not have ended this way. They had enough time here; if they were lovers, I would have seen them kiss each other. But I heard them lamenting and know they are innocent. Why did I believe such outrageous rumors? I regret it now and repent: he is a fool who believes what everyone says. I should have established the truth about the two before accepting this foolish notion. This evening was a fortunate one for them: listening to them taught me never again to be suspicious of them. Tomorrow morning Tristan will be reconciled with me, and he will have permission to be in my chamber whenever he wishes. And he will not have to flee tomorrow, as he planned."

The hunchback dwarf Frocin was outdoors, looking up at Orion and Venus. He knew the course of the stars and observed the planets. He knew the future, and when a baby was born he could foretell its entire life. The malicious dwarf Frocin had taken great pains to deceive the king, who one day would kill him. Observing the ascent of the stars, he bristled with rage, for he knew that the king was threatening him and would not give up until he had killed him. The dwarf reddened, then turned pale. He fled as quickly as he could to Wales. The king looked everywhere for the dwarf but, to his great sorrow, could not find him.   [338]

Isolde came into her room. Brangain saw that she was pale and knew that she had heard something distressing; she asked her what it was. Isolde answered: "My dear lady, I have good reason to be pensive and sad. Brangain, I will not lie to you: I don't know who wants to betray us, but King Mark was in the tree, near the marble stone. I saw his shadow in the fountain. God gave me the presence of mind to speak first. I said not a word about what brought me there, I assure you: just sighs and laments. I blamed Tristan for sending for me, and he begged me to reconcile him with his lord, who had false suspicions about us. I told him that his request was foolish, that I would never meet him again and that I would not speak to the king. I don't think I need to tell you more. There were many laments. The king never saw or suspected the truth, and I escaped from the trap."

Brangain rejoiced at these words: "Isolde, my lady, God had mercy on us when he let you conclude the conversation without going further, for the king saw nothing that could not be interpreted in your favor. God has performed a great miracle for you. He is our great Father, and He does not want harm to come to those who are good and true."

Tristan, too, told Governal everything that had happened. When he finished the story, he thanked God that he and Isolde had not done more.

The king, unable to find his dwarf (God! that does not bode well for Tristan!), returned to his chamber. Isolde saw him and said fearfully: "Sir where have you been? What makes you come here alone?"

"My queen, I have come to speak with you and to ask you a question. Do not conceal anything from me, for I want to know the truth."

"Sir, I have never lied to you. May I be struck dead if a single word of what I say is not true."

"My lady, have you seen my nephew?"

"Sir, I am telling you the truth. You will not believe it, but I will tell you the truth, without deceit. I saw him and spoke with him. I was under the pine tree with your nephew. Go ahead and kill me, king, if you wish. Yes, I saw him. It is a great pity that you think I am Tristan's mistress, and that grieves me so much that I don't care if you kill me. But have mercy on me this time! I told you the truth; if you do not believe me, but instead believe a foolish lie, my faith will protect me. Tristan, your nephew, asked me to meet him under the pine in the garden. He said nothing else, but I could not treat him cruelly: it is because of him that I am your queen. Certainly I would willingly show him proper respect, were it not for those who tell you lies. Sir you are my husband, and he is your nephew; it is for your sake that I have loved him. But those who are evil and jealous, who want him gone from the court, make you believe lies. So Tristan is going away. May God cover them with shame! I spoke with your nephew yesterday evening. He desperately implored me to reconcile him with you, sir. I told him to leave and never to send for me again; for I would never again come to meet him, and I would not intercede for him. I assure you that nothing else happened. Kill me if you wish, but it would be unjust. Tristan is going away because of this dissension; I know he is leaving the country. He wanted me to pay for his lodging; I did not want to do that or to talk with him any longer. Sir, now I have told you the whole truth. If I have lied, you can cut off my head. Sir, I would gladly have paid his debt if I had dared, but because of your slanderous entourage I did not even want to slip four besants into his purse. He is going away poor; may God care for him! You are wrong to make him flee. Wherever he goes, God will be his true friend!"

The king knew she was telling the truth, for he had overheard the conversation. He embraced her and kissed her repeatedly. She wept, and he comforted her. Never again would he mistrust them because of what a slanderer said; and they could come and go at will. What was Tristan's would be his, and what was his would belong to Tristan. Never again would he believe Cornishmen. Then the king told the queen how the evil dwarf Frocin had informed him of the meeting, and how he had climbed the tree to spy on them.

"What! You were in the tree, sir?"

"Yes, my lady. I heard every word that was said. When I heard Tristan talk about the battle that he fought for me, I felt great pity for him. I almost fell out of the tree! And when I heard you recount his suffering at sea, because of the dragon's wound from which you cured him, and the care you took of him; and when he asked you to pay his debts—you did not wish to do so, and neither of you approached the other—I felt great pity up there in the tree. I smiled to myself, but did nothing else."

"Sir, I am very happy. Now you know that we had enough time. If we were lovers, you would have seen evidence of it. But you didn't see him approach me or make any advances or kiss me. That proves that he does not love me improperly. Sir, if you had not seen it for yourself, you would surely not believe it."

"That is true," replied the king. "Brangain, go to my nephew's lodging and bring him to me; and if he hesitates or does not want to come with you, tell him I command it."

Brangain told him: "Sir, he hates me! God knows he is wrong! He says that it is my fault that he has quarreled with you. He desperately wants to see me dead. I will go; and perhaps, because of you, he will not harm me. Sir, for God's sake, reconcile him with me when he arrives!"

Listen to the cunning woman! She was being deceitful and lying when she complained about Tristan's hatred. "King, I am going for him," said Brangain. "Reconcile us; that will be a noble act."

The king answered: "I will do my best. Go now and bring him back."

Isolde smiled at this, and the king too. Brangain left at once. Tristan was waiting by the wall and had heard them talk with the king. He seized Brangain by the arm, embraced her, and gave thanks to God. From now on he could be with Isolde whenever he wished.

Brangain told Tristan: "Sir, there in his chambers the king spoke at length about you and your dear lady. He has pardoned you, and now he hates those who oppose you. He asked me to come to you; I told him you were angry with me. Pretend that I had to beg you to come with me and that you were reluctant. If the king intercedes for me, pretend to be angry."

Tristan embraced and kissed her. He was happy because now he would again be able to live as he wished. They entered the room that was decorated with murals. The king and Isolde were there, and when Tristan entered, the king said: "Nephew, come in! Forgive Brangain, and I will forgive you."

"Uncle, good sir, listen to me. You are taking this too lightly, for you have brought this upon me, and my heart is breaking! What an injustice! If we were guilty, I should be damned and disgraced. But God knows, we never had any sinful thoughts. And you should know that anyone who makes you believe such a thing surely hates you. From now on I advise you not to be angry with the queen or with me, your own relative."

"I will not, dear nephew, I assure you."

Tristan was reconciled with the king. Mark gave him permission to be in the royal chamber, and now he was happy. Tristan was free to come and go at will, and the king saw no harm in it.   [572]

God! Who could keep love secret for any period of time? For love cannot be hidden. Often one lover nods to the other, or they meet to speak together, in private or in public. They cannot easily postpone their happiness, and they cannot resist frequent trysts.

There were at the court three barons—never have you seen such evil men!—who had sworn that, if the king did not banish his nephew, they would no longer tolerate it; rather, they would withdraw to their castles and make war on Mark. The other day, in a garden, under a tree, they had seen the fair Isolde with Tristan in a compromising position; and several times they had seen them lying naked in King Mark's bed, for whenever Mark went into the forest, Tristan would say: "Sir, I'm leaving." But then he would stay behind, enter Isolde's chamber, and remain a long time with her.

"We will tell him ourselves. Let's go to the king and talk to him. Whatever he may think of us, we want him to banish his nephew." Together they decided on this course. They took the king aside and spoke to him. "Sir," they said, "there is trouble. Your nephew and Isolde love each other. It is obvious to anyone who cares to look, and we will no longer tolerate it!"

The king heard them, sighed, and bowed his head. He paced back and forth, not knowing what to say.

"King," said the three barons, "we will not permit this any longer, for we know for a fact that you are fully aware of their crime and that you condone it. What are you going to do about it? Think about it carefully. If you do not send your nephew away permanently, we will no longer remain loyal to you and will never leave you in peace. We will also persuade others to leave your court, for we cannot tolerate this any more. We have now offered you a choice; tell us your decision."

"Sirs, you are my faithful servants. May God help me, I am shocked that my nephew has tried to shame me; he certainly has a strange way of serving me! Please advise me. That is your duty, and I do not want to lose your services. You know that I am not proud!"

"Sir, send for the dwarf who foretells the future; he is versed in many arts. Let his advice be heard. Send for him, and let this matter be settled."

The hunchback dwarf—may he be cursed!—came quickly. One of the barons embraced him, and the king explained his dilemma to him. Alas! Listen to the deceitful and evil advice the dwarf Frocin gave the king! May all such diviners be damned! Who could even imagine such villainy as the cursed dwarf conceived? "Order your nephew to go tomorrow to Arthur, at the fortified city of Carlisle. Have him take Arthur a message, closed and sealed with wax. King, Tristan sleeps near your bed. I know he will want to speak with Isolde tonight, before he has to leave. King, leave the room early during the night. I swear by God and the Church of Rome, if Tristan is her lover, he will come to speak with her. And if he does so without my knowing it or without you and all your men seeing him, then kill me. Otherwise their guilt will be obvious. King, let me take care of things and do what is necessary, and do not tell him of his mission until bedtime."

The king answered: "Friend, it shall be done." Then they separated, and each one went his own way.

The dwarf was crafty, and he did a terrible thing. First he went to a bakery and bought four deniers' worth of flour, which he hid in his apron. Who could have imagined such treachery! That night, when the king had eaten and the others had gone to bed, Tristan went into the king's chamber. "Good nephew," said Mark, "I want you to do me a service. Ride to King Arthur, at Carlisle, and deliver this letter to him. Nephew, give him my greetings, but stay only one day with him."

Tristan heard the message and told the king that he would deliver it: "Sir, I will leave early tomorrow—yes, before the night is through."

Tristan was very distressed. His bed was a lance's length away from the king's. Tristan had a foolish plan: he decided that he would speak to the queen, if he could, after the king was asleep. God! What a shame that he was so foolhardy!

The dwarf was in the room that night. Here is what he did during the night: he sprinkled flour between the two beds, so that footprints would be visible if one of the lovers joined the other that night. The flour would preserve the form of the prints. Tristan saw the dwarf busily spreading the flour. He wondered what was happening, for this was most unusual behavior. Then he thought: "Perhaps he is spreading flour on the floor in order to see our tracks if one of us should go to the other. I'd have to be a fool to take that chance now; he'll certainly see if I go to her."

The day before, in the forest, Tristan had been wounded in the leg by a large boar, and the wound was very painful and had bled heavily. Unfortunately it was unbandaged. Tristan, of course, was not sleeping. The king arose at midnight and left the room, and the hunchback dwarf left with him. It was dark in the room; there was no lit candle or lamp. Tristan stood up. God! he would regret this! Listen: he put his feet together, estimated the distance, jumped, and fell onto the king's bed. His wound opened, and the blood flowing from it stained the sheets. Although the wound was bleeding, he did not feel it, for he thought only of his pleasure. And the blood accumulated in several places.

The dwarf was outside. By the light of the moon he clearly saw the two lovers lying together. He trembled with joy and told the king: "If you can't catch them together now, you can have me hanged!"

The three evil barons, who had conceived this plot, were there. The king came back to the room. Tristan heard him coming; he got up, frightened, and quickly jumped back into his bed. But when he jumped, the blood (alas!) dripped from his wound into the flour. Oh, God! What a pity that the queen did not remove the bedsheets; if she had, nothing could have been proved against them. If she had thought of that, she could have protected her honor.

God performed a great miracle, which saved their life according to his will. The king came back to the room; the dwarf, holding the candle, came with him. Tristan pretended to be asleep and snored loudly. He was alone in the room, except for Perinis, sleeping soundly at his feet, and the queen in her bed. The warm blood could be seen in the flour. The king noticed the blood on the bed: the white sheets were red, and blood from Tristan's leap was visible on the floor.

The king threatened Tristan. The three barons, who were now in the room, angrily seized Tristan in his bed. They hated him because they were jealous of his great prowess, and they hated the queen too. They vilified and threatened her; they would not fail to see justice done. They saw Tristan's bleeding leg. "This is conclusive evidence; your guilt is proved," said the king. "Your denials are worthless. Tristan, tomorrow you will be put to death."

Tristan cried out: "Sir, have mercy! In the name of God, who was crucified, sir, take pity on us!"

The barons said: "Sir, avenge yourself!"

"Good uncle, I do not care about myself; I know I am doomed. If it were not for fear of angering you, this condemnation would be paid dearly. Never would it have occurred to them to lay a hand on me. But I bear you no ill will. Now, for better or for worse, do what you will with me. I am ready to suffer punishment at your hands. But sir, in God's name, take pity on the queen!" Tristan bowed to him and added: "And anyone at your court who accuses me of being the queen's lover should have to face me immediately in armed combat."

The three barons had Tristan and the queen seized and bound: hatred had triumphed. If Tristan had known that he would not have the opportunity to defend himself, he would have let himself be torn limb from limb before allowing either of them to be bound. But his faith in God was so strong that he was convinced that if he were permitted to defend himself, no one would dare take up arms against him; he knew he could defend himself well on the battlefield. For that reason he did not want to take any action in the king's presence; but if he had known how this had come about and what was still to come, he would have killed all three of them, and the king could not have saved them. Oh, God! Why did he not kill them? Justice would have been better served.   [826]

News spread quickly through the city that Tristan and the queen Isolde had been found together and that the king wanted to have them put to death. The people wept and said to one another: "Alas, we have good reason to weep! Oh, Tristan, you are such a worthy knight. What a pity that these villains betrayed and trapped you. Oh, good and honored queen, what land will ever have a princess who is your equal? Ah, dwarf, this is the result of your divination! May anyone who has an opportunity to kill the dwarf be damned if he does not do so! Oh, Tristan, dear friend, we will mourn bitterly when you are put to death. Alas, what grief! When Morholt came to this land and demanded our children, our barons remained silent, for not one of them was courageous enough to oppose him. You undertook the battle for us, the people of Cornwall, and you killed Morholt. He wounded you with a lance, sir, and you nearly died. We should not allow you to be put to death now."

The noise and confusion increased, and people came running to the palace. The king was furious; there was no baron so strong or courageous that he dared urge the king to pardon this crime. The night passed, and day broke. The king gave orders for thorny bushes to be gathered and a trench to be dug. Then he commanded that vine-shoots be found and piled up with haw-thorns and blackthorns that had been pulled up by the roots. It was already early morning. A proclamation that was announced throughout the land sum-moned everyone to court. People came as quickly as they could; the people of Cornwall were all gathered there. There was great noise and commotion, and everyone grieved—except the dwarf of Tintagel.

The king announced that he intended to have his nephew and wife burned to death. All his subjects cried: "King, it would be a terrible injustice to put them to death without trying them first. Sir, have mercy!"

The king angrily responded: "Even if I should be disowned by God, the Creator of the world and everything in it, I am determined to have them burned, regardless of what anyone says. Now let all of my orders be carried out."

He commanded that the fire be lit and that his nephew be brought there: he wanted to burn him first. They went to get him, and the king waited. They led him back—God, this is too disgraceful! He wept, but to no avail; they took him away shamefully. Isolde wept, almost beside herself with despair: "Tristan," she said, "what a shame for you to be bound! I would willingly die if you were spared, dear friend; you would be able to avenge us."

Now hear how great is God's pity; He does not want a sinner to die. He heard the poor people's cries and pleas for the condemned couple. On the road they were taking there stood a chapel, built on the edge of a cliff, beside the sea, facing north. The part of the chapel called the chancel was on the edge of the rock; there was nothing beyond, except the cliff. The hill was of slaty stone. If a squirrel had jumped from it, it would certainly have been killed. In the apse was a purple window, the work of a pious man.

Tristan spoke to his guards: "Lords, here is a chapel; in God's name, let me go in. My life is about to end; I will pray to God that He have mercy on me, for I have sinned greatly. Lords, there is only this one door, and I see that each of you has a sword. It is obvious that I cannot escape, for I have to come out this way. And after I pray to God, I will return to you immediately."

They said to each other: "We can surely permit him to go in."

They untied him, and he entered. Tristan wasted no time, but went past the altar and came to the window. He opened it and jumped out. Jumping was better than being burned alive in public! Now, halfway down, a large flat rock extended out from the cliff, and Tristan landed nimbly on it. The wind caught in his clothes and broke his fall. In Cornwall the stone is still called "Tristan's Leap."

The chapel was filled with people. Tristan jumped down and fell to his knees in the soft sand. The guards were waiting in front of the church, but in vain: Tristan was gone, and God had generously granted him mercy. He ran away along the shore. He could hear the fire crackling, and he had no desire to go back; he ran as fast as he could.

But now listen to what Tristan's master Governal did. Armed, he rode out of the city. He knew that if he were caught, he would be burned in Tristan's place; fear made him run away. He did Tristan a great service by not leaving his sword behind; he picked it up where it lay and brought it with him, along with his own. Tristan saw his teacher and recognized him; he called to him, and Governal approached.

Tristan exclaimed joyfully: "Master, God had mercy on me! I escaped, and now here I am. But alas! What good is that? Since I do not have Isolde, nothing matters to me. I am so miserable! Why was I not killed when I jumped? I will surely regret having survived! I escaped—but, Isolde, they are going to burn you! Surely there was no reason for me to escape. They will burn Isolde because of me, and I will then die because of her!"

Governal said: "Good sir, in God's name, take comfort; don't despair. Here is a thicket surrounded by a trench. Sir, let's conceal ourselves in there. Many people pass here, so we should be able to hear news of Isolde. And if they burn her, then take to your saddle immediately to avenge her! You will have ample help. Never, in the name of Jesus, the son of Mary, will I rest until the three villainous barons who destroyed your lady Isolde have met their deaths. And if you should be killed, sir, before vengeance is taken, I could never be happy again!"

Tristan answered: "You are making too much of this, good master, for I do not even have a sword."

"Yes, you do, for I brought it."

Tristan said: "That pleases me, master, and now I fear nothing, except God."

"I also have something else that you will find most useful: a strong and light hauberk. You will surely need it."

"Give it to me," said Tristan. "By God, if I can get there before my lady is thrown into the flames, I would rather be torn limb from limb than fail to kill her captors."

Governal said: "Do not hurry. God will give you a better way to take vengeance. Then you will not have the obstacles you now face. I see nothing you can do now, for the king is angry with you, and he controls all the inhabitants of the city. He swore that he would hang anyone who passed up a chance to capture you. Everyone is more concerned about himself than about you: if you were accused, there are many who would like to save you but would be afraid even to consider it."

Tristan wept bitterly. If his master had not urged him not to go, he would have returned in spite of all the people of Tintagel, without fear for his life.

A messenger ran into Isolde's room and told her not to cry, for her friend had escaped. "Thanks be to God," she said; "now I do not care if they kill me, or whether I am bound or free."

The king, at the urging of the three barons, had her bound, and she was tied so tightly that her wrists were bleeding. She said: "If I felt pity for myself, now that my friend—thank God!—has escaped from his enemies, I would not be deserving of respect. I know that the evil dwarf and the jealous barons, who want to have me killed, will some day get what they deserve. May they be damned!"

The news came to Mark that his nephew, whom he was to burn, had escaped through the chapel. His face darkened with rage; he could hardly control himself. He angrily commanded that Isolde be brought to him. She left her room, and the clamor increased in the street. When they saw that the queen's hands were shamefully bound, the people were shocked. You should have heard them grieving and imploring God's mercy: "Oh, noble and honorable queen, what grief has been spread throughout the land by those who are responsible for this scandal! And a very small purse would hold all the profit they have gained. May they be cruelly punished!"   [1082]

The queen was brought to the pyre. Dinas, the lord of Dinan, who loved Tristan dearly, fell at the king's feet. "Sir," he said, "listen to me. For a long time I have served you honestly and loyally; you will not find anyone in this kingdom, not even a poor orphan or an old woman, from whom I have profited because of my position as seneschal, a position I have held my whole life. Sir, have mercy on the queen! You want to have her burned without a trial; that is not honorable, since she has not confessed the crime. It will be a tragedy if you have her burned. Sir, Tristan has escaped. He knows the plains, the forests, the trails, and the fords, and he is to be feared. You are his uncle, he your nephew. He would not attack you directly, but if he captured or assaulted the barons, your land would be ravaged. Sir, I can assure you: if a king who ruled over seven countries killed or burned even one of my squires, all his kingdoms would be endangered before I would have fully settled accounts. Do you think Tristan will simply stand by and permit the death of such a noble woman, whom he brought here from a distant kingdom? No, there will be serious trouble. King, entrust her to me, in recognition of my long service to you."

The three who had arranged all this had fallen silent and left; they knew that Tristan was free and were afraid that he was lying in wait for them. The king took Dinas by the hand; angrily he swore by St. Thomas that he would not fail to see justice done and the queen thrown into the flames. Hearing that, Dinas was very sad, because he did not want her to die. He rose, his head bowed: "King, I am going back to Dinan. In the name of God, who created Adam, I would not watch her being burned for all the wealth of all the richest men who have lived since the glory of Rome." Then he mounted his horse and turned away, sad and bereaved, with his head bowed.

Isolde was led to the fire. She was surrounded by people who screamed, cried, and cursed the traitors who had advised the king. Tears flowed down her face. She was dressed in a tunic of dark silk, finely stitched in gold. Her hair reached to her feet and was held by a golden net. One would have to have a very hard heart to see her and not feel pity for her. Her arms were tied very tightly.

There was a leper named Ivain, from Lantyan, and he was terribly deformed. He had come to witness the punishment. With him were a hundred of his companions, with their crutches and staffs. Never have you seen people so ugly, tumorous, and deformed! Each one carried a rattle to warn people of his approach. Ivain cried out to the king in a shrill voice: "Sir, you want to see justice done and have your wife burned! That is cruel punishment, of course, but it would not last long. The fire would quickly consume her, and the wind would scatter her ashes. The fire would die out soon, and the punishment would not outlast the embers. But if you will take my advice, you can punish her in such a way that she will live on in disgrace and will wish to be dead, and everyone who hears about that will respect you all the more. King, would you like to do that?"

The king heard him and answered: "If you tell me how she can live and be dishonored, I assure you I will be grateful to you, and I will reward you if you wish. In God's name, he who can select the worst and most painful punishment of all will have my eternal gratitude."

Ivain answered: "I will tell you my idea. Just look, I have a hundred companions here. Give Isolde to us, and she will be our common property. No woman ever had a worse fate. Sir, our desire is so strong that no woman in the world could bear a whole day with us. And see how our ragged clothes stick to our bodies? With you she was accustomed to luxury: furs, festivities, fine wines, and spacious marble chambers. If you give her to us lepers, when she sees our 'court,' when she lives in our small huts and eats out of our dishes and has to sleep with us, and when, instead of your fine food, she has only some of the scraps that are given to us, then she will despair and will prefer death to such a life! That viper Isolde will then know how terrible her actions were, and she will wish she had been burned."

The king listened to him and then stood there a long time without moving. He understood what Ivain had said. Then he ran to Isolde and took her by the hand. She cried: "Sir, have mercy! Don't give me to them! Have me burned here!"

The king gave her to Ivain, and he took her. There were fully a hundred lepers, and they all crowded around her. Everyone who heard their cries and wails was filled with pity. But if others were sad, Ivain was delighted! He immediately led her away down the hill. All the lepers, on their crutches, were heading directly toward the place where Tristan was lying in wait.

Governal cried loudly: "My son, what will you do? There is your lady!"

"God," said Tristan, "what good fortune! Oh, beautiful Isolde, you who were to die for me, as I for you! Your captors can be sure that if they do not release you immediately, I will make them regret it." He spurred his horse and rode out of the thicket. He cried at the top of his voice: "Ivain, that's far enough. Let her go, or I will cut off your head with this sword!"

Ivain, taking off his cloak, cried loudly: "Attack with your crutches! Show me who is on my side!"

You should have seen the lepers panting and tearing off their cloaks! They all brandished their crutches, threatening and cursing Tristan. He had no desire to injure them, but Governal, attracted by the shouts, came running with a green limb in his hand and struck Ivain, who was holding Isolde. Ivain started bleeding heavily. Tristan's master served him well; he recovered Isolde. Storytellers say that they drowned Ivain, but they are wrong; they do not know the true story, and Béroul remembers it better than they. Tristan was too valiant and courtly to kill lepers!

Tristan went away with the queen. They left the plain and, along with Governal, passed through the woods. Isolde was very happy. They were in the forest of Morrois, and that night they slept on a hill. Now Tristan was as safe as he would have been in a fortified castle.   [1278]

Tristan was an excellent archer, skilled with the bow. Governal had taken one from a forester, and he had brought two feathered and barbed arrows. Tristan took the bow and set out through the woods. He saw a buck, drew his bow, and shot, striking the animal directly in the right side. It cried out, leapt up in the air, and fell back to the ground. Tristan brought it back with him.

He prepared his shelter, using his sword to cut branches and making a bower. Isolde spread leaves around thickly; Tristan and the queen settled in it. Governal, who was a skilled cook, made a fire of dry wood. They were certainly well equipped for cooking: they had no milk or salt in their lodging! The queen was exhausted from the fear she had experienced. She became drowsy and wanted to sleep, she wanted to go to sleep beside her lover. Thus they lived deep in the forest; they remained in the wilderness for a long time.

Now hear how the dwarf served the king! The dwarf knew a secret about the king, and no one else knew it. He foolishly revealed it, and as a result the king cut off his head. The dwarf was drunk one day, and the barons asked him why he and the king spoke together so often in private, and what they said. "I have always loyally concealed one of his secrets. I see that you want to know it, but I don't want to betray my word. I will take the three of you to the ford called the Gué Aventuros. There is a hawthorn there, with a hollowed-out trench underneath the roots. If I put my head in there, you can overhear me from outside, and what I say will be about the secret that only I share with the king."

The barons followed the dwarf to the hawthorn. The dwarf was short, but he had a large head, so they enlarged the hole and then stuck his head and neck into it. "Now listen, lords! Hawthorn, I am talking to you, and not to any man: Mark has ears like a horse!" They heard the dwarf.

It happened that, one day after dinner, King Mark was talking with his barons, and in his hand he had a bowl of laburnum. The three to whom the dwarf had told the secret came to the king and said to him: "King, we know your secret."

The king laughed and said: "It is the fault of that diviner that I have horse's ears; believe me, this will be the end of him!" He drew his sword and cut off the dwarf's head. That pleased many people who hated the dwarf Frocin for what he had done to Tristan and the queen.

You have heard how Tristan had jumped down on the rocky ledge, and how Governal had fled on horseback, because he feared he would be burned if Mark captured him. Now the lovers were together in the forest, and Tristan fed them with venison. They remained in the woods, but every morning they left the place where they had spent the night. One day, by chance, they came to the hermitage of Brother Ogrin. They were leading a hard and painful life, but their love was so strong and true that both of them were oblivious to their suffering.

The hermit recognized Tristan and, leaning on his staff, addressed him: "Sir Tristan, throughout Cornwall it has been sworn that whoever delivers you to the king will receive a reward of one hundred marks. There is not a baron in the land who has not pledged to turn you over to him dead or alive." Then Ogrin told him kindly: "By my faith, Tristan, whoever repents of his sin through faith and confession will be pardoned by God."

Tristan answered him: "Sir, by faith, you do not know why she loves me deeply. If she loves me, it is because of the potion. I cannot leave her, nor can she leave me, I tell you truly."

Ogrin said: "And what comfort could be given to a dead man? For any man is as good as dead who lives for a long time in sin and does not repent. Absolution cannot be given to a man who does not repent." The hermit Ogrin preached to them at length and urged them to repent. He explained to them the prophecies of scripture and spoke often of their isolation. He said fervently to Tristan: "What will you do? Think about it carefully!"

"Sir, I love Isolde so much that I cannot sleep! My mind is made up. I would rather be a beggar with her and live on grasses and acorns than to have the kingdom of King Otrant. There is no point in even talking about leaving her, because I cannot do it."

Isolde, at Ogrin's feet, was weeping. The color drained from her face, and she repeatedly implored him to grant them mercy: "Sir, by omnipotent God, we love each other only through the power of a potion we drank. That was our tragedy, and that is why the king drove us away."

The hermit answered: "May God, Creator of the world, lead you to repent."

For their sake Ogrin gave up the hermit's life that night, and the couple spent the night at the hermitage. In the morning they left. Tristan stayed in the woods and avoided the open fields. They lacked for bread, and life was hard. He managed to kill enough stags, does, and bucks to keep them alive. Wherever they stopped, they made a fire and cooked, and they never stayed more than a single night in the same place.

The king had a warrant issued for Tristan: in every corner of Cornwall the terrible news is spread that whoever finds Tristan must turn him in.

[1436]

Anyone who would now like to hear a story that shows the benefits of training an animal should listen to me well. You will hear about Tristan's good hunting dog. No king or count ever had one like it. He was fast and alert; he was beautiful and he ran well, and his name was Husdent. He was leashed, and he kept watch from the dungeon. He was unhappy because he missed his master, and he refused all food. He whined and pawed the ground, tears in his eyes. What pity people felt for the dog! They all said: "If he were mine, I would let him go; it would be a shame if he went mad. Oh, Husdent, there will never be another hunting dog who grieves so much for his master. No animal ever loved anyone so much. Solomon correctly said that his dog was his best friend. You are proof of that, because you have refused to eat since your master was captured. King, release the dog!"

The king, thinking the dog was going mad because he missed his master, said to himself: "This dog is most discerning, for in all of Cornwall I do not think that in our time we could find a knight the equal of Tristan."

The three barons of Cornwall urged the king: "Sir, unleash Husdent. Then we will see whether he is grieving for his master; for if he is mad, he will bite somebody or something as soon as he is free, and his tongue will hang out of his mouth." The king called a squire to have Husdent released. Everyone climbed up on benches and stools for fear of the dog. Everyone said: "Husdent is mad!" But he paid no attention to them. As soon as he was released, he ran past them without hesitation; he raced out the door and ran to the house where he used to meet Tristan.

The king and the others watched him. The dog barked and whined and appeared to be very sad.

Then he picked up his master's trail, and he followed every step that Tristan had taken when he was captured and was to be burned. Everyone urged the dog on. Husdent entered the room where Tristan had been betrayed and arrested; he bounded out of the room, barking, and ran toward the chapel, with the people close behind. Now that he was finally free, he did not stop until he reached the church built on the cliff. The faithful Husdent ran into the chapel without pausing; he jumped onto the altar and, not seeing his master there, jumped out the window. He fell down the cliff and injured his leg. He sniffed the ground and barked. At the edge of the woods where Tristan had taken refuge Husdent paused briefly, then plunged into the forest. Everyone who saw him felt pity for him. The knights said to the king: "Let's stop following the dog. We might not be able to get back easily from where he is leading us."

They left the dog and turned back. Husdent found a trail, and the sound of the happy dog barking filled the woods. Tristan was deep in the forest, with the queen and Governal. They heard the sound; Tristan listened and said: "I am sure that is Husdent I hear." They were frightened. Tristan jumped up and grabbed his bow, and they hid in a thicket. They were afraid of the king and thought he might be with the dog. Husdent, following the trail, wasted no time. When he saw Tristan and recognized him, he raised his head and wagged his tail. Anyone who had seen him weep with joy would have said that no one had ever witnessed such happiness.

Husdent ran to the blonde Isolde, and then to Governal. He was happy to see all of them—even the horse. Tristan felt pity for the dog. "Oh, God," he said, "it is unfortunate that the dog followed us. People in hiding have no need for a dog that will not remain silent in the forest. We have to stay in the woods, hated by the king. Lady, Mark has people searching for us on the plains, in the forest, everywhere! If he found us and captured us, he would have us burned or hanged. We don't need a dog. We can be sure that if Husdent stays with us, he will bring us nothing but trouble. It is better to kill him than to let ourselves be captured because of his barking. I regret that such a noble animal came here only to die; it was his noble nature that made him do it. But what else can I do? It grieves me that I have to kill him. Help me make the decision; we have to protect ourselves!"

Isolde told him: "Sir, take pity on him! A dog barks while hunting as much from training as from instinct. After Arthur became king, I heard of a Welsh forester who had trained his hunting dog so that when he wounded a stag with an arrow, the dog would follow the stag anywhere without barking or making any sound. Tristan, it would be wonderful if we could train Husdent not to bark while hunting."

Tristan stood and listened to her. He took pity on the animal; he thought a moment and then said: "If I could train Husdent not to bark, he would be of great value to us, and I will try to do it before the week is out. I don't want to kill him; but I am afraid of his barking, because some day when I am with you or Governal, his barking might cause us to be captured. So I will do my best to train him to hunt without barking."

Tristan went hunting in the forest. He was a skilled hunter, and he shot a buck. Blood flowed from its wound; the dog barked, and the wounded buck fled. The barking of the excited dog echoed through the forest. Tristan struck him violently. Husdent stopped by his master's side, ceased barking and abandoned the chase. He looked up at Tristan, not knowing what to do. Tristan forced the dog forward, using a stick to clear the path. Husdent wanted to bark again, but Tristan continued to train him. Before the month was up, the dog was so well trained that he followed trails without a sound. Whether on snow, on grass, or on ice, he never abandoned his prey, however fleet or agile it might be.

Now the dog was a great help to them, and he served them well. If he caught a deer or buck in the woods, he would hide it carefully, covering it with branches. And if he caught it in the open, as he often did, he would throw grass over it. He would then return to his master and lead him to the place where he had killed the deer. Indeed dogs are very useful animals!

Tristan remained in the forest for a long time, and he suffered greatly. He did not dare remain long in one place. He knew that the king's men were searching for him and that Mark had ordered anyone who found him to capture him. They lacked for food: they lived on meat and ate nothing else. Is it any surprise that they became pale and thin? Their clothes, torn by branches, became ragged. For a long time they fled through Morrois. Each of them suffered equally, but because they were together, neither was aware of pain. The fair Isolde greatly feared that Tristan would repent because of her; and conversely, Tristan worried that Isolde, disgraced on his account, would repent of her irresponsible actions.   [1655]

Listen now to what happened to one of the three whom God has cursed, and through whom the lovers were discovered. He was a powerful man who was highly respected. He loved to hunt with dogs. The people of Cornwall were so afraid of the forest of Morrois that none of them dared enter it. They had good reason to be afraid, for if Tristan could capture them, he would hang them on trees. They were right to avoid the forest!

One day Governal was alone with his horse, beside a stream that flowed out of a little spring. He had unsaddled his horse, and it was grazing on the tender grass. Tristan was lying in his hut, with his arms tightly around the queen, for whom he had suffered such hardship and torment; they were both asleep. Governal was hidden, and by chance he heard dogs that were pursuing a stag at full speed. They were the dogs of one of the three whose advice had incited the king's wrath against the queen. The dogs ran, and the stag fled. Governal followed a path and came to a heath; far behind him he saw the man whom his lord hated more than anything, and he was approaching alone, without a squire. He spurred and whipped his horse sharply, so that it sprang forward. The horse stumbled on a stone. Stopping beside a tree, Governal hid and waited for the baron, who was approaching rapidly but would be slow to flee! The wheel of fortune cannot be turned backward: he was not on his guard against the anger that he had inspired in Tristan. Governal, under the tree, saw him coming and waited resolutely. He told himself he would rather have his ashes scattered in the wind than pass up a chance for revenge, for it was because of this man and his actions that all of them nearly perished.

The dogs were following the fleeting stag, and the man came after them. Governal jumped out of hiding, and thinking of all the evil the man had done, he cut him to pieces with his sword. He took the head and rode away. The hunters, who had flushed out the frightened stag, were still pursuing it when they saw the headless body of their lord under the tree. They fled as quickly as they could. They were sure that this had been done by Tristan, the object of the king's proclamation.

Throughout Cornwall it was known that one of the three who had caused trouble between Tristan and the king had had his head cut off. All the people were afraid, and they avoided the forest, rarely hunting there any more. Anyone who did enter the forest to hunt feared that the valiant Tristan would find him; Tristan was feared on the plains and even more on the heath.

Tristan lay in his bower; the weather was hot, and the bower was covered with leaves. He was asleep and didn't know that the man who had nearly cost him his life had been killed: he would be happy when he learned the truth. Governal approached the hut, holding the dead man's head in his hand. He tied it to a forked limb by the hair. Tristan awoke, saw the head and jumped up, frightened. His master cried out: "Stay there; don't be alarmed! I killed him with this sword. You see that it is your enemy." Tristan was happy at what he heard: the man he feared most was dead.

Everyone in the country was so terrified of the forest that no one dared enter it. The lovers had the woods to themselves. While they were there, Tristan invented the Unfailing Bow. He set it up in the woods in such a way that it killed everything that came in contact with it. If a deer came through the woods and touched the branches where the bow was set up and drawn, the bow shot high if the animal touched it high, low if it touched it near the ground. Tristan rightly called it the Unfailing Bow, for it never failed to strike anything, low or high. It served them very well, and enabled them to eat a good many stags. They had to live on wild game in the forest, since they had no bread, and they did not dare show themselves outside the woods. This exile lasted a long time. Tristan provided well for them, and they had an abundance of venison.

It was a summer day, during the harvest season, soon after Pentecost. It was early morning, and the birds were greeting the dawn. Tristan, girding on his sword, left the hut alone to go to the Unfailing Bow. He went hunting through the woods. Before going, he was in great distress—did anyone else ever suffer so much? But because of their pleasure together both were oblivious to pain. Never, since they had come to the forest, had two people ever tasted such sorrow. Nor, according to the story that Béroul has read, did two people ever love each other so much or pay so dearly for their love.

The queen came to meet him. The heat was oppressive. Tristan kissed her and said: [". . ." She asked:] "Where have you been?"

"I have been hunting a stag, and I am tired. I chased it until I was exhausted. Now I want to sleep."

The bower was made of green branches, with foliage added here and there, and the floor was covered with leaves. Isolde lay down first. Then Tristan lay down, drew his sword, and placed it between them. Isolde was wearing a chemise—if she had been naked, tragedy would have befallen them that day!—and Tristan had his trousers on. The queen wore her emerald wedding ring, but her finger had become so thin that the ring would scarcely stay on.

Notice how they were lying: she had one arm under Tristan's head, and the other one lay over him, so that she was embracing him closely, and he also had his arms around her. Their love was not feigned! Their mouths were close together, but not touching. No breeze was blowing, and the leaves were motionless. A ray of sunshine fell on Isolde's face, which shone brightly. Thus the lovers were sleeping and were not expecting trouble. There were only the two of them, for Governal had ridden down into the woods to see the forester.

Now listen to what happened: they had a narrow escape! A forester had found the bowers where they had stayed, and now he followed their trail until he came to the thicket where Tristan had made his shelter. He saw them sleeping and recognized them. He turned pale and left quickly, trembling with fear: he knew that Tristan, if he should wake up, would take no hostage except his head. It is no wonder that he fled! He ran out of the woods at full speed.   [1850]

Tristan and Isolde slept on: they barely escaped death! The place where they slept was two leagues away from where the king was holding court. The forester ran quickly to the king, because he had heard the proclamation about Tristan: whoever gave the king news of him would be handsomely rewarded. The forester knew it, and that was why he ran so swiftly.

King Mark was holding court with his barons in his palace; the hall was filled. The forester ran down the hill and rushed into the palace. Do you think he even paused before coming to the steps in the room? He ran up the stairs. The king saw the forester run in and called to him: "Are you in such a hurry because you have some news? You are running like a man pursuing an animal with his dogs. Are you here to lodge a complaint against someone at court? You give the impression of being in trouble and of having come a long way. If you have something to say, tell me. Did someone refuse to pay a debt or drive you out of my forest?"

"King, please listen to me! Throughout the land it has been announced that whoever finds your nephew should risk his life to capture him or to come and inform you. I have found him! But I am afraid of angering you. If I tell you, will you kill me? I will lead you to the place where he and the queen are sleeping. I saw them together, just now, and they were sound asleep. I was terrified when I saw them."

The king heard him. He sighed, then became agitated and angry. He asked the forester privately: "Where are they? Tell me."

"They are sleeping together in a hut in the forest of Morrois. Come quickly, and we will have our revenge. King, if you do not take cruel vengeance, you have no rightful claim on this land."

The king told him: "Leave here. If you value your life, tell no one what you know, whether he be a stranger or one of my men. Go to the red cross, at the fork in the road by the cemetery. Don't leave there; wait for me. I will give you all the gold and silver you want, I swear it."

The forester left the king, went directly to the cross and remained there. May God curse him, who so wanted to destroy Tristan! He would have been better off leaving, for he would die a terrible death, as you will hear later.

The king entered the room; he convened his retinue and forbade them to be so bold as to follow him. Everyone said: "King, are you serious about going somewhere alone? Kings never travel without an escort. What news have you heard? Don't act on the word of a spy!"

The king answered: "I know nothing. But a maiden asked me to come and speak with her and not to bring anyone with me. I will go by myself, on horseback, without any companion or squire; I will be completely alone."

They answered: "This worries us. Remember, Cato ordered his son to avoid deserted places."

He replied: "I know that, but let me do what I must do."

The king had his horse saddled; he girded on his sword, all the while lamenting the evil Tristan had done by abducting the beautiful, fair Isolde, with whom he had fled. If he found them, they would not be safe: he would not fail to kill them. The king was bent on destruction—what a pity! He left the city, saying to himself that he would rather be hanged than fail to avenge himself on those who had sinned so against him.

He came to the cross, where the man was waiting for him. The king told him to go quickly and lead him to the lovers. They entered the shadowy woods, the spy leading the king. Mark followed him, trusting in the sword at his side, for it had served him often and well. But he was too presumptuous; for if Tristan awoke and the nephew and uncle fought, one of them would surely have died before the battle was over. King Mark said to the forester that he would give him twenty marks of silver to lead him to the right place, as he had promised. The forester (may he be shamed!) said that they were near their destination. The spy held the king's stirrup and had him dismount from his good Gascon horse, and they tied the horses' reins to a green apple tree. They had advanced only a short distance when they saw the bower they were seeking.

The king opened the golden clasps of his cloak and took it off, revealing his strong body. He drew his sword and advanced angrily, telling himself that if he didn't kill them he himself deserved to die. With his sword drawn he entered the bower. The forester had been following closely behind the king, but Mark signaled for him to leave.

The king raised his sword in anger, but then hesitated. He was on the point of striking them; what a tragedy it would have been if he had killed them! Then he saw that she was wearing her chemise, and he saw that there was a space between them, and that their lips were not touching; and when he saw the naked sword separating them and the trousers that Tristan wore, he said: "God, what can this mean? Now that I have seen how they behave together, I do not know what to do. Should I kill them or leave? They have been in the woods a long time. Surely, if they were lovers, they would not be dressed, and they would not have a sword between them. They would be lying together in quite a different way! I wanted to kill them; I won't touch them, but will calm my anger. They have no illicit desires. I won't strike either of them. They are asleep. It would have been terrible if I had touched them; and if I awoke Tristan and either of us killed the other, people would condemn my actions. Before they awaken, I will leave them proof that they were found asleep and that I took pity on them. I do not want them killed, either by me or by any of my men. I see on the queen's finger the fine emerald ring I gave her. I have another one that was once hers. I will take mine off her finger. I have with me some fur gloves which she brought with her from Ireland; I will use them to block the sunlight falling on her face and making her hot. And when I am ready to leave, I will take the sword that now lies between them, and with which Morholt was beheaded."

The king took off his gloves. He looked at the two sleeping together and gently placed the gloves so as to block the sun's ray from Isolde's face. The ring was visible on her finger; he pulled at it without disturbing her. Although it had once been very tight, her fingers were now so thin that it came off easily. The king took it from her without difficulty. Then he gently removed the sword that was between them and replaced it by his own. He then left the bower, mounted his horse, and told the forester to leave immediately; and he did so. The king departed also, leaving the lovers asleep. On that occasion he did nothing more: he returned to the city. Everyone asked him where he had been for so long, but the king lied to them, not admitting where he had been, what he had been seeking, or what he had done.

Now we return to the sleeping couple, whom the king had left in the forest. The queen was dreaming that she was in a rich pavilion in a large wood. Two lions approached her, intending to devour her; she was about to beg for mercy when each of the famished lions took her by the hand. Her fear made Isolde cry out, and she woke up. The gloves, trimmed in white ermine, had fallen on her breast. Her cry awoke Tristan. With his face flushed he sprang to his feet and grabbed the sword like a man enraged. Looking at it, he saw that there was no notch in the blade; he then noticed the golden hilt and recognized the sword as the king's.

The queen saw on her finger the ring he had left her, and saw that he had taken the other one. She cried: "Alas, sir, the king has discovered us!"

He answered: "That is true, my lady. Now we must leave Morrois, for he is surely convinced of our guilt. He has taken my sword and left me his. He could easily have killed us!"

"Sir, I agree with you."

"My love, there is nothing for us to do except flee. He left us only to come back and capture us later. He was alone, and he has now gone back for help. I'm sure he plans to capture us. Lady, let us flee toward Wales. I am faint!" He became pale.

At that moment their squire was returning with the horse. He saw that his lord was pale and asked him what was wrong. "Alas, master, Mark found us sleeping here. He left his sword and took mine. I'm afraid he is arranging a violent punishment. He took the beautiful ring from Isolde's finger and left her his. Master, from those actions we can only conclude that he means us harm. He was alone when he found us; he was afraid, and he went back for help, for he has many courageous and able men. He will bring them back, and he wants to destroy the queen Isolde and me. He wants to capture us, burn us in public, and scatter our ashes to the wind. Let's flee; we cannot stay any longer."

It is true that they could not stay; they could not help being afraid, for they knew the king was of a violent and angry nature. Fearing him because of what had happened, they left quickly. They passed through Morrois, and their fear kept them going day after day; they fled toward Wales. Love has caused them great pain. For three full years they have suffered, and they have become pale and weak.   [2132]

*   *   *

You have heard about the wine they drank, which caused them so much torment; but you may not know how long the love potion was supposed to last. Isolde's mother, who brewed it, made it to be effective for three years of love. She made it for Mark and for her daughter; someone else drank it and suffered because of it. For the full three years the wine so dominated Tristan, and the queen too, that neither was unhappy.

On the day after the feast of St. John the three years of the potion's effect were ended. Tristan got up, leaving Isolde in her bower. He saw a stag and shot an arrow at it, wounding it in the side. The stag fled, and Tristan followed it; he pursued it until evening. As he was running after it, the hour came that was the exact anniversary of his drinking the love potion.

Suddenly he repented, saying to himself: "Oh, God, I am suffering so much; for three full years I have had nothing but pain, day in and day out! I have forgotten chivalry, court life, and baronage. I am in exile, deprived of furs and fine clothes, no longer living at court with other knights. God! My uncle would have loved me so much if I had not betrayed him! Oh, God, I am so miserable! I should be at the royal court, attended by a hundred young men who serve me in order to become knights themselves. I should be leading profitable missions to foreign lands. And it distresses me that I have given the queen a hut in the woods instead of a rich chamber at court. She lives in the forest, when she with her attendants could be in beautiful rooms decorated with silk. Her life has been ruined, and it is my fault. I ask mercy from God, ruler of the world. May He give me strength to leave my uncle and his wife in peace! Before God I swear that I would do it if I could, so that Isolde might be reconciled with King Mark, who married her—alas!—publicly and in accordance with the rites of the Christian religion."

Tristan leaned on his bow, regretting the king's enmity, which he had caused by coming between Mark and his wife. That evening Tristan was still lamenting; and Isolde kept repeating to herself: "Alas, I am so miserable! I have wasted my youth, living in the forest like a serf, with no one to wait on me. I am a queen, but I have lost that title because of the potion we drank at sea. That was Brangain's fault; she was in charge of it, and she was so careless! But there was nothing she could do after I had drunk so much of it. I should be surrounded by well-bred young women, the daughters of worthy vassals, and they would serve me in my chambers, and I would arrange for them to marry noble men. Dear Tristan, she who brought us the love potion to drink led us astray, and we could not have been more cruelly betrayed."

Tristan told her: "Noble queen, we are wasting our youth. My dear, if only I could reconcile us with Mark, so that he would forget his anger and accept our assurance that never, by act or word, did we do anything to disgrace him! Then if any knight between Dinan and Durham claimed that my love for you was less than honorable, he would have to face me on the battlefield. And if Mark admitted me to his household, once you are cleared of the charge, I would serve him faithfully as my uncle and my lord; he would have no soldier who would serve him better in war. But if he wished to take you back and refuse my services, I would go to the king of Dumfries, or to Brittany, with no companion except Governal. Good queen, wherever I may be, I will always be yours. I would never leave you, if we could stay together without the deprivation that I have made you endure so long in the wilderness. Because of me you have lost the title 'queen.' You could be living honorably in the palace with your lord, if it had not been for the potion given to us at sea. Noble, beautiful Isolde, tell me what we should do!"

"Sir, thanks be to God that you wish to repent of your sin! Friend, remember the hermit Ogrin, who preached to us about the scriptures and spoke to us at length when you visited the hermitage at the edge of the forest. Dear friend, if you decided to repent, it could not come at a better time. Sir, let's hurry back to him. I trust him completely; he will give us honorable advice, which will let us spend our lives in happiness."

Hearing her, Tristan sighed and said: "Noble queen, we will go back to the hermitage tonight or early tomorrow. With the advice of Master Ogrin let's write to Mark to tell him of our intentions."

"Tristan, I agree. And let us implore our great heavenly King to have mercy on us, dear Tristan."

The lovers set out through the woods, walking until they came to the hermitage. They found Ogrin there, reading. When he saw them, he greeted them warmly. They sat down in the chapel. "Poor outcasts, love has caused you so much suffering! How long will you continue your sinful ways? You have led this life too long; I beg you to repent."

Tristan said to him: "Listen to me. It has been our fate to live this way. We have suffered constantly for three years. If we could only find a way to reconcile the queen with King Mark, I could accept my own exile from his court; I would go away to Brittany or Lothian. But if my uncle will permit me to serve him at court, I will do it faithfully. [. . .] Sir, my uncle is a powerful king. Give us the best advice you can about what you have heard, and we will do your will."

Now the queen threw herself at the feet of the hermit and urgently implored him to reconcile them with the king, assuring him: "Never again will I even think of yielding to sinful desires. Please understand that I am not regretting having loved him honorably and as a friend; but we have both rejected carnal love."

The hermit listened to her and wept. He praised God for what he had heard: "O God, great omnipotent King, I give thanks to You with all my heart for having let me live long enough for these two to come to me for advice about their sin. May You be forever praised! I swear on my faith that I will give you both good counsel. You have come here for advice; now listen to me, Tristan, and you, queen, hear me well, and take my words to heart. When a man and a woman sin with each other and then leave each other and sincerely repent, God will forgive them, however horrible and ugly their crime may have been. Tristan and Queen Isolde, now listen to me carefully: in order to avoid shame and conceal evil, it is often useful to lie a bit. Since you asked me for advice, I will give it to you without delay. I will give you parchment for a letter. First you will greet the king; you will address it to him at Lantyan. Tell the king, with due respect, that you are in the forest with the queen, but that, if he wants to take her back and forget his anger, you will then do the same and will return to his court. Tell him that if anyone, however wise or foolish, accuses you of an illicit love, may Mark have you hanged if you do not defend yourself in battle. Tristan, I can give you that advice, because you have no equal at court who would dare stand up to you. I am advising you in good faith.

"Mark cannot deny this: when he wanted to burn you to death because of the dwarf, everyone—nobles and commoners alike—saw that he refused to permit a trial. When God had mercy on you and let you escape, as everyone has heard, only His power kept you from perishing in disgrace. The leap you took would have terrified any man alive. You fled because of fear; you rescued the queen, and since that time you have lived in the wilderness. You brought her from her native land and gave her to him in marriage. All that is true, and he knows it. She was wedded at Lantyan. You did not want to leave her in trouble, so you thought it better to flee with her. If he will hear your defense, you will offer to present it in court, so that everyone will witness it. And if it seems proper, once your loyalty to him is established, he should take back his noble wife on the advice of his barons. And if he agrees, you will be his willing and faithful servant; but if he does not want your service, you will leave for Scotland to serve another king. That is what should be in the letter." [Tristan said:] "And I approve. But with your permission, good Ogrin, I wish to add something, because I do not dare trust him: he issued a warrant for me. I therefore ask him, as a lord whom I love and respect, to have another letter prepared to make his pleasure known. He is to have the letter left at the red cross in the middle of the heath. I don't dare tell him where I am, for fear that he will harm me. I will be reassured only when I have the letter, and then I will do whatever he wishes. Master, let my letter be sealed now, and write a greeting on the ribbon: *Vale!* I have nothing more to add."   [2426]

Ogrin the hermit got up; he took pen and ink and parchment, and wrote the letter. When he had finished, he took a ring and pressed the stone into the wax seal. When it was sealed, he handed it to Tristan, who took it gratefully. "Who will deliver it?" asked the hermit.

"I will."

"Don't say that, Tristan!"

"Yes, sir, I will do it. I know Lantyan. Kind sir, with your permission, the queen will stay here. Soon, when it is dark and the king is sleeping, I will mount my horse and take my squire with me. There is a hill outside the town; I will dismount there and continue on foot. My master will hold my horse for me."

That evening, after sunset, when the sky began to darken, Tristan set out with his master. He was familiar with the area. They rode until they came to Lantyan, where they dismounted and entered the city. Guards sounded the alarm. Ducking into a trench, Tristan kept going until he reached the great hall. Anxious and frightened, he came to the window where the king was sleeping and called to him softly—for he certainly had no desire to speak loudly! The king awoke and said: "Who are you, coming here at this hour? What do you want? Tell me your name!"

"Sir, I am called Tristan. I am bringing a letter, and I will leave it here in the window. For a long time now I have not dared speak with you. I am leaving the letter for you, and I don't dare stay any longer."

Tristan turned away, and the king jumped up, calling to him aloud three times: "In God's name, dear nephew, wait for your uncle!"

The king picked up the letter. Tristan left without pausing: he was eager to be gone! He returned to his master, who was waiting for him. He jumped nimbly on his horse. Governal said: "Hurry now; let's escape by taking the side-roads!"

They rode through the wilderness until they reached the hermitage at dawn. Ogrin was fervently praying that God would protect Tristan and

Governal, his squire. When he saw him, he was overjoyed, and thanked his Creator. There is no need to ask how Isolde reacted when she saw them: from the time they left at night until she and the hermit saw them again, she had not stopped crying. The wait had seemed interminable to her. When she saw him arriving, she asked them what had happened [. . .]: "Friend, tell me, for God's sake, did you go to the king's court?"

Tristan told them everything: how he was in the city and how he spoke with the king, how the king called to him to come back, and how he had left the letter and the king had found it.

Ogrin said: "May God be praised! Tristan, you can be sure that you will soon hear from King Mark." Tristan dismounted and put down his bow.

They stayed on at the hermitage. Meanwhile the king had his barons awakened. First he sent for his chaplain and handed him the letter he was holding. The chaplain broke the wax seal and read the letter. At the top he saw the name of the king, to whom Tristan sent greetings. He read the whole letter and explained the contents to the king. The king listened attentively; he was overjoyed, because he loved his wife so much. The king awoke his barons and sent for those he valued most; and when they were all there, the king spoke, and they listened quietly:

"Lords, I have received this letter. I am your king; you are my vassals. Let the letter be read and listened to, and when that is done, I ask you to advise me, as it is your duty to do."

Dinas arose first and said to the others: "Lords, listen to me, and heed my advice only if you consider it wise! Anyone who can give better counsel should do so: let him do good and shun foolishness. We do not know from what country this letter came to us. Let it be read first, and then, depending on what it says, whoever can give sound advice should do so. I want to remind you that the worst offense anyone can commit is to give bad advice to his rightful lord."

The men of Cornwall told the king: "Dinas has spoken nobly. Chaplain, read the letter to all of us, from beginning to end."

The chaplain arose, untied the letter, and, standing before the king, said: "Now listen, and hear me well. Tristan, our lord's nephew, first sends greetings and love to the king and all his barons. Then he writes:

> "King, you know how the marriage of the daughter of the king of Ireland came about. I went to Ireland by sea; by my prowess I won her, by killing the great crested dragon; and as a result she was given to me. I brought her to your country, king, and you took her as your wife in the presence of your knights. Hardly had you married her when malicious gossips in your kingdom made you believe a lie. If anyone should make accusations against her, I am prepared to take up arms and defend her on foot or on horseback, to prove that she never loved me dishonorably, nor I her. If I cannot establish her innocence and my own, then have me judged before your barons—all of them. Any one of them who wanted to destroy me could have me condemned or burned. Sir, dear uncle, you know that in your rage you wanted to have us burned. But God took mercy on us, and we praise the Lord. Fortunately the queen escaped.

That was only just, because (God help me!) you were wrong to want to put her to death. I too escaped, by leaping from the top of a high cliff. Then, as punishment, the queen was given to the lepers. I rescued her from them, and since that time we have not ceased to flee. I could not fail her, since she nearly died, unjustly, because of me. Since then I have remained with her in the woods, for I was not so daring as to show myself on the plain. You ordered that we be captured and delivered to you. You would have had us burned or hanged, and thus we had to flee. But if it should now be your wish to take back the fair Isolde, no baron in the country would serve you better than I. However, if anyone should convince you not to accept my service, I will go to the king of Scotland. I will go abroad, and you will never hear from me again. Consider these matters carefully, king. I can no longer bear such torment. Either I will be reconciled with you, or I will take the king's daughter back to Ireland, and she will be queen in her own country."

The chaplain said to the king: "Sir, the letter ends there."

The barons had heard that Tristan was willing to do battle with them for the daughter of the king of Ireland. Every baron of Cornwall said: "King, take back your wife. No sensible person could ever have said about the queen what we have heard. But I cannot advise you to let Tristan stay in this country. Let him go serve the powerful king in Galloway, on whom the Scottish king is waging war. He can remain there, and you will have occasional news of him. If you send for him, he can come back; otherwise we will know nothing about him. Send him a letter telling him to bring the queen back to you immediately."

The king called his chaplain: "Write this letter quickly; you have heard what you are to put in it. Hurry now! I am impatient, for I have not seen the noble Isolde for such a long time. She has suffered too much in her youth! And when the letter is sealed, hang it upon the red cross. Do it tonight. Add my greetings to the letter."

When the chaplain had written it, he attached it to the red cross. Tristan did not sleep that night. Before midnight he had passed through the Blanche Lande, carrying the sealed letter. He knew the Cornwall countryside well. He came to Ogrin and gave him the letter. The hermit took it and read it. He learned of the generosity of the king, who was willing to forget his anger against Isolde and take her back, and he learned when the reconciliation was to occur. Then he spoke as his duty and his faith dictated: "Tristan, what joy has come to you! Your plea has been heard, and the king is taking his wife back. All his men advised him to do so. But they do not dare advise him to retain your services. Instead, go spend a year or two serving a foreign king who is involved in a war. If the king wishes, you will then come back to him and Isolde. The king will be ready to receive her three days from now. The meeting will take place at the Gué Aventuros. There you will give her up, and he will take her back. That is all the letter says."   [2680]

"God," said Tristan, "what a painful separation! He who loses the woman he loves is unhappy indeed! But it must be done, because of the suffering you have endured on my account. You do not have to suffer any more. When we have to separate, we will pledge our love to each other, dear one. As long as I live, in war or peace, I will not fail to send messages to you, and dear friend, send me news of yourself."

With a great sigh Isolde said: "Tristan, listen to me. Leave me Husdent, your hunting dog. No one ever cared for a dog as well as I will for him, dear friend. When I see him, he will remind me of you. However sad I may be, the sight of him will make me happy again. Never in the world will an animal have such fine shelter or such a rich bed. Dear Tristan, I have a ring, a green jasper with a seal. Sir, for love of me, wear the ring, and if you wish to send me a message, send the ring as well, for unless I see the ring, I assure you I will not believe the message. But if I do see it, no king's command can prevent me from doing anything the messenger tells me, as long as it is honorable. And I promise that with all my heart. Friend, will you give me Husdent as a gift?"

And he answered: "My dear, I will give you Husdent as a sign of my undying love."

"Sir, thank you for giving him to me. Take the ring in exchange." She took it off her finger and placed it on his. Tristan kissed the queen, and she kissed him, to symbolize their agreement.

The hermit went to the Mount, because of the rich market held there. He bought various furs, silk, rich scarlet, and cloth whiter than lilies; and he bought a gentle riding-horse with a harness of brightest gold. By cash, credit, and trade, he acquired precious cloth and furs until he had enough to dress the queen richly.

Throughout Cornwall it was announced that the king was to be reconciled with his wife: "Our reconciliation will take place at the Gué Aventuros." The news spread everywhere, and every knight and lady came to the gathering. They had long desired the queen's return, for she was loved by all (except the evil ones—may God curse them!). All four of them later got what they deserved. Two were killed with swords, the third by an arrow; they died a violent death in their own country. And the forester who denounced the lovers did not escape a cruel death, either, for the valiant Perinis killed him in the forest with his sling. God, who wanted to subdue their sinful pride, took vengeance on all four of them.

On the day of the assembly King Mark was surrounded by a great crowd. Many pavilions and barons' tents had been raised there, as far as the eye could see. Tristan, with his lady, rode toward the place until he saw the stone marking the ford. Under his tunic he had worn his hauberk; he feared for his safety because he had wronged the king. He caught sight of the tents on the meadow, and he recognized the king and the men with him. He spoke gently to Isolde:

"Lady, in God's name I ask you to keep Husdent and care for him well. If you ever loved me, love him now. There is the king, your lord, and his subjects with him. We have very little time left to talk. I see knights approaching, and the king and his soldiers are coming to meet us. In the name of God, our great glorious King, if at any time I should make a request of you, lady, do my will."

"Listen to me, dear Tristan. By the faith I owe to you, I will believe what I am told only if you send me the ring that is on your finger. But as soon as I see the ring with my own eyes, no tower or wall or castle could hold me and prevent me from doing the bidding of my lover, if it is honorable and good, and I know it is your will."

"Lady," he said, "may God bless you." He drew her to him and pressed her in his arms.

Isolde spoke thoughtfully: "Friend, listen to what I have to say."

"I am listening."

"You are bringing me back to give me to the king, on the advice of the good hermit Ogrin; I beg you, dear sweet friend, not to leave the country until you know whether the king is angry or reasonable with me. As your true love, I ask you, once the king has taken me back, to go stay at the home of Orri the forester. Please do that for me. We spent many a night there in a bed made for us. [. . .] My friend, go into the cellar under the cabin. I will send you news of the royal court by Perinis. May God keep you, my friend! Please don't refuse to stay there. My messenger will come to you often; by way of my servant and your master, I will send you news of myself. [. . .] I know the three who wanted to destroy us will some day pay for their actions. Their bodies will be found lying in the forest. But until then, dear friend, I am afraid of them. May Hell open up and swallow them! I fear them because they are completely evil."

"My love, whoever accuses you of impropriety should beware and consider me his enemy!"

"Sir," said Isolde, "thank you. Now I am happy, for you have put my mind at ease."

They rode on, and the others approached them; they exchanged greetings. The king, along with Dinas of Dinan, rode well ahead of his men. Tristan held the reins of Isolde's horse and led her forward. He greeted the king respectfully: "King, I am returning the fair Isolde to you. No one ever gave up anything so precious. I see here the men of your land; and in their presence, I ask your permission to establish my innocence and prove before your court that never in my life have she and I been lovers. You have been made to believe a lie; but, as God is my witness, there was no trial. Let me do battle in your court, on foot or otherwise, sir. If I am thus condemned, then burn me in sulphur. But if I can survive unharmed, let no one [accuse me again]. Now keep me with you, or I will go away to Lothian."

While the king was speaking with his nephew, Andrew, a native of Lincoln, urged him: "King, keep him with you, and you will be more respected and feared because of him." Mark was tempted to grant this request, for his heart had softened toward his nephew. The king took him aside, leaving the queen with Dinas, who was true, loyal, and faithful. Dinas chatted and joked with the queen and helped her remove her rich scarlet cape from her shoulders. She was wearing a tunic over a silk chemise. What can I tell you of her mantle? The hermit who bought it never regretted the expense! The robe was rich, and Isolde was beautiful. Her eyes were green, her hair golden.

The seneschal obviously enjoyed her company, to the great displeasure of the three barons (may they be cursed for their viciousness!). They drew near the king and said: "Sir, listen to us, and we will give you sound advice. The queen was accused and fled from your country. If they are together again in your court, it is our opinion that people will say you condone their crime. Everyone will say so! Send Tristan away from your court, and after a year, when you are certain that Isolde is true to you, you can send for him. We are advising you in good faith."

The king answered: "Whatever anyone else may say, I will not fail to heed your advice." The barons moved away and, in the name of the king, announced his decision.

When Tristan heard that he would not be pardoned, and that the king wanted him to go away, he took leave of the queen. They looked at each other tenderly. The queen blushed, embarrassed before all those gathered there. Tristan then rode off, and many hearts were saddened that day.

The king asked Tristan where he was going and told him he would give him anything he wanted: gold, silver, furs, or anything else. Tristan replied: "King of Cornwall, I will not accept anything from you. As soon as possible I will happily go offer my services to the great king who is embroiled in war."

Tristan had an impressive escort composed of Mark's barons and the king himself. The young man set out toward the sea. Isolde saw him go, and she did not move until he was out of her sight. Tristan left, and those who had accompanied him returned. Dinas, who was still with him, embraced him again and again and begged him to return safe and sound. The two swore fidelity to each other, and Tristan said: "Dinas, listen to me. I have to leave here; you know why. If I send word by Governal that I need something, look after it properly."

They embraced over and over. Dinas told him not to fear: he would do whatever Tristan asked. He lamented their separation, and he promised to look after Isolde—not for the king's sake, but for his love of Tristan. Thereupon Tristan left him, and both of them were sad.

Dinas returned to the king, who was waiting on a heath. The barons all rode quickly back to the city. More than four thousand people—men, women, and children—rushed out of the city, all rejoicing for Isolde and Tristan. Bells rang throughout the city. But when they learned that Tristan was leaving, there was not a one who did not feel bitter grief. They rejoiced about Isolde, however, and all wished to serve her; and every street was hung with brocaded cloths in celebration. Wherever the queen went, the streets were strewn with flowers.

The queen and all the barons went down the road to the monastery of St.

Samson. Bishops, clerics, monks, and abbots all came out to greet her, dressed in cassocks and copes. The queen, dressed in dark blue, dismounted; the bishop took her by the hand and led her into the church, up to the altar. The valiant and noble Dinas brought her a garment worth a hundred silver marks, a rich cloth embroidered in gold, such as no count or king ever owned. Queen Isolde took it and placed it reverently on the altar. Later on it was made into a chasuble, which never left the treasure except on feast days; and those who have seen it say it is still at St. Samson.

Then Isolde left the church. The king, the princes, and the counts accompanied her to the palace, where there was great rejoicing. No one was forbidden to enter; anyone who wanted to come in was fed, and no one was refused. Isolde was greatly honored that day, more than at any time since her wedding day. The king freed one hundred serfs and dubbed twenty young men as knights and gave them arms and hauberks.

Now listen to what Tristan did. Having made restitution to Mark, he went away. He left the road and set out on a small path; he followed trails and paths until he came to the forester's lodging by a secret way. Orri led him into the cellar, and there he had everything he needed. Orri was extremely generous. He caught boars and took wild sows in his nets, and trapped stags and does, deer and bucks. He unselfishly gave much of it to his servants. Tristan lived there secretly with him, in his cellar, and he received news of his mistress from Perinis, the queen's kind young servant.   [3027]

*   *   *

Now you will hear about the three barons—may God curse them!—who tormented the king so much. Before a month had passed, Mark went out hunting, accompanied by the traitors. Now listen to what they did! The peasants had burned part of the underbrush on a heath. The king was standing in the burned area, listening to the cries of his dogs. The three barons came and spoke to him: "King, listen to us. The queen has never proved by oath that she remained faithful to you, and people condemn you for that. Your barons have often asked you to require her to clear herself of the charge that Tristan was her lover. She must prove that people were lying. Make her undergo a trial; demand it as soon as you are alone with her tonight. If she is not willing to be judged, banish her from your empire."

The king listened, and his face reddened. "For God's sake, lords, will you never stop denouncing the queen? She is again being accused of something that should have been put to rest. If you want me to exile the queen to Ireland, tell me so! What do you want of her? Didn't Tristan offer to defend her? But you did not dare take up arms against him. It is your fault he is gone; it was your idea! I sent him away; shall I now send my wife away too? Cursed be the one who persuaded me to make him leave! By the martyr St. Stephen, you are going too far, and I am angry. I am astonished at your persistence. If he did wrong, he is suffering for it. You care nothing for my happiness; I can no longer have peace with you. By St. Trechmor of Carhaix, I warn you: today is Monday, and before Tuesday is finished you will see Tristan here!"

The king frightened them so much that they dared do nothing except flee. King Mark said: "May God curse you for trying to bring me shame! It will do you no good: I will summon the man you drove away."

When they saw Mark's rage, the three of them dismounted in a nearby clearing, leaving the angry king in the field. They said to each other: "What can we do? King Mark is very perverse; he will indeed send for his nephew and will not keep his promise or vow. If Tristan returns, we are finished; if he finds any of us in the forest or on the road, he will not leave a drop of blood in our bodies. Let's tell the king he will now have peace, and we will never mention the subject again."

They came back to the king in the field, but he brushed them aside, for he had no desire to listen to them. He swore frequently under his breath: they should never have spoken to him! He told himself that if his men had been there, he would have had all three barons arrested.

"Sir," they said, "listen to us. You are upset and angry because what we say affects your honor. It is our obligation to advise our lord, but our advice offends you. It is proper that someone who hated you and dared speak to you should have to flee! But we, who are your faithful servants, give you loyal counsel. Since you don't believe us, do as you wish; we will say no more. Pardon us for displeasing you!"

The king listened silently. He leaned on his saddle-bow and said, without turning toward them: "Lords, not long ago you heard my nephew's denials in regard to my wife. At that time you had no desire to take up arms or to mount your horses; I will not permit you to cause trouble now. Leave my land! By St. Andrew, for whom pilgrims journey to Scotland, you have caused me great pain, which will last a year; because of you I have banished Tristan."

The traitors came before Mark. They were named Godoine, Ganelon, and the evil Denoalen. In spite of their pleas the king would not change his mind, and he departed without further delay. Resentfully they left the king for their fortified castles, which were surrounded by palisades and built on rocks high in the hills. If something could not be done about it, they would cause their lord serious trouble!

The king did not delay long. Without waiting for anyone, he dismounted at Tintagel, before his tower, and entered alone. He came into their chamber, still wearing his sword. When he entered, Isolde arose, came to meet him, took his sword, and then sat at his feet. He took her hand and raised her up; she bowed toward him. When she looked into his face, she noticed that his expression was fierce and cruel. She saw that he was angry and that he had come alone.

"Alas," she said to herself, "my friend has been discovered, and my lord has captured him!" Her blood rushed to her face, and her heart froze in her breast. She fell back in a faint before the king, and she became pale. Mark lifted her up in his arms and embraced and kissed her; he thought she had fallen ill.

When she regained consciousness, he asked: "My dear, what is wrong?"

"Sir, I am afraid."

"There is no reason for you to be afraid."

When she heard his assurance, her color returned, and she became calm. She was again self-assured. She spoke cleverly to the king: "Sir, I can see by your expression that your hunters have made you angry. You should not get upset because of a hunt."

At that the king laughed, kissed her, and replied: "Friend, I have three evil men who for a long time have been jealous of my accomplishments. If I don't do something about it now, if I don't drive them out of my land, I will never again have any power over them. They have pushed me too far, and I have given in to them too many times. Now my mind is made up. Because of their words—their lies!—I sent my nephew away from me. I no longer want anything to do with them; but Tristan will soon return, and he will take revenge on the three traitors for me. They will be hanged by him."

When the queen heard him, she almost cried out, but didn't dare. Wisely, she composed herself and said: "God has worked a miracle, arousing my lord's anger against those responsible for the scandal. I pray to God that they may be shamed." She spoke those words softly, so that they could not be heard.

The fair Isolde, who knew the proper words to use, said to the king: "Sir, what evil have they said of me? Everyone is free to say what he thinks. Except for you I have no one to defend me, and that is why they continue to attack me. May God, our heavenly Father, curse them! They have frightened me so often!"

"Lady," said the king, "listen to me. Three of my most valued barons have left me in anger."

"Why, sir? For what reason?"

"They made accusations against you."

"Why, sir?"

The king answered: "Because you never established your innocence in regard to Tristan."

"Suppose I do it? [. . .] I am ready to do so."

"When will you do it? Today?"

"Give me a little time."

"A great deal of time has already passed."

"Sir, in God's name, listen and advise me. What does all this mean? Why can they never leave me in peace? May God help me, I will make no defense except one of my own choosing. Sir, if I took an oath in your court, before your men, before three days were up they would say they want some other proof. King, I have no relative in this country who would undertake a war or revolt on account of my troubles. But I don't care, because I no longer take notice of what people say. If they want my oath, or if they demand a trial by judgment, let them choose the date. They cannot think of a judgment so cruel that I will not submit myself to it. However, I want King Arthur and his entourage to be there. If I am declared innocent before him, and if anyone makes accusations against me later, those who witnessed my judgment will defend me, whether it is against a Cornishman or a Saxon. For that reason I want them to be there and witness my defense with their own eyes. If King Arthur is there, and his most noble nephew Gawain, and Girflet and Kay the seneschal, and a hundred other vassals of the king, they will not shrink from doing battle to defend me from my accusers. King, for that reason, my defense should take place before them. The Cornishmen are liars and deceivers! Choose a date and ask everyone, poor and rich alike, to come to the Blanche Lande. Announce that you will confiscate the inheritance of anyone who does not come; that way you will have no trouble with them. And I am sure that King Arthur will come as soon as he receives my message, for his compassion is well known to me."

The king answered: "You are right." Then the date, set for two weeks from that time, was announced throughout the country. The king also sent the word to the three who had left the court in anger: whatever the outcome might be, they were happy to hear the news.

Now everyone in the country knew the date chosen for the trial, and they knew that King Arthur would be there, accompanied by most of the knights of his court. Isolde wasted no time. She had Perinis tell Tristan of the pain and suffering she had endured on his account. She asked him to repay her for that suffering; for if he were willing, he could save her from further torment: "Tell him to remember a marsh at the end of the bridge, at Mal Pas, where I once soiled the hem of my dress. There is a small hill near the ford, just this side of the Blanche Lande. He is to go there, dressed as a leper, and take with him a leper's wooden goblet with a bottle tied to it by a leather thong. In his other hand he should have a crutch. And here is our scheme: he will be sitting on the hill at the appointed hour. Have him make his face appear tumorous and hold the goblet in front of him; from those who pass by, he is to ask for alms—nothing more. They will give him gold and silver. He is to keep the money for me, until I can see him alone, in a private room."   [3312]

Perinis said: "Lady, I will tell him all that, in confidence." He left the queen and went into the forest, passing through it all alone. At evening he came to Tristan's refuge in Orri's cellar. They had just finished eating. Tristan was happy to see Perinis, for he knew that the noble man had brought him news of his mistress. They grasped each other by the hand, and they sat together. Perinis related the queen's message. Tristan bowed his head and swore by all the saints that those responsible for this could not fail to lose their heads. They would hang high from the gallows! He said: "Tell the queen this, word for word: I will go at the appointed time; she should have no doubt about that. Tell her to be happy and not to worry. I will not rest until I have taken revenge with my sword on those who have made her suffer. Their treachery is now exposed! Tell her to have everything arranged to save herself when she swears her oath. I will see her soon. Go, and tell her not to worry. She cannot doubt that I will go to the trial disguised as a beggar. King Arthur will see me seated at the entry to Mal Pas, but he will not know me, and I will make him give me alms if I can. You can tell the queen what I have related to you here, in this place she herself had so beautifully constructed. Take her more greetings from me than I will have tumors on my body."

"I will tell her," replied Perinis. Then he left by the stairs, saying: "Sir, I am going to King Arthur, for I have to ask him to come to hear the oath and to bring with him a hundred knights who can defend the lady if the traitors ever again question her loyalty. Do you approve?"

"God be with you!"

Perinis ran up the stairs, jumped on his horse, and rode directly to Caerleon. All his efforts to carry out his duty were not well rewarded, for at Caerleon he was told that the king was at Stirling. So the servant of fair Isolde set out for that city. Meeting a shepherd who was playing pipes, he asked: "Where is the king?"

"Sir," the shepherd answered, "he is sitting on his throne. There you will see the Round Table, which rotates like the earth. And his men are seated around it."

Perinis said: "Let us go find him." When he got there, the young man dismounted and went in. There were at court many counts' and vassals' sons, who served others in order to earn their armor. One of them left the others and came running to the king, who said to him: "Where have you come from?"

"I bring you news. Out there is a rider who is urgently looking for you."

Then, watched by many nobles, Perinis came in and stepped up before the king at the dais where all his knights were seated. The young man said in a firm voice: "May God save King Arthur and all his company. That is the wish of his friend, the fair Isolde!"

The king arose and said: "And may God save and protect her, and you too, friend. I have wanted to hear from her for so long! Young man, here in the presence of my barons, I grant her whatever she may request. And I will knight you, along with two others, for bringing me a message from the most beautiful woman from here to Tudela."

"Sir," he said, "thank you. Now hear why I have come. And may these barons hear it too, and Sir Gawain in particular. The queen was reconciled with her lord, as everyone knows. Sir, all the barons of the kingdom were present at the reconciliation. There Tristan offered to defend his honor and prove the queen's fidelity before the king. No one cared to take up arms to dispute her loyalty. But now, sir, they have convinced Mark that she must take an oath. But there is no one of her lineage at court, neither Frenchman nor Saxon, who could defend her. A proverb says that a person can swim easily if someone holds up his chin! King, if I am lying about all this, you can punish me for slander. The king constantly changes his mind, now believing one thing, now another. The fair Isolde answered him that she would take an oath before you. She asks you to take pity on her, as your dear friend, and come to the Gué Aventuros, with one hundred of your friends, at the designated time. She knows that your court is loyal and your company sincere; she will be proven innocent before you, and may God protect her from misfortune. If she ever asks you to defend her, you will surely not fail her. The date has been set for a week from now."

Those who heard this wept bitterly, there was not a one of them who did not shed tears of pity for her. They all said: "God! What do they want from her? Mark does whatever they wish, and Tristan has left the country. May no one enter Heaven who does not go to the trial and help her, if that is the king's will."

Gawain stood up and said graciously: "Uncle, if you give me your permission, the trial that is to take place will turn out badly for the three traitors. The worst of them is Ganelon; he and I know each other well. Once, during a violent joust, I knocked him into a mudhole. If I could get my hands on him again, by St. Richier, there would be no need for Tristan to be there! I would make him suffer, and then I would have him hanged on the highest hill!"

Girflet stood up and took Gawain by the hand. "King, Denoalen and Godoine and Ganelon have hated the queen for a long time. May God not preserve me, and may I never again have the pleasure of a woman's private embrace, if I ever meet Godoine and the point of my lance does not pierce his body!"

Perinis listened, his head bowed. Yvain, the son of Urien, said: "I know Denoalen well. He is interested only in slander, and he knows how to manipulate the king, repeating his accusations until they are believed. If our paths ever cross, as they did once before, may I be cast out of our faith if I have the power to hang him with my own two hands and do not do so! Traitors deserve to be punished. And the king is easily manipulated by those hypocrites."

Perinis said to King Arthur: "Sir, I am confident that the traitors who caused trouble for the queen will be properly punished. Threats made at your court, against people from whatever land, are never idle; you pursue the matter, and those who deserve it are eventually punished."

The king was pleased; he blushed a little and said: "Young man, let us go eat. My knights will make plans to avenge her."

In his heart the king felt great joy. He spoke so that Perinis would hear him: "Noble and honored company, take care to see that, on the day of the trial, your horses are well fed, your shields new, your clothing rich. We will joust before the fair lady whose message you have all heard. Anyone who shrinks from bearing arms is lacking in pride and self-respect!"

The king had summoned all of them, but they regretted that the day was still so far off; they would have preferred it to be the next day! When Perinis asked permission to leave, the king mounted his horse, Passelande, for he wanted to escort the young man. They rode along, deep in conversation about the beautiful woman for whom many a lance would be splintered. Before leaving Perinis, the king offered him all the equipment a knight should have, but Perinis did not want to accept it.

The king rode with him a while longer, in honor of the beautiful, blonde noble, and virtuous Isolde; they spoke of her at length. The young man had a fine escort, made up of the king and his knights. They separated with regret, and the king said to him: "Good friend, go now; do not stay any longer. Greet your lady on behalf of her faithful servant, who will come to make peace for her. I will zealously do her will, and I will gain glory by serving her. Remind her of an incident that occurred once, when a lance that was thrown remained stuck in a post; she will know where that was. I want you to tell her that."

"King, I will do it, I promise." Then he spurred his horse, and the king turned back. Perinis left; he had taken pains to serve the queen well, and he had delivered his message. He rode on at full speed, returning to the queen without a day's rest. He told her about his journey and about Arthur and Tristan, and she was happy. They spent that night at Dinan.   [3562]

It was the tenth night of the moon, and the day of the queen's trial was approaching. Tristan, her friend, was not idle: he had devised a strange costume and was dressed in rough wool, without a shirt. His tunic was of ugly coarse cloth, and his boots were pieced together from patches. He had made a cloak of coarse, threadbare wool. He had a marvelous disguise, and he looked exactly like a leper. However, he had his sword girded tightly around his waist.

He secretly left his lodging, accompanied by Governal, who gave him instructions: "Tristan, conduct yourself wisely. Pay close attention to the queen, for she will make no sign to you."

"Master," he said, "I will do as you say. Now take care to do what I want. I am afraid of being recognized. Take my shield and lance; bring them to me, Master Governal, and saddle my horse. In case I need them, you should be at the ford, hidden but nearby. You know which ford, for you have been familiar with it for a long time. Since the horse is as white as flour, cover him all over so that he cannot be seen or recognized by anyone. Arthur and his entourage will be there, and Mark too. Knights from foreign lands will joust to win praise, and for the love of my Isolde, I may do something reckless. Attach to my lance the pennon given to me by my fair Isolde. Now go, master, and I beg you to do all this discreetly." He picked up his goblet and crutch, and he asked and received permission to leave.

Governal came to his lodging, gathered up his equipment, and set out. Taking care that no one saw him, he rode until he came to Mal Pas, where he concealed himself near Tristan. At the edge of the marsh Tristan sat down on a mound. In front of him was his rattle, suspended from his neck by a cord. There were mudholes around him. As he climbed the hill, he did not appear to be sick, for he was large and solidly built; he was certainly not a dwarf, an invalid, or a hunchback! He heard the noise of the people approaching, and he sat down. He had lumps and sores on his face, and whenever someone passed him, he moaned: "I am so miserable! I didn't want to be a beggar and spend my life this way. But what else can I do?"

Tristan's laments made them all take out their purses and give him something. He accepted the alms without comment. Even a man who had been another man's minion for seven years could not have been so successful in extracting money! With his head bowed, Tristan asked for alms in God's name, even from servants and disreputable vagabonds. Some of them would give him something; others would strike him. Unsavory people passed by and taunted him, calling him parasitic and worthless. Tristan listened but did not respond, except to say that he forgave them in God's name. Insolent young men insulted him, but he behaved prudently. He responded to some of his tormentors by helping them on their way with his crutch. At least fifteen of them went away bleeding profusely.

Well-bred young men gave him farthings and silver half-pennies, and he accepted them. He told them that he would drink to them; he explained that he had such a burning in his body that he could not relieve it. All who heard that were moved to tears; they could have no doubt that the man they were looking at was a leper.

Servants and squires hastened to find lodgings for themselves and to set up their lords' tents and pavilions of many colors. Every wealthy man there had his own tent. Knights arrived by all the roads and paths, and there was a great crowd on the marshy ground. The mud there was soft, and the horses sank up to their flanks; many of them fell and struggled to extricate themselves. Tristan laughed and remained unconcerned about it; instead he told all of them:

"Hold your reins by the knots, and use your spurs. Spur sharply, for there is no mud up ahead." But when they tried to advance, the marshy ground gave way under their feet, and they sank into the mud. Those who had not thought to wear boots regretted their error. When the leper saw someone fall into the mud, he would hold out his hand and shake his rattle. And when he saw them sink further, he would cry: "Think of me, and may God save you from Mal Pas. Help me buy new clothes!" He struck his goblet with the bottle. It was a strange place to beg alms; but he was doing it mischievously: he wanted his lady, the blonde Isolde, to be pleased and happy when she passed by.

There was great tumult at Mal Pas. Those who crossed the ford soiled their clothes, and their cries could be heard from far away. The crossing was dangerous for all of them.

And then Arthur arrived. He and many of his barons looked warily at the ford, fearful that they would be mired in the soft mud. All the knights of the Round Table had come to Mal Pas, with new shields and strong horses, and displaying their coats of arms. They were fully equipped from head to foot. Many silk pennons were raised there, and the knights began to joust near the ford.

Tristan recognized King Arthur easily and called to him: "Good King Arthur, I am sick—a weak, deformed leper covered with sores. My father is poor and never had anything. I came here to seek alms. I have heard many good things about you, and you should not turn your back on me. You are dressed in fine grey cloth from Regensburg and from Reims, I see, and underneath the cloth your skin is white and smooth. Your legs are covered with rich brocade and green net, and you are wearing leggings of scarlet. King Arthur, do you see how I scratch myself? I have chills even when others are hot. In God's name, give me your leggings!"

The noble king took pity on him. He had two young men take off his leggings, and he gave them to the leper. Tristan took them, immediately walked back to the hill, and sat down. The leper spared no one who passed by him, and soon he had many fine clothes, including King Arthur's leggings.

As Tristan was sitting near the marsh, an intense and regal King Mark came riding rapidly toward the ford. Tristan decided that he would try to obtain something of Mark's. He shook his rattle loudly and cried out in a hoarse, nasal voice: "In God's name, King Mark, give me something!"

Mark took off his hood and said: "Here, brother, put this on your head; you have suffered too often from the weather."

"Sir," he responded, "thank you. Now you have protected me from the cold." He put the hood under his cloak, folding it to conceal it from view.

"Where are you from, leper?" asked Mark.

"From Caerleon, sir; I am the son of a Welshman."

"How long have you been an outcast from society?"

"Truthfully, sir, three years. While I was healthy, I had a most courtly lady. Because of her my body is now covered with these ugly sores, and it is because of her that I have to use this rattle day and night, making noise that startles those from whom I seek alms in God's name."

The king said: "Tell me how she made you sick."

"Good king, her husband was a leper, and she transmitted the disease to me when we made love. But there is only one woman more beautiful than she in the world."

"Who is that?"

"The beautiful Isolde! And the two of them even dress alike."

The king, hearing that, laughed as he went away. Arthur, who had been happily jousting, came to meet him and asked him about the queen. Mark replied: "She is coming through the woods, good king. She is with Andrew, who is escorting her and looking after her." Then they said to each other: "I don't know how she will be able to cross Mal Pas. Let's stay here and watch for her."

The three traitors—may they burn in Hell!—came to the ford and asked the leper where those who were least soiled had crossed. Tristan pointed with his crutch to the softest part of the crossing, saying: "See the peat-bog at the end of the marsh? That's the best way: I have seen a good many people cross there."

The traitors entered the marsh, and where the leper had indicated, they immediately sank into mud up to their saddle-bows. All three of them fell off their horses. The leper, on the hill, cried to them: "Use your spurs if you are getting dirty in there! Let's go, lords! Now, by the holy apostle, give me something of yours."

The horses became mired in the soft mud, and the three men began to panic because they could not get their footing or a hand-hold. Those who were jousting nearby came quickly to them. Now listen to the leper's lie! "Lords," he said, "hold on to your saddle-bows firmly. May this soft marsh be cursed! Take off your mantles and paddle through the mud. I tell you, and I am sure of it, that other people have crossed today." He struck his goblet so hard he almost broke it. Brandishing it, he struck the bottle with the thong, while using his other hand to shake his rattle.

Then Isolde arrived. She saw her enemies in the mud and her friend sitting on the hill. That made her happy, and she laughed and rejoiced. She dismounted near the bank. Across from her were the king and the barons who had come with him, and they watched those who were flailing and wallowing in the mud. And the leper was urging them: "Lords, the queen has come to swear her oath; let us go hear the trial." There were few people there who were not happy to hear that.

Now listen to what the poor sick leper did! He said to Denoalen: "Grab this stick in both hands and pull hard." He held it out, and the traitor took hold. But the leper let go, and the other man fell back, sinking into the mud until only his hair could be seen. And when he was finally pulled out, the leper said to him: "I couldn't help it! My nerves and joints are numb, my hands were stiffened by the illness called the Mal d'Acre, and my feet are swollen from gout. Sickness has drained my strength, and my arms are weak and shriveled."

Dinas, who was with the queen, understood the ruse and winked at him; he knew it was Tristan beneath the cloak. He saw the three scoundrels caught in Tristan's trap, and he was delighted to find them so discomfited. The queen's accusers had great difficulty climbing out of the mudholes; it would take a long bath to get them clean! In front of everyone they undressed and put on other clothes.

Now you will hear about noble Dinas, who was on the other side of Mal Pas. He spoke to the queen, saying: "Lady, your silk garment will be heavily soiled. This marsh is full of filth, and I would be sorry to see any of it on your clothes." Isolde laughed, for she was not afraid; she winked and looked at him, and he knew what she had in mind. A little farther down, beside a thorn bush, Dinas and Andrew found a ford, where they crossed without getting dirty.   [3878]

Isolde was now on the other side, alone. There, across the ford, was a great crowd, composed of the two kings and all their barons. Isolde was very crafty. She knew that she was being watched by all those who were on the other bank of the Mal Pas. She walked over to her horse, lifted the fringes of the rich material covering the saddle, and knotted them together above the saddle-bows. No squire or servant could have protected them any better from the mud. Then she tucked the stirrup-strap under the saddle and took off the horse's harness and reins. She lifted the hem of her dress with one hand, holding the whip in the other. She guided the horse to the edge of the ford; then she struck him with the whip, and he crossed over the marsh.

The queen had been watched closely by those on the other side. The two great kings marveled at her, as did all the others who were watching. The queen was wearing clothing of Bagdad silk, trimmed in white ermine. Her mantle and tunic formed a train behind her. Her hair, tied in linen ribbons over a fine gold net, fell softly on her shoulders. Her head was encircled by a golden band, and her face was fresh and fair, with rosy cheeks.

She stepped toward the little bridge and said to Tristan: "I have an affair to discuss with you."

"Noble and worthy queen, I will come to you willingly. But I do not know what you want."

"I do not wish to stain my clothes. You will be my packhorse and carry me carefully across the boards."

"What?" he exclaimed. "Noble queen, don't ask me to do that. I am a sick, deformed leper."

"Hurry up and get in position! Do you think I am going to catch your illness? I assure you I won't."

"Oh, God!" he said. "Come what may, I never tire of talking with my lady." He leaned heavily on his crutch.

"My goodness, leper, you are large! Turn your face away so that your back is toward me, and I will straddle you the way a man rides a horse."

Then the leper smiled. He turned around, and she mounted. Everyone, kings and counts alike, watched them. Her thigh pressed against his crutch. He plodded on, pretending to stumble several times. He made a great pretense of suffering. The beautiful Isolde was riding him like a horse, with one leg on each side of him.

People said to one another: "Just look. [. . .] Look at the queen astride a leper who is sick and limping. With his crutch against her thigh, he is nearly falling off the planks. Let's go meet this leper as he comes out of the marsh."

The young men ran toward him. [. . .] King Arthur and all the others followed them. The leper kept his head down as he reached solid ground.

Isolde let herself slide off his back. Preparing to leave, the leper asked Isolde to give him food for that night. Arthur said: "He deserves it. Queen, give it to him."

Beautiful Isolde said to the king: "By the faith I owe you, this scoundrel is strong and has enough to eat. He won't even be able to eat what he already has. I felt what he has under his cloak! King, his pouch is completely full. I felt loaves of bread, and half-loaves and other pieces. He has food and clothing. If he can sell your leggings, he can have five pennies sterling. And with my husband's hood he can buy sheep and become a shepherd, or he can buy a donkey to carry people across this marsh. He is no good; I know it. He made a good profit today, for he found people who are to his liking. But he will not leave here with anything of mine, not even a farthing." The two kings laughed at that. They brought the queen's horse and helped her into the saddle. Then they rode off, while those who had armor engaged once again in jousts.

Tristan left the crowd and returned to his master, who was waiting for him. He had brought two fine Castilian horses, with saddle and bridle, and two lances and two shields; and it was impossible to identify any of them. And what of the riders? Governal had covered his face with a hood of white silk, so that only his eyes were visible. He had a fine, strong horse, and Tristan had his, named Bel Joeor, the best horse there was. He had covered his saddle, horse, shield, and clothes with black wool. His face was covered by a black mask, and his hair too. He had attached to his lance the pennon given to him by his lady.

They both mounted their horses and girded on their steel swords. Thus armed and mounted, they passed through a green meadow between two valleys and rode onto the Blanche Lande. Gawain, the nephew of Arthur, said to Girflet: "Look at those two riding toward us at full speed. I don't recognize them; do you know who they are?"

"I know them well," responded Girflet. "The one with the black horse and black pennon is the Black Knight of the Mountain. I recognize the other by his mottled arms, for there are few like them in this country. I'm sure the two of them are bewitched."

The two strangers rode out of the crowd, shields at the ready, lances raised, pennons fastened to the metal. They wore their equipment as easily as if they had been born in it. King Mark and King Arthur spoke far more of these two than of their own men down on the wide plain. The two knights were seen again and again in the front ranks of knights, and many others watched them. They rode through the front lines, but did not find anyone who would joust with them.

The queen recognized them. She and Brangain stood off to one side. Andrew, fully armed, rode up on his horse, with his lance raised and his shield firmly in his hand. He charged headlong at Tristan and attacked him. He did not recognize Tristan, but Tristan knew who he was. He struck his shield, knocking him off his horse and breaking his arm. Andrew lay on his back, motionless at the queen's feet. Goveral saw a knight riding forth from the tents: it was the forester who wanted to have Tristan killed while he was sleeping. Now the forester did not have long to live. Goveral attacked him without hesitation, thrusting his lance into his enemy's body so powerfully that it emerged from his back. The forester fell dead so quickly that a priest could not have been summoned. Isolde, who was noble and candid, smiled with satisfaction beneath her wimple.

Girflet, Cinglor, Yvain, Taulas, Coris, and Gawain saw their companions humbled. "Lords," said Gawain, "what can we do? The forester is lying here dead. Those two knights surely have magical powers. We do not know them, but they are making fools of us. Let's attack and capture them." The king added: "Whoever can deliver them to us will have served us well indeed!"

Tristan and Goveral rode down to the ford and crossed it. The others did not dare follow them, but stayed where they were. They were afraid, thinking the two were phantoms. They wanted to return to their lodgings, for they had had their fill of jousting. Arthur rode at Isolde's right, and the journey seemed very short to him. [. . .] The road branched off to the right, and they dismounted at their tents. Many tents stood on the heath, and even the tent-cords themselves were very expensive. The tent floors were strewn with flowers instead of reeds and rushes. All the roads and paths were filled with people coming to the Blanche Lande, and many of the knights had brought their ladies. Those who were camped on the meadow had been hunting stags. They spent the night on the heath. Each of the kings held an audience, and all those who were wealthy distributed gifts.

After eating, King Arthur went to visit King Mark in his tent, and he took his closest associates with him. Very few of them were wearing woolen clothes; most were dressed in silk. What else is there to say of their clothing? What wool there was had been dyed a rich scarlet color. There were many finely dressed people there. Never had anyone seen two richer courts; they could have satisfied any need. There was much celebration in the pavilions, and that night everyone talked about what was to come: how the noble lady was about to exonerate herself before the kings and all their barons.

King Arthur, his barons, and his friends retired for the night. Anyone who had been in the woods that night would have heard the music of pipes and trumpets coming from the pavilions. Before dawn it began to thunder, no doubt because of the heat. The sentinels announced the new day, and people arose without delay.

The sun shone hot soon after daybreak. The fog and the dew had disappeared. The Cornishmen gathered in front of the two kings' tents, every knight accompanied by his lady. On the grass in front of the king's tent they spread out a silken cloth, lined with dark brocaded material and embroidered delicately with figures of animals. The cloth had been bought in Nicaea. All the relics in Cornwall—whether in treasures or phylacteries, in chests or trunks, in reliquaries or jewel-cases or shrines, in gold or silver crosses or maces—were set out on the cloth and arranged in order.

The kings withdrew to one side, for they wanted to render a careful and impartial judgment. King Arthur spoke first, as was his custom: "King Mark," he said, "whoever advised you to take such an outrageous action committed a monstrous and disloyal act. You are easy to manipulate. You should not believe slander! Whoever caused you to convene this gathering made you swallow a bitter pill, and he should suffer and pay for it. The noble and good Isolde is eager to proceed with the trial. All those who have come to witness her defense can be sure that I will hang anyone who, after the trial, accuses her of infidelity. Such a person would be richly deserving of death. Now listen, king: whoever is at fault, the queen will come forward, before everyone gathered here, and she will raise her right hand and swear on relics, to God in Heaven, that never was there any love between her and your nephew which would result in dishonor to her, and that she never yielded to carnal passion. Mark, this has gone on too long; when she has sworn her oath, command your barons henceforth to leave her in peace."

"Alas, King Arthur, what can I do? You are right to reproach me, for only fools listen to accusations made because of jealousy. I believed them in spite of my better judgment. If she is exonerated here, anyone so foolish as to question her honor thereafter will pay dearly for it. Arthur, noble king, I assure you that I did not want this to happen; and from now on, her enemies will have to be on guard!"   [4181]

Their conversation ended there. Except for the two kings, everyone sat down. Isolde stood between the kings, who held her by the hand. Gawain was beside the relics, and the rest of Arthur's most prized knights surrounded the cloth on which they were arranged. Arthur, who was closest to Isolde, spoke first:

"Listen to me, beautiful Isolde. This is why you are summoned: you must swear that Tristan's love for you was never debauched or carnal, but only the kind of love owed to an uncle and his wife."

"Lords," she said, "praise be to God; I see many holy relics here. Now hear my oath, which I am swearing to reassure King Mark. In the name of God and of St. Hilaire, and on these relics and this reliquary and all the relics anywhere in the world, I swear that no man has ever been between my thighs, except the leper who turned himself into a beast of burden to carry me over the ford, and my husband King Mark. I exclude these two from my oath, but no one else. I cannot swear it about those two: the leper and my lord, King Mark. The leper was between my legs [. . .]. If anyone should require further proof from me, I am ready to provide it here and now."

All who heard her swear the oath could bear it no more, and they cried: "God! Who could doubt her oath! She has thoroughly justified herself! She did far more than she was asked to do, and more than the traitors demanded: she has no need to swear any oath other than the one you have heard, concerned with the king and his nephew. She swore and vowed that no one has ever been between her legs except the leper, who carried her across the ford yesterday morning, and her husband, King Mark. May anyone be cursed who ever again doubts her!"

King Arthur arose and spoke to King Mark in the hearing of all the barons: "King, we have seen and heard the defense. Now let the three traitors Denoalen, Ganelon, and the evil Godoine see to it that they never speak of this again. As long as they live, whether I am at peace or war, nothing can prevent me from coming immediately to defend Isolde, if I learn that she needs me."

She said: "Thank you, sir." The three villains were now detested by everyone. The two courts separated, and the people left. The beautiful blonde Isolde repeatedly thanked King Arthur.

"Lady," he said, "I guarantee you that as long as I am alive and healthy, no one will ever speak to you disrespectfully. The traitors will regret their actions. With respect and affection I ask the king, your husband, never to believe slander about you."

Mark replied: "If I ever do again, you should punish me for it."

They separated, and each one returned to his kingdom, King Arthur going to Durham, King Mark remaining in Cornwall. Tristan stayed where he was, his mind at ease.

* * *

The king now had peace in Cornwall, and he was respected by all, from far and near. He included Isolde in all his activities and took care to show his love for her. But in spite of this harmony the three villains had not abandoned their malicious schemes. A spy, hoping for a handsome profit, came to talk with them. "Lords," he said, "listen to me, and may I be hanged if I am lying. The king was resentful and angry with you the other day about his wife's trial. I am ready to be hanged or tortured if I cannot lead you to Tristan and let you see him with your own eyes as he waits to speak to his dear mistress! He is hidden, but I know where. When the king's activities take him elsewhere, Tristan is as sly as a fox; he goes into the royal chamber to say farewell. You can have me burned to death if you go to the back window on the right side and do not see Tristan come in, wearing his sword, holding a bow in one hand and two arrows in the other. You can see him tomorrow morning before dawn."

"How do you know this?"

"I have seen him."

"Tristan?"

"Yes, and I recognized him clearly."

"When was that?"

"Yesterday morning."

"And who was with him?"

"His friend."

"What friend? Who?"

"Lord Governal."

"Where are they staying?"

"They have fine lodgings."

"With Dinas?"

"Perhaps."

"They certainly aren't staying there without his knowledge!"

"Surely not."

"Where will we see him?"

"Through the bedroom window, and I am telling you the truth. If I show him to you, I will expect to be richly rewarded."

"Name your price."

"One silver mark."

"Agreed! And you will have much more than that: if you show him to us, you will add handsomely to your wealth."

"Now listen to me," said the scoundrel. "In the wall of the queen's chamber there is a small opening covered by a curtain. Outside the room there is a wide stream, and rushes grow thickly beside it. One of you three should go there early in the morning. Take the path through the new garden, and go directly to the opening; let no one pass by the window. Cut a stick and sharpen it. Use it to pull the curtain back carefully from the opening—it's always left unfastened—so that you will be able to see clearly when he comes to talk with her. If you keep watch that way, may I be burned to death if, in three days or less, you do not see what I have described."

Each of them said: "I promise that we will keep our agreement." Then they sent the spy on his way. They discussed which one of them would go first to witness Tristan's passionate encounter with his mistress. They agreed that Godoine would go first. Then they separated and went their own ways. By the next day they would know about Tristan's conduct. Alas! The noble lady was not on her guard against the villains and their scheme. She had sent word by Perinis, one of her servants, that Tristan should come to her the following morning: the king was going to St. Lubin.

Now listen to what happened! The next night was very dark. Tristan had set out through a thicket, and as he emerged from it, he looked around and saw Godoine coming out of his hiding place. Tristan lay in wait for him, hiding in the grove. He said: "O God, look after me; and may the man coming this way not see me until he is upon me."

Tristan waited with his sword drawn. But Godoine turned off on another path, leaving Tristan there, distressed and angry. He came out of the brush and ran toward the other road, but it was in vain, for the man who had evil intentions was already far away. Only a few minutes later, in the distance,

Tristan saw Denoalen coming toward him with two enormous hounds. He hid behind an apple tree. Denoalen rode down the path on a small black horse. He had sent his dogs to flush out a wild boar in a thicket. But before they could do it, their master would receive a blow from which no physician could cure him!   [4380]

The noble Tristan had removed his cloak. Denoalen was riding along fast, suspecting nothing. Tristan jumped out of hiding. Denoalen wanted to flee, but could not: Tristan was right in front of him. Tristan killed him. What else could he have done? The man would have killed him, but he was on his guard, and he cut off his enemy's head before the traitor could say: "I am hurt!" With his sword Tristan cut off the dead man's hair and put it in his pocket. He wanted to show it to Isolde to convince her that the villain was dead.

Tristan left the place without delay. "Alas," he said, "what became of Godoine, who was coming this way so quickly and then just disappeared? Where did he go? Is he gone? If he had waited for me, he would have met the same fate as the traitor Denoalen, whose head I cut off."

Tristan left the bloody body lying on its back on the heath. He wiped his sword and replaced it in his scabbard. He picked up his cloak and put his hood over his head. He covered the corpse with a large branch and left for his mistress's chamber. Now hear what happened to him!

Godoine rode hurriedly and arrived before Tristan. He had pierced the curtain so that he could see into the room. He looked at everything in the room, and Perinis was the only man he saw. The maid Brangain came in. She had just combed Isolde's hair, and she still had the comb in her hand. The traitor, pressed against the wall, looked and saw Tristan enter, holding a laburnum bow. The good man held his two arrows in one hand, and two long braids of hair in the other. He removed his cloak, revealing his handsome body.

The beautiful blonde Isolde came toward him and greeted him, and then, through the window, she saw the shadow of Godoine's head. The queen trembled with rage, but reacted wisely. Tristan spoke to her: "May God protect me, here is Denoalen's hair. I took revenge on him for your sake. He will no longer be buying or using shields and lances!"

"Sir," she said, "what is that to me? But I ask you to stretch your bow and see how well it bends." Tristan drew it and then hesitated. He gathered his thoughts, made a decision, and drew the bow. He asked news of King Mark, and Isolde told him what she could. [. . .] If Godoine could escape from there alive, he would incite a deadly war between King Mark and his wife Isolde. But Tristan (may God grant him honor!) would prevent him from escaping.

Isolde, intensely serious, said: "Friend, put an arrow in your bow, and be sure that the cord is not twisted. I see something that disturbs me greatly. Tristan, stretch your bow as far as possible."

Tristan stood thinking for a moment. Knowing that she had seen something that displeased her, he looked around. He was trembling with fear. Against the light, through the curtain, he saw Godoine's head. "O God, true King, I have made wondrous shots with bow and arrow; grant that this one not fail! I see one of the three villains of Cornwall, hiding outside treacherously. God, whose most holy body was put to death for all people, let me take vengeance for the evil these traitors have directed at me."

Then he turned toward the wall, drew the bow, and shot. The arrow flew so swiftly that nothing could have moved quickly enough to avoid it. It struck Godoine squarely in the eye, piercing his head and brain. Neither merlins nor swallows could fly half as fast; nor would the arrow have passed any faster through a ripe apple. The man fell back against a post and did not move again. He did not even have the time to cry out: "I am injured! God! Confession [. . .]"

Chapter XI

MARIE DE FRANCE: *THE LAY OF CHIEVREFUEIL (THE HONEYSUCKLE)*

RUSSELL WEINGARTNER

The lay entitled *Chievrefueil* is next-to-last in the unified group of lays found in Manuscript Harley 978 of the British Museum. Because this group of lays contains a number of references to its author, Marie, the consensus of scholars has been to declare *Chievrefueil* a work of Marie de France, a noblewoman of French origin who wrote three works in England during the last half of the twelfth century. From a statement of one of her contemporaries and from the fact that her lays exist in a number of manuscripts, we know that Marie was a popular poet in her day. Understandably she was quite proud of her reputation, and, in addition, she was something of a feminist, revealing a strong sympathy for neglected and unloved wives.

Of the twelve lays of Marie, *Chievrefueil* is the shortest. Apparently it is Marie's contribution to the long legend of Tristan and Isolde, which was extremely popular in her lifetime. Where she encountered the tale is unknown and probably undiscoverable, although she informs us that many persons had related it to her and that she had found a written text of it. In saying this, she is probably referring to the entire Tristan narrative, not merely the tale she is relating. This tale is not found in any of the various fragmentary manuscripts that scholars have used to reconstruct a hypothetical original of the Tristan legend. Possibly Marie's tale had been part of the oral tradition and had simply escaped the notice of poets who recorded this material. If so, the *Chievrefueil* incident probably was found in what is called the second division of the *roman*, a segment in which Tristan was temporarily banished from the court of King Mark.

Marie has summarized the longer tale in a brief eight verses, certain that her audience could fill in the details. She can therefore arrive very quickly at the beginning of her own contribution to the legend. In much the same way that she identified her lay *Lanval* with the Arthurian tradition, she seems once again to be assuring herself an audience by her use of the Tristan story. We see her utilize the same device, that of stating the irrelevant presence of a well-known character in order to give a kind of legitimacy to the tale. Just as, in *Lanval*, we notice "Yvain" among a group of knights, in *Chievrefueil* the queen stops the procession along the road and calls to her maid "Brangain," about whom we hear nothing more, but whose loyalty to Isolde was known to every reader.

The Tristan story was no doubt interesting to Marie because it is one more example of lovers who are kept apart by society's laws. But she must also have been charmed by the central symbol of the work, the honeysuckle entwined with the hazel tree. She may even be responsible for this traditional way of describing the two lovers.

Bibliographic note: For a good edition of all the Harleian lays, giving the Old French text, see Jean Rychner's edition, *Les Lais* (Champion, 1981). All the Harleian lays have been translated into English by Robert Hanning and Joan Ferrante, *The Lais of Marie de France* (Dutton, 1978), which contains a good selective bibliography.

Chievrefueil (The Honeysuckle)

It pleases me greatly and I truly wish
To tell you the truth
About the lay that they call *Chievrefueil,*
Why it was composed and about whom.
Several persons have recounted and told it to me,
And I found it written down,
About Tristan and the queen,
About their love that was so tender,
From which they had much suffering,
Then died from it on the same day.   10

King Mark was angry;
He was furious with his nephew Tristan.
He banished him from his kingdom
Because of the queen, whom Tristan loved.
He went off to his native land;
In South Wales, where he had been born,
He remained for an entire year;
He could not return.
But then he cast aside all restraint,
Heedless of death and destruction.   20
Don't be at all surprised at this:

For one who loves loyally
Is very sad and melancholy
When his wishes are denied.
Tristan was sad and dejected;
For that reason he left his country;
He went straight to Cornwall,
Where the queen lived.
He stationed himself in the forest, all alone,
Wanting no one to see him.   30
In the evening he emerged
When it was time to seek lodging.
With the peasants, with the poor people,
He took shelter for the night.
He asked them for news of the king
And what he was doing.
They told him that they had heard
That the barons were being convened;
They were to come to Tintagel;
The king wanted to hold his court there.   40
At Pentecost they would all be there;
There would be much joy and merriment,
And the queen would be there too.

      Tristan heard this; he was overjoyed.
She would surely not be able to go there
Without him seeing her pass by.
The day on which the king set out,
Tristan returned to the wood
On the road that he knew
The procession was to take.   50
He cut a hazel tree in half,
Split it so that it was squared.
When he had peeled the bark from the stick,
He wrote his name with his knife.
If the queen noticed it,
If she gave it her full attention,
She would understand well, when she saw it,
That the stick was from her beloved—
It had happened to her once before,
And she had indeed noticed it.   60
This was the meaning of the message
That he had imparted and told to her:
That he had been there a long time,
Had waited and remained

To keep watch and to find out
How he could see her,
For he could not live without her.
It was exactly the same with the two of them
As it was with the honeysuckle
That has attached itself to the hazel tree: 70
When it has so entwined itself and taken hold
And completely surrounded the trunk,
Together they can survive quite well;
But if someone then tries to sever them,
The hazel tree quickly dies,
And the honeysuckle as well.
"My beloved, it is the same with us:
Neither you without me, nor I without you!"

The queen came riding along.
She looked a bit ahead;   80
She saw the stick, noticed it well,
Recognized all the letters on it.
She ordered the knights who were accompanying her
And who were traveling with her
To stop immediately:
She wished to dismount and rest.
The knights obeyed her command.
She went far away from her party;
She called her servant,
Brangain, who was very loyal.   90
She moved a little distance off the road;
Inside the woods she found the one
She loved more than anything living;
Together they knew very great joy.
He spoke to her with great freedom,
And she told him whatever she wished.
Then she explained to him how
He would be reconciled with the king,
That it had greatly saddened the king
That he had banished Tristan in that way: 100
He had done it because of the accusation.
Then she pulled herself away, she left her love,
But when it came time to separate,
They began to weep.
Tristan returned to Wales
To wait until his uncle summoned him.

For the joy that he had known,
For his beloved whom he had seen,
And for what he had written down
Just as the queen had said it,   110
In order to commemorate these words,
Tristan, who knew well how to play the harp,
Composed a new lay about it.
I shall name it quite briefly:
In English they call it *Gotelef,*
The French call it *Chievrefueil.*
I have told you the truth about it,
About the lay that I have here recounted.

Chapter XII

THOMAS OF BRITAIN: *TRISTAN*
("THE DEATH SCENE")

JAMES J. WILHELM

Thomas of Britain is important because the ending of his version of the
Tristan and Isolde love story (which he would have titled *Tristan)* has survived, unlike those of Béroul or the German poet Gottfried von Strassburg.
But even though Thomas's *Tristan* has supplied an ending, it has not supplied
a beginning. The work is unfortunately fragmentary, consisting of only a
handful of segments that make up no more than one-sixth of the total story.
To get the whole Tristan tale, we have to piece these fragments together.
Here, at the ending, we have used the Douce Manuscript from Oxford University for lines 1487 to 1815, and the Sneyd Part 2 from Oxford for the last
few lines of the conclusion.

As for Thomas himself, we have no idea who he really was. Even his
name is taken largely from his German successor, Gottfried von Strassburg,
who says, in writing his own *Tristan*, that he followed "Thomas von Britanje";
"Britanje" could refer to either Britain or Brittany, since the Plantagenet
kings like Henry II (whom Thomas probably knew) had bound the Normandy–
Brittany area with the British Isles. In any case, it seems evident that Thomas
knew the Celtic legends well, was sympathetic to the English (as he shows in
a description of London preceding the part where this selection begins), and
had mastered the art of writing French romances in a sophisticated but marvelously artless way.

Thomas is often considered the initiator of the "courtly," as opposed to
the "heroic," school of romances. He concentrates on the psychology of love
and plays down the role of the warrior in medieval narrative. There are long
monologues in his work, and some of them are rhetorical almost to the point
of foolishness, as when Isolde says in the following selection that she hopes
that some sea creature may devour her body and Tristan's so that they may be

found together and then placed in a common grave. Despite these "unnatural" flourishes, there is a vigor in Thomas's writing that captures some of the powerful force that has kept this story alive for many centuries. It is obvious that Richard Wagner was inspired by Thomas in writing the "Love-Death" or *Liebestod* final scene of his opera *Tristan und Isolde*. As a result Thomas (quite unknown to himself) serves as an important link between medieval romance and nineteenth-century romanticism.

> *Bibliographic note:* The text translated here is that of Bartina H. Wind (Droz, 1960). For criticism see Joan M. Ferrante, *The Conflict of Love and Honor* (Mouton, 1973), and Gertrude Schoepperle, *Tristan and Isolt: A Study of the Source of the Romance* (2nd ed. R.S. Loomis: Franklin, 1959). Other translations have been made by A.T. Hatto (Penguin, 1967), R.S. Loomis (Dutton, 1951), and Dorothy Sayers (Benn, 1929).

Tristan

[After finally deciding that he cannot remain in Cornwall, Tristan (Tristran, as Thomas calls him) returns to Brittany, where he was born. He soon becomes involved in local warring, siding with the young heir of a neighboring duchy whose name is Caerdin (Kaherdin). This young man has a lovely sister named Isolde (Ysolt) of the White Hands, who proceeds to fall in love with the hero. Although he is still very much in love with Isolde of Cornwall, Tristan decides finally to marry this girl; he will never consummate the marriage, however. He tells the girl on her marriage night that he has been castrated, and so he preserves his chastity toward all women other than the "true" Isolde.

Back in Cornwall an evil knight named Cariado tells Isolde that her erstwhile lover has now taken a wife, and she is consumed with jealousy. Tristan meanwhile builds a special hall where he sculpts a statue of the absent Isolde so that he can commune directly with her figure.

When Caerdin learns that his sister is still a virgin despite her marriage, he is infuriated and confronts Tristan with this fact. Tristan calms him down and then shows him his statue of his beloved; Caerdin is overcome by Isolde's beauty. Soon the two vow to return to Cornwall, where Tristan introduces his brother-in-law to Brangain, Isolde's confidante. After several amatory misadventures Tristan and Caerdin decide to return to Brittany, where they immediately are involved in a variety of heroic exploits. A certain Tristan-the-Dwarf pleads with the hero to help him against a giant, but when Tristan aids him, the giant inflicts a poisoned wound upon him. Languishing helplessly, Tristan remembers Isolde's cure of him in the past when he was wounded by her uncle, and so he calls on Caerdin to go to London to beg Isolde to return and heal him. Tristan allows Caerdin forty days for this mission, telling him to hoist a white sail if he is successful and a black one if he is not.]

When Isolde had heard this message,   1487
She felt anguish in her heart
And pain and sympathy and sorrow—
Never had she felt any greater.
Now she thinks deeply, now she sighs;
She longs for Tristan, her dear friend,
But knows not how to reach him.
She goes to speak with Brangain.
She tells her about the misadventure
By which he got the poisoned wound,
About all his pain and his suffering,
And how and by whom he sent for her—
Otherwise his gash won't be healed.   1500
She revealed all of his torments,
Then asked her friend what she should do.
Now there are numerous sighs between them,
And lamentations and tears,
And pains and heaviness,
And grieving and depression.
In the talk they have together,
They express their sadness for him,
And thus after their conversation
They arrive at this decision: 1510
They will make the journey together;
They will go and see Caerdin first
To learn some more about Tristan's plight
And to help him in his hour of need.
Toward vespers-time they prepared themselves,
Taking with them everything they needed
While everyone else was sleeping;
And on the sly they crept carefully
In the pitch darkness with auspicious luck
Through a secret gate in the fortifications   1520
That loomed over the River Thames
Just as the rising tide swept in.
A little boat was waiting for them there,
And the two women quickly got aboard.
Rowing, drifting as the tide now ebbed,
Quick on the winds, they floated away,
Bending every effort to achieve their end.
They never ceased from steady rowing
Until they reached their flagship.
Then they raised the sails, and off they went.   1530
As long as the wind could billow them,

They scoured over the languorous deep,
Then followed the coastline abroad
On which the port of Wissant stands;
Then past Boulogne, past Treport.
The wind was brisk and beneficial,
And the ship that bore them nimble.
They sailed in front of Normandy,
Drifting with joy and gaiety,
Since the breeze was at their beck and call.   1540
Tristan meanwhile tossed with his wound,
Languishing gravely on his bed,
Finding no comfort in anything offered.
No medicine could help him—
Nothing anyone did was of avail.
He was longing for Isolde's arrival,
With no appetite for anything else;
Without her, he found nothing good;
He lived only with the thought of her.
So he languished there on his bed   1550
In the hope that she would come
And would remedy his illness;
He was sure he couldn't live without her.
Every day he sent someone down to the shore
To see if Caerdin's ship was coming back;
He had no other thought upon his mind.
Often he had himself carried down
On a litter to the side of the sea,
Where he waited to see if the ship
Was coming and what sails it bore.   1560
His heart was set on nothing else
Except for her arrival;
Toward this all his thoughts were aimed,
His longing and his will.
All that the world offers he counted
As nothing if the queen did not come.
Then he would have himself carried back
Because of the inner doubts he feels,
Since he's afraid that she may not come,
That she may prove disloyal to him;   1570
And he prefers to hear this from someone else
Rather than to see it with his own eyes.
He wants to keep a lookout for the ship,
But does not want to hear that he's failed.
He feels anxious deeply inside himself

Yet is still very passionate to see her.
He often complains to his wife, Isolde,
But never tells her about his longing—
Only about Caerdin, who isn't coming.
The longer Caerdin's absent, the more he fears   1580
That his friend has failed him at his task.
Ah, you should hear his terrible torment,
The profundity of his suffering,
Which is pitiful to all who love.
Never have you heard of a greater grief
From such a love, from such a longing.

Meanwhile as Tristan awaited Isolde,
The lady herself was anxious to land
After drawing in sight of the Breton coast,
So that she could survey the whole coastline.   1590
How happy all are, how gaily they sail—
Till suddenly a swell leaps from the south
And strikes the middle of the mainsail,
Making the whole ship stop in its course.
The crew rush to turn the sails around,
But despite their effort it starts to move back.
The wind grows stronger, kicking up waves;
The waters from the deep are welling up;
The sky is turbulent, the air is dense;
Swells are surging, the water's black.   1600
It rains, it hails, a storm is raging.
Bowlines break and staylines snap.
They lower the mainsail and run adrift,
Dipping on waves battered by winds.
They send out the landing-boat on the brink
Because they seem close to the friendly shore,
But this is done inauspiciously
For the waves soon smash the boat to bits.
By this time they have lost so much
And the tempest has risen to such a pitch   1610
That no skipper—not even the ablest—
Can steady himself upon his feet.
All the crew are sobbing and wailing
And venting their sorrow out of fear.
Then said Isolde: "Alas, poor me!
God does not mean for me to live
To cast my eyes on my beloved Tristan.
He wants to drown me here in the deep!

Tristan, if I could just talk with you,
It wouldn't bother me if I died.   1620
Dearest lover, when you learn of my death,
I know you'll never again be happy.
You'll feel so desolate about my demise
That you'll lapse into deep, deep suffering,
And you'll never again be cured.
My arrival lies beyond my hands.
If God so wills it, I shall come,
And I'll nurse you out of your illness,
Since I don't think you have other pains,
Except that now you don't have the right help.   1630
This is my only sorrow and grief,
And in my heart I feel such distress
Because, my love, you'll never be able,
Once I am dead, to ward off your death.
I don't care a thing about dying myself.
Whenever God wills it, I will it too;
But as soon as you learn of my fate,
I know that you shall also perish;
Such is the nature of our love:
I can't feel any sorrow unless you're there;   1640
You can't die unless I die too,
And I can't perish without your loss.
If I have to face my end here at sea,
Then you will have to drown on land.
Since you can't drown there on the land,
You'll have to join me out at sea.
I foresee your death looming before me,
And I know that soon I shall have to die.
Lover, I'm failing in my desire.
I wanted very much to die in your arms   1650
And to be buried with you in the same tomb,
But we have not succeeded in this at all.
Yet—it still might happen—
For if I should drown out here
(Since you, I am sure, will drown then too),
Some sea creature might devour us both
And so, by sheer chance, we could enjoy
A single grave, my dearest love,
For someone might catch that creature
And recognize our bodies inside,   1660
And then join us in great honor,
As is appropriate for our love.

But this is nonsense that cannot be—
Unless, O God! You make it so!
Lover, what could you do here on the sea?
I know that you can never come here.
Yet I am here, and here I'll die—
Drown without you, Tristan my love,
And to me, it's a very great comfort, darling,
That you won't even know about my death.   1670
From this point on it will not be heard;
I don't know, dearest, who could report it.
You will survive me by a long time
And keep on expecting my sudden arrival
If it pleases God that He may heal you—
And that is the only thing I pray for.
I'm more anxious now about your health
Than I am about my own coming to shore
Because of my fine, true love for you.
But, friend, after my death I fear   1680
That, once you are cured,
You'll drop me completely from your memory,
Finding some comfort in another woman,
Tristan, my dear, after my death.
Surely I fear or at least I suspect
Isolde of the White Hands, my love.
I don't know if I should be so distressed,
But if death should come to me first,
I wouldn't live very much longer than you.
Ah me, I don't know what to do!   1690
But above all else, I love you.
I pray that God wills that we shall meet
And, my beloved, that I can cure you;
Otherwise let us both perish of grief!"
As long as the tempest lasts,
Isolde complains and loudly laments.
The winds and the brutal weather
Endure on the ocean for about five days;
Then the winds yield to fairer weather.
The crew hoists up the sail of white,   1700
And they skim along with rapid grace
Until Caerdin again sees his Brittany.
Everyone's happy, gay, and glad;
They raise the mainsail on high
So that all on the coast can perceive
Whether the color is white or black.

Caerdin wants to show off the color white
Because it was now the very last day
Of the forty-day period Tristan had set
For them to return to their native land.   1710
But just as they were skimming gaily,
A hot swell hit and the wind died down,
And suddenly they couldn't sail any more.
The sea was all calm and glassy smooth.
Their ship didn't budge an inch,
Except with the bobbing of the tide,
And they didn't have their landing boat.
Now they all suffered terrible misery.
They could see the shoreline up ahead,
But they had no wind to push them there.   1720
So up and down they bobbed on the waves,
Drifting forward and drifting back.
They couldn't advance their voyage a bit
Because they were so impeded.
Isolde was now bitterly distressed;
She could see the land she coveted,
And yet she couldn't disembark;
Desire impelled her to the brink.
Everyone on ship yearned for the land,
But the wind was too weak to project them.   1730
Often poor Isolde let out a shriek.
Everyone on the shore yearned for the ship
Which they still hadn't exactly spied.
The delay made Tristan sad and depressed;
Often he was moaning, and often he sighed
For Isolde, whom he desired with all his heart.
Some tears trickle down; he twists his body,
Almost driven to death by desire.
While he suffers this anguish and pain,
His wife Isolde appears before him   1740
Carefully contriving a clever ruse;
She says: "My love, Caerdin's coming now.
I've spied his ship out on the sea,
And I assume that it has trouble sailing;
And yet I can see it with my own eyes
And I'm certain that it is his.
God grant that he may bring the news
That will give some comfort to your heart!"
Tristan leaped up on hearing this
And said to Isolde: "My lovely wife,   1750

Are you absolutely certain it's his?
If so, then describe the mainsail."
Isolde replied: "I know it for sure.
I can tell you frankly the sail is black.
They've hoisted it up very high
Because the wind is failing them."
Then Tristan suffered a complete collapse—
Greater than any past or to come;
Turning his face now toward the wall,
He whispered: "God save us, Isolde!   1760
Since you won't be coming to see me,
My love for you forces me to die.
I can't hold on any longer to life.
For you I die, Isolde, my love,
Though you feel no pity for my suffering,
But you'll feel grief about my death.
My friend, it's a very great comfort to me
That you'll feel pity about my death."
Three times he uttered: "My love Isolde,"
And on the fourth, he gave up the ghost.   1770

Then all his knights and companions
Ran wailing around the castle.
Their cries were loud, their passion great.
Knights and sergeants leapt to the task
And bore him nobly from his bed,
Laying him out on a cloth of silk,
Covering him with a shroud that's striped.
The wind then rose up on the sea
And billowed out the middle of the sails,
Bearing the ship at last to shore.   1780
Isolde clambered down from the bark
And heard the wailing in the streets
And the bells clanging in churches and chapels.
She asked some people what had happened:
Why all this clamor of the bells
And for whom everyone was weeping?
An aged man replied to her then:
"Milady, may the Good Lord help me!
We've suffered such an awful loss
That no people will ever suffer more.   1790
Tristan the valiant, the grand, lies dead.
He was the mainstay of all our realm.
He was generous to those in need

And helpful to those under stress.
He has died just now in his bed
From a wound he received in battle.
Never has such a catastrophe
Fallen upon our kingdom."
As soon as she heard this news,
Isolde was rendered mute with grief.   1800
She was so stricken by his death
That she ran up the street in disarray
Ahead of the others into the palace.
Never in their lives had the Bretons seen
A lady of such stunning beauty.
All were wondering throughout the city
Where she came from, who she was.
Isolde went inside to view the body
And, turning toward the Orient,
She prayed for him in a pitiful way: 1810
"Dear lover, Tristan, as I see you dead,
Reason tells me I can't live any more.
You died out of your great love for me,
And I'll die, darling, out of compassion,
Since I was unable to come here in time
And cure your body of its wound.
Dearest, dearest, because of your death
I'll never know any comfort again—
Any joy or happiness or delight.
Curses on that storm that made me   1820
Delay so long out there at sea
So that I couldn't come to see you!
If I had only come here in time,
I could have given you back your life;
I could have spoken to you very softly
About the great love we once shared;
I could have bemoaned our current fate,
Mentioning our happiness and ecstasy,
Our pain as well as the sorrow
That we've had throughout our affair;   1830
I could have reminded you of all this
And kissed you and embraced you.
If I couldn't cure you entirely myself,
Then we might have died together!
But since I couldn't come in time
And didn't know the true outcome,
Arriving only to find you dead,

I'll now take solace from the same drink.
You surrendered your life because of me,
And now I'll do the same for my beloved; 1840
For you I want to die the very same way."
Lying beside him, she hugged him tightly,
Pouring kisses over his mouth and face,
And drawing him closely to her breast;
Body to body, mouth to mouth,
She rendered up her spirit completely
And suffered death there at his side
Out of her sorrow for her true love.
Tristan perished because of his love,
And Isolde because she did not come in time; 1850
Tristan perished from his deep passion
And Isolde from her compassionate love.

[*According to popular mythology, the two lovers were buried side by side, and out of Tristan's grave there sprang a rose bush, while out of Isolde's came an entwining vine; others claimed that the two plants were a hazel tree and a honeysuckle vine.*]

Chapter *XIII*

CANTARE ON THE DEATH OF TRISTAN

JAMES J. WILHELM

Although Italy has not bequeathed us the wealth of Arthurian literature that one can find in France and Germany, it has left us several jewels, such as the lengthy fourteenth-century *La Tavola Ritonda* (The Round Table), an elaborate retelling of the Tristan and Isolde love story in prose. Also, from about 1250 to 1500, there flourished a popular form of art known as the *cantare* or folk-ballad. These were narrative poems sung in the city squares about Arthurian and other themes. The compositions, whose music has not survived, were divided into 8-line stanzas *(ottava rima)* and were frequently rhymed *ababababcc*.

Tristan was always one of the most popular heroes in this tradition. His love affair with Isolde, especially their tragic ending, held a grasp on Italian audiences that Arthur himself could not equal. This version of their death probably derives from Thomas of Britain's *Tristan* and the lengthy French *Prose Tristan*.

Although most folk-ballads are rather primitive in their diction and handling of plot and character, this one, despite some lapses in geographic and temporal continuity, conveys the tragic ending of the lovers in a way that is far more moving than most other versions. But it lacks two features that we otherwise associate with the love-death or *Liebestod*, as Richard Wagner called it: Tristan mistakes the color of the sails bringing Isolde to cure him (usually through the lies of his wife, Isolde of the White Hands), and two plants spring up over the double graves (usually a rose or hazel tree and a honeysuckle vine).

Like most *cantari*, this one exists in multiple versions. I have selected the more archaic one, which was printed by Giulio Bertoni in his edition of the *Cantari di Tristano* (Modenese, 1937). Very often this is joined with another *cantare* called *Le Ultime Imprese di Tristano* (The Last Deeds of Tristan), which is referred to below in stanza 2. I have omitted this earlier tale because it is not directly fused to the death scene and lacks the dramatic power of the ending.

Although Bertoni's version is archaic in its diction, I have not tried to duplicate this in my translation; nor have I attempted to follow the standard rhyme scheme. The names of the major characters in the original Italian are: Tristano, Isotta–Ixolta, Marco–Marcho, Arturo–Artuxe (from French Artus), Lancilotto–Lanziloto, and Zenevra–Ginevra.

> *Bibliographic note:* Besides Bertoni, one should consult the modernized and normalized version of this *cantare* by Armando Balduino, *Cantari del Trecento* (Marzorati, 1970). See the articles on "Italian Arthurian Literature" by Christopher Kleinhenz and "Cantari" by Susan J. Noakes in the *Arthurian Encyclopedia*, edited by Norris J. Lacy et al. (Garland, 1991).

Cantare on the Death of Tristan

1. At the time when flower and fruit flourish
    And every lover makes a beautiful expression
    Of fervent love for his chosen lady
    And desires with charming and gracious ploys
    To achieve the object of his will,
    I have come here to relate to you
    How Tristan through his beautiful love affair
    Underwent death with great remorse.

2. As you know from another *cantare*,
    Tristan had left the company of good Astor [Estor, Hector de Maris]
    And he wanted to travel all by himself
    Until he arrived at the shore of England.
    Then he found Sagramor, without a doubt,
    And they left for Castle Dinas in their own land
    And were received there with hospitality;
    At this point Tristan felt the need for repose.

3. When he and Sagramor had finally arrived
    At the fort of Dinas in Cornwall,
    And when Tristan had sufficiently relaxed,
    He was gripped again by love in a feverish way,
    Since he had languished alone for a long, long time
    Without his Isolde—may Christ lend me aid!—
    And he could not suffer the longing any further.
    He sent the queen a note, desiring to speak with her.

4. As soon as Queen Isolde realized
    That Tristan was in this sorry state,
    She sent him back a message that said clearly
    That he should come to see her without delay.
    Tristan immediately took himself to the road
    And traveled without a pause to the waiting queen,
    But in such a way that nobody heard or knew
    A thing about it—only his fair-faced love.

5. It was nighttime when he arrived there,
    And Sir Tristan stole immediately to the queen.
    He propped his lance up outside her chamber—
    Showing very little good sense in doing this.
    As soon as Queen Isolde saw him again,
    Overwhelmed with joy, she clasped him tightly,
    Since she had not seen him for a long, long time,
    Although the current hour was hardly propitious.

6. When Sir Tristan came to this rendezvous,
    He was not wearing any protective armor
    Except for a bright sword and the discarded lance,
    Which had been given to him by Morgan the Fay—
    A lance that could kill anyone without a doubt
    Because it had been charmed with an enchantment.
    And so as Tristan went to meet the queen,
    He carried along the tool that would cost his life.

7. Innumerable were the joys and the delights
    That Tristan felt at the side of the noble queen,
    As they constantly held each other in their arms
    All that first night through until the morning.
    No third person offered them any hindrance.
    They basked for eight whole days in this blessed joy
    Without King Mark's hearing or knowing that
    Sir Tristan was dallying with his lovely wife.

8. Finally there came a day when noble Tristan
    Was amusing himself along with Isolde the queen:
    He was strumming a harp, but very softly,
    While she was dancing to the musical sounds.
    Outside her room there passed one of her cousins
    Who heard this music and attached himself to the door;
    Peering through the keyhole, he saw Sir Tristan
    And then dashed off to King Mark and said these words:

9. "O noble sire, you simply have to know
    That Tristan is in Milady Isolde's boudoir,
    And they are pleasuring each other in love,
    Without showing any respect for your majesty."
    The king, on hearing this, changed his color,
    Feeling the sudden terrible weight of sorrow
    And saying: "My God! My life—how grim!
    Now I see clearly that he doesn't respect me!"

10. From that point on, King Mark enjoyed no rest;
    He strode to the boudoir that held Sir Tristan
    And grabbed the lance and stuck it through a window
    With frenzy, dealing his nephew a deadly blow.
    Tristan felt the stroke upon his right side,
    Which made him wobble and then—fall down.
    When the king saw that he had pierced his nephew,
    Without a pause, he quickly ran away.

11. When Tristan knew that he was badly wounded,
    He said at once to the loving queen:
    "Dear lady, I've been dealt a very bad hand;
    I'm afraid that very soon I'll have to leave you."
    The queen did not have a courageous enough heart
    To doctor him, since she saw that he was failing,
    And so he decided to leave her at once.
    And off he went to neighboring castle Dinas.

12. When he arrived at Dinas, he threw
    Himself on a bed and began at once to cry:
    "O cursed and unfortunate, unhappy me!
    I'm truly dead; I can no longer live.
    King Mark has wounded me so severely
    That no one except God can help me now!"
    Sirs Dinas [Dinadan] and Sagramor, full of grief,
    Poured out tears from their eyes and their hearts.

13. Dinas and Sagramor then had called
    Many fine doctors to the bed of Tristan,
    But the wound began to fester and show pus,
    And nobody could make a promise to heal it.
    Then it began to smell so putridly
    That everyone abandoned Tristan indeed,
    Except for his friends Dinas and Sagramor,
    Who never left his side—I'm telling the truth.

14. When King Mark received the report
    That Tristan was lying on the verge of death,
    He went to his queen and said these words:
    "From now on, I'll be safe in my own court,
    And won't have to bear any more evil gossip!"
    He chided her always with very probing words:
    "Queen, now separate yourself from Tristan,
    Who has held your love too long in his hands."

15. The queen did not deign to reply to this talk
    But kept on weeping welling tears.
    King Mark did not commiserate with her,
    But kept on rebuking her continually.
    The queen, who truly wanted to die herself,
    Said, "King Mark, if dear Tristan should perish,
    Those subjects who now honor you with love
    Will show you dishonor once he is dead."

16. And then the queen kept weeping on,
    Revealing to Mark her profound sorrow.
    Finally the king began to feel remorse
    For what he'd done, and from the heart
    He confessed: "Our royal majesty now
    Has lowered itself, Isolde, in value.
    Tristan may die—I can do nothing more!"
    And then he began to cry along with her.

17. Tristan, who kept failing and clearly saw
    That he could never escape from this woe,
    Said to Sir Dinas: "O my brave companion,
    Go at once to Mark, my royal lord,
    And tell him to come and see this poor sick soul,
    Since every sense I own is weakening;
    Before I make my exit from this life,
    He should come, by God, to witness my end!"

18. Those grieving friends, Sagramor and Dinas,
    Traveled together to see King Mark
    And told him that he should visit poor Tristan.
    King Mark came, along with many courtiers,
    Arriving at the castle with funeral pace.
    All of the people then reproached the monarch,
    Shouting: "If Tristan dies, everyone here
    Will offer indignities against your crown!"

19. The king, after dismounting in the stable,
    Rushed up to the chamber where Tristan lay
    And there he issued a sorrowful sigh
    And began to beat his body with his hands;
    And then he began to pray to Christ
    That He would make his nephew whole again.
    When the king saw Tristan, he greeted him,
    And Tristan at once returned the salutation.

20. When Tristan saw that Mark had arrived,
    He tried to lift himself up from his bed,
    But he lacked the strength and the power,
    And could do nothing but fall back.
    With lowered voice, he began to say:
    "Mighty King Mark, please feel welcomed!
    My death, which you have coveted so long,
    Has finally been dealt me as you planned!"

21. King Mark was weeping then with all abandon
    And said: "O my son, please pardon me!
    I have given you an egregious offense
    That will always be a cause for misery!"
    As soon as he let loose these words,
    Tears sprang forth out of his eyes
    So fervently that everyone around him
    Also wept bitterly for Sir Tristan too.

22. Sir Tristan said to Mark: "Please don't cry.
    Indeed I beg you: please pardon me.
    And furthermore, I beg, if you can will it,
    That you should offer me one last great gift:
    Please send to me your queen, Isolde,
    Whom you hold as your own beloved spouse,
    So that she may see me before my life is over."
    Said the king: "I shall see it's done."

23. Then the king had summoned Isolde the queen,
    Telling her to come and see her Tristan.
    Isolde, whose weeping now was without pause,
    Did exactly what the messenger asked.
    And on the way she said: "Alas, poor me!
    If God only willed that I could die with you!
    If I died now, my sorrow would be single,
    But if I live, I'll live in constant grief."

24. When Isolde arrived at Castle Dinas,
    She was crying so passionately
    In the midst of all the women-servants
    That they began crying with her too.
    Queen Isolde, bent over with grief,
    Went weeping as she made her way
    Until she found Tristan, who was suffering
    From a pain now approaching the final end.

25. When Tristan saw his lover coming toward him,
    He said: "My queen, bright star of the sky,
    My lady, I soon shall have to part from you.
    There is little life left for me in this world."
    Hearing these words, the queen then threw
    Herself with abandon upon his chest,
    So that Tristan, in the midst of his pain,
    Now lost even more strength and force.

26. Noble Tristan was veering on death's edge
    In the arms of his beloved Lady Isolde,
    While King Mark, with his great royal power,
    Was not uttering a word all this time.
    During the rest of that day, Tristan was silent,
    But at last he issued a cry that startled all
    As he said: "I'm going now to my death!
    Prepare for me my shield and also my sword."

27. With great lamentation, the sword was brought
    Along with the shield, and everyone wept;
    Milord Tristan took his sword in hand
    And with tearful words entrusted it
    To the others: "O sword, how I have loved you!
    For a very long time I showed you my love!
    But now I'm dying and you'll stay here;
    You'll never strike anyone again in my name!"

28. Then the shield was laid upon his breast
    As he was fast losing his last breath:
    "O shield of mine, I want to thank you,
    For you have spared me plenty of pain and death!
    Now I have no more power even to hold you,
    For my every vein is drained of strength."
    Then he lowered his helmet onto his head,
    Causing the viewers to vent more grief.

29. Then he said to Sagramor: "My dear friend,
    When I have passed beyond this age,
    Please go to Camelot with your sad tale
    Before the court of Arthur the King
    And give my long-proved, trusted weapons
    To him, and have it bruited all around
    About my death to all his barons—
    And especially tell Milord Lancelot."

30. The queen then began to utter some words,
    Saying: "Tristan, heart of my life,
    If you die now, whatever shall I do?
    I want to beg you, for the love of God,
    Not to abandon me here behind you,
    Since my heart will always suffer grief
    And pain and deep-felt sorrow
    If I have to live without my beloved lord."

31. Sir Tristan answered this way to the queen:
    "Milady, I am truly dying now!"
    Isolde, who had never stopped her weeping,
    Hurled herself directly on his form
    As Milord Tristan was dipping now toward death,
    Clutching lovely Isolde to him fiercely
    So that the hearts of both truly burst apart,
    And thus, in a last embrace, they perished in love.

32. King Mark, who was witnessing all this—
    How his queen and nephew Tristan had expired—
    Said mournfully to his surrounding men:
    "This bitter act has cost me much too much!"
    All of them then voiced a loud lament
    With heartfelt wailing and copious tears.
    It seemed as if the air and earth were issuing
    Floods of sorrow for this loving pair.

33. The grief and torment felt for poor Isolde
    And charming Tristan grew and grew
    Until both were finally laid to rest
    With noble honors in a single monument,
    With an inscription engraved in silver and gold
    That could be read by any viewer:
    HERE LIE ISOLDE AND POOR TRISTAN
    WHO THROUGH LOVE TOGETHER PASSED AWAY.

34. After Tristan and Isolde were interred,
    Dinas and Sagramor, abounding with grief
    And both stricken to the heart with sorrow,
    Carried the sword of Tristan and his helmet
    Polished bright, along with his precious shield,
    And crossed the sea when the weather was fine,
    Arriving at Castle Camelot in Britain,
    Where King Arthur lived with all his court.

35. Here there were wailings and woeful tears
    When the people heard about Tristan's death;
    Everyone was denuded of every joy
    As good King Arthur led the lamentations.
    Seeing his people in such misery,
    The king began to rend his royal vestments;
    And above all others, those who wept
    The most were Guinevere and Lancelot.

36. Many there were who swore that they
    Would wreak a vengeance upon King Mark.
    Queen Guinevere said with bitter grief:
    "Lovely Isolde, you've left me alone!"
    And Lancelot said, "Our dearest lord,
    Sir Tristan, unless Death rushes on me
    I'll show King Mark a very grievous end."
    Milords, this *cantare* ends in your honor!

[*Another cantare tells how Lancelot avenged Tristan's death by killing Mark.*]

A water-surrounded castle in Sussex of the type that may have suggested the castle of the Lady of the Lake. (Courtesy of the British Tourist Authority)

Chapter XIV

THE PROSE MERLIN AND THE SUITE DU MERLIN

SAMUEL N. ROSENBERG

The great seer of western Europe is a creature of Celtic legend, to whom Geoffrey of Monmouth gave literary life in his Latin *Historia regum Britanniae (History of the Kings of Britain)* and *Vita Merlini (Life of Merlin)*. He then appeared in Wace's *Roman de Brut*; but as a fully developed figure in vernacular literature he emerged only around 1200, in the poem *Merlin*, composed by the Burgundian cleric Robert de Boron. Robert had already written a lengthy verse narrative on Joseph of Arimathea and the origin of the Grail. His Merlin poem was intended as a continuation of the story, to be followed in its turn by a Grail romance built around the figure of Perceval. How far Robert actually succeeded in his endeavor is not quite clear, for the surviving *Merlin* is a mere fragment consisting of the five hundred opening verses, and there is no remnant of the Perceval poem. In both instances, however, as in the case of the Joseph poem, we have prose "translations" that may have been prepared by Robert himself and seem, in any event, to constitute a realization of his great plan for a Grail trilogy.

Among the versions of the Prose *Merlin* is one joined to a sequel known as the *Suite du Merlin*, an anonymous work over twice as long as Robert's, dating from the second quarter of the thirteenth century. The *Suite* makes mention of Robert de Boron as its author, but the claim is surely spurious. Together, these works were apparently envisaged as forming part of an even greater, more complex Romance of the Grail than Robert had conceived. Merlin—to a great extent reinvented in comparison with the models in Geoffrey—is the dominant character in the combined narrative, which opens with the demonic circumstances of his conception in pre-Arthurian times and leads, through many episodes, to his death at the hands of the Lady of the Lake. At the same time that he participates importantly in the action, he stands back and shapes it, influencing the behavior of characters and the course of events through his special powers. Dominant at a still further re-move from the action itself, he is all the while concerned to have the events chronicled in an abiding written record. Yet the two-part narrative extends its scope beyond Merlin and makes it clear that the limits of his life are insuffi-cient to define the work's purpose or coherence. Certainly the countless characters and sometimes bewildering adventures bespeak an intention that surpasses an interest in Merlin himself. Thus Robert concludes his story with the accession of Arthur to the royal throne; the *Suite*, moreover, pursues its tale past the death of Merlin and explicitly reminds the reader in its final sentence, as elsewhere, that the subject of overarching and continuing signifi-cance is the Grail. However different the two parts may be—and they are—they share that vision.

The selection of excerpts presented here, accounting for about one-fifth of the original, concentrates on the intriguing and commanding figure of Merlin. Spanning his whole life, it includes material from both Robert de Boron and the *Suite*, and allows their different conceptions and emphases to be seen: the prophetic Merlin of the first giving way to the sorcerer of the second; the historical and political interest of the one contrasting with the chivalric and supernatural bent of the other.

The translation attempts to convey the texture as well as the message of the original. It deliberately relies on a rather colorless, restricted vocabulary, along with the considerable repetition and limited syntactic variation that reflect the formative stage of French literary prose at the beginning of the thirteenth century.

> *Bibliographic note:* The text translated here was edited by Gaston Paris and Jacob Ulrich (Firmin Didot, 1886). For the *Merlin* proper I found occasional clarification in the texts edited by Alexandre Micha (Droz, 1980) and Bernard Cerquiglini (Bibliothèque Médiévale, 1981). For both parts I consulted the Modern French translation by Emmanuèle Baumgartner (Stock, 1980). Useful bibliographic references are included in all these volumes. In addition one might consult Chapters 19, 23, and 24, among others, in *Arthurian Literature in the Middle Ages*, edited by R.S. Loomis (Oxford University, 1959).

From the Prose Merlin

1. The Plot to Create Merlin

According to the tale, the Enemy was very angry when our Lord went down into Hell and freed Adam and Eve and as many others as He wished. When the demons found out, they were astonished; they gathered together and said: "Who is this man who has crushed us and smashed our defenses so that we can hide nothing from him and he can do whatever he likes? We never thought that a man could be born of woman and yet escape our grasp. This one, though, was born independent of us, and batters and torments us as much as he likes. If he was born of woman, how is it that we have no earthly pleasure in him and he ruins us so?"

Then one of the demons answered: "Lords, we have been ruined by what we thought would benefit us most. Remember the words of the prophets, who said that the son of God would come down to earth to save the sinners descended from Adam and Eve. And we went and seized those who said that the man who would come to earth would deliver them from the torments of Hell. Everything the prophets said has now come true. He has taken away all those that we had taken hold of, and we are powerless against him. He has taken away from us all those who believe in his special birth, who believe he was born of woman in such a way that we had no part in the event and were not even aware that it was going to happen."

"Don't you know, then," said another, "that he has them washed in water in his name? They are washed in the name of the Father, of the Son, and of the Holy Spirit, so that we can never again have them as we used to. We have now lost them all through this washing, so that we have no power over them unless they choose to come back to us. Thus the man who has taken them away has reduced our power. Moreover he has left ministers on earth who will save them, no matter how great a part they have had in our works; they have but to repent and renounce our works and do as the ministers say. We have thus lost them all. Our Lord has offered them a great spiritual gift: to save mankind, he came to earth and deigned to be born of woman and suffer all the torments of the world; and he was born of woman unbeknownst to us and without committing any sin of the flesh. When at last we came along, we tried and tested him in every way we knew, but he resisted all our efforts and chose instead to die in order to save mankind. He must surely love all men, if he was willing to suffer such great pain to take them away from us. We now have to seek a way to win them back so that they cannot repent or even speak to the ministers who could grant them the pardon that he paid for with his death."

Then all together they said: "We have lost everything, since he can pardon sinners up to the last moment. Whoever embraces him will be saved. Even someone who has always performed our works is now lost to us if he repents. We have now lost them all."

They went on: "Those who have harmed us most are those who kept predicting his coming to earth. Those are the ones from whom the greatest harm has come. The more insistent they were, the more we tormented them; so it seems he hastened to their rescue, to deliver them from the torments we were making them suffer. But how can we now find a spokesman of our own who could speak to men and tell them of our intelligence and our achievements and everything we do and how we have the power to know all things that have ever happened? If we had a man with such power, a man who could relate all that and live with all other men on earth, he could certainly help us with his teachings like those sorcerers and wizards who used to be with us, whose prophecies we knew were false. He would thus reveal everything said and done both long ago and recently, and he would be believed by many people."

Then they all said together: "It would be a great accomplishment to father such a man, for he would be widely believed."

Then one of them said: "I do not have the power to make a woman pregnant, but if I had, you could count on me: I know a woman who says and does whatever I want."

Another said: "There is one among us who is able to take on the appearance of a man and make a woman conceive. But he has to do it as discreetly as possible."

In this way the demons decided that they would engender a man who could lead the others astray. What fools, though, to think that our Lord would remain unaware of their scheming! But thus the Enemy undertook to create a man in his image, using his memory and his intelligence to deceive both mankind and Jesus Christ. (You can see how foolish the Devil is to think that he can deceive the One who is master over him and all the world.) With that agreement, then, the council ended. The demon who claimed power over a woman did not delay in coming to the place where she lived and making her do his will. And everything that she and her husband possessed she dedicated to the Enemy.

[The Devil gradually destroys the woman and most of her family. A surviving daughter, despite her virtuous behavior, falls victim to him one night in her sleep and conceives a child, whose father she is clearly at a loss to identify. She faces being burned at the stake for fornication. A worthy priest befriends her and persuades her judges to let the young woman live at least long enough to give birth. The judges agree, confining her to a tower with two women there to guard her.]

2. Merlin's Birth and the Defense of His Mother

She remained for a long while in the tower. The judges had prepared whatever was needed and delivered it to the two women who were with her. There she remained, as you have heard, and gave birth when God wished. When the child was born, he had the intelligence and the power of the Enemy, whose offspring he was. But the Enemy had been senseless to father him, for our Lord had redeemed with His death those who repent truly, and He had pardoned their sins, while the Enemy had seduced the young woman with a trick. She, though, as soon as she realized that she had been deceived, begged mercy of the One who mattered and then placed herself under the authority of God and the Holy Church, and she obeyed all the orders of her confessor. Nevertheless God did not want the Devil to lose what he had desired and what he had created the child for, and so, as the Devil wished, the child received his ability and his power to know all things said and done in the past. But our all-knowing Lord knew that the mother had confessed and repented and had done so sincerely, that she had not, moreover, been to blame for what had happened, and that in any case she had been washed pure by baptism. He did not wish the sin, then, to harm the child, and so God gave him the power to know all things to come. In this way the boy knew the things of the past through the Devil, and the knowledge of the future came to him from God, who thus wanted to counterbalance the other's work. Let the boy, then, decide which way to turn: to choose the Devil's path or our Lord's! For the Devil creates only the body, while our Lord confers the breath of life and, according as it pleases him to grant intelligence and memory, the ability to see and hear and understand; and more than to any other he gave the ability to this child, whose need was greater. We shall soon see which side the boy would choose.

When the two women saw the child and picked him up, they were both frightened, because he was all covered with hair, more than any other child they had ever seen. They showed him to his mother, who, seeing him, crossed herself and said: "This child frightens me!"

The other women said: "He does us, too. We can hardly hold him."

The mother said: "Send him down from the tower and have him, baptized."

They asked: "What name do you wish to give him?"

She said: "I want to name him Merlin, for my father."

After the baptism Merlin was entrusted to his mother for nursing, which she did for nine months. At that point the boy looked as if he were a year old.

When he reached the age of eighteen months, the two women said to his mother: "Lady, we would like to leave here and go back to our families. It seems to us we have been here for a long time, and we cannot stay forever."

She answered: "Of course. I cannot stop you." But she began to weep and to beg them, for the love of God, to remain a bit longer. With her child in her arms she went over to a window and kept crying. She said: "Dear son, I am going to die because of you, though I have done nothing to deserve it. No one knows who your father was, and I cannot be believed, whatever I say. I am doomed to die."

As she was bemoaning her death and the torment she expected, the child looked at his mother and said: "Dear mother, do not be afraid; you will never die on my account."

When his mother heard him speak, her heart almost failed her; her arms suddenly dropped from the child, and she let him fall to the floor. The women, sitting near a window, heard the noise and jumped up, convinced that she was trying to strangle him. "What are you doing to your child? Do you want to kill him?" they said.

She answered, stunned: "No. I was just stunned by the incredible thing he said to me, and my heart and my arms failed me."

They asked: "What did he say to you?"

"He said," she answered, "that my death will never come because of him."

The women said: "He is going to say something else." They picked up the child and listened closely for any further words, but he gave no sign of speaking any more.

After a long wait the mother said to the two women: "Threaten me, and you'll see if he tries to speak again." Then the mother took him in her arms and began to weep; she would truly have liked him to speak in front of the women.

They said right away: "Lady, what a horror that a beautiful woman like you should be burned at the stake because of such a creature! It would have been much better if he had never been born."

The child then spoke: "That's a lie. My mother made you say it."

The women were startled to hear him speak and said: "This is no child, but a devil! He knows what we have said and done!"

And they spoke to him and put many a question to him, but he said only: "Let me be! You are fools, and greater sinners than my mother."

The women were astonished and said: "This can't be kept hidden! Let's tell it to the people down below." The two women then went to the window and told the crowd what the child had said.

At this remarkable news they agreed it was time to let the mother face her punishment, and a letter was written summoning her to punishment forty days later. When the mother received the summons and learned the date of her ordeal, she was filled with fear and sent word to her good confessor. Many days passed, until only seven were left before she was to go to the stake. Whenever she thought of that day, she felt bewildered and terrified and burst into tears. The child, though, moving around in the tower and seeing his mother crying, began to laugh and look delighted. The women said to him: "You have no thought for what is on your mother's mind. She is going to be burned at the stake this week, because of you! What a curse that you were ever born, for thanks to you—unless God puts it right—she is going to suffer a dreadful end."

The child answered: "Dear mother, that is not the truth. As long as I live, no man will dare to kill you or touch you or deliver you to the stake, unless God wishes."

Hearing these words from the boy, the mother and two women were overjoyed and said: "A child who can say such things will be a wise and virtuous man, God willing."

That is where matters stood until the appointed day. That day the two women were released and the mother appeared before the judges with the child in her arms. But the judges first spoke in private to the women who had been with her, asking whether it was true that the child had spoken as reported. When the women related everything they had heard him say, the judges were greatly surprised and said that he would need to know a good many words if he were to save his mother from death. Then they came back. Meanwhile the good man who was the mother's confessor had arrived.

One of the judges said: "Young woman, have you any final request? Prepare yourself now, for your end is near."

She answered: "My lord, if you please, I should like to speak with this good man." She was allowed to do so and went into a side chamber, leaving the child outside. Many people put questions to him, but to no effect.

Meantime the woman spoke to her confessor, shedding bitter tears all the while. When she had finished, the good man asked: "Is it true, then, that your child speaks as they claim?"

She answered: "Yes, my lord" and recounted what she had heard him say.

The good man said: "Something extraordinary is going to come of this."

Then they left the chamber, and the woman picked up her child and stood once more before the judges. Seeing her, they said: "Young woman, will you state who the father of this child is? Beware of keeping it a secret."

She answered: "My lords, I see clearly that I am doomed. May God show me no mercy if I ever saw the father or ever even let a man come close enough to make me pregnant."

The judges answered: "We do not believe that that can be true, but we will ask other women if what you claim is possible, for we have never heard such an extraordinary thing."

With that the judges went aside to speak to a number of women about the young woman's claim. "Ladies," said one of the judges, "has any of you, or anyone you know of, ever been able to conceive a child and give birth without first having relations with a man?"

The women said it was impossible. Then the judges returned to Merlin's mother and told her what they had heard from the other women. "And now it is right that justice be done."

Then Merlin, angered by these words, jumped in front of the judges and said: "Lords, such justice is not about to be done! If you put to death all the men and women who have been guilty of adultery, you would have to burn two-thirds of all the people present here! I know everyone's secrets, and if I wanted to reveal them, I could make them all confess. You may be sure that many have behaved worse than my mother. In fact she is not guilty as charged. Or if she is, this good man here has taken the guilt upon himself. If you don't believe me, ask him."

The judges called up the priest and asked him if Merlin had just stated the truth. The good man then retold word for word everything that Merlin's mother had said to him. Asked whether everything had truly happened as she claimed, he answered: "I told her that she need fear neither God nor man and that justice would be done. She herself has told you how she was seduced and how she bore this extraordinary child without knowing who had fathered him or how; she came to confess and repent, and I ordered her penance."

The boy then said to the good man: "You wrote down the night and the hour I was conceived, and you can easily find out when I was born. In that way you can be sure of much of what my mother says."

The good man answered: "That is true, but I cannot tell where your knowledge comes from. Somehow you know more than all the rest of us."

Then the women were called up who had been in the tower with Merlin's mother. They compared the length of the pregnancy and the date of birth with the confessor's note on the time of conception, and it all fitted together.

One of the judges said: "Nevertheless she shall not be acquitted unless she states who the father is."

That angered the boy, and he said: "I know my father better than you do yours. And your mother knows who fathered you better than mine knows who fathered me."

That angered the judge, and he said to Merlin: "If you have any charge to make against my mother, I shall examine it."

Merlin answered: "I could readily say that, if you sent her to the stake, her death would be more justified than my mother's. If I make her admit that to you, acquit my mother, because she is not guilty as charged and everything she has said about my conception is true."

The judge was much annoyed by Merlin's words and said: "Merlin, if you are right, your mother will be spared the stake. But understand this: if you cannot prove your charge against my mother well enough to persuade me and save your own, you too shall be burned at the stake."

Then the judge and Merlin agreed to adjourn for two weeks. The judge sent for his own mother, while he had Merlin and his placed under guard; and he himself stayed with the guards all the time. The boy was often questioned about his mother and other persons, but throughout the two weeks no answer could be drawn from him.

On the appointed day the judge's mother arrived, and Merlin and his mother were led out of their prison. Before all the people the judge said: "Merlin, here is my mother, against whom you have an accusation to make. Say to her what you wish to say."

The child answered: "You are far from being as wise as you think. Go take your mother to a secluded house and take along your closest supporters, and I shall call upon my mother's supporters: all-powerful God and her confessor."

The people who heard these words were so dumbfounded that they could hardly respond, but the judge realized that there was wisdom in them. The child turned to the other judges: "Lords, if I can convince this man of my mother's innocence, will you all acquit her?"

They answered: "If she is deemed innocent by him, she will have no further problem."

As proposed, then, Merlin and the judge went off to a private place. The judge took his mother and two of his most upright friends, and the child took along his mother's confessor. When they were all gathered, the judge said: "Now you can tell my mother what you will in order to win your mother's release."

"My wish," said Merlin, "is less to champion my mother against a wrong than it is to defend the right, both God's and hers. You may be sure that my mother did nothing to deserve the death you want to put her to, and if you listen to me, you will acquit her and give up any inquiry concerning your own mother."

The judge answered: "You can't get by with that. You will have to say more."

Merlin said: "Are you assuring my mother and me that, if I can defend her successfully, you will release her?"

The judge answered: "That is true."

Merlin answered: "You want to send my mother to the stake because she gave birth to me without knowing who my father was. But if I wished, she could more easily say whose son I am than you can say who your father was, and your mother can more easily say whose son you are than my mother could now say whose son I am."

The judge said: "Dear mother, am I not the son of your true husband?"

"Yes, dear son," said the judge's mother.

Merlin responded: "My lady, you will have to tell the truth if your son does not acquit my mother and me. But if he were willing to do so with no further discussion, I would gladly keep quiet."

The judge answered: "I will do nothing of the sort."

"In that case you shall have the advantage of learning from your mother's testimony who your father was!" Those present were astonished at Merlin's words and crossed themselves. Merlin said to the judge's mother: "My lady, you must tell your son whose son he is."

And the lady said: "You devil! Haven't I told him?"

Merlin answered: "You know perfectly well that he is not the son of the man he thinks."

The lady was frightened and said: "Of whom then?"

He answered: "You know that he is the son of your priest. The first time you had relations with him, you told him that you were afraid you would become pregnant, and he told you that you wouldn't be, and he said that every time he went to bed with you he would make a note of it, because he was afraid you might go with some other man as well—though not with your husband, since the two of you had a falling out in any case. When the child was conceived, you were quick to complain to the priest that you were pregnant. If what I am saying is true, admit it. Otherwise I shall have to go on."

The judge was angry and asked his mother: "Is it true, what he says?"

In her fright the mother answered: "Dear son, do you really believe what this devil is saying?"

Merlin said: "If you do not admit it, I will tell you something else that you know to be true." The lady kept silent. Merlin went on: "I know everything that happened. The truth is that when you realized you were pregnant, you asked your priest to reconcile you with your husband, because you wanted to disguise the fact that you were with child by him. He managed to reconcile the two of you, and you went to bed together. In that way you gave the good man to understand that the child was his. Many other people believe so, too. And this very man here firmly believes that he is the son of your good husband. Afterward you persisted in such behavior, and you still do. The very night before coming here you were with the priest, and in the morning he escorted you quite far along the way. When he turned back, he whispered to you with a smile: 'Make sure you obey all the wishes of our son.' He knows, thanks to his notes, that this man is his son!"

When the judge's mother thus heard Merlin speak the truth, she felt greatly distressed and sat down. She realized that she would have to confess. Her son looked at her and said: "Dear mother, whoever my father may be, I am your son and will behave as your son. But tell me the truth: is this boy's statement true?"

The mother answered: "Dear son, in the name of God, forgive me! I cannot hide it from you: everything he has said is true."

At those words the judge said: "So the child was telling the truth! And he knew more about his father than I knew about mine! It is not right that I should punish his mother if I am not punishing my own." And he said to Merlin: "Merlin, I ask you for God's sake, so that I can clear your mother's name and your own in public: tell me who your father is."

Merlin said: "I will tell you, more out of love for you than out of fear of your authority. I want you to know that I am the son of a demon who seduced my mother. He is from that race of demons known as Incubi, who live in the air. He gave me the ability to know all things said and done in the past, and that is how I know what life your mother has always led. Our Lord, moreover, wanted me to have that memory because of my mother's virtue and her true repentance; and because of my own submission to the commandments of the Holy Church, He granted me the power to know the things that are to come." Then Merlin took him aside and said: "Your mother will go tell what I have said to the man who fathered you, and when he hears that you know the truth, he will be so frightened of you that he will run away. And the Devil, whose works he has always performed, will lead him to a river, and he will drown there. You can see, then, how well I know the things that are to come."

The judge answered: "Merlin, if what you have told me is true, I will never again fail to believe you."

There ended their private conversation; they reappeared before the crowd, and the judge announced: "This child has saved his mother from the stake.

Let all who ever see him know that they have never seen and will never see a man more wise than he."

They all cried: "God be praised if she is saved from death!"

At this point, according to the tale, Merlin remained with the judges. The judge sent his mother home, along with two men who would test the truth of Merlin's prediction. As soon as she was back, the mother spoke in private to the priest about the extraordinary thing she had heard. He was so terrified that he could not utter a word in reply, and it occurred to him that the judge would come to kill him. With this thought in mind he went out of the town and soon came to a river. He thought it would be better to drown himself than to be made to die a horrible death by someone else. Thus did the Devil, whose works he had performed, lead him to jump into the river and drown, which was witnessed by the two men who had accompanied the judge's mother. As the tale says, a man should not flee the company of other people, for the Devil more easily takes hold of a man alone than with a group.

The two witnesses returned to the judge and reported the deed, which had taken place on the third day of their stay, as they had seen it. The judge marveled at their news. He told it to Merlin, who laughed and said: "Now you can see whether I speak the truth!" He added: "Please repeat everything I have told you to Blaise, my mother's confessor."

The judge then related to Blaise the extraordinary fate of the priest. Then Merlin went off with his mother and Blaise, and the judges went on their way.

3. Merlin's Instructions to Blaise

Blaise, now, was a worthy man and had a sharp mind under his tonsure. Hearing such intelligent words from Merlin, who was at that time no more than two and a half years old, he wondered how the boy could be so wise. He probed and tested, until one day Merlin said: "Stop probing. The more you probe, the more you will wonder. Instead do what I ask you and accept everything I tell you, and I will teach you how to receive the love of Jesus Christ."

Blaise said to Merlin: "I heard what you said about being fathered by the Devil, and I believe it. I am afraid, then, that you may lead me astray."

Merlin said: "It is a habit of all faint-hearted people to see their own behavior in everyone else and more readily take note of the bad than the good. Just as you heard me say that I was a son of the Devil, you heard me say, too, that God had given me knowledge and awareness of the things that are to come. With that in mind, if you were wise, you would surely understand which direction I was bound to take. You may be sure that it is God who wants me to know these things, because the demons never gained my allegiance. True, I have not ceased to share their skill in ruse and trickery, but I have only as much of it as I need to have and I certainly do not use it for their benefit. Nor were they very wise in choosing a mother for me, for they put me into a womb that was not meant to be theirs, and my mother's virtue harmed their cause. If they had placed me instead in my grandmother, I would not have had the capacity to know God and would have belonged to them: it was through her that came all the trouble that my mother inherited from her father, all the disasters that you have heard her recount. But now believe what I shall tell you about faith in Jesus Christ. I shall tell what no one else, save God alone, could tell you. Make it into a book; and many people, hearing it read, will be better for it and save themselves from sin, and you will thus be performing an act of great charity."

Blaise answered: "I shall gladly write the book, but I beg you, in the name of the Father and the Son and the Holy Spirit, in the name of the dear Lady who bore our Lord, and in the name of all the angels and archangels and apostles and everything that comes from God, that you should not deceive me or lead me astray or do anything that is not according to the will of God."

Merlin answered: "May all the creatures that you have just named speak ill of me to God, if I ever do anything to you that is not in accordance with His will!"

"Tell me, then," said Blaise, "whatever you wish for our good, and I will do it from now on."

Merlin said: "Then go find a good supply of ink and parchment, and I will tell you many things to write in your book."

When Blaise was prepared, Merlin gave him a faithful account of the love that Jesus Christ and Joseph [of Arimathea] had shown each other, and told him the story of Alain and his companions, and how Joseph had relinquished the Grail and then died; and he recounted how the demons, after all these events, realized that they had lost their power over men, and how, since the prophets had harmed them, they all agreed to engender a man. "And you have heard from my mother and from others the effort and the cunning that they put into that. But in their mad excess they never gained my allegiance."

Merlin thus dictated the whole story to Blaise. Blaise marveled at the extraordinary things he was hearing, but they seemed right and true to him, and he wrote them down with great care.

While he was busily at work, Merlin said to him: "What you are writing down is going to bring me great suffering."

Blaise asked him to explain, and Merlin said: "Men from the west will come in search of me. They will have sworn to their lord to kill me and take my blood back to him, but as soon as they see me and hear me speak, they will no longer want to. When I go off with them, you leave for those parts where the keepers of the Holy Grail live, and from then on all people will be eager to hear or read this book, the fruit of your pains. Still, it will have no final authority, since you are not and cannot be an apostle: the apostles never wrote anything about our Lord that they themselves had not seen and heard, while everything that you are writing you can see or hear only through me.

Just as I live hidden, and always shall, from those to whom I do not wish to reveal myself, so, too, the book will remain obscure and only rarely will anyone reap all its benefit. You will take it with you when I leave with those who come in search of me. And so the book of Joseph, the book of the lineages that I have told you about, will be put together with your book and mine; your labor will have been completed and you will be worthy of their company. Your book, then, will be joined to that of Joseph, as clear evidence of the work that you and I have done. If they like it, they will show their thankfulness and pray for us to our Lord. The two books together will make a single fine book and will be of equal worth—except in this respect: that I cannot and must not relate the private words that passed between Joseph and Jesus Christ."

[*The throne of England falls into the hands of the usurper Vertiger, or Vortigern, who, trying to build an impregnable tower, finds that the walls keep collapsing. Merlin, coming to be recognized as a seer, offers to solve the problem: under the foundation there are two quarrelsome dragons that need to be released. Brought to light, the white one kills the red one and then dies himself. The tower is completed, but Merlin explains to Vertiger that, as prefigured by the dragons' combat, he, the usurper, will soon be defeated in battle by the sons of the late king. This occurs, and the elder son, Pendragon, accedes to the throne. With the help of Merlin's wizardry Pendragon and his brother, Uther, make progress against the Saxon invaders of their land, killing their king, Hangus, or Hengist. The brothers are happy to have an ally in Merlin.*]

4. The Testing of Merlin's Prophetic Wisdom

Then the two brothers, in the name of God and with the promise that they would defer to him in all matters, appealed to Merlin to remain with them. Merlin answered: "My lords, you must both know that I have all the knowledge of hidden things that I want to have. And you, my lord," he said to the king, "you know, don't you, that I have told you the truth about whatever you have asked me?"

The king answered: "I have never caught you in a lie."

"And you, Uther, did I not tell you the truth about a certain lady when you thought that no one could know it?"

Uther answered: "You have been so open with me that I can never lose my confidence in you. And it is because I know how worthy and how wise a man you are that I wish you would stay with us."

Merlin answered: "I shall gladly stay. But I want to share a secret of mine with the two of you: I am compelled, from time to time, to go off by myself, far away from people. Be assured, though, that wherever I am I shall have you uppermost in my mind, and if I ever learn that you are facing some problem, I shall do everything possible to come to your aid. But if you want to keep my friendship, please do not be disturbed whenever I go away, and every time I come back, give me a warm welcome in public. Worthy men will love me all the more, and the wicked, who will never be friends of yours, will hate me, but if you treat me well, they will never dare let it be seen. Let me add that except for you, in private, I will not disguise my appearance. I shall soon come to your palace, and those who have already seen me will run to tell you of my arrival. As soon as you receive the message, make it obvious that you are delighted, and they will tell you that I am an excellent seer. Then do not hesitate to ask me whatever your counselors suggest, and I shall advise you concerning anything you ask."

At this point, according to the tale, Merlin took leave of Pendragon and Uther and, taking on the appearance by which the people of the land would recognize him, he went to see the men who had been Vertiger's counselors. They were very happy and hurried to tell the king that Merlin had come. The king was delighted by the news and went out to meet him. Those who were well disposed toward Merlin said: "Merlin, here comes the king to meet you!"

The king gave Merlin a joyful welcome and led him to the palace, where his counselors immediately drew him aside and said: "My lord, Merlin here is the best seer alive. Ask him to tell you how you can capture Hangus's castle and how the war between you and the Saxons will end. If he wants to, he will tell you!"

The king agreed, and they then left the matter for the moment because the king wanted to show Merlin proper honor. Two days later, in front of his assembled counselors, he asked Merlin for his advice, as had been suggested: "Merlin, dear friend, I have heard that you are very wise. I beg you to tell me, then, how I can capture Hangus's castle and whether I can drive the Saxons out of our land."

Merlin said: "My lord, now you can see just how wise I am! I can assure you that ever since Hangus died, the Saxons have yearned for nothing better than to run away from this land. In fact your messengers will bring you that news tomorrow, and you will send them back with a peace proposal. Then the Saxons will send word that they are prepared to leave you this land that was your father's, and you will have them escorted away and will give them ships to ensure their departure."

The king said: "Merlin, that is very good. But I will send them a peace proposal beforehand by other means, simply to see how they respond."

He dispatched King Urfin, one of his counselors, along with two other men. They rode to the castle and were met by the Saxons, who asked the knights what they wanted. Urfin answered: "Lords, in the name of the king, we are asking for a three-month truce."

"We shall consider it," said the Saxons. They drew aside to deliberate and agreed: "The death of Hangus has left us sorely pressed, and we do not have enough food to remain here through the king's three-month truce. Let us ask him to lift the siege and leave us the castle as a fief held from him, and each year we shall give him as tribute ten knights, ten damsels, ten falcons, ten hares, and one hundred riding horses."

That was the outcome of their deliberations, which they conveyed in just those terms to the messengers. The messengers relayed it to the king and Merlin and all the barons, whereupon the king asked Merlin what he would do. Merlin answered that he would not intervene, for great harm to the kingdom would come from it. "But send them word right now that they should leave the castle with no delay—since they have nothing to eat, they will do so gladly—and that if they do not leave, they will have no truce. Tell them that you will give them ships and boats to enable them to go and, if they refuse, capture as many of them as you can and put them all to a harsh death. I assure you, though, that they will be only too happy to escape alive, for they now believe that they are going to die."

The next morning the king did as Merlin had said and dispatched his envoys with that message. When those in the castle received it and realized that their lives would be saved, they were overjoyed as never before, because since the death of Hangus they had not known where to turn. Word of it was sent throughout the land, and the king had them escorted to the port and given ships to sail away.

As you have heard, then, Merlin understood what was in the Saxons' hearts, and through his advice the king sent them on their way. Thus the Saxons left Pendragon's kingdom, and Merlin retained the full confidence of the king.

So things remained for a long time, until one day, when Merlin had spoken to the king about an important matter, one of the barons, who felt slighted, came to the king and said: "My lord, it is extraordinary how you rely on that man! All his knowledge, I tell you, comes from the Devil. Allow me to put him to the test, and you will be convinced that I am right."

The king answered: "I agree, provided you do not anger him."

The other said: "My lord, I promise not to do or say anything to displease him."

So the king agreed, and the baron was delighted. A powerful man by reason of fortune and family, he was regarded by everyone as both very wise and treacherous. One day he came up to Merlin at court, made a great display of friendliness, and drew him aside into a conversation with the king and two other men. He said to the king: "My lord, this is one of the wisest men in the world. I have heard that he predicted Vertiger's death to him, that Vertiger would die in a fire set by you, and he did. That is why I ask you all, in the name of God, since you know that I am sick, to ask him to tell you what kind of death I shall have. I am sure that, if he wants, he can say that."

The king and the others put the question to Merlin, but Merlin, who had heard the baron's words and understood perfectly well what envy and ill will they expressed, turned to the king and said: "My lord, you have asked me to predict his death, and I will: on the day of his death he will fall from his horse and break his neck. That is how his life will end."

At those words the man said to the king: "My lord, you have just heard him! May God protect me!" Then he drew the king aside and said: "My lord, remember what he said, for I am going to make a change and put him to another test."

With that he went home and disguised himself; then he returned as quickly as he could and pretended to be sick. He asked the king in secret to bring Merlin to him, but without telling Merlin whom he was going to see. The king agreed and promised not to tell. Then the king came to Merlin and said: "Merlin, come to town with me to visit a sick man."

Merlin answered with a laugh: "My lord, a king must not ride out without an escort of at least twenty men!"

Then the king picked some men to escort him and they went to see the baron. As soon as they arrived, the sick man's wife, as planned, fell to her knees before the king and said: "My lord, in the name of God, have your seer tell me whether my husband will recover!"

The king, with an innocent look on his face, turned to Merlin and said: "Merlin, could you answer this woman's question about her husband?"

"My lord," said Merlin, "please be assured that this man lying here will not die of his illness."

The sick man, pretending to speak with difficulty, asked Merlin: "My lord, how will I die, then?"

And Merlin answered: "On the day of your death, you will be found hanging." With these words Merlin, looking irritated, turned away and walked out of the house, in order to let the sick man speak to the king in private: "My lord," he said, "now you see that Merlin is a madman and tells lies, since he has predicted for me two different deaths that are incompatible. I will test him once more in front of you. I shall go to an abbey and there pretend to be sick. I shall have the abbot ask you to come, saying that I am one of his monks, and that he is extremely fearful that I may die, and he will ask you to bring your seer with you. I assure you that this is the last test."

The king agreed to this plan and then returned home. The baron went to an abbey, proceeded as he had said, and sent the abbot to fetch the king. Together with Merlin the king then rode out to the abbey and, when he had heard mass, the abbot and fifteen monks invited him to come see their sick brother and to bring along his seer. The king asked Merlin whether he would accompany him, whereupon Merlin called both him and his brother Uther before an altar and said to them: "Lords, the better I know you, the more foolish I find you. Do you believe that I do not know how this fool will die? So help me God, I know perfectly well! I shall tell you how, and you will be even more surprised by what I am going to say than by the two predictions I have already made."

The king said: "Merlin, can it be that a man can die in two ways?"

Merlin answered: "My lord, if he does not die as I have predicted, never again believe anything I say! I know for certain how he will die; and when you have seen it happen, you will ask me to foretell your death as well. And let me say to Uther that I shall yet see him king before I go."

With that the king, Uther, and Merlin rejoined the abbot. "My lord," said the abbot to the king, "in the name of God, have your seer tell me whether the monk lying there will ever be able to recover."

The king conveyed the question, and Merlin, looking irritated, said to the abbot: "My lord, he can get up whenever he wishes. There is nothing wrong with him; it is pointless for him to put me to any test, because he is bound to die in the two ways I have already predicted, and in a third, also, even more surprising than the others. After breaking his neck and hanging, he will drown. All three things will happen to him. And now let him put an end to his playacting! I know quite well what evil purposes he harbors in his heart."

The man sat up and said to the king: "My lord, now you can recognize how mad he is and see that he does not know what he is saying! How could he be speaking the truth? He says that on the day of my death I will break my neck and be hanged and drown, and all of that is supposed to happen at the same time! You know as well as I that no one could die like that. You need to wonder, then, whether you are being wise to have confidence in such a man and to let him rule over your counselors and yourself."

The king said: "I will not act before seeing how you die."

The baron was very angry to hear that Merlin would not be ousted from the king's council until after his death. But that is where matters remained, except that everyone learned what Merlin had foretold about the death and was curious to see what would happen.

One day, a long time afterward, the good baron who was supposed to die in three ways was riding along with a great retinue, when he came to a river. There was a wooden bridge over the river, and his horse stumbled and fell to its knees. The man was pitched forward and fell in such a way that his neck broke. He rolled over and fell into the water in such a way that his clothes caught on one of the piles of the old bridge, leaving his body dangling upside down, with head and shoulders immersed in the water. When they saw this, the men in the escort raised a great cry, and the people of the nearby town heard it and hurried over as fast as possible on foot or by boat. The good people said to those who were pulling the body out of the water: "Lords, see whether his neck is broken!"

They looked and said that there was no doubt of it. They all marveled at that, saying: "He really spoke the truth, Merlin did, when he said that this man would break his neck and hang and drown. Anyone who does not trust whatever he says is out of his mind, because it is obvious to us that he tells the truth."

Merlin did not need to be told of the event to know of it. He came to Uther, who held him very dear, and recounted the man's death just as it had occurred, and then told him to report it to the king, which Uther did.

The king marveled at the news and said to his brother, Uther: "Who told you that?"

Uther said: "It was Merlin."

The king sent Uther to ask Merlin when it had happened. Merlin answered: "It happened yesterday, and messengers will come to report it to the king in six days. I, though, am leaving, because I do not want to be here when they come. They would ask me many questions that I would not care to answer. From now on, moreover, I shall speak in public only in veiled terms, so that people will understand what I foretell only when they see it happen."

Now, the tale tells us that, once Merlin had spoken, he left for Northumberland to see Blaise. Uther, for his part, reported to the king what Merlin had said to him, and the king, thinking that Merlin was angry, asked where he had gone. Uther answered: "My lord, I do not know, but he said that he did not want to be here when the news arrived."

At this point the tale takes leave of Pendragon and Uther and speaks of Merlin in Northumberland relating all these events and many others to Blaise as material for his book.

On the sixth day the witnesses to the death of the baron arrived at the king's court and related the extraordinary event just as they had seen it. Whereupon the king said, and everyone else agreed, that no man was wiser than Merlin, and they decided to put down in writing from then on every prediction that they would hear Merlin make. Thus was begun a book called the *Book of the Prophecies of Merlin*, which contains what he foretold about the kings of England and about later events. Yet the book does not say who Merlin was or where he came from, because they wrote down only what he predicted.

5. The Battle of Salisbury and the Erection of Stonehenge

Merlin remained away a long time. Meanwhile he had won the full confidence of King Pendragon (whom the English called by his baptismal name of Aurelius Ambrosius) and his brother, Uther. When he became aware of their decision to put all his pronouncements down in writing, Merlin told this to Blaise, who asked him: "Merlin, will their book be just like mine?"

Merlin answered: "Not at all. They will write down only what they can understand before the fact." With that Merlin came back to the king's court, where he was given the news of the baron's death, as if he had known nothing about it. Merlin then began to make the veiled statements that were recorded in the book: prophecies that could be truly understood only after the event. Somewhat later Merlin very movingly told Pendragon and Uther how much he loved them and wanted to work for their power, their good, and their fame. They were delighted with this avowal and said to Merlin that he should feel free to tell them whatever he liked and that he should not hide anything of concern to them.

Merlin answered: "I will never hide anything that I should tell you. Moreover I am going to tell you something now that you will find extraordinary. Do you remember the Saxons, whom you drove out of your land after the death of Hangus?"

"Of course," they answered.

"They took home with them the news of Hangus's death. Hangus, now, came from a very noble line, and when the family received the news of his death and the expulsion of the others, they all came together and agreed to seek vengeance, with the idea of conquering this kingdom."

Pendragon and Uther were greatly surprised to hear this and asked Merlin: "Have they so many men under arms that they can think of attacking us?"

Merlin answered: "For every man of yours they will have two, and if you do not behave very wisely, they will destroy you and conquer your kingdom."

They said: "We shall follow your counsel faithfully and do exactly as you say." Then they asked Merlin: "When do you think their army will arrive?"

Merlin said: "The eleventh day of July; and no one here will know it, except you. I ask the two of you not to speak of it but to do as I say. Summon all your men, all your knights, rich and poor, and give them the warmest welcome you can; it is always wise to keep your men happy—and keep them with you at court. Then ask them to do their utmost to spend the last week of June with you at the entrance to Salisbury Plain. There you must assemble all your forces near the river in order to fight off the enemy."

"What!" said the king. "Are we then to let them sail so far inland?"

"Yes, if you listen to me. Let them disembark and then march away from the riverbank, unaware that you have your troops assembled there. Once they are at some distance, you will send men of yours down to the ships to make it clear that you are cutting off their retreat. When they see what has happened, they will be bewildered, and one of you must then pursue them so closely with his troops that they will be forced to camp far away from the river. In that camp they will lack water, and the boldest of them will be panic-stricken. Keep them cut off like that for two days, and attack them on the third day. If you do that, I assure you that your men will win."

The two brothers then said: "For God's sake, Merlin, please tell us, too, whether we are going to die in that battle."

And Merlin said: "My lords, nothing begins that does not come to an end, and no man should fear death if he receives it properly. Everyone living must realize that he will die, and you must realize that you will as well, and that neither nobility nor fortune can spare you from death."

Pendragon said: "Merlin, you once told me that you could predict my death just as you had predicted the death of the baron who was testing you, and you were right about his. Tell me then, please, about mine."

Merlin said: "I should like the two of you to send for the best reliquaries that you possess and to swear, both of you, by the holy relics that you will do whatever I command for your good and your fame. When you have sworn, I shall feel free to tell you what it will profit you to know."

They did as Merlin had stated, and when they had taken the oath, they said: "Merlin, we have followed your order. Now we ask you, please, to tell us why you had us do it."

Merlin answered the king: "You asked me about your death and the outcome of the battle, and I am going to tell you. But do you know what you have just sworn to each other? You have sworn that in the coming battle you will behave honorably and loyally both to God and to each other. And I will show you how. Make your confession, which is more fitting now than at some other time, because you are about to go into combat. If you do as I say, be assured that you will win, for the Saxons do not believe in the Trinity or in the fact that Jesus Christ appeared on earth; besides, you are defending your lawful inheritance, yours by right. One of you will die in the struggle, at peace with Jesus Christ according to the commandments of the Holy Church: he need hardly fear death. I want you to know that never, since the Holy Church was established on this island, has there been so great a battle as the one about to come, nor in your time will there ever be. Each of you has sworn to the other that he will fight for his honor and his fame. I want you to know, even if I do not speak more specifically, that one of you is to depart from this life. On the site of the battle the one surviving will, under my guidance, build the finest and most imposing monument he can. And I promise to offer so much help that this work of mine will last as long as Christendom. I have told you that one of you is to die. Now see that you show your valor!"

After a while the day of the convocation came. The two brothers had done as Merlin had ordered, and at Pentecost they came to the river to hold court, and everyone assembled there. They were generous with gifts and unstinting in their hospitality. There they still were in the first week of July, when they learned that the enemy ships had arrived. At this news Uther was convinced that Merlin had told him the truth, and he ordered the prelates of the Holy Church to see that all the men in the army confessed their sins and forgave one another their wrongs. Meanwhile the invaders had disembarked. They remained in their camp for eight days and on the ninth rode out. King Pendragon, who had spies in their army and knew what they were doing, told Merlin, and Merlin said that it was indeed true. Then the king asked him how to proceed. Merlin said: "You will dispatch Uther tomorrow, together with a large company of men. Once he is sure that the Saxons are far from their ships, let them bar their way back to both the river and the sea and force them to camp out in the fields. Let him pull back then, and in the morning, when the Saxons try to push ahead, let him attack them and keep so close that they will not be able to ride on their way. Then they will all regret that they had not stayed at home! Uther and his men should keep this up for two days. On the third day, as soon as the sky is bright and clear, you will see a red dragon dashing through the air between heaven and earth. You must then attack. When you see that sign, you can fight with no fear, because it will be a sign of your name, and your side will win."

With that they separated, and Merlin came to Uther and said: "See that you show your valor, for you need not fear death in this battle." Merlin then went to join Blaise in Northumberland and related everything that had happened. Blaise put it into writing, and thanks to his book we know it today. But here the tale falls silent about him and Merlin and returns to the deeds of Uther and Pendragon in their battle with the Saxons.

Now, according to the tale, the two brothers did exactly as Merlin had prescribed. Uther chose a great company of horsemen, the strongest and the best that he could find, and rode with them until they could see the camp that the Saxon army had set up on open ground. They spread out between the ships and the tents and thus forced the enemy to spend that night out in the fields with no water and far from the ships where their food supplies were. For two days Uther held them in such a grip that they could not move in any direction. On the third day King Pendragon came with a great company of men, whom he commanded to prepare and take their places for battle. When the Saxons saw the two armies around them, they were panic-stricken. Uther and his troops attacked them so fiercely that they were thrust back toward Pendragon's army. There was such noise, such shouting, such clamor, that you couldn't have heard God thundering. Pendragon's men were all prepared to strike as soon as the king ordered, but he was waiting for the monster to appear, as Merlin had said. And in fact the monster appeared with almost no delay. They saw a red dragon come flying through the air, spewing fire and flame through its nose and mouth, and roaring directly over the army of the Saxons. At the sight the Saxons were panic-filled and terrified. Pendragon and Uther told their men that their foe was surely destroyed: had they not just seen the sign foretold by Merlin? And so Pendragon's troops charged with all the speed their horses were capable of, and when Uther saw the king's men joined in battle, he and all his troops charged the enemy as well, and with even greater boldness. They all fought with great violence, and the battle was terrible and fierce. And in that ruthless battle King Pendragon met his death.

The Battle of Salisbury took place as you have just heard: Pendragon died, and Uther won. Many men were killed; and the Saxons all died, without exception, either drowned or slain. So ended the Battle of Salisbury. After the death of Pendragon Uther became king. He had all the bodies of the Christians brought together in the same place for burial; everyone brought bodies of friends, one after another. Uther had the body of his brother buried along with his men; and on each tomb he had the soldier's name inscribed and the name of his lord. Pendragon's tomb he built higher than the others, and he said that he would have no name inscribed upon it, for only fools could ever see that tomb and not understand who lay buried there.

After that Uther went to London with all his men, as did all the prelates of the Holy Church who were his vassals. And there Uther was crowned. Two weeks later Merlin came to court, and the king received him with great joy. Merlin said: "Uther, I want you to tell your people about my prediction that the Saxons would invade, about the agreement that you and Pendragon made with me, and about the oaths that the two of you swore to each other."

Uther reported to his people how he and Pendragon had acted in all matters in accordance with Merlin's words, but he did not speak of the dragon, which he understood no better than anyone else. Merlin, however, went on to reveal the meaning of the dragon. He said that it signified the death of Pendragon and the elevation of King Uther. Uther was then given a surname: to honor his brother, and to remember the appearance of the dragon and its meaning, he was from then on called Uther Pendragon. The barons thus learned with what firmness and steadiness Merlin had guided the two brothers.

Some time then went by. Merlin was on the best of terms with both Uther Pendragon and his counselors. One day, well into the king's reign, Merlin asked him: "What will you do to honor Pendragon, who lies in Salisbury Plain?"

The king answered: "I shall do whatever you wish."

"You swore to me that you would build a monument, and I told you that I myself would help you as much as possible. I now pledge to you that we will create something that will last as long as the world. You keep your word, and I shall keep mine."

The king said to Merlin: "What can I do?"

He answered: "Undertake something never imagined before, and it will be spoken of forever."

The king said: "Gladly."

"In that case send to Ireland for the large blocks of stone they have there; send your ships to fetch them. Whatever their size, they can be lifted with my help, and I will even go along to point out to your men which ones I want brought back."

The king then dispatched a great number of ships. Once they arrived, Merlin pointed out some enormous boulders and said to the men: "These are the stones to take." But at the sight of such size they thought this was sheer madness and said that even all of them together could not roll one of those stones over and that, please God, they were not about to load them onto their ships. Merlin said: "Then you have come here for nothing."

The men returned to the king and told him what an extraordinary thing Merlin had commanded them to do, a feat they were sure no one in the world could perform. The king answered: "Just be patient till Merlin comes. "

When Merlin came, the king told him what his men had said, and Merlin answered: "I shall keep my promise even without their help."

Thereupon Merlin brought the great stones from Ireland by magic, and they still stand in the burial ground at Salisbury.

Once they had been transported, the king took a great number of people and went to see that extraordinary accomplishment. Looking at the stones, they said they had never yet seen such large blocks and did not believe that human power could move even one of them. They marveled at Merlin's ability to transport them without anyone's seeing or knowing. Then Merlin said that the stones needed to be set up.

The king said: "Merlin, no one but God could do that, except you!"

And Merlin said: "Leave now, for I am going to honor my promise concerning Pendragon. I shall create something for the king that could never be accomplished by any other mortal man."

Thus Merlin set up the blocks of stone that still stand in the burial ground at Salisbury, and his accomplishment has lasted all this while.

6. The Creation of the Round Table

Merlin had great affection for the king and served him for a long time. One day he drew him aside and said: "Now that I see the whole country is safely under your control, I must reveal to you the greatest secret that I know. I have great love for you, as I showed when I saved you from being killed by Hangus, and you should feel the same way toward me. That is why I want to tell you something."

The king answered: "There is nothing you might want for which I would not do my utmost."

Merlin answered: "If you do it, the benefit will be yours, for I shall show you the way to God's love."

The king answered: "Merlin, don't hesitate to tell me what you want. You cannot ask for anything a man might do that I would refuse."

Then Merlin said: "My lord, what I am going to say will sound very strange to you. Please keep it a secret, as I want the good and the fame that it will bring to be yours alone."

The king promised Merlin never to speak of it. Then Merlin said: "My lord, I wish you to know that I have knowledge of all things done and said in the past and that it comes to me from my demonic origin. Our Lord, who is all-powerful, has also given me the wisdom to know the things that are to come. Through that gift the demons lost their hold over me, so that I shall never carry out their will. Now you know where I find the power to do what I do. Our Lord wants you to know something else as well. When you know it, be sure to carry out His will. Sire, you must believe that our Lord came to earth to save mankind and that at the Last Supper He said to His apostles: 'There is one among you who will betray me.' And the guilty one left His company, just as He had foretold. After that, sire, our Lord suffered death for our sake. Then a knight appeared who asked for the body and removed it from the cross. After that, sir, our Lord was resurrected, and the knight [who was named Joseph of Arimathea] went away to a wilderness with a great part of his family and many other people. A great famine occurred, and they complained to the knight, who was their leader. He asked God to show him why they were enduring such suffering. Our Lord commanded him to build a table, in memory of the table of the Last Supper, and to place on it a certain bowl that he had, from which Jesus and the apostles had eaten at that Supper; the table was to be covered with a white cloth, as was the bowl, except in front of his place. Bron, a brother-in-law of his, then caught a fish, which was put in the center of the table next to the bowl in front of Joseph. Through the power of that bowl the wicked at the table were separated from the good. My lord, whoever could sit at that table had the fulfillment of his heart's desire. Sire, there was always an empty place there, representing the place where Judas had sat at the Last Supper until he heard the words our Lord spoke for him and he withdrew from His company. His place remained empty until our Lord put another man there in order to bring the number of apostles back to twelve. The two tables were thus perfectly matched. And so our Lord fulfills man's heart's desire at the second table. The people who sit there call that bowl, which bears His grace, the 'Grail.' Now, if you trust me, you will establish the third table, in the name of the Trinity, which the three will represent. I assure you that if you do it, much good will come of it to both your body and soul, and things will happen in your lifetime that will make you truly marvel. If you agree, I shall help you, and if you do it, I assure you that it will be one of the things that the world will speak about most. If you trust me, you will do it and, believe me, it will make you very happy." That is what Merlin said to the king.

The king answered: "I do not want our Lord to be deprived of anything on my account, and so I agree to rely upon you completely."

Merlin said: "Consider, then, my lord, where you would best like to have the table."

The king answered: "I want it to be where you would like to have it."

Merlin said: "At Carduel, in Wales. Gather all the people of your kingdom there at Pentecost and prepare to give away many fine gifts; give me men, too, to carry out my orders. When you are ready, I shall choose the knights who are worthy of being seated at the table."

The king then sent out word to everyone, and Merlin went away to have the table made. That is how things remained until Pentecost, when the king went to Carduel. There he asked Merlin how his work had progressed, and Merlin said: "Very well, my lord."

On the day of Pentecost, then, everyone gathered at Carduel. There were many knights and ladies. The king said to Merlin: "Which men are you going to choose to sit at the Table?"

Merlin said: "Tomorrow you will see something you would never have imagined seeing. I shall choose fifty of the most worthy men in this land, and once they have taken their seats, they will never want to return home from here. Then, too, you will see the meaning of the empty place and of the other two tables reflected in your own."

The king said: "I am eager to see that."

Merlin chose fifty of the most worthy men he could identify and seated them at the Table; he called the king and showed him the empty place; many others saw it too, but only the king and Merlin knew why it was empty and what it signified. Then Merlin said to the king that he should take his seat, but the king declined to sit until he could see the others served, which he ordered to be done before he would take a step toward the Table. Once they had been served, he sat down as well.

In that way a week passed, during which the king gave many beautiful gifts and fine presents to the ladies, young and old. When it came time for the crowd of guests to take their leave, the king came to the worthy knights who were sitting at the Table and asked them what they had in mind to do. They answered: "Sire, we have no wish to move away from here. We would rather send for our wives and children, and live in this town at the pleasure of our lord. That is how we feel."

The king asked them: "Lords, is that how you all feel?"

And they all answered: "Yes, although we certainly wonder how that can be! Some of us had never even seen one another before coming here, and few were acquainted with any of the others; yet now we have as much love for one another as a son has for his father, or even more! We will never willingly separate; only death can part us."

The king marveled to hear them speak like that, as did everyone else who heard them. It made him happy, and he ordered that they be shown as much honor in the town as he himself was shown. Once everyone was gone, the king said to Merlin: "You did indeed speak the truth. I am now convinced that our Lord wanted the Table to be established; but I still wonder about the empty place, and I do wish that you would tell me, if you know, who will one day sit there."

Merlin said: "I can tell you that the place will not be taken in your lifetime. The man who will take it will be born in due time, but to a father who has not yet married and does not know that he is to sire him. It must happen, too, that the man who is to take this place will first occupy the empty seat at the Table of the Grail (something that the guardians of the Grail will have never seen before). It will happen not in your lifetime but during the life of the king who comes after you. Meanwhile I should like you to hold your assemblies and maintain your court in this town, and to live here yourself and gather your people here for the annual feasts."

The king said: "Gladly, Merlin."

Merlin said: "I shall be away, and you will not see me for a long time."

Then the king asked him: "Merlin, where are you going? Do you mean you will not attend all the great gatherings that I shall have here?"

Merlin said: "No, I cannot be present. I want your people to credit everything they are going to see happen, and not simply dismiss it as my work."

At this point, according to the tale, Merlin took leave of Uther Pendragon and went to rejoin Blaise in Northumberland. He told him about the establishment of the Table and all the other things that you have heard or will hear in this book. And for more than two years Merlin stayed away from the king's court.

7. Uther Pendragon's Desire for Ygerne

The king had long been in the habit of holding his court at Carduel when one day he decided to summon all his barons and have them bring their wives with them. He sent letters throughout the land summoning them for Christmas, and the barons did as he commanded. There came to court a great number of ladies, maidens, and knights. I cannot name all the people who came, but can tell you about those who are spoken of in my tale. I want you to know, then, that the duke of Tintagel was present, together with his wife, Ygerne. When the king saw her, he fell passionately in love with her, but he never let it show, except that he tended to look at her more than at the other women. She became aware of it and realized that the king liked to look at her. With that knowledge she avoided as much as possible coming into his presence, for she was no less virtuous than beautiful. The king, in order to express his love, but also to keep anyone from noticing it, sent presents to all the ladies, and to Ygerne he sent those that he thought she would like the best. Seeing that he sent presents to all the other women as well, she neither wished nor dared to refuse his gifts.

Before the court dispersed, the king invited all his barons to come back at Pentecost together with their wives, just as they had come to this feast. They all agreed very gladly. When the duke of Tintagel took his leave, the king accompanied him a long way and showed him great honor. Just before turning back, the king whispered to Ygerne that he wanted her to know that she was carrying off his heart with her. She, though, offered no acknowledgment, and with that the two parted.

The king remained in Carduel and saw to the entertainment and comfort of the worthy men at the Table, but his heart was always with Ygerne. He waited like that until Pentecost, when the barons and their ladies returned. The king was very happy when Ygerne came back, and he gave her many presents in the course of those days. When he sat down to dinner, he had the duke and Ygerne sit beside him. So generous were his gifts and his attentions that Ygerne could no longer deny that the king loved her. Everyone, meanwhile, enjoyed the celebration very much, and the king showed his barons great honor. When the feast was over, they all made ready to take their leave and return home. The king urged them to come back when he would invite them, and they all agreed. With that the court dispersed.

The king endured his pain for a whole year. Finally he complained to two of those closest to him and told them what torment he was suffering on account of Ygerne. They said: "Sire, what would you have us do? There is nothing you can order that we will not do if we possibly can."

The king said: "How could I see more of Ygerne?"

They said that if he went to her land, people would suspect something and he would be blamed for it.

"Then what advice," said the king, "would you give me?"

They said: "The best we can. Proclaim a great gathering at the court of Carduel and make it clear to everyone coming that he is to plan to stay for two whole weeks and that he is to bring his wife. That will allow you to win the love of Ygerne."

The king summoned his barons, and they all came to Carduel. Once again he greeted them with many fine presents. He was very glad to see them all again, but to a counselor of his named Urfin [Ulfin] the king confided that he did not know what to do about his love for Ygerne, which was killing him. He could not go on living without seeing her: when he saw her, his pain grew lighter; yet he could not live without some further remedy for his love and would surely die.

Urfin answered: "There is something wrong with you if desire for a woman can make you think of dying! Has anyone ever heard of a woman who has not yielded when she has been wooed and begged the right way, especially with gifts to her and to the people around her? And you are giving up?"

The king answered: "You are right; you obviously know what is needed in such a situation. Please help me, then, in every way you know. Take whatever treasure of mine you want and give it to the people around Ygerne, and speak to her in whatever way you know will be helpful to me."

Urfin said: "I shall do whatever I can."

That brought their conversation to a close, but then Urfin added: "You be sure to remain on good terms with the duke, and I shall see to speaking with Ygerne."

The king agreed, and they undertook to act. The king behaved very graciously toward the duke throughout the week and gave many a fine gift to his retinue. Urfin spoke to Ygerne, telling her what he believed would please her most, and a number of times he presented her with very beautiful gifts. She protested and did not want to accept any of them, but one day she drew Urfin aside and said to him in private: "Why do you want to give me all these beautiful presents?"

He answered: "Out of admiration for your mind and your great beauty. But I cannot really give you anything, for everything the king possesses is already yours, and his very person awaits your pleasure."

She answered: "You mean . . . ?"

He said: "That you are the sole possessor of his heart and he is utterly yours."

She answered: "Whose heart do you mean?"

And he said: "The king's."

She crossed herself and said: "God! What a traitor the king is, just pretending to be a friend to the duke so that he can disgrace me! Urfin," she said, "do not ever speak to me about this again. You may be sure that I would tell my husband, and once he knew, your death would be sure to follow. I am telling you, I will keep it quiet only this time."

He answered: "My lady, it would be an honor to die for my lord. But what lady has ever before refused to accept the king as her lover! And he does love you more than anyone else. Surely you are fooling? By God, do take pity on the king! Be assured, besides, that you may face great problems if you do not, and that neither you nor the duke can prevail against the king's will."

She answered, with tears in her eyes: "I shall resist him perfectly well, please God. I will never again come near any place where he may be."

With those words Urfin and Ygerne parted. Urfin came to the king and told him everything Ygerne had said. The king answered that that was the way a virtuous lady should respond, but added: "Do not let that stop you from pursuing her."

The next day the king was sitting at the dinner table, with the duke beside him. In front of the king stood a very beautiful gold cup, which Urfin whispered to him he should send to Ygerne. The king raised his head and said to the duke: "My lord, ask Ygerne to take this cup and drink from it for love of me. I shall have one of your knights take it to her filled with good wine."

The duke answered in all innocence: "My lord, thank you very much. She will be glad to accept it." The duke called over one of his knights and said: "Brethel, take this cup to your lady from the king and tell her to drink from it for love of him."

Brethel [Britaelis] carried the cup to Ygerne in the room where she was dining and said to her: "My lady, the king sends you this cup, and my lord asks that you take it and drink from it for love of him."

When Ygerne heard that, she turned red with embarrassment, but she took the cup and drank and then held it out for Brethel to take back. But he said: "My lady, my lord asks that you keep it."

She kept it. Brethel went back to the king and thanked him on Ygerne's behalf, even though she had not said a word about thanks. Then Urfin went to see what Ygerne was doing and found her quiet and thoughtful. At the end of the ladies' meal, once the tables had been removed, she turned to him and said: "Urfin, it was dishonorable for your lord to send me that cup. Have no doubt that I shall tell my husband how you and the king are plotting to disgrace me."

Urfin answered: "My lady, you are surely sensible enough to know that once a woman has said such a thing to her husband, he will never trust her any more. And for that reason you won't do it."

Ygerne answered: "How wrong you are!"

And with that Urfin left Ygerne.

Dinner was over, and the king was feeling very cheerful. He took the duke by the hand and said: "Let us go see the ladies."

The duke said: "With pleasure, my lord."

The king and duke then went to the room where Ygerne was with all the other ladies, but the king was there to see her alone, and Ygerne knew it. She suffered through his presence until night fell and she could return to her own quarters.

When the duke joined her, he found her in tears. At the sight he was extremely surprised and took her in his arms as any truly loving man would do. He asked her what was wrong, and she said: "I won't hide it from you, for there is no one I love as much as you."

Then she told him, as you have heard, what the king was trying to do and said that all the ladies he invited and all these gatherings at court were simply his way of reaching her. "And now you have made me accept his cup and drink from it for love of him. I tell you, I can no longer hold out against him or against that counselor of his, Urfin. And yet I know that, having told you as much, I can only expect something terrible to happen. Please take me away from here, for I do not want to remain in this town any longer."

When the duke heard these words, he was very upset, as he loved his wife deeply. He sent through the town for all his knights. As soon as they gathered, they realized how angry he was. The duke said to them: "Lords, prepare to leave in total secrecy, and do not ask me why until I am ready to tell you."

They all said: "As you command."

The duke said: "Leave all your baggage and take only your arms and your horses. The rest will follow tomorrow. I do not want the king to know that I am leaving, or anyone else that I can hide it from."

Everything was done as the duke ordered. He had his horses brought for the departure, and he and Ygerne rode off as secretly as they could. And so the duke withdrew to his own land, taking his wife with him.

In the morning word of the departure spread very quickly through the town from those of the duke's men who had remained. When the news reached the king, it pained him greatly, and he was very troubled that the duke had taken Ygerne away. He sent for all his barons and informed them of the shame and scorn to which the duke had subjected him by leaving the court without his permission. They answered that they were all extremely surprised and that the duke had acted very rashly. They did not know, of course, why the duke had left. The king said: "My lords, how shall I get him to make amends? Advise me!"

They said: "Sire, just as you wish."

The king said: "With your agreement I shall send him word to come back and right the wrong that he has done. And he must return just as he went away!"

They all agreed. Two of the king's men rode off to Tintagel bearing the message. When they reached the duke, they told him that the king had sent for him. Hearing that he was to return to the court exactly as he had left it, he understood full well that he was to go back with Ygerne, and he answered the messengers: "You may tell the king that I will not go back to his court, because he has behaved toward me and my household in such a way that I am bound not to trust him or to go to his court. I will not say anything further, but, as God is my witness, he has made it impossible for me to trust him any more." At that the messengers turned back toward the king's court.

When the messengers had gone, the duke sent for the worthy men of his privy council and explained to them why he had come away from Carduel and how the king was disloyally pursuing his wife. They responded that, please God, he would never succeed and that a king who so betrayed his own vassal deserved to be punished. Then the duke said: "My lords, in the name of God and because it is your duty, I ask you to help me defend my land if the king attacks."

They answered that they would gladly do so and would help him as fully as they could. Thus did the duke take counsel with his vassals.

The messengers, back at court, gave the king the duke's reply. The king said that he was extremely surprised by the rashness of the duke, whom he had always considered a very wise man. He asked his barons to help him in erasing the shame that the duke had brought upon his court. They answered that they would not refuse him, but they all asked that in loyal fashion he not take action against the duke for another forty days. The king agreed and asked them to be at Tintagel in forty days, ready to do battle. They said that they would be there, and the king then sent his messengers to the duke to issue the challenge. The duke said that he would defend himself if he could and, once the messengers had left, he made ready for the defense. The messengers reported to the king that the duke would defend himself if he were attacked.

The king was very vexed to hear that. Summoning his barons from throughout the land, he met them all at the edge of the duke's estates and from there started to ravage his towns and castles. Then the king heard that the duke was in one castle and his wife in another. He gathered his counselors and asked them which one they thought he should attack first, and they advised him to attack the duke, for if he defeated him, he would have the whole land under his control.

The king accepted their unanimous advice, but as he was riding toward the duke's castle, he said to Urfin: "Urfin, what shall I do about Ygerne?"

Urfin answered: "My lord, we must be patient when it comes to something we cannot have right away. You need to put all your efforts into defeating the duke. Once you have done that, you can see about the other matter."

At this point, according to the tale, the king laid siege to the duke's castle. A long time went by with no success, and the king's spirits sagged. He was heartsick for Ygerne, and all the while he was in his tent he wept. When his men saw him weeping one day, they withdrew and left him alone; but when Urfin, who was outside, heard about it, he came in. He was sorry to find him in tears and asked why he was crying. The king said: "Urfin, you must know why! You know that I am dying of love for Ygerne. It is clear to me that I am bound to die, for I have lost all the peace of mind that a man needs. Without it, all I can do is die. I do not see any remedy."

Urfin said: "My lord, how feeble-hearted you are, if you can think of dying because of a woman! But let me give you some good advice. If you sent word to Merlin to come here, he would surely be able to counsel you. Of course, you would give him whatever he might want."

The king answered: "There is nothing I would not do, but I know perfectly well that Merlin is aware of my distress. I am afraid I must have made him angry when I let someone try to take the empty seat at the Round Table. For a long time he has stayed far away from me. Or else it may disturb him that I love the wife of a vassal of mine. But there is nothing I can do about it! My heart just can't let go! Besides, I remember that he told me I should not send for him."

Urfin answered: "My lord, there is one thing I am certain of: if he is safe and sound and still loves you as he used to, then, knowing what distress you feel, he will not delay in coming to you."

With those words Urfin consoled the king. He added that if he made an effort to show good cheer and spend some time with his men, he would in fact feel much better. The king said that he would gladly follow that advice but he could hardly forget his love for Ygerne. For a while he did find comfort in that way; and he attacked the castle once again but could not capture it.

One day, as he was riding through the camp, Urfin came upon a man whom he did not know. The man said to him: "Urfin, sir, I should like to speak with you in private."

Urfin said: "And I with you."

Then they both rode out of the camp. Urfin dismounted and asked the man who he was. He said: "I am an old man. I was considered wise when I was young, but now they say I just speak drivel. But I'll tell you in confidence that I was recently in Tintagel and met a good man there who told me that your king was in love with the wife of the duke and that he destroyed the duke's land because the duke had taken her away from Carduel. If you trust me and give me a good reward, I know someone who could arrange a meeting with Ygerne and advise the king about his love."

When Urfin heard the old man speak this way, he wondered, with surprise, where he could have learned such things and he asked him to direct him to the man who could help the king. The old man answered: "I should like to know first what reward the king would give me."

Urfin said: "Can I find you back here once I have spoken with the king?"

The man said: "Yes, me or my messenger."

Urfin bade him goodbye and rode off. He came to the king and told him about the encounter. The king laughed and asked: "Urfin, do you know that man?"

He answered: "My lord, he was an old man."

The king asked: "When are you to meet again?"

Urfin said: "In the morning; and he told me I should be able to say what reward you will give him."

The king said: "I shall go with you."

The next morning the king followed Urfin and, once outside the camp, came upon a cripple. The king rode right past him, and the cripple cried out: "King, give me something I can be grateful for, and may God satisfy your heart with what you love best in the whole world!"

The king laughed and said to Urfin: "Urfin, will you do something for me?"

He answered: "Yes, my lord, whatever I can."

"Then go," said the king, "and hand yourself over to the cripple, and tell him that I have given you to him, since you are the most valuable thing I have with me."

Urfin rode straight back to the cripple and sat down beside him. The man said: "What do you want of me?"

He answered: "The king wants me to be in your service."

Hearing that, the cripple laughed and said: "The king saw right through me! He knows me better than you do! But go back to the king now and tell him that he would be leading you into a serious mistake in order to have his way. Tell him, too, that I realize he recognized me and that that will be to his benefit."

Urfin came back to the king and reported these words. The king and Urfin then galloped back to the spot where they had seen the man, but he was no longer there. The king said to Urfin: "Do you know who the man is who spoke to you yesterday in the guise of an old man? He is the same one you have seen today as a cripple."

Urfin answered: "Can a man really change his appearance like that? Who can he be?"

The other answered: "I tell you, it is Merlin, playing a little joke on us. And when he wants to speak to us, he will let us know!" That is where they let the matter stand. Merlin, meanwhile, went to the royal tent in his normal appearance and asked where the king was. A messenger then came to the king and told him that Merlin was asking for him. Uther Pendragon was delighted to hear this and, along with Urfin, hurried to Merlin as fast as he could. He said to Urfin: "Now you will see what I have been telling you: Merlin has come! I knew it would be pointless to send for him."

Urfin said: "My lord, now it will be clear whether you have ever shown enough respect for his will, for no man alive could be of greater help to you in winning the love of Ygerne."

Then Merlin approached Urfin with these words: "If the king were willing to swear on holy relics that he would grant me what, with no offense to his honor, I would ask of him, I would help him obtain the love of Ygerne. But you must swear this likewise before returning to him."

Urfin answered: "It can't happen too soon!"

The king agreed, and Urfin reported to Merlin: "It is time to bring an end to his suffering."

But Merlin laughed and said: "When the oaths have been sworn, I shall tell you how it can be done." Then the king had the relics brought in, and together with Urfin he swore, as Merlin instructed, that he would give Merlin what he wanted. After swearing the oath, the king said: "Now Merlin, I ask you please to give me your help. No man in the world needs it more than I do!"

Merlin answered: "My lord, to reach Ygerne you will have to take on a very different appearance, for she is a very virtuous woman and faithful to both God and her husband. But now you are going to see what power I have to help you achieve your goal." He went on: "My lord, I shall make you look like the duke, so that no one will recognize you. The duke moreover, has two knights, Brethel and Jordan, who are extremely close to him and Ygerne. I shall disguise Urfin as Jordan and myself as Brethel. I shall open the gate of the castle where Ygerne is staying and let you in, and you will be able to share her bed. Urfin and I shall come in after you, thanks to our disguised appearance. But you will have to leave very early the next morning, because, while we are there, we shall receive some very unexpected news. Now give the necessary orders to your troops and barons, and forbid anyone to go near the duke's castle before we have come back. And be sure to tell no one where you are planning to go."

Urfin and the king answered that they would do as instructed, and Merlin said: "Now prepare to leave; I shall change your appearance on the way."

The king hurried to do what Merlin had said and, as quickly as he could, returned and asked: "Are you ready?"

The other answered: "We have only to go!"

With that they set out and rode along until they came close to the castle.

Then Merlin said to the king: "My lord, you stay here, while Urfin and I go off for a moment."

They left, and Merlin disguised himself and Urfin. Coming back, Merlin handed the king an herb and said: "My lord, rub your hands and face with this herb."

The king did so and unmistakably took on the appearance of the duke. Merlin said: "My lord, you remember seeing Jordan, don't you?"

The king said: "Yes, I know him quite well."

Merlin then went to fetch Urfin, disguised as Jordan, and brought him back to the king. Urfin said: "I would not take you for anyone but the duke!" And the king said of Urfin that he looked just like Jordan, and, looking at Merlin, they were both convinced that they were seeing Brethel.

They went on speaking as they waited for nightfall. Then, in the early darkness, they approached the gate of Tintagel. Merlin called to the gatekeeper, who, just like the guards, was sure that he was looking at Brethel and the duke and Jordan. They opened the gate and let the three men in. Once inside, "Brethel" forbade the guards to tell anyone else that the duke had arrived, but there was no question of keeping the news from the duchess. The three men rode up to the palace. When they had dismounted, Merlin and the king spoke in private for a moment, and Merlin reminded the king to show the same cheerfulness as the duke. The three then came to Ygerne's chamber, where they found the lady in bed, and, as quickly as they could, Merlin and Urfin helped the king prepare to join her there.

The king and Ygerne thus spent that night together, and that night they engendered the good king who was to be known as Arthur. The lady received Uther Pendragon with all the passion she felt for her husband the duke, whom she loved very much, and they stayed together until dawn. At that point news came to the town that the duke was dead and his castle taken. The news was not confirmed, but when it reached "Brethel" and "Jordan," who were already awake, they rushed to their lord, still in his bed, and said: "Sir, get up! Hurry back to your castle, because your men think you are dead!"

He answered: "No wonder they think so, since I left the castle without anyone knowing!" In the presence of the others he took leave of Ygerne with a tender kiss, and the three men left the castle as quickly as they could. No one took notice of them, and the king was delighted. Merlin said to him: "My lord, I have kept my promise to you. Now keep yours to me."

The king said: "You have done me the best favor and shown me the greatest friendship a man is capable of, and, God willing, I shall keep my promise faithfully."

Merlin said to the king: "I trust so. Now I can tell you that you have fathered an heir. He will be the gift you have promised me, for you are not to keep him yourself, and you will grant me all your authority over him. We can write down the night and the time when he was conceived, and so you will know whether I have told you the truth."

"I gave you my word," said the king, "and I will do just as you have said. I grant you the child."

They all rode on until they came to a stream. There Merlin had them wash, and they all regained their normal appearance. Then they rode on to the king's camp as quickly as they could. At their arrival the vassals gathered around and reported that the duke was dead. The king asked how it had happened, and they replied that when he had left, the camp was very quiet and calm. "The duke realized that you were not here. He ordered his men armed, and they came out on foot and on horseback, and struck our camp and did much damage before we were armed. But the cry went up, and our men rushed to their arms, counterattacked, and pushed the enemy back to the castle gate. There the duke turned and fought bravely, but his horse was killed and he was struck down, and there the duke died among our foot-soldiers, who did not recognize him. We threw ourselves against the enemy at the gate, but, with the duke gone, there was very little resistance."

The king said that he was grieved by the death of the duke.

And so the duke of Tintagel died, and his castle was taken. The king spoke to his barons and told them how grieved he was by the duke's misfortune, and he asked their help in deciding how to make amends, for, not having hated the duke or sought his death, he did not want to be blamed for what had happened. "I shall make whatever amends I can."

Then Urfin, who was an intimate of the king, said: "My lord, the damage has been done, and we must repair it as well as possible."

Urfin then took aside a number of the barons and said to them: "Lords, how do you advise the king to make amends to the duchess and her family for the death of her lord? He is asking for your counsel, and it is your duty to offer it."

They answered: "We shall gladly counsel him, but you should counsel us about the best recommendation to make, for we know that you are very close to him."

Urfin answered: "Do you think, because I am an intimate of his, I advise him differently in public and in private? Do you take me for a traitor? If, in any case, it were up to me to advise him on settling matters with the lady and her relatives, I would recommend something that you would not even dare imagine."

They answered: "Do tell us. We know that you are a man of good counsel, and we ask you to state what you think."

He said: "I shall tell you what I think, and if you know any better, say so. I would advise the king to summon all the relatives of the duke and duchess to Tintagel, where he could have them appear before him and he could offer them a settlement—such that, if they rejected it, they would receive the blame and he would be praised for his good will."

The barons then came before the king and gave him their counsel, but they did not say that it had come to them from Urfin, since he had forbidden them to do so. The king answered: "Lords, I accept your counsel and will proceed as you have explained."

And so the king sent word throughout his lands that the relatives of the duke should come to Tintagel, because he wanted to make amends for the wrongs that they imputed to him. Then Merlin came to the king in private and said: "My lord, do you know who thought of this plan?"

The king said: "No, only that the barons have recommended it."

Merlin said: "My lord, all of them together would never have been able to devise it. It was wise and loyal Urfin who found in his heart the best and the most honorable way to peace, and he believes that no one knows it. And no one does, except me and now you!"

The king asked Merlin to tell him the plan, which Merlin then did. The king was overjoyed and said: "How do you advise me?"

Merlin said: "I have no better or more loyal counsel to give you than what you have heard. It will let you accomplish everything you most fervently desire. Now I am going to leave, but I want to speak to you in front of Urfin. Once I have left, you can ask him how he came to devise this settlement."

The king agreed. Urfin was called in, and in his presence Merlin said: "My lord, you promised to give me the heir that you have fathered and cannot recognize as your own son. You have in writing the date and hour of his conception, and you know that only through me was it all possible. Yet the sin would be yours if I did not now lend my aid, for his mother might well find the child a source of shame, and by herself a woman is defenseless against a growing problem that she cannot hide. I want Urfin, too, to put down in writing the time of the child's conception. Neither you nor the child will see me before the night he is born. Meanwhile I ask you to trust whatever Urfin tells you. He is utterly devoted to you and will never advise anything that is not to your benefit and your honor. I shall not speak with you for the next six months, but will speak with Urfin between now and then. Trust whatever word I send you through Urfin and act accordingly, if you wish to keep my affection and his, and if you wish to behave in good faith."

And so Urfin noted the time of the child's conception, and Merlin said to the king in private: "My lord, you must take care not to let Ygerne know that you went to bed with her. That more than anything else will put her at your mercy, so that if you ask her about her pregnancy and who the father is, she will not be able to tell you, and she will be very embarrassed. That is how you can best help me to obtain the child."

Merlin thereupon took leave of the king and Urfin. While the king rode off toward Tintagel, Merlin left for Northumberland. There he related all these events to Blaise, who wrote them down, and that is how we know them.

8. The Birth of Arthur

At Tintagel the king gathered his vassals and asked them what he should do. They said: "Sire, we advise you to make peace with the duchess and her family and the family of the duke."

The king told them to go speak with her and tell her that she could not hold out against him but that, if she wanted peace, he would abide by her wishes. As the barons left for the castle, the king took Urfin aside and said: "What do you think of this way of settling the matter?"

The king gave Urfin to understand that he knew that he had devised the plan, and Urfin said: "My lord, the idea was mine. It is for you to say whether you like it."

The king answered: "I like it, and I wish the duchess were already here."

Urfin said: "My lord, do not intervene in the discussion. Leave it in my hands." Their conversation ended there.

At Tintagel Castle the messengers found the duchess and the duke's relatives and told them how the duke had died through his own rashness. They said that the king was grieved and that he was ready to make peace with the lady and her family, who could no doubt see that it was pointless to resist him, and so the good men advised the lady and all her relatives to accept the royal offer. They answered that they would discuss it, and withdrew. "The messengers are right when they say that we cannot hold out against the king, but let us hear what kind of settlement he would offer us. The king may well propose a peace that we can hardly reject. That, lady, is our view."

The lady answered: "I never declined the advice of my husband, and I shall not decline yours."

They returned to the messengers, and one of the wisest in the group spoke: "Lords, my lady would like to know what amends the king is prepared to make."

The messengers answered: "We do not know the king's wishes, but he has said that he would abide by the recommendations of his barons."

The others answered: "If that is true, the settlement will be a good one. You are such worthy men that, God willing, you will give him good and honorable advice."

They decided that two weeks later the lady and her family would come before the king to hear his offer. The messengers then returned to the king and told him what they had learned, and he said that the lady and all those accompanying her would have safe conduct and should not hesitate to come. During the next two weeks the king and Urfin spoke of many things. Then, on the appointed day, just as the barons had advised, he sent for the duchess. When she reached the camp, the king gathered all her barons together with his own and asked them what peace settlement they wanted to request for the lady. Her advisers answered: "Lord, the lady has not come here to make a request, but to hear what you will offer as compensation for the death of her husband."

The king was struck by the wisdom of these words. He drew his counselors aside and asked them: "Lords, how do you advise me?"

They answered: "Sire, only you can know what sort of settlement you have it in your heart to offer them."

The king answered: "I'll tell you: You are all my vassals and all such worthy men that you will never give me poor counsel. I leave the matter entirely in your hands."

They said: "It is a heavy burden, sire. Order Urfin to join our group, for without his help we could never reach a decision."

When the king heard them ask for Urfin to advise them, he made it clear that he was delighted, and he said to Urfin: "I brought you up, and I have made you a powerful man, and I know how wise you are. Go help them in their deliberations."

Urfin said: "Yes, of course, just as you say. But let me leave you with this word: that no lord can ever be too greatly loved by his vassals and that, if they are worthy men, he can never humble himself too much to win their hearts." With that Urfin went to join the counselors.

Once they were all together, they asked him: "Urfin, what is your advice to us?"

Urfin answered: "You have heard that the king leaves the matter in your hands. Let us now go to the duchess and her relatives and find out whether they agree to do the same."

They all answered that he had spoken well, and then went to see the lady and her advisers. They told them that the king was leaving the matter in their hands and would accept whatever settlement they proposed; they had come, they went on, to ask whether the lady's side would do the same. Her counselors answered: "We need to confer about this."

They conferred and then said that the king could do no better than to leave the matter in the hands of his barons. The lady, her advisers, and the relatives of the duke then agreed to do the same, and the king's counselors acknowledged their decision. Then they withdrew and discussed the question, and when each man had spoken his mind, they turned to Urfin for his views. Urfin said: "I shall tell you what I think. As you know, my lords, the duke did not do anything to deserve to die, and it is the king's fault that he is dead. Isn't that true? His wife remains with children to support, but you know that the king has laid waste to all her lands; moreover she is the best lady in the world—the most beautiful, wise, and virtuous. You know, too, that the duke's death has meant a great loss to his relatives, and it is only right that, in order to win their friendship, the king should compensate them for some part of their loss. Furthermore you know that the king has no wife. I conclude, then, that the only way the king can redress the wrong that he has done is by marrying the duchess. It seems to me that he should do it to repair the harm, to ensure our affection, and for the sake of everyone in the kingdom. Having done that, he should marry off the duke's daughter to King Lot of Orkney, who is here with us, and he should similarly treat the other relatives of the duke, so that they will regard him as their friend, their lord, and their rightful king. Now you have heard my counsel; suggest something else if you are not in agreement."

They all answered: "You have made the best proposal that anyone could imagine. If you actually present it to the king and he accepts, we will all support it."

Urfin answered: "My lords, that is not enough. I must be able to tell the king that the plan already has your full support. I see the king of Orkney here. The settlement depends to a great extent on him. Let him say what he thinks of it."

Lot responded: "Whatever you may once have said about me, I do not want to stand in the way of peace."

Having heard that, the rest all fell into agreement. They returned to the king and sent for the lady and her advisers. When all were assembled, Urfin stated the peace terms as planned and then asked the barons: "Are you in favor of this agreement?"

And they all answered yes. Urfin turned toward the king and said: "My lord, what is your wish? Do you accept the terms proposed by these worthy men?"

The king answered: "I do, provided the lady and her family agree and King Lot is willing to marry the duke's daughter."

Then King Lot spoke: "My lord, for the sake of your friendship and for peace, I shall do whatever you think right."

Then Urfin addressed the lady's spokesman, asking: "Do you accept this agreement?"

And the man answered wisely. He looked around at the lady and her counselors, who were so moved that all had tears in their eyes, and some, from both sadness and joy, were actually weeping. He himself was weeping as he answered: "No lord has ever before made amends with such generosity."

Urfin asked the lady and the duke's family: "Do you accept this agreement?"

The lady remained silent, but her relatives all answered: "There is no one who cannot; we accept it! We consider the king to be so worthy and so honorable a man that we place all our trust in him."

The peace was thus ratified by both sides, and Uther Pendragon took Ygerne as his wife, and gave her daughter to King Lot of Orkney. The wedding of the king and Ygerne took place on the twenty-eighth day after the settlement, which had taken place three weeks after the death of the duke; almost two months had thus passed since the night when the king had been with the duchess in her chamber. The daughter who became the wife of King Lot later gave birth to Mordred, to my lord Gawain, to Agravain and Gareth and Gaheris. Another daughter, a bastard, was married to King Neutre of Sorhaut. Finally, on the recommendation of the whole family, the king sent the daughter named Morgan to school at a convent. She was so gifted that she learned the seven arts and quite early acquired remarkable knowledge of an art called astronomy, which she used all the time. She also studied nature and medicine, and it was through that study that she came to be called Morgan the Fay. The king provided all the other children, too, with good guidance, and he showed the duke's relatives great friendship.

And so Uther Pendragon won Ygerne. After some time her pregnancy became apparent, and the king, lying with her one night, placed his hand on her stomach and asked who had made her pregnant. It was clear that it could not be he, for, ever since they had married, he had written down every time he had gone to bed with her; and it could not have been the duke, for he had been away from her for a long time before his death. When the lady heard the question, she felt ashamed and began to weep. With tears in her eyes, she said: "My lord, I cannot tell you a lie when you already know so much, and I shall not try, but, in God's name, take pity on me! If you assure me that you will not leave me, I shall tell you something extraordinary but true."

He assured her that he would never leave her, whatever she might say. Delighted with his reassurance, she went on: "My lord, I shall tell you an extraordinary story." And she told him how a man looking just like her husband the duke had been to bed with her in her chamber. "And he brought with him two men whom my husband loved most dearly, and right before my servants he came into the room and entered my bed. I had no doubt at all that it was my husband. The man fathered the child that I am now carrying, and I now know that it was the very night my husband died. He was lying with me when the news of the death reached the castle. He let me go on believing he was my husband, saying that his men simply did not know what had become of him, and with that he went away."

When the queen had told her story, the king answered: "My dear love, take care to keep your condition a secret from as many people as you can, because you would be disgraced if it were known. I hope you understand that, when the child is born, we cannot reasonably acknowledge it as ours, and we shall not keep it for ourselves. I am asking you, then, to give it, as soon as it has been born, to a certain person that I shall point out to you, and in that way we shall never hear anything further about it."

She answered: "My lord, you may do as you wish with me and whatever is mine."

Then the king came to Urfin and repeated the conversation he had had with the queen, to which Urfin replied: "My lord, now you know how virtuous and loyal she is, for she did not attempt to lie about that extraordinary occurrence. You have also been of great help to Merlin, since he could not obtain the child in any other way."

That is how matters remained until the sixth month, when Merlin had promised to return. He came and spoke in private with Urfin, asking for news of whatever interested him, and Urfin told him truthfully whatever he knew. After the conversation the king had Urfin bring Merlin to him, and when all three were together, he told Merlin how he had behaved toward the queen and how he had brought about the peace agreement that allowed him to marry her. Merlin answered: "My lord, Urfin is absolved of his sin in bringing you together with the queen. But I am not yet absolved of mine in helping him to deceive her and facilitate the conception of a child whose father she does not know."

The king answered: "You are so wise that you will find a way to free yourself of the sin."

Merlin said: "My lord, you must help me."

The king said that he would help in any way he could and that he was in any case going to give him the child. Merlin said: "In this town lives the most worthy man in the land, and his wife is the most worthy and honorable woman, with the finest qualities imaginable. She has given birth to a son, and her husband is a man of only modest means. I want you to send for him and to give him money on this condition: that he and his wife swear on holy relics that they will raise a child who will soon be brought to them and nourish him with the lady's own milk, and that they will have their son nursed by another woman but treat this child as their very own."

The king said: "Merlin, I shall do everything you say."

Then he said goodbye, and Merlin went back to Master Blaise.

The king sent for the good man and received him very warmly. As the man was greatly surprised by such a warm welcome, the king said to him: "Dear friend, I must reveal to you an extraordinary thing that has happened to me. You are my liegeman; I ask you, then, by the loyalty you owe me, to help me in a certain matter that I shall explain to you and that you must keep hidden as well as you can."

The man answered: "My lord, there is nothing you may command that I will not do if I am at all able; and if not, I will at least keep it a secret."

The king said: "An extraordinary thing happened to me in a dream. A good man appeared to me in my sleep, who told me that you are the most worthy and loyal man in the kingdom. He told me, too, that your wife has just given you a son. Then he ordered that I ask you to remove the boy from your wife's breast and give him over to another woman, so that your wife, for my sake, could nurse another child soon to be brought to her."

The worthy man answered: "My lord, that is quite a lot to ask! But please tell me when this child will be brought to us."

The king said: "So help me God, I am not sure!"

The good man said that he would do as the king wished, and he was then given so generous a gift that he was astonished. He left the king and went back to tell his wife what had been said. It seemed to her a very strange thing, and she said: "How can I give up my own child and start nursing another?"

He said: "There is nothing we can refuse to do for our lord. He has given us so much and promised so much that we must do as he pleases. I insist that you agree."

She said: "I am yours, just as the child is, and you may do as you wish both with me and with him. I agree, then, for I am bound to accept what you want."

The good man was delighted to have the consent of his wife. Then he told her to find a nurse for their child even before the other one was brought to them, and so he took the boy from his mother's breast. Meanwhile the time approached for the queen to give birth. The day before the delivery Merlin came to the court in secret and spoke to Urfin: "Urfin, I am very pleased with the king for having so effectively given my message to Auctor [Hector]. Now tell him to go to the queen and announce to her that she will have the child tomorrow evening after midnight, and let him order her to surrender it right away to the good man who will be waiting just outside the room."

At these words Urfin said: "Merlin, are you, then, not going to speak to the king?"

Merlin said: "Not this time."

Then Urfin came to the king and told him what Merlin had ordered.

The king welcomed the news with delight and said: "Urfin, won't he speak to me before he leaves?"

And Urfin said: "No, but do what he orders."

The king then came to the queen and said: "My lady, listen to what I have to tell you; trust me and do as I say."

The queen said: "My lord, you have all my trust, and I shall do whatever you order."

The king said: "My lady, tomorrow evening after midnight you will give birth, with God's help. I want you, please, as soon as the child has been born, to have one of your personal maids give it to the first man she finds just beyond the door of the room. And order all the women who are present at the birth never to say that it took place, because the news would bring great shame to both you and me: many people would say the child was not mine, and they would apparently not be wrong."

The lady answered: "My lord, what I recounted to you earlier is true. I shall do as you command—but I find it remarkable that you already know the time of my delivery."

The king said: "My lady, please do as I order."

She answered: "My lord, of course I will, please God."

With that the king left the queen. The next day, as God wished, the lady's labor began after vespers and continued until the time the king had predicted; she gave birth between midnight and dawn. As soon as she had delivered, she called over a woman in whom she had especial trust and said to her: "Dear friend, take the child out of the room. At the door, if you find a man who asks for it, give it to him. But try to find out, too, who he is."

The woman did as ordered; she wrapped the child in the finest linens she had and carried it to the door, where she saw a man who looked remarkably decrepit. She said to him: "Good man, what are you waiting for here?"

He answered: "I am waiting for what you bring me."

She asked: "Who are you? To whom can I tell my lady I gave her child?"

"He answered: "That is not for you to ask; just do what you have been told."

The woman handed him the child and, once he had taken it, she had no idea of what became of him. She went back to her lady and said: "My lady, I gave the child to an old man; that's all I know about him."

The queen was greatly pained and wept. Meanwhile the man to whom the child had been given went as quickly as he could to Auctor. He found him in the morning just as he was going to mass, called to him and said: "Auctor, I want to speak to you."

Auctor looked at him, thought him a very honorable man, and said: "My lord, what is it you wish?"

The old man said: "Auctor, I have this child to give you. I ask that you bring him up with more care than your own. You may be sure that, if you do so, great good will come of it for you and your offspring, but if anyone were to tell you more now, you would not believe it."

Auctor said: "My lord, is this the child that the king has asked me to raise?"

The man answered: "Yes indeed. Both the king and all good men should ask you to do it. And you may be sure that my request has at least as much weight as that of a powerful baron."

Auctor took the child and saw how beautiful it was; he asked whether the boy had been baptized. The man said no, but that Auctor should have him baptized right away. Auctor gladly agreed and asked what name he should be given. The other answered that he should have the name Arthur. "Now I am leaving, since I have nothing more to do here. Great good will come to you from this child, as you will soon realize. In a short while you and your wife will be unable to say which you prefer, this one or your own."

Auctor answered: "My lord, who shall I tell the king gave me the child? Who are you?"

The man said: "You cannot know any more for the time being."

At this point, according to the tale, Merlin took leave of Auctor. Auctor had the child baptized without delay and gave him the name Arthur. Then he took the boy home to his wife and said: "My lady, here is the child that I asked you to take in."

She answered that he was welcome and took him into her arms. She asked her husband whether the child was baptized, and he answered that he was named Arthur. Then the lady gave him her breast.

[*With Merlin's help Uther Pendragon reigns effectively for many years. When he dies with no apparent heir, Merlin assures the great lords of the realm that God will soon designate his successor. This is Arthur, now grown to manhood, who proves himself the rightful new king by pulling the Sword from the Stone. The Prose* Merlin *concludes with Arthur's coronation. The* Suite du Merlin, *opening one month later, presents a series of important episodes in Arthur's life which continually*

*bring into play the prophetic and necromantic powers of Merlin. The often inter-
twined episodes include, among others, the birth of Mordred, the disclosure of Arthur's
true parentage, the magical appearance of the sword Excalibur, the fateful tale of
Balin and his brother, the combats with Pellinor, the first hints of the treachery of
Morgan the Fay, Arthur's marriage to Guinevere, the renewal of the Round Table,
the adventures of Gawain, and the appearance, abduction, and rescue of Niviane the
Huntress. Meanwhile many years have passed, and Merlin is now an old man.*]

From the Suite du Merlin

9. Merlin's Love for Niviane the Huntress

There was great joy at court. The king asked the Huntress, as soon as she had
given him her hounds, her pointer, and the stag's head: "Well, my young
lady, what do you say? Have we kept our word to you?"

"Yes indeed, my lord," she said. "I would never have thought you could
be so successful. And since I am not missing any of the things that I had when
I first came to your court, I shall now take my leave to return to my country
as quickly as I can."

"My lady," said the king, "do stay a while, if you like, together with all
the ladies who are companions to my lady the queen. I assure you that you
will receive as much honor and respect as the noblest lady at court, or even
more. You well deserve it, God knows!"

"Indeed, my lord, as God is my witness!" said Merlin. "And you don't
even know as much as I do!" Then he whispered to him: "I can assure you
that she is extremely worthy and intelligent and has all the nobility of the
daughter of a king and queen. If you do her honor, everyone will be grateful
to you."

The king said that he was quite ready to do her honor, now and as long
as she remained at court. Then he asked the queen to keep her in her company and to show her greater respect and friendship than any of her other
young ladies. The queen gladly agreed, and so urged the Huntress that she
consented to stay at court for a while. The queen asked her what her baptismal name was, and she answered that she was named Niviane and was the
daughter of a nobleman in Brittany, but she did not say that she was the
daughter of a king. Let all those who listen to the tale of my lord Robert de
Boron know, however, that this young lady was the one who would later be
called the Lady of the Lake, and would raise Lancelot of the Lake in her
dwelling, just as the great *Story of Lancelot* makes clear. But the present *Story
of the Holy Grail* does not speak much of that and instead goes on as follows.

[*Merlin tells Arthur about certain inescapable misfortunes that are to come: Pellinor's death at the hands of Gawain and the destruction of the realm through Mordred.*]

Merlin happily spent much time with Niviane the Huntress, so much time, in fact, that he fell deeply in love with her, for she was extremely beautiful and was no more than fifteen years old. The girl was very wise for her age, and she was frightened by Merlin's attention; she was afraid that he might dishonor her by means of a magic spell or take advantage of her during her sleep. He, though, had no such desire, not wishing to do anything that might vex her.

Now, according to the tale, the young lady remained at court for a good four months. Merlin, much in love with her, came to see her every day. Seeing him so taken with her, she said to him: "I won't ever love you unless you swear to teach me some of the spells that you know."

He began to laugh then and said: "There is nothing I know that I would not teach you, because you are the only woman I love or could love."

"Since you love me so much," she said, "I want you to swear with your bare hand that you will never do anything, either by magic or otherwise, that you think might displease me."

He took the oath immediately. So it was that the girl became an intimate of Merlin, although not in the sense that she admitted him to her bed—but he was waiting and hoping to have his way with her, to know her in the flesh and deflower her (for he knew that she was still a virgin); and so he began to teach her sorcery and enchantment, and she learned rapidly.

During that time the king of Northumberland—the Northumberland that borders Brittany—sent a letter to King Arthur, saying: "King Arthur, I greet you as my friend and ask, in friendship and courtesy, that you bid farewell to my daughter Niviane, who, I have been informed, has been staying at your court, and send her back to my country in the company of the messengers that I have sent you. Be assured that I am most grateful to you for the honor and hospitality that you have shown her."

When the king had seen the letter, he sent for the girl and said: "My lady, your father has sent messengers here for you. What do you wish? Will you leave us or stay?"

"My lord," she said, "I will leave, since I have been sent for."

"That is certainly a wise and worthy answer," he said. "Yet I must say that if I did not know the desire of your royal father, I should prefer to have you stay here. I have very much enjoyed your company."

"My lord," she said, "I am very happy to hear that, and if I wished to live away from my father's house, there is no court in the world where I would more gladly stay than at yours, which deserves more praise than any other. But since it is my father's wish that I return home, I cannot fail to do so, even if only out of obedience."

"That is the best decision you can make," said the king, "and I respect you all the more for it."

So it was that the girl had to leave the court to return to her own country. I can tell you that the queen and the other ladies were all saddened by it, since everyone had come to be very fond of her. On the eve of her departure Merlin came to her and said: "Ah, young lady, are you really going?"

"Yes indeed, Merlin," she said; "and what will you do? Won't you come along with me?" (She said that because she could not imagine he might in fact come along!)

"Certainly, my lady!" he said. "I won't let you go without me but will keep you company all the way back to your country. And once there, I shall stay if you wish me to and, if you do not, I shall leave. Whatever you like, I shall be sure to do."

When she heard that he would come with her, she felt struck to the quick, because she hated no one else so much as Merlin. She did not dare let it show, however. She pretended instead to be delighted and thanked him very much for offering to accompany her.

The horses were saddled and the young lady bade farewell to the king and queen; and in the morning, as soon as she had heard mass, she left. Merlin did not tell anyone at court that he too was going, as he well knew that the king would not be pleased to grant him leave, should he ask for it. From Camelot they rode straight down to the sea and there boarded a ship for Brittany. They arrived safely and then rode into the land of King Ban of Benwick. There, if they had not had Merlin with them, the girl and her party would have been frightened, as the war raging between King Ban and King Claudas of the Wasteland left no one safe. That night the girl turned for shelter to a castle of King Ban's that sat high atop a remarkable pinnacle and was one of the strongest castles in the entire land; it was called Trebe. King Ban was not at the time in the castle, being engaged not far away in his war with King Claudas, but the queen, his wife, was there: Helaine, the most beautiful woman in all of Brittany and the most worthy known to either God or man. She and the king had only one child, a boy not yet one year old, but already the most beautiful creature in the world. He was affectionately known as Lancelot, but his baptismal name was Galahad.

Queen Helaine, as soon as she recognized the young lady of Northumberland, gave her a joyous welcome. (You must not think, you who are listening to this tale, that the Northumberland that I mean was the kingdom of Northumberland in Britain, which lay between the kingdoms of Logres and Gorre; that would be a gross mistake, for the one I mean was in Brittany.) Queen Helaine, as I was saying, welcomed the girl with great delight and warm hospitality. When they had eaten, the queen had her son brought in for the girl to see. After a long look the girl said: "Beautiful boy, if you can only live to the age of twenty, you will be the handsomest of all men!"

At that Merlin laughed, together with everyone else who had heard it. He whispered to the girl: "He will live more than fifty years, but he will gain even more fame for his knightly valor than for his beauty. You cannot imagine another knight, either before him or after, who could be his peer."

She answered with thanks to God that He had let her see such a beautiful creature, and she kissed him more than a hundred times. Then the child's nurses took him back to their chambers, and the queen said to the girl: "My lady, it would be of great help to us if the boy were older than he is! There is a relentless war going on every day with a neighbor of ours, who is doing us as much harm and damage as he can."

"My lady," said the girl, "what is the name of this neighbor of yours?"

"He is," she said, "Claudas of the Wasteland, the most treacherous man in the world. I wish God would one day let me have my revenge. I would be overjoyed, because I have never hated any other man as much as I hate him."

"My lady," said Merlin, "you will hate him even more. But you will see the day, well before the death of Lancelot, when Claudas will have no inch of land left in this country and will slink off with just a few followers, defeated and humbled, all his possessions gone, to seek some poor refuge in another land."

"Ah, God!" said the queen, "if I could see that day, I would never ask for any other happiness in this life, for there is nothing I hate as much I do him. And it's no wonder if I hate him: I owe him my poverty!"

"Take heart, my lady," said Merlin. "Be assured that what I have predicted will come true."

"May God grant that!" she said; "I would be very happy."

That, then, is what Merlin said about Claudas, and everything happened eventually just as he had foretold. The lady did not inquire who he was, as she could never have imagined that Merlin would come near her castle.

The next day, as soon as the girl had heard mass, she and her party left Trebe, riding on until they reached a wood. It was small, but for its size it was the most beautiful and the most delightful in all of France or Brittany; the wood was called En Val, because most of it lay in a valley. When they were in the wood, Merlin said to the girl: "My lady, would you like to see the Lake of Diana, which you have heard of so often?"

"Yes indeed," she said, "I should be very pleased to see it. Nothing about Diana could fail to please me or could leave me indifferent, since throughout her life she enjoyed hunting in the woods just as much as I do, or even more."

"Let us go, then," he said, "and I shall show it to you."

Then they went down through the valley until they found a very large, deep lake. "There," said Merlin, "is the Lake of Diana." And they continued on their way until they came to a place on the shore where there was a marble tomb. "My lady," said Merlin, "do you see this grave?"

"Yes," she said, "of course."

"Here, let me tell you," said Merlin, "is where Faunus, Diana's lover, is buried. He was deeply in love with her, but she was so cruel to him that she brought about his death in the most treacherous way possible. That was his reward for loving her faithfully."

"Really, Merlin," said the girl, "did Diana kill her lover?"

"Really," he said. "There is no doubt of it."

"Do tell me how it happened," she said; "I want to know."

"Of course," said Merlin; "I shall tell you. Diana, as you know, lived in the time of Vergil, a long time before Jesus Christ came to earth to save sinners, and above all else she loved hunting in the woods. She had hunted in all the forests of France and Brittany, but nowhere had she found a wood as pleasing to her as this one, and so she settled here and built her manor on the shore of this lake. In that way she could go hunting in the woods during the day and come back to her lake at night. She spent a long time here, concerned only with the hunt, until one day the son of a king who held this entire country saw her and fell in love with her. He was struck not only by her beauty but also by such courage and swiftness and agility as no man could match. The young man was not yet knighted, but he was very handsome and bright. He pursued Diana so ardently that she at last granted him her love, but on condition that he never return to his father or seek any company but hers. He consented and so remained with her. And she, for his sake and also because the place pleased her so much, built a very beautiful impressive manor on the shore of the lake. Faunus was thus cut off from the world, separated by his love for Diana from his father, his friends, and all other sorts of companions.

"When he had been with her for two years, Diana met another knight while she was out hunting, just as she had earlier met Faunus, and she fell passionately in love with him. This was Felix, who had been born into a poor and humble family but through his prowess had become a knight. He knew that Faunus was Diana's lover and knew too that if Faunus discovered him, he would leave him in sorry shape or even kill him. He said to Diana: 'You say you love me . . .'

"'It is true,' said Diana; 'more than any other man I have ever seen.'

"'No good,' he said, 'can ever come to me of that. Even if I loved you very much, I would not dare to come near you, because I know that if Faunus found out, he would destroy not only me but my whole family as well.'

"'Don't be concerned by that,' she said. 'You must not let that stop you from coming to me.'

"'On the contrary,' he said; 'either you rid yourself of him once and for all, or I can never stay with you.'

"'I cannot rid myself of him as long as he is sound and fit,' she said. 'He loves me far too much ever to allow it.'

"'You must do it,' he said, 'in one way or another.'

"Diana loved Felix so much that she would have paid with her life to have him in her bed, and so she decided to kill Faunus, either with poison or in some other way. Now this grave that you see here was already in existence at the time; it was ordinarily full of water, and there was a stone slab covering it. An evil sorcerer named Demophon, who lived in this land, had given the water the power to heal the wounds of all those who bathed in it; it was a feat of black magic. One day, then, Faunus came home from hunting with a wound that a wild animal had inflicted on him, and Diana, who could think of nothing but harm and misfortune for him, decided, as soon as she had heard he was wounded, to have the grave drained of its water so that he could not be healed in it. When he came near and saw that the healing water was gone, he felt sudden panic and said to Diana: 'What shall I do? I am very badly wounded!'

"'Have no fear,' she answered. 'I can heal you. Take off all your clothes and lie down in the grave, and I shall put the stone slab back in place over you. Then, through the slit in the slab, I shall strew herbs over your body, herbs of such great power that you will be healed as soon as you have felt their warmth.'

"Faunus, who would never have thought that she intended to betray him, said that he would do whatever she ordered. He lay down naked in the grave, and the stone was placed over him; it was so heavy that he could not possibly have pushed it back without help from above.

"Then Diana, who was determined to be done with him, flooded the tomb with molten lead that she had ready, so that he died instantly, burned to the very entrails. Once she had put Faunus to death, she came to Felix and said: 'I have freed myself of the man whom you have feared,' and she told him how she had done it.

"When she had finished, he said: 'The whole world should hate you for that! No one could love you now, and certainly not I!' With that he drew his sword, seized Diana by her hair, and cut off her head. Because Diana had enjoyed this place so much during her life and because at her death, her body was thrown into the lake, the lake came to be named the Lake of Diana, and it will bear that name as long as the world lasts. Now you have heard how Diana killed her lover and why this is called the Lake of Diana."

The girl said: "You have certainly told the story well, Merlin! But now tell me what became of the buildings that she had built here."

"The father of Faunus," said Merlin, "destroyed them as soon as he learned how Faunus had died; he smashed everything that Diana had built."

"That was wrong of him," answered the girl, "for her manor stood in a very lovely and charming place. I find this place so beautiful and appealing that, so help me God, I will never leave it. I shall have a house built as great and fine as any here before and live here in it for the rest of my life. And I ask, Merlin," she went on, "that, out of love for me, you take charge of the project."

He said that, since she asked him to, he would gladly do it. Merlin thus undertook to build the dwelling beside the Lake of Diana.

The young lady said to the men in her party: "My lords, I should be delighted if you cared to stay here with me, as I could hardly remain in this forest alone. You must understand that I wish never to leave this place but rather spend my whole life hunting here, always coming back to my house to rest for a day or two or more before returning to the hunt."

The men to whom she spoke were noblemen and close relatives of hers; they answered: "If you prefer to remain here rather than go back to our lord your father, we shall remain too. We dare not return home without you."

She said that she was happy with that decision. "Let me add," she said "that Merlin has given me so much gold and silver that you will have enough to spend for a lifetime."

"Lady, if you had no resources, we would do everything possible to support you ourselves, which would only be our duty."

Then Merlin hired masons and carpenters from throughout the land and had them construct along the shore a great house and outbuildings so fine and so lavish that in all Brittany you could not have found a royal or princely dwelling that was any finer. When the work was finished and the masons and carpenters gone, Merlin said to the young woman: "This manor will be worthless to you if I do not make it invisible to everyone except the people who live in it." Then he cast a spell over all the buildings, so wondrously closing them off from every side that nothing was visible but water. If you stood outside, however closely you looked, all you could see was the lake. When he had accomplished this wonder, Merlin showed it to the girl and said: "Is your manor safe enough? No one will ever see it, no matter how close he comes, unless he belongs to the household. And if anyone who does belong tries, out of envy or hatred, to show it to an outsider, he will immediately fall into the lake and drown."

"My God, Merlin!" said Niviane. "I have never before heard of such clever protection!"

Merlin remained with the young lady. He stayed at the manor night and day, feeling a greater love for her than he had ever felt for anyone or anything else in the world. And because of his great love, he did not dare to seek any favor of her, lest he vex her. All the same, he thought that one day, somehow or other, he would take his pleasure with her. He had already taught the girl so many spells and so much magic that she knew more than anyone alive, apart from Merlin himself, and no one could imagine any game or pleasant distraction that she could not produce through sorcery. There was no one in the world, though, whom she hated as fiercely as she did Merlin, because she was well aware that he was eager to deflower her, and if she had dared attempt to kill him, whether by poison or in some other way, she would have done it with fury. But she did not dare, since she was afraid that he would realize what was about to happen, he who was so much more alert than other people. Nevertheless she had so enchanted him with the very spells that he himself had taught her, that she could say whatever she wanted and he would not grasp her meaning.

10. The Journey Toward the Perilous Forest

One day, when Merlin was walking through the manor, he noticed, sleeping in the main hall, a knight who was a relative of the girl's. She, the mistress of the household, was present, and Merlin exclaimed: "Ah, God! He is much more at ease, this knight, than King Arthur has been today!"

"What has happened to Arthur?" said the young lady. "Tell me!"

"Today," Merlin said, "he came so close to death that he was terrified he might not escape; nor would he have, if not for the boldness of Kay, his seneschal, who with two blows killed two kings. That is how King Arthur was saved and his enemies defeated."

"Really," said the girl, "it is wrong of you to let him fall into such danger! You should always be at his court to protect him, not far away as you are."

"The truth is," said Merlin, "that I am staying away from Britain for two reasons. One is that I am so in love with you that I could not possibly live without you. The other reason is that my power as a seer tells me I should no sooner be back there than I would be poisoned or killed in some other way."

"What!" she said. "Can you not protect yourself?"

"No," he answered. "I am already so spellbound that I cannot tell who is planning my death."

"You mean," she said, "that all your claims to see into the future have now come to naught?"

"Apart from my own life and death," he said, "I can still foretell almost everything. But where I myself am concerned, I am so bound by enchantments that I am helpless, for I cannot undo the spells unless I am willing to lose my soul. But I would much rather let my body be destroyed through someone's treachery than let my soul be damned."

This revelation made the young lady very happy, as she longed for nothing else so much as Merlin's death, and now it was clear that, with all the magic she had been practicing against him, he was indeed unable to grasp what she had in mind. One day not long afterward Merlin was sitting beside her at the table and said to her: "Ah! Lady of the Lake, if you only felt some affection for Arthur! If you only knew what is being plotted against him! His sister Morgan, whom he trusts completely, has just stolen his good and trustworthy sword Excalibur, together with the scabbard, and she has replaced it with one that looks identical but is worthless. And tomorrow he is to meet a knight in single combat! That means that his life is in danger, because his sword will fail him when he needs it. The other man, meanwhile, will be using the best sword that a knight could use and will be wearing a scabbard that has the power to keep its wearer from losing any blood."

"How terrible!" said the girl. "What a risk for the king! Now I should very much like the two of us to be present at the combat, for if Arthur is undone, it will surely be the worst thing that could happen in our time."

"He will be defeated and die," said Merlin, "unless our Lord decides otherwise. And it will happen because of a sin that I know he committed after our Lord had raised him to his kingly rank." The young lady asked what the sin was. "I may not reveal that to you," he answered; "it does not concern you or me. It is only for God to take vengeance, as He wishes, for great sins."

"That's right," she said, "and it was very wrong of me to ask. But tell me: could you in any way delay the battle long enough for us to reach Britain?"

"Yes, of course," he answered.

"And how many days," she asked, "would it take us to reach the site of the battle?"

"Twelve days," he said.

"I ask you, please, then," she said, "to delay the combat. Let us leave tomorrow morning and ride straight there without a stop. If it is God's will to let us arrive in time, I am sure that King Arthur will not lose a hair in battle."

"The truth is, Lady of the Lake," said Merlin, "there is nothing I would more gladly do than go to Britain, if I were not fearful of being betrayed and killed."

"You must not have any such fear," she answered. "You may be sure that I will watch over you as carefully as I watch over my very self, for I love you more than any other man in the world—and rightly so, since you have taught me everything I know, and my happiness depends on you."

"My lady," he said, "do you wish me, then, to go to Britain with you?"

"Yes, please," she said.

"Then I shall go," he answered, "since you wish me to. All the same, I believe it is a rash mistake."

Then the young lady decided who would stay at home and who would go with her. The next day, as soon as it was light, she and Merlin set out, together with two knights and four squires. The knights were cousins of hers and knew for a fact that there was nothing she hated more than she did Merlin. When they reached the coast, they set sail and, with a good wind, crossed very quickly to the British side. Once they were off the boat and on their horses, Merlin said: "Let us turn toward the kingdom of Logres. That is where we can find what we have come for."

One of the knights objected: "If we go in that direction, we shall have to pass through the Perilous Forest."

"True," said Merlin, "but that is where our road takes us."

Thereupon they all took the direction that he showed them. That day they rode on in peace, without any incident worth recording. The next morning they left the impressive, well-fortified castle where they had spent the night and continued to ride until the hour of tierce. Then they came to a beautiful, open plain where the only trees that grew were two extraordinary, huge elms. The two elms stood halfway down the road, and a cross stood between them. Near the cross there were a hundred or more graves. Beside it were two thrones beautiful and magnificent enough for an emperor, and each one had an ivory arch over it that protected it from the rain. On each of the thrones sat a man with a harp in his hand, playing whenever he wished. There were also many other instruments lying about, as if the men had nothing to do but play. Now, according to the tale, as the travelers were approaching them, Merlin halted and said to the others: "Do you see the two men who are sitting on those thrones with harps in their hands?" They answered that they did. "And do you know what they are doing?" They said that they did not and asked him to tell them.

"I shall tell you, then," said Merlin, "the most extraordinary thing that you have heard in a long time. The melody coming from those harps has the power to enchant any man or woman who hears it, except the two players. The spell is so overpowering that the hearers immediately lose all control of their limbs, fall down as if dead, and lie on the ground as long as the harpers want them to. Many people have suffered from this enchantment. Besides, if some good man came through here and had with him a wife or mistress of any beauty at all, the sorcerers would force themselves on her in the man's presence and then kill him, whoever he might be, so that he would not talk. That is how the two sorcerers have long behaved, and they have caused the death of many a worthy man and the shame of many a virtuous and beautiful lady. But if I have ever been able to cast a magic spell, I will now make sure that no good man or lady will ever again be subjected to their cruelty."

Then he stopped his ears as best he could in order not to hear the sound of the harps: he acted like the serpent that lives in Egypt, the asp, which stops one of its ears with its tail and presses the other against the ground in order not to hear the sorcerer's incantations. That is how Merlin approached the sorcerers, since he was fearful of their magic; and, protected as he was, the spell had no effect on him. To the girl and to the others, though, it proved so harmful that they could no longer remain in their saddles; they fell to the ground as if dead and lay in a faint. When Merlin saw his lady in such a state, he was not a little upset, and he said: "My love, I promise to take such revenge that no one will ever forget it. And through you all people will benefit who pass by here in the future, for if they are bound by some spell when they arrive, they can free themselves at once simply by touching one of these two trees."

Then he uttered the magic words that he knew to be fitting, and hurried on toward the sorcerers. When he came up to them, he found them already unconscious and stiff-limbed, so that a child would have had enough strength to kill them then and there. They could do nothing but sit and stare at Merlin, and their harps had fallen to the ground. At this point, according to the tale, Merlin looked at them in their helplessness and said: "Ah, evil outcasts that you are! If anyone had stunned you like this in the past, it would have been an act of charity, for you have caused great suffering and been guilty of great treachery ever since you came into this land! But now your wickedness and crimes have come to an end!" Then he returned to the young woman and her party and succeeded with his magic in restoring them to their normal state. He asked them: "What was it like?"

"My lord," they answered, "we felt all the pain and all the dread that a human being can imagine, for we clearly saw the princes and ministers of Hell. They bound up all our limbs so tightly that we were powerless to do anything and thought we were dead in body and soul."

"Now you can put aside your fear," said Merlin. "Once I have finished with these two, no man alive will ever again be tormented by them." Then he had two large pits dug in the ground, one beside each tree. When they were deep enough, he took one of the sorcerers, still sitting as he was on his throne, and lowered him into the first pit; that done, he did the same with the other. Next he quickly took and lighted a great quantity of sulphur and threw it into the pits, so that in no time at all the sorcerers were dead, choked by the hot fumes and the smell of the sulphur. Merlin then asked his fellow travelers: "What do you think of such vengeance? Is it great enough to match the crime?"

"Yes indeed," they all said, "and everyone who ever hears of it, sir Merlin, will bless you for it! You have done a great good deed by freeing the road of those two devils, for they would only go on doing evil as long as they lived."

"Still," said Merlin, "I cannot consider myself satisfied unless my vengeance is known to all the people who come here even long after my death." Then he himself went over to the graves of the good men whom the sorcerers had slain and removed three slabs of stone for each of the pits. These he arranged over the pits in such a way as to let onlookers clearly see the flames that burned within. When he had finished, he showed his work to the girl and her companions and said: "Do you think that this fire can last a long time?"

"Sir," they said, "we don't know, but you do. Tell us, please."

"I shall tell you," he said, "because I want you to know what a wonder this is. I tell you, this fire will burn as long as Arthur reigns, and that will be a long time. All that while it will never fail, but on the very day when Arthur leaves this world the flame, too, will die. And something else will happen here, an even greater wonder: the bodies of the sorcerers will be preserved just as they are right now, without burning up or rotting, as long as King Arthur lives; they will remain as intact as they are today. Nor will the thrones burn or fall apart until Arthur leaves this life. I am doing this so that all good men who live after me, when they see this wonder, can bear witness that I was the greatest wizard of all who ever breathed in the kingdom of Logres. It is true that, if I thought I still had long to live, I would not trouble with such a thing, since I would then have ample time to demonstrate my powers. But I know that I am bound to die soon, and I have done this extraordinary thing for that reason, for I want it to stand after my death as proof of my great craft."

The others answered: "Indeed, my lord, this will make it clear that you are the wisest of the wise, for a greater wonder has never been heard of." At that point they left the spot and took their way straight toward the Perilous Forest. But at this point the tale leaves off speaking of them and returns to Arthur and his court.

[*Here are narrated the adventures that constitute the background of Arthur's imminent battle. They include the king's defeat of an invading army, the seating of several new knights at the Round Table, and, most pertinently, the machinations of Morgan the Fay to destroy her brother Arthur.*]

11. The Death of Merlin

Now, according to the tale, when Merlin left the sorcerers whom he had brought to a dreadful end (as our book has already recounted), he rode on together with his companions for the rest of the day and then spent the night with a very worthy vavasor who offered them all the warmest welcome he could. But Merlin was dying of love for the young Lady of the Lake. He did not dare make any advance to her, because he well knew that she was still a virgin. Nevertheless he did not expect to wait too long before becoming intimate with her and doing what a man does with a woman. He had taught her so much magic, though, that she knew hardly less than he did. She also understood very well that he was only interested in deflowering her; she hated him for it with all her being and sought his death in every way she could. As I told you a while ago, she had already cast so many spells over him that he was by now quite unable to discern what she was plotting. She had revealed to one of the knights in her company, who was a cousin of hers, that she was going to kill Merlin as soon as she saw the right moment. She could not wait any longer! "Even if he made me sovereign over all the riches of the world, I would not be able to find it within me to love him, because I know that he is a son of the Devil and is not like other men."

The Lady of the Lake spoke like that quite often, since she thoroughly hated Merlin for being a son of the Enemy. One day, as they were all riding through the Perilous Forest, night came on rather suddenly while they were in a deep valley full of rocks and boulders and far from any town or castle or people of any sort. The night was so utterly dark that they could not proceed, but had to halt right where they were. With tinder that they had and very dry wood that they could gather, they lit a big fire and prepared food that they had brought with them from a castle where they had stopped earlier that day. After the meal Merlin said to the young lady: "My lady, nearby among the rocks I could show you the most beautiful little chamber that I know of. It was carved entirely out of the rock, and it has iron doors so strong that if anyone were trapped inside, I believe he could never get out."

"What an extraordinary thing you are telling me!" said the girl. "A beautiful and charming room here among the rocks—and I thought there could be nothing here but demons and wild beasts!"

"Yet it is true," said Merlin. "Not a hundred years ago there was a king in this land named Assen, a very worthy man and a fine knight. He had a son, Anastew, who was a knight of great valor and prowess. The young man loved the daughter of a certain poor knight with a love as great as any mortal man could feel for a woman. When King Assen found out that his son loved a girl of such low and poor circumstances, he rebuked him for it and tried to dissuade him. But the young man loved the girl no less for all that, and he went on seeing her. When the king saw that his pleas were in vain, he took the boy aside and said: 'If you do not give her up at once, I will kill you!'

"The other answered: 'I shall never give her up but will love her as long as I live.'

"'In that case,' said the king, 'you may be sure that I shall separate you from her. I will kill her, and then you.'

"When the knight heard these words, he decided to carry off and hide the girl so that his father could not find her. Then he went looking for a remote and hidden place, where no one lived or passed through; there he would withdraw with the young lady and stay for the rest of their lives. He had oftentimes hunted in this forest, so that he knew this valley well. He came here right away, bringing along the companions he loved best and men who knew something about building. Out of the bare rock they carved a beautiful dwelling. When it looked just as he wished, so splendid that you would almost need to see it in order to believe it, he hurried back to where he had hidden his lover and he brought her here. He provided their home in the rock with everything he thought necessary, and there he spent his entire life with his lover, in happiness and joy. They died on the same day and were buried together in the chamber itself. Their bodies are still there and will not decay as long as I am alive, because they were embalmed."

When the young lady heard that story, she was thoroughly delighted and decided immediately that, if she could, she would shut Merlin away in the lovers' room. And if ever spells or incantations could help a woman, she was sure that they would help her. She said to Merlin: "Really, Merlin, those two lovers must have loved each other truly, if they could give up everything and everyone just to enjoy each other!"

Merlin then whispered to her: "That is what I, too, have done, lady. To be with you, I have given up King Arthur and all the great men of the kingdom of Logres, who looked up to me as their master. But I have gained nothing by following you."

She answered quickly: "Merlin, if you could have had your way at the very start, you would no doubt have considered yourself fortunate and fulfilled. So would I, if I could have my way."

"Indeed, my lady," said Merlin, "there is nothing in the world, however difficult, that I am not prepared to do, if only you want it done. I beg you to tell me what it is that you cannot do yourself!"

"I will not tell you now," she said, "but you shall know soon enough. . . . Now that chamber of the two lovers that you told me about—I want to see it. We can spend the night there together. The true love that they filled it with makes me love the place."

Very glad to hear those words, Merlin said that since she wanted to see the room, she would see it; besides, it was not at all far. He told two squires to come along with torches, and they all started down a narrow path that ran off from the road. It was not long before they came to a rocky cliff, where they found a very narrow iron door. Merlin opened it and stepped inside, and the others followed. There they found themselves in a chamber covered with mosaics so splendidly crafted that the best workman in the world might have devoted twenty years to them. "Really," said the girl, "what a beautiful, splendid place this is! It was obviously created for the delight of pleasure-loving people."

"And this is not even their bedroom!" said Merlin. "This is where they often ate, but now I shall show you where they slept together." Then he went over to an iron door and opened it. He stepped inside and called for some light. When the others were at the threshold, he said: "Now you can see the chamber where the two lovers lived and the place where their bodies lie."

With that, they went in and began to look all around. When they had thoroughly examined the room and all the art that it contained, they said that never had there been so beautiful a dwelling in the whole world.

"Truly," said Merlin, "it is beautiful, just as they were who made it this way." Then he showed the girl, on the other side of the chamber, a beautiful, splendid tomb that was covered with a rich, red cloth expertly embroidered in gold with figures of animals. "My lady," said Merlin, "under this stone lid are the bodies of the two lovers whom I have told you about."

She eagerly picked up the cloth and looked closely at the slab that covered the tomb. She recognized it as made of red marble. "Really, Merlin," she said, "this is a beautiful, splendid place. It seems clear that it was planned and built for the delight and enjoyment of cheerful, pleasure-loving people."

"So it was, indeed," said Merlin. "If you knew how much effort and how much care went into it, you would be amazed."

"What about this stone slab?" she asked. "Can anyone lift it?"

"No one," said Merlin, "except me. However, I advise you not to look at the bodies, because bodies that have lain in the ground as long as these have are ugly and horrible, not fit to see."

"Even so," she said, "I want the lid raised."

He agreed and, grasping it at the edge, he raised it on one side. It was so heavy that ten men would have had great trouble moving it, so that we can only believe the power of his mind was of greater avail than the strength of his body. But that was true of everything he did.

Then he laid the slab down on the ground alongside the tomb. The young lady looked in and saw that the two bodies were wrapped in a white shroud, which prevented her from seeing faces or limbs. Realizing that that was all she would see, she said to Merlin: "Merlin, you have told me so much about these two lovers that if I were God for a moment, you can be sure I would unite their souls in everlasting joy. In fact I find it such a pleasure to think about their life together that for their memory's sake I want to stay right here, without moving, all through the night."

"I shall stay with you," said Merlin, "to keep you company."

As she spoke, so she did. The girl ordered her bed to be made in that very room, and as soon as it was done, she lay down to sleep. Merlin did likewise, but in a different bed. That night Merlin had been feeling a great torpor rather than his usual alertness and cheer, and he fell asleep as soon as he had closed his eyes. He was like a man under a spell, and he had indeed lost all the craft and all the knowledge that had always been his. The young lady, who was well aware of his state, left her bed to come over to him and place him under an even greater spell than before. When she had numbed him to such an extent that he would be powerless to move even to save his neck from the ax, she threw open the door to the room and called to her men to come in. She led them over to the bed where Merlin lay and began to turn him over and around in every direction, like a lump of earth. He showed no more response than if his soul had already departed from his body. She then said to the men standing there: "Well, what do you think of him now, my lords? Look how the enchanter is enchanted!"

In their astonishment they crossed themselves and said that they would never in the world have imagined such a thing could happen. "Now tell me," she said, "what shall we do with him? He followed me on this journey not for the sake of my honor but in order to disgrace me and take away my maiden-hood. I should rather see him hang than let myself be touched by him, for he is a son of the Devil and I could never, for anything imaginable, love a son of the Devil. I must decide, then, how to free myself of him. If I do not make sure right now that I am free of him forever, I shall never again find as good an opportunity."

"My lady," said one of the squires, "you have no need to wonder or to hesitate. I am ready to get rid of him for you at this very moment."

"How would you do it?" she asked.

"Kill him," he said. "What else is there to do?"

"God never forgive me," she said, "if he is slain in front of me! I could not bear to watch him killed. But I shall find a better way to take revenge than you propose!" At that she told the men to pick him up by the head and feet and throw him into the tomb where the two lovers lay. Then she had them replace the stone slab. When, with great effort, that was done, she began her incantations, and with her spells and magic words she so tightly bound and sealed the slab in place that there was no one afterward who was able to move it or open it or look at Merlin, dead or alive, until she herself returned at the request of Tristan (as is recounted in the true story of Tristan, and the very *Tale of the Cry* speaks of it, though not in detail). Nor was there anyone afterward who heard Merlin speak, except Bademagu, who arrived four days after he had been entombed. At that point Merlin was still alive and spoke out when Bademagu, wanting to know who was in the tomb lamenting so bitterly, attempted to raise the stone slab. Merlin said to him: "Bademagu, do not struggle to raise the slab! Neither you nor anyone else will succeed, until the lady returns who has buried me here. No strength and no stratagem will be of any avail, for I am trapped here by such powerful charms and magic spells that no one could release me except my enchantress herself."

I shall not recount any more of this episode in the present book, because the *Tale of the Cry* recounts it in detail. You may know, though, that the cry that Master Helie has written about is the last cry that Merlin ever uttered in that grave in which he lay trapped. His cry came from the sharp pain he felt when he realized that he was being killed by a woman's cunning and that a woman's craft had defeated his own. The echo of the cry was heard throughout the length and breadth of the kingdom of Logres, and it gave rise to many extraordinary events, as the *Tale* recounts in detail. And since it is all explained there, we shall not speak of it in the present book, but instead go back now to our own story.

When Niviane had sealed Merlin in the tomb, as I have explained, she closed the door to the chamber behind her as securely as she could, though without using any magic spell, and then spent the rest of the night in the front room with her men. In the morning, when day broke, she left the dwelling, closing the door behind her but not in such a way as to bar entry to anyone whom chance might lead to it. Once she and her party were mounted, they rode directly from the rocky cliff toward the site where she understood that Arthur's battle was to take place. She reached it on the appointed day. The tale does not speak of any adventure that may have occurred on the way, but only of the fact that she arrived at the field of combat. With that our tale falls silent about her and turns back to King Arthur, recounting how he achieved victory in his battle and how he learned that that trap had been laid for him by his sister Morgan.

[*Niviane arrives in time to save Arthur from his foe by magically restoring to him his sword Excalibur and its enchanted scabbard. Morgan, undeterred, persists in her efforts to destroy Arthur, but the Lady of the Lake again rescues him. The work ends with the following sentence:*]

Now the tale ceases to speak of the Lady of the Lake and King Arthur and the entire life of Merlin, and goes on to the subject of the Holy Grail, which is the point of this book.

Chapter *XV*

THE RISE OF GAWAIN, NEPHEW OF ARTHUR

Mildred Leake Day

The Rise of Gawain, Nephew of Arthur tells the story of Gawain's birth, boy-hood, and early adventures. It ends with Gawain being received by King Arthur and acclaimed as the pre-eminent knight of the realm. Other Arthurian works tell of Gawain's parentage and training in Rome—Geoffrey of Monmouth's *Historia Regum Britanniae*, Wace's *Roman de Brut*, Layamon's *Brut*, *Enfances Gauvain*, *Perlesvaus*—but *De ortu Waluuanii* is the only complete source.

The Rise of Gawain is written in Medieval Latin. The single remaining manuscript is a copy made in the early fourteenth century. Its date has been debated, but it was written after Geoffrey of Monmouth (mid-twelfth century) because the plot and many specific passages, are borrowed from Geoffrey. Although J.D. Bruce and R.S. Loomis propose a date of composition in the thirteenth century, several details of costume and ship construction suggest an earlier date.

The work is anonymous, but the catalog tradition as recorded by John Bale in the sixteenth century lists Robert of Torigny as author. Robert was the renowned abbot of Mont St. Michel in France from 1154 to 1186. Al-though no other evidence indicates that Robert was the author of this ro-mance or of *The Story of Meriadoc (Historia Meriadoci)*, a second romance by the same hand, the two romances with their learned style must have been composed by a cleric with a similar background and range of interests.

One of the most interesting episodes in the series of adventures concerns the making of the explosive known as Greek fire. The description is a bizarre combination of folklore, literary passages about Medea's magic from Ovid's *Metamorphoses*, and a layman's description of the method of processing and projecting the petroleum mix. The method described would have produced a flame-weapon of thickened gasoline, much like a primitive napalm. This description, odd as it is, is one of the earliest documents on Greek fire from a European source.

Although most of the work is concerned with serious adventures, some passages are funny, as when Gawain forces Arthur into the River Usk. Arthur's explanation to his wife Gwendoloena (Guinevere) about why he is so cold and wet is one of the most delightful bits of humor in Arthurian literature. Equally funny is the scene on the next day when the proud Gawain presents horses to Gwendoloena and the King and meets the angry face of Arthur. Arthur opens a packet from the Emperor of Rome, but keeps the enclosed knowledge of Gawain's lineage to himself. The trick now is how Arthur can manage to save face, yet retain this remarkable kinsman in his service. So the King rebuffs Gawain until the frustrated knight makes the rash promise that if he can perform an exploit beyond the capability of Arthur's entire band of knights, then Arthur must accept him into their number. Arthur, delighted, agrees.

The theme of establishing one's identity gives *The Rise of Gawain* its structure and plot. Gawain first must learn who he is as an individual: a knight of incomparable prowess but known only as "Knight of the Surcoat." Then he must learn who he is by lineage. The reader, like the Emperor, holds the true knowledge from the beginning.

Bibliographic note: Scholarly work on *De ortu Waluuanii* has not been as extensive as that on many other Arthurian romances. James Douglas Bruce prepared two editions, the first for *PMLA*, 13 (1898), 365–455; the second as part of his volume *Historia Meriadoci* and *De ortu Waluuanii, Hesperia 2,* Göttingen: Dandenhoed & Ruprecht, 1913. The most recent edition is by Mildred Leake Day, *The Rise of Gawain, Nephew of Arthur (De ortu Waluuanii nepotis Arturi)*, Garland Library of Medieval Literature, 15, Series A (1984), which contains a full bibliography. The version that follows is slightly revised.

The Rise of Gawain, Nephew of Arthur

King Uther Pendragon, father of Arthur, subjugated the kings of all the provinces bordering Britannia to his authority; in order to insure their subjection he held their sons in his court, partly in the position of hostages, partly to be trained in nobility of conduct and military discipline. Among these hostages was Loth, nephew of King Sichelm of Norway, a young man of striking appearance, who was strong of body and manly of spirit. For these qualities Loth was held in higher esteem than others of his age by Uther and his son Arthur, and he frequently visited their private living quarters. King Uther also had a daughter named Anna, an incomparable beauty, who still lived with her mother, the queen, in her chambers.

As Loth would often tease her playfully and engage in merry words with her quite privately, they were both seized with love for one another. Yet for a long time, from shyness and shame, their mutual affections were hidden from each other. Truly, "love is like a flame, the more it is concealed the hotter it burns," and from hasty suppression it becomes intensified. Not being able to contain so great a love within themselves, they revealed to each other what possessed their hearts. With both their prayers answered, they yielded to their desires, and soon Anna conceived a child. When she was near the time to bear the child, she feigned illness and retired to a private bedchamber, with only her lady-in-waiting knowing why.

At last the time came for the delivery of the infant, and she gave birth to a male child of rare beauty. Earlier, Anna had made a contract with certain wealthy men who had come from beyond the seas seeking trade, confirming a pact with them under oath that as soon as the infant had come into the world, lest anyone should find out, they would carry the child away to their own land and bring it up with care. So with no one knowing of the child's birth, the merchants accepted the infant son along with an untold wealth of gold, silver, and rich vestments that the mother had provided. In addition, she entrusted to them an immensely valuable cloak embroidered with jewels worked in gold over its entire surface, as well as a signet ring set with an emerald that she had received in trust from the king, a ring which he himself was accustomed to wear only on feast days. She added also a document impressed with the king's seal, the text of which identified with irrefutable proofs that the child, whom she had named Gawain, was the son of the nephew of the King of Norway and of the sister of Arthur; the document explained further that he had been sent to a foreign land out of fear of the king. Thus these items—the cloak, the ring, and the document—she wanted the child to have, foreseeing that whenever he returned, if he was not recognized by his parents and they rejected him, these would display proof of his identity, and through their evidence he would attain the acknowledgment of his parents.

The merchants, accordingly, boarded ship carrying the infant committed to them for fostering. Hoisting the canvas to the winds and plowing a wake across the sea, at last on the eighth day they were sailing toward the coast of Gaul, and reaching shore, they came to land two miles from the city of Narbonne. From here, once they had heaved to, all the men, dripping salt and sea-water, hastened on foot to the city, leaving the ship in port with only a single serving-boy to look after their merchandise and the nursling in the cradle. Actually, they had steered under a steep cliff quite a distance from the city and thought that no one would come near the ship in the meantime. But after they had gone, by chance a certain fisherman from the neighboring region, who was called Viamundus (a man poor in possessions but noble by birth and bearing), came walking along the shore with his wife, as was his daily routine, searching if he might find a fish stranded on the shore by the ebb of the sea, with the price of which he could buy food. When he saw the keel drawn to the shore, abandoning his other plan, he at once set out in that direction. On boarding, he found that no one except a boy had been left to guard it and, what is more, he was asleep. Seeing an infant of great beauty and an unguarded ship filled with all riches, and considering his own poverty which, with fortune favoring, he would be able to relieve (as the proverb says, "opportunity of place and time makes the thief"), he plundered whatever seemed to him of greatest value in silver and gold and various furnishings. He handed the infant to his wife as well as the coffer placed at his head that contained the cloak, the ring, and the document. Laden with riches, they escaped quickly to their dwelling, the affair being observed by no one.

When the merchants, though, returned later to the mooring-place, they discovered the theft of their property. They were shocked by the unexpected turn of events, and overwhelmed by the great loss, they began weeping and groaning. They continued all day in deep despair, particularly for the kidnaped infant who had been entrusted to their safekeeping. In a short time they sent carefully chosen agents through the neighboring shores and fields to investigate the matter thoroughly and to find out who had inflicted such a loss on them. But since "that which lies hidden from the knowledge of all is with difficulty discovered," those who had been sent returned sadly to the ship without having discovered any trace of the infant or the treasure.

Viamundus, meanwhile, hid the stolen wealth that he had carried to his cottage, along with the infant boy. He cared for the child, exerting great concern, as if the boy were his son, since he had none of his own. He was afraid to reveal the riches which he now had in his control, lest by ostentatious display the ugly truth of the crime he had perpetrated would become known, because not only was the poverty which had burdened him up to this time quite obvious, but also the investigation of his theft was still in progress.

After a period of seven years had elapsed, he decided to make a pilgrimage to Rome, led both by repentance for his deed and by the fact that he did not doubt that he would be able to spend his wealth without fear of the law in a region where he was not known. When everything necessary for the journey had been prepared, he set out with his wife and adopted son, with his household staff accompanying him with all his possessions. By good fortune he arrived in a short time safely at the walls of Rome. When he entered, he walked around the city all day through every section and scrutinized the entire area. He shrewdly inquired about the conditions of the place, the customs of the citizens, and the names of the senators and the most distinguished men.

In fact, Rome at this period had been captured by the barbarians and sacked, ravaged almost to the point of utter destruction—walls thrown down, buildings burned, and citizens captured, driven out, or slain by various means of torture. But a new emperor had succeeded to the throne who, although grieving over the ruin of the city, was rebuilding the destroyed sections, gathering together the scattered citizens, redeeming the captives, striving with all his might to bring Rome back to her former good fortune. Viamundus perceived this and, since he was astute, saw that the situation was favorable to his own goals, and so without delay he dressed himself in an impressive style and acquired servants and as many slaves as possible from the neighboring towns, fitting them out magnificently. Escorted by a numerous train of servants, he proceeded through the center of the city to the palace, creating a spectacle for all to behold. Coming before the emperor, he was received with honor.

When at last he had the opportunity of speaking with the emperor, Viamundus stated in his petition that he came from a very noble family of Romans and had been the military leader of a region of Gaul until he heard about the destruction of the city of Rome; he had hastened there to swell the ranks of his fellow citizens, and he now begged the emperor to grant a place in the city for him and his people to live in together. The emperor, judging him to be of no minor nobility, not only from his venerable gray hair and the elegance of his many possessions, but also from his numerous followers, gave thanks because he had come to him and promised that if he remained in the city he would be endowed with many honors. He also gave him a marble residence of remarkably good design located in front of the gates of his own palace, a home that allegedly had belonged to the great Scipio Africanus. The emperor also conferred on him towns, vineyards, and fields outside the city which were to provide for his expenses.

Viamundus, having obtained these favors of good fortune beyond all estimation, conducted himself so fitly and nobly and charmingly that he earned the admiration of the emperor, senate, and people, and the much repeated story of his lavish generosity spread privately and publicly throughout the city. Daily the senators and nobles of Rome gathered about him—not only these men, but out of regard for his young son, boys wearing the toga of noble birth and a number of knights from the imperial court, all of whom Viamundus honored with many delicacies, sumptuous banquets, and rich gifts. Meanwhile, as the boy grew, he increased both in manly spirit and physical skill, and he strove hard for courtesy and prowess, emerging as the equal of his supposed father. He frequented the palace and was considered a friend to the emperor and to those under him. Truly something of excellence flourished naturally in that young man and with this he ravished the hearts of the perceptive and drew them to love him. He had a tall and noble stature, a graceful bearing, and a handsome face, and he was endowed with remarkable strength.

When the boy had reached his twelfth year, Viamundus took to his bed, stricken with a serious illness. Then because of increasing weakness, he realized that the end of his life was imminent, and he begged earnestly that the emperor and the pope—Sulpicius occupying at that time the papal throne—should come to him and hear his words. Those men, not wishing to spurn the entreaties of this great man, whom they esteemed so much because of his generous character, came, bringing with them high-ranking men of the city who gathered before him with heavy hearts. Viamundus first gave thanks to those present for the benefits they had shared with him; then consulting with them in private, he revealed his former life, how by chance he had obtained such great wealth and the boy whom he had raised as his son; and he laid bare his whole life in proper order.

He concluded: "I resolved often with a burning desire to reveal this to your highnesses, but I delayed, always waiting for the opportune moment; I put it off till the present. Now, however, since my ultimate fate is imminent, I am compelled to confess these things. Though what I ask may be summarily granted to a man of my lowly estate by you masters of the entire world, still I believe that you, remembering our friendship and fellowship, will not deny my petition. It is specifically for this reason that I summoned you: to commit to the protection of your highnesses this boy whom I have nurtured as my son and with whom all these material things fell to my lot, so that you may advance him, educating him for the order of knighthood when he comes of age. From the proof I will give you, you will learn that he is the nephew of Arthur, King of Britannia" (by this time, Uther had died and Arthur had succeeded him), "the man whose fame for great prowess flies everywhere. I do not doubt that this boy, outstanding in nobility, will show this quality without dishonor. I recommend, nevertheless, that the matter be held secret from everyone and from the boy himself; don't even let his name be revealed until he is acknowledged by his parents because the terms of the document that attests to his origin prohibit it. But when he comes to manhood, I beg you to let him be sent back with this letter offering the sure evidence of his lineage." And summoning the boy, who until that time had been called the "Boy with No Name," because it was not known by what family name he should be registered, Viamundus embraced the feet of the emperor and commended the boy to his care with humble pleas and solemn vows. Ordering the coffer which contained the proofs assembled by his mother to be brought out, he presented it to the emperor.

When the emperor had inspected it, he praised the man's generosity toward his foster-son, and he accepted the boy, throwing his arms around him and promising that he would fulfill Viamundus' desire in all respects. Thus Viamundus, having achieved to his satisfaction what he had striven for so intensely, with the emperor sitting by his bedside, died happy. With great mourning, he was buried among the tombs of the nobility in a monument of marvelous workmanship erected by the emperor.

So it was that, after the death of Viamundus, the nameless boy was conducted to the palace by order of the emperor and included among the royal children. When three years had passed—that is to say, when the boy had reached fifteen—and his prowess met the test, he was granted arms by the emperor. As a mark of favor, the emperor also granted arms to twenty other young men in military training with him. Then from the palace with the other new knights and young Romans still in training they proceeded to the Circus, where the racing of horses was customarily practiced. On this day so great was the valor with which the new knight conducted himself, and so vigorous were his exploits that the cheers of all the people served as a testimony. No one in that spectacle could withstand him, no one could match his strength; in truth, whomever he encountered in a single combat he overthrew.

Later at the festival of Equirria, the new knight, wearing the golden circlet which the emperor had promised to the victor, was led into the emperor's presence, with a cheering procession of people escorting him. The emperor, praising him in no small way for his outstanding prowess, granted him any reward he would ask for, but the young man replied, "I desire nothing of your bounty, O emperor, unless that I may take part in the first combat that you wage against your enemies."

The emperor assented and placed him in the first Order of Equestrians. On the day when he received his knighthood, before he went out to combat on horseback, he wore a crimson tunic to cover his armor. He called it a "surcoat for armor." When asked by the knights why he had put it over his armor—since no one before this time had worn a tunic while dressed in armor—he replied that he wanted a splendid attire. After that reply, everyone chanted: "New knight with a surcoat for his armor, New knight with a surcoat for his armor"; and so "Knight of the Surcoat" became his name.

This man, who was advanced by the emperor to very high honor, strove always for even higher achievements in valor and prowess. A distinguished reputation and singular daring were attributed to him in every encounter of every tournament. While this was going on in Rome, war broke out between the King of Persia and the Christians in Jerusalem. When the day came for battle, the besieging formations of both cavalry and infantry produced a spectacle of terror as they drew near to battle. While the trumpets were being sounded, the bowstrings tautened, the lances couched, and the chief centurions tensed to join in hand-to-hand combat, those more mature in age and wisdom on both sides were meeting in council. When these men considered that the clash of such multitudes could not take place without great disaster, they proceeded between the lines, restrained the first attack, and then sent officials to discuss the conditions of peace with each side. After talks between them went on for some time, all parties agreed to this: from each side one man should be chosen to duel, and victory would go to the man who won, as would the final decision on those matters over which the war had broken out. But because the Jerusalemites did not dare to agree without the assent of the emperor, they bound themselves to a truce to be granted until they could send a delegation to the emperor and ascertain his will. They swore an oath that they agreed in principle to this procedure if it was affirmed by him. Therefore, when the truce had been granted, they selected those who were to act as delegates, and without delay they sent them on their way. When instructing these men, they emphasized that if the emperor did not deny their petition, they were also to entreat him earnestly for a man capable of handling the proposed deal. The emissaries made a hurried journey to the emperor, and when they were brought into the senate, they explained in their most eloquent manner why they had come.

The emperor, after taking counsel concerning their pleas, considered agreeing to their petition but was undecided about whom he should send on their behalf. When the talk had dragged on with a diversity of opinions, the substance of it reached the ears of the Knight of the Surcoat. Without delay, he burst into the presence of the emperor, exclaiming, "O emperor, I want you to remember the honor you so graciously bestowed on me at the arming of the new knights when you promised me the first single combat that would be undertaken by you against your enemies. Now war is declared by the infidels not only against you and the Roman people, but also against the Christian faith. I beg your highness to allow me what you granted, so that I may not only receive your reward but may also avenge the honor of the Roman people and their religion."

Although it required a parting with this excellent knight in assigning him to this duel, because fulfilling his promise compelled it and because he knew no better man for such a mission, the emperor granted that it be done according to the rules of the senate. The emperor directed that the knight, along with the delegation, be well equipped, and that a hundred knights with a centurion in command escort them, so that not only would the knight go forth with honor, but also whatever dangers might confront him through the expanses of land or sea, he could thwart them with their help. Without delay they began the journey, and reaching the Adriatic Sea they boarded ships. There were sixteen other vessels along with theirs, some of which were merchantmen, others fast ships bound for the Holy Land which had joined their convoy because of the savage pirates who roamed the wide seas. The ships formed up, left the harbor, and set sail for deep water.

For twenty-five days they were tossed on huge waves, unable either to seek haven or to steer a straight course. Beset by mounting gales and driven in great circles, they were brought to shore on an island with barbarous people. The inhabitants were so savage that they would arrange no safe conduct for anyone either for sex or for age, but would inflict punishment on all landing from outside, whether guilty or innocent. For this reason they were approached by no one seeking trade, and were branded with a reputation for such cruelty that they were shunned by all, remaining cut off from the society of all others. They were said to consume voraciously the meat of all cattle and fowl; and since they were so dominated by passions of the flesh, the fathers did not know their own sons, nor the sons their fathers. Their stature ranged to three cubits, and their life expectancy was fifty years. Rarely did anyone die before the tenth year or live beyond fifty. Accustomed to hard work, they were known for their cultivation and production of food, abounding in wealth and with many children.

The news had spread through all the pagan lands that a knight whose passage at arms no one could withstand was being sent by the emperor to undertake the duel. For that reason, to all the islands in the Aegean Sea under pagan control near which the knight would have to pass, secret orders were sent to keep a constant watch over the ports and shores and, if by chance the knight should come to land, they should overpower him, so that he would not be able to arrive on the designated day. They also directed pirates to blockade the open reaches of the sea in different areas so that if the men escaped unharmed by those on guard at the ports, they might be taken by others patrolling the seas.

Reigning at this time on that island was a man named Milocrates, an enemy of the Roman people, who had captured and abducted by force the emperor's niece, whom the emperor himself had betrothed to the King of Illyricum. Since the stratagems above had been made known to him, he fortified the cities and towns that lay near the sea so that his soldiers could attack them as they approached, or the guards could capture them if they landed.

However, the shores by which the Romans did land were lined with dense forests in every direction—not the best land for animals of the field. Because of this scarcity, the wild beasts were protected quite carefully and strictly from the local people as well as from any outsiders who might land. According to the law, no one was to have the pleasure of eating this game, except the king himself or his princes. So it happened that when the centurion mentioned earlier and the fleet under his command landed on this island, the Knight of the Surcoat disembarked with a few companions to hunt. Six stags were soon slain, and with dogs set loose, he began to pursue the seventh, when suddenly the keeper of the preserve, stationed in the interior of the forest, heard the baying of the hounds and the blasts of the horns. The keeper summoned his companions and commanded them to arm themselves. As ordered, these men went out to confront the hunters, who were already in possession of the quarry. The foresters demanded by whose authority they poached on the royal game preserve, where no one was allowed entrance even with peaceful intent. They ordered the hunters to lay down their weapons and go before the king to submit to his judgment for the rash act they had committed.

To this our knight responded, "We have come for these deer which we took because of our need, and we will not sheathe our weapons anywhere except in your guts."

> He spoke, and brandishing spears with a powerful arm,
> He hurled cold steel into the arrogant throat;
> With his powerful right arm he stopped the mouth of the
>   menacing one.

The wounded keeper of the preserve groaned, so enraged by the intensity of the pain that when he had wrenched the spear from his wound, with supreme effort he flung it back at the Knight of the Surcoat; yet because his arm shook, it went awry and struck a tree.

At once the rest of the men from both sides attacked; grappling in close conflict, hand to hand they slashed at each other, and from a distance they fought by hurling spears. Actually the Knight of the Surcoat had more men, but none of them were wearing armor, while all their adversaries were fully protected. But the Knight of the Surcoat, when he saw his own men giving way before the enemy, drew his sword, and rushing at their leader, knocked him to the ground, grabbed the noseguard of his helmet, dragged him toward his own men, and stripped him of his life and his armor together. Having equipped himself with this armor, shouting for his men, he then attacked the enemy, and although some fled, he alone slew thirteen of them.

The hunting party followed the fugitives through the forest and sent to the Underworld all they could overtake. Only one man was left as a survivor to be the messenger of this great defeat. He had hidden himself out of sight within the dense foliage until his adversaries stopped searching for him and went away. When the Romans had left, he rose up quickly and went to the king and related what had happened. King Milocrates was staying at that time in a nearby city that he had founded in a delightful setting three miles from the sea. When he learned of the landing of the enemy and the slaying of his knights, he at once dispatched messengers and ordered the princes of all the provinces to come together as quickly as possible with as many men as they could muster. They complied with the command and came with a vast army. Those arriving were lodged throughout the neighboring countryside because the king's city was not able to hold them. Then King Milocrates deliberated with his princes about what they must do.

Meanwhile, the Knight of the Surcoat, having overcome the foresters, returned to the ships. The entire contingent, rewarded with the spoils of victory, congratulated him. Then on the third day they attempted to get on with the voyage they had begun, but because the winds continued to be unfavorable, they were forced to remain where they were. The centurion, quite disturbed by the delay, assembled the leaders of the knights and sought counsel from them about what could be done toward proceeding with their mission. He assumed that the king of that island and his princes were now moving against them in retaliation for their resistance, and that they had by now mobilized to crush them in vengeance for those deaths— and would do so, unless they could quickly get under way. He contended that unless the wind abated for them, they lacked the strength to row the ships from that place, and it would not be safe to remain there, since they had too few knights to fight off the great numbers of the enemy, and their provisions of food and fodder would not last much longer. "It is necessary then," the centurion began, "for some of our men to go spy on the manpower and plans of the enemy so that when we know how he usually deploys his forces, we may see more practically what must be done."

The words of the leader were well received, and two of the men were chosen to perform the task. One of them was the Knight of the Surcoat; the other, named Odabel, was a blood relative of the centurion. They were known in uncertain situations to be careful and prudent, and in danger to be stronger and more skillful than the others. Protected with armor, they began the journey as ordered and made their way through the forest to the city. At the entrance to the king's forest an enormous boar rushed upon them, its neck covered with bristles like shafts, its gaping jaws armed with curved tusks, thunder roaring from its mouth, and saliva spewing over its forequarters. It charged at an angle to the attack. Seeing it, the Knight of the Surcoat leaped from his horse and, brandishing a flashing hunting-spear in his right hand, struck a blow before it had a chance to strike. The spearhead pierced into its foreskull between the brows; forced on through the body, it came out above the flank. Yet not only did the boar not fall immediately, but with the wound it seemed to gather fury, so that although its strength was diminished greatly by the loss of blood, with all the might it could muster, it could still attack him with its tusks. While blocking the slash, the Knight of the Surcoat took the blow on his shield, unsheathed his sword, cut off the head of the beast as it was raging at him, and left it rolling around in its own blood. The beast was lifted onto the armorbearer's horse, and the armorbearer delivered it to the centurion on their behalf.

Returning quickly to the path, the Knight was waiting for Odabel at the gates of the city by midday. When they entered the city, they proceeded to the palace and mingled with the king's men as if they belonged with them. Actually the very large number of men made it possible for them to go unnoticed as strangers, while as an additional safeguard, they had a practical knowledge of the language of that country. They scoured the city and also the rural regions in every direction, noting the strength and number of military groups. By no means had the entire army assembled. Actually, the day before, King Milocrates had sent some men to spy on the fleet of the Romans, and when they returned to the city, they had terrified him by reporting a multitude of armored men. As a result, Milocrates feared that the fleet had invaded with an overwhelming force. Through messengers he summoned his brother, Buzafarnan, who reigned over a nearby kingdom, so that he might bring him help in his great need as fast as he could. While he waited for his brother's arrival, the action of the attack was postponed. On the day that the Knight of the Surcoat came to the city, Milocrates had called an assembly of the nobility, discussing with them what steps to take in this emergency. The consensus was that when his brother Buzafarnan arrived, the army should be divided into two parts—one for ship and the other for land—so that when they engaged the enemy in battle, no route would be open for escape. The

Knight of the Surcoat, who remained unrecognized among them and listened intently, noted what each man said and committed the plan to memory.

When the sun had set, King Milocrates hurried to his evening meal. The Knight of the Surcoat, placing himself in his company, entered the royal palace while his companion waited outside for his return. When the rest of the king's men had reclined to eat, the Knight slipped out unnoticed toward the bedchamber where the niece of the emperor—that is, the queen, whom Milocrates had stolen from her lawful husband—resided alone with her maidens. The rather late hour had dimmed visibility; still it was said that the chamber was unapproachable. He began to deliberate what in his judgment should be done and to plan carefully, picturing in his mind how he would have the strength to meet whatever traps he might encounter. If, for instance, he was to hide in the bedchamber and kill the king while he was asleep, as he had originally planned, he knew that if he was caught in the act of murder, he would suffer the same punishment. On the other hand, if he returned to the ship with no deed accomplished, he would be rightfully considered a slacker and a coward. While he turned such things over in his mind, a knight named Nabaor (who had been taken prisoner by the Romans but later released) came along, having been sent by the king to the queen. The Knight of the Surcoat could see him clearly, but he himself remained unnoticed by the man. (Those standing in the shadows see clearly those in the light while they themselves remain unseen by others.) While this man was being held captive earlier with other spies, the Knight of the Surcoat had struck up a strong friendship with him; for remembrance sake, he had shared with him a ring and a crimson mantle.

Recognizing him now and gambling on his friendship, the Knight of the Surcoat called Nabaor over secretly, embraced him, hinted at the reason for his coming, and by some preliminary remarks tested his feelings. When he perceived that Nabaor would protect him, forsaking all pretense, he asked the man to help him accomplish what he had in mind. Nabaor, for his part, wondered greatly about his presence there and when he learned why he had come was delighted to have found the chance to return his generosity. After leading him to a private chamber, Nabaor said: "My beloved friend, what you desire is greater than what you can accomplish, and it ought not to be undertaken by you alone. For thirty very strong men, always on watch, surround the couch of the king; no one is allowed access to him until daylight, not even his servants. Besides, you know that on the whole you have to use more care than strength, because what is longed for is often accomplished successfully by careful planning in support of strength. Strength without cunning never gets the job done. Follow this advice as you approach your venture, but with me to guide you in what order it is to be carried out. The queen is greatly attracted to you; she desires most ardently to make your acquaintance either by addressing you in person or through intermediaries. She has often inquired of me, after I returned from my duty as a spy, what form and stature you have, and I, replying that you are incomparable in both, kindled her heart with love for you, so that she is more concerned with your welfare than with the king's. Though doubtlessly the queen of this country has been raised to the highest degree of honor and glory by King Milocrates, still because she has not forgotten that she was abducted from the marriage bed by plunder, the shame of captivity constantly torments her, and she would even now prefer to be free with a poor man than to live on here with ostentation as a captive. Hearing that you have landed here on a mission for the emperor, she yearns desperately to have a chance to speak to you. For she hopes that if she gains your attention, she can be freed from the yoke of captivity and restored to her own husband, whose marriage was approved by the emperor. You know without doubt that this venture will require effort and cunning; from her it will require commitment with sagacity, so that your strength and courage may allow you to prevail against King Milocrates. Yet because a woman's mind is always changing with random moods more quickly than the wind, one must first discreetly test in which way her disposition is inclined. If this woman has learned you are here, neither fear of the king nor shame of gossip will keep her from coming to you; she will still speak with you. I shall go to her, then—being sent to carry her the king's messages—and among other things I mention, I'll speak of you artfully and learn where her will is inclined. You, meanwhile, stay hidden here until I know the outcome."

Nabaor accordingly approached the queen. Between them, as various topics of conversation were discussed, there was talk concerning the Knight of the Surcoat. As Nabaor narrated his marvelous deeds with much praise, the queen replied, "How happy I'd be if I could tell such a worthy man my heartfelt distress! Certainly if only because of the emperor whose niece I am and whose knight he is, he would rescue me from this man's tyranny. I desire, therefore, to find someone trustworthy to send as a messenger to him, so that in one way or another he may be given the opportunity of seeing and talking with me." Nabaor was also one of those whom Milocrates had captured with her and forced into chains of servitude. Thus to this man as a fellow-conspirator of her secrets, she safely committed the confidences of her heart.

He replied to her, "My queen, there is no impediment to your wishes, nor will there be need of a messenger. Only let yourself be free from deceit; only let your wishes agree with your words, and he whom you desire will be present as you command."

When she had sworn in reply that she wanted this to be done more eagerly than she had dared to confess, Nabaor led the Knight of the Surcoat into her presence, and he laid open to her the purpose for which he had come. Moreover, as was earlier understood, he loomed handsome to her sight with a manly build that drew glances from people who were amazed at his beauty. The queen, greeting him as he entered, bade him sit down, and having contemplated him intensely for some time, finally burst into tears, brought forth a deep sigh from her breast and explained the distress by which she was burdened, adding that he could offer her, if he were willing, the remedy for her great ills.

He replied, "If my desire could be joined by equal ability, without doubt there would be no delay in obeying your will. But it is plain that the king exceeds us in the number and strength of his soldiers, and it is uncertain for that reason what conclusion awaits us. If you know anything that could help us bring this undertaking to a successful end, tell me and you will not find me either slack or slow in carrying it out."

While the queen, pausing for a moment, considered what she would say to this, Nabaor spoke: "It is by no means hidden from you, my queen, that the king is summoning the army against these men for what will be a pitched battle. In the great mass of this army I see the best opportunity for taking action. If, therefore, you are burdened with such concern, you have the means both to remove him and his comrades from the impending disaster and also to accomplish what you have longed for so intensely. The king's attention, fixed on the strategies of war, will be less concerned with other matters. Command, then, through this knight that the centurion should select forty armed men and send them here tomorrow through the forest in secret, so that the day after, when the king advances against him in battle, they will occupy the city, which you will betray to them; and when they have set it on fire, the horrible spectacle for the king and his men will provide the means of victory."

She begged him with many prayers to carry out the proposed plan. She then bestowed on the Knight of the Surcoat the king's sword and his gilded armor, on which lay the curse that the king, having been overcome, would be stripped of the royal crown by the one who first wore it other than the king himself. In addition she gave him abundant gifts of gold, silver, and gems of great value and, above all, sealed the pact with friendship. With these matters settled, the Knight of the Surcoat quickly rejoined his comrades and, leading them from the city, came upon the centurion at the first light of dawn. Displaying the gifts he had been given, he also reported what he had done, what he had seen, and what he had heard.

The centurion, exhilarated beyond all expectation by hope of victory, assigned selected knights to go to the queen. When they were chosen, he made his kinsman Odabel the ranking officer, and having urged him to lead those under him with care and foresight, he sent them off toward the vineyard close to the palace as soon as it was dusk, to wait there hidden all night. On the following day Nabaor would admit them by order of the queen.

The next day was dawning when Milocrates marched out of the city with his army to meet the centurion in battle. The larger part of his army he had committed under his brother's leadership to attack the enemy from the rear by ship, so that, having been surrounded on both sides by the fighting, they would surrender more quickly. But the centurion, knowing their plan in advance, had relocated the ships side by side around the camp, so that later if it became necessary, they would form a rampart for those retreating to them. From the camp set up in a secure place a short distance from the sea, the centurion himself led forth his band of knights. He divided the knights and their units into five squadrons. He himself was the commanding officer of the center. They were openly moving forward face to face against the king, who was surrounded in the front line by a thousand armored men. But however superior in number and strength of warriors the king might be, he held little hope of victory: the armor upon which he thought rested the protection of himself and his kingdom had been stolen. When he looked for it as he was preparing to go into battle and could not find it anywhere, all hope of success for his plan left him, even though he did not know for certain that the Knight of the Surcoat had it until finally he saw the man himself clad in it on the field as he was about to begin the battle. On seeing this he shrieked in terror. Supposing only too truly that what later did happen would happen to him, he was panic-stricken. Still, he was unable to stop what he had begun, and he realized that, to advance his own personal glory, he must either conquer courageously or die bravely.

The blare of trumpets sounded then from both sides, a call which traditionally inspires a fighting spirit and signals the attack on the enemy. The foot-soldiers had already begun to make contact when the smoke rising from the city indicated plainly what was happening there. For as planned, once the king had led his troops from the city in haste to battle, immediately those waiting in hiding had risen up and seized control, and they had set aflame the structures below the walls by throwing fire. As the flames reached skyward, the catastrophe of the city was revealed to the citizens already stationed at some distance; so also ashes carried by the south wind flew into the faces of the men fighting. The heart of the king was so aghast at the impending disaster that, disregarding the battle already engaged, he turned quickly to the aid of the city:

> You could see the lines in confusion, hands without spears,
> Men urging dispersal and flight.
> They go a thousand ways, no two together;
> Thus flees the enemy like cattle from a barking dog.
> The avengers press on, charge the enemy in flight,
> Settle accounts by slaughter of those overtaken.
> Rocks bury some, some lie vanquished;
> He who suffers neither endures the harsh chains.

The Knight of the Surcoat, seeing the formations of the enemy dissolving and suddenly turned to flight, regrouped his own men and pursued and inflicted mass destruction. Not only had the blast of flame that was consuming the buildings of the city terrified them, but the very flight they attempted made them for the most part mentally and physically helpless. Scattered throughout the declivities of the mountains, through the unfrequented places of the forests, like a flock attacked by the fury of wolves, they headed toward the city walls, and they received ceaseless vengeance from the swords of their pursuers. The knights who had set fire to the outskirts of the city, meeting the fugitives, kept them away from the walls, and driving them back into the field of battle, forced them to fall into the hands of those from whom they fled. On either hand there was the horrible slaughter, and they were impeded by the very numbers of their own men so that they had recourse neither to flight nor to skillful defense. They were shaken and without a protector, like an unarmed rabble, and no one thought it right to give help to him who sought it.

Finally King Milocrates, realizing that he was surrounded on all sides by the enemy, reckoned infamy upon himself if he died without some worthy action. He gathered his scattered men into a unit and, advancing bravely against his challengers, restrained the force of the enemy in their first encounter and even compelled them to give way before him. With his own right hand he attacked as many as possible and turned the rest to flight, until at length the Knight of the Surcoat, seeing his comrades hard pressed by that man, gave rein to his horse and bore down upon the king. Milocrates daringly met the charge of the challenger, and as they exchanged blows, each in turn unhorsed the other. But the Knight of the Surcoat, rising more quickly, drew his sword and rushed the king the moment he was struggling to get up. He would have inflicted a fatal wound, had not the king blocked the blow with his shield. No great injury resulted, but it so stunned the king's brain that he collapsed and lay for about an hour as if asleep.

At that moment, the nephew of the king, a skillful young knight, bore down upon the Knight of the Surcoat as he was about to dispatch the king with a second thrust of his sword, and with threats and blows the horseman attacked the Knight of the Surcoat from the left. The knight on foot repelled the attack with his own shield and, grasping a javelin that had by luck fallen near him, flung it back by the thong. It was not stopped by either shield boss or iron lorica, but passing through the horseman's saddlebow, it pierced deeply under the belly of that one who had made threats beyond his power.

Once he had eliminated that attacker, the Knight of the Surcoat again sought out the king, but he was received with a boldness of greater intensity than he expected. For shame and wrath had brought back to the king's memory his former dignity and prowess and given him strength as he regained his breath. He was inspired to avenge himself on the enemy, reckoning that he should not be punished like some commoner, especially since there was no hope of rescue. He was determined to expend every effort to prevent the joy of victory from falling to his enemies. First, then, he attacked the approaching Knight of the Surcoat, slashed a swordcut across his forehead where it was unprotected by the helmet, and had not the nosepiece projecting from the helmet blunted it, would have brought death from the gash. The Knight of the Surcoat, wounded, became frantic with fear that his sight would be dimmed by the flowing blood, and striving to exact revenge for the injury, he rushed the king and, swinging his sword with a sidelong blow to the nape of the neck, severed the head along with the right arm.

When he fell, those who were with him took flight, their only hope of safety. The centurion, wishing to spare the multitude, signalled the knights by trumpet not to pursue the fugitives, knowing that with their leader dead, those under him would surrender without a fight. After collecting the spoils of the enemy, they entered the city with triumphant pomp, and an arch was built in their honor. The queen, niece of the emperor, met them, led them into the palace, and with every attention refreshed those most exhausted by the fighting. She directed that the dead be buried and the wounded cared for with healing remedies, and she showed herself most bountiful to all and rewarded each man according to the prize deserved.

The centurion, staying on at the island for fifteen days, allowed the country to be plundered by the army. Prominent men and administrators, because they had collaborated with the enemy of the Roman people, he had executed and dismembered. He punished the common people by a harsh levy of reparations. Leaving some of the knights there to protect the island and choosing others to accompany the queen, he returned the niece of the emperor to her rightful husband, the King of Illyricum, from whom she had been forcibly seized.

With two hundred additional knights enlisted from that province, he boarded the refurbished fleet with his companions in order to complete the mission that they had undertaken. When he had already completed a day's journey through the waves of the sea, the brother of King Milocrates, whose kingdom he had conquered, appeared with no small fleet. For, as stated earlier, he had been sent by King Milocrates before the battle to surprise the fleet of the centurion so that, surrounded on all sides, flight for him would be cut off, whether by land or sea. Although he had reached the fleet, or rather the landing area of the centurion's ships, he found neither the ships nor the men. The centurion had hurriedly fortified the camp at some distance from the sea and set up the ships as a rampart for his people, prows pointing outward on all sides. King Egesarius (so the brother of Milocrates was called) assumed they had already escaped. Turning his ships about, he sailed back into deep water, where he was storm-tossed for three days. When he wanted to come about to seek port again, the winds blowing from every direction drove him farther off toward distant lands for a five-day voyage. Now with a lighter wind behind him, he had returned, and he was confronted by the fleet of the centurion in the midst of the sea.

By chance, however, the centurion himself was seated in the tower-like structure which he had erected in the stern as a defense, and with the Knight of the Surcoat sitting near him, he was scanning the horizons of the sea from this vantage point. At first he had given attention to figures contrived in the likeness of a cock or some such thing placed on the masts, doubtless to test by which wind the keel was being propelled. For toward whatever corner of the earth the wind of the region is inclined, these always face into it. The banners, devices carried on the masts of the approaching fleet, were tossed higher and then lower by the action of the wind.

The centurion, thinking he saw birds—kingfishers—on the horizon, shouted to the ship's captain, "Ahoy," and said, "I think a mighty storm is upon us. For as these birds direct their course, beating their wings and wheeling through the empty air, so they taste their joys almost with a knowledge of the future, with our corpses about to be food for their crops. Indeed it is said that with a storm imminent, these birds, wheeling about, now together, now separated, circle into mass flight and foretell by their behavior coming disaster."

The Knight of the Surcoat, however, standing by him at that moment and perceiving things as they really were, said, "Sir, your concept is in error. For those are not birds which you think you see, but standards mounted on mastheads. You must realize that it is without doubt the enemy fleet approaching, which was sent to pursue us some time ago by the king already subjugated by your forces. Perhaps they were driven by some storm and forced to seek a foreign harbor—the reason, it seems to me, for the delay. Now since the wind favors their plans, they have returned. Order the knights to put on their armor so that the enemy will not find us unarmed."

At the command of the centurion, those who were aboard that ship armed themselves; and to the rest of the ships (for there were thirty, fifteen of which he had led there and just as many others he had acquired later from the conquered island) the ship's trumpets gave a signal to do the same. The ships were placed in battle order: some to attack the enemy from the front, others from the left or right, and still others to remain in the rear as a trap. Moreover, five ships that had rams, in the first of which he was himself, he ordered ahead to attack the advancing enemy vessels with sudden force. Those experienced in naval battle use this particular type of ship fully rigged for piracy, the armament of which is so strong that whatever ship it strikes, it rips the planking open from top to bottom. Because all the area projecting between the prow and keel is covered with iron, the ridge armed with iron hooks, the vertex of the extension of the ram carrying iron points and armed like the crested beak of the cock, these ships are termed "rostrated." Towers are also erected on which are stationed the strongest men ready to stop the impetus of the enemy defense by hurling stones and javelins from above. The merchant ships were placed toward the rear so that if the ships carrying knights yielded, these could withdraw and might at least escape the hands of the pillagers.

When everything necessary was done, dropping anchor, they awaited the coming of the enemy. The sighting of the hostile fleet brought quick confirmation to the words of the Knight of the Surcoat. What he had reasoned had not been false. The men observed for themselves the fleet in formation and foresaw with no less astuteness the tactics required for such a battle. The Knight of the Surcoat, observing the pirates to be prepared for battle and closing in, immediately ordered the anchors raised and, as soon as the sails caught the winds, the ships to be driven forward by oars. With armed men in place on deck, he rushed the foremost galley on which the commander of the enemy fleet was sailing. The knight, smashing first with his single ship, drove home a blow by the force of its ram with such power all the way through to the mast that when the ram struck with its iron vertex, it forced the crippled vessel to seek the depths.

The other ships came up and surrounded the shattered vessel as reinforcement for the Knight of the Surcoat, and even though the enemy soldiers defended themselves vigorously, the knight's men overcame those who resisted. Some of them were thrown overboard; others were cut down by battleaxes and swords. Those remaining they restrained with chains. They slew the commander, who fought valiantly lest he fall living into the hands of his enemy. Then they seized the riches and arms and sank the ship beneath the sea.

After overthrowing these men, the Knight of the Surcoat advanced even more daringly into the remaining ships. With a battlecry these ships regrouped; he was intercepted, surrounded, cut off from his companions, and attacked fiercely from all sides. You could see the air darkened by the hurling of javelins and the surface of the sea covered with their great numbers. From one side and the other, a huge piece of stone-throwing equipment was manipulated in a circular course, the din of which produced no less horror than the danger. The contenders pressed with every kind of weapon trying to destroy the ship of the Knight of the Surcoat, but the planking, each board individually fastened with iron, did not separate from the blows. Hemmed in as he was by the formations of the enemy, he still did more damage than he received. When the enemy saw his determination, that he preferred to die rather than be conquered, and he could not be forced to submit nor lower his defense for an instant, they hurled their fire, that is to say "Greek fire," into the ship.

Fire of this kind may in fact be made in several ways. But the power of the formula that produces the fiercest fire and continues burning longest is prepared in this way. Those who possess the knowledge of preparation first make ready a brass vessel, and they collect poisonous toads of the kind called "rubetae," as many as needed, and they force-feed them with dovemeat and honey for three months. After this period has elapsed, they allow the toads to fast for two or three days; then they put the little beasts to the teats of some prolific creature, recently delivered and lactating, whose milk they suck for such a long time that they fall off from complete satiety. Swollen by poisonous fluid, they are laid upon a small vessel, and a fire hot enough to consume them like a funeral pyre is set under it. To these also are added water snakes, "chelyndri," which for ten days preceding their inclusions on the pyre are fed on a human cadaver.

There is in addition an asp (whose name escapes me), poisonous and deadly, bearing three heads upon one gullet, a venomous creature able to corrupt with incurable disease whatever it touches. At the touch of it the field loses its vegetation, the sea its fish, the trees their fruit, and so it is a very great marvel. Even if the most minute distillation infects a tree, no matter how huge, at that spot where it drops, it is absorbed inwardly, and like a chancer it will corrode, felling the tree to the earth. It has been learned that no remedy can stop the destruction; and even worse, if men or beasts are touched even slightly on the surface of the skin by this poison, it penetrates and they are slain instantly. How great its power is can be determined from the flame spewing intensely from the creature's mouth; and while it is itself burning with greatest heat, very often the forest it inhabits is set afire. From the venomous slaver that flows from its triple gaping mouths, three extracts are produced, doubtless a trace from each. The first of these, if consumed by anyone in meat or drink, will drive him mad; the second also brings death with but a taste; the juice of the third infects with the king's evil by swallowing or rubbing it. This monstrous beast, if one comes upon it when the poisons are fully developed, will destroy itself. If indeed it is captured, before it can be added to the above process, it must be fattened for a week on the proper food for these creatures.

In addition there must be included the gall bladder and testicles of a wolf that does not lack the ability to change its nature, a creature engendered by air and wind so that whatever it touches, by contact it receives that form. Also a "ligurius," obtained from the end of the earth, occupies no small place among the other ingredients, the same stone that is believed to be both endowed with virtue and to originate from the solidified urine of the wolf. For nothing interrupts the concentrated staring of the lynx; even the inner matter, which surely must be excreted, hardens while it contemplates the light. Also the head, the heart, and the liver of a crow which has measured out its ninth generation are added to increase the strength of the formula. Sulphur, also, and pitch, resin, olive oil, tartar, and petroleum are not in the least withheld from these things already mentioned; they feed the fire quickly when the flame is applied; they are set aside until later.

When these items have been collected in the order I have stated, they are enclosed in a heating vessel made of the purest bronze, and the vessel is filled to the brim with the blood of a red-haired man and a dragon. Indeed, a fiery nature is attributed to the blood of the red-haired man because of both the color of the hair and the great vigor these men usually have, a vivacity that openly attests their nature. A youth, then, whose beard and hair are red, with skin eruptions of the same color sprinkling his face, is led into a fine bedroom, and for the space of one month he is fattened sumptuously on every prepared delicacy. During this time, each day a hearth-fire is kindled before him, and he is made drunk with wine in order to increase the blood; and he is carefully kept from the embraces of women. When the month has come to an end, in the middle of the room charcoal fires of a man's length are lighted; he is exposed between these when he is full of food and drink and his clothing is removed; in the way meat is turned on the spit, he is turned before the fire. Warmed sufficiently, the veins on his entire body soon become swollen, and he is bled: that is, the veins of both arms are cut transversely. In the meantime, while he loses blood, he receives wafers in wine to sustain his spirit, lest because of weakness or a trance, the desired liquid be clotted. For a long time, then, the blood is allowed to flow, until it brings on death by its deficiency and casts the soul from the body. Next, having been mixed with the blood of the dragon, it is heated separately for a long time. Finally poured over the other substances, it blends the mixture together.

If one is asked how a dragon may be caught, first stalwart men are chosen to search out the dragon's cave, the den where it lurks, and when they have found it, they sprinkle sleep-inducing drugs moistened with various spices across the rim of its entrance. When the dragon, leaving the mouth of the cave, smells these fragrances, it consumes them voraciously and is at once overcome by sleep. The men, who have been hidden in a safe place not far away, surround the beast and slaughter it. The men carry off the dragon blood, along with the dragon gem that they shake loose by smashing its brain. The gem may then be used in many sorts of undertakings.

The vessel in which these substances are placed is a tripod whose handled upper section with its lid of bronze is constructed to fit the narrow neck snugly. Closed by this, it is so tightly fitted on all sides that not even the least wisp of smoke escapes from it. When everything has been placed in this vessel, fire is immediately kindled under it, and for seven days and seven nights the flames are fed with pitch and naphtha so that it will boil intensely. There is, in addition, a copper tube, the uppermost end of which has been bent, that is attached in the manner of a valve. By means of this a small hole on top of the lid of the vessel is kept closed for the first six days. On the seventh day, when the flame in the heating vessel is ignited, a tremendous roar inside can be heard, like an earthquake, or as if at a distance you heard the rumblings of a raging sea. When the attendant has observed the familiar signs of the ignited fire, he pours into the valve on the outside some very sharp vinegar; penetrating its mass, it checks the force of the fire now striving to burst out.

Bellows are constructed of bronze, as many as suffice, by which the fire is drawn out; their connectors are screwed together so tightly that the series of connections is penetrated by the fire under the blast of air as though made of wood and leather. For they are indeed so meshed that you would more easily believe them composed of leather than bronze. Once the fire has been moderated from its intense heat by the vinegar dousing, the valve is released and the ductile pipe projecting forward in the bellows is applied to the small opening of the vessel. By the suction of the air flow of this, the fire is pumped out of the heating vessel. Immediately, lest the flames rise up, the mouth of the tube is closed by the valve. Thus the fire is received into other containers to be held for later use. A small part, it is true, is retained in the heating vessel; the heat by which it is nourished must be applied daily. Small openings with a leaf in the middle like a small shutter are provided through which fuel is fed lest the flame go out. By this routine is Greek fire prepared. If you ask what power it has, no military machine is so strong, no ship so great but that if the fire is thrown it penetrates defenses and consumes everything on every side. It has the strength to resist being extinguished by anyone until the matter that it consumes is exhausted. What is more astounding, it burns also among the waves; and if it is mingled with common fire, it will continue to hold itself in a separate fireball and will consume common fire like wood.

When the enemy discovered that the Knight of the Surcoat was unconquerable by arms, one of them seized the bellows in which the baleful fire was contained and, removing the valve from the tube, pressing down one of the boards with his left hand and raising the other with his right, he compressed them by turns with the greatest exertion. As the flaming fuel streamed forward, he sprayed the centurion's galleon amidship, consuming four oarsmen with flames. Quickly everything was enveloped in fire, and panic spread among the men on board. Surrounded by the flames aboard and the enemy outside, the Romans did not know what to do; they had no power to defend themselves nor to attack. If they wanted to consider flight, neither to the waves nor to the enemy was it safe to commit themselves. Either way, death was imminent for those remaining on the ship. The Knight of the Surcoat, considering the crisis, drove himself forward with renewed determination. Alone, he leaped onto the ship of the attackers, cutting down some of the enemy, throwing others to the waves. He transferred his companions over to the other ship, rescuing them from a threefold threat: the balls of fire, the shipwrecking waves, and the fury of the enemy. Enraged with an increasing fury, as soon as the fleet again came together, he immediately avenged himself. After having sunk every tenth ship and broken the enemy's power, he captured thirty of the pirate vessels.

When, not without grave peril, the naval battle was finally over, the Romans completed the journey with good fortune, arriving safely in Jerusalem at the appointed time. After being received with unbelievable acclaim by everyone, the men, exhausted, restored their bodies with rest and leisure. Meanwhile mighty hosts of warriors had assembled, and facilities were prepared for these men by the local and foreign commanders of the knights. They also ordered knights to be chosen throughout the entire region, which was to be put into a state of defense by the strongest men, with weapons and stores of provisions and fodder adequate for siege made ready. Prayer was offered daily to God by all the people through various relics of the saints, and devotion to prayer with fasting and almsgiving was continued so that He might confer the desired triumph to those who served Him, and so that destruction would await the adversary.

The day dawned that had been set for the duel, and when the vast army of armored Christians and, of course, pagans had been drawn up in formation on either side, the two men who were to render judgment by combat, sheathed in armor, proceeded according to the agreement to the center. Here the Knight of the Surcoat, by boldness of spirit, courage, prowess, habit of winning, and the more righteous cause, filled his allies with the hope of victory. His opponent, Gormundus, because of his remarkable limbs, huge stature, glowering face, war experience, much-touted courage, and the horror and din of his weapons, seemed to promise that triumph would be accorded to him. Both of them came on foot; because of his immense height Gormundus could find no horse strong enough to bear him.

With shields opposing and right arms raised, they met boldly in attack. However much strength each had and however great the force that anger directed, each went after the other with naked blade. A thousand thrusts were returned and in a thousand ways they pressed on with their exchange of bloodletting and wounding. They strike and are stricken; they advance and are driven back. The wheel of Fortune favors them with various turns. Nothing whatever is omitted that may be summed up in courage and strength; everyone's eyes are fixed on them. If either is more prepared for dealing death or if either is braver in endurance, this is not known; between these men such frequent thrusts and severe blows are unceasingly exchanged that who gives and who receives them is hard to discern. You cannot tell which man has greater strength. The more they press the fight, the more they hunger for battle. At times they intersperse their blows with clever taunts; at times they inflame each other with witty obscenities. Now they withdraw, out of breath; now refreshed, they more eagerly rush together. With renewed strength they join in a more heated attack; and as if nothing had yet been done fiercely, their spirits rage with greater ferocity.

You could see them facing each other like two ferocious boars in mortal combat who now attack each other with curved tusks in sidelong slashes, now strike their flanks, now trample hoof under hoof; their jaws are now foaming with smoky spume, now sparking forth fire. If one presses more violently, the other, yielding, is forced back; then with the other prevailing, the first is forced to retreat. This one, as if setting a trap, strives to inflict a wound. The other, if anything lies open to the point of his sword, skillfully makes a thrust; but the first, with equal skill, mocks the other's effort and blocks it. The clash of arms echoes loudly far and wide, and the density of the armor blunts and dulls their sharp blades. From the striking of the arms sparks leap up. Because of the intense effort salty sweat pours off their limbs from top to toe. It was uncertain to whom victory would fall; everyone thought that the strength of the two was evenly matched. With remarkable courage and remarkable prowess the fight was fought; from the first hour till sunset, nothing during the fighting gave preference to one over the other. So when evening fell, they were drawn apart with no deep wounds. In the morning they would fight again, and again the struggle would begin from the beginning.

At Aurora's rising the helmeted phalanxes came together in a twofold battle-line, and the contending factions led their men to the arena. They clashed; there was a shout; each man intended to inflict death on the other. The man-to-man fight was repeated with greater rivalry because the more one made trial of the other, the more the other conducted himself with care and bravery. It was a source of shame that men who in everyone's judgment were definitely proven to be of equal strength should yield in the smallest degree. For if on that day you had watched the battle of these two, you would have sworn that they had merely played the day before. You would have been astounded, considering these repeated blows and severe buffets, how the keenness of the sword blades could have lasted without dulling, how the solidity of the armor could have remained intact, and particularly how they themselves, unwearied and uninjured, could have stood as long as they chose to. Indeed with such vigor and such bravery the swords clashed against helmets and pounded against shields that the air glowed with bursting sparks, and steel repelled clashed steel and then sprang back at the one who had wielded it.

With frequent gasps they agitate the air, throwing weapon against weapon, blow upon blow. With one mind they stand; they wage a valiant fight, and the prolonged battle produces a lust for conflict. Chest expands to chest, and they strive with every effort to attack and to resist. The boldness of one provokes the wrath of the other; and the stubbornness of that one increases a bolder intensity in this one. Each man's strength offers stimulus to the other's courage; and the vigor of one advances as it is matched by the other.

Most of the day the odds between them were considered equal until the Knight of the Surcoat contrived a particular feint: while he pretended to cut down Gormundus above the left knee and drew Gormundus to lower his bronze shield, with his right hand turned to the right of the other, the Knight's sword unexpectedly struck into the middle of Gormundus' mouth, which was unprotected, knocked out four front teeth, and broke the jawbone on the left side. The wound was not grave, and it seemed to act more powerfully as a goad to fury than as an incitement to despair, as the strength of a wounded man may seethe with more fury than that of one unharmed. Enraged by the wound inflicted, Gormundus shouted no more words; he had to conserve his strength. Like a wild beast he lunged at the Knight of the Surcoat, and with his right arm high, he slammed his sword on the shield with such force that the row of set jewels, sharply jarred, flew piecemeal in different directions, as the boss tore off, and the upper edge of the shield hit the Knight's forehead hard enough to cause an effusion of blood.

Even more enraged, the Knight of the Surcoat again drew him out, and with redoubled savagery, the contest was pressed fiercely till the duel reached a crisis. The Knight of the Surcoat, seeking a weak spot, ran with sword raised at the unprotected flank of his enemy. But since Gormundus was experienced and parried the thrust, when the Knight pressed his effort, his sword was caught by the blocking of the shield and broke down to a small shaft. Neither the density nor the resistance of Gormundus' shield was able to withstand the force of that blow, with the result that it was smashed through the middle, and splitting under the boss, flew into pieces.

At this a great shout rose from all the assembled armies, with cheers from one side, and from the other insults. The greater danger to the Knight of the Surcoat was apparent: since his sword was shattered, nothing at all was at hand by which he could defend himself or by his own effort keep the enemy at bay. For Gormundus, although his shield was smashed, his blade was intact; he was pounding his adversary with the rigid two-edged sword without a moment's pause. The Knight of the Surcoat then faced the attack and was skillfully blocking with his shield in every direction. If the setting sun had not ended the duel, he would without doubt have incurred the most severe loss. The end of the match had been decided so that at the time the shadow of the setting sun reached a determined mark, it fulfilled the agreement that the men were to be separated, without regard to advantage or disadvantage. The shadow reached the mark then, and although the pagans were unwilling and barely held themselves from revolt, the two combatants were in fact separated. Whatever remained of the fight would be postponed till the next day.

When the radiance of the sun had put to flight the darkness of the night, the lines from both sides assembled, and the seasoned warriors presented themselves strengthened and grim, with arms repaired. A bitter, almost fatal quarrel arose between the two armies over whether the sword should be conceded to the Knight of the Surcoat or the shield to Gormundus, or to both, to neither, or to one and not the other. After the dispute had continued for some time, and the main disagreements had been aired, the consensus was that the combatants should be made equal; both sides agreed that the Knight could not defend himself without a sword, nor could the other, with his shield destroyed, be strong enough to protect himself from attack.

When the multitude was assembled, the duelists—protected by loricas and crested helmets, horrible to see—once again challenged each other and attacked and assailed with powerful hands. The thunder of battle arose, the clash of arms rang out, the sound of blows increased, and the fiery shock grew fearfully hot. The air rebounded and resounded with terrible noise, and, as the bronze was struck, the hollows of the mountains re-echoed that noise. As the duel was demanding, no rest was given to the weary nor breathing space allowed for the winded. They fought wholeheartedly, and wholeheartedly they struggled until one would fall and the other achieve the victory. Neither the hot summer sun nor the continuous strain hindered them, yet no decision was reached because they resisted always more boldly, each one throwing himself against his ever more unconquerable opponent. Thus the participants were inspired by ferocity and were invigorated by animosity.

When most of the day had passed, Gormundus began to waver from the heat and also from the constant harrying of his adversary. The attack was increased against him vehemently, and the whole weight of the clash fell on him. He weakened in spirit and fought less effectively. Perceptibly drawing back from the Knight of the Surcoat, he retreated, not defending himself with such courage as before; by no means was he pressing his opponent. The Knight of the Surcoat, aware of this, stood his ground more boldly and caused the anxious man's spirit more anxiety. He did not stop till he had pushed him beyond the boundary of the circle that surrounded them. The noise and murmurs, the shouts and screams of the incredulous people rose to the stars, and dismayed groups shouted: "Back, Gormundus; come back, Gormundus! What are you trying to do? Where do you think you're going, great knight? Making others run—not running yourself—has always been your style. Come back, or in the end shame will erase all the winning you've ever done. You can't run away from here! Here you must either conquer or be conquered!"

At these shouts, Gormundus, overcome by shame and gasping somewhat, took his stand more bravely and weathered the charge of his adversary more manfully. Brandishing his sword, he dealt a blow that felled the Knight, whose legs folded under him. Gormundus forced him to his knees by the force of his thrust. But his breastplate remained impenetrable. Then the Knight of the Surcoat, wild and enraged, sprang to his feet, drew himself up in his armor, brandished his right arm and shouted, "Here is the blow that ends the game!" Striking with his double-edged sword on the top of Gormundus' helmet while the armor was hot and thus less resistant, he guided the blow, fracturing, splintering, and penetrating everything all the way to the breastbone. (Hardly a desirable stomach remedy!) When he drew the sword from the wound, the skull split into two parts, with the brains oozing out. The victor kicked it away with his foot.

When they saw their champion vanquished and cruelly slaughtered, the pagans united in the grief of death, mourning over him with interminable wailing; and as they gathered his armor, they would have attacked the Knight of the Surcoat in vengeance, had they not been restrained by their inviolable laws. Once their defender had been given over to death, the pagans yielded to the pact with the Romans according to the agreed conditions: peace confirmed, hostages given, heavy reparations imposed. The enemy then retired in confusion to their own country.

The Knight of the Surcoat, having been awarded the trophy for his supreme victory, while the highborn Jerusalemites then honored him with many rewards, in the fullness of time returned to Rome. He was received by the emperor and the Senate with a triumphal procession. The emperor, restoring him to the company of his closest companions, resolved to raise him to the highest honors and to grant him high rank. Once these deeds had been accomplished, since no one was presuming to move against the Roman Empire by sword, the Knight of the Surcoat, disdaining a peaceful life and desiring military action, eagerly inquired what region was torn by the tumults of war.

When the name of Arthur, the famous King of Britannia (his uncle, though he did not know it), who was acclaimed for prowess around the world, was brought to his attention, unmoved by all that the emperor had given him, the Knight of the Surcoat humbly begged permission to leave time and again. Although the emperor had already decided to promote him to the highest position, and he had no doubt that the departure of so worthy a man would be to his own loss, he gave assent to the petition in order that the Knight might learn about his lineage, and also because he felt confident that through him the Kingdom of Britannia, so long separated from the Roman Empire, might be regained for himself. The emperor bestowed on him rich, sumptuous, and priceless gifts, and gave him the coffer in which the proof of his parentage remained, with orders that it must be presented to King Arthur, adding his own letter as testimony that everything the documents stated was established and confirmed. Further, the emperor forbade him to look inside the coffer before he entered the presence of King Arthur. He ordered, then, that the first citizens of the Gauls, through whose lands the Knight must pass, should receive him with honor, serve him, provide him with necessities, and escort him safely through their territories all the way to the sea. So, farewells were spoken and the Knight departed, leaving the ruler behind.

With everyone grieving over his departure, the Knight of the Surcoat began the journey as planned. He crossed the Alps and after having made his way through Gaul, arrived safely in Britannia. Inquiring where King Arthur was in residence, he learned that he was staying at the city of Caerleon in Demetia [South Wales], where he was accustomed to spend more of his time than in his other cities. That charming place was laid out with groves, abounding in animals, rich in treasures, pleasant for its green meadows, and watered by the Usk River, and not far away the Severn River offered a dwelling place of the utmost delight. Here was the metropolitan city of the province of Demetia; here the legions of Rome used to spend the winters; here King Arthur celebrated the high feasts, wore the crown, and convened all the barons of Britannia for his assembly. As soon as the Knight found out where Arthur was residing, he made his way in that direction, traveling swiftly in high spirits, pressing on day and night without a break. When he was almost there, on the last night before he expected to reach Caerleon, he was just outside the town of Usk, six miles away, when a sudden, violent storm struck with a driving rain. Everyone with him either left the high road or was unable to continue.

That same night, King Arthur and Gwendoloena, his queen, were talking to each other about many things while resting in bed. (Because of the length of the night they had had enough sleep.) Queen Gwendoloena was indeed the most beautiful of all women, but she had been initiated into sorcery, so that often from her divinations she could read the future. Among other things, she said, "Lord, you boast and greatly extol your prowess, and you assume that no one is your equal in strength."

Arthur replied, "That's so. Doesn't your own heart feel the same about me?"

The queen answered, "Of course it does—but there is at this very hour of the night a knight from Rome who is passing through the town of Usk on his way here. Have no doubt that you will find him pre-eminent in courage and prowess. He is mounted on a steed to which no other can be compared in vigor, value, or grace. His armor is impenetrable, and no one withstands the blow of his right arm. Lest you think I declare this to you lightly, look for this sign: he will send me a gold ring and three thousand-piece coins, as well as two horses, by mid-morning."

Arthur, aware that she had never deceived him in any prediction whatever, still decided to test this information without her knowledge. For it was his custom that whenever he heard about any strong man, he would challenge him, so that by single combat he could display the greater valor. So a little later when the queen had drifted off to sleep, he got up, armed himself, mounted his horse, and took as his companion for the encounter only Kay, his seneschal.

He came upon the Knight of the Surcoat halting at a little stream flooded by the storm, looking for the ford and cursing the delay. Actually because the Knight was confused by the foul fog of the night, he had decided to cross through the deep channel of the river. Sighting him by the gleam of his armor, Arthur shouted, "Where do you come from, you who wander over this countryside in the dead of night? Are you an exile, a bandit, or a spy?"

To him the Knight replied, "I wander because I do not know the roads. No flight of an exile drives me, no pillage of a bandit tempts me, nor does any deceit cover any trickery." Arthur answered, "You rely on a quick tongue. I see your game. I know very well that you have to be one of those three I named. So without more ado, lay down your arms. Unless you give yourself up to me entirely, you will learn immediately that I am the scourge of your wickedness."

The Knight responded, "Anybody is foolish and fainthearted who starts to run before the fight, or who gives in to his enemy before he has to. If, however, you still want my arms, I swear to their power; I'll match you for them, blow for blow."

So words exchanged between them erupted into threats and abuses, and Arthur, goaded to fury, got ready to cross the river, spurred his horse to the encounter, and rushed blindly at him. The Knight of the Surcoat, waiting for him with drawn and couched lance, drove at him in the ford itself and knocked him into the middle of the river. Backing up, he caught hold of his struggling horse by the reins. Kay the Seneschal, wanting to avenge his lord, spurred his horse and met the Knight of the Surcoat, but just as before, with the first blow he was piled on top of Arthur in a single heap. The knight, using the point of his lance, pulled the horse toward him. The darkness of the night saved Arthur and Kay from being harmed. Those two who had come to this place as knights returned home as foot-soldiers with no little disgrace. Arthur, in fact, climbed back into bed. Queen Gwendoloena asked him, stiff as he was with cold and soaked not only by the rain but also by the river-water, where he had been for so long and why he was so wet.

Arthur replied, "I thought I heard some sort of commotion outside in the courtyard. I figured it might be some of my men fighting, so I went out. It took a while to settle, and I was drenched in the rain."

The queen answered, "Whatever you say. Truly, wherever you went and whatever took place, my messenger will tell me in the morning."

The Knight of the Surcoat, having crossed the shallowest part of the water and not realizing with whom he had done battle, turned toward the nearby village and found lodging. At the first light of day, he hurried on toward Caerleon. About two miles down the road he noticed a boy and asked who employed him. The boy told him, "I am a messenger of the queen, whose personal instructions it is my duty to carry out."

And the Knight said, "Will you do what I ask of you?"

The boy replied, "I am at your service."

The Knight said, "Take these two horses and lead them for me to the queen as my gift so that she may gladly accept the proof of my prowess in pledge for requesting friendship." Handing him the gold ring and the three pieces of gold to be carried to her as well, he told him his name and declared that he would follow him on the road. The messenger did what had been asked of him. He accepted the gold items and led the horses with him.

Meanwhile, Queen Gwendoloena, aware of what was going to happen, stood on the wall of the castle watching the road that led to the town of Usk. When she observed from a distance her messenger returning, leading two horses with all their trappings, she understood the situation and, descending quickly, met him as he entered the hall. The boy transacted the business gracefully, revealed his instructions, delivered the things sent, and announced that the Knight of the Surcoat was about to arrive. The queen, smiling at the name, accepted the gifts and thanked him. She ordered that the horses should be led into the bedroom right to the couch of the king, who was still resting, since he had spent the whole night being active. Having roused him from his sleep, she said, "Lord, lest you accuse me of fabricating what I know, see the ring and the gold which yesterday I promised would be sent to me today. Furthermore, the knight I told you about last evening has given me these two horses which, having thrown their riders into that river, he commandeered for himself."

King Arthur, recognizing his own horses and seeing disclosed what he had hoped would be kept secret, was consumed with shame. Then he went to the assembly of nobles he had ordered to come together on that day for pressing concerns. As he sat outside the hall under the shade of an ash tree with his people, the Knight of the Surcoat entered the gates on horseback. Approaching King Arthur, he greeted him along with the queen and knights sitting nearby.

Arthur, not unaware of who he was, turned a grim face toward him and responded quite bluntly. He asked about his origin, where he traveled, what he sought in these regions. The man replied that he was a Roman knight, and that, since he had heard Arthur was pressed by war and in need of knights, he had come to offer his services, and that furthermore he had brought imperial mandates. He then handed the sealed coffer and letter to the king. When Arthur had received the emperor's letter, he withdrew from the assembly and ordered it to be read. On receiving the testimony of the document along with the records of proof and the cloak and the signet ring offered in evidence, he was greatly astonished. All this he strove to regard as truth. Despite his immense joy, he simply could not believe that this man was indeed his nephew. He remained incredulous about the matter till both parents had been summoned—Loth, King of Norway, and Anna, the Queen—who, it happened, were there. He exacted the truth from them and rigorously tested the facts. They confessed that this was all true, that he was indeed their son, and their testimony was sworn by special oaths. Arthur was exhilarated with incredible joy that the man upheld in so many ways by the emperor's commendations and by a great reputation for exalted prowess was, as a final surprise, related to him by close kinship. Nevertheless, he purposely ordered that none of this should be revealed to the Knight till he had accomplished some outstanding exploit in his presence.

So returning to the assembly and calling the Knight before everyone, Arthur said, "Your help, friend, I do not need at the present time. I do not know precisely whether prowess or awkwardness is stronger in you. I have a band of knights of such incomparable prowess, endowed with such strength and courage that to include a clumsy and cowardly man among the skillful and daring is to risk weakening their spirit from its customary boldness and aggressiveness. An enormous number of knights like you serve me voluntarily without stipend, among whom, unless you first show that you deserve it, my decision stands that you should not even be enrolled."

To this the Knight of the Surcoat, goaded by his words, replied, "By offering to serve you, I have incurred from you a grave rejection and an unexpected injury—I, who up to now was deemed worthy to come to your aid, inasmuch as I was not influenced by others' entreaties nor by great wealth. I do not doubt that I will find someone whom I may serve; yet even if I do, I will not easily find your equal. Indeed, since a desire for military challenge brought me here, on the following condition you might consider me worthy to be one of your knights: if I alone can accomplish something in which your whole army has failed."

Arthur answered, "My reply is this decree: if you should accomplish what you have bargained for, I shall not only enroll you among my men but indeed set you to be loved above them all." The plan pleased the king and all his nobility as well, and he kept the Knight at his court for the present under the agreed condition.

Not twice six days had passed when an occasion of this sort compelled Arthur to send out an expedition. In the northern part of Britannia was a place called "the Castle of the Maidens," which a young woman, who was noted for her grace and nobility, governed by right of lordship. She was allied to Arthur by the deepest obligations of friendship. A certain pagan king, captivated by her graceful bearing and great beauty and having in turn been rejected by her, had besieged her in her fortified town. Since the siege machinery had been constructed and transported to the site and the mounds to support it built up, he was threatening to storm the castle and seize her. Since she knew she could not bear up under the unremitting attacks and daily assaults, she sent a messenger and begged Arthur to come to her aid. As she was barricaded in her tower and the farther wall had already been breached, she deemed it necessary to surrender very soon to the enemy unless Arthur brought up reinforcements immediately.

So Arthur, fearing the peril of the young woman in her castle, at once mustered, armed, and drew up the ranks of his knights; and fully prepared, though consumed by great dread, he began the march to the place where he had been summoned. Many times, it is true, he had encountered and fought this very king, but it had always resulted that he was repulsed and beaten. As he was approaching the siege, a second messenger arrived, running with hair loose about his cheeks, who reported that the pagan king had razed the city and had seized and carried off the lady. The messenger continued to plead for his mistress that the love King Arthur had held for her in prosperity he would now show her in adversity. Arthur pursued the enemy, which was burdened with plunder. He fell furiously upon their rear guard, where he thought them least protected, but because of an unfortunate omen, he was intercepted by them. Having been thus warned of his approach, they repulsed him. To protect themselves, they had placed their more experienced warriors in the rear guard, which would not easily be thrown into confusion by sudden attack.

Arthur's front ranks, instead, were brought to confusion by the unexpected strength of the enemy's rear guard, which, surrounding Arthur's men on all sides, contained them, pressed them, and shattered them. Here the bitterest battle was fought, and bloody slaughter was inflicted on both sides. Arthur, in the very lap of the enemy, was being pressed back, demoralized and exhausted; and unless by cutting his way out he could immediately retreat, he would be slain, and his entire army cut down. He therefore gambled on flight, guessing that it would be wiser to run to safety than to succumb to the disaster hanging over him.

At the beginning of the engagement, the Knight of the Surcoat had withdrawn to a high, remote lookout in order to see what happened to the fellowship of knights during the course of battle. When their retreat revealed the disaster to him, he met Arthur fleeing with the first wave, and laughing at him, shouted sarcastically, "Tell me, O King, are you hunting deer or perhaps rabbits as you go scattered this way along the paths?"

Arthur replied indignantly, "I see your great prowess, since you, while others are involved in battle, have removed yourself to the hiding-places of the forest!" Without further words, he rode off, with the enemy in pursuit.

The Knight of the Surcoat, taunting every one of the knights he encountered with jeers and slurs, turned to attack the pursuing enemy. He rushed raging upon the advance patrols, penetrating through the tight and strong formations into their very midst like a winter storm, injuring all those who offered him resistance. When he saw the pagan royal guard, he instantly spurred his horse forward; with lance couched, the unexpected assailant ran the gleaming point into the hollow of the pagan king's chest. Having thrown the dying man to the ground, he seized the young woman by her horse's bridle and at once set out to return the way he had come.

But the guard which surrounded the pagan king, thrown into disorder on seeing their lord struck down in their midst, with a shout cut the invader off, and, with swords drawn, they charged upon him. They rushed at him together, and he at all of them. From a distance some threw spears at him; from all sides others struck at him ceaselessly with their blades. Like a rainstorm a multitude of blows beat upon him. Still, he continued on his way, leaving them cut down. But he was greatly hampered because he had to defend not only himself but the lady. Not far distant was a broad and deep fosse marking the boundary between two provinces. It had a narrow access since its bridge allowed only one person to cross at a time. To this place, then, the Knight of the Surcoat raced, and arriving there, he sent the lady to safety within the fortifications of the fosse, ordering her to remain hidden from sight until he returned. Once more plunging into the ranks of the pursuing enemy, he turned them back and put them to flight. Roaring like a lion bereft of its cubs, he inflicted cruel slaughter on them without mercy. Not one of them bore up under the attack and none who came into contact with the massive power of his right arm went away uninjured. Wherever he turned, they were scattered, as from the blast of a tempest. The powerful one continually slashed them to death without pity. Not withdrawing until all of them had been routed, he marked them all for death: some flung themselves from the steep banks, some by choice threw themselves into the obstructing waters, and the remainder he himself cut to pieces in a massacre.

The Knight of the Surcoat, having gained victory without injury to himself, cut off the head of the pagan king with the royal diadem still in place, fastened it onto his standard and, raising it on high, returned to King Arthur with the lady by his side. Exulting, he entered the hall where King Arthur, depressed and grieving at the misfortune of war, was seated. He cried out, "Just where, O King, are your famous champions about whom you so long boasted that no one was their equal in courage? See the head of the man I alone conquered and laid low, along with the entire force of his knights! He was the king who with a handful put to flight so many thousands of your men that it is shameful! Do you consider me worthy now to be your knight?"

Arthur, joyously recognizing the head of the king who was hateful to him beyond all others and the young woman so dear to him rescued from the hands of the enemy, ran to embrace the Knight and replied, "You are truly worthy to be one of us and you must be granted special honors! Nevertheless, since till now we have been uncertain as to who you are, I ask you to explain where your native land is, from whom you trace your lineage, and what family name you bear."

The other replied, "The truth of what I have told you holds. I was born in Gaul, fathered by a Roman senator. I was educated in Rome, and 'Knight of the Surcoat' is what I happen to be called."

Arthur returned, "You are plainly mistaken. What you have thought true cannot be confirmed. In a word, you have been deceived by this information."

The knight asked, "How so?"

Arthur explained, "I shall show you your true lineage. This knowledge shall be the reward for your deeds." Then with both of his parents present (to wit, Loth, King of Norway, and Anna, the Queen) Arthur ordered the letter written by the emperor to be brought to him and, when it was brought, to be read in the hearing of the common people and the nobles. When the documents were read, amazement and incredible joy arose with the comprehension of it all, and everyone proclaimed the parents blessed for such an offspring.

Then King Arthur, gazing at him with joy, said: "I acknowledge you, dear friend, as my nephew. You are the son of my sister, to whom Fortune gave such a child not for disgrace but for honor." He added, "Indeed at an early age you were called 'Boy with No Name,' and from the time you entered knighthood till the present, 'Knight of the Surcoat.' From now on you will be known as 'Gawain,' your real name."

When Arthur announced this, three times, then four times the entire assemblage repeated and echoed, "Gawain, nephew of King Arthur."

When the son had been acknowledged by his father and the nephew by his uncle, the magnitude of joy doubled, not only for the recovery of a lost loved one, but also for this man's incomparable courage and strength. What other outstanding exploits fell to Gawain, anyone who desires to know must ask from one who knows these things. Realizing that just as it is harder to take part in a battle than to record one, it is even more difficult to compose a history in an eloquent style than to present it orally in the words of common speech.

Beaumaris Castle of Anglesey in North Wales, in country associated with the wanderings of Gawain in Sir Gawain and the Green Knight. (Courtesy of the British Tourist Authority)

Chapter *XVI*

SIR GAWAIN AND THE GREEN KNIGHT

James J. Wilhelm

Sir Gawain and the Green Knight is not only the finest Arthurian romance in English literature, but also a work of commanding literary merit. This four-teenth-century tale deals with the timeless themes of love, honor, heroism, and the human will to survive in a world that is often perplexing, changeable, and violent.

In his *Anatomy of Criticism* Northrop Frye suggests that all literature can be grouped under headings of religious affirmation, romantic fantasy, or realistic presentation. *Sir Gawain* simultaneously exhibits all three modes of expression. On the one hand it can be read as a religious parable that extols humility and integrity against the vices of pride, lust, and recklessness. Cer-tainly the dominant symbol of the green sash must be viewed as a token of Gawain's humble acceptance of his all-too-human flaw of wanting to survive at any price.

The fantastic element is also conspicuous in the story, since the tale contains magical acts and unreal creatures, such as trolls and fairies. Morgan the Fay, who is herself a member of the mythic world, is the presiding genius of the story. Her desire to test Arthur's court and to shock Guinevere (sup-posedly because the Queen exposed her love affair with the knight Guiomar) impels the action, in which the Green Knight is in many ways simply her tool. Behind Morgan is the wizard Merlin (Part Four, Stanza 19) and the entire world of Celtic myth.

Realistic elements also abound, especially in the basic vocabulary, with its highly precise words for butchering an animal or dressing a knight in armor. No novelist of the nineteenth century ever showed a firmer handling of detail. In its outlook, too, the poem celebrates the "real" every bit as much as it does the ideal or the imaginary. What causes Sir Gawain to abandon his rigid code of morality is simply his desire to save his own skin—and this frank simplicity is also the thing that saves him. For, as the Green Knight says at the last encounter, Gawain's lack of integrity "didn't arise for an artful object or amorous fling—/ No! You just loved your life! And I blame you the less for it" (2367–68).

By employing these three very different modes of expression almost simultaneously, the poet is able to establish striking juxtapositions. The blood and gore of the hunting scenes alternate with the slick French manners of the boudoir. Prayers to Christian divinities are uttered in heathen places. The poet is able to hold these diverse strands together because of the strict unity that he employs. Part One sets up the motif of the beheading challenge and its first enactment. Part Two introduces the motif of the exchange of presents between a host and a guest. Part Three alternates panels showing the overt aggression of the hunt with the suppressed sensuality of the beautiful hostess's temptations. Part Four brings together the two central motifs, which can be found widely in folklore, as the violence of the hunt finds its last echo in the abortive beheading, and the potentially lascivious secrets of the boudoir are finally revealed as merely the innocent acceptance of a sash.

Everything ends happily in *Sir Gawain*, as it should in a fairy tale. The hero also learns a lesson, as he should in a religious parable. And finally the reader is exposed, along with the hero, to a series of traumatic experiences that lead to a catharsis that brings one close to the true meaning of humility. If we read the poem correctly, surely we feel pity for the once-unassailable Gawain, that paragon of virtue, and terror toward the mysteries that threaten him and us all, whether they spring from supernatural sources or the human heart.

Only a very great writer could achieve a successful conclusion for so complex a design. Unfortunately we do not know the author's name, since none is appended to the single fourteenth-century manuscript in which the poem survives. There it occurs with two other works written in alliterative verses (*Patience* and *Purity*) and another composed in rhymed stanzas (*The Pearl*). These three poems are also written in a dialect of the Midlands of England, probably from around Stafford, and treat moral or religious themes.

The so-called "Gawain-poet" may well have written all four pieces, but he made of *Sir Gawain and the Green Knight* something greater than a traditionally moral work of art. The dangerous ramifications of the courtly game of love are clearly delineated (in contrast to Chrétien's *Lancelot*, where they are exalted), and Arthur's court is portrayed as refined to the point of effeteness. To Gawain, his sash at the end of the story is a religious icon, but to the other courtiers it is little more than the latest French fashion. Still, the morality of the work never intrudes upon the poem's esthetic structure, and *Sir Gawain* transcends a literature that is merely didactic to join the mainstream of the imaginative literature of all times.

Bibliographic note: The following book contains a complete summary of criticism and scholarship to 1977: Malcolm Andrew, *The "Gawain"-Poet: An Annotated Bibliography, 1839–1977* (Garland, 1979). Three important critical studies are: Larry D. Benson, *Art and Tradition in "Sir Gawain and the Green Knight"* (Rutgers, 1965); John Burrow, *A Reading of "Sir Gawain and the Green Knight"* (Barnes and Noble, 1966); and Donald R. Howard, *The Three Temptations* (Princeton, 1966). See also Marie Borroff, *"Sir Gawain and the Green Knight": A Stylistic and Metrical Study* (Yale, 1962). For analogues with earlier literature, see Chapter 39 of R.S. Loomis, ed., *Arthurian Literature in the Middle Ages* (Oxford, 1959).

The text translated here was edited by J.R.R. Tolkien and E.V. Gordon, rev. Norman Davis (Oxford, 1967). I have consulted almost every previous translation, but especially those of Marie Borroff (Norton, 1967) and John Gardner (Chicago, 1965). For the many cruxes I tend to follow the Oxford text and its notes. In the translation I do not try to reproduce the alliteration of the original exactly; I frequently reduce it, just as I suppress one of the rhymes in the so-called "wheel of the bob," the last five lines of every stanza. No other poem that we know of contains this unique construction, and the work is similarly unique in its free handling of meter, alliteration, and diction.

Note on the opening stanza: Following the tradition established by Latin chronicles and the Anglo-Norman *Roman de Brut*, by Wace, in the 1100s, the poet links Britain to a founder named Felix Brutus, whose roots reach back through Rome to Troy. The traitor in line 3 is apparently Antenor, while the Ticius of line 11 is unknown (sometimes the name is emended to Tirius, for whom the Tyrrhenian Sea was supposedly named).

Sir Gawain and the Green Knight

Part One

1.

After the siege and the assault had ceased at Troy,
The citadel was shattered and burned to cinders and shards,
And the traitor who wove out his tapestry of treason
Was tried for his treachery, which was proved beyond doubt;
Then Aeneas the kingly and his high-born kinsmen
Prevailed over many powers, becoming the possessors
Of well-nigh all of the wealth of the western lands.
Next royal Romulus reached out ambitiously for Rome;
With pomp and with pride, he founded that place first,
Honoring it with his own name, which it even now bears.   10
Ticius went into Tuscany and erected some towers;
King Longbeard in Lombardy lifted up dwellings,
And over the French flood-waves great Felix Brutus

Established Britain with eagerness upon its many
    Spreading hills,
Where war and ruin and wonder
At times have overspilled;
And there have been swift turnings
Of the blissful and the ill.

2.

And when Britain had been built by this noble baron,   20
Bold men were bred there who relished their battling,
Who incited insurgence in many times gone by.
More miracles have occurred more often on British meadows
Than on any others that I've heard tell of till now.
And of all the British founders who have ever flourished here,
Surely Arthur was the most heroic, as I have heard.
And so I aim to narrate an earthly adventure
That many men consider a marvelous thing to view,
An otherworldly exploit of Arthurian wonder.
If you will listen to this lay just a little while,   30
I shall tell it at once, as I have heard it told round,
    In my own song,
The way it was set and established
In a story stout and strong,
That's been locked in loyal letters
Through our land for very long.

3.

This king lay at Camelot around Christmastime
With many a gracious lord, the best of his liegemen,
Assuredly all royal brethren of the Round Table,
With rich revels and innumerable games arranged.   40
There tussled many champions in tourneys at times;
They jousted, these gentle knights, with great jocularity,
Then crowded into court to sing and dance to carols.
And then the feast flowed unbroken for a good fifteen days
With all of the fun and the food that one could fancy;
Such noise and enjoyment were invigorating to hear,
Delightful all the day long, with dancing during the night.
The height of happiness was attained in those chambers and halls
By those lords and ladies—the loveliest of lives, they thought.
With all the delights of the world they dwelled together,   50
The most celebrated knights to recognize Christ himself,

And the loveliest ladies who have ever enjoyed their lives,
And the most courteous king who ever controlled a court.
All of these fair-haired people still had their precious primes
    To fulfill—
The happiest folk under heaven,
With the king of greatest good will.
It would be far too taxing to number
All the hardy host on that hill.

4.

While the New Year was young, having just now entered,   60
Double portions that day were served to all of the diners.
When the king came in with his counts into the hall
As the chanting in the chapel had hushed to its close,
An outcry was uttered by the clerics and by others:
"Noel!" they announced, calling it again and again.
Then the regal party ran around to pass out their gifts,
Hawking them with high-pitched calls, giving them out by hand,
Debating very busily about all their barterings.
The ladies laughed loudly—even when they were losers—
While the winners felt no wrath, *that* you may well trust.   70
They made all this merriment right up until mealtime,
When they washed themselves well and then went on to their seats,
With the grandest barons above, for so it seemed best.
Queen Guinevere very gaily was gathered among them,
Dressed up on the dais, which was decked all around
With expensive silk sidings, and a ceiling above
Made of drapes from Toulouse and Turkestan—indeed!
They were embroidered and embellished with the best of gems
That could be purchased with pounds to meet the price
    On any selling day.   80
The prettiest lady that one may describe,
She gleamed there with eyes of grey;
To have seen one fairer to the sight—
That no one could truly say.

5.

But Arthur would not sit down until they were served:
He was so jolly in his youthfulness—and just a bit juvenile.
He wanted life to be lighthearted, liking much less
To loll around for very long, or a long time to sit.
This way his young blood and restless brain kept him busy.

Then also, another affair concerned him as much: 90
For he had established the noble custom that he never would sup
On a high and holy day until he had first heard
An unusual account of some adventuresome affair,
Or some major miracle in which he might believe:
About aristocrats and arms and other such achievements;
Or unless somebody begged him for some brave-hearted knight
To join in a joust, with each to lay in jeopardy
A life for a life, thereby allowing the other
To have the fairer share if Fortune should so favor him.
This was always the king's custom when he was in court,   100
At every fancy feast among the finest fellows
  In his hall.
He stood firm in his place
Appearing proud and tall,
But early in this New Year,
He loosed merriment for all.

6.
So he appeared in that place, the proud king himself,
Talking before the High Table about delicate trifles.
And there Gawain the good was seated next to Guinevere,
While Sir Agravain Hard-hand on the other side was sitting—   110
Both sons of the king's sister and stout knights for sure.
Bishop Baldwin led off the guests on the board up above,
While Yvain, the son of Urien, ate with him there.
They were seated this way on the dais, and scrupulously served,
With many a sterling sire set along the sideboards.
In came the first course to the crackling sound of trumpets,
While many a bright-colored banner was furling close by.
The kettledrums clamored, accompanied by courtly pipes,
Blending wild warblings with loudly awakened alarms
That lifted hearts high as they heard those crescendoes.   120
Dainties were doled out with other dearly bought foods—
A harvest of wholesomeness, heaped high on so many platters
That scarcely were places found before all those people
To set down the silver vessels with the various entrees
  Upon the cloth.
Every person reached as he pleased,
Not feeling one bit loath.
No—twelve dishes for every pair;
Good beer and bright wine both!

7.

Now of the service I'll supply no further details,   130
But well you might wager that there was no want there.
Then another noise, all new, drew suddenly nigh
That now might allow noble Arthur to gather some nurture.
For scarcely had the music ceased for a single second
And the first course been courteously doled around to the court,
When there rushed through the door an extremely awesome rider,
One of the greatest on earth, in measure enormous,
From his neck to his nates looking nearly square and thick,
While his loins and his limbs were long and very huge.
Half a giant from the ground up I'd guess him to be,   140
But still wholly human I'd have to declare him—
The grandest master in girth who ever galloped!
For the back and the breast of his body were very broad,
Though his stomach and his waistline were supremely slim;
And his facial features were like his figure—very neat
     And clean.
Yet one truly wondered at the hue
Of his countenance when seen;
For he acted like a thing bewitched
And was, head to toe, ink-green.   150

8.

All colored green were this creature and his clothes.
He sported a very tight straight-coat that stuck to his sides,
With a lovely mantle on top and a lining within
Whose fur clearly was trimmed with a facing that was fair,
And with elegant ermine embellishing it and the hood,
Which hung loose from his locks, lying over his shoulders.
He also sported tight stockings of the very same color,
Which clung to his calves, and below, cleanly polished spurs
Of burnished gold set on bases of richly barred silk;
And shoeless beneath his shanks this chevalier rode.   160
All of his gear was, I swear, a gorgeous green:
Both the bosses on his belt and the brilliant, shiny stones
That were elaborately arranged on the noble array
Of his saddle and on his own clothes spun from silk.
It would be much too tiring to tell even half the details
That were embroidered above: the birds and the butterflies,
With the gay, gaudy green and the gold interwoven
On the hangings from the breast-band, the horse's crupper,

The bosses on its bit, with their enameled metal,
The stirrups that he stood on, stained the same color,   170
And the bows and the panels of his princely saddle,
Which always gleamed and glimmered with its greenish stones.
The steed that he sat on shared the same color,
    It's true:
A green horse, huge and heavy,
A stallion hard to subdue;
In its bordered bridle, it was quick
Its master's will to pursue.

9.

Very gaily was this gallant man decked out in green,
The hair of him and his horse having the same sheen.   180
Beautifully flowing tresses folded over his shoulders.
A beard as big as a bush spread out over his breast
That with the heavy hair falling down from his head
Was clipped all around just a bit above the elbows,
So that half of his arms were hidden underneath,
The way a king's heavy coat may cover his torso.
The mane of that mighty horse resembled it very much;
It was nicely curled and well-combed, with many a knot
Of golden thread twisted in among the fair green:
Here a strand of green hair, and there a strand of gold.   190
Its tail and its tuft were twins in their coloring,
And both were bound with bands of bright-shining green,
Which adorned the tail's point with preciously priced stones.
Then a thong was bound tight with a high triple knot
From which many bright bells of burnished gold were ringing.
Such a foal in a field or a fellow to ride upon it
Was never observed in that open hall before that hour
    By any man alive.
He looked as lithe as lightning,
Said those who saw him arrive.   200
It seemed no mortal might
His deadly blows survive.

10.

And yet he had no helmet, and no hauberk either,
No breastplate or other parts pertaining to armor,
No shaft or no shield to shove or to strike with,
But in one of his hands he was holding a branch of holly,

Which is greatest in its greenery when all the groves are bare.
In his other he held an ax, immense and appalling,
A battle-ax quite awful to describe—if anyone could.
The large head measured the full length of an ell-yard;   210
Its handle had the hues of green steel and of gold;
That blade had a bright burnish, and also a broad edge
As well-shaped for shearing as any sharpened razor.
The stern one gripped it by its stiff and steely shaft,
Which was wound around with iron down to the wand's end,
And all engraved with enchanting designs in emerald.
A lacing was looped around it and locked at the head,
And down the shaft it swept in tight-clinging circles,
With innumerable, intricate tassels attached to it
On buttons of emerald that were embroidered most elegantly.   220
This horseman hurtled up and hove into the hall,
Dashing forward to the dais and fearing no danger,
Not saluting a single soul, but surveying them all.
The very first word that he hurled out then was: "Where
Is the commander of this crowd? I would quite gladly
Summon him to my sight, and with His Honor speak words
    Rational and sound."
On the knights he beamed his eyes,
Rolling them all around;
He paused—to ascertain   230
Who claimed the seat of renown.

11.

The group there kept gawking a long time to gather more,
For everyone was marveling at exactly what it might mean
That a champion and his charger could acquire such a sheen,
Growing green as the grass—even greener, it seemed—
Glowing brighter than green enamel gleaming upon gold.
All who stood there were stupefied; they stepped a bit nearer,
With all the world's wonder as to what works he'd perform.
For they'd witnessed a lot of weird things, but never one like this!
Many of the followers charged it to phantoms and fairies,   240
And so these aristocrats were a bit anxious about answering;
Yes, astonished by that voice, they sat there all stone-still,
While silence like a swoon swept through that hall,
As if everyone was slipping into slumber. They censored
    Any words coming out,
And because of courtesy, I think—
Not because of fear or doubt—

So the king whom they all obeyed
Could speak up to that lout.

12.
Then Arthur before the dais acknowledged the adventurer   250
And warmly welcomed him, for he was never weak-kneed,
Saying, "Good sir, I extend a greeting to my gathering.
I'm the head of the household here; Arthur's my name.
Step down now gently, and stay a while, I ask you;
And whatever you want—we shall see that it's fulfilled."
"No!" said the stranger. "So help me He who rules on high!
It was not my intention to interrupt your amusements;
But because the praise of you, prince, is puffed so high,
And your manor and your men are considered so magnificent,
The most stalwart ever to ride on steeds in steel-gear,   260
The most valiant and virtuous of the variety of humans,
Tough lads to try one in a gentleman's many tests,
And politeness is practiced here—so it's been prated—
Your celebrity summons me here now in this season.
Please be assured by the branch that I am bearing
That I'm passing in peace, wanting no prickly words.
For if I'd come here with comrades in a quarrelsome mood,
I wouldn't have left my hauberk at home—or my helmet either—
And my shield and my sharp spear shining all bright,
And other weapons to wield—please know this well.   270
No, because I want no warfare, I wore my soft garments.
And if you're as bold as all the barons bandy it,
You'll graciously grant me the little game that I ask
       By right."
Arthur then responded,
Saying, "Sir kindly knight,
If true battle is your care,
You will not lack your fight."

13.
"No, in full faith! I'm not spoiling for any fight!
Why, around on these benches I see just beardless babies!   280
If I were suited in my armor, on top of my strong steed,
There'd be no man here to match me; their muscles are too weak.
No, in this court I crave just a little Christmas pastime,
For it's New Year and Yuletide—and the people here are young.
If any human here considers himself husky enough

With a bold brain in his head—as well as some boiling blood—
So that he'd exchange with me one stiff stroke for another,
I'll give him as a gift this gorgeous battle-ax—
This haft, which is heavy indeed, to handle as he chooses.
And I'll undergo the first thrust, unarmed as I am now.   290
And if any churl is so childish as to challenge what I say,
Let him leap down lightly here and latch on to this tool.
I'll quit-claim it forever; he can keep it as his catch.
And I'll suffer his swiping—standing stiff on this floor—
If you'll grant me the chance to give him another glance
     My way.
Yet he can have a little respite
For twelve months and a day.
Now hurry, and let's see quickly
If someone will have his say."   300

14.

If they were astonished at first, they now acted even stiller,
Those householders in the hall, the high and the low.
The man on his stallion swung around on his saddle
And roguishly rolled his red eyes all about,
Bending his bristly brows, which were beaming all green,
And, wagging his beard, while waiting for someone to answer.
When no one would counter his charge, he coughed just a bit,
And, pulling himself up pompously, he proclaimed:
"What! Is this Arthur's house," said the accuser then,
"Whose fame goes flowing throughout so many fiefdoms?   310
Well, where's your derring-do now, your dashing conquest?
Your bluster and bravado, your big-sounding words?
Now all the revel and renown of the Table Round
Are overwhelmed by the words of one creature's speech,
And from fear, all fierceness fades without a blow!"
With this he guffawed so loud that the good king grieved.
The blood shot for shame up into Arthur's cheeks
     And hair.
He grew as angry as the wind,
As did all those who were there.   320
But the king, always keen to act,
Answered that tough man's dare,

15.

Saying, "My fond fellow, by God, your asking is foolish,

But he who requests what's wrong shall reap his will.
I'm sure that no person here is put off by your proud words.
Give me your great-ax, for the sake of our Lord God,
And the boon that you beg for soon shall be bestowed."
Lightly Arthur leaps down and lunges toward that hand,
While fiercely the other fellow falls to his feet.
Now Arthur grabs the great-ax, gripping it by the haft,   330
And swinging it sternly, takes some practice swipes.
The grim one stands his ground, in all of his grandeur,
Huger than any thane in the house by a head-length or more.
With an unsmiling face, he stands there, stroking his beard,
And with a deliberate look, he draws down his collar,
No more nervous or unsettled by Arthur's warming strokes
Than if some buddy from the benches had brought him a draught
    Of wine.
Gawain, who sat by the queen,
To Arthur's ear inclined: 340
"I beg you, sir, here and now:
Please let this match be mine."

16.
"Would you please, kindly sir," said Gawain to the king,
"Let me jump up from this bench and join you over there?
Without breaking protocol, I'd abandon this board
And if my liege-lady here doesn't greatly dislike it,
I'll come share your counsel before this courtly throng.
For I find it unthinkable, if the truth may be told,
That when such a weird request is raised in your halls,
You alone should have the yearning to undertake it yourself,   350
While so many bold warriors are warming these benches,
Who, I know, stand second to none in fighting spirit
And who cut the finest figures on the fields in the fray.
I'm the weakest of all, I'm aware—the feeblest in wit.
The loss of my life would surely be the least important.
My only claim to fame is that I call you my close kin.
My body has no blessing except what comes from your blood;
And since this is all a foolish fuss, it shouldn't fall upon you.
For since I've asked for it first, it is fittingly mine.
And if I annoy you by my nagging, this noble court should   360
    Give me the blame."
The nobles whispered together;
And since they felt the same,
To spring their sceptred king,

To Gawain they gave the game.

17.

Then the king commanded the knight to come and join him;
And the knight arose all ready and reached him fast,
Kneeling down to his lord, laying hands on the lethal weapon.
Arthur lightly yielded it, and then lifted up his hand,
Bestowing God's blessing, and bidding him urgently   370
To employ heart and hands in a very hardy way:
"Take care, my cousin," said the king; "make just one carving.
For if you deal with him deftly, I know, without a doubt
That you'll absorb any tap that he'll administer later."
Gawain approached the adversary with ax in hand,
Facing him most fiercely—not the least bit afraid.
Then the Giant in Green muttered grimly to Sir Gawain:
"Let's reformulate our agreement before we go further.
First, I'll query you, kind sir, as to how you are called,
And please tender me a retort in a way I can trust."   380
"In God's faith," said the good knight, "Gawain is my name.
I'll be handing you a hack soon—whatever happens after—
And twelve months from this Yuletime, I will take another
By whatever weapon you want, and without any second
    Alive."
The other one responds:
"Sir Gawain—God let me thrive!—
I am wonderfully content
To take any dent you drive."

18.

"Bigod," said the Green Knight, "Sir Gawain, I am glad   390
To acquire from your armed fist what I asked for here,
And you've already recited with a reasoning that's right
And careful all of the clauses I claim from your king—
Except for promising me, good sir, by your sworn pledge,
That you'll search for me yourself wherever you suspect
You'll find me on earth's face, to gather such fees
As you'll pay me here today before this powerful party."
"Where will I find you?" asked Gawain. "Where do you live?
I don't know your homestead—by Him who created me!—
No, I don't know, knight, either your court or your name.   400
Tell me this truly; tell me what you are called,
And I'll use all my wits to wend my way toward you.

This I openly swear on my own self-assured oath!"
"That's enough for a New Year. You need say no more,"
Said the vassal shining verdant to Gawain the valiant;
"To tell you the truth, when I've taken your tap,
And you've had your swift swipe, I'll instruct you then
About houses and homesteads and how I am called;
Then you can question my customs—and keep to your promise.
And if my spirit's snuffed, you'll surface all the safer,   410
For you can tarry on this turf without traveling any farther—
    So relax!
It's time to take up your tool
And show how you can hack."
"Yes, indeed, milord," said Gawain,
Stroking upon the ax.

19.
The Green Knight got ready right away on that ground,
Bending his neck a bit forward to lay bare the flesh,
Stringing his long, lovely strands up over his scalp,
Exposing his naked nape to the need at hand.   420
Gawain gathers up the ax, gripping it tightly,
And placing his left foot before him on the floor,
He brings it down brusquely upon the bare-skinned neck,
So that the sharpened blade shatters through the bones.
It shears the shaft of the neck, splitting it in two,
With the edge of bright iron biting into the earth.
The fair head flips from its foundation to the floor,
And the crowd begins to kick it as it caroms their way.
Blood spurts from the base, shining bright upon the green,
But the fellow doesn't fail or falter one bit.   430
No, he starts up swiftly upon his solid shanks
And reaches out roughly where the courtiers are ranked
To gather back his head, which he heaves then on high.
Then he strides to his stallion, snatching at its bridle,
Stepping up into the stirrups and standing aloft.
Then, dangling the head by its hairs in one of his hands,
The stranger sits very steadily in his saddle,
As if nothing had bothered him one bit—but yet he had
    No head.
He twisted his torso around,   440
That ugly trunk that bled.
The onlookers had some doubts
Before the next words were said.

20.

Holding the head straight outward in one hand,
He directed the face toward the great dons on the dais.
It opened its eyelids and ogled them all around,
Then muttered from the mouth these words that you must hear:
"All right, Gawain! Be so good as to go as you promised
And try faithfully to find me, my fine fellow,
As you have sworn in this hall, and these knights have heard.   450
Come to the Green Chapel, I command you, to suffer
A dent like the one you've dealt me—for you deserve
To be promptly repaid on the approaching New Year's morn.
Numerous people know me as the Knight of the Chapel Green.
So if you want faithfully to find me, you shall not fail.
And so, come! Or else, be called a craven coward!"
With a violent jerk, he veered away on the reins
And hurtled through the hall-door with his head in his hand,
While a fire, as from flint, flickered up from his horse's hooves.
To what land he launched out—nobody there could learn;   460
Nor did they have any notion as to his native place.
        What then?
The king and Gawain next
Laughed and grinned again;
The affair was widely proclaimed
A marvel by all men.

21.

Though Arthur, the artful king, felt a bit anxious at heart,
He let no semblance be seen, but loudly issued instead
To his most becoming queen this courteous speech:
"My dear lady, you should not be dismayed today;   470
This cleverness is customary at Christmastime,
With performances of plays, pastimes, and songs,
As well as the deft dances of knights and damsels.
And so to my supper I shall now address myself,
For a wonder I have witnessed—*that* no one will deny."
He glanced over at Gawain and graciously said to him,
"Hang up your hatchet, sir; you have hewn quite enough."
The tool was tied to a tapestry over the throne,
Where all men might marvel at it with great amazement
And prattle about the prodigy, having viewed the living proof.   480
Then they fell to their food, these fond friends together,
This king and his companion, where men catered carefully
With the plentiful portions that to princely men fall!

With all manner of fine meats—and minstrelsy to boot—
In good spirits they spent that day, till its end sped
    Through the land.
Now be very mindful, Sir Gawain,
That, if in danger you stand,
You see to the very end
Any enterprise at hand.   490

Part Two

1.

This exchange of exploits Arthur experienced early
In the young year; how he yearned to hear such vaunts!
Though words once were lacking, as they went to their seats,
The court now swelled with serious talk—overspilled!
Gawain was glad to begin those games in that hall,
But if this story turns serious, you shouldn't feel surprised,
For though men have merry minds when they've drunk very much,
The seasons run rather swiftly and experience many shiftings:
The outset and the outcome are seldom in one accord.
And so the Yuletide rolled by, and the young year came on,   500
And one season, as established, succeeded another.
After Christmas there came the cold of crabby Lent,
Which tests the human flesh with fish and simpler foods.
And then the world's weather wrestles against the winter.
Chill clings to the earth, while clouds go billowing upward.
Sheerly sprinkles the rain in showers that are warm,
Falling upon fair plains where the spring flowers swell,
And the ground and the groves burgeon under gowns of green.
Birds busy themselves with their building and beautifully warble
In the solace of the soft summer that slowly steals in   510
    Over hill and shore.
Then blossoms sprout on boughs
That are lined with blooms galore,
While all throughout the woodland
Bird-notes show that birds adore.

2.

Next comes the season of summer with its softened winds,
When Zephyrus sighs over the seedlings and the sedges;
Full of pleasure are the plants that spring up all around,
As the dampening dew drops gently from their leaves,

And then they bask in the blissful blush of the sun.   520
Ah, but then Harvest comes hurrying, making all things harsh,
Warning them that, against the winter, they must wax all ripe.
He drives up the dust in the middle of a drought,
Making it fly up over the fair face of the earth.
Wrathful winds wrestle with the sun high up in the heavens;
Leaves fall, loosened from lindens, then drift to the ground,
And all grey is the grass that was green just a bit before.
Then everything ripens and rots that once rose high,
And so the year yields, with the passing of yesterdays,
And winter winds round again, as the world-order demands—   530
     No lie!
Now the moon of Michaelmas
Hangs with wintry pledges high.
His own voyage most annoying
Gawain ponders by and by.

3.
Up to All Hallows Day with Arthur he abided,
When the king arranged a great revel for his relative's sake,
With plenty of pomp and partying at the Table Round.
Courtiers acting courteous and very becoming women
Felt a sympathy inside, out of love for that fond sire,   540
But nevertheless, they accentuated their amusement,
And, though joyless, invented jests for that gentleman.
After dinner, Sir Gawain dolefully addressed his dear uncle
About the perilous passage; he very plainly explained:
"My liege, the lord of my life, I now must leave you.
You know the terms of my trial. I'm not going to try
To tell you a lot about it—just a trifle.
You know that I'm bound to bear up my burden tomorrow,
To seek out the knight in green—and may God guide me!"
Then the select of that circle sequestered a bit: 550
Sir Yvain and Sir Erec, and many another aristocrat:
Sir Dodinal the Savage, with the Duke of Clarence,
And Lancelot and Lionel along with Lucan the good,
Sir Bors and Sir Bedivere—both mighty barons—
And many another manly one, like Mador of the Gate.
All of this courtly company drew closer to the king
To advise the arch-ruler with anxiousness at heart.
A somber sorrow was stealing through that inner sanctum
That a gallant man like Gawain should go on that errand

And suffer some baleful blow, feeling his brave hand   560
    Fall weak.
But Gawain feigned a happy face
And asked, "Should I now retreat?
Whether destiny looms dear or dark,
What can a man do but seek?"

4.

He stayed there all of that day, getting dressed in the morning,
Asking early for his arms, all of which were conveyed to him.
The servants spread a silken carpet over the floor,
Which had many a gold garment there gleaming upon it.
The stalwart one stepped onto the rug and took hold of the steel,   570
Slipping into a jacket that was spun from rich Turkish silk,
And donning a fancy hood that was fastened tight at the throat,
Which had a brilliant fur lining bound up inside.
Then they fitted some footwear over the hero's feet.
His legs were lined with lovely greavings of steel,
Which had kneeplates appended, polished all bright,
That were knit around the kneecaps with knots of gold.
Then costly cuisse-pieces craftily enclosed
His thick, brawny thighs, with many a thong attached.
Next body-armor embroidered with burnished rings   580
Circumscribed that courtier with very costly material.
He had beautifully shining bracers on both his arms,
And wore strong, gaudy elbow-guards and gloves of iron;
And all of that gorgeous gear was guaranteed to help
    Turn any tide.
With a fashionable overcoat
And gold spurs to jab with pride,
He was girded by a silken belt
With a trusty sword at his side.

5.

When he was suited in his steel, his armor looked superb.   590
The slightest lacing or loop was lustrous with gold.
Fully harnessed this way, he heard the high mass sung,
As it was offered and honored at the high altar.
Then he went to the king and all his courtly companions,
And lovingly took his leave from those ladies and lords.
They kissed him, walked with him, commending him to Christ.
Then Gringolet was geared up, girt round with a saddle

That glistened all gaily with many a golden fringe;
It was all newly nailed, newly furbished for that mission.
The bridle was barred around and bound with the brightest gold.   600
The sheen of the breast-cloth and its haughty side-skirts,
The crupper and caparison accorded with the saddle-bow,
For a rich field of red was arrayed with golden studs
That glittered and glistened like the glints of the sun.
Then our hero grabbed his helmet and hastily kissed it;
It was strongly stapled together and stuffed within.
He put it high on his head and hooked it behind,
Letting a band of cloth cover over the visor,
Which was embroidered and bound with the best of all gems
Set on broad, silken borders with birds at the seams,   610
Such as popinjays that were painted among periwinkles
And turtledoves entangled with true-loves so thickly
That it would take a seamstress seven winters to sew them
  In any town.
The band was of even greater price
That circumscribed his crown,
With diamonds that were finely cut
And glittered brightly around.

6.

Then they showed him the shield that was of shiny scarlet
With the pentangle depicted in pure golden hues.   620
He swung it by its strap, slung it over his shoulders,
And it seemed to fit that fighter perfectly.
Now why the pentangle is proper for this noble prince
I intend to inform you, despite the interruption:
It's a sign that Solomon established some time ago
As a token of truthfulness, which it bears title to,
For it is a figure that is formed out of five points,
And every line overlaps and locks in another
In a way that's entirely endless; therefore Englishmen
Call it everywhere, I hear, "the endless knot."   630
And so it was appropriate for this knight and his armor,
For Gawain was famous as a good man, as pure as is gold,
Always faithful in five things, each in a fivefold way,
Always devoid of villainy, and endowed in the finest virtues
  Most duly;
He carried on his shield and coat
This pentangle painted newly—
That man who was gentle in his speech

And who kept his word most truly.

7.

First of all, he was always faultless in his five senses,   640
And secondly he never failed in using his five fingers,
And his earthly faith was founded upon the five wounds
That Christ suffered on the Cross, as the Creed informs us;
And whenever this baron was embroiled in a battle,
His every thought was on that, above all other things.
Indeed, all of his daring he derived from the five delights
That the charming queen of heaven had from her boy-child.
And for this reason the royal man quite rightly had the queen
Embellished in her image on the inside of his shield,
So that when he viewed it, his vigor never wavered.   650
And the fifth group that I find the fighter employing were:
Free-giving and Good Fellowship, before all of the others;
His Chastity and his Courtesy were never corrupted;
And his Pity surpassed all the rest. These five points
Were more firmly fixed in him than in any other fellow.
Yes indeed, all of these fives were ingrained in this knight,
And each one linked to the next, so that there was never an end;
They were fastened securely by the five points that never failed,
And they never swerved to one side or broke asunder.
No ending at any nook do I find anywhere,   660
Wherever the design began or glided to an end.
And so on this shiny shield, that knot stood painted
Royally with reddish gold upon a red-gules field.
This is the Pentangle Perfect—which is known to every person
        Of good lore.
Now Gawain the gay was fully geared
And his lance he lightly bore.
He issued them all a fond "Good day"—
He thought: for evermore.

8.

He stuck his spurs into his steed, and they sprang on the way   670
So fast that sparks went flashing, as from flint, out behind.
And all who saw him depart sighed sincerely within,
And uttered indeed the same old saws to one another
In compassion for the courtier: "By Christ! it's a shame
That you, my lad, shall be lost, who lived so nobly.
In faith, it's not easy to find your equal here on earth.

It would have been wiser if you'd waited more warily,
And later on, you'd be dubbed a dashing duke.
I believe you'd have made an unsurpassed leader of legions
And would have shone brightly instead of being snuffed out,   680
Beheaded by some beast because of unbridled pride.
Who'd ever think that our Arthur would embark on such an exploit
As to yield to the gibberish of knights in a Yuletide jest!"
A great deal of warm water was wept from those eyes
As that handsome young hero ambled away from their haunt
     That day.
He didn't make any stops,
But went swiftly on his way.
Many a winding road he took,
As I've heard the old books say.   690

9.
Now this regal noble rides through the realm of Logres,
Sir Gawain, the champion of God—no mere gamester he!
Usually solitary, he sleeps alone with the stars
And seldom does he find any food one might call the finest.
He had no friend except for his foal in those forests and hills,
And no creature except the Creator there to converse with,
Until he drew near to the northernmost part of Wales.
All of the islands of Anglesey he bore on his left hand
As he passed by the fords that fork into the foothills
Over toward Holy Head; then he gained the higher ground   700
In the Wilderness of Wirral, where few men are dwelling
Who show a humane heart toward God or any human.
And always, as he went, he asked those whom he encountered
If they'd heard any gossip about some gallant in green
Or if, in the environs, might exist some emerald chapel.
Everyone nodded no. They said that they'd never seen
In all their careers any creature with such a coloring
     Of green.
The knight took many pathways strange
In terrain both bleak and mean;   710
And his visage suffered many a change
Before that chapel was seen.

10.
Many a cliff he climbed over in that strange country
Where he rode as a foreigner, far removed from his friends.

At every creek and crossing where that fellow coursed,
He found—quite fantastically—some foe before him,
One who was foul and fierce, with whom he had to fight.
In those mountains he met with such a host of marvels
That it would be too trying to tell even the tenth part.
Sometimes with serpents he struggled, sometimes with wolves,   720
Sometimes with troll-like creatures who camp in the crags,
Also with bulls and with bears—and even with boars—
And giants who jumped out at him from the jags.
Had he not been strong and unstinting and served his Maker,
He would doubtlessly have been utterly dashed, and then died.
Yet danger was not what worried him; the weather was worse,
For the cold, clear water kept dropping down from the clouds
And freezing even before it fell on the frigid earth.
Almost slain by the sleet, he slept in his iron clothes
More nights than he had need for among the naked rocks,   730
Where cold torrents came crashing down from the crests
And hard icicles were hanging over his head.
And so in peril and pain, and in pitiful danger,
This chevalier coursed the countryside till Christmas Eve,
    All alone.
Then the horseman at that time
To good Mary made a moan
That she should direct his wanderings
And guide him to some home.

11.

By a mountain the next morning he merrily rode   740
Into a wood that was deep and wonderfully wild,
With towering hills on each side and high trees below
Containing a hundred or more huge, hoary oaks
And hazels and hawthorns heavily gnarled together,
While rough, ragged moss ran rampant everywhere.
Above, bevies of down-hearted birds on bare twigs
Were pitifully peeping because of the painful cold.
The rider on the back of Gringolet glided in below them
Through all of the mud and the mire—that lonely man—
Caring about his condition, fearing he might not come back   750
To see again the services for that Sire who on that Eve
Was born from a maiden to mollify all of our miseries.
And so, breathing hard, he begged: "I beseech thee, Lord,
And Mary, who is the mildest mother and dear,
For some haven where I might devoutly hear my mass,

And tomorrow hear matins—very meekly I ask this—
And now I promptly offer my Our Father and my Ave
    And Creed."
He rode on, deep in prayer,
Crying for his misdeeds,   760
And blessed himself several times,
Saying, "Christ's Cross grant me speed!"

12.

The cavalier had just crossed himself for the third time
When quickly through the trees he caught sight of a moated castle
Perched on a mound above a meadow, enmeshed in the boughs
Of tough-rooted tree-trunks that grew around the main trench.
It was the most charming chateau that a chevalier ever saw!
It lorded high on its towering lawn with a park below it,
Where pointed palisades kept everything in their pen,
Enfolding a forest for more than a fine two miles.   770
The hero simply stared at the façade of that stronghold
As it shimmered and shivered among the spangling leaves.
Then he humbly bared his head, and he heartily thanked
Lord Jesus and St. Julian, who are both gentle men,
Who had heard his cry and compassionately conveyed him:
"Now for a lovely lodging," said he. "I long for that still!"
Then he goaded on Gringolet with his gilded spurs
And he chose by chance to approach the chief portcullis.
This course carried him quickly to the head of the bridge
    At last.   780
The drawbridge was sharply lifted,
And the main gate bolted fast;
The walls looked very heavy
To withstand the winter's blast.

13.

The noble stayed on his steed, which drew short at the shore
Of the deep double ditch that fully encircled the dwelling.
The walls reached down into the water wondrously deep
And conversely they climbed to a dizzying crest above
As their hard, well-cut rocks created the cornices
That bulged underneath the battlements in the best of styles;   790
And over them towered the turrets neatly interspersed
With lots of useful loopholes to look through clearly.
Our baron had never laid eyes on a better barbican!

Then inside he could see the impressive inner keep,
Where towers extended tall between thick pinnacles
Whose fancy finials reached fittingly up, fine and long,
Culminating in carved caps that were craftily fashioned.
Then the champion noticed a host of chalk-white chimneys
That were sparkling snow-white upon the citadel's roof.
So many painted pinnacles were pointing up everywhere   800
And clambering in clusters among the crenellations
That the palace appeared indeed to be cut out of paper.
The stolid lord on his steed thought it all quite splendid
If he could just gain entrance into that enclosure
And, while the holidays lasted, find haven in that hostel
     Clean and bright.
He called, and soon there answered
A porter most polite,
Who assumed his place on the wall
And saluted the errant knight.   810

14.

"Kind sir," answered Gawain, "could you convey this message
To the lord of the house: I would deeply like some lodging."
"By Saint Peter, yes!" said the porter. "I can almost promise
You'll be summoned, good sir, to stay as long as you like."
Then he rushed away rapidly, and returned again as fast,
Bringing waves of well-wishers to welcome the knight.
They let down their drawbridge and then they all dashed out
And fell on their knees upon that freezing earth
To welcome that warrior in a way that was most worthy.
They guided him then to the main gate, which was soon yanked open,   820
And he graciously urged them to rise as he rode over the bridge.
Inside, the servants took his saddle as he dismounted,
And many stout-hearted men then stabled his steed.
A drove of mighty dons and squires then descended
To lead the lord lightheartedly into the hall.
When he took off his helmet, there hurried up a group
To hoist it out of the hands of this handsome man.
They also took his sword and his shining shield.
Then he greeted those gracious men most gratefully,
While many proud people pressed forward to honor that prince.   830
They whisked him, still clad in his armed coat, into the court,
Where a fine fire was kindling fiercely upon the hearth.
Then the great duke of that land descended from his den
To face with good manners the foreigner on his floor.

He said, "You are welcome to take whatever you wish
Of what is here; it's your own to have and to hold
 At your own pace."
"Many thanks," returned Sir Gawain;
"May Christ grant you equal grace!"
Like humans who are happy,   840
The two men then embrace.

15.
Gawain glanced at the lord who had greeted him so kindly
And considered him capable of guarding that castle—
An enormous fellow, by the way, exactly at his prime.
Broad and bright was his beard, with a beaver's color;
Sturdy and straight was his stance upon his strong shanks.
He was frank in his speech, with a face as ferocious as fire,
And he seemed in all truth (or so Sir Gawain supposed)
Just right for leading a lordship with its liegemen.
The host then conducted his guest to a chamber, commanding 850
A servant to be sent to wait sedulously upon him.
A whole host of boys were bound to his beck and call.
They led him into a boudoir where the bedding was splendid,
With curtains of sheerest silk and shiny gold hems,
And coverlets quaint with the most becoming panels,
Brightly lined on the top, with embroidery on the sides.
The draperies ran on ropes with red-gold rings,
And tapestries from Toulouse and Tarsia spread on the walls,
While the floor was covered with fancy rugs for the feet.
There Sir Gawain was stripped of his iron suit   860
And his shiny garments, surrounded by humorous speeches.
Carefully educated esquires gave him expensive robes
To experiment with or exchange or elect the best.
As soon as he selected one, he slipped it on,
And it suited him beautifully with its swirling skirt.
"Primavera" he truly appeared from his springlike expression
To almost all the aristocrats; his limbs were absolutely
Dazzling and adorable as they reflected those hues,
So that Christ never created a more radiant creature,
 They thought.   870
Wherever in the world he went,
It seemed that Gawain ought
To be a prince without a peer
In the fields where menfolk fought.

16.

Before the chimney, where charcoals were burning, a chair
Was prepared for Sir Gawain, made plush with pillows.
Little cushions were placed on the quilt, both carefully sewn,
And then a magnificent mantle they threw over that man
Made of the finest fabric, and embroidered most fancily
With lovely furs inside to serve as a soft lining,   880
And they were made entirely of ermine, as was his hood.
He sat on that settee that seemed very royal indeed
And warmed himself well—and soon his mood waxed brighter.
Then a table was tossed up on the finest trestles,
Covered with a clean cloth that appeared clear white,
Along with linens and a salt-cellar and some silver spoons.
Gawain washed as he wanted, and then went on to dine.
The servants certainly set themselves to serving him well,
With several fine soups, which were seasoned with the best,
With double servings, as was suitable, and many species of fish—   890
Some baked in bread, some broiled over the coals,
Some boiled, some cooked in stews with savory spices,
And always with subtle sauces that the connoisseur adores.
Very often and freely, that fellow proclaimed it a feast
With great courtesy, while the courtiers teased in a chorus:
      "Be comforted!
Just suffer this penance now,
For soon you'll be better fed!"
Their guest responded with laughter
As the wine went to his head!   900

17.

Then they queried and questioned—but always courteously—
Placing before that prince some private inquiries,
And finally he confessed that he came from the court
Where Arthur the admirable monarch held sway alone—
The rich, royal ruler of the Table Round.
Ah yes, Sir Gawain himself was sitting right there!
He had come to them at Christmastime as chance befell.
When the overlord was informed who this invited man was,
He laughed very loudly, for he liked it a lot;
And all the men of his mansion amused themselves too   910
By partaking of Gawain's presence right then and there.
Soon virtue and valor and the very finest manners
Were attributed to his person. He was always praised.
Before every human on earth, he was hailed as the highest!

Every man very softly then muttered to his mate:
"Soon we'll be seeing the most subtle behavior,
The most sophisticated standards of civilized speech,
And we'll be learning the lore of effortless language,
For we have in this place the paragon of perfect manners.
God has graciously granted us a gift indeed,   920
That a guest such as Gawain is given to us now
When gentlemen, overjoyed at the Savior's birth, join together
     And sing.
An education in etiquette
This knight shall surely bring;
And those who listen well
May gain love's mastering."

18.

When the dinner drew to an end, the dear guest arose;
It was nearing nighttime, for evening had now descended.
Chaplains to the chapel began wending their way   930
To ring the bells roundly, as rightly they should,
In the solemn evensong of that most sacred season.
The great lord attended there, along with his lady,
Who passed by with beauty en route to her private pew.
Gawain jumped up all jovially and went over to join them.
The lord seized his lapel and led him to a seat,
Then kindly took care of him, calling him by name,
Saying that he was the most welcome guest in all the world.
Gawain thanked him thoroughly; they embraced each other
And sat there soberly throughout the high service.   940
Then it intrigued the lady to entertain the invited one;
She departed from her pew, trailed by her pretty maids.
She was the fairest of all in her figure, flesh, and face,
As well as her contour, complexion, and conduct—
Even more gorgeous than Guinevere, so Gawain thought.
She crossed over the chancel to encounter the chevalier,
With another lady leading her by the left hand
Who was far more aged—an ancient one, she appeared—
And highly honored by all those high-born around her.
I must tell you that these two were totally unalike,   950
For if the younger had spirit, the senior one was seared.
A perfect pink complexion suffused the one,
While rough, wrinkled cheeks rolled down upon the other.
The younger wore a kerchief clustered with clearest pearls;
Her breast and her bright throat were laid all bare,

Shining more splendidly than the snow adrift on the hills.
The senior wore a scarf that was encircling her throat,
And her swarthy chin was concealed under chalky veils;
Her forehead was burrowing under silk folds and frills
With laces and lattices and lots of little ornaments,   960
So that only the black brows of that beldame were bared,
With her nose, her naked lips, and her two eyes—
And those two, sour to see, were most sorrowfully bleared.
She was one of the world's most wonderful women, you'd say—
    By God!
Her body was squat and thick,
Her buttocks bulging and broad;
Far lovelier was the lady
Who just behind her trod.

19.

When Gawain glances at that lady who looks so lovely,   970
He takes leave of her lord and lounges over to the two.
He salutes the senior first, scraping very low,
While the lovelier one he locks for a little in his arms,
Kissing her very courteously and chatting cavalierly.
They ask for his acquaintance, and he readily asserts
That he'll act as their obedient if they find this opportune.
They entwine him between them and, talking, they propel
Him into a chamber with charcoals, where they chiefly
Call for some spices that the serving-boys speedily bring
And the most wanted wines—all that they could wish for.   980
The host most hospitably kept hopping all around,
Reminding them that mirth should be made on every side.
He shucked off his hood and hung it upon a hook,
Then prodded them all to compete for its possession
By trying to raise the greatest revelry during that Yule:
"And I shall try, by my faith, with the help of my fond friends
To hustle with the happiest so my hood will not be lost."
And so, with these lighthearted words, the lord enlivened
And gladdened Sir Gawain's heart with gaming in his hall
    And great delight.   990
And when the hour rolled by
To call for the candlelight,
Sir Gawain climbed the stairs,
Bidding them all good night.

20.

On that morning when every mortal mulls over the time
When our Divine Lord for our destiny was born to die,
Joy wells up in everyone in the world on His behalf.
So did it there on that day with its countless delights,
Both at buffet and at the broad board spread on the dais,
Where caterers were serving courses of the finest cuisine.   1000
The aged harridan was sitting there highest in honor,
With the baron attentively by her, so I believe.
Gawain and the gay first lady were grouped together
About in the central section when supper was served,
While others were placed in the hall as was appropriate,
Since every diner was dealt with according to his degree.
There was food, there was fun, there was great frivolity—
So much that it would be tiring to tell the sum
Or to document the details, if I even dared.
Yet I think that our champion and his choice companion   1010
Were drawing such comfort from their company together,
From their sweet sophistication with subtle words,
With their nice and courteous talk—indeed, nothing nasty—
That their pastime surpassed any other palatial game—
     I declare!
Trumpets and kettledrums
And pipings filled the air;
Everyone tended his own thing,
And these two looked after theirs.

21.

Much merriment was made there that day and the next,   1020
And the third one impelled itself as intensely after.
The enjoyment of St. John's Day was a joy to behold,
But that was the end of entertaining—or so each thought.
The guests were planning to go away in the grey morning;
And so they remained wide-awake, imbibing their wine,
And all night long, they danced their devoutly loved carols.
At last, in the wee, wee hours, they whispered good night,
With each one wending his way to his own bedroom.
Gawain bade all goodbye; then the baron grabbed him,
Pulling him into his private chamber by its fireplace,   1030
And there he detained him a while, thanking him deeply
For the very precious privilege that he had provided
By honoring that house with his presence during the holidays,
Enchanting the whole chateau with his lively cheer:

"Indeed, royal sir, for as long as I breathe, I shall relish
The fact that you've been my friend for God's birthday feast."
"Many thanks, good sir," said Gawain, "but in all good faith,
The honor is yours—and may the Yule spirit bless you!
However, I'm here at your will to fulfill your behest
As I'm surely beholden, in matters either high or low,   1040
    With all due right."
The baron takes special pains
To further detain the knight,
But Gawain answers no:
He can't stay another night.

22.

The kindly castellan then inquired concernedly
What dire need had driven him out during this time
To travel so courageously out of the king's court alone
Before the holiday's holly was hauled out of town.
"Indeed, sir," said Gawain, "you certainly speak the truth.   1050
A high mission and a hard one bears me from those halls,
For I've been summoned to search alone for a site
Whose location I don't know where in the world to find.
For all of the land of Logres—may the Lord lend me aid!—
I'm bound to be there by daybreak on New Year's Day.
And so, sir, I'm asking you for assistance now:
Please tell me in all truth if you have ever been told
About any soil where a green sanctuary stands,
Or a knight who keeps it, who is clothed in the color green.
A pact was established with statutes set between us   1060
That I should meet that man at that monument if I could
On New Year's Day, which is now very nearly upon us,
And I'll face up to that fellow, if our Father allows me,
More gladly, by Jesus' grace, than have any other good thing!
And so, if you please, I have a long passage to travel
And I have only three more days to carry it through.
But I affirm I'd rather fall dead than fail in my errand!"
Then laughingly the lord replied, "Linger awhile!
For I'll teach you how to get there before your time is up.
The whereabouts of the church will worry you no longer.   1070
Instead, you can loll in your loft, my lord, at your ease
Till day flushes on the First, and then you can venture forth,
Coming there close to mid-morning, to clear what you
    Have to clear.
Stay awhile! And then rise up

And go on the First of the Year.
We'll direct you to your journey's end,
Which is not two miles from here."

23.

Then Gawain was full of joy and jovially rejoined,
"Now I thank you for this thoroughly—above everything else.   1080
I've accomplished part of my action, and I'm all at your command,
So I'll stay and perform any service that may please you."
Then the sire seized him and set him down at his side,
Paging the ladies to help them prolong their pleasure,
And they all participated in telling pleasant, private jokes.
The lord, who was brimful of friendship, acted frenzied at times
And nobody knew what he'd say, so out of his wits he was.
Suddenly, in a stentorian voice, he said to his guest,
"You've already agreed to do anything that I ask;
And will you verify your vow at this very time?"   1090
"Yes sir, in all truth," said the trusty knight in return;
"As long as I bask in your bower, I'm bound to your will."
"You've had a terrible trip," said the host, "traveling far,
And been kept awake by me. You're not fully caught up
Either in eating or sleeping—of this I'm sure.
So linger awhile aloft; yes, lie up there and rest
Tomorrow until mass-time, and then meander down
Whenever you want; my wife will be here beside you,
Comforting you with her company till I come back to court.
        Yes, take it slow.   1100
But *I* shall get up early
And to my hunting go."
Gawain assents to this,
Bowing, as knights bow low.

24.

"And still," said the host, "let's set up one stipulation:
Whatever I win out in the woods shall revert to you,
And whatever you gain, be so good as to give it to me.
Let this be our swap, my sweet friend, truly sworn,
Whichever way fortune falls, my partner—fair or foul."
"By God," declared Gawain the good, "I grant it all!   1110
And I think it's great that this gentleman likes to gamble!"
"Somebody bring us a drink and this bargain is sealed,"
Said the master of the manor, and the masses laughed.

They drank and they flirted and they frolicked freely,
These lords and these ladies, for as long as they liked.
And finally with French mannerisms and many fine words,
They stood and secretly exchanged subtle words,
Kissing very courteously and casting their adieux.
With several servants holding bright, shiny torches,
Everybody was escorted at the end to his chamber,   1120
    Soft and neat.
But before they go to bed,
Their bargains they repeat;
The old keeper of that castle
Surely kept them on their feet!

Part Three

1.

In the gloom before daybreak, the guests who would journey
Stirred from their slumber and summoned their grooms
And busied themselves with saddling their stallions.
They tended to their gear, tying up their trunks,
And arrayed themselves royally for their riding away.   1130
They leaped on their mounts lightly, lifting the reins,
And they all departed to their desired destinations.
The overlord of that land was far from the last one
To be ready to ride off with his many retainers.
He hurried through his breakfast and then heard his mass
And briskly breezed to the fields at the bugle's cry.
As the morning's glow was glimmering along the horizon,
The man and his minions sat high upon their mounts.
The crafty kennelmen then leashed up their canines
And pulled the pound's doors open, letting them pour forth,   1140
While the bugles kept blaring some solitary blasts.
The beagles bounded out, all barking and baying;
They were chastised and whipped if they strayed in that course
By about a hundred hunters, I've heard—the best
    Who ever might be.
The trainers took their stations
As the bloodhounds were set free;
Bugles blared throughout the wood,
And a roar rose through the trees.

2.

At the chase's first cries, nature's creatures were quaking;   1150

Deer rushed down to the dales, darting with fear,
Then hurtled back to the heights, where they were hastily
Turned around by the beaters with their bold bellowings.
They let the harts with their high heads pass safely by,
As well as the bucks with their broadly branched antlers,
Since the free-giving lord had forbidden in the off-season
Any man to molest one of the masculine deer.
The hinds were hemmed in with a "Hey!" and a "Ho!"
While the does were driven with a din to the glades.
There you could see arrows slipped out and slicing   1160
As the shafts whizzed up under the bends of the boughs,
Then dipped and bit those brown hides under those broad heads.
Ah! they bray and they bleed; they die on those banks!
For the hounds always follow them hot and heavy,
While hunters with high-pitched horns pursue ceaselessly,
With a shrill-sounding cry, as if the steep hills were crumbling.
Any wild ones who managed to get away from the archers
Were pursued and pulled down at the lower posts,
For they were harried on high, then herded to the water.
The kennelmen were very cunning at catching them below,   1170
And the greyhounds were great at getting them quickly
And finishing them off as fast as you could focus
    Your sight.
Our lord was a very merry boy;
He'd ride, and then he'd alight;
Yes, he rode all that day with joy
Till on came the darkening night.

3.

This lord we leave bantering by the lindenwood's borders,
While Gawain the good-hearted lies in his gaudy bed,
Lolling there while daylight is lengthening on the walls,   1180
Safe in his curtained bed with its costly cover.
And while he wallowed in slumber, a wee little noise
He heard at his door, which was delicately opened.
He perked his head up from his pillow and peeked
Around the curtain's corner, which he caught up a bit,
And he warily watched to see who it might be.
It was Madam herself, so marvelous to meditate,
Who slipped past the door, which she stealthily shut
And headed for the bed. How our boy did blush!
He precociously fell back and pretended a profound sleep.   1190
She stepped up silently, stealing toward his side,

Slipped up the curtain's edge, then sidled inside,
Perching very pertly and close beside him,
Lingering on awhile, waiting for him to waken.
Our warrior, however, wallowed on a bit longer,
Mulling in his mind what her actions might mean
Or portend—he pronounced it a bit preposterous;
So he said to himself, "I think it's suitable
To ask very openly just what she is after."
Then he started, and stretched, and turned to her side,   1200
Unlocking his eyelids and looking astonished;
And, to make himself safe with a prayer, he crossed himself
    Right on that bed.
Her chin and cheeks were prettily flushed
As whiteness blended with red
Through lips both small and laughing
These gentle words she said:

4.

"Good morning, Sir Gawain," was her lilting greeting;
"You're not a smart sleeper! I slipped in here with ease!
And I've caught you right here! If you don't cry surrender,   1210
I'll bind you to this bed—and that you may believe!"
Very teasingly the lady tossed out these taunts.
"Good morning, my charmer," answered Gawain quite graciously,
"I'll do what you please—that I promise you fully.
Yes, I'll yield myself easily, and sue for your mercy.
It's the safest course, I'm sure; so I'm bound to that."
In this way he joked back with some jolly laughter:
"But would you, sweet lady, kindly lend me some leave,
Freeing your fettered guest to allow him to rise—
Then I'll bolt from this bed and be quickly dressed   1220
And prepared to pursue a polite conversation."
"O no, milord!" said that lighthearted lady,
"You'll not get out of bed; here I'll handle you better
By trussing you in tightly on that other side;
Then I can talk with milord, whom I now have trapped,
Since I'm quite assured that you're the great Sir Gawain
Whom the whole world worships wherever you go.
Your gentility and graciousness are grandly sounded
By all lords and all ladies and everyone alive.
And now you are here—ah! and we're all alone!   1230
My husband and his hangers-on are hunting far away.
The servingmen are sleeping downstairs with the maids.

The door is slammed shut, and the bolt has been sprung;
Now I have in my house the hero whom all the world adores
And I'll employ my time while it endures, with an eye
        Toward gathering tales.
My person is at your pleasure,
Your every wish to avail;
Hospitality makes me your servant,
And in nothing shall I fail."   1240

5.

"In good faith," said Sir Gawain, "I feel greatly flattered,
But I'm surely not the person about whom you are speaking.
I'm an unworthy creature—and I know this full well—
Without that perfection that you've just portrayed.
But by God, I'll be glad, if you think it is good,
To arrange some pleasure for your most prized person
Like some speeches or services—it would be sheer joy!"
"In good faith, dear Gawain," replied the gay lady,
"If I scorned or reviled the virtue and the valor
That infatuate the others, it would be most improper,   1250
But there are lots of high ladies who would love to have you
In their clutches, my handsome one, as I have you here:
To dally in delight of your delicate words,
Gaining some consolation to quell their cares—
That they would treasure more than a trove of gold.
But as surely as I adore the Lord in heaven above,
I have wholly in my hands what every woman desires
        By His grace."
She flashed him a merry look,
That lady with her fair face;   1260
And the knight with words immaculate
Parried in every case.

6.

"Madam," said the gentleman, "may Mary reward you!
I've found in all faith a refined spirit in you.
Some men have received fancy favors for their actions,
But my deserts have never matched their great doles.
It's your own great virtue that makes you see virtue in others."
"By Mary," said milady, "I believe that it must be different.
For if I were as worthy as all the women alive,
And all of the wealth of the world were in my hands,   1270

Then I'd shop and search around to find me a sire
With the qualities I've come to admire in you, dear knight:
Your beauty, your debonairness, your smart behavior—
Things I've heard tell of before but never observed—
And so I would choose before all other challengers—*you!*"
"Mercy, dear madam!" said he. "You have a man who's much better!
Still, I'm proud of the price that you put on my worth;
I swear to be a servant, with you as my sovereign,
Your own cavalier, and may Christ kindly guard you!"
So they trafficked in trivia till mid-morning passed,   1280
And the lady allowed as to loving him a lot.
The knight was very gracious—and also on his guard.
The lady said inside, "Even if I were the very loveliest,
He'd show little tenderness because of the terror he faces
    On New Year's Day—
A stroke that will surely stun him
And cannot be waved away."
She begged to leave him then
Since they had had their say.

7.

Then she wished him good cheer and chuckled with a side-glance   1290
As she stood and perplexed him with some very pointed words:
"May He who protects all speech repay you for this pleasure!
Yet to think that you're the brilliant Gawain boggles my mind!"
"But why?" asked the bed-dweller, blurting it out
And fearing he had failed in his flawless behavior.
The lady gently blessed him, and then she said, "It's because
Sir Gawain is considered a knight who's constantly correct,
Who's the paragon of courtly perfection himself;
He couldn't linger very long or engagingly with a lady
Without craving for a kiss with all due courtesy,   1300
And saying so with some trifling phrase at the end of his talk."
Then Gawain retorted, "Is that it? Well, take what you want!
I shall kiss at your command in the best knightly custom,
And more, lest it displease you, so plead no further!"
At that she came nearer, catching him into her arms,
And leaning lovingly over, she kissed his lordly face.
Then they courteously commended each other to Christ,
And she whisked out of the chamber without another word.
He reachèd out and rose up, rushing into his underwraps,
Calling for his chamberlain and selecting his clothing.   1310
Then, all dressed, he descended to hear the mass;

Later he enjoyed a dinner that was elegantly arranged,
Making merry all day long till the moon at last was rising,
    With jest and game.
Never was a gentleman received
More fairly by more worthy dames,
The old one and the young;
And their happiness matched their fame.

8.
Meanwhile the overlord rode on and on at his pleasure,
Looking for fawnless hinds in the holts and the heaths.   1320
By the time the sun was setting, he had slain such a sum
Of does and other deer that it was dazzling to behold.
Toward evening the hunting-folk eagerly flocked together
And hastily made a heap of the hewn-down game.
The highest hurried up with their henchmen around them
And collected the plumpest corpses piled up there,
And had them cleanly cut up as custom demanded;
At the assaying, they searched for some select innards,
Finding a good two fingers of fat on even the thinnest.
Then they slit the slot and seized the gullet,   1330
Scraping it with a sharp knife and tying it into a knot;
Then they hacked off the legs and stripped away the hide,
Breaking open the belly and scooping out the bowels
Deftly, so as not to destroy the duly tied knot.
Then they seized the gullet and scrupulously separated
The esophagus from the pipe, gouging out the guts;
With sharp knives, they sheared through the hide
And pulled out the shoulders, leaving the skin intact.
Then they broke the breast into two separate bits
And they began to hack again back at the gullet,   1340
Slitting it swiftly right down to the front legs,
Clipping away the clavicle pieces and very cleanly
Removing the membranes rapidly from the rib-cage;
Then, as was customary, they cleaned the ridge of the spine,
All the way to the haunches, which hung together;
Those parts which were pulled up and then completely detached
Have the special and well-suited name of "the numbles,"
    So I find.
At the breaching of the thighs,
They cut the skin behind;   1350
And to separate it swiftly,
The backbone they unbind.

9.

Both the head and the neck they disconnected then
And they swiftly severed the sides away from the chine,
Tossing "the raven's reward" into a rugged thicket.
Then they ran the thick flanks through by the ribs
And hung them up by the hocks of the haunches,
As every fellow claimed the fee that fell to him.
And on the dearly priced pelts they fed the pet hounds,
Letting them feast on livers and lungs and tripe   1360
Blended with bits of bread that were soaked in blood.
Then the bugle's "sound of the kill" blared over the dog-bays,
And they folded their harvest of flesh and headed for home,
Striking strident note after note on their silvery horns.
By the time the daylight had run, the rout had returned
To the comfortable castle, where our cavalier was resting
    By the fire's side
In perfect bliss and ease.
The lord bounced up with a stride,
And Gawain hailed him home;   1370
Their joy was unqualified.

10.

Then the lord commanded his court to convene in the hall,
And the high-born damsels to descend with their domestics,
And before all that assembled audience, he asked his men
To place the venison before all the palace's people.
And he summoned Gawain the goodly to his games,
Tallying for him the total of his great take,
Showing him the fine cutlets that had once fleshed flanks:
"How does our sport please you? Have I won your praise?
Do I have your cordial approval for covering my craft?"   1380
"Yes, indeed," said the invited one, "it's the finest game
That I've spied in seven years in the winter season."
"Well, I give it all to you, Gawain," said he to his guest,
"In accordance with our agreement; it is yours alone."
"Correct and proper," said the guest, "and I'll repay you right now
With everything I've earned in earnest inside your walls.
It shall all be surrendered with the very same good will."
Then Gawain took his host's great neck in his grasp,
And kissed him as courteously as he could do it:
"Here! Take my paltry gain—I've won no further profit.   1390
I'd freely give you something greater if it was here to grant."
"No, that's fine!" replied the host. "A thousand thanks!

But I'd like it even better if you'd just brief me
As to where you garnered this gain with your ingenuity."
"That's not a part of our pact!" replied the knight. "No more!
You've cornered what was in our covenant; no further claim
    Accrues to you."
They chuckled, and they were cheerful;
Their talk was sincere and true.
Very soon they went to dine on   1400
 Some delicacies fresh and new.

11.

Afterward by the hearth in a heated hall they lounged
As chamber-boys carried out the choicest of wines,
And once more in their merriment they agreed the next morning
To enact again the agreement that they had earlier made;
Whatever fortune might fling them, what newfangled thing they won—
That earning they'd exchange the ensuing evening.
They came to this accord before all the other courtiers;
Beverages were brought out for a toast at that time;
Then they lovingly uttered their good-nights at last   1410
And everyone bustled off to bed with briskness.
When the cock had crowed and cackled just three times,
The high lord leaped out of bed, along with his lieges;
The morning meal and the mass were duly taken care of,
And the courtiers dressed for the woods before the dawn sprang,
    Off to their chase.
The hunters high with horns
Passed through an open place,
Unleashing among the thorns
The hounds to run their race.   1420

12.

The dogs soon barked after a scent along a bog-side
And the hunters howled out the names of the hounds who sniffed it,
Shouting encouraging cries with strident sounds;
Hearing this, the hounds hurtled forward in haste,
Falling fast on the track, about forty at once;
Then such a yelping and yowling of yappers
Rose up that the rocks all rang around with the sound.
The chasers urged them onward with cheers and with horns.
The pack pushed forward together in a great press
Between a fen in the forest and a fiendish-looking crag;   1430

On a mound by a cliff at the quagmire's side,
Where some rough rocks had once come rumbling down,
They raced after the quarry as the hunters rushed behind;
The men encompassed the mound and the cliff together,
Knowing full well that within it was lurking
A beast that the bloodhounds were now baying out.
The men beat the bushes and bellowed: "Come out!"
It ferociously lunged from the lair on attack—
One of the biggest boars you have ever seen!
It had wandered all alone because of its great age;   1440
And it was grim-looking and quite gigantic,
And ghastly when it grunted; the men soon groaned,
Because at that first thrust, it threw three to the ground,
Then sped away at full speed without further spite.
The men shouted "Hi!"; they yelled "Hey, hey!"
Holding horns to their mouths and recalling the hounds.
Many were the merry mouths of the men and the dogs
Who coursed along after this boar to catch it with cries
        To kill and fell.
The pig often stood at bay   1450
And maimed the pack pell-mell;
It hurt the hounds, and they
Very painfully yowl and yell.

13.

Archers fully armed stepped up then to aim at him,
Showered him with shafts that struck him repeatedly;
But the points couldn't penetrate his powerful shoulders,
And the barbs didn't take a bite away from his brows.
No, the soft-wooded arrows simply split into splinters,
And the arrowheads hopped away harmlessly after a hit.
But as the storm kept stinging him with fiery strokes,   1460
Raving wildly for revenge, he rushed at his tormentors
And gored them most grimly wherever he would go.
Most of them shivered, and then they slinked back.
But the lord on his lithe horse lunged after the boar,
Blowing his bugle like a man who is bent on battle.
He rallied the hounds, riding through the rough brushwood,
Pursuing that pig till the sun began to plummet.
All day long they engaged in activities of this kind
While our kindly courtier lay comfortably in bed:
Sir Gawain safely at home, swaddled in his   1470
        Wealthy gear.

The lady didn't forget
To bring him some morning cheer.
Bright and early she was up
To add spice to his career.

14.

She tiptoed over to his curtain and took a peek in.
Sir Gawain at once offered her a gracious greeting,
And she immediately embarked on another eager talk.
Sitting softly by his side and chuckling at the start,
She addressed him in this way with an amiable look: 1480
"Sir, I find it somewhat strange, since you indeed are Gawain,
A man always genuinely geared toward doing the good,
That you don't pursue the practices of polite society;
If somebody teaches you something, you seem to toss it away;
Certainly you've already let slide my lesson of yesterday,
Where I used the most masterful methods I could employ."
"How's that?" he asked; "indeed, I'm not quite aware of it.
But if what you tell me is true, the transgression's mine."
"I lectured you on kissing," said the lovely lady then;
"And to quickly claim a favor that's been clearly conferred.   1490
This is necessary for a knight concerned with nice behavior."
"My dear," said the dashing man, "do away with such talk.
I dare not ask for any favors, for fear I'd be refused.
If I were denied, I'd be all dismayed about my daring."
"Mercy!" said the merry wife, "but you may not *be* refused!
And you're large enough to latch on to whatever you like—
Provided some woman is plebeian enough to refuse you."
"By God, yes," answered Gawain, "your reasoning is good.
But force is not favored by the people where I come from—
And neither is a gift that is given without gladness.   1500
But I'm at your command, to kiss whenever you please;
You may take it when you want, and whenever you think best,
    Withdraw a pace."
The lady leaned over a bit
And gently brushed his face;
Much speech they then dispensed
About love's grief and grace.

15.

"I would like some wisdom," the worthy woman then said,
"Provided you aren't provoked, to learn about the practices

Of a young and energetic creature such as you are—   1510
As courteous and courageous as you're known to be.
In chivalric affairs, the chief thing that's well chosen
Is the game of love, the true lore of every lord;
For to speak of the striving of all stalwart knights,
Love is the title taken and text of their deeds:
Valiant lords have ventured their very lives for love
And endured for their dowry many doleful hours,
Then later won vengeance with their valor and voided their cares,
And brought bliss into their bower through love's bounty.
You are the knight of your age most known as accomplished;   1520
Your words and high worth are whispered about everywhere;
Yet I have sat by your side now for two whole sessions
And I haven't heard one single syllable slip from your lips
That mentions the art of love, neither more nor less.
Yet you, who are so fine and fastidious in your vows
Ought to be eager to educate some tender young thing
And teach her the tools of the trade of noble love.
Or are you, who are praised for ingenuity, ignorant?
Or maybe you think I'm too slow for your subtleties?
        For shame!   1530
I've come here alone to sit
And bask in your great fame;
Come! Teach me a little wit
While my husband's at his game."

16.
"In good faith," said Gawain, "may God take care of you!
Great is my enjoyment and gigantic my pleasure
To think that one as worthy as you are should come
And expend so much energy on a poor man like me; it encourages
Me that you dawdle away your time with a dull-wit like me;
But to take on the trouble of expounding true love   1540
And teach the terms of that text with its tales of arms
To you, who, I'm sure, have twice the knowledge
Of that art than I do or a hundred like me
Have now or ever will have, as long as I live—
That would be sheer stupidity, my lady, I swear!
I'll strive to satisfy your desires with all my strength,
Since I'm really devoted to you, and forever shall remain
A servant to your person, so save me our Creator!"
In this way the lady tried him and tested him often
To win him over to wooing—whatever else she wanted;   1550

But he put her off so politely there was no improper move
Or no evil expressed on either side. No, there was nothing
    But bliss.
They laughed and sported a long while,
And then she gave him a kiss;
Then she took her gracious leave
When the gentleman granted this.

17.

The hero then stirred and straggled down to his mass,
And next his supper was ready and was superbly served.
He amused himself all day long with the able lady,   1560
While her husband was hunting over the homeland turf,
Pursuing the ill-fated swine, which was sweeping the slopes,
Biting the backs of his finest beagles in two.
When the boar was at bay, the bowmen would break his stance
And, despite his persistence, force him to change position
As fierce arrows kept falling while a following gathered.
Still the swine often forced the stalwart into wavering,
Till finally he was so exhausted, he could escape no more.
Summoning what might he could muster, he managed to reach
A crevice in a cliff where a cold creek was flowing.   1570
He put the slope at his back and scraped the soil,
With froth foaming out of his fierce-looking mouth.
He whet his white tusks; this wait permitted the men,
Who were weary from wearing him down at a distance,
To enclose him in a crowd—yet no one had the courage
    To draw near;
He had hurt so many before
That all were filled with fear
Of being torn apart by those tusks;
He was savage and severe.   1580

18.

Then up swept the seigneur, spurring on his steed,
Spied the standing boar with his men spread in a circle.
He leapt down lightly from his courser's back
And, brandishing a blade, he boldly strode forward,
Wading right through the water to where the beast waited.
The wild one was aware of that weapon in his hand,
He heaved up his bristles and then he horribly snorted.
Many feared that the felon would gore their friend.

The swine then hurtled straight off toward his adversary,
So that baron and boar both fell in one big tumble   1590
In the wild-rushing water. And the boar got the worst.
The man hit the mark well at the shock of their meeting,
Plunging his sword in the soft slot over the breastplate
All the way down to the hilt. It split open the heart.
The snarling one snapped, then slipped away into the water
    Upon his back.
A hundred hounds splashed in,
Biting him blue and black;
Lads bore him then to the shore,
Where the dogs finished off the attack.   1600

19.

Then blasts were blown from several blaring horns;
There was a high hallooing as loud as they could make;
The bloodhounds bayed their best as they were bid
By the chief men who presided over the challenging chase.
Then a man who was wise in the ways of woodcraft
Began the skillful butchering of that boar.
First he sliced off the head and set it on a stake;
Then he slit the body roughly straight down the spine;
He scooped out the bowels and broiled them over the embers,
Blending them with breadcrumbs as a boon for his hounds.   1610
Then he carved some broad cuts away from the carcass,
Removing the entrails in a way that was just right;
Then he stitched the two sides securely together
And slung them over a strong and sturdy pole.
With the swine swinging, the men then started home.
The boar's head was borne in front of the baron
Who had felled him in that forest, using the force
    Of his strong hand.
Until he could reach Sir Gawain
The time seemed too long to stand;   1620
Crying hello, he rushed in,
His day's fee to demand.

20.

Loud with mirth and merry with laughter, the lord,
On seeing Sir Gawain, spoke very sincerely.
He gathered the great ladies and the servants together,
And he showed them his choice cuts and recounted his tale

Of the strength and the size and the savagery
Of the wild pig's struggle away off in those woods.
The courteous guest commended these acts as courageous
And proclaimed he had acted in a manner worthy of praise,   1630
Saying that never in his life had he ever laid eyes
On a beast that had such big and such brawny sides!
When the head was exhibited, the guest expressed his awe
At its huge proportions, and he further praised his host.
"Now, Gawain," said the good man, "the game is all yours
By our covenant fixed and fast, as you know for sure."
"That's God's truth," said the guest, "and you'll certainly get
All the wages I've won once more—upon my word!"
Then he grabbed the man's neck and graciously kissed him,
And very soon after he served him a second smack.   1640
"Now we're even," said the guest, "right up to this evening
By the agreement arranged when I arrived, with all respect
     To the law."
"By Saint Giles!" exclaimed the host;
"A finer man I never saw!
You'll shortly be a millionaire
If this is the pay you draw!"

21.

Then they tilted up the tables upon their trestles,
Which were covered with cloths, while candlelight flickered
Over the walls, which was cast by torches of wax.   1650
Men set down food and served all around the salon;
Gossip and glee could be found in every group
By the fire and across the floor, and before
And after supper there were many ceremonious songs,
Such as Christmas carols, as well as fresh chansons,
With all the well-mannered mirth a man could imagine,
And always our loyal knight lingered by the lady's side.
She kept glancing at her stalwart guest as if to suggest
That she wanted to please him in some sly, secret way,
So that he was quite agitated and angry within,   1660
But because of his breeding, he could never be boorish;
So he dealt with her delicately, even though this dallying
     Could go awry.
After that parrying in the hall,
The gaming hour passed by;
The lord summoned him to his chamber,
Where the flames were leaping high.

22.

There they dawdled and they drank and discussed once again
The continuance of their covenant till the New Year should come.
The guest regretted he'd have to say goodbye in the morning,   1670
Since the agreed-on hour for departing was approaching.
But the host wouldn't hear of it; he tried to hold him back,
Saying, "I swear on my word, I fully assure you
You'll arrive at the Chapel to carry out your chores,
My dear friend, on New Year's Day before dawning.
So loll around in your bed and enjoy your leisure
While I scour the countryside, keeping our contract,
And hand over whatever winnings I can carry home.
I have tested you twice and found you trustworthy.
But remember for tomorrow: the third time is the best!   1680
Let's be merry while we can and remember our pleasures,
For the losses may fall to us whenever they like."
Gawain graciously agreed to this, and so he stayed on.
Chalices were cheerfully filled, and then they climbed to bed
        By candlelight.
Sir Gawain lay and slept
Soft and sound all night;
While the lord, keeping to his craft,
Arose very early and bright.

23.

After mass he and his men took a very brief meal.   1690
The morning was magnificent as he mounted on his steed,
And the hunters who would go with him got on their horses,
Sitting tall in their saddles before the tower gates.
The fields were beautifully blanketed under a film of frost,
While the sun with ruddy streaks soared up through the cloud-puffs,
Then coasted with radiance along the cumulus crests.
The hunters unleashed their hounds alongside a thicket,
And the rocks around rang clear with the clarion cries.
Some hit on the scent that was left by the hiding fox;
They pursue a tortuous track that tests their wiles.   1700
A small dog was yelping, and his master yelled after;
All sniffing, the fellow hounds now followed his lead.
They rushed in a rabble, having found the right track.
The fox flashed before them; they dashed after him fast;
Once they perceive him, they pursue all the harder,
Cursing at him cruelly with crass indignation.
He twisted and turned through the tangle of thickets,

Hurtling backward to hear alongside the hedgerows.
At last, at the side of a little ditch, he leapt over a fence,
Then stole out stealthily inside a small copse,   1710
Half-outwitting by his wiles those pursuers in the woods.
But he wandered, unaware, right into a pack of whelps,
And three in one throw thrust themselves upon him
    In their coats of grey.
He swerved again most swiftly
And unfailingly got away;
To the woods he ran a-racing,
Filled with woe and with dismay.

24.

What a heavenly thing it was to hear those hounds,
As the whole pack picked up his scent and pursued again!   1720
Such swears the men growled whenever they got a glimpse of him,
As if the clambering cliffs would come crashing down!
The hunters hollered "Halloo!" whenever they met him,
Loudly haranguing him with their howls of scorn;
They threatened him dourly; they dubbed him a thief;
They tailed him continuously, not allowing any tarrying;
They hounded him endlessly, till he headed for the open,
And then he reeled back again, for Reynard has his ruses.
He led them every which-way, that lord and his lieges,
Over hill and hollow till half the afternoon was gone.   1730
Meanwhile our hero at home was wholesomely sleeping
Inside his cozy curtains throughout that cold morning.
But because of love, the lady was unable to languish
Or control the purpose that kept pricking her heart,
And so she got up early, and she went to see him
In a gorgeous gown that swished along the ground
And was lined with pieces of the most precious pelts.
She wore no hood on her head, and yet her hairnet
Was set with rich stones in sections of twenty;
Her enchanting face and throat were entirely exposed,   1740
And her breasts and her back were also remarkably bare.
She slipped through the door and closed it very softly,
Swinging open a window and suddenly addressing the sleeper,
Rebuking him roundly with her regal-sounding words
    And cheer:
"What, sir! How can you sleep
While the morning shines so clear?"
He still drooped deep in slumber,

But every word he could hear.

25.

From the depths of darkened dreams the hero mumbled,   1750
Like one who is gripped by many grievous thoughts:
How destiny would deal him his fate the very next day
At that meeting-place where he would face his match
And have to suffer a swipe with no forswearing;
But as the queenly one came there, he collected his wits,
Swept free of his slumber and swiftly said hello.
The lovely lady swished toward him, laughing sweetly,
Leaned over his handsome face and kissed him lovingly.
He spoke in a friendly way, presenting his finest face.
To him she seemed so gorgeous, so gloriously attired,   1760
So faultless in her features and fair complexion
That a warm joy came welling up within him.
With merry and subtle smiles, they melted in mirth,
And all was bliss and bonhomie that passed between them—
        Full of delight.
They bandied some delicate words
Replete with sweetness and light;
Yet a peril was lurking around them—
Unless Mary took care of her knight!

26.

Because that prized princess was pressing him so far,   1770
Almost to the edge of the hem, it was now essential
To either embrace her love or emphatically deny it.
He was concerned with courtesy, not wanting to be callous,
And even more with sinning or misbehaving, with standing
As traitor to the man who controlled that territory.
"God help me," he vowed, "but that shall never happen!"
With cheerful chuckles, he was able then to check
All those splendid phrases that kept springing from her lips.
For example, she said, "I feel that you deserve censure
If you don't love the lady whom you're lying next to,   1780
Who's more wounded than any other woman in the whole world.
But if you have a lover already—some lass you like better—
And are faithful to that girl and fastened to her so firmly
That you don't want to be loosed—then I'll believe you.
If that's the case, then tell it to me please, I beg you.

In the name of all human love, don't keep hiding the truth
    With guile."
"By St. John," replied the knight
With a very genial smile,
"Right now I don't love a soul,   1790
And I won't for quite a while."

27.

"Ah, *those* words," she answered, "are the wickedest of all!
But your retort is truthful—this I painfully think.
Now just kiss me once sweetly, and I'll steal away,
Lamenting my fate like some lovelorn maiden."
With a sigh, she swooped over and kissed him quite suavely,
Then severing quickly, she said as she stood up,
"Now, precious, please grant me a favor on parting.
Please offer me a little gift—a glove, if you have one—
For memory's sake, my sweet man, to lessen my sorrow."   1800
"Ah, indeed," sighed the hero, "I wish that I had here
The loveliest thing on the earth to offer your love,
For in all sincerity, you have surely deserved
A far greater reward than I can rightly grant.
But to hand you some token that's only a trifle
Would not be to render you a reward that's right—
A mere glove as a show of Sir Gawain's generosity!
Besides, I'm on errand in these strange parts of the earth,
Having no servants with sacks full of civilized presents;
I'm deeply sorry, sweet lady, for your sake right now.   1810
Every person must do what he can. Please don't take it poorly
    And pine."
"Heavens no, my honored guest,"
Said that lady fair and fine,
"But if I can't have a keepsake of yours,
At least you'll have one of mine!"

28.

She held out a ring that was made of reddish gold,
With a sparkling stone that shone high on the band,
Casting brilliant beams resembling the blazing sun.
And you can rest fully assured it was worth a fortune.   1820
But the baron drew back very brusquely, saying,
"For God's sake, good woman, no gifts at this juncture!

I don't have any to offer, and so I can't take any."
She extended it more eagerly; he eluded her offer,
Swearing on his oath that he simply couldn't accept it.
Rueful about his rejection, she very quickly rejoined,
"If you won't take my ring because it's too rich,
And you rebel against being beholden to me,
Then I'll give you my girdle—a much humbler gift."
She loosened a sash that was lightly locked around her,   1830
Circling her waist underneath her shiny chemise;
It was sewn out of green silk with stitchings of gold,
Embroidered around the edges by the most expert hands.
This she offered the hero, earnestly exhorting him
To take it if he would, insignificant as it might be.
But he kept refusing—he could in no way receive
Keepsakes or gold until God sent him grace
To accomplish the act that he was attempting there:
"So therefore, I beg you, without any further bother,
Let's ignore this whole idea; it's a thing that I can't   1840
    Grant you.
I am dearly beholden to your grace
For all the things you do,
And I promise through thick and thin
To remain your servant true."

29.
"Now, is this silk unsatisfactory," the lady asked,
"Because it is so simple? Or so it seems to you?
Well! It's a paltry thing, not appearing very precious,
But if you were aware of the worth contained within it,
You'd place a much higher price on it, I suspect;   1850
For whoever is girded by this green-colored sash
And wears it tightly wrapped around his waist,
No creature under the heavens may cut him down,
And he can't be killed by any earthly cunning."
This made the knight think; the thought sprang to mind
That here was a magic gem against the jeopardy ahead
When he'd arrive at the Chapel to challenge a checkmate.
If he could escape intact, this trick would not be ignoble!
He acquiesced to her alluring, allowing her to speak,
And she beckoned with the belt, begging him to take it.   1860
He surrendered; and so she handed it to him swiftly,
Urging him for her sake to keep the matter secret,
To conceal it carefully from her lord; Gawain concurred:

Except for the two, no human would ever have it
    In his sight.
He thanked her most emphatically,
With all his heart and might;
After that for three straight times
She kissed that stalwart knight.

30.

Then she asked for her leave, and she left him there,   1870
Knowing that there was no more enjoyment to be had from him.
When she had departed, Gawain quickly got dressed,
Putting on some garments that looked grand indeed,
But laying aside the love-token the lady had left for him;
He concealed it carefully where he could find it later.
Then he went very quickly on his way to the chapel,
Where he privately approached a priest and asked him
To listen to his confession and to lend him some learning
About saving his soul when he should abandon this earth.
Then he confessed sincerely, revealing his sins,   1880
Both major and minor, and, begging for mercy,
He prayed to the priest to purify them all.
The cleric absolved him and cleansed him so completely
That the Day of Doom might have dawned the next morning.
Then he went and enjoyed himself with the elegant ladies,
With singing and dancing and every sort of sweetness
On into the darkness, with a delight he'd never known
    Before that day.
All the courtiers were amused
By Gawain; they were heard to say,   1890
"Ah, he was never so happy
As he has been on this day!"

31.

Now let's leave him at his idyll with love all around him.
The lord of that land was still leading on his men,
And had overtaken that fox he had followed so ferociously.
As he darted over a hedge on the track of that dodger,
And heard the hounds bearing down heatedly on the prey,
He saw Reynard come running out of a rugged thicket,
And all of that rabble were riotously hot on his heels.
The baron, aware of the wild one, craftily waited,   1900
Then flashed out his shiny sword and skillfully struck.

The fox flinched away from the blade and would have fled,
But before he could bolt, a hound came bounding after him,
And right in front of the horses' feet, the pack fell on him,
Attacking the wily one with a wild-sounding roar!
The lord swooped in swiftly and scooped him up,
Saving him for a second from those savage jaws;
He held him over his head and called loud halloos
Over the howling chorus of those ravening hounds.
Hunters hastened there with blares of their horns,   1910
Sounding the recall until they reached their master.
As this courtly company were all convening together,
They blared on the bugles that they were bearing at once,
While the hunters without any horns merely shouted halloos.
It was the merriest melody that a man ever heard—
The riotous racket that was raised for Reynard's soul
        With royal notes!
The men reward their hounds then;
They fondle them and they dote;
And then they take old Reynard   1920
And off they strip his coat.

32.

Then finally they hurried homeward, for the night was hovering,
Blowing boisterously upon their blaring horns.
At last the lord leaped down at his much-loved home,
Finding flames in the fireplace inside, his guest beside it,
Gawain the good, who was glad-hearted in every way,
Enjoying the entertainment of the elegant ladies!
He was wearing a robe of blue that brushed the ground,
And his surcoat with its soft fur lining suited him well,
While a hood of similar stuff hung over his shoulders;   1930
Both had borders that were embroidered with bright ermine.
Gawain went over and met his host in the middle of the hall,
And good-heartedly he greeted him, saying graciously,
"Let me first carry out the main clause of the covenant
That we've already agreed on and drunk to as well."
Then he hugged his host, kissing him three whole times,
As energetically and as earnestly as he had ever done.
"By Christ," said his companion, "you've been quite successful
In conducting your business if you won a bargain like that!"
"Yes, but let's forget the terms," retorted the traveler,   1940
"Since I've openly repaid you the whole debt that I owed."
"Mary!" said the other man, "I'm missing all your luck,

Since I've been out chasing all day and all I've achieved
Is this foul little fox-fur—may the Fiend take it!
Now that's a paltry repayment for the precious things
You've so kindly conferred on me—those three kisses
    That are sweet and good."
"Enough!" replied Sir Gawain.
"I thank you by the Holy Wood!"
Then the baron explained to all   1950
How the fox was dispatched for good.

33.

With music and amusements and all the meat one required,
They carried on as contentedly as any human can;
With the laughter of ladies and great lightheartedness,
Gawain and his goodly host both acted very gleeful.
Unless some bore in the crowd was besotted or boorish.
Both the master and his minions cracked many a joke
Till the hour arrived for their saying adieu,
And it was finally the best thing to be off to bed.
Then the hero quite humbly begged leave of his host,   1960
The first to give him fond thanks for all of the fun:
"May the Good Lord repay you for all of the pleasures
I've enjoyed here during your genial holiday feast!
I'll count myself one of your court, if you choose,
But tomorrow morning, as you know, I have to move on;
So please lend me some servant who can show me the way,
As you agreed, to the Green Chapel, where God demands
That I suffer on the First the fulfillment of my fate."
"In good faith," said the gentleman, "very gladly
I'll provide you with whatever I promised in the past."   1970
Then he assigned him a servant to set him on the road
And conduct him through the downs to avoid all delay
In ferreting through the forest, so he could arrive favorably
    At the appointed site.
Gawain thanked his host
With all the respect that was right;
And then to the ladies fair
He uttered a fond good-night.

34.

He spoke then with sincerity and offered sad kisses,
Wishing them all his warmest, most well-meaning thanks;   1980

They willingly replied that they all wished him the same,
Recommending him to Christ with great sighs of care.
Then he politely separated himself from the party,
Extending his thanks to all the people he encountered
For their service and solace and the separate pains
They had taken in trying to comfort him by their care.
Every serving-person was sorry for his separation,
As if they had lived with this lord their whole lives through.
Then the lads with their lights led him up to his chamber,
Guiding him to his bed for a good night's sleep.   1990
I won't venture to vouch for a sound sleep or a vexed one,
For he had much to mull over concerning the morning, if he
     Gave it any thought.
So let him lie quietly there,
Close to what he has sought,
And if you'll just be patient,
I'll tell you what daybreak brought.

Part Four

1.
Now the New Year draws near, and the night passes on
As the day drives away the dark as the Deity commands.
But wild weather had wakened and raged through the world;   2000
Clouds cast their cold drops down upon the earth,
As bitterness from the north bit whatever lay bare.
The snow fell ferociously, flailing wild creatures;
A blustery blizzard blew down out of the heights
And drove up mountainous snowdrifts in every dale.
Our hero listened to all this as he lay in his bed,
And, though his lids were locked, he slept very little,
Counting away the hours by every crow of the cock.
He got dressed very deftly before the daylight broke,
Since a lamp had been left for him to light his chamber.   2010
He summoned his manservant, who swiftly answered,
Asking him for his armor and his riding apparel.
The man got moving and produced his many garments,
Outfitting Gawain in a fashion that was fitting.
First he wrapped him in underclothes to ward off the cold,
Then his other equipment, all cleaned and cared for,
Then his pauncer and breastplate, polished all clean,
With the rust removed from the rich rings of mail.

Everything was as fresh as at first, and he was grateful,
    Of course.   2020
The man had shined up every piece
Without neglect or remorse
To make it the best from here to Greece;
Then Gawain called for his horse.

2.

While he dressed himself in his most dapper clothing—
His coat with its crest showing the finest craft
Sewn over velvet, with stones of great virtue
Bound and embroidered to the seams and the borders,
With a fine fur lining inside with fancy pelts—
He did not let slip the sash, the lady's souvenir.   2030
No, Gawain did not omit it because of his own good.
After he had circled his strong hips with his sword-belt,
He wrapped her reminder doubly around his waist,
Swiftly and spryly encircling his central part
With the girdle of green that neatly suited that gay one
Over his rich-looking and royal clothing of red.
But he wasn't garbed in the girdle because of its gaudiness,
Or out of pride for its pendants, which were neatly polished,
With glittering gold gleaming at the ends of their tips—
No, he did this to save himself when the time came to suffer   2040
A malicious swipe without any answer of sword
    Or knife.
And so the bold man, dressed,
Descended to the castle life,
And to all that famous household
His gratitude ran rife.

3.

Gringolet, great and huge, was standing all geared up
After his long stabling in a safe and suitable way.
He was prancing in healthy pride, that powerful horse,
While his master stepped up and inspected his sleek coat,   2050
Saying most soberly and swearing on his oath,
"Now here's a staff that understands what is civilized!
Their man maintains them well—may he joyously thrive
And may his adorable lady enjoy love all her life!
If they cherish their guests with such Christian charity
And govern so generously, may the Good Protector above
Treat them this way too—and the same thing to you all!

And if I live my life for a good while longer,
I'll rightly repay you some reward if I can!"
Then he stepped into his stirrups and sat on high.   2060
His servant handed him his shield, which he slung over his shoulder.
He goaded Gringolet onward with his gilded heels,
And the steed sprang over the stones, no longer content
    To prance.
The master rode on his horse,
Holding his spear and his lance:
"I commend this castle to Christ!
May He keep it from mischance!"

4.

The drawbridge was let down, and the doors of the gates
Were unbolted and unbarred; they both were gaping open.   2070
The hero blessed himself quickly and hurried across the boards,
Praising the porter, who was praying on his knees
That God would protect Gawain and send him a good day.
Then the hero went on his way with his one assistant,
Who had to direct him toward his terrible destination,
Where he would have to suffer that very serious stroke.
They rode along by some banks where the boughs were all bare;
They climbed over cliffs where the cold was closely clinging.
The heavens were holding back, but the low haze was ugly.
Mist swarmed over the moors, then merged with the mountains.   2080
Every hill wore a hat, and a hanging mantle of haze.
Brooks boiled up and then broke free from their banks,
Spattering spume against the slopes before cascading.
The road they took through the woods was weaving along at random,
And soon it was time for the sun in that wintry season
    To rise.
They were riding on a high ridge
With snow all before their eyes.
The man who was guiding Gawain
Said, "It's time now for goodbyes.   2090

5.

"I've guided you this far, Gawain, up to this point,
And now you're not very far from that fabulous spot
That you've asked about and sought with special care;
And I'll tell you sincerely, since I now know you somewhat,
And you're a man whom I admire most assuredly,

If you follow my words, things will work out well for you:
The place you're approaching is indeed very perilous.
A wild man inhabits that waste—the worst in the world.
He is savage and strong and loves to swoop down upon you,
And is mightier than any man on this massive earth.   2100
His physique's more formidable than the finest four
In Arthur's house or in Troy or anywhere else.
He governs the games down at his Green Chapel,
A place that nobody passes scot-free on parade
Without being dashed to death by a dent from his hand.
He's a man who acknowledges no mercy or no mean.
If either a chaplain or a churl rides by his chapel,
A monk or a mass-priest or any other mortal,
He'll wipe him out as easily as he'd just walk away.
And so I say, as surely as you sit in that saddle,   2110
If you keep going, you'll be killed by this creature's whim.
That you can trust, even if you had twenty lives
    To dispense.
He has lived here a long, long time
On a field full of violence,
And against his bitter blows
There is never any defense.

6.

"Therefore, good Sir Gawain, let this ogre go!
Ride on some other route, in the Redeemer's name!
Travel through some other turf, where Christ will take care of you,   2120
And I shall hurry home, but I promise you right here
That I shall swear by God and all of his sacred saints,
By the Lord Himself and his holy realm and a hundred oaths
That I'll truly watch over you and never whisper a word
That you ever wanted to run from anyone I know of."
"A great many thanks," answered Gawain, adding grouchily,
"I wish you luck, sir, since you're worried about my welfare,
And I sincerely believe you'd support me if I escaped.
But even if you kept that secret, and I got away safely,
Fleeing out of fear in the fashion you just mentioned,   2130
I'd be a crass-hearted coward and could never be excused.
No! I'm on my way to the Chapel, whatever chance lets fall;
And I'll tell your cherished monster whatever I choose,
Whether Destiny decides to deal me my destruction
    Or to save.

Your man may have a mighty club
That makes him an awesome knave,
But Our Master is good at shaping
Salvation for the brave!"

7.
"Mary," said the other man, "you've made it very clear   2140
That you're intent on dealing destruction for yourself.
Well, if you want to lose your life, I have to let you.
Have here a helmet for your head and a spear for your hand,
And just ride down this road past that rocky slope there,
And you'll come at last to the bottom of the broad vale below.
Then look around a little, and on your left side
You'll spy that very same chapel you've been searching for,
As well as the massive master who maintains it.
Now, on behalf of God—goodbye, my noble Gawain!
I wouldn't go on with you for all of the gold in the ground.   2150
Not one step further will I take in this forest as your friend!"
With that, the guide bent his horse's bridle backward,
Hitting his horse with his heels as hard as he could,
And it leapt with a sudden lunge, leaving our hero
     All alone.
"For God's sake," said Sir Gawain,
"I'm not going to weep or moan.
To God's will I'm obedient,
For I call myself His own."

8.
Then he goaded Gringolet, going onward down the road,   2160
Skirting the stony slopes along the sheer sides,
Riding over rugged ridges that reached down to the dale.
There he carefully eyed the environs and found them eerie.
There was no sign of civilization on any side—
Just slopes that were slanting up steeply everywhere
With roughly crenellated crags bearing ragged rocks;
It seemed to him that their stones scraped against the sky.
Then he hove in his reins, holding his horse back,
And shifted his eyes, searching for the sanctuary.
Strangely to say, he could see nothing on any side   2170
Except a little nob on the land, like a knoll,
A bulge that was swelling slightly on the bank of a brook,

Where a freshet was flowing freely in its furrow,
Bubbling as if it was boiling upon its bed.
The knight nudged his steed forward, approaching the knoll.
Then he leaped down lightly and attached to a linden's
Ragged branches the reins of his royal steed.
Next he meandered over to the mound and moved slowly around it,
Mulling over in his mind exactly what it might mean.
It had one hole at one end, and there was one at the other.   2180
It was overgrown with globs of grass everywhere;
It was concave and hollow within—just some old cavern
Or a crevice in a crag—he couldn't really be
    Very clear.
"Whew, Lord!" said the gentle knight,
"This might be the Chapel, I fear.
The Devil along about midnight
Might mumble his matins here."

9.

"Dear God!" muttered Sir Gawain, "but this place is grim!
This is an ugly oratory, all overrun with weeds!   2190
It's perfect for that weird person who appears all green
To deal out his devotions in the Devil's camp.
Now I'm confident in my five senses that it's the Fiend
Who arranged this appointment for my undoing here!
It's the Chapel of Bad Chance—may a checkmate fall to it!
It's the most cursed cathedral that I've ever come upon!"
With his helmet on his head and a lance in his hand,
He clambered up on the dome of that dismal edifice.
Then from that hillock he could hear, from behind a rock
On the bank beyond the brook, a barbaric sound: 2200
Whzzz! it echoed against the cliff as if to cleave it—
The sound of somebody grinding a scythe at a grindstone.
Whzzz! it whirred and it whirled like water over a mill.
Whzzz! it scraped and it scratched, offensive to the ear.
"By God," exclaimed Gawain, "these goings-on, I believe,
Are arranged, my dear friend, as a very royal reception
    For me!
Ah, well. Let God's will be done!
No good to act cowardly.
I may lose my life, but still   2210
No noise will make me flee."

10.

Then the knight started to shout out very stridently:
"Who's the agent who arranges the appointments here?
Gawain the gallant has now arrived on your ground!
If anyone wants a word with him, let him appear
Either now or never, and say what he will need."
"Wait awhile," said someone above from the other shore,
"And you'll get very promptly everything that I promised!"
That person didn't stop his scraping for a single second,
But kept whetting and whirring on for a little while;   2220
Then around a rock and out of a burrow he rambled,
Hurtling from his hiding-place with his hideous weapon—
A Danish ax, all neatly honed and ready for an attack,
With a broad-cutting blade that was bent upon the shaft,
Filed by a sharpener, about a good four feet wide
And no less, as you could tell by the lace at its haft.
The strange apparition was appareled in green as at first,
His face and his legs and his locks and his beard,
Except that he now loped along on his own two legs,
Using the shaft as a staff, as it swung at his side.   2230
When he came to the water, he did not want to wade,
And so he hopped over on his ax, then haughtily strode forward,
Looking fierce and grim, onto the field that was filled
      With snow.
Gawain the knight stepped down to meet him,
In no way bending low;
The green one said, "My dear sweet sir,
You have come where you said you'd go."

11.

"Gawain," said the green one, "may God protect you!
Indeed, you are welcome, my man, to my mansion.   2240
And you've timed your travel as a true fellow should,
Acknowledging the agreement arranged between us.
Twelve months ago at this time you took what fell to you,
And promptly on this New Year I'm prepared to repay.
We're all alone in this valley, I assure you;
Not a soul here to separate us from our happy sport.
So take that helmet off your head and have your pay.
Don't try to dicker around any more than I did
When you swiped off my head with a single stroke."
"No, by God," said Gawain, "who granted me my life,   2250
I won't begrudge you a grain for any grief that follows.

But steady yourself to strike, and I'll stand still,
Offering no obstruction to your operation
    In any way."
He bared his neck and bent it,
Pulling his clothes away,
Resolved not to let his fear
At any point hold sway.

12.

Then the man in the green got himself quickly ready,
Lifting his loathsome tool to strike Lord Gawain.   2260
With all the brute force in his body, he bore it up,
As if he meant to maim the hero mercilessly.
If he'd driven it downward as direly as he threatened,
That priceless prince would have perished from the blow.
Gawain glanced up at that gruesome thing that hovered,
And as it started its swoop to split him in two,
His shoulders shrank back from the razor-sharp iron.
With a sudden swerve, his adversary checked his stroke,
Reproaching the prince with some very pompous words:
"You're certainly not Gawain, who's considered so gallant,   2270
And who never feared any fighter either far or wide.
Why, you're flinching out of fear for a harm you only fancy!
I never heard that this hero had such a faint heart!
I didn't flinch or fail when you aimed at me, friend.
I offered you no obstruction in King Arthur's house.
My head flew to the floor, yet I never once faltered.
But before you're hurt, you show you have a cowardly heart.
And so I claim that I'll have to be called the superior knight
    On every score."
Gawain replied, "I did flinch once,   2280
But I won't flinch any more.
Yet if *my* head hits the stones,
It will be hard to restore."

13.

"But be brisk in your business, man; bring this to a head!
Deal out my destiny and do it right away!
I'll suffer your stroke without any further shudder
Till the ax-head hits me; here now is my pledge."
"Get ready then," replied the other, raising his tool
And appearing as angry as if he were half-mad.

He started to swing wildly—yet grazed no skin,   2290
Withholding his heave before it could bring any harm.
Gawain suffered it stoically, not swerving an inch,
Standing as still as a stone or like a stump
That is anchored in the rocky soil by a hundred roots.
Then the man in the green was mocking him merrily:
"Now that you've got your heart again, I can hit you.
Show me some of that chivalry that Arthur showered on you,
And recover your neck from this cut now if you can!"
Gawain very acidly answered him with anger:
 "Come on, brave one, strike! You're bragging much too long!   2300
I suspect somehow that your spirit is cringing inside!"
"Ah, so," said the other, "you're talking so sordidly now
That more mincing on your mission is a thing
     I can't allow."
He moved as if to strike,
Twisting both lips and brow;
No wonder if Gawain was grieving,
Since there was no rescue now!

14.
He lifts his ax lightly and then allows it to fall,
With the barb on the blade just grazing the bare neck;   2310
Though he hammers down hard, he inflicts no harm,
Just nicking one side and lightly slicing the skin.
But as the blade brushes against the bright flesh on the neck,
Some scarlet blood spurts downward onto the soil.
When Sir Gawain sees his stains of blood on the snow,
He springs with a sudden leap the length of a spear,
Hastily grabbing his helmet and covering his head.
He swings his shield around from behind his shoulders,
Brandishes his bright sword and speaks up very bravely
(Never since he was a baby born to his mother   2320
Has he been so wholly happy in all this world!):
"Stop blustering, my baron; don't bother me any more!
I've suffered your swing without showing any resistance,
But if you molest me once more, I'll meet you headlong
And fiercely pay back—I promise—with promptness
     Every blow.
I agreed to a single stroke;
The covenant said so
That we formed in Arthur's halls.
Now away, my friend! Yes, go!"   2330

15.

The regal one relaxed, resting upon his ax-blade,
Leaning on the sharp part, with the haft set upon the soil,
And studying the man who was standing there before him.
He observed how that stalwart one stood there unshivering,
Armed and unawed, and he found it very admirable.
Then he spoke sympathetically in a rather stentorian voice,
Addressing that aristocrat with far-echoing words:
"Don't frown so fiercely, my fellow, here on this field.
No man misbehaved here or was unmannerly toward you.
I just carried out the clauses we set at the king's court.   2340
I promised a stroke, which you got; consider yourself paid.
I release you now from all of the rest of my rights.
If I'd been busier, I could have given you a buffet
That was far more aggressive and made you more angry!
My first blow was simply a feint that I made for fun
And caused you no deep cut; I simply carried out
That agreement that we arranged that original evening.
You have truly and trustily maintained your troth,
Giving me all that you gained, like a very good man.
The second feint, my friend, I fashioned for the morning   2350
When you kissed my charming wife—but counted back those kisses.
For those two fond acts I offered you two feints
    Without any mishap.
One true man is true to another
And needs never fear any trap.
But you failed at my third testing
And therefore took my tap.

16.

"It's all because of my beautiful girdle you're bearing,
Which my own wife formed—I know this for a fact;
For I'm conscious of your kisses and other conduct,   2360
Playing games with my spouse. I was the planner myself.
I sent her to tempt you, and truly I've come to think
You're one of the finest fellows to set foot on the earth:
A pearl more precious than any simple white pea
Is our Sir Gawain, by God, next to other gallants.
But you have a small flaw, my friend: you lack some faithfulness.
It didn't arise for an artful object or amorous fling—
No! You just loved your life! And I blame you the less for it."
The other stern knight stood there studiously for a while,
Shuddering inside himself with a shameful rage.   2370

The blood in his body blushed upward into his cheeks,
And he shrank back shamefaced from what was being shown.
The first words then that the fair-haired knight let fly
Were "Curses on cowardice and a covetous heart!
For in that way villainy and vice destroy all virtue."
Then he grasped at his girdle and roughly grabbed it free,
Flinging it frantically over to that foe himself:
"There! That's for falsehood! May it meet a foul fate!
I cringed at your cuts, and my cowardice induced me
To make an accord with avarice, abandoning my nature,   2380
Which always leaned toward loyalty and knightly largess.
Now I'm false and flawed, I who always was fearful
Of treachery and lack of truth; may sorrow overtake them,
     As well as care.
I confess to you, my dear knight,
The wrongs I committed there,
But let me regain your good will,
And from now on, I'll beware."

17.

Then the other party laughed, proclaiming politely,
"Any wrong that you wreaked I now consider repaid.   2390
You've confessed very freely, acknowledging your flaws,
And you've performed your penance at the point of my sword.
I consider you cleansed of your sins, as immaculate
As if you'd never fallen since your very first day;
And I give you, kind sir, this golden-hemmed girdle
Which is as green as my gown, Gawain, so that you may
Meditate on this meeting whenever you move
Among rulers of renown—this is a fine remembrance
Of our affair at this abbey for other adventurous knights.
But come again in this New Year, come back to my castle,   2400
Where for the rest of this rich holiday you can revel
     In a glorious show."
The lord invited him thus,
Saying, "My wife, I know,
Will welcome you most warmly,
Though she was your bitter foe."

18.

"No, I'm sorry," said Sir Gawain, seizing his helmet
And holding it in his hands while he thanked his host;

"I've lingered here far too long; I hope you enjoy good luck
From God, who governs all men with magnanimous grace!   2410
And give my goodbye to your gentle, gracious lady,
And that other aged one, her most honored confidante,
For they cunningly waylaid this warrior with their wiles.
But it's no great wonder whenever a woman outwits
A man and leads him away to mourning or to madness,
For Adam himself was led astray by a woman,
And Solomon by several, and so too was Samson
(Who was doomed by Delilah), not to mention David,
Who was blinded by Bathsheba and suffered a bitter fate.
These were all laid low by women's lies. What great luck   2420
If a lord could simply love them and not believe them!
These former men were the finest who ever followed
The leisurely fates of lovers or lived under heavenly
    Skies of blue.
Yet they were all beguiled
By the women whom they knew;
And if I have been defiled,
Let me be forgiven too.

19.
"But may God repay you for your girdle!" said Sir Gawain.
"I'll wear it with good will—not for its genuine gold   2430
Or the silk in its sewing or the pendants at its side;
Not for its wealth or worthiness or elegant weaving—
But as a sign of my excess, I shall survey it often
Whenever I ride with renown, rehearsing to myself
The frailties and faults of this fickle flesh,
How it eagerly embraces every taint of corruption.
And so whenever pride propels me toward prowess in arms,
One look at this love-token will make my heart feel lowly.
But one thing I beg you, if it doesn't bother you:
Since you're the lord of this land where you have lodged me   2440
Beside you in perfect pleasure—may God repay you
From heaven and the heights where He upholds His throne—
What is your right name? The rest I will ignore."
"Then I'll tell you that truly," said the other there:
"Bertilak de Hautdesert is the name I have around here.
The mighty Morgan the Fay, who lives on my manor,
Whose mastery of magic is manipulated with craft,
Learned to a large degree from the lore of great Merlin—
For indeed she had a long and a lasting love

With that crafty wizard, who is known to your country's knights   2450
    As one of fame;
Therefore Morgan the Goddess
Rightly is her name;
Nobody's so wild against her
That she can't make him tame—

20.

"Well, she guided me in this disguise to your gay halls,
So that I could see if you were all as superb and splendid
As the fame of the Round Table runs with renown.
She produced this paradox in order to puzzle and perplex you,
And to goad poor Guinevere halfway to her grave   2460
As she gaped while I spoke in my most ghastly manner
From the head that I held in my hands right out before her!
She is actually resting at home, that aged lady,
And she's truly your aunt, being Arthur's half-sister,
The daughter of the Duchess of Tintagel, by whom
Uther fathered Arthur, your great ancestral lord.
Now I ask you, dear sir, to come back and see your aunt,
And be merry in my house; my serving-men adore you,
And I wish you well too with all truth, dear sir,
As do all who inhabit God's earth—for your integrity."   2470
But Gawain said no—in no way would he go back.
So, embracing and kissing, they commended each other
To the Prince of Paradise, and they parted right there
    In the cold.
Gawain rides away rapidly
To the fort of Arthur bold,
While the gent in inky green
Slips off to a place untold.

21.

Now Gawain wandered the wild highways of the world
On Gringolet, having regained the grace of life;   2480
Often he accepted lodgings in houses, or slept outside,
And was a victor in many adventures in many vales,
Though I don't have the time to tell them in this tale.
The nick that he had on his neck had healed like new
And he bore his brilliant belt about his body
Obliquely like a baldric that was bound at his side,
Locked under his left arm and laced tightly with a knot

To show that he had slipped badly in some misdeed.
And this way he came to the court, completely sound,
Arousing great revelry when the royal Arthur heard   2490
That Gawain the good was safely home; he considered it grand.
Then the king kissed the knight, as did the queen,
And many a staunch fellow stepped up to salute him,
Asking about his adventures; he answered fascinatingly,
Documenting the dangerous discomforts he'd endured,
The chance he took at the Chapel with its chaplain,
The loving acts of the lady, and lastly her lace.
He exposed for them the nick on his neck all naked,
Which he carried for those connivings that had corrupted
      His fame.   2500
He was troubled when he told this,
Groaning grievously for his blame;
The blood suffused his cheeks
When he showed his mark of shame.

22.
"Look, my lord," said Sir Gawain, fingering the lace,
"This band symbolizes the blame I bear on my neck;
It signifies the sorrowful loss that I have suffered,
Caught by cowardice and covetousness there;
It is a token of the untruthfulness that trapped me,
And I have to wear it for as long as I may live;   2510
For a man can hide his hurt, but never hurl it away,
Since once it is attached, it will not disappear."
The king comforted the knight, and all of the court—
Those lords and ladies who were loyal to the Table—
Laughed loudly at him; very lovingly they agreed
That every member of their brotherhood should wear a baldric,
A slanted belt about him of burnished green,
Out of sympathy for the sake of their sweet friend.
And so the renown of the Round Table was recorded
In this way, and heroes were honored who wore the belt,   2520
As is recounted in the choicest books of romance.
And in this way in Arthur's day this adventure occurred,
As the books about Felix Brutus all bear witness,
That bold baron who, as I've said, established Britain
After the siege and the assault had ceased among
      The Trojan men.
Many adventures of this kind
Have happened long since then.

May He who wore the crown of thorns
Bring us to His bliss. AMEN!   2530

Chapter XVII

THE WEDDING OF SIR GAWAIN AND DAME RAGNELL

JAMES J. WILHELM

This amusing romance, written about 1450 at the end of the Middle Ages, treats the Loathly Lady theme that medieval readers know well from Geoffrey Chaucer's *Wife of Bath's Tale*. In essence, this familiar folklore motif concerns the transformation of an ugly hag into a beautiful woman after a man has placed himself under her "sovereynté" (sovereignty, power). To this is added the theme of A Riddle Asked and Answered; both here and in Chaucer, the riddle asks what women most desire. In both cases, the answer is that very same sovereignty that transforms the harridan into a lady of beauty and grace. In Chaucer, the tale is didactic, enforcing the Wife of Bath's own selfish desires and dreams of wish fulfillment; here, without the Wife as a narrator, the tale has a whimsical charm that makes it one of the most delightful of Middle English romances.

Peculiarly enough, the story does not end on a humorous note. At line 841 the otherwise unidentified narrator suddenly steps out of his creation and informs the reader that he is "besett withe gaylours" (beset with jailers), and he ends by praying for deliverance. This is like *Le Morte Darthur*, where Malory in his ending indicates that he too is a prisoner who dreams about being liberated from his inhibiting earthly condition. Both Malory and the anonymous author here are thus like the enchanted Loathly Lady, hoping for some miracle to transform them into creatures of happiness.

The dialect of the poem is East Midland, and is easy to read with a few simple transformations. The scribe frequently uses *y* for *i* ("lyf" for "life," "wyf" for "wife") and either *y* or *i* for *e* in preterite situations: "lyvid, belovyd" for "lived, beloved." Terminal *e* is often added where it does not exist in Modern English. The scribe doubles terminal *t* throughout. In my editing, I have doubled the vowel on "thee" (meaning "you") and in a few other cases

where it does not influence the pronunciation; I have also made a few nor-
malizations.

Bibliographic note: A standard edition of the Oxford manuscript (Bodleian
Library, Rawlinson C 86) was made by Laura Sumner (Smith College Studies
in Modern Languages, 1924), which was reprinted by B.J. Whiting in his
commentary on the *Wife of Bath's Tale* in *Sources and Analogues of Chaucer's
"Canterbury Tales,"* ed. W.F. Bryan and Germaine Dempster (Humanities,
1941), pp. 223–268, which also mentions John Gower's "Tale of Florent" in
Confessio Amantis.

The Wedding of Sir Gawain and Dame Ragnell

Lythe* and listenythe* the lif of a lord riche,	*hark/listen to*
The while that he lyvid* was none hym liche,*	*lived/like*
Nether in bowre ne* in halle;	*neither in chamber nor*
In the tyme of Arthoure thys adventure betyd,*	*happened*
5 And of the greatt adventure that he hymself dyd,	
That kyng curteys* and royalle.	*courteous*
Of alle kynges Arture berythe* the flowyr,	*beareth*
And of alle knyghtod he bare* away the honour	*bore*
Where-so-evere he wentt.	
10 In his countrey was nothyng butt chyvalry,	
And knyghtes were belovid by that doughty,*	*valiant one*
For cowardes were everemore shent.*	*disgraced*
Nowe wylle ye lyst* a whyle to my talkyng,	*if you will listen*
I shalle you telle of Arthowre the kyng,	
15 Howe ones hym befelle.*	*once it befell him*
On huntyng he was in Ingleswod*	*Inglewood*
Withe alle his bold knyghtes good;	
Nowe herken to my spelle.*	*tale*
The kyng was sett att his trestylle-tree*	*hunting-station*
20 Withe hys bowe to sle* the wylde venere,*	*slay/deer*
And hys lordes were sett hym besyde;	
As the kyng stoode, then was he ware*	*aware*
Where a greatt hartt was and a fayre,	
And forthe fast dyd he glyde.	
25 The hartt was in a braken ferne,*	*fern thicket*
And heard the groundes,* and stoode fulle derne;*	*earth-sounds/very still*
Alle that sawe the kyng:	
"Hold you stylle, every man,	
And I wolle goo myself, yf I can,	
30 Withe crafte* of stalkyng."	*the skill*
The kyng in hys hand tooke a bowe,	

	And wodmanly he stowpyd* lowe,	*woodmanlike he stooped*
	To stalk unto that dere;*	*deer*
	When that he cam the dere fulle nere,*	*near*
35	The dere lept forthe into a brere,*	*briar patch*
	And evere the kyng went nere* and nere.	*nearer*
	So kyng Arthure went a whyle	
	After the dere, I trowe,* half a myle,	*believe*
	And no man withe hym went;	
40	And att the last to the dere he lett flye,*	*fly [arrow]*
	And smote hym sore and sewerly*—	*hard and surely*
	Suche grace God hym sent.	
	Down the dere tumblyd so deron,*	*wounded*
	And felle into a greatt brake of feron;*	*fern thicket*
45	The kyng folowyd fulle fast.	
	Anon* the kyng bothe ferce and felle*	*at once/savage*
	Was withe the dere and dyd hym serve welle,*	*killed him*
	And after the grasse he taste.*	*tasted (bit the dust)*
	As the kyng was withe the dere alone,	
50	Streyghte* ther cam to hym a quaynt grome,*	*straightway/straight fellow*
	Armyd welle and sure:	
	A knyghte fulle strong and of greatt myghte,	
	And grymly wordes to the kyng he sayd:	
	"Well i-mett,* Kyng Arthour!	*met (welcome)*
55	Thou hast me done wrong many a yere,*	*year*
	And wofully I shalle quytte* thee here;	*repay*
	I hold thy lyfe-days nyghe* done;	*almost*
	Thou hast gevyn* my landes in certayn*	*given/indeed*
	Withe greatt wrong unto Sir Gawen.	
60	Whate sayest thou, kyng alone?"	
	"Syr Knyghte, whate is thy name withe honour?"	
	"Syr Kyng," he sayd, "Gromer Somer Joure,*	*Summerday Man*
	I telle thee nowe withe ryghte."	
	"A! Sir Gromer Somer, bethynk thee* welle:	*consider*
65	To sle* me here, honour getyst thou no delle;*	*slay/part*
	Bethynk thee thou artt a knyghte;	
	Yf thou sle me nowe in thys case,	
	Alle knyghtes wolle refuse thee in every place.	
	That shame shalle nevere thee froo;*	*go away from thee*
70	Lett be thy wylle* and folowe wytt,*	*anger/reason*
	And that* is amys,* I shalle amend itt,	*what/amiss*
	And thou wolt, or that* I goo."	*if you wish, before*
	"Nay," sayd Sir Gromer Somer, "by hevyn* kyng!	*heaven's*
	So shalt thou nott skape,* withoute lesyng;*	*escape/a lie*
75	I have thee nowe att avaylle;*	*my advantage*

Yf I shold lett thee thus goo withe mokery,*   *only banter*
Anoder* tyme thou wolt me defye;   *another*
Of that I shalle nott faylle."
Now sayd the kyng, "So God me save,
80 Save my lyfe, and whate thou wolt crave,
I shalle now graunt itt thee;
Shame thou shalt have to sle me in venere,*   *while hunting*
Thou armyd and I clothyd butt in grene, perde."*   *par Dieu, by God*
"Alle thys shalle nott help thee, sekyrly,*   *surely*
85 For I wolle nother lond ne* gold truly,   *want neither land nor*
Butt yf* thou graunt me att a certayn day   *unless*
Suche as I shalle sett, and in thys same araye."*   *attire*
"Yes," sayd the kyng, "lo! here my hand."
"Ye,* butt abyde, kyng, and here me a stound;*   *yea/while*
90 Fyrst thow shalt swere upon my sword broun,*   *burnished*
To shewe* me att thy comyng whate wemen*   *tell/women/field*
    love best in feld* and town;
And thou shalt mete* me here withouten send,*   *meet/my sending for you*
Even att this day xij monethes end;
And thou shalt swere upon my swerd* good   *sword*
95 That of thy knyghtes shalle none com with
    thee, by the rood,*   *cross*
Nowther fremde* ne freynd.   *neither stranger*
And yf thou bryng nott answere withoute faylle,
Thyne hed thou shalt lose for thy traveylle*—   *trouble*
Thys shalle nowe be thyne othe.*   *oath*
100 Whate sayst thou, kyng? Lett see; have done."
"Syr, I graunt to thys, now lett me gone;*   *be gone*
Though itt be to me fulle lothe,*   *loathsome*
I ensure thee, as I am true kyng,
To com agayn att thys xij monethes end,
105 And bryng thee thyne answere."
"Now go thy way, Kyng Arthure;
Thy lyfe is in my hand, I am fulle sure;
Of thy sorowe thow artt nott ware.
Abyde, Kyng Arthure, a lytelle whyle;
110 Looke nott today thou me beguile,
And kepe alle thyng in close;*   *secret*
For and* I wyst,* by Mary mylde,   *if/knew*
Thou woldyst betray me in the feld,
Thy lyf fyrst sholdyst thou lose."
115 "Nay," sayd Kyng Arthure, "that may nott be;
Untrewe knyghte shalt thou nevere fynde me;
To dye yett were me lever.*   *preferable*

Farwelle, Sir Knyghte and evylle mett:
I wolle com, and I be on lyve* att the day sett,   *If I'm alive*
120 Thoughe I shold scape nevere."
The kyng his bugle gan* blowe,   *did*
That hard* every knyghte and itt gan knowe;*   *heard/they recognized*
Unto hym can they rake;*   *they did hasten*
Ther they fond* the kyng and the dere   *found*
125 Withe sembland* sad and hevy chere,*   *semblance, face/spirit*
That had no lust to layk:*   *desire for sport*
"Go we home nowe to Carlylle;*   *Carlisle*
Thys huntyng lykys* me nott welle"—   *pleases*
So sayd King Arthure.
130 Alle the lordes knewe by his countenaunce
That the kyng had mett withe some
        dysturbaunce.
Unto Carlylle then the kyng cam,
Butt of his hevynesse knewe no man;
Hys hartt was wonder hevy;
135 In this hevynesse he dyd abyde,
That many of his knyghtes mervelyd that tyde,*   *wondered at that time*
Tylle att the last Sir Gawen
To the kyng he sayd then,
"Syr, me marvaylythe ryghte sore,*   *I wonder very strongly*
140 Whate thyng that thou sorowyst fore."*   *for*
Then answeryd the kyng as tyghte,*   *immediately*
"I shalle thee telle, gentylle Gawen knyghte.
In the forest as I was this daye,
Ther I mett withe a knyghte in his arraye,
145 And certeyn wordes to me he gan sayn,
And chargyd me I shold hym nott bewrayne;*   *betray*
Hys councelle must I kepe therfore,
Or els I am forswore."*   *forsworn, perjured*
"Nay, drede* you nott, lord, by Mary flower,*   *fear/the flowering Virgin*
150 I am nott that man that wold you dishonour,
Nother by evyn ne by moron."*   *evening nor morning*
"Forsoothe I was on huntyng in Ingleswod;
Thowe knowest well I slewe an hartt, by the rode,*   *cross*
Alle myself alon;
155 Ther mett I withe a knyghte armyd sure;
His name he told me was Sir Gromer Somer Joure;
Therfor I make my mone.*   *moan, lament*
Ther that knyghte fast* dyd me threte,*   *much/threaten*
And wold have slayn me withe greatt heatt,*   *anger*

160 But* I spak fayre agayn;*   *except that/back well to him*
    Wepyns* withe me ther had I none.   *weapons*
    Alas! my worshypp* therfor is nowe gone."   *honor*
    "What therof?"* sayd Gawen;   *why*
    "What needys more?* I shalle nott lye,   *what more to say*
165 He wold have slayn me ther withoute mercy,
    And that me* was fulle lothe;   *to me*
    He made me to swere that att the xij monethes end,
    That I shold mete hym ther in the same kynde;*   *way*
    To that I plyghte my trowithe.*   *pledged my faith*
170 And also I shold tell hym att the same day
    What wemen desyren moste, in good faye;*   *faith*
    My lyf els shold I lese.*   *lose*
    This othe I made unto that knyghte,
    And that I shold nevere telle itt to no wighte;*   *person*
175 Of thys I myghte nott chese.*   *choose*
    And also I shold com in none oder arraye,
    But even as I was the same daye;
    And yf I faylyd of myne answere,
    I wott* I shal be slayn ryghte there.   *know*
180 Blame me nott thoughe* I be a wofulle man;   *if*
    Alle thys is my drede and fere."
    "Ye, Sir, make good chere;
    Lett make your hors redy
    To ryde into straunge contrey;
185 And evere wheras* ye mete owther* man   *everywhere/either*
        or woman, in faye,
    Ask of them whate they therto saye.
    And I shalle also ryde anoder waye
    And enquere of every man and woman, and gett whatt I may
    Of every man and womans answere,
190 And in a boke I shalle them wryte."
    "I graunt," sayd the kyng as tyte,*   *right away*
    "Ytt is welle advysed, Gawen the good,
    Even by the holy rood."
    Soone were they bothe redy,
195 Gawen and the kyng, wytterly.*   *indeed*
    The kyng rode on* way, and Gawen anoder,   *one*
    And evere enquyred of man, woman, and other,
    Whate wemen desyred moste dere.
    Somme* sayd they lovyd to be welle arayd,*   *some/arrayed, dressed*
200 Somme sayd they lovyd to be fayre prayed;*   *gallantly courted*
    Somme sayd they lovyd a lusty man
    That in theyr armys can clypp* them and kysse   *embrace*

	them than;*	*then*
	Somme sayd one; somme sayd other;	
	And so had Gawen getyn* many an answere.	*gotten*
205	By that* Gawen had geten whate he maye	*by the time that*
	And come agayn by a certeyn daye,	
	Syr Gawen had goten answerys so many	
	That had made a boke greatt, wytterly;	
	To the courte he cam agayn.	
210	By that* was the kyng comyn withe hys boke,	*that time*
	And eyther on others pamplett* dyd loke.	*pamphlet*
	"Thys may nott faylle," sayd Gawen.	
	"By God," sayd the kyng, "I dred me sore;*	*I'm much afraid*
	I cast me* to seke a lytelle more	*intend*
215	In Yngleswod Forest;	
	I have butt a monethe to* my day sett;	*till*
	I may happen on somme good tydynges to hitt—	
	Thys thinkythe me* nowe best."	*seems to me*
	"Do as ye lyst,"* then Gawen sayd;	*please*
220	"What-so-evere ye do, I hold me* payd;	*consider myself*
	Itt is good to be spyrryng;*	*inquiring*
	Doute* you nott, lord, ye shalle welle spede;*	*doubt/succeed*
	Some of your sawes* shalle help att nede;	*answers*
	Els itt were ylle lykyng."*	*otherwise it would be bad luck*
225	Kyng Arthoure rode forthe on the other* day,	*next*
	Into Yngleswod as hys gate* laye,	*way*
	And ther he mett withe a lady;	
	She was as ungoodly* a creature	*unattractive*
	As evere man sawe, withoute mesure.*	*exceedingly so*
230	Kyng Arthure mervaylyd securly.*	*indeed*
	Her face was red, her nose snotyd withalle,*	*all snotty*
	Her mowithe* wyde, her teethe yalowe over alle,	*mouth*
	Withe bleryd eyen* gretter then a balle;	*bleary eyes*
	Her mowithe was nott to lak;*	*mouth lacked nothing (was huge)*
235	Her tethe hung over her lyppes;	
	Her cheekys syde* as wemens hyppes;	*broad*
	A lute she bare upon her bak.	
	Her nek long and therto greatt,	
	Her here cloteryd on an hepe;*	*hair clustered in a heap*
240	In the sholders she was a yard brode;*	*broad*
	Hangyng pappys* to be an hors lode;*	*paps big enough to/horses' load*
	And lyke a barrelle she was made;	
	And to reherse the foulnesse of that lady,	
	Ther is no tung* may telle, securly:	*tongue*
245	Of lothynesse inowghe* she had.	*loathliness enough*

She satt on a palfrey was gay begon,*   *that was gaily decorated*
Withe gold besett and many a precious stone;
Ther was an unseemely syghte;
So foulle a creature withoute mesure
250 To ryde so gayly, I you ensure,
Ytt was no reason ne ryghte.
She rode to Arthoure, and thus she sayd:
"God spede, Sir Kyng, I am welle payd*   *very pleased*
That I have withe thee mett;
255 Speke withe me, I rede or* thou go,   *I advise before*
For thy lyfe is in my hand, I warn thee so;
That shalt thou fynde, and I itt nott lett."*   *if I don't defend it*
"Why, whatt wold ye, lady, nowe withe me?"
"Syr, I wold fayn nowe speke withe thee,
260 And telle thee tydynges good;
For alle the answerys that thou canst yelpe,*   *boast of*
None of them alle shalle thee helpe—
That shalt thou knowe, by the rood.
Thou wenyst* I knowe nott thy councelle,*   *thickest/secret*
265 Butt I warn thee I knowe itt every dealle.*   *bit*
Yf I help thee nott, thou art butt dead.
Graunt me, Sir Kyng, butt one thyng,
And for thy lyfe, I make warrauntyng,*   *I'll give a guarantee*
Or elles thou shalt lose thy hed."
270 "Whate mean you, lady, telle me tyghte,*   *quickly*
For of thy wordes I have great despyte;
To* you I have no nede.*   *of/need*
Whate is your desyre, fayre lady?
Lett me wete* shortly;   *know it*
275 Whate is your meanyng,
And why my lyfe is in your hand,
Telle me, and I shalle you warraunt*   *guarantee*
Alle your own askyng."
"Forsoothe," sayd the lady, "I am no qued;*   *villain*
280 Thou must graunt me a knyghte to wed;
His name is Sir Gawen;
And suche covenaunt I wolle make thee,
Butt thorowe* myne answere thy lyf savyd be;   *if through*
Elles* lett my desyre be in vayne.   *otherwise*
285 And yf myne answere save thy lyf,
Graunt me to be Gawens wyf.
Advyse thee nowe, Sir Kyng;
For itt must be so, or thou artt butt dead;
Choose nowe, for thou mayste soone lose thyne hed.

290   Telle me nowe in hying."*   *haste*

      "Mary,"* sayd the kyng, "I maye nott graunt thee   *by Mary!*

      To make warraunt Sir Gawen to wed thee;

      Alle lyethe in hym alon.

      Butt and* itt be so, I wolle do my labour   *so that*

295   In savyng of my lyfe to make itt secour;*   *secure*

      To Gawen wolle I make my mone."*   *lament*

      "Welle," sayd she, "nowe go home agayn,

      And fayre wordes speke to Sir Gawen,

      For thy lyf I may save;

300   Thoughe I be foulle, yett am I gaye;*   *lusty*

      Thourghe* me thy lyfe save he maye,   *through*

      Or sewer* thy dethe to have."   *ensure*

      "Alas!" he sayd, "nowe wo is me,

      That I shold cause Gawen to wed thee,

305   For he wol be lothe to saye naye.

      So foulle a lady as ye ar nowe one

      Sawe I nevere in my lyfe on ground gone;*   *to go*

      I nott* whate I do may."   *know not*

      "No force,* Sir Kyng, thoughe I be foulle;   *matter*

310   Choyce for a make* hathe an owlle;   *mate has (even an ugly) owl*

      Thou getest of me no more;

      When thou comyst agayn to* thyne answere,   *for*

      Ryghte in this place I shalle meete thee here,

      Or elles I wott* thou artt lore."*   *know/lost*

315   "Now farewelle," sayd the kyng, "lady."

      "Ye, Sir," she sayd; "ther is a byrd men calle an owlle,

      And yett a lady I am."

      "Whate is your name, I pray you telle me?"

      "Syr Kyng, I highte* Dame Ragnelle, truly,   *am called*

320   That nevere yett begylyd* man."   *beguiled a*

      "Dame Ragnelle, now have good daye."

      "Syr Kyng, God spede thee on thy way;

      Ryghte here I shalle thee meete."

      Thus they departyd fayre and welle.

325   The kyng fulle soone com to Carlylle,

      And his hartt hevy and greatt.

      The fyrst man he mett was Sir Gawen,

      That unto the kyng thus gan sayn,*   *did say*

      "Syr, howe have ye sped?"*   *fared*

330   "Forsoothe," sayd the kyng, "nevere so ille.

      Alas! I am in* poynt myself to spylle,*   *at the/kill*

      For nedely* I must be ded."   *of necessity*

      "Nay," sayd Gawen, "that may nott be;

I had lever* myself be dead, so mott I the;*   *rather/may I thrive!*
335   Thys is ille tydand."*   *bad news*
"Gawen, I mett today withe the fowlyst lady
That evere I sawe certenly;
She sayd to me my lyfe she wold save,
Butt fyrst she wold thee to husbond have;
340   Wherfor I am wo-begon;
Thus in my hartt I make my mone."
"Ys this alle?" then sayd Gawen.
"I shalle wed her and wed her agayn,
Thoughe she were a fend;*   *fiend*
345   Thoughe she were as foulle as Belsabub,*   *Beelzebub*
Her shalle I wed, by the rood;
Or elles were nott I your frende,
For ye ar my kyng withe honour,
And have worshypt* me in many a stowre;*   *honored/time*
350   Therfor shalle I nott lett;*   *hesitate*
To save your lyfe, lorde, itt were my parte,*   *would be my duty*
Or were I false and a greatt coward;
And my worshypp is the bett."*   *better*
"Iwys,* Gawen, I mett her in Inglyswod.   *indeed*
355   She told me her name, by the roode,
That itt was Dame Ragnelle;
She told me butt* I had of her answere,*   *unless/an answer from her*
Elles alle my laboure is nevere the nere;*   *nearer (to a solution)*
Thus she gan me telle.
360   And butt yf* her answere help me welle,   *unless*
Elles lett her have her desyre no dele*—   *not a bit*
This was her covenaunt;
And yf her answere help me, and none other,
Then wold she have you; here is alle togeder;*   *that's the whole story*
365   That made she warraunt."
"As for this," sayd Gawen, "it shalle nott lett.*   *hinder (me)*
I wolle wed her att whate tyme ye wolle sett;
I pray you make no care;*   *don't worry*
For and* she were the moste fowlyst wyghte*   *if/person*
370   That evere men myghte see withe syghte,
For your love I wolle nott spare."
"Garamercy,* Gawen," then sayd Kyng Arthor;   *many thanks*
"Of alle knyghtes thou berest the flowre,
That evere yett I fond;*   *found*
375   My worshypp and my lyf thou savyst forevere;
Therefore my love shalle nott from thee dyssevyr,*   *be served*
As I am kyng in lond."

Then within v or vj days,

The kyng must needys* go his ways   *of necessity*

³⁸⁰ To bere his answere.

The kyng and Sir Gawen rode oute of toun,

No man withe them, butt they alone,

Neder ferre ne nere.

When the kyng was within the forest:

³⁸⁵ "Syr Gawen, farewell, I must go west,

Thou shalt no furder* goo."   *further*

"My lord, God spede you on your jorney.

I wold* I shold* nowe ryde your way,   *wish/should (could)*

For to departe I am ryghte wo."*   *woeful/sorry*

³⁹⁰ The kyng had rydden butt a while,

Lytelle more then the space of a myle,

Or* he mett Dame Ragnelle.   *ere, before*

"A, Sir Kyng, ye are nowe welcum here;

I wott* ye ryde to bere your answere   *know*

³⁹⁵ That wolle avaylle you no dele."*   *not a bit*

"Nowe," sayd the kyng, "sithe* itt wolle none other be,   *since*

Telle me your answere nowe, and my lyfe save me:

Gawen shalle you wed;

So he hathe promysed me my lyf to save,

⁴⁰⁰ And your desyre nowe shalle ye have,

Bothe in bowre* and in bed.   *chamber*

Therfor telle me nowe alle in hast,

Whate wolle help now att last—

Have done; I may nott tary."*   *tarry*

⁴⁰⁵ "Syr," quod* Dame Ragnelle, "nowe shalt thou knowe   *said*

Whate wemen desyren moste of highe and lowe;

From this I wolle nott varaye.*   *vary, deviate*

Somme* men sayn* we desyre to be fayre;   *some/say*

Also we desyre to have repayre*   *the company*

⁴¹⁰ Of* diverse straunge men;   *with*

Also we love to have lust* in bed,   *pleasure*

And often we desyre to wed;

Thus ye men nott ken.*   *don't understand*

Yett we desyre anoder manner* thyng: *kind (of)*

⁴¹⁵ To be holden* nott old, butt fresshe and yong,   *considered*

Withe flattryng and glosyng* and quaynt gyn;* *complimenting/clever ploys*

So ye men may us wemen evere wyn,

Of* whate ye wolle crave.   *for*

Ye goo fulle nyse,* I wolle nott lye;   *very foolishly*

⁴²⁰ Butt there is one thyng is alle oure fantasye,

And that nowe shalle ye knowe:

We desyren of men, above alle manner thyng,
To have the sovereynte,* withoute lesyng,*   *sovereignty/lying*
Of alle, bothe hyghe and lowe.
425 For where we have sovereynte alle is ourys,*   *ours*
Thoughe a knyghte be nevere so ferys,*   *fierce*
And evere the mastry wynne;*   *mastery we gain*
Of the moste manlyest is oure desyre;
To have the sovereynte of* suche a syre,   *over*
430 Suche is oure crafte and gynne.*   *conniving*
Therefore wend, Sir Kyng, on thy way,
And telle that knyghte, as I thee saye,
That* itt is as* we desyren moste;   *what/that*
He wol be wrothe* and unsoughte,*   *angry/harsh*
435 And curse her fast that itt thee taughte,
For his laboure is lost.
Go forthe, Sir Kyng, and hold promyse
For thy lyfe is sure nowe in alle wyse*—   *ways*
That dare I well undertake."*   *vouch for*
440 The kyng rode forthe a greatt shake*   *distance*
As fast as he myghte gate*   *go*
Thorowe mire, moore, and fenne,*   *bog*
Whereas* the place was sygnyd* and sett then,   *where/assigned*
Evyn there* withe Sir Gromer he mett.   *right there*
445 And stern wordes to the kyng he spak withe that:*   *spoke then*
"Com off, Sir Kyng, nowe lett see
Of thyne answere whate itt shal be,
For I am redy grathyd."*   *all prepared*
The kyng pullyd oute bokes twayne:*   *two books*
450 "Syr, ther is myne answer, I dare sayn,
For somme wolle help att neede."
Syr Gromer lookyd on them everychon;*   *every one*
"Nay, nay, Sir Kyng, thou artt butt a dead man;
Therfor nowe shalt thou bleede."
455 "Abyde, Sir Gromer," sayd Kyng Arthoure;
"I have one answere shalle make alle sure."
"Lett se," then sayd Sir Gromer,
"Or els so God me help, as I thee say,
Thy dethe thou shalt have with large paye;*   *violently*
460 I tell thee nowe ensure."*   *for sure*
"Now," sayd the kyng, "I see, as I gesse,
In thee is butt a lytelle gentilnesse,
By God, that ay is helpand.*   *ever is helping*
Here is oure answere, and that is alle,
465 That* wemen desyren moste specialle,   *to what*

Bothe of fre and bond.*   *from freemen and bondsmen*
I saye no more, butt above al thyng
Wemen desyre sovereynte, for that is theyr lykyng,
And that is theyr moste desyre:
470 To have the rewlle of* the manlyest men,   *rule over*
And then ar they welle;* thus they me dyd ken:*   *happy/teach*
To rule thee, Gromer Syre."
"And she that told thee nowe, Sir Arthoure,
I pray to God, I maye see her bren* on a fyre,   *burn*
475 For that was my syster, Dame Ragnelle;
That old scott,* God geve* her shame;   *hag/give*
Elles* had I made thee fulle tame;   *otherwise*
Nowe have I lost muche travaylle.
Go where thou wolt, Kyng Arthoure,
480 For of me thou mayste be evere sure;
Alas! that I evere se* this day;   *saw*
Nowe, welle I wott,* myne enime* thou wolt be,   *know/enemy*
And att suche a pryk* shalle I nevere gett thee;   *on such a note*
My song may be welle-awaye!"*   *alas*
485 "No," sayd the kyng, "that make I warraunt;
Some harnys* I wolle have to make me defendaunt,*   *armor/defensible*
That make I God avowe;*   *I swear to God*
In suche a plyghte shalt thou nevere me fynde,
And yf thou do, lett me bete and bynde,*   *be beaten and bound*
490 As is for thy best prouf."*   *advantage*
"Nowe have good day," sayd Sir Gromer.
"Farewell," sayd Sir Arthoure, "so mott I the,*   *may I thrive*
I am glad I have so sped."
Kyng Arthoure turnyd hys hors into the playn,
495 And soone he mett withe Dame Ragnelle agayn,
In the same place and stede.*   *spot*
"Syr Kyng, I am glad ye have sped welle;
I told howe itt wold be every delle;
Nowe hold that* ye have hyghte.*   *keep what/promised*
500 Syn* I have savyd your lyf, and none other,   *Since*
Gawen must me wed, Sir Arthoure,
That* is a fulle gentille knyghte."   *who*
"No, lady; that* I you hyghte* I shalle nott faylle;   *what/promised*
So* ye wol be rulyd by my councelle,*   *if/advice (for secret wedding)*
505 Your wille then shalle ye have."
"Nay, Sir Kyng, nowe wolle I nott so;
Openly I wol be weddyd, or* I parte thee fro;*   *before/from*
Elles shame wolle I have.
Ryde before, and I wolle com after

510 Unto thy courte, Syr Kyng Arthoure;
    Of* no man I wolle* shame;   *from/want*
    Bethynk you* howe I have savyd your lyf.   *consider*
    Therfor withe me nowe shalle ye nott stryfe,*   *quarrel*
    For and* ye do, ye be to blame."   *if*
515 The kyng of her had greatt shame;
    Butt forthe she rood,* thoughe he were grevyd;   *rode/grieved*
    Tylle they cam to Karlyle forth they mevyd.*   *moved*
    Into the courte she rode hym by,*   *by his side*
    For no man wold she spare, securly—
520 Itt likyd* the kyng fulle ylle.   *pleased*
    Alle the contraye* had wonder greatt,   *country, people*
    Fro whens she com, that foule unswete;*   *ugly thing*
    They sawe nevere of so fowlle a thyng;
    Into the halle she went, in certen:
525 "Arthoure, kyng, lett fetche me Sir Gaweyn
    Before the knyghtes, alle in hying,*   *haste*
    That I may nowe be made sekyr;*   *secure, sure*
    In welle and wo trowithe plyghte us* togeder   *pledge our troth*
    Before alle thy chyvalry.
530 This is your graunt; lett se, have done;
    Sett forth Sir Gawen, my love, anon,*   *right away*
    For lenger tarying kepe* nott I."   *care*
    Then cam forth Sir Gawen the knyghte:
    "Syr, I am ready of that I you hyghte,*   *pledged*
535 Alle forwardes* to fulfylle."   *promises*
    "God have mercy," sayd Dame Ragnelle then;
    "For thy sake I wold* I were a fayre woman,   *wish*
    For thou art of so good wylle."
    Then Sir Gawen to her his trowthe plyghte,*   *pledged his troth*
540 In welle and in wo, as he was a true knyghte.
    Then was Dame Ragnelle fayn.*   *pleased*
    "Alas!" then sayd Dame Gaynour;*   *Guinevere*
    So sayd alle the ladyes in her bower,
    And wept for Sir Gawen.
545 "Alas!" then sayd bothe kyng and knyghte,
    "That evere he shold wed such a wyghte!"*   *creature*
    She was so fowlle and horyble.
    She had two teethe on every syde,
    As borys* tuskes, I wolle nott hyde   *like a boar's*
550 Of lengthe a large handfulle;
    The one tusk went up, and the other down;
    A mouthe fulle wyde, and fowlle i-grown*   *grown*
    With grey herys many on;*   *hairs many a one*

Her lyppes laye lumpryd* on her chyn;	*lumped*
555 Nek forsoothe on her was none i-seen—	
She was a lothly on!*	*loathly one*
She wold nott be weddyd in no maner	
Butt* there were made a crye in all the shyre,	*unless*
Bothe in town and in borowe.*	*borough*
560 Alle the ladyes nowe of the lond,	
She lett cry to com to hand,	
To kepe that brydalle thorowe.*	*proper*
So itt befelle after on a daye	
That marryed shold be that fowlle lady,	
565 Unto Sir Gawen.	
The daye was comyn* the day shold be;	*came when*
Therof the ladyes had greatt pity;	
"Alas!" then gan they sayn.	
The queen prayd Dame Ragnelle sekerly*	*earnestly*
570 To be maryed in the mornyng erly,	
"As pryvaly* as we may."	*privately*
"Nay," she sayd, "by Hevyn Kyng,	
That wolle I nevere for no-thyng,	
For oughte* that ye can saye;	*aught, anything*
575 I wol be weddyd alle openly,	
For with the kyng suche covenaunt made I;	
I putt you oute of dowte,*	*doubt*
I wolle nott to churche tylle highe masse-tyme,	
And in the open halle I wolle dyne,	
580 In myddys* of alle the rowte."*	*the midst/company*
"I am greed,"* sayd Dame Gaynour,	*agreed*
"Butt me wold thynk more honour,	*I'd think (the other) more honorable*
And your worshypp moste."*	*and to your benefit*
"Ye, as for that, lady, God you save;	
585 This daye my worshypp wolle I have;	
I telle you withoute boste."*	*boast*
She made her redy to churche to fare,	
And alle the states* that there ware,*	*ranking people/were*
Syrs, without lesyng.*	*a lie*
590 She was arrayd in the richest maner,	
More fressher than Dame Gaynour;	
Her arayment was worthe iij mlle. mark,*	*three thousand marks*
Of good red nobles styff and stark,*	*gold coins sturdy and strong*
So rychely she was begon.*	*adorned*
595 For* alle her rayment she bare the belle*	*despite/bore the (highest) prize*
Of* fowlnesse that evere I heard telle;	*for*
So fowlle a sow sawe nevere man,	

For to make a shortt conclusion.
When she was weddyd, they hied them home;
600 To mete* alle they went.   *meat, dinner*
This fowlle lady bygan* the highe dese;*   *sat at the head of/dais*
She was fulle foulle and nott courteys,
So sayd they all verament.*   *truly*
When the servyce* cam her before,   *servings*
605 She ete* as muche as vj that ther wore,*   *ate/were*
That mervaylyd* many a man;   *so that marveled*
Her nayles were long ynchys iij;
Therwithe she breke her mete ungoodly;*   *broke (cut) her food uncouthly*
Therfore she ete alone.
610 She ete iij capons and also curlues* iij,   *curlews (large wading-birds)*
And greatt bake-metes she ete up, perde;*   *by God*
All men therof had mervaylle;
Ther was no mete cam her before
Butt she ete itt up lesse and more,
615 That praty,* fowlle dameselle.   *odious*
Alle men then that evere her sawe
Bade the deville her bonys* gnawe,   *bones*
Bothe knyghte and squyre;
So she ete tylle mete was done,
620 Tylle they drewe clothes* and had wasshen,*   *took towels/washed*
As is the gyse* and maner.   *custom*
Many men wold speke of diverse service;*   *various meats*
I trowe* ye may wete inowghe* ther was,   *believe/know enough*
Bothe of tame and wylde;
625 In King Arthours courte ther was no wontt*   *want*
That* myghte be gotten withe mannys* hond,   *of what/man's*
Noder in forest ne in feld.
There were mynstralles of diverse contry.

[About 70 lines are lacking here.]

"A, Sir Gawen! syn* I have you wed,   *since*
630 Shewe me your cortesy in bed;
Withe ryghte itt may nott be denyed.
I-wyse,* Sir Gawen," that lady sayd,   *indeed*
"And* I were fayre, ye wold do anoder brayd,*   *if/act a different way*
Butt of wedlok ye take no hed,*   *heed*
635 Yett for Arthours sake kysse me att the leste;*   *least*
I pray you do this att my request;
Lett se howe ye can spede."*   *manage*
Sir Gawen sayd, "I wolle do more

Than for to kysse, and God before!"
640 He turnyd hym her untille.*   *toward her*
He sawe her the fayrest creature
That ever he sawe without mesure.
She sayd, "Whatt is your wylle?"
"A, Jhesu! " he sayd, "what ar ye?"
645 "Sir, I am your wyf, securly;
Why ar ye so unkynde?"
"A, lady! I am to blame;
I cry you mercy, my fayre madame—
Itt was nott in my mynde.
650 A lady ye are fayre in my syghte,
And today ye were the foulyst wyghte
That ever I sawe withe myne ie.*   *eye*
Wele is me,* my lady, I have you thus";   *happy am I*
And brasyd* her in his armys, and gan her kysse,   *he embraced*
655 And made greatt joye, securly.
"Syr," she sayd, "thus shalle ye me have;
Chese of* the one, so God me save   *choose*
(My beauty wolle nott hold):
Wheder ye wolle have me fayre on nyghtes,*   *at night*
660 And as foulle on days to alle men sightes,
Or els to have me fayre on days,
And on nyghtes on the fowlyst wyfe;*   *one of the foulest women*
The one ye must needes have;
Chese* the one or the oder,*   *choose/other*
665 Chese one, Sir Knyghte, whiche you is levere,*   *to you is dearer*
Your worshypp for to save."
"Alas!" sayd Gawen, "the choyce is hard;
To chese the best, itt is froward;*   *difficult*
Wheder* choyse that I chese—   *whichever*
670 To have you fayre on nyghtes and no more—
That wold greve my hartt ryghte sore,
And my worshypp shold I lese.
And yf I desyre on days to have you fayre,
Then on nyghtes I shold have a symple repayre.*   *lean time*
675 Now fayn* wold I choose the best;   *gladly*
I ne wott* in this world whatt I shalle saye,   *do not know*
Butt do as ye lyst* nowe, my lady gaye: *please*
The choyse I putt in your fist.
Even as ye wolle, I putt itt in your hand;
680 Loose* me when ye lyst, for I am bond;*   *relieve/bound*
I putt the choyse in you;
Bothe body and goodes, hartt, and every dele*   *part*

Ys alle your own, for to buy and selle—
That make I God avowe!"
685 "Garamercy, corteys knyghte," sayd the lady;
"Of alle erthly knyghtes blyssyd mott* thou be,   *blessed may*
For now am I worshyppyd;
Thou shalle have me fayre bothe day and nyghte,
And evere whyle I lyve as fayre and bryghte;
690 Therfore be nott grevyd.*   *grieved*
For I was shapen by nygramancy,*   *transformed by magic*
Withe my stepdame,* God have on her mercy,   *by my stepmother*
And by enchauntement,*   *enchantment*
And shold have beene oderwyse understond,*   *taken differently*
695 Evyn tylle the best of Englond
Had weddyd me verament.*   *truly*
And also* he shold geve me the sovereynte   *so that*
Of alle his body and goodes, securly,
Thus was I disformyd;   *misshapen*
700 And thou, Sir Knyghte, curteys Gawen,
Has gevyn me the sovereynte certeyn,
That wolle nott wrothe* thee erly ne late.   *disturb*
Kysse me, Sir Knyghte, evyn now here;
I pray thee: be glad and make good cheere,
705 For welle is me begon."*   *all turned out well for me*
Ther they made joye oute of mynde,
So was itt reason and cours of kynde,*   *reasonable and nature's way*
They two themself alone.
She thankyd God and Mary mylde,
710 She was recovered of that that she was defoylyd;*   *what she was defiled of*
So dyd Sir Gawen;
He made myrthe alle in her boure,*   *bower, chamber*
And thankyd of alle oure Savioure,
I telle you, in certeyn.
715 Withe joye and myrthe they wakyd tylle daye,
And then wold ryse that fayre maye.*   *maid*
"Ye shalle nott," Sir Gawen sayd;
"We wolle lye and slepe tylle pryme,*   *late morning*
And then lett the kyng calle us to dyne."
720 "I am greed,"* then sayd the mayd.   *agreed*
Thus itt passyd forth tylle mid-daye.
"Syrs," quod* the kyng, "lett us go and asaye*   *said/find out*
Yf Sir Gawen be on lyve;*   *alive*
I am fulle ferd of* Sir Gawen,   *afraid for*
725 Nowe lest the fende* have hym slayn;   *fiend*
Nowe wold I fayn preve.*   *gladly find out*

Go we nowe," sayd Arthoure the Kyng;
"We wolle go see theyr uprisyng,
Howe welle that he hath sped."
730 They cam to the chambre, alle in certeyn.
"Aryse," sayd the kyng to Sir Gawen;
"Why slepyst thou so long in bed?"
"Mary," quod Gawen, "Sir Kyng, sicurly,
I wold be glad and* ye wold lett me be,   *if*
735 For I am fulle welle att ease;
Abyde, ye shalle see the dore undone;*   *unlocked*
I trowe* that ye wolle say I am welle goon;   *believe/in good shape*
I am fulle loathe to ryse."
Syr Gawen rose, and in his hand he toke
740 His fayr lady, and to the dore he shoke,*   *hurried*
And openyd the dore fulle fayre;
She stod in her smok alle* by that fyre;   *smock right*
Her her* was to her knees as red as gold wyre: *hair*
"Lo! this is my repayre,*   *refuge, pleasure*
745 Lo!" sayd Gawen, Arthoure untille,*   *unto*
"Syr, this is my wyfe, Dame Ragnelle,
That savyd onys* your lyfe."   *once*
He told the kyng and the queen hem beforn*   *before them*
Howe soddenly from her shap she dyd torne:*   *turn*
750 "My lord, nowe be your leve."*   *by your leave*
And whate was the cause she forshapen* was,   *transformed*
Syr Gawen told the kyng both more and lesse.
"I thank God" sayd the queen;
"I wenyd,* Sir Gawen, she wold thee have myscaryed;*   *thought/harmed*
755 Therfore in my hartt I was sore agrevyd;
Butt the contrary is here seen."
Ther was game, revelle, and playe,
And every man to other gan saye:
"She is a fayre wyghte."
760 Then the kyng them alle gan telle
How did held hym att* neede Dame Ragnelle,   *save him at the time of*
"Or my dethe had beene dyghte."*   *prepared*
Ther the kyng told the queen, by the rood,
Howe he was bestad* in Ingleswod   *beset*
765 Withe Sir Gromer Somer Joure;
And what othe* the knyghte made hym swere,   *oath*
"Or elles he had slayn me ryghte there
Without mercy or mesure.
This same lady, Dame Ragnelle,
770 From my dethe she dyd help me ryght welle,

Alle for the love of Gawen."
Then Gawen told the kyng alle togeder
Howe forshapen she was withe* her stepmother   *by*
Tylle a knyghte had holpen her agayn;
775   Ther she told the kyng fayre and welle
Howe Gawen gave her the sovereynte every delle,
And what choyse she gave to hym;
"God thank hym of* his curtesye;   *for*
He savid me from chaunce and villony
780   That was fulle foulle and grym.
Therfore, curteys knyghte and hend* Gawen,   *gracious*
Shalle I nevere wrathe* thee, serteyn;   *upset*
That promyse nowe here I make—
Whiles that I lyve, I shal be obeysaunt;
785   To God above, I shalle itt warraunt,
And nevere withe you to debate."
"Garamercy, lady," then sayd Gawen;
"With you I hold me fulle welle content,
And that I trust to fynde."
790   He sayd, "My love shalle she have;
Therafter* neede she nevere more crave,   *for it*
For she hathe bene to me so kynde."
The queen sayd, and the ladyes alle,
"She is the fayrest nowe in this halle.
795   I swere by Seynt John!
My love, lady, ye shalle have evere
For that ye savid my lord Arthoure,
As I am a gentilwoman."
Syr Gawen gatt* on her Gyngolyn,*   *begot/Guinglain, Gingelein*
800   That was a good knyghte of strengthe and kynn,*   *nobility*
And of the Table Round.
Att every greatt fest* that lady shold be   *festival where*
Of fayrnesse she bare away the bewtye,*   *beauty-prize*
Wher she yed* on the ground.   *walked*
805   Gawen lovyd that lady Dame Ragnelle;
In alle his lyfe he lovyd none so welle,
I telle you withoute lesyng;
As a coward* he lay by her bothe day and nyghte: *lazy lover*
Nevere wold he haunt justyng* aryghte   *engaged in jousting*
810   Ther-att mervayled Arthoure the kyng.
She prayd the kyng for his gentilness,
"To be good lord to Sir Gromer, i-wysse,*   *indeed*
Of that to you* he hathe offendyd";   *about that (in which) you*
"Yes, lady, that shalle I nowe for your sake,

815 For I wott* welle he may nott amendes make;   *know*
   He dyd* to me fulle unhend."*   *acted/ungraciously*
   Now for to make you a short conclusyon,
   I cast me* for to make an end fulle soone,   *intend*
   Of this gentylle lady.
820 She livyd with Sir Gawen butt yerys v;*   *only five years*
   That grevyd Gawen alle his lyfe,
   I telle you securly;
   In her lyfe she grevyd hym nevere;
   Therfor was nevere woman to hym lever;*   *dearer*
825 Thus leves* my talkyng;   *ends*
   She was the fayrest lady of alle Englond
   When she was on lyve, I understand,
   So sayd Arthoure the kyng.
   Thus endyth the adventure of Kyng Arthoure,
830 That oft in his days was grevyd sore,
   And of the weddyng of Gawen.
   Gawen was weddyd oft in his days,
   Butt so welle he nevere lovyd woman always,
   As I have heard men sayn.
835 This adventure befelle in Ingleswod,
   As good Kyng Arthoure on huntyng yod,*   *went*
   Thus have I hard men telle.
   Nowe God, as thou were in Bethleme born,
   Suffer nevere her* soules be forlorne   *their*
840 In the brynnyng* fyre of Helle!   *burning*
   And, Jhesu, as thou were borne of a virgyn,
   Help hym oute of sorowe that this tale dyd devyne,*   *compose*
   And that nowe in alle hast,   *haste*
   For he is besett withe gaylours* many   *jailers*
845 That kepen* hym fulle sewerly,*   *hold/very securely*
   Withe wyles wrong and wraste.*   *hard*
   Nowe God, as thou art veray* kyng royalle,   *true*
   Help hym oute of daunger that made this tale,
   For therin he hathe bene long;
850 And of greatt pity help thy servaunt,
   For body and soulle I yeld* into thyne hand,   *yield*
   For paynes he hathe strong.

   Here endythe the weddyng of
   Syr Gawen and Dame Ragnelle
   For helpyng of Kyng Arthoure.

Chapter XVIII

THE ALLITERATIVE MORTE ARTHURE

VALERIE KRISHNA

The *Alliterative Morte Arthure*, like *Sir Gawain* an anonymous narrative poem and one of the masterpieces of the English alliterative tradition, is nevertheless unique in Arthurian literature. It depicts King Arthur as a warlord, emphasizing his great military victories, in particular his defeat of the fictional Roman emperor "Lucius Iberius," his vast continental conquests, and finally his betrayal and death at the hands of a very human and political Mordred. In its vigorous and enthusiastic celebration of the warlike virtues the *Morte Arthure is* closer in spirit to *Beowulf*, the *Iliad*, or the *Song of Roland* than to most of the Arthurian romances. Unlike Chrétien's knights, who serve the cause of love and display their knightly prowess in a magical enchanted, or picturesque setting, the knights in the *Morte Arthure* are preoccupied with a more political type of heroism. Loyalty to their overlord, not deference to ladies, motivates them, along with a desire for fame, which is gained not in tournaments but through heroic deeds on the battlefield.

But the poem does not sentimentalize war. Though the poet glorifies his heroes through exaggerated descriptions of superhuman assaults and victories over enormous odds, he is unblinking in his descriptions of the ghastliness of hand-to-hand combat and the finality of death on the battlefield. This is no fairy world in which knights are brought back to life by magic. Arthur's death is real, with no promise or hint of his return.

Also reminiscent of the *Iliad* or *Roland* are the poem's heroic speeches—exhortations to battle and boasts or threats addressed to the enemy (humility is not a strong point with these knights!), elaborate descriptions of knightly costume and armor, and passionate laments for the fallen warriors. Gawain, the greatest of Arthur's warriors, courageous to the point of rashness, is very much like Roland, and in spite of the disastrous consequences of his rashness, his death, like Roland's, is accompanied by stirring elegaic tributes that proclaim the passing of an irreplaceable glory.

Though Gawain is important, the character who dominates the work from beginning to end is King Arthur, and in this the poem is also unusual, since Arthur occupies only a background position in many other Arthurian works. Furthermore, this Arthur is more than a simple heroic warrior-king. He is an ambiguous and not wholly laudable figure, perhaps the most complex Arthur in all of literature. In recent years critics have begun to see this Arthur as a tragic hero—flawed and guilty of hybris—and to consider the poem a kind of primitive tragedy with a strong moral tone. According to this view, the king begins his military campaigns as a just defender of his lands against an oppressor but eventually becomes carried away with his victories, enlarges his ambitions, and becomes in turn an aggressor, who finally contributes to his own downfall through the overextension of his ambitions and conquests.

The work has a symmetrical, rise-and-fall structure resembling that of tragedy, rather than the loose, episodic structure of many medieval works. This "pyramid" shape is underscored throughout by parallel passages, the most notable being Arthur's two prophetic dreams. The first dream, of a battle between a dragon and a bear with the dragon victorious, marks the beginning of the king's rise. The second, of Lady Fortune and her wheel, marks the turn of his fortunes and the beginning of his fall. Similarly, Arthur's altruistic motives in battling the giant of Mont St. Michel (St. Michael's Mount) contrast with the belligerent and aggressive nature of his campaign against the Duke of Lorraine. Yet the poet is careful not only to tie Arthur's fall to the change in his character but to make this change credible by foreshadowing it, giving the story a sense of tragic inevitability. From the beginning Arthur shows traces of pride and incipient rashness, which, fed by his victories, finally overcome the king's prudence, and are the source not only of his aggressive wars in the second part of the poem but also of his final reckless and disastrous battle with Mordred.

Like all Arthurian narratives, the *Alliterative Morte Arthure* is a retelling. Its immediate source is uncertain, but in general outline its story, like other tales in the *Morte* tradition, is another segment of the chronicle version of Arthur's life recounted first by Geoffrey of Monmouth and retold by Wace, Layamon, and other earlier chroniclers. (The *Brut* in the last line probably refers to the Englishman Layamon's poem but might refer to the Norman *Roman de Brut*, by Wace.) The poet has ornamented this basic story with additions from many sources, the most striking being Arthur's dream of Lady Fortune, a combination of two popular medieval motifs—the Wheel of Fortune and the quasi-historical theme of the Nine Worthies (lines 3218 ff.). The *Morte Arthure* is in turn the source of one of the central episodes in *Le Morte Darthur*, and is the most important English work used by Malory in his monumental compilation.

Bibliographic note: Two works that supply more information about the poem are William Matthews's *Tragedy of Arthur: A Study of the Alliterative Morte Arthure* (California, 1960) and Karl Heinz Göller's compilation of essays *The Alliterative Morte Arthure* (Brewer, 1981). For the complete poem see the author's *Alliterative Morte Arthure: A New Verse Translation* (1983); the editors wish to thank the University Press of America for permission to reprint the sections included here. The author's edition of the text was published by Burt Franklin in 1976.

The Alliterative Morte Arthure

Invocation

May great, glorious God, through His singular grace,
And the precious prayers of His peerless Mother,
Help us shun shameful ways and wicked works,
And grant us grace to guide and govern us here,
In this woeful world, through virtuous ways,
That we may hurry to His court, the Kingdom of Heaven,
When the spirit must be split and sundered from the body,
To dwell and abide with Him in bliss forever;
And help me to pour forth some words here and now,
Neither empty nor idle, only honor to Him,   10
And pleasing and helpful to all people who hear.
      You who like to listen and who love to hear
Of lords of the old days and of their dread deeds,
How they were firm in their faith and followed God Almighty,
Hear me closely and hold your silence,
And I shall tell you a tale lofty and true
Of the royal ranks of the Round Table,
The flower of knighthood and all noble lords,
Prudent in their deeds and practiced men-in-arms,
Able in their actions, ever fearful of dishonor,   20
Proper men and polished and versed in courtly ways;
How they gained by battle glories abundant,
Laid low Lucius the wicked, Lord of Rome,
And conquered that kingdom by prowess in arms—
Hark now closely and hear out this tale.

[King Arthur, conqueror and overlord of Britain and of vast territories on the continent, holds court in splendor at Carlisle. A delegation from the Roman emperor Lucius Iberius interrupts the festivities with a demand that Arthur pay tribute to Rome as a vassal of Lucius. Arthur, supported by his prominent nobles, defies the summons, declaring that the emperor is his own vassal.

After sending the messengers back with a contemptuous message, Arthur rallies his armies, bids a tender farewell to Guinevere, appoints a reluctant Mordred as regent, and sets sail for the continent to do battle with Lucius (lines 26–755).]

Arthur's First Dream and the Battle with the Giant

The king was in a great craft with a full force of men,
In a closed cabin, snugly equipped;
Inside on a royal bed he rested awhile,
And with the sighing of the sea he fell into a slumber.
He dreamed of a dragon, dreadful to see,   760
Who came driving over the deeps to drown all his people,
Winging straight out of the western wastes,
Wandering wickedly over the wide waves;
His head and his neck all over the surface
Were rippled with azure, enameled most fair;
His shoulders were scaled in the same pure silver
Spread over all the beast's body in sparkling points;
His belly and his wings of wondrous colors,
In his glittering mail he mounted most high,
And all whom he smote were forfeit forever.   770
His feet were blazoned a beautiful black,
And such a deadly flare darted from his lips
That the sea from the flecks of fire seemed all aflame.
        Then out of the east directly toward him
Up in the clouds came a savage black bear,
With each shank like a pillar and paws most enormous,
Their talons so deadly—all jagged they looked;
With legs all crooked and filthily matted,
Most vilely snarled, and foaming lips,
Rough and repulsive he looked, and worse,   780
His form the foulest that ever was framed.
He stomped, he sneered, then swaggered about;
He bounded to battle with brutal claws;
He bellowed, he roared, so that all the earth rocked,
So lustily he smote it for his own sheer delight.
        Then from afar the dragon charged toward him,
And with his thrusts drove him far off toward the heavens.
He moved like a falcon, fiercely he struck;
He fought all at once with both fire and claw.
Still, the bear seemed the stronger in battle,   790
And savagely slashed him with venomous fangs;
He gave him such blows with his great paws

That his breast and his belly were all bathed in blood.
The bear raged so wildly he rent all the earth,
Which ran with red blood like rain from the heavens.
He would have brought down that serpent by sheer brute force,
Were it not for the fierce fire with which he fought back.
    Then soared the serpent away toward his zenith,
Swooped down from the sky and struck full straight:
Smote the bear with his talons, tore open his back,   800
Which was ten feet in length from the top to the tail.
Thus the dragon crushed the bear and drove him from life;
May he fall in the flood and float off to his fate!
The beasts so wrung the brave king there in the ship's hold,
That he near burst for bale as he lay in his bed.
    Then, worn out with suffering, the good king awoke,
And summoned two sages who attended him always,
In the seven studies the wisest to be seen,
The cleverest of clerics known in all Christendom.
He told them of his torment during the time he slept: 810
"Wracked by a dragon, and such a dread beast;
He has made me most weary—so help me dear God,
Interpret my dream, or I die at once!"
    "Sire," said they presently, these sage men of knowledge,
"The dragon you dreamed of, so dreadful to see,
Who came driving over the deeps to drench—not drown—your folk,
Truly and for certain symbolizes you yourself,
Who here sail over the sea with your steadfast knights;
The colors that were painted upon his brilliant wings
Must be all the kingdoms that you have justly conquered;   820
And the tentacled tail with tongues so huge
Signifies these fair folk who in your fleet go forth;
The bear that was vanquished high up in the clouds
Betokens the tyrants who torment your people,
Or that a day of battle must be braved by you alone,
In single-hand combat with some kind of giant,
And you shall gain victory through the grace of our Lord,
As you in your vision were vividly shown.
Of this fearful dream dread you not any more;
Be not troubled, Sir Conqueror, but hearten yourself,   830
As well as these who sail the sea with your steadfast knights."
    To trumpets then briskly they trice up their sails,
And row over the wide waters, this troop, all together;
The fair coast of Normandy they fetch straightway;
Smoothly at Barfleur the stalwarts are landed,
And find there a fleet of friends in abundance,

The flower and the fair folk of fifteen realms;
For kings and chieftains attended him duly,
As he himself had commanded in Carlisle at Christmas.
    Soon as they had reached land and set up their tents,   840
Straightway came a Templar and spoke to the king:
"Near this place is a monster who is plaguing your people,
A huge giant of Genoa, engendered by fiends;
He has devoured more than five hundred folk,
And as many children of freeborn knights;
This has been his sustenance all these seven winters,
And still the sot is not sated, so much it delights him.
In Cotentin country not a clan has he left
Outside the great castles surrounded by walls,
Of which he has not slain fully all the male children,   850
Carried them off to the crag and cleanly devoured them.
The Duchess of Brittany today has he seized
As she rode beside Rennes with her royal knights,
Carried her off to the crag where that creature dwells,
To lie with that lady as long as life lasts.
We pursued them afar, more than five hundred,
Barons and burgesses and high-born knights,
But he gained the crag—she cried out so loud,
I shall never get over my grief for that creature!
She was flower of all France, of full five realms,   860
And one of the fairest that ever was framed;
Lauded by lords as the loveliest gem
From Genoa to Garonne, by Jesu in Heaven!
She was your wife's cousin—own it if you will—
Born of the royalest blood that reigns on this earth.
As a righteous king take pity on your people,
And undertake to avenge them who thus are outraged."
    "Alas!" cries King Arthur, "that so long I have lived!
Had I known of this, things would have gone better.
It befalls me not well, but ill me betides,   870
That thus this fair lady this fiend has destroyed.
I wish rather than own all France these fifteen winters,
I had been close to that creature a furlong's space,
When he captured that lady and carried her off to the crag;
I would have given my life before she had met grief!
Still, will you show me the crag where that cruel creature dwells?
I wish to go to that place and speak face to face,
To come to terms with that tyrant for abuse of these lands,
And make truce for a time till things may go better."
    "Sire, do you see yon headland with those two fires?   880

There lurks that fiend—seek him out when you choose—
On the ridge of the crag, by a cold river,
That guards the cliff with cataracts sheer;
There you can find fated folk beyond number,
And more florins, in faith, than there are in all France,
And more gold which that wretch has guilefully got
Than was in Troy, I swear, at the time it was conquered."
    Then the great king cries out, in pity for the people,
Makes straight for a tent and is tranquil no longer.
He tosses, he writhes, he wrings his hands—   890
Not another living soul could know how he suffered.
He summons Sir Kay, who carries his cup,
And Sir Bedivere the bold, who bears his great sword:
"See that by evensong you be properly armed,
On steeds, by yon thicket, near those soft streams,
For I wish to go on pilgrimage secretly anon,
At the time of supper, when the men are served,
To seek out a saint by yon salt strands,
On St. Michael's Mount, where miracles are made."
    After evensong, King Arthur, alone,   900
Withdrew to his wardrobe and cast off his garb,
And dressed him in a doublet embroidered in gold,
Above that a tunic of Acre on top,
And above that a hauberk of fine chainmail,
And a surcoat of Jerodyn, scalloped in gold.
He clamps on a helmet, gleaming with silver,
The best from Basel, with magnificent trim:
The crest and the coronal compassed so fair
By clasps of pure gold, encrusted with gems,
The vizard, the ventail, enameled so fair,   910
Free of all flaw, with slits framed in silver;
His gauntlet brightly gilded and trimmed at the edge
With seed-pearls and gems of a glorious hue.
He straps on a great shield and calls for his sword,
Saddles him a bay and bounds to the field;
He springs to his stirrup and straddles atop him,
Bridles him firmly and skillfully guides him,
Spurs the bay steed and rides off to the wood,
And there his men await him, all fully armed.
    Then they ride along that river that rapidly rushes   920
Which the banks overhung with royal boughs;
There the roe and the deer lightheartedly leap
Through brakes and briers to frolic themselves;
The friths were embellished with blooms in abundance,

And with falcons and pheasants of fabulous hues;
There flashed all the birds that fly upon wing,
There sang the cuckoo full clear in the copse—
They give vent to their joy with all manner of mirth.
Sweet was the sound of the nightingales' notes:
They vied with the thrushes, three hundred at once,   930
That such sighing of water and singing of birds
Might soothe the sorrow of one who had never been sound.
    So these folk fare on, alight from their steeds,
And fasten their fine mounts a fair distance off;
With that the king bravely bade his knights
To stay by their steeds and go forward no further:
"I want to search out this saint alone, by myself,
And settle with the master who holds sway on this mount,
And after, you shall do homage, each in turn,
Solemnly, to St. Michael, most mighty in Christ."   940
    The king reaches the crag with its chasms so steep;
He climbs aloft to the crest of the cliff;
He casts up his visor and looks about keenly,
To brace himself, breathes in the cold wind.
Two fires he spies, flaming full high;
He stalks between them a quarter furlong away.
The way by the spring waters he traverses alone,
To find out that fiend in his home ground.

*   *   *   *

    On the side of the smoke straightway he stalked,
And crossed himself faithfully with solemn words,
When, from the side of that creature he reached the sight,
How gruesomely that sot sat gorging himself!
He lay stretched out full length, loathsomely lolling,
The haunch of a man's leg held up by the hip;
His back and his buttocks and his big loins
He baked at the blaze, and breechless he was;
There were such brutal roasts there and pitiful meats,
Human beings and beasts, spitted together,   1050
A cauldron crammed full of christened children,
Some skewered like meat—and the maidens revolved them.
As for this noble king, for the sake of his subjects,
His heart bleeds for pain as he stands there on that plain.
Then he straps on his shield and stands still no longer,
Brandishes his burnished blade by the bright hilt,

Stalks straight toward that sot with a stout heart,
And loudly hails that hulk with haughty words:
"May Almighty God, who is worshiped by us all,
Give you sorrow and suffering, sot, where you lie,   1060
The foulest freak that ever was formed!
Foully you feed yourself—the Fiend have your soul!
This is food unclean, clod, on my oath,
Refuse of all creatures, you cursed wretch!
Because you have murdered these christened children,
And you have made martyrs and sundered from life
Those stabbed here on the heath and crushed at your hands,
I shall mete you out your reward, since you have served well,
Through the might of Saint Michael, who reigns over this mount;
Also for this fair lady, whom you have left lifeless,   1070
And thus befouled in the dust for the sake of your filth:
Get you ready now, dog's son—the Devil take your soul—
For you shall die this day, by dint of my hands!"
Then that sot glared and gruesomely glowered,
Bared his teeth like a hound with hideous fangs;
He gnashed, he snarled fiercely, with scowling face,
In rage at the good king, who confronts him in wrath.
    His hair and his forelock were tangled together,
And from his face spouted foam a half-foot out;
It was flecked all over his features and forehead,   1080
Like the skin of a toad, so that speckled he seemed;
Hook-beaked like a hawk and with a hoar beard,
And furred to his hollow eyes with hanging brows;
Rough as a houndfish to whoever looks hard,
So was the hide of that hulk wholly all over;
Ears had he most huge and hideous to look at,
With eyes full fearsome, and flaming in fact;
Flat-mouthed as a flounder, with fleering lips,
And hunks of flesh in his fangs, foul as a bear;
His beard was bristly and black and hung down to his breast;   1090
He was fat as a sea-hog, with carcass full huge;
And so contorted the flesh of his foul lips,
That the wrinkles, like rebels, writhed out every which-way.
Bull-necked was that being and broad in the shoulders,
Skunk-striped like a swine with bristles full big,
Huge arms like an oak with gnarled sides,
Limbs and loins all loathsome, believe it for sure;
Shovel-footed was that creature and shuffling he seemed,
With legs misshapen, shoved up together,
Thick thighs like a monster, even huger in the haunch,   1100

Fat-swollen as a swine, so unsightly he looks;
He who faithfully gauges the height of that hulk
Will find him five fathoms from forehead to foot.
    Then springs he up wildly on two stout shanks,
And quickly clutches a club of full solid iron;
He would have killed the king with his keen weapon,
But, by Christ's might, in the end the clod failed.
The crest and the circlet, the clasps all of silver
At one clip with his club he struck clean to the ground.
The king throws up his shield and shelters him nimbly,   1110
And with his stout blade he strikes him a blow:
Point-blank in the forehead the savage he smites,
So the bright blade sank into the brain.
The creature clutched at his countenance with his foul claws;
Then fiercely with full force flung out at his face.
The king shifts his footing, gets clear by a hair—
Had he not dodged that stroke, evil had triumphed.
He follows up fiercely and fastens a blow
High up in the haunch with his hardy weapon,
So he buried the blade half a foot in,   1120
And the hot blood of that hulk gushed over the hilt.
Right to the innards of the ogre he thrusts,
Straight up to the genitals, and slashed them asunder.
    Then he bellowed, he roared, and frenziedly swung
Full fiercely at Arthur, but struck into the ground.
A sword's length in the sod swiftly he smote,
So that Arthur near swoons from the sweep of his strokes.
But swiftly the king strains himself fiercely,
Thrusts in with the sword so it punctured the groin:
Both the guts and the gore gush out together   1130
And enslime all the grass on the ground where he stands.
Then he casts down the club and lays hold of the king,
On the crest of the crag clutches him in his arms,
Wraps him right round, to rupture his ribs;
So hard he hugs that hero, his heart nearly bursts.
    Then the mournful maidens fell to the earth,
Kneeling and crying, and clasped their hands:
"Christ deliver this knight and keep him from grief,
And let not that fiend fell him from life."
Yet is the monster so mighty he hurls him under;   1140
Wildly they writhe and wrestle together,
Welter and thrash out through the thornbush,
Swiftly tumble and turn and tear their garb;
Ungently from the crest they struggle together—

Sometimes Arthur on top and other times under—
From the height of the mount down to the rough rock,
They slack not till they fall at the shore of the sea.
Then Arthur with a dagger savagely strikes,
And stabs the hulk straight up to the hilt;
The wretch in his death-throes wrings him so hard,   1150
Three ribs in his side he squeezes to splinters.
　　Then Sir Kay the courageous rushes up to the king,
Cries, "Alas, we are lost! My lord is laid low!
Felled by a fiend! Evil befalls us!
We will be finished, by my faith, and exiled forever!"
Then they lifted his hauberk and felt underneath it,
His flesh and his thigh and on up to his shoulders,
His flank and his loins and his fair sides,
His back and his breast and his fine arms;
They were happy when they found no flesh torn,   1160
And rejoiced for that day, these noble knights.
　　"To be sure," says Sir Bedivere, "it strikes me, by God,
One must seek saints, but seldom to grip them so tight
And to drag down such a relic from these high cliffs
And carry forth a corpse like this to enclose all in silver.
By Michael, of such a fellow I marvel much
That ever our sovereign Lord allows him in Heaven!
If all saints be such who serve our Lord,
I shall never be a saint, by my father's soul!"
　　The bold king banters back at Bedivere's words: 1170
"This saint have I searched out, so save me our Lord,
So haul out your sword and thrust him through to the heart;
Be sure of this servant—he has troubled me sore;
I fought not with such a fellow these fifteen winters;
Only on Mount Snowdon have I met such a match;
He was the strongest by far that ever I found;
Had not my fortunes been fair, I had fallen to my fate.
 Swiftly strike off his head, set it up on a stake,
And give it to your squire, for he is strong-horsed;
Bear it to King Howell, who is in harsh bondage,   1180
And bid him hearten his spirit, for his foe is felled.
Then carry it to Barfleur and enclose it in iron,
And put it up on the parapet for people to see.
My sword and my great shield lie on the sod,
At the crest of the crag, where first we clashed,
And nearby the club, of full solid iron,
That has killed many Christians on the Breton coast;
Go to that headland and get me that weapon,

And let us set forth for our fleet where it waits on the water;
If you wish any treasure, take what you please;   1190
If I have kirtle and club, I crave nothing else."
Then they climb to the crag, these goodly knights,
And bring him the great shield and his shining sword;
Sir Kay himself bears the club and also the kirtle,
And they set out with the conqueror to show to the kings
What in secret the king had kept hidden to himself,
As bright morn from the mountain mounted on high.
     By then to court had come clamor full great,
And before the noble king the people knelt together:
"Welcome, our liege lord, too long have you been away,   1200
Ruler under God, most great and grand,
To whom grace has been granted and given at God's will;
Now your happy arrival has heartened us all!
In your kingliness you have avenged your vassals:
By the force of your hand the foe is felled,
Who oppressed your people and deprived them of children;
Never was realm in disarray so readily set right!"
     Then the conqueror piously spoke to his people:
"Thank God for this blessing, and no other being,
For it was never man's making, but only God's might,   1210
Or a miracle of His Mother, who is merciful to all."
And with that he swiftly summoned the seamen
To go forth with the townsmen to share out the goods,
All the great treasure that tyrant had taken,
To the folk of that country, clergy and all.
"See it be divided and dealt out to my dear people,
So none complain of their portion—on pain of your lives!"
Then he commanded his kinsman with kingly words
To build a church on the crag where the corpse lay,
And a convent within it for the service of Christ,   1220
In memory of that martyr who rests on the mountain.

[The Emperor Lucius, having raised a great army of barbarians and Saracens, has marched into France. After some initial skirmishes, the armies prepare to face each other (1222–2005).]

The Battle with Lucius

     Then the emperor soon after, with his able knights
And earls, enters the valley in quest of adventure,
And comes on King Arthur, with his armies arrayed.
And at his arrival, to worsen his woe,

Our fair, fearless king comes forth on the field,   2010
With battalions spread full and banners flying.
He had barred the city from every side,
And all the chasms and cliffs with good men-at-arms,
The marsh and the morass and the mountains so high,
With a great multitude of men to bar him the ways.

                    *   *   *   *

        Then Lucius loudly spoke lordly words: 2032
"Think on the wide fame of your great fathers,
And the ravagers of Rome, who ruled with their lords;
And how our ranks overran all that reigned on this earth,
And captured all Christendom by courage in arms—
With every campaign a conquest was gained;
And subdued all the Saracens within seven winters,
All the land from Port Jaffa to the Paradise gates.
For a realm to be rebel, we reck it a trifle: 2040
It is just and right for such a man to be quelled.
Therefore, to arms, and hold back no longer,
For, dread not, without doubt the day shall be ours!"
        After these words were spoken, the Welsh king himself
Spotted the foe who had warred on his knights,
And fiercely through the vale he shouts his defiance:
"Viscount of Valence, venomous of deeds,
That feat at Viterbo today shall be avenged;
Unvanquished from this field flee shall I never!"
Then the valiant viscount, noble of voice,   2050
Withdrew from the vanguard that surrounded his steed;
He took up a stout shield, serrated in black,
With a huge dragon, dreadful to see,
Devouring a dolphin, with doleful looks,
As a sign that our leader would be laid low,
And with sweeps of swords done out of his days;
For there is nothing but death where the dragon is raised.
        Then the worthy Welsh king readies his weapon,
And with a stern lance he smites him straight,
A span's length of that shaft right in the small ribs,   2060
So both steel and spleen are impaled on the spear.
Blood spurted and splattered as the horse sprang;
The man suddenly sprawls and speaks nevermore.
And thus has Sir Valiant kept to his vows
And vanquished the viscount, who had been called victor.

Then Sir Ewain fitz Urien eagerly rides
In a rush to the emperor to rip down his eagle;
Through his stout troop he swiftly charged,
Hauls out his sword and with a happy face
Promptly cuts down the eagle and gallops away,   2070
Comes back with that bird in his fair hands,
And safely lines up on the front with his fellows.
    Now Sir Lancelot makes ready and rushes straight
To Sir Lucius the lord and gruesomely smites him;
Through armor and plate he pierces the mail,
So the proud pennon impales his paunch,
And the point projects behind a half-foot span.
Through hauberk and hip with his hardy weapon,
The steed and the stalwart he strikes to the ground,
Also cuts down a banner and bounds back to his band.   2080
    "I am pleased," says Sir Lot, "yonder lords are dispatched!
It is my turn now, with my lord's leave;
Today my name be laid low and my life henceforth
If some do not fall to their fate who await on the field!"
Then the stalwart stretches his body and strains his bridle,
Strikes into the struggle on a stout steed,
Takes on a giant and slashes him through;
Then boldly this warrior runs down another,
Cuts wide ways, wreaking ruin on knights,
And wickedly wounds all who get in his way.   2090
He fought all the force and in a flash
Felled scores on the field with his fine weapon,
Vanquished and laid low valiant knights,
Charged through the whole valley and withdrew when he chose.
    Thereafter then boldly the bowmen of Britain
Fought with foot-soldiers from afar on those fields;
With flitting arrows they fearlessly forced back the foe,
With feathers fiercely pierce the fine mail;
Such fighting is foul that so rends the flesh,
And that flashes from afar into flanks of steeds.   2100
The Dutchmen hurled their darts against them:
With dread deathblows they slice through shields;
Shafts so swiftly shear through knights,
Cut with iron so clean they cannot even wink.
They so shrink before the sweep of the sharp shafts
That all the troop turned back and scattered at once.
The great stallions spring up and rush right onto weapons,
And soon a whole hundred are stretched out on the heath.
    Still, swiftly the strongest, heathens and all,

All hurtled forth headlong to wreak their woes;   2110
With all the giants in front, engendered by fiends,
They attack Sir Jonathal and other fine knights.
With clubs of hard steel they hammered in helms,
Struck down crests and smashed in skulls,
Slaughtered coursers and caparisoned mounts,
Sliced straight through stalwarts on snow-white steeds;
Neither steel nor stallion could stand up against them,
For they stunned and struck down all who stood in our host,
Till the conqueror came with his keen knights,
And with a fierce countenance lustily cried: 2120
"I expect no Briton to be daunted by so little,
By barelegged boys who have entered the battle!"
     He whips out Caliburn, all freshly whetted,
Hastes to Golapas, who had hurt the most men,
And cleaves him just at the knees cleanly in two.
"Come down," cries the king, "and speak to your comrades!
You are too high by half, I tell you in truth;
You will be handsomer soon, with the help of my Lord."
And with his steel sword he struck off his head.
Stoutly into that struggle he strikes at another,   2130
And sets on seven with his stalwart knights—
Till sixty were so served, ceased they never.
And thus in that skirmish the giants are slain,
Laid low in that battle by lordly knights.
     Then the Romans and the ranks of the Round Table
Arranged themselves in array, rearguard and all,
And on helms went to work with stout weapons of war;
With strong steel they sundered splendid mail,
They arrayed themselves well, these royal men,
And thrust in skillfully on steel-grey steeds,   2140
Fiercely flourished with flashing spears.
Sliced away ornaments fastened on shields;
So many battle-fated are fallen on the field
That each brook on the forest floor flows with red blood.
     Thus swiftly lifeblood is left on the sod,
Swords are broken in two, and dying knights
Loll full length, lurching on lunging steeds;
Worthy warriors' wounds, ruptured ribs,
Faces gruesomely framed in tangled locks
Were all trampled, trod down by steeds in their trappings.   2150
The fairest on earth that ever were framed
Stretched as far as a furlong, a thousand all told.
     By then the Romans were somewhat subdued,

And lingered no longer, but fearfully fled;
Our king with his force follows fast on their heels,
And bears down on the bravest with his best knights;
Sir Kay, Sir Clegis, Sir Cleremond the noble
Take them on at the cliff with skilled men-at-arms,
Fight hard in the forest, hold back no weapon
And fell at the first rush five hundred at once.   2160
When they saw they were surrounded by our stern knights,
And that, outmatched, our men battled even better,
They fought with all the troop and flourished with spears,
And battled the bravest belonging to France.
Then Sir Kay the keen levels his lance,
Gives chase on a courser and charges a king;
With a spear of Lithuania he rips through his ribs,
So both liver and lungs are impaled on the lance;
The shaft shivered and sailed toward the great lord,
Ripped clear through the shield and came to rest in the man.   2170
But on entry Sir Kay was ignobly attacked
By a coward knight from that great land;
Just as he turned, the traitor struck
Right through the flesh and into the flank,
So the brutal lance ripped open the bowel,
And burst on impact, and broke in the center!
Sir Kay knew full well by that infamous wound
He was doomed by that stroke and done out of his life.
He moves into array and rides into their ranks,
To avenge his own death on that proud man;   2180
Crying, "Guard yourself, coward!" he calls him forth quickly,
And with gleaming sword cleaves him cleanly in two!
"Had you so well dealt that dint with your hands,
I had forgiven you my death, by Christ up in Heaven!"
    He goes to the good king and graciously greets him:
"I am grievously wounded and will never get well;
Do now your rites, as the world demands,
And bring me to burial—I beg nothing more.
Greet well my lady, the queen, if fortune befall you,
And all those fair ladies who belong to her bower;   2190
And my gracious wife, who grieved me never,
Bid her, as worthy woman, to pray for my soul."
The king's confessor came, with Christ in his hands,
And to solace that soul spoke over him prayers;
With a noble heart the knight got to his knees,
And received his Creator, who comforts us all.
    Then the great king cries out with grief in his heart,

And rides into the rout to avenge Sir Kay's death,
Pushes into the press and encounters a prince,
Known as heir of Egypt in those eastern lands,   2200
And with Caliburn cleaves him cleanly asunder;
Slices right through the man, splits the saddle in two,
And right there on the steed's back burst open the bowel.
In his fury he fiercely takes on another,
And the middle of that mighty man, who maddened him mightily,
Through the mail he slits it asunder at center,
So that half of the man falls on the hill,
And the other half, haunch down, is left on the horse—
Of that hurt, I vow, he will never be healed.
He then rushed through the ranks with his rugged weapon,   2210
Slashed through men and shredded mail,
Struck down flags and shattered shields,
Fiercely vented his fury with flashing steel.
He twists and turns madly with all might and main,
Wounded his foes and wreaked ruin on knights,
Fought through the throng thirteen times,
Thrusts fiercely into the thick of it and strikes straight through.
    Then Sir Gawain the good, with his gallant knights,
Moves up to the vanguard by the verge of the wood,
Catches sight of Sir Lucius where he waits in a clearing,   2220
With the lords and the liegemen loyal to him.
The emperor then eagerly asks him at once,
"What do you want, Gawain? Work for your weapon?
I can tell by your trembling you are craving for trouble!
I shall be avenged on your wrath, for all your proud words!"
He whipped out a long sword, and like lightning lunged out,
Like a lord in that glade at Sir Lionel he strikes,
Smites so hard on his head that he shatters his helm,
And laid open the skull a good hand's breadth.
He pitched into the press and highhandedly served them,   2230
Wondrously wounded worthy knights,
Fought with Florent, the finest of swords,
Till the foaming blood flowed clear over his fist.
    Then the Romans rallied, who had been rebuffed,
And on rested steeds put our men all to rout;
When they see their chieftain so hotly aroused,
They chase and chop down our noble knights.
Sir Bedivere was thrust through and his breast gored,
With a hard blade, broad at the hilt;
The noble stout steel sank into his heart,   2240
And he pitched to the earth—pity is the more.

The conqueror caught sight and came with his force
To rescue the royal ranks of the Round Table,
And to finish the emperor, if fortune allow it;
They ride straight to the eagle, and "Arthur!" they cry.
The emperor then eagerly strikes out at Arthur,
Backhanded at the visor and viciously smites him;
The naked sword wounds him sore on the nose,
And the blood of the brave king gushed over his breast,
And bloodied the broad shield and the bright mail.   2250
The bold king turns his horse by the rich reins,
And with his stout sword deals Lucius a stroke;
Through both armor and breast with his bright blade,
Aslant through the throat with one stroke he slices,
And thus ends the emperor at Arthur's hands.
With that, his fierce force all become frightened,
And they flee to the forest, the few that are left,
In fear of our folk, toward the fresh streams;
The flower of our stalwarts, on steel-grey steeds,
Chased down those men who had never known fear.   2260

*   *   *   *

Then heralds hastily, at behest of the lords,
Hunt up the heathens who lie on the heath:
The Sultan of Syria and his steadfast lords,
And sixty of the foremost senators of Rome.
They anoint and array these honored kings,
Then lap them in sixty layers of linen,
And encase them in lead, so they might the less   2300
Decay or crumble, if they could prevent it.
Then enclosed in caskets they will ride clear to Rome,
With their banners above, their badges beneath,
So in all countries they cross men could know
Each king by his colors, in his native land.

*   *   *   *

The king himself the coffins consigned to the captives,   2340
And right before his stalwart men spoke these words:
"These are the coffers," said the king, "that will cross the mountains:
The full measure of wealth that you have much craved,
The tax and the tribute of ten score winters,

That was grievously lost in our ancestors' day.
Say to the Senator who governs the city
That I send him the whole sum—assess it as he please!
And bid them never be so bold, so long as my blood reigns,
To wrangle a second time for my spacious lands,
Nor demand tribute or tax by any manner of title,   2350
Save such treasure as this, as long as my day endures!"

[After his victory over Lucius, King Arthur decides to make war on the Duke
of Lorraine, claiming that he is a disloyal vassal. During Arthur's siege of the
city of Metz, Gawain goes off on a foraging expedition and encounters and
fights Priamus, a Saracen knight, in a joust that ends with the two knights
becoming friends and Priamus's mercenary followers deserting the duke's
service. A battle against the duke's forces and the siege of the city end in
victory for the king. Arthur then marches down into Italy, conquering city
after city, in a campaign that ends with the Romans, including an emissary of
the Pope, who offers him the imperial crown. Arthur glories in his triumph,
vowing to become "overlord of all that belongs to this earth" (2279–3217).]

Arthur's Second Dream and the News of Mordred's Treachery

Then this noble king, so chronicles say,
Bounds briskly to bed with a blithe heart;
He undresses with ease and loosens his girdle,   3220
And with sleepy languor slips into a slumber.
By the hour after midnight his mood changed completely,
And toward morning he saw wondrous strange dreams
And when his dread dream had drawn to an end,
The king is frozen with fright as if he should die.
He sends for his sages and tells of his terror:
"Since I was formed, by my faith, so afraid was I never.
So quickly search and translate my dream,
And I shall readily and rightly recount the true story:
    "It seemed I was in a wood, lost and alone,   3230
And knew not at all which way I should go,
For wolves, wild boars, and bloodthirsty beasts
Stalked that wasteland, searching for prey;
There hideous lions were licking their fangs,
In their lust to lap the blood of my loyal knights.
Through that forest I fled to where flowers grew high,
To hide me, in fear of those foul things.
I came on a meadow, surrounded by mountains,
Most delightful on earth that men might behold;

That valley all round was covered all about   3240
And clad clear over with clover and blooms;
The vale was circled with vineyards of silver,
All hung with gold grapes (there never were grander),
Trimmed with arbors and all types of trees,
Fine, fair groves, with flocks grazing beneath.
There were furnished all fruits that flourish on earth,
Nicely fenced in upon those fair boughs;
With no dropping of damp that could damage the blooms,
In the warmth of the day all dry were the flowers.
    "Down from the clouds descended into that dale   3250
A lady dressed richly in damasked robes,
In a surcoat of silk of such a rare hue,
All fretted with fur full to the hem,
And with elegant lappets as long as a yard,
All lovingly lined with layers of gold;
Jewels, gold coins, and other bright gems
On her back and her breast were embroidered all over;
With headdress and coronal richly arrayed,
Another so fair of face could never be found.
    "With her white hands she whirled round a wheel   3260
As if she might suddenly upset it completely;
The rim was red gold set with rare royal stones,
Arrayed with richness and rubies aplenty;
The spokes were all plated with splints of pure silver,
And splendidly spread out a full spear's span.
At the summit was a seat of snow-white silver,
Fretted with rubies, flashing with fire.
Round the rim there clung kings, one after another,
With crowns of pure gold, all cracking apart.
Six from that seat had been struck down abruptly,   3270
Each one in turn, and they cried out these words:
'That I reigned on this wheel I shall rue it forever!
Never monarch mighty like me had ruled on this earth.
When I rode with my retinue I recked nothing more
But to hunt and revel and ravage the people;
And thus I drew out my days, as long as I could endure,
And for that I am ruthlessly damned forever.'
    "The lowest was a little man, who had been thrown beneath;
His loins lay there all lean and loathsome to look at,
His locks grey and long, the length of a yard,   3280
His flesh and his form full foully disfigured;
And one of his eyes was brighter than silver,
And the other was yellower than the yolk of an egg!

'I was lord,' cried that man, 'of lands beyond measure,
And all the men bowed before me who drew breath on this earth!
Now not a rag is left me to lay on my body,
And I am suddenly forsaken—let all men see the truth!'
    "The second lord, I swear, who came along in that line,
Seemed more stalwart to me and stronger in arms;
Many times he sighed sadly and these words he spoke: 3290
'On that throne have I sat as sovereign and lord,
And all ladies loved to twine me in their arms;
Now my glories are all lost and laid low forever!'
    "The third was right sturdy and stout through the shoulders,
A tough man to threaten, even thirty together.
His diadem had slipped down, all studded with stones,
And bedecked all with diamonds, adorned to perfection:
'I was dreaded in my day in lands far and wide,
But now am doomed to downfall and death—dole is the more.'
    "The fourth was a fair man, forceful in arms,   3300
The fairest of form that ever was framed:
'I was heroic, by my faith, when I reigned on earth,
Famed in far lands and the flower of all kings;
Now my face has all faded and fate treats me foully,
For I am fallen from far heights and left without friends.'
    "The fifth was a fairer man than most of the others,
A man strong and fierce, with foam at his lips;
He clutched tight at the rim and flexed his arms,
But he faltered and fell from a fifty-foot height;
Still he sprang up and sprinted and spread out his arms,   3310
And, sprawled on those spear-length spokes, speaks these words:
'I was a lord in Syria, set up by myself,
As sovereign and lord of sundry kings' lands;
Now I am abruptly fallen from bliss,
And because of my sins, that seat is bereft me!'
    "The sixth bore a psalter, beautifully bound,
With a cover of silk, splendidly stitched,
A harp, a handsling, and hard flint stones,
And of the sorrows he suffers he soon sent up a cry:
'I was deemed in my day, for deeds of arms,   3320
One of the ablest who ever lived on earth;
But at the peak of my powers I was dropped in the dust
By this meek maid, who moves the whole world.'
    "Two kings were clambering and clawing at the heights,
At the crest of the wheel, which they frantically crave:
'This ruby throne,' they cried, 'henceforth we claim,
As two of the greatest ever graced on this earth!'

Those warriors waxed white as chalk, faces and all,
But that chair at the top they never achieved.
The higher was handsome, with a high brow,   3330
The fairest of face that ever was framed,
And was garbed in a shade of glorious blue,
Flourished all over with gold fleurs-de-lis.
The other was clad in a coat all of pure silver,
With a graceful cross engraved in gold;
Four perfect crosslets surround that cross,
And thus I could tell that king was a Christian.
     "Then I went toward that fair one and greeted her warmly,
And she said, 'Welcome indeed, it is well you are come;
If you were wise, you would worship my will,   3340
Of all the worthy men there ever were in this world,
For all your glory in war through me have you won;
I have been friendly to you, sir, and hostile to others,
Whom you have fought, in faith, and many of your folk,
For I felled Sir Frollo, for all his fierce knights,
And thus the fruits of France are all freely yours.
You shall achieve this chair; I choose you myself
Above all other chieftains honored on earth.'
     "She lifted me smoothly in her slim hands,
And set me gently in the seat and presented me the scepter;   3350
And with a comb deftly she dressed my hair,
So the waving locks curled up round my crown,
Put on me a diadem, dazzling fair bedecked,
Then offered me an orb, all studded with fair stones,
And enameled with azure, earth blazoned thereon,
Encircled with the salt sea on every side,
As a symbol that I truly was supreme on all the earth.
Then she brought me a sword with a most splendid hilt,
And bade me 'Brandish the blade; this sword is my own;
Many a man by its stroke has shed his life's blood,   3360
And while you work with this weapon it will fail you never.'
     "Then she goes off in peace to rest at her pleasure,
To the edge of the forest—a more fruitful was never;
No orchard was so planted for any prince on earth,
And no array so splendid but in Paradise itself.
She bade the boughs bow down and yield to my hands
The best that they bore on their branches so high;
They heeded her behest, the whole lot at once,
The tallest of each grove, I tell you in truth.
She bade me spare not the fruit but sample at will: 3370
'Taste of the finest, you worthy man;

Reach for the ripest and revel yourself;
Rest, royal king, for Rome is your own.
And I shall willingly whirl the well-wheel straightway,
And reach you rich wine in clear-rinsed cups.'
     "Then she went to the well by the edge of the wood,
That welled up with wine and wondrously flowed,
Dipped a cupful, and drew it up deftly,
Then bade me draw deeply and drink it to her.
And thus she led me about the space of an hour,   3380
With all the fondness and love any man could desire;
But exactly at midday her mood changed completely,
And she turned on me with terrible words.
When I entreated her, she drew down her brows:
'King, you cry to no use, by Christ who created me!
You must lose this game and later your life;
You have lived with delight and lands long enough!'
Round she spun the wheel and whirled me under,
So all my limbs then and there were pounded to pieces,
And with the chair my spine was broken asunder.   3390
And I have shivered with chill since this thing befell me.
Then I wakened, truly all worn down with these dreams;
And now you know my woe, speak out as you wish."
     "Sire," said the sage, "your good fortune is passed:
You shall find her your foe—test her out as you wish;
You are now at your zenith, I tell you in truth;
Take what challenge you wish, you will achieve nothing more.
You have spilled much blood and destroyed many men,
All sinless, by your pride, in sundry kings' lands.
Shrive you of your sins and prepare for your end;   3400
You have had a sign, sir king; please you, take heed,
For you shall fall fearfully within five winters.
Found abbeys in France—her fruits are your own—
For Frollo, for Ferrant, and for all those fierce knights
Who in France you have savagely felled on the field.
Take heed of the other kings and search your own heart:
They were renowned conquerors, crowned on this earth.
The most ancient was Alexander, whom all earth bowed before;
The next Hector of Troy, that hardy hero;
The third Julius Caesar, renowned as a giant,   3410
Acclaimed by knights in all battles as mighty;
The fourth was Sir Judas, a jouster most noble,
That unconquered Maccabee, mightiest of strength;
The fifth was Joshua, that gallant man-at-arms,
Who much joy brought to Jerusalem's host;

The sixth, David the peerless, deemed by kings
One of the noblest who ever was knighted;
For with a sling he slew with a stroke of his hands
Goliath the giant, most ferocious on earth,
Then composed in his day all those beloved psalms,   3420
That in the psalter are set down in such a strange tongue.
Of the two clambering kings, I know it in truth,
One shall be called Charlemagne, the great king of France;
He shall be stern and keen, and as conqueror acclaimed,
And shall gain by conquest countries in hosts;
He shall achieve the crown that Christ himself wore,
And the very spear that plunged into His heart,
When He was crucified on the cross, and all those cruel nails
He shall carry like a king into Christian men's keeping.
The other shall be Godfrey, who shall avenge God   3430
On a Good Friday, with his gallant knights.
He shall be made lord of Lorraine, by leave of his father,
And later in Jerusalem achieve great joy,
For he shall win the Cross by his prowess in war,
And then be crowned king and anointed with chrism.
No other duke in his day shall have such a destiny,
Nor suffer such woe when the truth shall be judged.
    "And so Fortune has fetched you to fill out the number:
The noblest nine ever known on the earth.
This shall be read in romance by royal knights,   3440
Renowned and reckoned among ruthless kings,
And you deemed at Doomsday, as deeds of arms go,
One of the ablest ever living on earth.
So many scholars and sovereigns shall speak of your deeds
And preserve your conquests in chronicles forever.
But the wolves in the wood and those wild beasts
Stand for wicked men who wage war on your realms,
And who have dared in your absence to arm against your folk,
With heathens and hosts from barbarous lands.
You will have tidings, I tell you, within ten days,   3450
That some tragedy has taken place since you turned from home.
I urge you: reckon and recount your outrageous deeds,
Or you will too soon repent all your ruinous works.
Mend your heart, king, before you meet with misfortune,
And humbly seek mercy for the sake of your soul."
    Then the great king arose and drew on his garments:
A doublet red with roses, most royal of flowers,
A gorget and a breastplate and a precious girdle;
And he pulls on a hood of most splendid scarlet,

And a round helm from Pavia, preciously set   3460
With jewels from the Orient and magnificent gems,
His gloves gloriously gilded and engraved at the edge
With beads of ruby, bright to behold;
With hunting hound and sword and no other man,
He hastes over a wide mead, with rage in his heart.
He steps softly over a path by the still wood's edge,
And halts on a high road, brooding all alone.
Off in the sunrise he espies there approaching,
Proceeding toward Rome by the readiest way,
A man in a coarse cloak, with clothes rather loose,   3470
With hat and high boots, humble and round;
With flat farthings the man was flourished all over,
And many rags and tatters hung at his hems;
With pouch and with mantle and scallop shells in plenty,
And with staff and with palm, a pilgrim he seemed.
    The man greeted him readily and bade him good morn,
And the king himself, proudly, in the language of Rome,
In Latin all rude he addresses him grandly:
"Where do you wish to go, sir, wandering all alone?
I think it a danger when the world is at war.   3480
Hidden in that vineyard is a foe with his host;
If they see you, I swear, sorrow befalls you;
Unless you have safe-conduct from the king himself,
Knaves will slay you and seize what you have;
And if you keep to the high road, they will catch you as well,
Unless you get help at once from his gallant knights."
    Then Sir Cradok speaks up straight to the king:
"I shall forgive him my death, so help me God,
The lowest groom under Heaven who walks the ground.
Let the fiercest come forth who follows the king: 3490
I shall face him like a knight—may Christ take my soul.
For you will never seize me, or take me yourself,
Though in splendid robes you be richly arrayed;
And for no war will I turn from traveling where I wish,
Nor for no man of this world made on this earth.
But I shall pass in pilgrimage at this pace unto Rome,
To get me a pardon from the Pope himself,
And of the penalties of Purgatory be perfectly absolved.
Then I shall go straight in search of my sovereign lord,
King Arthur of England, that able man;   3500
For he is in this empire, so honest men tell me,
Warring in these eastern parts with his awesome knights."
    "Whence come you, keen man," cried the king then,

"That you know King Arthur and also his knights?
Were you ever in his court when he dwelt in his country?
Your speech is so familiar, it gladdens my heart.
Well are you come and with wisdom you search;
I know you as British knight by your bold speech."
    "I should know the king—he is my kinsman and lord,
And I was named in his court a knight of the chamber;   3510
Sir Cradok was I called in his splendid court,
Chieftain of Caerleon, next to the king.
Now I am harried from my homeland with distress at my heart,
And that castle is captured by barbarous men."
Then the fair king caught him up in his arms,
Threw off his kettle-helm and kissed him straightway,
Cried, "Welcome, Sir Cradok, so help me Christ!
Dear kinsman in blood, you turn my heart cold.
How fares it in Britain with all my brave men?
Are they slaughtered, or burnt, or sundered from life?   3520
Tell me fully what fate has befallen;
I need seek no credentials; I know you as true."
    "Sire, your regent is wicked and wild in his ways,
For he has wrought woe since you went away;
He has captured your castles and crowned himself king,
And raked in all the revenues of the Round Table.
He has carved up the kingdom, passed it round as he wished.
Proclaimed the Danes as dukes and earls,
And dispersed them far and wide to sack your cities;
Joined to Saracens and Saxons on every side,   3530
He has brought together a band of barbaric men,
Sovereigns of Surgenale and hirelings in hosts:
Picts and paynims and practiced knights,
From Ireland and Argyle—outlaw men;
All those louts are now lords who belong to the mountains,
And all have lordship and lands, as much as they like.
And there is Sir Childrik held up as a chieftain;
And that same brutal man is plaguing your people:
They rob your monks and ravish your nuns,
And he rides ready with his rout to ravage the poor;   3540
Humber to Hawick he has in his hand,
And all the country of Kent by covenant bequeathed—
All the lovely castles that belonged to the crown,
The groves, the grey woodlands, and rugged shores,
The same that Hengist and Horsa seized in their time.
At Southampton on the sea are seven score ships,
Freighted full of fierce folk from faraway lands,

To stand up to your army as soon as you strike.
But one more word straight, for you know not the worst:
He has wedded Guinevere and calls her his wife,   3550
And lives in the wild lands of the west marches,
And has got her with child, so say those who have seen.
Of all the men in this world may woe fall on him,
Regent unworthy to watch over women!
Thus has Sir Mordred ruined us all.
So I betook me over these peaks to tell you the truth."
　　Then the worthy king, with wrath in his heart,
And with hapless grief, grew ghastly pale.
"By the Cross!" cries the king, "I shall pay him in kind!
He shall too soon repent all his ruinous works!"   3560
Sore wretchedly weeping he went to his tents,
And woefully the worthy king wakens his men,
Summoned with a clarion kings and all,
Calls them to council and makes known their plight:
　　"I am treacherously betrayed despite all my true deeds;
All my labor lies in ruins, and I am left none the better.
Woe will befall the man who wrought this betrayal,
If I can only lay hold of him, as I am a true lord.
It is Mordred, the man whom I trusted most.
He has captured my castles and crowned himself king,   3570
With the riches and revenues of the Round Table;
He has made up his retinues of renegade wretches,
And carved up my kingdom for countless lords,
For hirelings and Saracens from all sorts of lands;
He has wedded Guinevere and calls her his wife,
And if a child has appeared, our plight is no better.
On the sea they have gathered seven score ships,
Full of foreign folk to fight none else but me.
So back to Britain the Great it behooves us to hasten,
To crush the man who has caused such grief."   3580

[Upon hearing of Mordred's treachery, Arthur hastens back to Britain and,
on the coast, engages in a sea battle with Mordred's heathen allies. Victorious, he turns now to Mordred (3581–3711).]

Gawain's Last Battle

　　Still the traitor lurks on land, with knights tried and true,
And to trumpets they trot up on steeds in their trappings,
And come in sight behind shields on the bright shore:
Mordred shrinks not for shame, but shows off with pride.

King Arthur and Gawain both turned toward those men,
Toward sixty thousand men who rode into view.
After the folk were felled, the floodtide had passed,
And there was such sludge in shoals so wide,
The king was loath to land in the low water;   3720
So he stayed on the sea for fear his horses would sink,
And to look after his liegemen and his loyal knights,
So that any lamed or lost would live if they could.
    Then Sir Gawain the good seizes a galley,
And glides up at an inlet with his good men-at-arms;
When he landed, in his rage he rushed into the water,
Till he sank to his girdle, in all his gold garb.
He splashes up on the sound, right in sight of those lords,
All alone with his troop—my sorrow is the more.
With banners blazoned with his bearings, the best of his arms,   3730
He bounds up the embankment in his bright array;
He bids his flag-bearer, "Hie you in haste,
To that huge host that waits on the hill,
And I pledge you my word to be right at your heels;
See you shrink from no sword or glittering steel,
But lay low the lustiest and launch them from life!
Be not shaken by their show, but stand your ground.
You have borne my banners in battles so great;
We shall fell the false men—the Fiend have their souls!
Fight hard with this rout and the field shall be ours.   3740
If I overtake that traitor, woe will betide him,
Who contrived this treachery to my true lord;
From such a beginning can come little joy,
And from what in this skirmish is soon to be settled."
    Now straightway these men strike out over the sand,
Assail those warriors and lay on their strokes,
Right through shining shield smite those men,
With lances soon split their gleaming spears;
Dire strokes they dealt with stabbing darts:
In the dew's damp many lie dead,   3750
Dukes and peers and new-dubbed knights—
The ablest of Denmark are undone forever.
Then madly those men slash mailcoats asunder,
And lay into the lustiest with cruel blows.
They press into the throng and thrust to the earth
Of the hardiest men, three hundred at once.
    And Gawain, his blood boiling, could not hold back:
He grabs up a spear, gallops down on a man,
Who bore scarlet all splendid with droplets of silver,

And thrusts him through at the throat with his bloodthirsty blade,   3760
So the sharpened spear shatters to splinters,
And with that savage stroke, he sinks down to die.
The King of Gotland it was, a good man-at-arms;
And with that, his host all takes to its heels,
All routed for good by gallant knights.
Then they meet the middle ranks, which Mordred commands,
And our men gallop toward them—to their own grief.
For had Sir Gawain had the good luck to hold that green hill,
Doubt it not, he would have gained glory forever.
But then Gawain, in fact, watches and waits   3770
To wreak his wrath on the wretch who has wrought this war,
And he moves toward Sir Mordred among all his men,
Along with the Montagues and other great lords.
Then Sir Gawain waxed wroth and with iron will
He levels a stout lance and lustily cries,
"Foul-bred bastard, the Fiend have your bones!
A curse on you, wretch, and all your false works!
You shall be dead and undone for your dire deeds,
Or I shall die this day, if destiny have it!"
Then the foe, with a band of outlaw men,   3780
Drove into a corner our dauntless knights,
Whom that traitor had treacherously singled out himself.
Dukes of Denmark he swiftly disposes,
And Lithuanian leaders with legions in hosts
Surround our men with savage spears;
Hirelings and Saracens from all sorts of lands,
Sixty thousand men, precisely arrayed,
Thickly swarmed in on seven score knights,
Swiftly and slyly by those salt streams.
Then Sir Gawain dropped tears from his grey eyes,   3790
Out of grief for his good men whom he had to guide:
He knew they were wounded and worn out with fighting,
And, what with anguish and woe, he was at his wit's end.
And then, sorrowing, he spoke with streaming tears:
"We are beset with Saracens from every side;
I sigh not for myself—so help me our Lord—
But to see us caught off guard, my grief is the more.
Be brave this day and yonder dukes shall be yours;
For our dear Lord's sake, dread no weapon now;
We shall finish our fight as faultless knights,   3800
And go on to endless bliss with angels unblemished.
Though we have unwittingly wasted ourselves,
We shall turn it all to good in the glory of Christ.

With the help of these Saracens I give you my word,
We shall feast with our Savior solemnly in Heaven;
In the presence of that peerless Prince above all,
With prophets and patriarchs and apostles most noble,
Before that glorious Face that fashioned us all.
He who ever yields him to yonder sons of jades,
While he still has life and breath and is unbowed by battle,   3810
May he never be saved or succored by Christ,
But may Satan send his soul straight down to Hell!"
      Then grimly Sir Gawain grips his weapon,
And toward that huge host he suddenly hastes,
Swiftly straightens the straps of his stout sword,
Thrusts forth his shield and shrinks back no longer;
All reckless and rabid he rushed in straight,
And bloodied the foe with furious blows,
Till all welled with blood where he rushed by.
And, though in great grief, he wavers but little,   3820
But wreaks, to his glory, the wrath of his lord.
He stabs steeds in the struggle and stalwart knights,
So stout men are left standing stone-dead in their stirrups.
He sunders strong steel, he slashes chainmail—
No men there could stop him, for his sense was distraught.
With the force of his fury he falls into a frenzy,
Assails and strikes down all who stand in his way.
No doomed man on earth ever had such a destiny!
Through the whole host he rushes headlong,
And wounds some of the hardiest who dwell on the earth.   3830
Lashing out like a lion, he slashes them through,
Lords and leaders, who are left in the dust.
Still Sir Gawain wavers but little with woe,
But fells the foe with fearsome strokes,
As if he willfully wished to do away with himself.
Wild and bewildered, he was out of his wits,
And, mad as a wild beast, he rushed on those nearest,
Till all wallowed in blood wherever he went;
Each man could take warning from the wounds of another.
      Then he moves in on Mordred among all his knights,   3840
Smote him mid-shield and thrust him through.
But the traitor swerved slightly from the sharp weapon,
And he slashed him in the ribs a six-inch span.
The shaft shivered and sank into that splendid knight,
So the spurting blood streamed clear to his shank,
And gleamed on his greave, burnished so bright.
They so struggle and shove, Mordred sprawls in the dust;

With the force of the lance, he lands on his shoulders
A furlong off, on the ground, all gruesomely wounded.
Gawain flew after him and flung himself flat;   3850
As his grief was fixed, so followed his fortune:
He whipped out a short knife, sheathed in silver,
And would have slit his throat through, but no chink chanced;
His hand slipped and slid aslant down the mail,
And the other one slyly slung him under.
With a sharp knife the traitor struck,
Through helm and head, up into the brain.
Thus Sir Gawain is gone, that good man-in-arms,
With no rescue at all—rue is the more.
Thus Sir Gawain is gone, who led so many others;   3860
From Gower to Guernsey, all the great lords,
From Glamorgan, from Wales, all worthy knights
With that grievous stroke nevermore will know joy.
    Then King Frederick of Friesland, in faith,
Questions that felon about our fierce knight:
"Knew you ever this knight in your noble land,
And of what kin he came? Declare now the truth.
What man was this with these glorious arms?
With this golden griffon, sprawled now on the ground?
He has grieved us greatly, so help me God;   3870
Struck down our strong men and distressed us full sore.
He was the boldest in battle that ever bore blade,
For he has stunned our troop and destroyed it forever."
    Then Sir Mordred speaks with full fair words:
"He was unmatched on earth, sir, on my oath.
He was Gawain the good, most gracious of men,
And the greatest of knights who lived under God,
The man boldest of hand, most blessed in battle,
And the humblest in hall under all the wide heavens;
In leadership the lordliest as long as he lived,   3880
And lauded as a lion in lands far and wide;
Had you known him, sir king, in the country he came from,
His wisdom, his valor, his virtuous works,
His conduct, his courage, his exploits in arms,
You would weep for his death all the days of your life."
    Then the traitor freely let fall his tears,
Turned away suddenly and spoke no more,
Rode off crying and cursed the hour
That ever his fate was written to work such woe.
It wrung his heart when he thought on this thing;   3890
For the sake of his blood-ties sorrowing he rides.

When that fugitive wretch recalled to himself
The glory and the good times of the Round Table,
He railed and he rued all his ruinous works.
He rode off with his rout and rested no longer,
In fear of our great king, if he chanced to come.
He hurries to Cornwall, heavy at heart,
Because of his kinsman, who lies cold on the shore.

*   *   *   *

When our worthy king learned that Gawain had landed,
He writhes wildly with woe, wringing his hands,   3920
And bids his boats be launched upon that low water.
He lands like a lion with his lordly knights,
Slides aslant into the sludge, straight up to his girdle,
And swiftly splashes ashore with his sword drawn,
Arrays his host and hoists his banners,
And hurries over the wide sand, with rage in his heart.
He dashes quickly to the field where the dead lie,
And, of the traitor's men on mailed mounts,
Truth to tell, a full ten thousand were lost;
And, I swear, on our side just seven score knights,   3930
Along with their leader, lifeless are left.
      The king turned over carefully knights and all,
Earls of Africa and Austrian men,
From Argyle and Orkney, Irish kings,
The noblest of Norway, numbers most great,
Dukes of Denmark and new-dubbed knights,
And the Gotland king, in the bright arms,
Who lies groaning on the ground, gored straight through.
The royal king ransacks, with rue in his heart,
And hunts for the heroes of the Round Table,   3940
Spots them all in a heap, apart by themselves,
With mangled Saracens encircled all about,
And Sir Gawain the good, in his glorious arms
Sprawled face down and clutching the grass,
His banners struck down, emblazoned with scarlet,
His blade and his broad shield all bathed in blood.
Never was our goodly king so heavy at heart,
And nothing smote him so sore as that sight itself.
      The good king gazes and grieves in his heart,
Gruesomely groans through grinding tears,   3950
Knelt down to the body, caught it up in his arms,

Cast up his visor and kissed him at once,
Looked at his eyelids that now were locked fast,
His lips like lead and his face white,
And with that, the crowned king cries out aloud,
"Beloved kinsman in blood, cursed am I left;
For now my glory is gone and all my wars ended.
Here lies my promise of ease, my prowess in arms;
My heart and my strength hung wholly on him.
My counselor, my comfort, who carried all my hopes,   3960
King of all knights that lived under Christ,
You were worthy to be king, though I wore the crown.
My good and my glory throughout all this great world
Were won through Sir Gawain, through his wisdom alone.
Alas!" cries King Arthur. "Now swells my sorrow!
I am undone utterly in my own lands.
Ah, dire, dread death, you drag out too long.
Why draw on at such length? You ravage my heart!"
The good king, stricken, sinks into a swoon;
But he staggers up suddenly and kisses him fondly,   3970
Till his thick beard was all bathed in blood,
As if he had butchered beasts and dispatched them from life.
Had not Sir Ewain arrived and other great lords,
His great heart would have burst with grief then and there.
        "Have done!" cried these bold men, "you are losing your reason;
This is bottomless woe, for it will never be better;
It is not worthy, in truth, to be wringing your hands;
To weep like a woman is not deemed wise.
Be manly of mien, as a king must,
And cease this clamor, for love of Christ above!"   3980
"By Christ's blood," cried the king, "cease shall I never!
Till my brain or my breast burst all to bits!
Never did such sharp sorrow sink into my heart,
And grief is close kin to me—my care is the more.
Never was so sorrowful a sight seen by my eyes;
Unsullied, he is destroyed, and all for my sins."
        Down knelt the king and cried aloud;
With careworn countenance he calls out these words:
"Oh great, righteous God, look down on this grief!
See this royal, red blood run over the ground!   3990
It is fit to be shrouded and enshrined in gold,
For it is unstained by sin, so save me our Lord!"
Down knelt the sovereign with sorrow in his heart,
Caught it up carefully in his clean hands,
Placed it in a kettle-helm and covered it fast,

And rode forth with the body toward the place of his birth.
"Here and now I give my oath," cried the king then,
"To Christ and to Mary, Heaven's merciful Queen,
Never again shall I hunt or unleash my hounds,
At any roe or deer that runs about on the earth,   4000
Never let sprint my greyhound or let hunt my hawk,
Nor never see fowl felled that flies upon wing,
Neither falcon nor formel hold on my fist,
Never again with jarfalcon rejoice me on earth,
Nor reign in royal splendor, nor call my Round Table,
Till your death, dear one, be duly avenged.
But ever I'll languish and mourn as long as I live,
Till God and dread death have done their desire!"

[Arthur has Gawain's body conveyed to Winchester and orders it to remain
unburied until he has slain the traitor Mordred (4009–4059).]

Arthur's Last Battle

    Now his enemy emerges from out the wood's edge,   4060
With hordes of aliens, awesome to see;
Sir Mordred the Malebranch and a myriad men
Issue out of the forest on every side,
In seven big battalions, precisely arrayed:
Sixty thousand men—the sight was staggering—
All fighting folk from faraway lands,
Tightly formed up in the front line, along those fresh streams.
And all Arthur's army added up, in knights,
To just eight hundred men in all, entered in the rolls.
This was no even match—except for Christ's might—   4070
To take on that multitude in those open lands.
    Then the royal king of the Round Table
Rides round on a fine steed and readies his men:
Arranged his vanguard as he knew best,
And Sir Ewain and Sir Eric and other great lords
Manfully manage the middle-flank next,
With Merrak and Meneduke, mighty of strength;
Idrus and Alimere, able knights both,
Go along with Arthur, with seven score men;
He quickly arrayed his rearguard next,   4080
The rough-and-readiest men of the Round Table.
Thus he fits out his folk and shouts his defiance,
And fires up his men with fearless words:
"I beseech you, sirs, for the sake of our Lord,

That you do well today and dread you no weapon.
Fight fiercely now, and defend yourselves well,
Fell yonder doomed folk and the field shall be ours.
They are Saracens, this lot; may they soon be undone!
Lay into them lustily, for love of our Lord!
If we be destined to die today on this ground,   4090
We shall be hauled up to Heaven before we be half cold.
See you fail in no way to perform like lords:
Lay low this foe before the game finish.
Have no heed of me: hold me of no matter,
But tend to my banners with your bright blades,
So they be amply surrounded by stout men-at-arms
And held grandly on high for all to behold;
If any man rip them down, rescue them straight;
Now work to my glory, for today my war ends.
You have shared my wealth and my woe, now work to your credit;   4100
May Christ crowned in glory comfort you all,
The noblest creatures that ever a king led.
I bestow on you all my blessing with a blithe heart,
And on all brave Britons—may you find bliss."
    They strike out at sunrise and proceed toward the foe;
Esteemed men and noble put their strength to the test;
Boldly the buglers blazon the trumpets
And cornets grandly, as knights come together.
Thus boldly these brave knights ride out to battle;
A nobler day there never was known,   4110
As when these Britons bravely buckled on shields,
Crossed them as Christians and couched their spears.

           *   *   *   *

    Then Sir Mordred the Malebranch and a great mass of men
Engage our middle-rank and grapple together;
He had hidden in the rear, within the wood's edge,
With a whole host on the heath—woe is the more.
He had watched that clash clear to the end,
How our knights had fared by fortune in arms;
He knew our folk were fought out and fated to fall,
And he swiftly decides now to set on the king.   4180
But that churl's son had changed his charge:
His engrailed cross he had cast aside, I swear,
And instead seized three lions of burnished bright silver,
Passant on scarlet, richly studded with stones,

So the king might not know the cunning wretch.
On account of his cowardice he cast off his garb,
But our sovereign spotted him right from the start,
And spoke to Sir Cador these timely words:
"I see the traitor come yonder trotting all hot;
Yonder lord with the lions is like him exactly;   4190
Grief will befall him, if I seize him just once,
For all his treason and treachery, as I am a true lord!
Today Clarent and Caliburn, blade to blade, shall make clear
Which is cleaner of cut or keener of edge;
We shall size up fine steel against fine garb.
It was my great pride, so preciously prized;
It was kept for crownings of sanctified kings;
And on days when I dubbed dukes and earls,
It was borne in procession by the bright hilt;
I never ventured to damage it in deeds of arms,   4200
But kept it ever perfect, at my own pleasure.
Now that I see Clarent uncased, that crown of all swords,
My vault at Wallingford, I know well, is laid waste:
No one knew of that site, but Guinevere herself;
She herself had safekeeping of that splendid blade
And of sealed coffers that belong to the crown,
Holding rings and relics and the Regal of France,
That were found on Sir Frollo, when he was felled on the field."
    Then Sir Marrik, maddened, takes on Mordred straightway,
With a battered mace smites with full might and main;   4210
The edge of his helm he hews asunder,
So the bright red blood ran down his mail.
Mordred pulls back in pain, and his face goes all pale;
He turns at bay like a boar and brutally strikes:
He whipped out the sword that shone like silver,
That was Arthur's own, and Uther, his father's,
And in the vault at Wallingford was wont to be kept,
And with it the dread dog dealt such dire dints
That the other drew far back and dared do no more;
For Sir Marrik was a man scarred by age,   4220
And Sir Mordred was mighty and at the peak of his powers.
None came within range, knight nor other,
Of the sweep of that sword, but surrendered lifeblood.
    Our prince saw this and pressed on fast,
Pushed into the fray with full brute force,
Countered Sir Mordred and scornfully cried,
"Turn, untrue traitor; no more shall you thrive.
By the great God, you shall die by dint of my hands!

No man shall rescue you, nor all the riches on earth!"
And the king with Caliburn heroically smites: 4230
The corners of his shining shield shears right through,
Straight into the shoulder a six-inch span,
So the bright red blood gleamed on the mail.
Mordred shivered and shuddered, but shrank only little;
Then bounded back boldly in his bright garb;
The felon with that fine sword fiercely struck,
And the flesh on the far flank he slashes asunder.
Straight through surcoat and hauberk of splendid mail
He flaps open the flesh a half-foot span.
That dread blow was Arthur's death-wound—dole is the more   4240
That ever the gallant have to die except at God's will.
      Still with his sword Caliburn bravely he strikes,
Thrusts forth shining shield and shelters him well,
And swipes off Mordred's sword hand as he sweeps by!
An inch from the elbow he cleft it clean off—
So Mordred sprawls on the sod and sinks into a faint—
Through armplate of bright steel and shining chainmail,
So both hilt and hand lie on the heath.
Then in a flash he heaves that fiend to his feet,
Runs him through with his blade right to the bright hilt,   4250
So he sprawls on the sword and sinks down to his death.
"In faith," cries the doomed king, "it pains me sore,
For such a false felon to have so fair an end."
When they finished this fight, the field was won,
And the false folk on the field were left to their fate;
To a forest some fled and fell down in the thickets,
But our fierce fighting folk followed right after:
They hunted and hewed down the heathen hounds;
They finished off, in those mountains, Sir Mordred's knights;
No knight got away there, leader or other: 4260
They were cut down on the run—rue is the less.
      But when Arthur erelong comes on Sir Ewain,
And Eric the gracious and other great lords,
He clasped Sir Cador with grief in his heart,
And Sir Clegis and Sir Cleremond, keen men-in-arms,
Sir Lot and Sir Lionel, Sir Lancelot and Lowes,
Marrik and Meneduke, who ever were mighty;
Grieving, he lays them together in the glade,
Looked on their bodies and with a loud voice,
Like a man loath to live, who has lost all his joys,   4270
He stammers, distracted, and all his strength fails;
He casts his eyes to the heavens, and all his hue fades,

Down he sinks suddenly and falls in a swoon;
But he struggled to his knees and sorrowed over and over:
    "King crowned in glory, in care am I left.
All my lordliness down in the dust is laid low!
You who gave me gifts by Your own grace,
Upheld my honor by the might of their hands,
Made me honored near and far, the overlord of earth,
In a wicked time this woe was wrought,   4280
That, through a traitor, all my true lords are destroyed.
Here rests the royal blood of the Round Table,
Undone by a dog—dole is the more!
I can only make my home alone and hopeless on a heath,
Like a woeful widow in want of her man,
Waste away and weep and wring my hands,
For my greatness and my glory are all gone forever,
And I take leave of all lordship for what life I have left.
Here the blood of the Britons has been parted from life,
And here with this battle ends all my bliss."   4290
    Then the ranks of the Round Table all rally round;
To their royal king they ride all together;
Seven score knights assemble most swiftly,
In front of their sovereign, who lies there stricken.
The crowned king then kneels and cries out aloud,
"I gratefully thank Thee, God, for Thy grace,
That gave us strength and skill to surmount these men,
And has granted us the victory over these great lords.
He never sent us shame or stain on this earth,
But mastery evermore over all other monarchs.   4300
We have no leisure now to look out for our lords,
For that loathsome brute has gruesomely lamed me.
Let us go to Glastonbury—nothing else will do now—
Where we may peacefully rest and care for our wounds.
For this lofty day's labor, praise be to the Lord,
Though He has destined and doomed me to die all alone."
    Then at once they wholeheartedly heed his behest,
And proceed toward Glastonbury by the readiest route,
Reach the Isle of Avalon, and Arthur alights,
And goes to a manor there—he could move on no further.   4310
A surgeon of Salerno searches his wounds,
And the king sees from this he will never be sound,
And soon to his steadfast men he speaks these words:
"Do call me a confessor with Christ in his hands;
I must have the Host quickly, whatever else chance.
My kinsman Constantine shall wear the crown,

In keeping with his kinship, if Christ will allow it.
Sir, if you prize my blessing, bury those lords
Who in that struggle with swords were sundered from life;
And then sternly mark that Mordred's children   4320
Be secretly slain and slung into the seas:
Let no wicked weed in this world take root and thrive—
I warn you, by your worth, work as I bid.
I forgive all offenses, for Christ's love in Heaven:
If Guinevere has fared well, fair fortune be with her."
With all his strength, "Into Thy hands . . . ," he said with his last breath,
And gave up his spirit and spoke nevermore.
      The royal blood of Britain then, bishops and all,
Proceed toward Glastonbury, with hearts full of grief,
To bury the brave king and bring him back to the earth,   4330
With all the honor and majesty that any man could have.
Loudly bells they ring and requiem sing,
Intone masses and matins with mournful notes;
Monastics arrayed in their richest robes,
Pontiffs and prelates in precious attire,
Dukes and peers all dressed in mourning,
Countesses kneeling and clasping their hands,
Ladies forlorn and mournful to look at,
One and all were draped in black, damsels and all,
Who appeared at that sepulcher with streaming tears;   4340
A more sorrowful sight was never seen in their time.
      Thus ends King Arthur, so authors declare,
Of the blood of Hector, the King of Troy's son,
And of Sir Priam the Prince, praised all the earth over;
From Troy the Britons brought all his brave forebears
Into Britain the Greater, so says the *Brut*.

Chapter *XIX*

SIR THOMAS MALORY: *LE MORTE DARTHUR* ("THE DEATH OF ARTHUR")

JAMES J. WILHELM

Sir Thomas Malory is the last great Arthurian writer of the Middle Ages. The little we know about him comes from the end of his monumental work *Le Morte Darthur* (in French, "The Death of Arthur"), that is the end of the present selection: his name was Thomas Maleore or Malleorre, he was a knight (Sir), and he finished his enormous compilation of Arthuriana in the ninth year of King Edward IV's reign, which began on March 4, 1469, and ended on March 3, 1470. Numerous scholars have tried to track him down among the six or so Thomas Malorys alive at this time, and most have agreed that he is Sir Thomas Malory of Newbold Revel, Warwickshire, who was often in prison and died in 1471.

Malory's lengthy work was published by the early printer William Caxton at Westminster in 1485; a perfect copy of this edition exists in the Pierpont Morgan Library in New York and a slightly defective one in the John Rylands Library of Manchester. The relationship between Caxton and Malory is unclear. For example, Malory called his work *The Whole Book of King Arthur and of His Noble Knights of the Round Table*; Caxton, however, became confused and took the title of the last tale, which is printed here, as a title for the whole. Posterity has let it stand.

Actually, the whole work encompasses not only the story of King Arthur from his birth to his death, but also the stories of Merlin, Lancelot, Gareth, Tristan and Isolde, and the Grail. Malory's original version consisted of eight tales (not to be confused with Caxton's divisions into books or chapters), and they are almost all based on French sources, what Malory calls collectively "the French book." The first tale, for example, is taken from the French Prose *Merlin*, and the third from the French Prose *Lancelot*. Malory also used English sources: the eighth and last tale presented here is based on the English stanzaic *Le Morte Arthur* and the French *Mort Artu*. But Malory is in every sense an author rather than a translator or imitator, as the power of this tragic finale shows.

For years the Caxton version seemed to be the only one available until in 1934 a manuscript was discovered in Winchester College that was edited by Eugene Vinaver and published in 1947. The manuscript was often very different from Caxton's printing, and although Vinaver's edition was highly praised, there is still no agreement about the relationship between the two versions and therefore which one to use, since both have their strong points. It is generally agreed that there was an original version that superseded both of these.

One secret of Malory's success is that he is able to maintain a sense of the imaginative and emotional world of romance at the same time that he conveys a sense of psychological and dramatic realism. This is no mean feat, and it is in part what made him so attractive to twentieth-century writers like John Steinbeck (*The Acts of King Arthur and His Noble Knights,* 1976) and Marion Zimmer Bradley (*The Mists of Avalon,* 1982), as well as to the film producer John Boorman ("Excalibur," 1981), whose highly successful movie owed a great deal to the music of that devoted Arthurian Richard Wagner.

Bibliographic note: The text offered here is based on Oskar H. Sommer's edition (Nutt, 1889–91), the first complete edition of Caxton's version of Malory, with consultation of the copy in the Morgan Library. Other editions, such as that of Ernest Rhys (Dutton, 1906), have been consulted for normalization and modernization. Archaic words are glossed in brackets and occasional words are inserted in brackets for clarification. For a text based on the manuscript, see Eugene Vinaver's *King Arthur and His Knights: Selected Tales by Sir Thomas Malory* (Oxford, 1975), a popular version of his scholarly three-volume edition (Clarendon, rev. 1973).

For a bibliography, see Page West Life's *Sir Thomas Malory and the "Morte Darthur"* (Virginia, 1980). Important critical studies include: P.J.C. Field, *The Last Years of Sir Thomas Malory* (Rylands University Library, 1983); Larry D. Benson, *Malory's "Morte Darthur"* (Harvard, 1976); J.A.W. Bennett, ed., *Essays on Malory* (Clarendon, 1963). A good introduction is that of Edmund Reiss, *Sir Thomas Malory* (Twayne, 1966).

XX. The Piteous Death of Arthur

In May when every lusty heart flourisheth and bourgeoneth, for as the season is lusty to behold and comfortable, so man and woman rejoice and gladden of summer coming with his fresh flowers—for winter with his rough winds and blasts causeth lusty men and women to cower, and sit fast by fires—so in this season, as in the month of May, it befell a great anger and unhap [misfortune] that stinted not till the flower of chivalry of all the world was destroyed and slain; and all was long upon [caused by] two unhappy knights, the which were named Agravain and Sir Mordred, that were brethren unto Sir Gawain. For this Sir Agravain and Sir Mordred had ever a privy hate unto the queen, Dame Guinevere, and to Sir Lancelot, and daily and nightly they ever watched upon Sir Lancelot.

So it mishapped [that] Sir Gawain and all his brethren were in King Arthur's chamber. And then Sir Agravain said thus openly, and not in no counsel, that many knights might hear it: "I marvel that we all be not ashamed both to see and to know how Sir Lancelot lieth daily and nightly by the queen, and all we know it so; and it is shamefully suffered of us all, that we all should suffer so noble a king as King Arthur is so to be shamed."

Then spoke Sir Gawain, and said: "Brother Sir Agravain, I pray you and charge you: move no such matters no more afore me, for wit [know] you well," said Sir Gawain, "I will not be of your counsel."

"So God me help," said Sir Gaheris and Sir Gareth, "we will not be knowing, brother Agravain, of your deeds."

"Then will I," said Sir Mordred.

"I believe well that," said Sir Gawain, "for ever unto all unhappiness [mischief], brother Sir Mordred, thereto will ye grant [yield]; and I would that ye left all this, and made you not so busy; for I know," said Sir Gawain, "what will fall of it."

"Fall of it what fall may," said Sir Agravain, "I will disclose it to the King."

"Not by my counsel," said Sir Gawain, "for an [if] there rise war and wrake [strife] betwixt Sir Lancelot and us, wit you well, brother, there will [be] many kings and great lords [who] hold with Sir Lancelot. Also, brother Sir Agravain," said Sir Gawain, "ye must remember how ofttimes Sir Lancelot hath rescued the king and the queen; and the best of us all had been full cold at the heart-root, had not Sir Lancelot been better than we, and that hath he proved himself full oft. And as for my part," said Sir Gawain, "I will never be against Sir Lancelot for one day's deed, when he rescued me from King Carados of the Dolorous Tower, and slew him, and saved my life. Also, brother Sir Agravain and Sir Mordred, in like wise Sir Lancelot rescued you both, and threescore and two, from Sir Tarquin. Methinketh, brother, such kind deeds and kindness should be remembered."

"Do as ye list [please]," said Sir Agravain, "for I will layne [hide] it no longer."

With these words came to them King Arthur.

"Now brother, stint your noise," said Sir Gawain.

"We will not," said Sir Agravain and Sir Mordred.

"Will ye so?" said Sir Gawain. "Then God speed you, for I will not hear your tales or be of your counsel."

"No more will I," said Sir Gareth and Sir Gaheris, "for we will never say evil by that man." "For because," said Sir Gareth, "Sir Lancelot made me knight; by no manner owe I to say ill of him." And therewithal they three departed, making great dole [dolor].

"Alas," said Sir Gawain and Sir Gareth, "now is this realm wholly mischieved [destroyed], and the noble fellowship of the Round Table shall be disparply [dispersed]." So they departed.

And then Sir Arthur asked the others what noise they made.

"My lord," said Agravain, "I shall tell you that [which] I may keep no longer. Here is I, and my brother Sir Mordred, broke [disclosed] unto my brothers Sir Gawain, Sir Gaheris, and to Sir Gareth, how this we know all: that Sir Lancelot holdeth your queen, and hath done long. And we be your sister's sons, and we may suffer it no longer, and all we wot [know] that ye should be above Sir Lancelot. And ye are the king that made him knight, and therefore we will prove it, that he is a traitor to your person." "If it be so," said Sir Arthur, "wit you well he is none other; but I would be loath to begin such a thing but I might have proofs upon it. For Sir Lancelot is an hardy knight, and all ye know he is the best knight among us all; and but if he be taken with the deed, he will fight with him that bringeth up the noise, and I know no knight that is able to match him. Therefore an [if] it be sooth as ye say, I would he were taken with the deed [in act]." For as the French book saith, the king was full loath thereto, that any noise should be upon Sir Lancelot and his queen; for the king had a deeming [suspicion], but he would not hear of it, for Sir Lancelot had done so much for him and the queen so many times, that wit ye well the king loved him passingly well.

"My lord," said Sir Agravain, "ye shall ride to-morn on hunting, and doubt ye not Sir Lancelot will not go with you. Then when it draweth toward night, ye may send the queen word that ye will lie out all that night, and so may ye send for your cooks, and then upon pain of death we shall take him that night with the queen, and outher [either] we shall bring him to you dead or quick."

"I will [it] well," said the king. "Then I counsel you," said the king, "take with you sure fellowship."

"Sir," said Agravain, "my brother Sir Mordred and I will take with us twelve knights of the Round Table."

"Beware," said King Arthur, "for I warn you ye shall find him wight [strong]."

"Let us deal [act]," said Sir Agravain and Sir Mordred.

So on the morn King Arthur rode on hunting, and sent word to the queen that he would be out all that night. Then Sir Agravain and Sir Mordred got to them twelve knights, and hid themself in a chamber in the Castle of Carlisle, and these were their names: Sir Colgrevance, Sir Mador de la Porte, Sir Gingaline, Sir Meliot de Logris, Sir Petipace of Winchelsea, Sir Galleron of Galway, Sir Melion of the Mountain, Sir Astamore, Sir Gromore Somir Joure, Sir Curselaine, Sir Florence, Sir Lovel. So these twelve knights were with Sir Mordred and Sir Agravain, and all they were of Scotland, outher of Sir Gawain's kin, either well-willers to his brethren.

So when the night came, Sir Lancelot told Sir Bors how he would go that night and speak with the queen. "Sir," said Sir Bors, "ye shall not go this night by my counsel." "Why?" said Sir Lancelot. "Sir," said Sir Bors, "I dread me ever of Sir Agravain, that waiteth you daily to do you shame and us all; and never gave my heart against no going, that ever ye went to the queen, so much as now. For I mistrust that the king is out this night from the queen because peradventure he hath lain some watch for you and the queen, and therefore I dread me sore of treason."

"Have ye no dread," said Sir Lancelot, "for I shall go and come again, and make no tarrying."

"Sir," said Sir Bors, "that me repenteth, for I dread me sore that your going out this night shall wrath [hurt] us all."

"Fair nephew," said Sir Lancelot, "I marvel much why ye say thus, sithen [since] the queen hath sent for me; and wit ye well, I will not be so much a coward, but she shall understand I will see her good grace."

"God speed you well," said Sir Bors, "and send you sound and safe again."

So Sir Lancelot departed, and took his sword under his arm, and so in his mantle that noble knight put himself in great jeopardy; and so he passed till he came to the queen's chamber, and then Sir Lancelot was lightly [swiftly] put into the chamber.

And then, as the French book saith, the queen and Lancelot were together. And whether they were abed or at other manner of disports, me list [I wish] not hereof make no mention, for love at that time was not as is nowadays. But thus as they were together, there came Sir Agravain and Sir Mordred, with twelve knights with them of the Round Table, and they said with crying voice: "Traitor knight, Sir Lancelot du Lake, now art thou taken!" And thus they cried with a loud voice, that all the court might hear it; and they all fourteen were armed at all points, as they should fight in a battle.

"Alas," said Queen Guinevere, "now are we mischieved [ruined] both."

"Madam," said Sir Lancelot, "is there here any armour within your chamber, that I might cover my poor body withal? And if there be any, give it me, and I shall soon stint their malice, by the grace of God."

"Truly," said the queen, "I have none armour, shield, sword, nor spear; wherefore I dread me sore our long love is come to a mischievous end, for I hear by their noise there be many noble knights, and well I wot they be surely armed; against them ye may make no resistance. Wherefore ye are likely to be slain, and then shall I be brent [burnt]. For an ye might escape them," said the queen, "I would not doubt but that ye would rescue me in what danger that ever I stood in."

"Alas," said Sir Lancelot, "in all my life thus was I never bestad [beset] that I should be thus shamefully slain for lack of mine armour."

But ever in one Sir Agravain and Sir Mordred cried: "Traitor knight, come out of the queen's chamber, for wit thou well, thou art so beset that thou shalt not escape."

"O Jesu mercy," said Sir Lancelot, "this shameful cry and noise I may not suffer, for better were death at once than thus to endure this pain."

Then he took the queen in his arms and kissed her, and said: "Most noble Christian queen, I beseech you as ye have been ever my special good lady, and I at all times your true poor knight unto my power, and as I never failed you in right nor in wrong sithen the first day King Arthur made me knight, that ye will pray for my soul if that I here be slain. For well I am assured that Sir Bors, my nephew, and all the remnant of my kin, with Sir Lavain and Sir Urry, that they will not fail you to rescue you from the fire; and therefore, mine own lady, recomfort yourself, whatsoever may come of me, that ye go with Sir Bors, my nephew, and Sir Urry, and they all will do you all the pleasure that they can or may, that ye shall live like a queen upon my lands."

"Nay, Lancelot," said the queen, "wit thou well, I will never live after thy days, but an thou be slain, I will take my death as meekly for Jesu Christ's sake as ever did any Christian queen."

"Well, madam," said Lancelot, "sith it is so that the day is come that our love must depart, wit you well: I shall sell my life as dear as I may; and a thousandfold," said Sir Lancelot, "I am more heavier for you than for myself. And now I had liefer [rather] than to be lord of all Christendom, that I had sure armour upon me, so that men might speak of my deeds or [ere] ever I were slain."

"Truly," said the queen, "I would it might please God that they would take me and slay me, and suffer you to escape."

"That shall never be," said Sir Lancelot. "God defend me from such a shame, but, Jesu, be thou my shield and mine armour!"

And therewith Sir Lancelot wrapped his mantle about his arm well and surely; and by then they had gotten a great form [bench] out of the hall, and therewithal they rushed at the door. "Fair lords," said Sir Lancelot, "leave your noise and your rushing, and I shall set open this door, and then may ye do with me what it liketh you."

"Come off, then," said they all, "and do it, for it availeth thee not to strive against us all; and therefore let us into this chamber, and we shall save thy life until thou come to King Arthur."

Then Lancelot unbarred the door, and with his left hand he held it open a little, so that but one man might come in at once; and so there came striding a good knight, a much man and large, and his name was Colgrevance of Gore, and he with a sword struck at Sir Lancelot mightily. And he [Lancelot] put aside the stroke and gave him such a buffet upon the helmet that he fell grovelling dead within the chamber door. And then Sir Lancelot with great might drew that dead knight within the chamber door. And Sir Lancelot with help of the queen and her ladies was lightly armed in Sir Colgrevance's armour.

And ever stood Sir Agravain and Sir Mordred crying: "Traitor knight, come out of the queen's chamber!"

"Leave your noise," said Sir Lancelot unto Sir Agravain, "for wit you well, Sir Agravain, ye shall not prison me this night; and therefore an ye do by my counsel, go ye all from this chamber door, and make not such crying and such manner of slander as ye do. For I promise you by my knighthood, an ye will depart and make no more noise, I shall as to-morn appear afore you all before the king, and then let it be seen which of you all, outher [or] else ye all, that will accuse me of treason; and there I shall answer you as a knight should, that hither I came to the queen for no manner of mal engine [evil intent], and that will I prove and make it good upon you with my hands."

"Fie on thee, traitor," said Sir Agravain and Sir Mordred. "We will have thee maugre [despite] thy head, and slay thee if we list; for we let thee wit we have the choice of King Arthur to save thee or to slay thee."

"Ah sirs," said Sir Lancelot, "is there none other grace with you? Then keep [guard] yourself!"

So then Sir Lancelot set all open the chamber door, and mightily and knightly he strode amongst them, and anon at the first buffet he slew Sir Agravain. And twelve of his fellows after; within a little while after, he laid them cold to the earth, for there was none of the twelve that might stand Sir Lancelot's one buffet. Also Sir Lancelot wounded Sir Mordred, and he fled with all his might.

And then Sir Lancelot returned again unto the queen, and said: "Madam, now wit you well: all our true love is brought to an end, for now will King Arthur ever be my foe; and therefore, madam, an it like you that I may have you with me, I shall save you from all manner of adventures dangerous."

"That is not best," said the queen. "Meseemeth now ye have done so much harm, it will be best ye hold you still with this. And if ye see that as to-morn they will put me unto the death, then may ye rescue me as ye think best."

"I will well," said Sir Lancelot, "for have ye no doubt: while I am living I shall rescue you." And then he kissed her, and either gave the other a ring, and so there he left the queen, and went until his lodging.

When Sir Bors saw Sir Lancelot, he was never so glad of his homecoming as he was then. "Jesu mercy," said Sir Lancelot, "why be ye all armed? What meaneth this?"

"Sir," said Sir Bors, "after ye were departed from us, we all that be of your blood and your well-willers were so dretched [troubled] that some of us leapt out of our beds naked, and some in their dreams caught naked swords in their hands. Therefore," said Sir Bors, "we deem there is some great strife at hand; and then we all deemed that ye were betrapped with some treason, and therefore we made us thus ready, what need that ever ye were in."

"My fair nephew," said Sir Lancelot unto Sir Bors, "now shall ye wit all: that this night I was more harder bestad [beset] than ever I was in my life and yet I escaped." And so he told them all how and in what manner, as ye have heard tofore. "And therefore, my fellows," said Sir Lancelot, "I pray you all that ye will be of good heart in what need soever I stand, for now is war come to us all."

"Sir," said Bors, "all is welcome that God sendeth us, and we have had much weal [happiness] with you and much worship [praise], and therefore we will take the woe with you as we have taken the weal."

"And therefore," they said all (there were many good knights), "look ye take no discomfort, for there is no bands of knights under heaven but we shall be able to grieve them as much as they may us. And therefore discomfort not yourself by no manner, and we shall gather together all that we love, and that loveth us, and what that ye will [wish to] have done shall be done. And therefore, Sir Lancelot," said they, "we will take the woe with the weal."

"Grantmercy [many thanks]," said Sir Lancelot, "of your good comfort, for in my great distress, my fair nephew, ye comfort me greatly, and much I am beholding unto you. But this, my fair nephew, I would that ye did in all haste that ye may, or it be forth days [before long]: that ye will look in their lodging that be lodged here nigh about the king, which will hold with me and which will not, for now I would know which were my friends from my foes."

"Sir," said Sir Bors, "I shall do my pain [effort], and or [ere] it be seven of the clock I shall wit of such as ye have said before, who will hold with you."

Then Sir Bors called unto him Sir Lionel, Sir Ector de Maris, Sir Blamore de Ganis, Sir Bleoberis de Ganis, Sir Gahalantine, Sir Galihodin, Sir Galihud, Sir Menaduke, Sir Villiers the Valiant, Sir Hebes le Renoumes, Sir Lavain, Sir Urry of Hungary, Sir Neroveous, Sir Plenorius. These [last] two knights Sir Lancelot made, and the one he won upon a bridge, and therefore they would never be against him. And Harry le Fitz du Lake, and Sir Selises of the Dolorous Tower, and Sir Melias de Lille, and Sir Bellengere le Beuse, that was Sir Alexander's son Le Orphelin, because [of] his mother, Alice la Belle Pellerine, and she was kin unto Sir Lancelot, and he held with him. So there came Sir Palomides and Sir Safir, his brother, to hold with Sir Lancelot, and Sir Clegis, Sir Sadok, and Sir Dinas, Sir Clarrus of Cleremont.

So these two-and-twenty knights drew them together, and by then they were armed on horseback, and promised Sir Lancelot to do what he would. Then there fell to them, what [ever there was] of North Wales and of Cornwall, for Sir Lamorak's sake and for Sir Tristram's sake, to the number of a four-score knights.

"My lords," said Sir Lancelot, "wit you well: I have been ever since I came into this country well-willed unto my lord, King Arthur, and unto my lady, Queen Guinevere, unto [in all] my power. And this night because my lady the queen sent for me to speak with her, I suppose it was made by treason, howbeit I dare largely excuse her person, notwithstanding I was

there by a forecast [plot] near slain; but as Jesu provided me, I escaped all
their malice and treason." And then that noble knight Sir Lancelot told them
all how he was hard bestad in the queen's chamber, and how and in what
manner he escaped from them. "And therefore," said Sir Lancelot, "wit you
well, my fair lords, I am sure there is but war unto me and mine. And for
because I have slain this night these knights, I wot well, such as Sir Agravain,
Sir Gawain's brother, and at the least twelve of his fellows, for this cause now
I am sure of mortal war, for these knights were sent and ordained by King
Arthur to betray me. And therefore the king will in this heat and malice judge
the queen to the fire, and that may I not suffer, that she should be brent for
my sake. For an I may be heard and suffered and so taken, I will fight for the
queen, [to prove] that she is a true lady unto her lord. But the king in his heat,
I dread me, will not take [accept] me as I ought to be taken."

"My lord, Sir Lancelot," said Sir Bors, "by mine advice ye shall take the
woe with the weal, and take it in patience, and thank God of it. And sithen it
is fallen as it is, I counsel you keep yourself, for an ye will [guard] yourself,
there is no fellowship of knights christened that shall do you wrong. Also I
will counsel you, my lord Sir Lancelot, that an my lady, Queen Guinevere be
in distress, insomuch as she is in pain for your sake, that ye knightly rescue
her; an ye did otherwise, all the world will speak of you shame to the world's
end. Insomuch as ye were taken with her, whether ye did right or wrong, it is
now your part to hold with the queen so that she be not slain and put to a
mischievous death, for an she so die, the shame shall be yours."

"Jesu defend me from shame," said Sir Lancelot, "and keep and save my
lady the queen from villainy and shameful death, and that she never be destroyed in my default. Wherefore, my fair lords, my kin, and my friends," said
Sir Lancelot, "what will ye do?"

Then they said all: "We will do as ye will do."

"I put this to you," said Sir Lancelot: "that if my lord Arthur by evil
counsel will to-morn in his heat put my lady the queen to the fire there to be
brent, now I pray you counsel me what is best to do."

Then they said all at once with one voice: "Sir, us thinketh best that ye
knightly rescue the queen; insomuch as she shall be brent, it is for your sake;
and it is to suppose, an ye might be handled [captured], ye should have the
same death, or a more shamefuller death. And sir, we say all that ye have
many times rescued her from death for other men's quarrels, [and so] us
seemeth it is more [to] your worship that ye rescue the queen from this peril,
insomuch [as] she hath it for your sake."

Then Sir Lancelot stood still and said: "My fair lords, wit you well I
would be loath to do that thing that should dishonour you or my blood, and
wit you well I would be loath that my lady, the queen, should die a shameful
death; but an it be so that ye will counsel me to rescue her, I must do much
harm or [ere] I rescue her; and peradventure I shall destroy some of my best
friends; that should much repent [distress] me; and peradventure there be

some, an they could well bring it about or disobey my lord King Arthur, they would soon come to me, the which I were loath to hurt. And if so be that I rescue her, where shall I keep her?"

"That shall be the least care of us all," said Sir Bors. "How did the noble knight Sir Tristram, by your good will? Kept not he with him La Belle Isolde near three year in Joyous Gard? The which was done by your althers [unanimous] device [advice], and that same place is your own; and in like wise may ye do an ye list, and take the queen lightly away, if it so be the king will judge her to be brent; and in Joyous Gard ye may keep her long enough until the heat of the king be past. And then shall ye bring again the queen to the king with great worship; and then peradventure ye shall have thanks for her bringing home, and love and thank whether [even if] others shall have maugre [spite]."

"That is too hard to do," said Sir Lancelot, "for by Sir Tristram I may have a warning: for when by means of treaties, Sir Tristram brought again La Belle Isolde unto King Mark from Joyous Gard, look what befell on the end: how shamefully that false traitor King Mark slew him as he sat harping afore his lady La Belle Isolde; with a grounden glaive [sword], he thrust him in behind to the heart. It grieveth me," said Sir Lancelot, "to speak of his death, for all the world may not find such a knight."

"All this is truth," said Sir Bors, "but there is one thing shall [en]courage you and us all: ye know well King Arthur and King Mark were never [a]like of conditions, for there was never yet man could prove King Arthur untrue to his promise."

So to make short tale, they were all consented that, for better outher for worse, if so were that the queen were on that morn brought to the fire, shortly they all would rescue her. And so by the advice of Sir Lancelot, they put them all in an embushment [ambush] in a wood, as nigh Carlisle as they might, and there they abode still, to wit what the king would do.

Now turn we again unto Sir Mordred, that when he was escaped from the noble knight, Sir Lancelot, he anon got his horse and mounted upon him, and rode unto King Arthur, sore wounded and smitten, and all forbled [bloody]. And there he told the king all how it was, and how they were all slain save himself all only.

"Jesu mercy, how may this be?" said the king. "Took ye him in the queen's chamber?"

"Yea, so God me help," said Sir Mordred. "There we found him unarmed, and there he slew Colgrevance, and armed him in his armour." And all this he told the king from the beginning to the ending.

"Jesu mercy," said the king, "he is a marvellous knight of prowess. Alas, me sore repenteth," said the king, "that ever Sir Lancelot should be against me. Now I am sure the noble fellowship of the Round Table is broken forever, for with him will many a noble knight hold; and now it is fallen so," said the king, "that I may not [continue] with my worship, but [unless] the queen must suffer the death."

So then there was made great ordinance in this heat: that the queen must be judged to the death. And the law was such in those days that whatsoever they were, of what estate or degree, if they were found guilty of treason, there should be none other remedy but death; and either the menor [demeanor, evidence] or the taking with the deed [arrest in the act] should be causer of their hasty [quick] judgment. And right so was it ordained for Queen Guinevere because Sir Mordred was escaped sore wounded, and the death of thirteen knights of the Round Table. These proofs and experiences [evidence] caused King Arthur to command the queen to the fire, there to be brent.

Then spake Sir Gawain, and said: "My lord Arthur, I would counsel you not to be overhasty, but that ye would put it in respite, this judgment of my lady the queen, for many causes. One it is: though it were so that Sir Lancelot were found in the queen's chamber, yet it might be so that he came thither for none evil; for ye know, my lord," said Sir Gawain, "that the queen is much beholden unto Sir Lancelot, more than unto any other knight, for ofttimes he hath saved her life, and done battle for her when all the court refused the queen. And peradventure she sent for him for goodness and for none evil, to reward him for his good deeds that he had done to her in times past. And peradventure my lady, the queen, sent for him to that intent that Sir Lancelot should come to her good grace privily and secretly, weening [thinking] that it was best so to do, in eschewing [avoiding] and dreading of slander; for ofttimes we do many things that we ween it be for the best, and yet peradventure it turneth to the worst. For I dare say," said Sir Gawain, "my lady, your queen, is to you both good and true; and as for Sir Lancelot," said Sir Gawain, "I dare say he will make it good upon any knight living that will put upon him [charge him with] villainy or shame, and in like wise he will make good for my lady, Dame Guinevere."

"That I believe well," said King Arthur, "but I will not [act] that way with Sir Lancelot, for he trusteth so much upon his hands and his might that he doubteth [fears] no man; and therefore for my queen he shall never fight more, for she shall have the law. And if I may get Sir Lancelot, wit you well he shall have a shameful death."

"Jesu defend," said Sir Gawain, "that I may never see it."

"Why say ye so?" said King Arthur. "Forsooth ye have no cause to love Sir Lancelot, for this night last past he slew your brother, Sir Agravain, a full good knight, and almost he had slain your other brother, Sir Mordred, and also there he slew thirteen noble knights; and also, Sir Gawain, remember ye he slew two sons of yours, Sir Florence and Sir Lovel."

"My lord," said Sir Gawain, "of all this I have knowledge, of whose deaths I repent me sore; but insomuch I gave them warning, and told my brethren and my sons aforehand what would fall in the end, insomuch they would not do by my counsel, I will not meddle me thereof, nor revenge me nothing of their deaths; for I told them it was no boot [good] to strive with Sir Lancelot. Howbeit I am sorry of the death of my brethren and of my sons, for they are the causers of their own death; and ofttimes I warned my brother Sir Agravain, and I told him the perils the which be now fallen."

Then said the noble King Arthur to Sir Gawain: "Dear nephew, I pray you make you ready in your best armour with your brethren, Sir Gaheris and Sir Gareth, to bring my queen to the fire, there to have her judgment and receive the death."

"Nay, my most noble lord," said Sir Gawain; "that will I never do; for wit you well I will never be in that place where so noble a queen as is my lady, Dame Guinevere, shall take a shameful end. For wit you well," said Sir Gawain, "my heart will never serve me to see her die; and it shall never be said that ever I was of your counsel of her death."

Then said the king to Sir Gawain: "Suffer your brothers Sir Gaheris and Sir Gareth to be there."

"My lord," said Sir Gawain, "wit you well they will be loath to be there present, because of many adventures the which be like[ly] there to fall, but they are young and full unable to say you nay."

Then spake Sir Gaheris and the good knight Sir Gareth unto Sir Arthur: "Sir, ye may well command us to be there, but wit you well it shall be sore against our will; but an we be there by your straight commandment, ye shall plainly hold us there excused. We will be there in peaceable wise, and bear none harness of war upon us."

"In the name of God," said the king, "then make you ready, for she shall soon have her judgment anon."

"Alas," said Sir Gawain, "that ever I should endure to see this woeful day." So Sir Gawain turned him and wept heartily, and so he went into his chamber.

And then the queen was led forth without [outside of] Carlisle, and there she was despoiled into her smock; and so then her ghostly [spiritual] father was brought to her, to be shriven of her misdeeds. Then was there weeping and wailing and wringing of hands, of many lords and ladies, but there were but few in comparison that would bear any armour for to strength [support] the death of the queen. Then was there one that Sir Lancelot had sent unto that place for to espy what time the queen should go unto her death; and anon as he saw the queen despoiled into her smock, and so shriven, then he gave Sir Lancelot warning.

Then was there but spurring and plucking up [goading] of horses, and right so they came to the fire. And who that stood against them, there were they slain; there might none withstand Sir Lancelot; so all that bore arms and withstood them, there were they slain, full many a noble knight. For there was slain Sir Belliance le Orgulous, Sir Segwarides, Sir Griflet, Sir Brandiles, Sir Aglovale, Sir Tor, Sir Gauter, Sir Gillimer, Sir Reynolds' three brethren, Sir Damas, Sir Priamus, Sir Kay the Stranger, Sir Driant, Sir Lambegus, Sir

Herminde, Sir Pertilope, Sir Perimones, two brethren that were called the Green Knight and the Red Knight. And so in this rushing and hurtling, as Sir Lancelot thrang [dashed] here and there, it mishapped him to slay Gaheris and Sir Gareth, the noble knights, for they were unarmed and unware. For as the French book saith, Sir Lancelot smote Sir Gareth and Sir Gaheris upon the brainpans, wherethrough they were slain in the field. Howbeit in very truth Sir Lancelot saw them not, and so were they found dead among the thickest of the press.

Then when Sir Lancelot had thus done, and slain and put to flight all that would withstand him, then he rode straight unto Dame Guinevere and made a kirtle and a gown to be cast upon her; and then he made her to be set behind him, and prayed her to be of good cheer. Wit you well, the queen was glad that she was escaped from the death. And then she thanked God and Sir Lancelot; and so he rode his way with the queen, as the French book saith, unto Joyous Gard, and there he kept her as a noble knight should do. And many great lords and some kings sent Sir Lancelot many good knights, and many noble knights drew unto Sir Lancelot. When this was known openly, that King Arthur and Sir Lancelot were at debate, many knights were glad of their debate, and many were full heavy of their debate.

So turn we again unto King Arthur, that when it was told him how and in what manner of wise the queen was taken away from the fire, and when he heard of the death of his noble knights, and in especial of Sir Gaheris and Sir Gareth's death, then the king swooned for pure sorrow. And when he awoke of his swoon, then he said: "Alas, that ever I bore crown upon my head! For now have I lost the fairest fellowship of noble knights that ever held Christian king together. Alas, my good knights be slain away from me. Now within these two days I have lost forty knights, and also the noble fellowship of Sir Lancelot and his blood, for now I may never hold them together no more with my worship [honor]. Alas that ever this war began. Now fair fellows," said the king, "I charge you that no man tell Sir Gawain of the death of his two brethren, for I am sure," said the king, "when Sir Gawain heareth tell that Sir Gareth is dead, he will go nigh out of his mind. Mercy Jesu," said the king, "why slew he Sir Gareth and Sir Gaheris, for I dare say, as for Sir Gareth, he loved Sir Lancelot above all men earthly."

"That is truth," said some knights, "but they were slain in the hurtling as Sir Lancelot thrang [pushed on] in the thick of the press; and as they were unarmed, he smote them and wist [knew] not whom that he smote, and so unhappily they were slain."

"The death of them," said Arthur, "will cause the greatest mortal war that ever was; I am sure, wist Sir Gawain that Sir Gareth were slain, I should never have rest of him till I had destroyed Sir Lancelot's kin and himself both, outher [or] else he to destroy me. And therefore," said the king, "wit you well, my heart was never so heavy as it is now, and much more I am sorrier for my good knights' loss than for the loss of my fair queen; for queens I might have enow, but such a fellowship of good knights shall never be together in no company. And now I dare say," said King Arthur, "there was never Christian king held such a fellowship together; and alas that ever Sir Lancelot and I should be at debate. Ah Agravain, Agravain," said the king, "Jesu forgive it thy soul, for thine evil will that thou and thy brother Sir Mordred hadst unto Sir Lancelot hath caused all this sorrow." And ever among these complaints the king wept and swooned.

Then there came one unto Sir Gawain, and told him how the queen was led away with Sir Lancelot, and nigh a twenty-four knights slain. "O Jesu, defend my brethren," said Sir Gawain, "for full well wist I that Sir Lancelot would rescue her, outher else he would die in that field; and to say the truth, he had not been a man of worship had he not rescued the queen that day, insomuch she should have been brent for his sake. And as in that," said Sir Gawain, "he hath done but knightly, and as I would have done myself, an I had stood in like case. But where are my brethren?" said Sir Gawain, "I marvel I hear not of them."

"Truly," said that man, "Sir Gareth and Sir Gaheris be slain."

"Jesu defend," said Sir Gawain, "for all the world I would not that they were slain, and in especial my good brother, Sir Gareth."

"Sir," said the man, "he is slain, and that is great pity."

"Who slew him?" said Sir Gawain.

"Sir," said the man, "Lancelot slew them both."

"That may I not believe," said Sir Gawain, "that ever he slew my brother Sir Gareth; for I dare say my brother Gareth loved him better than me and all his brethren, and the king both. Also I dare say, an Sir Lancelot had desired my brother Sir Gareth with him, he would have been with him against the king and us all, and therefore I may never believe that Sir Lancelot slew my brother."

"Sir," said this man, "it is noised that he slew him."

"Alas," said Sir Gawain, "now is my joy gone!" And then he fell down and swooned, and long he lay there as [if] he had been dead. And then, when he arose of his swoon, he cried out sorrowfully, and said: "Alas!" And right so Sir Gawain ran to the king, crying and weeping: "O King Arthur, mine uncle, my good brother Sir Gareth is slain, and so is my brother Sir Gaheris, the which were two noble knights." Then the king wept and he, both; and so they fell on swooning. And when they were revived, then spake Sir Gawain: "Sir, I will go see my brother, Sir Gareth."

"Ye may not see him," said the king, "for I caused him to be interred, and Sir Gaheris both; for I well understood that ye would make over-much sorrow, and the sight of Sir Gareth should have caused your double sorrow."

"Alas, my lord," said Sir Gawain, "how slew he my brother Sir Gareth? Mine own good lord, I pray you tell me."

"Truly," said the king, "I shall tell you how it is told me: Sir Lancelot slew him and Sir Gaheris both."

"Alas," said Sir Gawain, "they bore none arms against him, neither of them both."

"I wot not how it was," said the king, "but as it is said, Sir Lancelot slew them both in the thickest of the press and knew them not; and therefore let us shape a remedy for to revenge their deaths."

"My king, my lord, and mine uncle," said Sir Gawain, "wit you well, now I shall make you a promise that I shall hold by my knighthood: that from this day, I shall never fail Sir Lancelot until the one of us have slain the other. And therefore I require you, my lord and king, [ad]dress you to the war, for wit you well: I will be revenged upon Sir Lancelot; and therefore, as ye will have my service and my love, now haste you thereto, and assay [try out] your friends. For I promise unto God," said Sir Gawain, "for the death of my brother Sir Gareth, I shall seek Sir Lancelot throughout seven kings' realms, and I shall slay him or else he shall slay me."

"Ye shall not need to seek him so far," said the king, "for as I hear say, Sir Lancelot will abide me and you in the Joyous Gard; and much people draweth unto him, as I hear say."

"That may I believe," said Sir Gawain; "but, my lord," he said, "assay your friends, and I will assay mine."

"It shall be done," said the king, "and as I suppose, I shall be big enough to draw him out of the biggest tower of his castle." So then the king sent letters and writs throughout all England, both in the length and the breadth, for to summon all his knights. And so unto Arthur drew many knights, dukes, and earls, so that he had a great host. And when they were assembled, the king informed them how Sir Lancelot had bereft him his queen. Then the king and all his host made them ready to lay siege about Sir Lancelot, where he lay within Joyous Gard.

Thereof heard Sir Lancelot, and purveyed him of many good knights, for with him held many knights; and some for his own sake, and some for the queen's sake. Thus they were on both parties well furnished and garnished of all manner of thing that [be]longed to the war. But King Arthur's host was so big that Sir Lancelot would not abide him in the field, for he was full loath to do battle against the king. But Sir Lancelot drew him to his strong castle with all manner of victual, and as many noble men as he might suffice within the town and the castle.

Then came King Arthur with Sir Gawain with an huge host and laid a siege all about Joyous Gard, both at the town and at the castle, and there they made strong war on both parties. But in no wise Sir Lancelot would ride out, nor go out of his castle, of long time; neither he would [allow] none of his good knights to issue out, neither none of the town nor of the castle, until fifteen weeks were past.

Then it befell upon a day in harvest time, Sir Lancelot looked over the walls, and spake on high unto King Arthur and Sir Gawain: "My lords both, wit ye well: all is in vain that ye make at this siege, for here win ye no worship but maugre [ill will] and dishonour; for an it list me to come myself out and my good knights, I should full soon make an end of this war."

"Come forth," said Arthur unto Lancelot, "an thou durst, and I promise thee I shall meet thee in midst of the field."

"God defend me," said Sir Lancelot, "that ever I should encounter with the most noble king that made me knight."

"Fie upon thy fair language," said the king, "for wit you well and trust it: I am thy mortal foe, and ever will to my death day; for thou hast slain my good knights and full noble men of my blood, that I shall never recover again. Also thou hast lain by my queen, and holden her many winters, and sithen like a traitor taken her from me by force."

"My most noble lord and king," said Sir Lancelot, "ye may say what ye will, for ye wot well: with yourself will I not strive. But thereas ye say I have slain your good knights, I wot well that I have done so, and that me sore repenteth; but I was enforced to do battle with them in saving of my life, or else I must have suffered them to have slain me. And as for my lady Queen Guinevere, except your person of your highness, and my lord Sir Gawain, there is no knight under heaven that dare make it good upon me that ever I was traitor unto your person. And where it please you to say that I have holden my lady your queen years and winters, unto that I shall ever make a large answer, and prove it upon any knight that beareth the life, except your person and Sir Gawain, that my lady Queen Guinevere is a true lady unto your person as any is living unto her lord, and that will I make good with my hands. Howbeit it hath liked her good grace to have me in charity, and to cherish me more than any other knight; and unto my power I again have deserved her love, for ofttimes, my lord, ye have consented that she should be brent and destroyed, in your heat, and then it fortuned me to do battle for her; and or I departed from her adversary, they confessed their untruth, and she [was] full worshipfully excused. And at such times, my lord Arthur," said Sir Lancelot, "ye loved me and thanked me when I saved your queen from the fire; and then ye promised me forever to be my good lord; and now methinketh ye reward me full ill for my good service. And, my good lord, meseemeth I had lost a great part of my worship in my knighthood an I had suffered my lady, your queen, to have been brent, and insomuch as she should have been brent for my sake. For sithen I have done battles for your queen in other quarrels than in mine own, meseemeth now I had more right to do battle for her in right quarrel. And therefore my good and gracious lord," said Sir Lancelot, "take your queen unto your good grace, for she is fair, true, and good."

"Fie on thee, false recreant [cowardly] knight," said Sir Gawain. "I let thee wit my lord, mine uncle, King Arthur, shall have his queen and thee, maugre [despite] thy visage, and slay you both wherever it please him."

"It may well be," said Sir Lancelot, "but wit you well, my lord Sir Gawain: an me list to come out of this castle, ye should win me and the queen more harder than ever ye won a strong battle."

"Fie on thy proud words," said Sir Gawain. "As for my lady, the queen, I will never say of her shame. But thou, false and recreant knight," said Sir Gawain, "what cause hadst thou to slay my good brother Sir Gareth, that loved thee more than all my kin? Alas, thou madest him knight with thine own hands; why slew thou him that loved thee so well?"

"For to excuse me," said Sir Lancelot, "it helpeth me not, but by Jesu and by the faith that I owe to the high order of knighthood, I should with as good will have slain my nephew, Sir Bors de Ganis, at that time. But alas that ever I was so unhappy," said Lancelot, "that I had not seen Sir Gareth and Sir Gaheris!"

"Thou liest, recreant knight," said Sir Gawain, "thou slewest him in despite of me; and therefore, wit thou well: I shall make war on thee, and all the while that I may live."

"That me repenteth," said Sir Lancelot, "for well I understand it helpeth not to seek none accordment while ye, Sir Gawain, are so mischievously set. And if ye were not, I would not doubt to have the good grace of my lord Arthur."

"I believe it well, false recreant knight," said Sir Gawain, "for thou hast many long days overlaid [oppressed] me and us all, and destroyed many of our good knights."

"Ye say as it pleaseth you," said Sir Lancelot, "and yet may it never be said of me and openly proved that ever I by forecast of treason slew no good knight, as my lord, Sir Gawain, ye have done; and so did I never, but in my defense that I was driven thereto, in saving of my life."

"Ah, false knight," said Sir Gawain, "that thou meanest by Sir Lamorak; wit thou well I slew him."

"Ye slew him not yourself," said Sir Lancelot. "It had been overmuch on hand for you to have slain him, for he was one of the best knights christened of his age, and it was great pity of his death."

"Well, well," said Sir Gawain to Lancelot, "sithen thou upbraidest me of Sir Lamorak, wit thou well I shall never leave thee till I have thee at such avail that thou shalt not escape my hands."

"I trust you well enough," said Sir Lancelot; "an ye may get me, I get but little mercy."

But as the French book saith, the noble King Arthur would have taken his queen again, and have been accorded with Sir Lancelot, but Sir Gawain would not suffer him by no manner of mean. And then Sir Gawain made many men to blow upon [defame] Sir Lancelot; and all at once they called him false recreant knight. Then when Sir Bors de Ganis, Sir Ector de Maris, and Sir Lionel heard this outcry, they called to them Sir Palomides, Sir Safir's brother, and Sir Lavain, with many more of their blood. And all they went unto Sir Lancelot, and said thus: "My lord Sir Lancelot, wit ye well we have great scorn of the great rebukes that we heard Gawain say to you. Wherefore we pray you, and charge you as ye will have our service, keep us no longer within these walls. For wit you well plainly, we will ride into the field and do battle with them; for ye fare as a man that were afeared, and for all your fair speech, it will not avail you. For wit you well, Sir Gawain will not suffer you to be accorded with King Arthur, and therefore fight for your life and your right, an ye dare."

"Alas," said Sir Lancelot, "for to ride out of this castle and to do battle, I am full loath." Then Sir Lancelot spake on high unto Sir Arthur and Sir Gawain: "My lords, I require you and beseech you, sithen that I am thus required and conjured [urged] to ride into the field, that neither you, my lord King Arthur, nor you, Sir Gawain, come not into the field."

"What shall we do then?" said Sir Gawain. "Is this not the king's quarrel with thee to fight? And it is my quarrel to fight with thee, Sir Lancelot, because of the death of my brother Sir Gareth."

"Then must I needs unto battle," said Sir Lancelot. "Now wit you well, my lord Arthur and Sir Gawain, ye will repent it whensoever I do battle with you."

And so then they departed either from other; and then either party made them ready on the morn for to do battle, and great purveyance was made on both sides; and Sir Gawain let purvey many knights for to wait upon Sir Lancelot, for to overset him and to slay him. And on the morn at undorne [nine o'clock] Sir Arthur was ready in the field with three great hosts. And then Sir Lancelot's fellowship came out at three gates, in a full good array; and Sir Lionel came in the foremost battle, and Sir Lancelot came in the middle, and Sir Bors came out at the third gate. Thus they came in order and rule, as full noble knights; and always Sir Lancelot charged [ordered] all his knights in any wise to save King Arthur and Sir Gawain.

Then came forth Sir Gawain from the king's host, and he came before and proffered to joust. And Sir Lionel was a fierce knight, and lightly he encountered with Sir Gawain; and there Sir Gawain smote Sir Lionel through-out the body, that he dashed to the earth like as he had been dead; and then Sir Ector de Maris and other more bore him into the castle.

Then there began a great stour [battle], and much people was slain; and ever Sir Lancelot did what he might to save the people on King Arthur's party, for Sir Palomides and Sir Bors and Sir Safir overthrew many knights, for they were deadly knights; and Sir Blamore de Ganis, and Sir Bleoberis de Ganis, with Sir Bellengere le Beuse, these six knights did much harm; and ever King Arthur was nigh about Sir Lancelot to have slain him, and Sir Lancelot suffered him, and would not strike again. So Sir Bors encountered with King Arthur, and there with a spear Sir Bors smote him down, and so he alit and drew his sword, and said to Sir Lancelot: "Shall I make an end of this war?" And he meant to have slain King Arthur.

"Not so hardy [violent]," said Sir Lancelot; "upon pain of thy head, that thou touch him no more, for I will never see that most noble king that made me knight neither slain nor shamed."

And therewithal Sir Lancelot alit off his horse and took up the king and horsed him again, and said thus: "My lord Arthur, for God's love, stint this strife, for ye get here no worship, and I would do mine utterance [utmost], but always I forbear [spare] you, and ye nor none of yours forbeareth me; my lord, remember what I have done in many places, and now I am evil rewarded."

Then when King Arthur was on horseback, he looked upon Sir Lancelot, and then the tears brast [burst] out of his eyen, thinking on the great courtesy that was in Sir Lancelot more than in any other man. And therewith the king rode his way, and might no longer behold him, and said: "Alas, that ever this war began!"

And then either parties of the battles withdrew them to repose them, and buried the dead, and to the wounded men they laid soft salves; and thus they endured that night till on the morn. And on the morn by undorne they made them ready to do battle. And then Sir Bors led the forward. So upon the morn there came Sir Gawain as brym [fierce] as any boar, with a great spear in his hand. And when Sir Bors saw him, he thought to revenge his brother Sir Lionel of the despite that Sir Gawain did him the other day. And so they that knew either [each] other feutred [fixed] their spears, and with all the mights of their horses and themselves, they met together so feloniously [fiercely] that either bare the other through, and so they fell both to the earth; and then the battles joined, and there was much slaughter on both parties. Then Sir Lancelot rescued Sir Bors and sent him into the castle; but neither Sir Gawain nor Sir Bors died not of their wounds, for they were all holpen [helped].

Then Sir Lavain and Sir Urry prayed Sir Lancelot to do his pain, and fight as they had done. "For we see ye forbear and spare, and that doth much harm. Therefore we pray you spare not your enemies no more than they do you."

"Alas," said Sir Lancelot, "I have no heart to fight against my lord Arthur, for ever meseemeth I do not as I ought to do."

"My lord," said Sir Palomides, "though ye spare them all this day, they will never conne you thank [be grateful]; and if they may get you at avail [disadvantage], ye are but dead." So then Sir Lancelot understood that they said him truth; and then he strained himself more than he did aforehand, and because his nephew Sir Bors was sore wounded.

And then within a little while, by evensong [sunset] time, Sir Lancelot and his party better stood, for their horses went in blood past the fetlocks, there was so much people slain. And then for pity Sir Lancelot withheld his knights and suffered King Arthur's party for to withdraw them inside. And then Sir Lancelot's party withdrew them into his castle, and either parties buried the dead, and put salve unto the wounded men. So when Sir Gawain was hurt, they on King Arthur's party were not so orgulous [eager] as they were toforehand to do battle.

Of this war was noised through all Christendom, and at the last it was noised afore the Pope; and he, considering the great goodness of King Arthur and of Sir Lancelot, that was called the most noblest knights of the world, wherefore the Pope called unto him a noble clerk that at that time was there present. The French book saith it was the Bishop of Rochester; and the Pope gave him bulls under lead unto King Arthur of England, charging him upon pain of the interdicting [excommunication] of all England that he take his queen Dame Guinevere unto him again, and accord with Sir Lancelot.

So when this Bishop was come to Carlisle, he showed the king these bulls. And when the king understood these bulls he nyst [knew not] what to do: full fain he would have been accorded with Sir Lancelot, but Sir Gawain would not suffer him; but as for to have the queen, thereto he agreed. But in no wise Sir Gawain would not suffer the king to accord with Sir Lancelot; but as for the queen, he consented. And then the Bishop had of the king his great seal, and his assurance, as he was a true anointed king, that Sir Lancelot should come safe and go safe, and that the queen should not be spoken unto of [badly by] the king, nor of none other, for no thing done aforetime past; and of all these appointments [agreements] the Bishop brought with him sure assurance and writing, to show Sir Lancelot.

So when the Bishop was come to Joyous Gard, there he showed Sir Lancelot how the Pope had written to Arthur and unto him, and there he told him the perils if he withheld the queen from the king. "It was never in my thought," said Lancelot, "to withhold the queen from my lord Arthur; but, insomuch she should have been dead for my sake, meseemeth it was my part to save her life, and put her from that danger, till better recover might come. And now I thank God," said Sir Lancelot, "that the Pope hath made her peace; for God knoweth," said Sir Lancelot, "I will be a thousandfold more gladder to bring her again, than ever I was of her taking away; with this [condition]: I may be sure to come safe and go safe, and that the queen shall have her liberty as she had before; and never for no thing that hath been surmised afore this time, she never from this day stand in no peril. For else," said Sir Lancelot, "I dare adventure me to keep her from an harder shower [battle] than ever I kept her."

"It shall not need you," said the Bishop, "to dread so much. For wit you well, the Pope must be obeyed, and it were not the Pope's worship nor my poor honesty to wit [think that] you distressed the queen, neither in peril, nor shamed." And then he showed Sir Lancelot all his writing, both from the Pope and from King Arthur.

"This is sure enough," said Sir Lancelot, "for full well I dare trust my lord's own writing and his seal, for he was never shamed of his promise. Therefore," said Sir Lancelot unto the Bishop, "ye shall ride unto the king afore, and recommend me unto his good grace, and let him have knowledging that this same day eight days [from now] by the grace of God I myself shall bring my lady, Queen Guinevere, unto him. And then say ye unto my most redoubted [noble] king, that I will say largely for [defend] the queen, that I shall none except [spare] for dread nor fear but the king himself and my lord Sir Gawain; and that is more for the king's love [sake] than for himself." So the Bishop departed and came to the king at Carlisle, and told him all how Sir Lancelot answered him; and then the tears brast out of the king's eyen.

Then Sir Lancelot purveyed him an hundred knights, and all were clothed in green velvet, and their horses [in the same] to their heels; and every knight held a branch of olive in his hand, in tokening of peace. And the queen had four-and-twenty gentlewomen following her in the same wise; and Sir Lancelot had twelve coursers following him, and on every courser sat a young gentleman, and all they were arrayed in green velvet, with sarpys [bands] of gold about their quarters, and the horse trapped [draped] in the same wise down to the heels, with many ouches [ornaments] set with stones and pearls in gold, to the number of a thousand. And she and Sir Lancelot were clothed in white cloth of gold tissue; and right so as ye have heard, as the French book maketh mention, he rode with the queen from Joyous Gard to Carlisle. And so Sir Lancelot rode throughout Carlisle, and so into the castle, that all men might behold; and wit you well, there was many a weeping eye.

And then Sir Lancelot himself alit and voided his horse, and took the queen, and so led her where King Arthur was in his seat; and Sir Gawain sat afore him, and many other great lords. So when Sir Lancelot saw the king and Sir Gawain, then he led the queen by the arm, and then he kneeled down, and the queen both. Wit you well, then was there many a bold knight there with King Arthur that wept as tenderly as though they had seen all their kin dead afore them. So the king sat still, and said no word.

And when Sir Lancelot saw his countenance, he arose and pulled up the queen with him, and thus he spake full knightly: "My most redoubted king, ye shall understand, by the Pope's commandment and yours, I have brought to you my lady the queen, as right requireth; and if there be any knight, of whatsoever degree that he be, except your person, that will say or dare say but that she is true and clean to you, I here myself, Sir Lancelot du Lake, will make it good upon his body that she is a true lady unto you; but liars ye have listened, and that hath caused debate betwixt you and me. For time hath been, my lord Arthur, that ye have been greatly pleased with me when I did battle for my lady, your queen; and full well ye know, my most noble king, that she hath been put to great wrong or this time; and sithen it pleased you at many times that I should fight for her, meseemeth, my good lord, I had more cause to rescue her from the fire, insomuch she should have been brent for my sake. For they that told you those tales were liars, and so it fell upon them; for by likelihood had not the might of God been with me, I might never have endured fourteen knights, and they armed and afore purposed [prepared], and I unarmed and not purposed. For I was sent for unto my lady your queen, I wot not for what cause; but I was not so soon within the chamber door, but anon Sir Agravain and Sir Mordred called me traitor and recreant knight."

"They called thee right," said Sir Gawain.

"My lord Sir Gawain," said Sir Lancelot, "in their quarrel they proved themselves not in the right."

"Well, well, Sir Lancelot," said the king, "I have given thee no cause to do to me as thou hast done, for I have worshipped [honored] thee and thine more than any of all my knights."

"My good lord," said Sir Lancelot, "so ye be not displeased, ye shall understand I and mine have done you oft better service than any other knights have done, in many diverse places; and where ye have been full hard bestad diverse times, I have myself rescued you from many dangers. And ever unto my power I was glad to please you, and my lord Sir Gawain, both in jousts, and tournaments, and in battles set. Both on horseback and on foot, I have often rescued you and my lord Sir Gawain and many more of your knights in many diverse places.

"For now I will make a vaunt," said Sir Lancelot: "I will that ye all wit that yet I found never no manner of knight but that I was overhard for [overcame] him, an I had done my utterance [utmost], thanked be God; howbeit I have been matched with good knights, as Sir Tristram and Sir Lamorak, but ever I had a favour unto them and a deeming [suspicion of] what they were. And I take God to record," said Sir Lancelot, "I never was wroth nor greatly heavy with no good knight, an I saw him busy about to win worship; and glad I was ever when I found any knight that might endure me on horseback and on foot. Howbeit Sir Carados of the Dolorous Tower was a full noble knight and a passing strong man, and that wot ye, my lord Sir Gawain; for he might well be called a noble knight when he by fine force pulled you out of your saddle, and bound you overthwart [crosswise] afore him to his saddle bow; and there, my lord Sir Gawain, I rescued you, and slew him afore your sight. Also I found his brother, Sir Tarquin, in like wise leading Sir Gaheris, your brother, bound afore him; and there I rescued your brother and slew that Tarquin, and delivered threescore and four of my lord Arthur's knights out of his prison. And now I dare say," said Sir Lancelot, "I met never with so strong knights, nor so well fighting, as was Sir Carados and Sir Tarquin, for I fought with them to the uttermost. And therefore," said Sir Lancelot unto Sir Gawain, "meseemeth ye ought of right to remember this; for, an I might have your good will, I would trust to God to have my lord Arthur's good grace."

"The king may do as he will," said Sir Gawain, "but wit thou well, Sir Lancelot, thou and I shall never be accorded while we live, for thou hast slain three of my brethren; and two of them ye slew traitorly and piteously, for they bare none harness [armor] against thee, nor none would bear."

"God would they had been armed," said Sir Lancelot, "for then had they been on life. And wit ye well, Sir Gawain, as for Sir Gareth, I love none of my kinsmen so much as I did him. And ever while I live," said Sir Lancelot "I will bewail Sir Gareth's death, not all only for the great fear I have of you but many causes cause me to be sorrowful. One is, for I made him knight; another is, I wot well he loved me above all other knights; and the third is, he was passing noble, true, courteous, and gentle, and well conditioned; the fourth is, I wist well, anon as I heard that Sir Gareth was dead, I should never after have your love, but everlasting war betwixt us; and also I wist well that ye would cause my noble lord Arthur forever to be my mortal foe. And as Jesu be my help," said Sir Lancelot, "I slew never Sir Gareth nor Sir Gaheris by my will, but alas that ever they were unarmed that unhappy day. But thus much I shall offer me," said Sir Lancelot, "if it may please the king's good grace and you, my lord Sir Gawain: I shall first begin at Sandwich, and there I shall go in my shirt, barefoot; and at every ten miles' end I will found and gar make [cause built] an house of religion, of what order that ye will assign me, with an holy convent, to sing and read, day and night, in especial for Sir Gareth's sake and Sir Gaheris. And this shall I perform from Sandwich unto Carlisle; and every house shall have sufficient livelihood. And this shall I perform while I have any livelihood in Christendom; and there is none of all these religious places, but they shall be performed, furnished and garnished in all things as an holy place ought to be, I promise you faithfully. And this, Sir Gawain, methinketh were more fairer, holier, and more better to their souls, than [for] ye, my most noble king, and you, Sir Gawain, to war upon me, for thereby shall ye get none avail."

Then all knights and ladies that were there wept as they were mad, and the tears fell on King Arthur's cheeks. "Sir Lancelot," said Sir Gawain, "I have right well heard thy speech, and thy great proffers, but wit thou well: let the king do as it pleaseth him; I will never forgive my brothers' death, and in especial the death of my brother Sir Gareth. And if mine uncle, King Arthur, will accord with thee, he shall lose my service, for wit thou well, thou art both false to the king and to me."

"Sir," said Lancelot, "he beareth not the life that may make that good; and if ye, Sir Gawain, will charge me with so high a thing, ye must pardon me, for then needs must I answer you."

"Nay," said Sir Gawain, "we are past that at this time, and that [was] caused [by] the Pope, for he hath charged mine uncle, the king, that he shall take his queen again, and to accord with thee, Sir Lancelot, as for this season, and therefore thou shalt go safe as thou camest. But in this land thou shalt not abide past fifteen days, such summons I give thee; so the king and we were consented and accorded ere thou camest. And else," said Sir Gawain, "wit thou well thou shouldst not have come here, but if it were maugre [to lose] thy head. And if it were not for the Pope's commandment," said Sir Gawain, "I should do battle with mine own body against thy body, and prove it upon thee, that thou hast been both false unto mine uncle King Arthur, and to me both; and that shall I prove upon thy body, when thou art departed from hence, wheresoever I find thee."

Then Sir Lancelot sighed, and therewith the tears fell on his cheeks, and then he said thus: "Alas, most noble Christian realm, whom I have loved above all other realms, and in thee I have gotten a great part of my worship, and now I shall depart in this wise. Truly me repenteth that ever I came in this realm, that I should be thus shamefully banished, undeserved and causeless; but fortune is so variant, and the wheel so movable, there is none constant abiding, and that may be proved by many old chronicles, of noble Hector and Troilus and Alexander the mighty Conqueror, and many more others; when they were most in their royalty, they alit lowest. And so fareth it by me," said Sir Lancelot, "for in this realm I had worship, and by me and mine all the whole Round Table hath been increased more in worship by me and mine blood than by any other. And therefore wit thou well, Sir Gawain, I may live upon my lands as well as any knight that here is. And if ye, most redoubted king, will come upon my lands with Sir Gawain to war upon me, I must endure you as well as I may. But as to you, Sir Gawain, if that ye come there, I pray you charge me not with treason nor felony, for an ye do, I must answer you."

"Do thou thy best," said Sir Gawain. "Therefore hie thee fast that thou were gone, and wit thou well we shall soon come after, and break the strongest castle that thou hast upon thy head."

"That shall not need," said Sir Lancelot, "for an I were as orgulous set [arrogant] as ye are, wit you well I should meet you in the midst of the field."

"Make thou no more language," said Sir Gawain, "but deliver the queen from thee, and pick thee lightly out of this court."

"Well," said Sir Lancelot, "an I had wist of this shortcoming [hassle], I would have advised me twice ere that I had come hither; for an the queen had been so dear to me as ye noise her, I durst [should] have kept her from the fellowship of the best knights under heaven."

And then Sir Lancelot said unto Guinevere, in hearing of the king and them all: "Madam, now I must depart from you and this noble fellowship forever; and sithen it is so, I beseech you to pray for me, and say me well; and if ye be hard bestad [ill beset] by any false tongues, lightly my lady send me word, and if any knight's hands may deliver you by battle, I shall deliver you." And therewithal Sir Lancelot kissed the queen. And then he said all openly: "Now let see whatever he be in this place that dare say the queen is not true unto my lord Arthur; let see who will speak an he dare speak."

And therewith he brought the queen to the king, and then Sir Lancelot took his leave and departed; and there was neither king, duke, nor earl, baron nor knight, lady nor gentlewoman, but all they wept as people out of their mind, except Sir Gawain. And when the noble Sir Lancelot took his horse to ride out of Carlisle, there was sobbing and weeping for pure dole of his departing; and so he took his way unto Joyous Gard. And then ever after he called it the Dolorous Gard. And thus departed Sir Lancelot from the court forever.

And so when he came to Joyous Gard, he called his fellowship unto him and asked them what they would do. Then they answered all wholly together with one voice, they would [do] as he would do. "My fair fellows," said Sir Lancelot, "I must depart out of this most noble realm, and now I shall depart, it grieveth me sore, for I shall depart with no worship, for a flemed [banished] man departed ever out of a realm with no worship; and that is my heaviness. Forever I fear after my days that men shall chronicle upon me that I was flemed out of this land; and else, my fair lords, be ye sure, an I had not dreaded shame, my lady, Queen Guinevere, and I should never have departed [parted]."

Then spake many noble knights, as Sir Palomides, Sir Safir his brother, and Sir Bellengere le Beuse, and Sir Urry, with Sir Lavain, with many others: "Sir, an ye be so disposed to abide in this land, we will never fail you; and if ye list not to abide in this land, there is none of the good knights that here be will fail you, for many causes. One is: all we that be not of your blood shall never be welcome to the court. And sithen it liked us to take part with you in your distress and heaviness in this realm, wit you well it shall like us as well to go in other countries with you, and there to take such part as ye do."

"My fair lords," said Sir Lancelot, "I well understand you, and as I can, thank you: and ye shall understand, such livelihood as I am born unto, I shall depart [share] with you in this manner of wise; that is for to say, I shall depart all my livelihood and all my lands freely among you, and I myself will have as little as any of you; for have I sufficient that [which] may [be]long to my person; I will ask none other rich array; and I trust to God to maintain you on my lands as well as ever were maintained any knights."

Then spake all the knights at once: "He [should] have shame that will leave you; for we all understand: in this realm will be now no quiet, but ever strife and debate; now the fellowship of the Round Table is broken; for by the noble fellowship of the Round Table was King Arthur upborne, and by their noblesse, the king and all his realm was in quiet and rest, and a great part they said all was because of your noblesse."

"Truly," said Sir Lancelot, "I thank you all of your good saying. How-beit, I wot well, in me was not all the stability of this realm, but in that I might, I did my devoir [duty]; and well I am sure I knew many rebellions in my days that by me were peaced, and I trow [believe] we all shall hear of them in short space, and that me sore repenteth. For ever I dread me," said Sir Lancelot, "that Sir Mordred will make trouble, for he is passing envious and applieth him to trouble."

So they were accorded to go with Sir Lancelot to his lands, and to make short tale, they trussed [equipped] and paid all that would ask them. And wholly an hundred knights departed with Sir Lancelot at once, and made their avows they would never leave him for weal nor for woe. And so they shipped at Cardiff, and sailed unto Benwick. Some men call it Bayonne, and some men call it Beaune, where the wine of Beaune is. But to say the sooth, Sir Lancelot and his nephews were lords of all France, and of all the lands that [be]longed unto France; he and his kindred rejoiced [possessed] it all, through Sir Lancelot's noble prowess. And then Sir Lancelot stuffed and furnished and garnished all his noble towns and castles. Then all the people of those lands came to Sir Lancelot on foot and hands [in submission].

And so when he had stablished all these countries, he shortly called a parliament; and there he crowned Sir Lionel King of France; and Sir Bors crowned him king of all King Claudas' lands; and Sir Ector de Maris, that was Sir Lancelot's youngest brother, he crowned him King of Benwick, and king of all Guienne, that was Sir Lancelot's own land. And he made Sir Ector prince of them all, and thus he departed.

Then Sir Lancelot advanced all his noble knights, and first he advanced them of his blood: that was, Sir Blamore, he made him Duke of Limousin in Guienne; and Sir Bleoberis, he made him Duke of Poitiers; and Sir Gahalantine, he made him Duke of Auvergne; and Sir Galihodin, he made him Duke of Santonge; and Sir Galihud, he made him Earl of Périgord; and Sir Menaduke, he made him Earl of Rouerge; and Sir Villiars the Valiant, he made him Earl of Béarn; and Sir Hebes le Renoumes, he made him Earl of Comminges; and Sir Lavain, he made him Earl of Armagnac; and Sir Urry, he made him Earl of Estrake; and Sir Neroveous, he made him Earl of Pardiak; and Sir Plenorius, he made Earl of Foix; and Sir Selises of the Dolorous Tower, he made him Earl of Marsan; and Sir Melias de Lille, he made him Earl of Tursar; and Sir Bellengere le Beuse, he made Earl of the Landes; and Sir Palomides, he made him Duke of the Provence; and Sir Safir, he made him Duke of Languedoc; and Sir Clegis, he gave him the Earldom of Agen; and Sir Sadok, he gave him the Earldom of Sarlat; and Sir Dinas le Seneschal, he made him Duke of Anjou; and Sir Clarrus, he made him Duke of Normandy. Thus Sir Lancelot rewarded his noble knights and many more, that meseemeth it were too long to rehearse.

So leave we Sir Lancelot in his lands, and his noble knights with him, and return we again unto King Arthur and to Sir Gawain, that made a great host ready, to the number of threescore thousand; and all thing was made ready for their shipping to pass over the sea, and so they shipped at Cardiff. And there King Arthur made Sir Mordred chief ruler of all England, and also he put Queen Guinevere under his governance; because Sir Mordred was King Arthur's son, he gave him the rule of his land and of his wife. And so the king passed the sea and landed upon Sir Lancelot's lands, and there he brent and wasted, through the vengeance of Sir Gawain, all that they might overrun.

When this word came to Sir Lancelot, that King Arthur and Sir Gawain were landed upon his lands, and made a full great destruction and waste, then spake Sir Bors, and said: "My lord Sir Lancelot, it is shame that we suffer them thus to ride over our lands, for wit you well, suffer ye them as long as ye will, they will do you no favour an they may handle [capture] you."

Then said Sir Lionel, that was wary and wise: "My lord Sir Lancelot, I will give you this counsel: let us keep our strong walled towns until they have hunger and cold, and blow on their nails; and then let us freshly set upon them, and shred them down as sheep in a field, that aliens may take example forever how they land upon our lands."

Then spake King Bagdemagus to Sir Lancelot: "Sir, your courtesy will shende [destroy] us all, and your courtesy hath waked all this sorrow; for an they thus over our lands ride, they shall by process bring us all to nought whilst we thus in holes us hide."

Then said Sir Galihud unto Sir Lancelot: "Sir, here be knights come of kings' blood, that will not long droop [cower], and they are within these walls; therefore give us leave, like as we be knights, to meet them in the field, and we shall slay them, that they shall curse the time that ever they came into this country."

Then spake seven brethren of North Wales, and they were seven noble knights; a man might seek in seven kings' lands or [before] he might find such seven knights. Then they all said at once: "Sir Lancelot, for Christ's sake, let us out ride with Sir Galihud, for we be never wont to cower in castles nor in noble towns."

Then spake Sir Lancelot, that was master and governor of them all: "My fair lords, wit you well I am full loath to ride out with my knights for shedding of Christian blood; and yet my lands I understand be full bare for to sustain any host awhile, for [because of] the mighty wars that whilom [previously] King Claudas made upon this country, upon my father King Ban, and on mine uncle King Bors; howbeit we will as at this time keep our strong walls, and I shall send a messenger unto my lord Arthur, a treaty for to take; for better is peace than always war."

So Sir Lancelot sent forth a damosel and a dwarf with her, requiring King Arthur to leave his warring upon his lands; and so she start[ed] upon a palfrey, and the dwarf ran by her side. And when she came to the pavilion of King Arthur, there she alit; and there met her a gentle knight, Sir Lucan the Butler, and said: "Fair damosel, come ye from Sir Lancelot du Lake?" "Yea sir," she said; "therefore I come hither to speak with my lord the king." "Alas," said Sir Lucan, "my lord Arthur would love Lancelot, but Sir Gawain will not suffer him." And then he said: "I pray to God, damosel, ye may speed well, for all we that be about the king would that Sir Lancelot did best of any knight living." And so with this, Lucan led the damosel unto the king, where he sat with Sir Gawain, for to hear what she would say.

So when she had told her tale, the water ran out of the king's eyen, and all the lords were full glad for to advise the king as to be accorded with Sir Lancelot, save all only Sir Gawain. And he said: "My lord mine uncle, what will ye do? Will ye now turn again, now ye are passed thus far upon this journey? All the world will speak of your villainy."

"Nay," said Arthur, "wit thou well, Sir Gawain, I will do as ye will advise me. And yet meseemeth," said Arthur, "his fair proffers were not good to be refused; but sithen I am come so far upon this journey, I will that ye give the damosel her answer, for I may not speak to her for pity, for her proffers be so large."

Then Sir Gawain said to the damosel thus: "Damosel, say ye to Sir Lancelot that it is waste labour now to sue [appeal] to mine uncle; for tell him, an he would have made any labour for peace, he should have made it or this time, for tell him now it is too late. And say that I, Sir Gawain, so send him word that I promise him by the faith I owe unto God and to knighthood, I shall never leave him till he hath slain me or I him."

So the damosel wept and departed, and there were many weeping eyen; and so Sir Lucan brought the damosel to her palfrey, and so she came to Sir Lancelot where he was among all his knights. And when Sir Lancelot had heard this answer, then the tears ran down by his cheeks. And then his noble knights strode about him and said: "Sir Lancelot, wherefore make ye such cheer? Think what ye are, and what men we are, and let us noble knights match them in midst of the field."

"That may be lightly done," said Sir Lancelot, "but I was never so loath to do battle, and therefore I pray you, fair sirs, as ye love me, be ruled as I will have you, for I will always flee that noble king that made me knight. And when I may no further, I must needs defend me, and that will be more worship for me and us all than to compare [contend] with that noble king whom we have all served."

Then they held their language, and as that night [came], they took their rest. And upon the morn early, in the dawning of the day, as knights looked out, they saw the city of Benwick besieged round about; and fast they began to set up ladders, and then they defied [chased] them out of the town, and beat them from the walls mightily.

Then came forth Sir Gawain well armed upon a stiff steed, and he came before the chief gate, with his spear in his hand, crying: "Sir Lancelot, where art thou? Is there none of your proud knights that dare break a spear with me?"

Then Sir Bors made him ready, and came forth out of the town, and there Sir Gawain encountered with Sir Bors. And at that time he smote Sir Bors down from his horse, and almost he had slain him; and so Sir Bors was rescued and borne into the town.

Then came forth Sir Lionel, brother to Sir Bors, and thought to revenge him; and either feutred [fixed] their spears, and ran together; and there they met spitefully, but Sir Gawain had such grace that he smote Sir Lionel down, and wounded him there passing sore; and then Sir Lionel was rescued and borne into the town.

And thus Sir Gawain came every day, and he failed not but that he smote down one knight or other. So thus they endured half a year, and much slaughter was of people on both parties. Then it befell upon a day, Sir Gawain came afore the gates armed at all pieces on a noble horse, with a great spear in his hand; and then he cried with a loud voice: "Where art thou now, thou false traitor, Sir Lancelot? Why hidest thou thyself within holes and walls like a coward? Look out now, thou false traitor knight, and here I shall revenge upon thy body the death of my three brethren!"

All this language heard Sir Lancelot [in] every deal [part]; and his kin and his knights drew about him, and all they said at once to Sir Lancelot: "Sir Lancelot, now must ye defend you like a knight, or else ye be shamed forever; for now ye be called upon [accused of] treason, it is time for you to stir, for ye have slept overlong and suffered overmuch."

"So God me help," said Sir Lancelot, "I am right heavy of Sir Gawain's words, for now he charged me with a great charge; and therefore I wot it as well as ye, that I must defend me, or else to be recreant."

Then Sir Lancelot bade saddle his strongest horse, and bade let fetch his arms, and bring all unto the gate of the tower; and then Sir Lancelot spake on high unto King Arthur, and said: "My lord Arthur, and noble king that made me knight, wit you well I am right heavy for your sake, that ye thus sue upon [pursue] me; and always I forbare [tolerated] you, for would I have been vengeable, I might have met you in midst of the field, and there to have made your boldest knights full tame. And now I have forborne half a year, and suffered you and Sir Gawain to do what ye would do. And now may I endure it no longer, for now must I needs defend myself, insomuch Sir Gawain hath appelled [accused] me of treason, the which is greatly against my will that ever I should fight against any of your blood, but now I may not forsake it; I am driven thereto as a beast till a [at] bay."

Then Sir Gawain said: "Sir Lancelot, an thou durst do battle, leave thy babbling and come off, and let us ease our hearts."

Then Sir Lancelot armed him lightly, and mounted upon his horse, and either of the knights got great spears in their hands, and the host without stood still all apart, and the noble knights came out of the city by a great number, insomuch that when Arthur saw the number of men and knights, he marvelled, and said to himself: "Alas, that ever Sir Lancelot was against me, for now I see he hath forborne me." And so the covenant was made, there should no man [draw] nigh them, nor deal with them, till the one were dead or yielded.

Then Sir Gawain and Sir Lancelot departed a great way asunder, and then they came together with all their horses' might as they might run, and either smote other in midst of their shields. But the knights were so strong, and their spears so big, that their horses might not endure their buffets, and so their horses fell to the earth; and then they voided [left] their horses, and dressed their shields before them. Then they stood together and gave many sad strokes on diverse places of their bodies, that the blood brast out on many sides and places.

Then had Sir Gawain such a grace and gift that an holy man had given to him, that every day in the year, from underne [nine o'clock] till high noon his might increased those three hours as much as thrice his strength, and that caused Sir Gawain to win great honour. And for his sake King Arthur made an ordinance that all manner of battles for any quarrels that should be done afore King Arthur should begin at underne; and all was done for Sir Gawain's love, that by likelihood, if Sir Gawain were on the one part, he should have the better in battle while his strength endureth three hours. But there were but few knights that time living that knew this advantage that Sir Gawain had, but King Arthur only.

Thus Sir Lancelot fought with Sir Gawain, and when Sir Lancelot felt his might evermore increase, Sir Lancelot wondered and dread him sore to be shamed. For as the French book saith, Sir Lancelot weened [thought] when he felt Sir Gawain double his strength, that he had been a fiend and none earthly man; wherefore Sir Lancelot traced and traversed [dodged back and forth], and covered himself with his shield, and kept his might and his breath during three hours. And that while Sir Gawain gave him many sad brunts, and many sad strokes, that all the knights that beheld Sir Lancelot marvelled how that he might endure him; but full little understood they that travail that Sir Lancelot had for to endure him.

And then when it was past noon, Sir Gawain had no more but his own might. When Sir Lancelot felt him so come down, then he stretched himself up and stood near Sir Gawain, and said thus: "My lord Sir Gawain, now I feel ye have done; now my lord Sir Gawain, I must do my part, for many great and grievous strokes I have endured you this day with great pain." Then Sir Lancelot doubled his strokes and gave Sir Gawain such a buffet on the helmet that he fell down on his side, and Sir Lancelot withdrew himself from him.

"Why withdrawest thou thee?" said Sir Gawain. "Now turn again, false traitor knight, and slay me, for an thou leave me thus, when I am whole I shall do battle with thee again."

"I shall endure you, sir, by God's grace, but wit thou well, Sir Gawain, I will never smite a felled knight." And so Sir Lancelot went into the city, and Sir Gawain was borne into King Arthur's pavilion, and leeches were brought to him that searched [examined] and salved him with soft ointments. And then Sir Lancelot said: "Now have good day, my lord the king, for wit you well ye win no worship at these walls; and if I would my knights outbring, there should many a man die. Therefore, my lord Arthur, remember you of old kindness; and however I fare, Jesu be your guide in all places."

"Alas," said the king, "that ever this unhappy war was begun; for ever Sir Lancelot forbeareth me in all places, and in like wise my kin, and that is seen well this day by my nephew Sir Gawain." Then King Arthur fell sick for sorrow of Sir Gawain, that he was so sore hurt, and because of the war betwixt him and Sir Lancelot. So then they on King Arthur's part kept the siege with little war without, and they within kept their walls, and defended them when need was. Thus Sir Gawain lay sick three weeks in his tents, with all manner of leechcraft that might be had.

And as soon as Sir Gawain might go and ride, he armed him at all points, and started upon a courser, and gat a spear in his hand, and so he came riding afore the chief gate of Benwick; and there he cried on high: "Where art thou, Sir Lancelot? Come forth, thou false traitor knight and recreant, for I am here, Sir Gawain, [and] will prove this that I say on thee!"

All this language Sir Lancelot heard, and then he said thus: "Sir Gawain, me repents of your foul saying, that ye will not cease your language. For ye wot well, Sir Gawain, I know your might and all that ye may do; and well ye wot, Sir Gawain, ye may not greatly hurt me."

"Come down, traitor knight," said he, "and make good the contrary with thy hands, for it mishapped me the last battle to be hurt of thy hands; therefore wit thou well, I am come this day to make amends, for I ween this day to lay thee as low as thou laidest me."

"Jesu defend me," said Sir Lancelot, "that ever I be so far in your danger [control] as ye have been in mine, for then my days were done. But Sir Gawain," said Sir Lancelot, "ye shall not think that I tarry long, but sithen that ye so unknightly call me of treason, ye shall have both your hands full of me." And then Sir Lancelot armed him at all points, and mounted upon his horse, and gat a great spear in his hand, and rode out at the gate. And both the hosts were assembled, of them without and of them within, and stood in array full manly. And both parties were charged to hold them still, to see and behold the battle of these two noble knights. And then they laid their spears in their rests, and they came together as thunder, and Sir Gawain brake his spear upon Sir Lancelot in an hundred pieces unto his hand; and Sir Lancelot smote him with a greater might, that Sir Gawain's horse's feet raised, and so the horse and he fell to the earth.

Then Sir Gawain deliverly [quickly] voided his horse, and put his shield afore him, and eagerly drew his sword, and bade Sir Lancelot: "Alight, traitor knight, for if this mare's son hath failed me, wit thou well a king's son and a queen's son shall not fail thee."

Then Sir Lancelot voided his horse, and dressed his shield afore him, and drew his sword; and so stood they together and gave many sad strokes, that all men on both parties had thereof passing great wonder. But when Sir Lancelot felt Sir Gawain's might so marvellously increase, he then withheld his courage and his wind, and kept himself wonder[fully] covert of his might; and under his shield he traced and traversed here and there, to break Sir Gawain's strokes and his courage; and Sir Gawain enforced himself with all his might and power to destroy Sir Lancelot. For as the French book saith, ever as Sir Gawain's might increased, right so increased his wind and his evil will. Thus Sir Gawain did great pain unto Sir Lancelot three hours, that he had right great pain for to defend himself.

And when the three hours were passed, so that Sir Lancelot felt that Sir Gawain was come to his own proper strength, then Sir Lancelot said unto Sir Gawain: "Now have I proved you twice that ye are a full dangerous knight, and a wonderful man of your might; and many wonderful deeds have you done in your days, for by your might increasing you have deceived many a full noble and valiant knight; and now I feel that ye have done your mighty deeds; now wit you well, I must do my deeds."

And then Sir Lancelot strode near Sir Gawain, and then Sir Lancelot doubled his strokes. And Sir Gawain defended him mightily, but nevertheless Sir Lancelot smote such a stroke upon Sir Gawain's helm and upon the old wound that Sir Gawain sinked down upon his one side in a swoon.

And anon as he did awake, he waved and foined [thrust] at Sir Lancelot as he lay, and said: "Traitor knight, wit thou well, I am not yet slain; come thou near me and perform this battle unto the uttermost."

"I will no more do than I have done," said Sir Lancelot, "for when I see you on foot, I will do battle upon you all the while I see you stand on your feet; but for to smite a wounded man that may not stand, God defend me from such a shame!"

And then he turned him and went his way toward the city. And Sir Gawain evermore calling him a traitor knight, and said: "Wit thou well, Sir Lancelot, when I am whole I shall do battle with thee again, for I shall never leave thee till that one of us be slain."

Thus as this siege endured and as Sir Gawain lay sick near a month, and when he was well recovered and ready within three days to do battle again with Sir Lancelot, right so came tidings unto Arthur from England that made King Arthur and all his host to remove.

XXI. The Last Departing of Arthur

As Sir Mordred was ruler of all England, he did make letters as though that they came from beyond the sea, and the letters specified that King Arthur was slain in battle with Sir Lancelot. Wherefore Sir Mordred made a parliament and called the lords together, and there he made them to choose him king; and so was he crowned at Canterbury, and held a feast there fifteen days. And afterward he drew him unto Winchester, and there he took the Queen Guinevere, and said plainly that he would wed her, which was his uncle's wife and his father's wife. And so he made ready for the feast, and a day prefixed that they should be wedded; wherefore Queen Guinevere was passing heavy. But she durst not discover her heart, but spake fair, and agreed to Sir Mordred's will. Then she desired of Sir Mordred for to go to London, to buy all manner of things that belonged unto the wedding. And by cause of her fair speech, Sir Mordred trusted her well enough, and gave her leave to go.

And so when she came to London, she took the Tower of London and suddenly in all haste possible she stuffed it with all manner of victual, and well garnished it with men, and so kept it. Then when Sir Mordred wist and understood how he was beguiled, he was passing wroth out of measure. And a short tale for to make, he went and laid a mighty siege about the Tower of London, and made many great assaults thereat, and threw many great engines unto them, and shot great guns. But all might not prevail, for Queen Guinevere would never for fair speech nor for foul, would never trust to come in his hands again.

Then came the Bishop of Canterbury, the which was a noble clerk and an holy man, and thus he said to Sir Mordred: "Sir, what will ye do? Will ye first displease God and sithen shame yourself and all knighthood? Is not King Arthur your uncle, no farther but your mother's brother, and on her himself King Arthur begat you upon his own sister; therefore how may you wed your father's wife? Sir," said the noble clerk, "leave this opinion or I shall curse you with book and bell and candle."

"Do thou thy worst," said Sir Mordred; "wit thou well I shall defy thee."

"Sir," said the Bishop, "and wit you well I shall not fear me to do that me ought to do. Also, where ye noise where my lord Arthur is slain, and that is not so, and therefore ye will make a foul work in this land."

"Peace, thou false priest," said Sir Mordred, "for an thou chafe me any more, I shall make off thy head."

So the Bishop departed and did the cursing in the most orgulist [proudest] wise that might be done. And then Sir Mordred sought the Bishop of Canterbury, for to have slain him. Then the Bishop fled, and took part of his goods with him, and went nigh unto Glastonbury; and there he was as priest hermit in a chapel, and lived in poverty and in holy prayers, for well he understood that mischievous war was at hand.

Then Sir Mordred sought on Queen Guinevere by letters and sondes [messengers], and by fair means and foul means, for to have her to come out of the Tower of London. But all this availed not, for she answered him shortly, openly and privily, that she had liefer [rather] slay herself than to be married with him.

Then came word to Sir Mordred that King Arthur had raised the siege from Sir Lancelot, and he was coming homeward with a great host, to be avenged upon Sir Mordred; wherefore Sir Mordred made write writs to all the barony of this land, and much people drew to him. For then was the common voice among them that with Arthur was none other life but war and strife, and with Sir Mordred was great joy and bliss. Thus was Sir Arthur depraved [defamed] and evil said of. And many there were that King Arthur had made up of nought, and given them lands, that might not then say him a good word.

Lo, ye all Englishmen, see ye not what a mischief here was! For he that was the most king and knight of the world, and most loved the fellowship of noble knights, and by him they were all upholden, now might not these Englishmen hold them content with him. Lo, thus was the old custom and usage of this land; and also men say that we of this land have not yet lost nor forgotten that custom and usage. Alas, this is a great default of us English-men, for there may no thing please us no term! And so fared the people at that time: they were better pleased with Sir Mordred than they were with King Arthur; and much people drew unto Sir Mordred, and said they would abide with him for better and for worse. And so Sir Mordred drew with a great host to Dover, for there he heard say that Sir Arthur would arrive, and so he thought to beat his own father from his lands; and the most part of all England held with Sir Mordred; the people were so new-fangled.

And so as Sir Mordred was at Dover with his host, there came King Arthur with a great navy of ships, and galleys and carracks. And there was Sir Mordred ready awaiting upon his landing, to let [prevent] his own father to land upon the land that he was king over. Then there was launching of great boats and small, and full of noble men of arms; and there was much slaughter of gentle knights, and many a full bold baron was laid full low, on both parties. But King Arthur was so courageous that there might no manner of knights let him to land, and his knights fiercely followed him; and so they landed maugre [despite] Sir Mordred and all his power, and put Sir Mordred aback, so that he fled and all his people.

So when this battle was done, King Arthur let bury his people that were dead. And then was noble Sir Gawain found in a great boat, lying more than half-dead. When Sir Arthur wist that Sir Gawain was laid so low, he went unto him; and there the king made sorrow out of measure, and took Sir Gawain in his arms, and thrice he there swooned. And then when he awaked, he said: "Alas, Sir Gawain, my sister's son, here now thou liest, the man in the world that I loved most. And now is my joy gone, for now, my nephew Sir Gawain, I will discover me unto [disclose] your person: in Sir Lancelot and you, I most had my joy, and mine affiance [trust], and now have I lost my joy of you both. Wherefore all mine earthly joy is gone from me."

"Mine uncle King Arthur," said Sir Gawain, "wit you well my death-day is come, and all is through mine own hastiness and willfulness; for I am smitten upon the old wound the which Sir Lancelot gave me, on the which I feel well I must die by noon. And had Sir Lancelot been with you as he was, this unhappy war had never begun; and of all this am I causer, for Sir Lancelot and his blood, through their prowess, held all your cankered enemies in subjection and daunger [control]. And now," said Sir Gawain, "ye shall miss Sir Lancelot. But alas, I would not accord with him, and therefore," said Sir Gawain, "I pray you, fair uncle, that I may have paper, pen, and ink, that I may write to Sir Lancelot a cedle [letter] with mine own hands."

And then when paper and ink was brought, then Gawain was set up weakly by King Arthur, for he was shriven a little tofore. And then he wrote thus, as the French book maketh mention: "Unto Sir Lancelot, flower of all noble knights that ever I heard of or saw by my days, I, Sir Gawain, King Lot's son of Orkney, sister's son unto the noble King Arthur, send thee greeting, and let thee have knowledge that the tenth day of May I was smitten upon the old wound that thou gavest me afore the city of Benwick, and through the same wound that thou gavest me I am come to my death-day. And I will that all the world wit that I, Sir Gawain, knight of the Table Round, sought my death, and not through thy deserving, but it was mine own seeking; wherefore I beseech thee, Sir Lancelot, to return again unto this realm, and see my tomb, and pray some prayer more or less for my soul. And this same day that I wrote this cedle, I was hurt to the death in the same wound, the which I had of thy hand, Sir Lancelot, for of a more nobler man might I not be slain. Also Sir Lancelot, for all the love that ever was betwixt us, make no tarrying, but come over the sea in all haste, that thou mayst with thy noble knights rescue that noble king that made thee knight, that is my lord Arthur. For he is full straitly bestad [harshly beset] with a false traitor, that is my half-brother, Sir Mordred; and he hath let crown himself king, and would have wedded my lady Queen Guinevere; and so had he done, had she not put herself in the Tower of London. And so the tenth day of May last past, my lord Arthur and we all landed upon them at Dover; and there we put that false traitor, Sir Mordred, to flight, and there it misfortuned me to be stricken upon thy stroke. And at the date of this letter was written, but two hours and a half afore my death, written with mine own hand, and so subscribed with part of my heart's blood. And I require thee, most famous knight of the world, that thou wilt see my tomb."

And then Sir Gawain wept, and King Arthur wept; and then they swooned both. And when they awaked both, the king made Sir Gawain to receive his Saviour. And then Sir Gawain prayed the king for to send for Sir Lancelot, and to cherish him above all other knights. And so at the hour of noon Sir Gawain yielded up the spirit; and then the king let inter him in a chapel within Dover Castle. And there yet all men may see the skull of him, and the same wound is seen that Sir Lancelot gave him in battle.

Then was it told the king that Sir Mordred had pyghte [pitched] a new field upon Barham Down. And upon the morn, the king rode thither to him, and there was a great battle betwixt them, and much people was slain on both parties; but at the last Sir Arthur's party stood best, and Sir Mordred and his party fled unto Canterbury.

And then the king let search all the towns for his knights that were slain, and interred them and salved them with soft salves that so sore were wounded. Then much people drew unto King Arthur. And then they said that Sir Mordred warred upon King Arthur with wrong. And then King Arthur drew him with his host down by the seaside westward toward Salisbury; and there was a day assigned betwixt King Arthur and Sir Mordred, that they should meet upon a down beside Salisbury, and not far from the seaside. And this day was assigned on a Monday after Trinity Sunday, whereof King Arthur was passing glad, that he might be avenged upon Sir Mordred.

Then Sir Mordred raised much people about London, for they of Kent, Sussex, and Surrey, Essex, and of Suffolk, and of Norfolk held the most part with Sir Mordred; and many a full noble knight drew unto Sir Mordred and to the king. But they [who] loved Sir Lancelot drew unto Sir Mordred.

So upon Trinity Sunday at night, King Arthur dreamed a wonderful dream, and that was this: that him seemed he sat upon a chaflet [platform] in a chair, and the chair was fast to a wheel, and thereupon sat King Arthur in the richest cloth of gold that might be made; and the king thought there was under him, far from him, an hideous deep black water, and therein were all manner of serpents and worms and wild beasts, foul and horrible; and suddenly the king thought the wheel turned up-so-down, and he fell among the serpents, and every beast took him by a limb; and then the king cried as he lay in his bed and slept: "Help!"

And then knights, squires, and yeomen awaked the king; and then he was so amazed that he wist not where he was; and then he fell on slumbering again, not sleeping nor thoroughly waking. So the king seemed verily that there came Sir Gawain unto him with a number of fair ladies with him. And when King Arthur saw him, then he said: "Welcome, my sister's son, I weened thou hadst been dead, and now I see thee on life, much am I beholden unto almighty Jesu. O fair nephew and my sister's son, what be these ladies that hither be come with you?"

"Sir," said Sir Gawain, "all these be ladies for whom I have foughten when I was man living, and all these are those that I did battle for in righteous quarrel; and God hath given them that grace at their great prayer, because I did battle for them, that they should bring me hither unto you. Thus much hath God given me leave, for to warn you of your death; for an ye fight as to-morn with Sir Mordred, as ye both have assigned, doubt ye not ye must be slain, and the most part of your people on both parties. And for the great grace and goodness that almighty Jesu hath unto you, and for pity of you, and many more other good men there shall be slain, God hath sent me to you of his special grace, to give you warning that in no wise ye do battle as to-morn, but that ye take a treaty for a month's day; and proffer you largely, so as to-morn to be put in a delay. For within a month shall come Sir Lancelot with all his noble knights, and rescue you worshipfully, and slay Sir Mordred, and all that ever will hold with him." Then Sir Gawain and all the ladies vanished.

And anon the king called upon his knights, squires, and yeomen, and charged them wightly [quickly] to fetch his noble lords and wise bishops unto him. And when they were come, the king told them his avision, what Sir Gawain had told him, and warned him that if he fought on the morn he should be slain. Then the king commanded Sir Lucan the Butler and his brother Sir Bedivere, with two bishops with them, and charged them in any wise, an they might: "Take a treaty for a month's day with Sir Mordred, and spare not; proffer him lands and goods as much as ye think best."

So then they departed, and came to Sir Mordred, where he had a grim host of an hundred thousand men. And there they entreated Sir Mordred long time; and at the last Sir Mordred was agreed for to have Cornwall and Kent, by Arthur's days; after[ward], all England, after the days of King Arthur.

Then were they condescended [consented] that King Arthur and Sir Mordred should meet betwixt both their hosts, and every each of them should bring fourteen persons; and they came with this word unto Arthur. Then said he: "I am glad that this is done." And so he went into the field. And when Arthur should depart, he warned all his host that, an they see any sword drawn: "Look ye come on fiercely, and slay that traitor Sir Mordred, for I in no wise trust him."

In like wise Sir Mordred warned his host that: "An ye see any sword drawn, look that ye come on fiercely, and so slay all that ever before you standeth; for in no wise I will not trust this treaty, for I know well my father will be avenged on me."

And so they met as their appointment was, and so they were agreed and accorded thoroughly; and wine was fetched, and they drank. Right soon came an adder out of a little heath bush, and it stung a knight on the foot. And when the knight felt him stung, he looked down and saw the adder, and then he drew his sword to slay the adder, and thought of none other harm. And when the host on both parties saw that sword drawn, then they blew beams [small horns], trumpets, and horns, and shouted grimly. And so both hosts dressed them together [faced each other].

And King Arthur took his horse and said: "Alas, this unhappy day!" and so rode to his party. And Sir Mordred in like wise. And never was there seen a more dolefuller battle in no Christian land, for there was but rushing and riding, foining [thrusting] and striking, and many a grim word was there spoken either to other, and many a deadly stroke. But ever King Arthur rode throughout the battle of Sir Mordred many times, and did full nobly as a noble king should, and at all times he fainted never; and Sir Mordred that day did his devoir [utmost] in great peril. And thus they fought all the long day, and never stinted till the noble knights were laid to the cold earth; and ever they fought still till it was near night, and by that time was there an hundred thousand laid dead upon the down. Then was Arthur wood wroth [madly angry] out of measure, when he saw his people so slain from him.

Then the king looked about him, and then was he ware [that] of all his host and of all his good knights were left no more on life but two knights: that one was Sir Lucan the Butler, and his brother Sir Bedivere, and they were full sore wounded. "Jesu mercy," said the king, "where are all my noble knights become? Alas, that ever I should see this doleful day, for now," said Arthur, "I am come to mine end. But would to God that I wist where were that traitor Sir Mordred, that hath caused all this mischief!"

Then was King Arthur ware where Sir Mordred leaned upon his sword among a great heap of dead men. "Now give me my spear," said Arthur unto Sir Lucan, "for yonder I have espied the traitor that all this woe hath wrought."

"Sir, let him be," said Sir Lucan, "for he is unhappy [brings misfortune]. And if ye pass this unhappy day ye shall be right well revenged upon him. Good lord, remember ye of your night's dream, and what the spirit of Sir Gawain told you this night, yet God of his great goodness hath preserved you hitherto. Therefore, for God's sake, my lord, leave off this, for, blessed be God, ye have won the field, for here we be three on life, and with Sir Mordred is none on life; and if ye leave off now, this wicked day of destiny is past."

"Tide me death, betide me life," saith the king. "Now I see him yonder alone; he shall never escape mine hands, for at a better avail shall I never have [of] him.

"God speed you well!" said Sir Bedivere.

Then the king gat his spear in both his hands and ran toward Sir Mordred, crying: "Traitor, now is thy death day come!" And when Sir Mordred heard Sir Arthur, he ran until him with his sword drawn in his hand. And there King Arthur smote Sir Mordred under the shield, with a foin of his spear, throughout the body, more than a fathom. And when Sir Mordred felt that he had his death-wound, he thrust himself with the might that he had up to the bur [hand-guard] of King Arthur's spear. And right so he smote his father Arthur, with his sword holden in both his hands, on the side of the head, so that the sword pierced the helmet and the brain-pan, and therewithal Sir Mordred fell stark dead to the earth; and the noble Arthur fell in a swoon to the earth, and there he swooned ofttimes.

And Sir Lucan the Butler and Sir Bedivere ofttimes heaved him up. And so weakly [gently] they led him betwixt them both to a little chapel not far from the seaside. And when the king was there, he thought him well eased. Then heard they people cry in the field. "Now go thou, Sir Lucan," said the king, "and do me to wit what betokens that noise in the field."

So Sir Lucan departed, for he was grievously wounded in many places. And so as he yede [went], he saw and harkened by the moonlight how that pillers [pillagers] and robbers were come into the field, to pill and to rob many a full noble knight of brooches and beads, of many a good ring, and of many a rich jewel; and [those] who that were not dead all out, there they slew them for their harness and their riches. When Sir Lucan understood this work, he came to the king as soon as he might, and told him all what he had heard and seen. "Therefore by my rede [advice]," said Sir Lucan, "it is best that we bring you to some town."

"I would it were so," said the king. "But I may not stand, mine head works [hurts] so. Ah, Sir Lancelot," said King Arthur, "this day have I sore missed thee. Alas, that ever I was against thee, for now have I my death, whereof Sir Gawain me warned in my dream."

Then Sir Lucan took up the king the one part, and Sir Bedivere the other part, and in the lifting, the king swooned; and Sir Lucan fell in a swoon with the lift, that part of his guts fell out of his body, and therewith the noble knight's heart brast. And when the king awoke, he beheld Sir Lucan, how he lay foaming at the mouth, and part of his guts lay at his feet. "Alas," said the king, "this is to me a full heavy sight, to see this noble duke so die for my sake, for he would have holpen me that [who] had more need of help than I. Alas, he would not complain him, his heart was so set to help me: now Jesu have mercy upon his soul!" Then Sir Bedivere wept for the death of his brother.

"Leave this mourning and weeping," said the king, "for all this will not avail me; for wit thou well: an I might live myself, the death of Sir Lucan would grieve me evermore; but my time hieth fast," said the king. "Therefore," said Arthur unto Sir Bedivere, "take thou Excalibur, my good sword, and go with it to yonder waterside, and when thou comest there, I charge thee: throw my sword in that water, and come again and tell me what thou there seest."

"My lord," said Bedivere, "your commandment shall be done, and lightly [I'll] bring you word again."

So Sir Bedivere departed, and by the way he beheld that noble sword, that the pommel and the haft was all of precious stones; and then he said to himself: "If I throw this rich sword in the water, thereof shall never come good, but harm and loss." And then Sir Bedivere hid Excalibur under a tree. And so, as soon as he might, he came again unto the king, and said he had been at the water, and had thrown the sword in the water. "What saw thou there?" said the king.

"Sir," he said, "I saw nothing but waves and winds."

"That is untruly said of thee," said the king; "therefore go thou lightly again, and do my commandment; as thou art to me lief [beloved] and dear, spare not, but throw it in."

Then Sir Bedivere returned again, and took the sword in his hand; and then him thought sin and shame to throw away that noble sword, and so eft [again] he hid the sword, and returned again, and told to the king that he had been at the water and done his commandment. "What saw thou there?" said the king.

"Sir," he said, "I saw nothing but the waters wappe [lap] and waves wan."

"Ah, traitor untrue," said King Arthur, "now hast thou betrayed me twice. Who would have weened that—thou that hast been to me so lief and dear? And thou art named a noble knight, and would betray me for the richness of the sword! But now go again lightly, for thy long tarrying putteth me in great jeopardy of my life, for I have taken cold. And but if thou do now as I bid thee, if ever I may see thee, I shall slay thee with mine own hands; for thou wouldst for my rich sword see me dead."

Then Sir Bedivere departed and went to the sword, and lightly took it up, and went to the waterside; and there he bound the girdle about the hilts, and then he threw the sword as far into the water as he might; and there came an arm and an hand above the water and met it, and caught it, and so shook it thrice and brandished, and then vanished away the hand with the sword in the water. So Sir Bedivere came again to the king, and told him what he saw. "Alas," said the king, "help me hence, for I dread me I have tarried over long."

Then Sir Bedivere took the king upon his back, and so went with him to that waterside. And when they were at the waterside, even fast by the bank hoved a little barge with many fair ladies in it, and among them all was a queen, and all they had black hoods, and all they wept and shrieked when they saw King Arthur. "Now put me into the barge," said the king. And so he did softly; and there received him three queens with great mourning; and so they set them down, and in one of their laps King Arthur laid his head. And then that queen said: "Ah, dear brother, why have ye tarried so long from me? Alas, this wound on your head hath caught overmuch cold."

And so then they rowed from the land, and Sir Bedivere beheld all those ladies go from him. Then Sir Bedivere cried: "Ah my lord Arthur, what shall become of me, now ye go from me and leave me here alone among mine enemies?"

"Comfort thyself," said the king, "and do as well as thou mayest, for in me is no trust for to trust in; for I will into the vale of Avalon to heal me of my grievous wound. And if thou hear nevermore of me, pray for my soul." But ever the queens and ladies wept and shrieked, that it was pity to hear.

And as soon as Sir Bedivere had lost the sight of the barge, he wept and wailed, and so took [to] the forest; and so he went all that night, and in the morning he was ware, betwixt two holts hoar [gray copses], of a chapel and an hermitage. Then was Sir Bedivere glad, and thither he went; and when he came into the chapel, he saw where lay an hermit grovelling on all fours, there fast by a tomb [that] was new graven [dug]. When the hermit saw Sir Bedivere, he knew him well, for he was but little tofore Bishop of Canterbury, that Sir Mordred flemed [banished]. "Sir," said Bedivere, "what man is there interred that ye pray so fast for?"

"Fair son," said the hermit, "I wot not verily, but by deeming [guessing]. But this night, at midnight, here came a number of ladies, and brought hither a dead corpse, and prayed me to inter him; and here they offered an hundred tapers, and they gave me an hundred besants."

"Alas," said Sir Bedivere, "that was my lord King Arthur, that here lieth buried in this chapel." Then Sir Bedivere swooned, and when he awoke, he prayed the hermit he might abide with him still there, to live with fasting and prayers. "For from hence will I never go," said Sir Bedivere, "by my will, but all the days of my life here to pray for my lord Arthur."

"Ye are welcome to me," said the hermit, "for I know ye better than ye ween that I do. Ye are the bold Bedivere, and the full noble duke Sir Lucan the Butler was your brother." Then Sir Bedivere told the hermit all, as ye have heard tofore. So there [a]bode Sir Bedivere with the hermit that was tofore Bishop of Canterbury, and there Sir Bedivere put upon him poor clothes, and served the hermit full lowly in fasting and in prayers.

Thus of Arthur I find nevermore written in books that be authorized, nor more of the very certainty of his death heard I never [nor] read, but thus was he led away in a ship wherein were three queens: that one was King Arthur's sister, Queen Morgan le Fay, the other was the Queen of Northgalis, the third was the Queen of the Waste Lands. Also there was Ninive, the chief lady of the lake, that had wedded Pelleas the good knight; and this lady had done much for King Arthur, for she would never suffer Sir Pelleas to be in no place where he should be in danger of his life; and so he lived to the uttermost of his days with her in great rest. More of the death of King Arthur could I never find, but that these ladies brought him to his burial; and such a one was buried there; that the hermit bare witness that sometime [once] was Bishop of Canterbury, but yet the hermit knew not in certain that he was verily the body of King Arthur. For this tale Sir Bedivere, knight of the Table Round, made it to be written.

Yet some men say in many parts of England that King Arthur is not dead, but had by the will of our Lord Jesu [gone] into another place; and men say that he shall come again, and he shall win the holy cross. I will not say it shall be so, but rather I will say, here in this world he changed his life. But many men say that there is written upon his tomb this verse: HIC JACET ARTHURUS REX, QUONDAM REXQUE FUTURUS [Here lies King Arthur, former King and future].

Thus leave I here Sir Bedivere with the hermit, that dwelled that time in a chapel beside Glastonbury, and there was his hermitage. And so they lived in their prayers and fastings and great abstinence.

And when Queen Guinevere understood that King Arthur was slain, and all the noble knights, Sir Mordred and all the remnant, then the queen stole away, and five ladies with her, and so she went to Amesbury. And there she let make herself a nun, and wore white clothes and black, and great penance she took, as ever did sinful lady in this land, and never creature could make her merry; but she lived in fasting, prayers, and alms-deeds, that all manner of people marvelled how virtuously she was changed. Now leave we Queen Guinevere in Amesbury, a nun in white clothes and black, and there she was abbess and ruler, as reason would [have it], and turn we from her, and speak we of Sir Lancelot du Lake.

And when he heard in his country that Sir Mordred was crowned king in England and made war against King Arthur, his own father, and would let [forbid] him to land in his own land—also it was told Sir Lancelot how that Sir Mordred had laid siege about the Tower of London, because the queen would not wed him—then was Sir Lancelot wroth out of measure and said to his kinsmen: "Alas, that double traitor Sir Mordred! Now me repenteth that ever he escaped my hands, for much shame hath he done unto my lord

Arthur; for I feel by the doleful letter that my lord Sir Gawain sent me, on whose soul Jesu have mercy, that my lord Arthur is full hard bestad. Alas," said Sir Lancelot, "that ever I should live to hear that most noble king that made me knight thus to be overset with his subject in his own realm! And this doleful letter that my lord Sir Gawain hath sent me afore his death, praying me to see his tomb, wit you well: his doleful words shall never go from mine heart, for he was a full noble knight as ever was born. And in an unhappy hour was I born that ever I should have that unhap [misfortune] to slay first Sir Gawain, Sir Gaheris the good knight, and mine own friend Sir Gareth, that full noble knight. Alas, I may say I am unhappy," said Sir Lancelot, "that ever I should do thus unhappily; and, alas, yet might I never have hap [the chance] to slay that traitor, Sir Mordred."

"Leave your complaints," said Sir Bors, "and first revenge you of the death of Sir Gawain; and it will be well done that ye see Sir Gawain's tomb, and secondly that ye revenge my lord Arthur and my lady Queen Guinevere."

"I thank you," said Sir Lancelot, "for ever ye will [promote] my worship." Then they made them ready in all the haste that might be, with ships and galleys, with Sir Lancelot and his host to pass into England. And so he passed over the sea till he came to Dover, and there he landed with seven kings, and the number was hideous to behold. Then Sir Lancelot spered [inquired] of men of Dover where was King Arthur become. Then the people told him how that he was slain, and Sir Mordred and an hundred thousand died on a day; and how Sir Mordred gave King Arthur there the first battle at his landing, and there was good Sir Gawain slain; and on the morn Sir Mordred fought with the king upon Barham Down, and there the king put Sir Mordred to the worse.

"Alas," said Sir Lancelot, "this is the heaviest tidings that ever came to me! Now, fair sirs," said Sir Lancelot, "show me the tomb of Sir Gawain." And then certain people of the town brought him into the Castle of Dover, and showed him the tomb. Then Sir Lancelot kneeled down and wept and prayed heartily for his soul. And that night he made a dole [wake], and all they that would come had as much flesh, fish, wine, and ale, and every man and woman had twelve-pence, come who would. Thus with his own hand dealt he this money, in a mourning gown. And ever he wept, and prayed them to pray for the soul of Sir Gawain.

And on the morn all the priests and clerks that might be gotten in the country were there, and sang mass of requiem. And there offered first Sir Lancelot, and he offered an hundred pound; and then the seven kings offered forty pound apiece; and also there was a thousand knights, and each of them offered a pound; and the offering [en]dured from morn till night, and Sir Lancelot lay two nights on his tomb in prayers and weeping.

Then on the third day Sir Lancelot called the kings, dukes, earls, barons, and knights, and said thus: "My fair lords, I thank you all of your coming into this country with me, but we came too late, and that shall repent me while I live; but against death may no man rebel. But sithen it is so," said Sir Lancelot, "I will myself ride and seek my lady, Queen Guinevere, for as I hear say, she hath had great pain and much disease [sorrow], and I heard say that she is fled into the west. Therefore, ye all shall abide me here, and but if [unless] I come again within fifteen days, then take your ships and your fellowship, and depart into your country, for I will do as I say to you."

Then came Sir Bors de Ganis, and said: "My lord Sir Lancelot, what think ye for to do, now to ride in this realm? Wit ye well: ye shall find few friends."

"Be as be may," said Sir Lancelot, "keep you still here, for I will forth on my journey, and no man nor child [squire] shall go with me." So it was no boot [use] to strive, but he departed and rode westerly, and there he sought a seven or eight days.

And at the last he came to a nunnery, and then was Queen Guinevere ware of Sir Lancelot as he walked in the cloister. And when she saw him there, she swooned thrice, that all the ladies and gentlewomen had work enough to hold the queen up. So when she might speak, she called ladies and gentlewomen to her, and said: "Ye marvel, fair ladies, why I make this fare. Truly," she said, "it is for the sight of yonder knight that yonder standeth; wherefore, I pray you all, call him to me."

When Sir Lancelot was brought to her, then she said to all the ladies: "Through this man and me hath all this war been wrought, and the death of the most noblest knights of the world; for through our love that we have loved together is my most noble lord slain. Therefore, Sir Lancelot, wit thou well: I am set in such a plight to get my soul-heal. And yet I trust through God's grace that after my death to have a sight of the blessed face of Christ, and at Doomsday to sit on His right side, for [those] as sinful as ever I was are saints in heaven. Therefore, Sir Lancelot, I require thee and beseech thee heartily, for all the love that ever was betwixt us, that thou never see me more in the visage; and I command thee, on God's behalf, that thou forsake my company and to thy kingdom thou turn again, and keep well thy realm from war and wrake [ruin]; for as well as I have loved thee, mine heart will not serve me to see thee, for through thee and me is the flower of kings and knights destroyed. Therefore, Sir Lancelot, go to thy realm, and there take thee a wife, and live with her with joy and bliss; and I pray thee heartily: pray for me to our Lord that I may amend my misliving."

"Now, sweet madam," said Sir Lancelot, "would ye that I should now return again unto my country, and there to wed a lady? Nay, madam, wit you well: *that* shall I never do, for I shall never be so false to you of that I have promised. But the self-same destiny that ye have taken you to, I will take me unto for to please Jesu, and ever for you I cast me [promise] specially to pray."

"If thou wilt do so," said the queen, "hold thy promise, but I may never believe but that thou wilt turn to the world again."

"Well, madam," said he, "ye say as pleaseth you, yet wist you me never false of my promise, and God defend but I should forsake the world as ye have done. For in the quest of the Sangrail I had forsaken the vanities of the world, had not your love been. And if I had done so at that time with my heart, will, and thought, I had passed all the knights that were in the Sangrail except Sir Galahad, my son. And therefore, lady, sithen ye have taken you to perfection, I must needs take me to perfection, of right. For I take record of God: in you I have had mine earthly joy; and if I had found you now so disposed, I had cast [resolved] to have had you [taken] into mine own realm. But sithen I find you thus disposed, I ensure you faithfully: I will ever take me to penance, and pray while my life lasteth, if I may find any hermit either gray or white that will receive me. Wherefore, madam, I pray you kiss me, and never no more."

"Nay," said the queen, "that shall I never do, but abstain you from such works." And they departed. But there was never so hard-an-hearted man but he would have wept to see the dolour that they made; for there was lamentation as [if] they had been stung with spears; and many times they swooned, and the ladies bare the queen to her chamber.

And Sir Lancelot awoke, and went and took his horse, and rode all that day and all night in a forest, weeping. And at the last he was ware of an hermitage and a chapel [that] stood betwixt two cliffs; and then he heard a little bell ring to mass, and thither he rode and alit, and tied his horse to the gate, and heard mass. And he that sang mass was the Bishop of Canterbury. Both the Bishop and Sir Bedivere knew Sir Lancelot, and they spake together after mass. But when Sir Bedivere had told his tale all whole, Sir Lancelot's heart almost brast for sorrow, and Sir Lancelot threw his arms abroad [apart] and said: "Alas, who may trust this world?" And then he kneeled down on his knee and prayed the Bishop to shrive him and assoil [absolve] him. And then he besought the Bishop that he might be his brother. Then the Bishop said: "I will gladly!" And there he put an habit upon Sir Lancelot, and there he served God day and night with prayers and fastings.

Thus the great host abode at Dover. And then Sir Lionel took fifteen lords with him, and rode to London to seek Sir Lancelot; and there Sir Lionel was slain and many of his lords. Then Sir Bors de Ganis made the great host for to go home again. And Sir Bors, Sir Ector de Maris, Sir Blamore, Sir Bleoberis, with more other of Sir Lancelot's kin, took on them to ride all England overthwart and endlong [up and down] to seek Sir Lancelot.

Sir Bors by fortune rode so long till he came to the same chapel where Sir Lancelot was; and so Sir Bors heard a little bell knell that rang to mass; and there he alit and heard mass. And when mass was done, the Bishop, Sir Lancelot, and Sir Bedivere came to Sir Bors. And when Sir Bors saw Sir Lancelot in that manner clothing, then he prayed the Bishop that he might be in the same suit. And so there was an habit put upon him, and there he lived in prayers and fasting.

And within half a year, there was come Sir Galihud, Sir Galihodin, Sir Blamore, Sir Bleoberis, Sir Villiars, Sir Clarrus, and Sir Gahalantine. So all these seven noble knights there abode still. And when they saw Sir Lancelot had taken him to such perfection, they had no list to depart, but took such an habit as he had. Thus they endured in great penance six year; and then Sir Lancelot took the habit of priesthood of the Bishop, and a twelvemonth he sang mass. And there was none of these other knights but they read in books, and holp for to sing mass, and rang bells, and did bodily all manner of service. And so their horses went where they would, for they took no regard of no worldly riches. For when they saw Sir Lancelot endure such penance, in prayers and fastings, they took no force [care] what pain they endured, for to see the noblest knight of the world take such abstinence that he waxed full lean.

And thus upon a night, there came a vision to Sir Lancelot, and charged him, in remission of his sins, to haste him unto Amesbury: "And by then thou come there, thou shalt find Queen Guinevere dead. And therefore take thy fellows with thee, and purvey them of an horse bier, and fetch thou the corpse of her, and bury her by her husband, the noble King Arthur." So this vision came to Sir Lancelot thrice in one night.

Then Sir Lancelot rose up or day, and told the hermit. "It were well done," said the hermit, "that ye made you ready and that you disobey not the vision." Then Sir Lancelot took his seven fellows with him, and on foot they yede [went] from Glastonbury to Amesbury, the which is little more than thirty mile. And thither they came within two days, for they were weak and feeble to go. And when Sir Lancelot was come to Amesbury within the nunnery, Queen Guinevere died but half an hour afore. And the ladies told Sir Lancelot that Queen Guinevere told them all, or she passed, that Sir Lancelot had been priest near a twelvemonth: "And hither he cometh as fast as he may to fetch my corpse, and beside my lord, King Arthur he shall bury me." Wherefore the queen said in hearing of them all: "I beseech Almighty God that I may never have power to see Sir Lancelot with my worldly eyen." "And thus," said all the ladies, "was ever her prayer these two days, till she was dead."

Then Sir Lancelot saw her visage, but he wept not greatly, but sighed. And so he did all the observance of the service himself, both the dirge at night, and on the morn he sang mass. And there was ordained an horse bier; and so with an hundred torches ever burning about the corpse of the queen, ever Sir Lancelot with his seven fellows went about the horse bier, singing and reading many an holy orison, and frankincense upon the corpse incensed. Thus Sir Lancelot and his seven fellows went on foot from Amesbury unto Glastonbury.

And when they were come to the chapel and the hermitage, there she had a dirge with great devotion. And on the morn the hermit that sometime was Bishop of Canterbury sang the mass of requiem with great devotion. And

Sir Lancelot was the first that offered, and then also his seven fellows. And then she was wrapped in cered [waxed] cloth of Raines [Rennes] from the top to the toe in thirtyfold; and after she was put in a web [sheet] of lead, and then in a coffin of marble.

And when she was put in the earth, Sir Lancelot swooned, and lay long still, while the hermit came and awaked him and said: "Ye be to blame, for ye displease God with such manner of sorrow making." "Truly," said Sir Lancelot, "I trust I do not displease God, for He knoweth mine intent. For my sorrow was not, nor is not, for any rejoicing of sin, but my sorrow may never have end. For when I remember of her beauty, and of her noblesse, that was both with her king and with her, so when I saw his corpse and her corpse so lie together, truly mine heart would not serve to sustain my careful [care-filled] body. Also when I remember me how by my default, mine orgule [arrogance] and my pride, that they were both laid full low that were [as] peerless that ever was living of Christian people, wit you well," said Sir Lancelot: "this remembered—of their kindness and mine unkindness—sank so to mine heart that I might not sustain myself." So the French book maketh mention.

Then Sir Lancelot never after ate but little meat nor drank till he was dead. For then he sickened more and more, and dried, and dwined [wasted] away. For the Bishop nor none of his fellows might not make him to eat, and little he drank, [so] that he was waxen by a cubit shorter than he was, that the people could not know him. For evermore, day and night, he prayed, but sometime he slumbered a broken sleep. Ever he was lying grovelling on the tomb of King Arthur and Queen Guinevere. And there was no comfort that the Bishop nor Sir Bors, nor none of his fellows could make him; it availed not.

So within six weeks after, Sir Lancelot fell sick, and lay in his bed; and then he sent for the Bishop that there was hermit, and all his true fellows. Then Sir Lancelot said with dreary steven [voice]: "Sir Bishop, I pray you give to me all my rites that longeth to a Christian man."

"It shall not need [be needed by] you," said the hermit and all his fellows, "it is but heaviness of your blood; ye shall be well mended by the grace of God to-morn."

"My fair lords," said Sir Lancelot, "wit you well: my careful body will [go] into the earth. I have warning more than now I will say; therefore give me my rites." So when he was houseled [given the Eucharist] and enelid [received extreme unction] and had all that a Christian man ought to have, he prayed the Bishop that his fellows might bear his body to Joyous Gard. Some men say it was Alnwick, and some men say it was Bamborough.

"Howbeit," said Sir Lancelot, "me repenteth sore, but I made mine avow sometime, that in Joyous Gard I would be buried. And because of breaking of mine avow, I pray you all, lead me thither."

Then there was weeping and wringing of hands among his fellows. So at a season of the night they all went to their beds, for they all lay in one chamber. And so after midnight, against [near] day, the Bishop that was hermit, as he lay in his bed asleep, he fell upon a great laughter. And therewithal the fellowship awoke, and came to the Bishop, and asked him what he ailed. "Ah Jesu mercy," said the Bishop, "why did ye awake me? I was never in all my life so merry and so well at ease."

"Wherefore?" said Sir Bors.

"Truly," said the Bishop, "here was Sir Lancelot with me with more angels than ever I saw men in one day. And I saw the angels heave up Sir Lancelot unto heaven, and the gates of heaven opened against [for] him."

"It is but dretching [confusion] of swevens [dreams]," said Sir Bors, "for I doubt not Sir Lancelot aileth [feels] nothing but good."

"It may well be," said the Bishop. "Go ye to his bed, and then shall ye prove the sooth."

So when Sir Bors and his fellows came to his bed, they found him stark dead, and he lay as [if] he had smiled, and [had] the sweetest savour about him that ever they felt. Then was there weeping and wringing of hands, and the greatest dole they made that ever made men. And on the morn the Bishop did his mass of requiem; and after the Bishop and all the knights put Sir Lancelot in the same horse bier that Queen Guinevere was laid in tofore that she was buried. And so the Bishop and they all together went with the body of Sir Lancelot daily, till they came to Joyous Gard; and ever they had an hundred torches burning about him.

And so within fifteen days they came to Joyous Gard. And there they laid his corpse in the body of the quire [chancel], and sang and read many psalters and prayers over him and about him. And ever his visage was laid open and naked, that all folks might behold him. For such was the custom in those days, that all men of worship should so lie with open visage till that they were buried. And right thus as they were at their service, there came Sir Ector de Maris, that had seven years sought all England, Scotland, and Wales, seeking his brother, Sir Lancelot.

And when Sir Ector heard such noise and light in the quire of Joyous Gard, he alit and put his horse from him, and came into the quire, and there he saw men sing and weep. And all they knew Sir Ector, but he knew not them. Then went Sir Bors unto Sir Ector, and told him how there lay his brother, Sir Lancelot, dead; and then Sir Ector threw his shield, sword, and helm from him. And when he beheld Sir Lancelot's visage, he fell down in a swoon. And when he waked, it were hard any tongue to tell the doleful complaints that he made for his brother.

"Ah Lancelot," he said, "thou were head of all Christian knights, and now I dare say," said Sir Ector, "thou Sir Lancelot, there thou liest, that thou were never matched of [by an] earthly knight's hand. And thou were the courteoust knight that ever bare shield. And thou were the truest friend to thy lover that ever bestrad horse. And thou were the truest lover of sinful men that ever loved woman. And thou were the kindest man that ever struck with sword. And thou were the goodliest person that ever came among press of knights. And thou were the meekest man and the gentlest that ever ate in hall among ladies. And thou were the sternest knight to thy mortal foe that ever put spear in the rest."

Then there was weeping and dolour out of measure. Thus they kept Sir Lancelot's corpse on loft [view] fifteen days, and then they buried it with great devotion. And then at leisure they went all with the Bishop of Canterbury to his hermitage, and there they were together more than a month.

Then Sir Constantine, that was Sir Cador's son of Cornwall, was chosen King of England. And he was a full noble knight, and worshipfully [honorably] he ruled this realm. And then this King Constantine sent for the Bishop of Canterbury, for he heard say where he was. And so he was restored unto his bishopric, and left that hermitage. And Sir Bedivere was there ever, still hermit to his life's end.

Then Sir Bors de Ganis, Sir Ector de Maris, Sir Gahalantine, Sir Galihud, Sir Galihodin, Sir Blamore, Sir Bleoberis, Sir Villiars le Valiant, Sir Clarrus of Clermont—all these knights drew them to their countries. Howbeit King Constantine would have had them with him but they would not abide in this realm. And there they all lived in their countries as holy men.

And some English books make mention that they went never out of England after the death of Sir Lancelot, but that was but the favour [whim] of makers [authors]. For the French book maketh mention, and is authorized, that Sir Bors, Sir Ector, Sir Blamore, and Sir Bleoberis went into the Holy Land, thereas Jesu Christ was quick and dead, and anon as they had stablished their lands. For, the book saith, so Sir Lancelot commanded them for to do, or ever he passed out of this world. And these four knights did many battles upon the miscreants or Turks. And there they died upon a Good Friday for God's sake.

Here is the end of the book of King Arthur, and of his noble knights of the Round Table, that when they were whole together, there was ever an hundred and forty. And here is the end of "The Death of Arthur." I pray you all, gentlemen and gentlewomen that readeth this book of Arthur and his knights from the beginning to the ending, pray for me while I am on life, that God send me good deliverance, and when I am dead, I pray you all pray for my soul. For this book was ended the ninth year of the reign of King Edward the Fourth [March 4, 1469 to March 3, 1470], by Sir Thomas Maleore, knight, as Jesu help him for his great might, as he is the servant of Jesu both day and night.

Bibliography

SOME GENERAL BOOKS FOR FURTHER READING

[*Readers should also refer to the bibliographic notes ending the introduction to each chapter.*]

Alcock, Leslie. *Arthur's Britain*. Penguin, 1971.

Ashe, Geoffrey. *A Guidebook to Arthurian Britain*. Longman, 1980; rev. Aquarian, 1983.

———. *Kings and Queens of Early Britain*. Methuen, 1982.

———, ed. *The Quest for Arthur's Britain*. Praeger, 1968; rev. Paladin, 1982.

Barber, Richard W. *Arthur of Albion*. Barnes and Noble, 1971; rev. as *King Arthur in Legend and History*, Cardinal, 1973.

———, ed. *Arthurian Literature*. 2 vols. Rowman and Littlefield, 1981–82.

Bromwich, Rachel, A.O.H. Jarman, and Brynley F. Roberts, eds. *The Arthur of the Welsh*. University of Wales, 1991.

Bruce, J.D. *The Evolution of Arthurian Romance*. 2 vols. Johns Hopkins University, 1923; rpt. Peter Smith, 1958.

Chambers, E.K. *Arthur of Britain*. Sidgwick and Jackson, 1927; rpt. Barnes and Noble, 1964.

Frappier, Jean, and Reinhold R. Grimm. *Le Roman jusqu'à la fin du XIIIe siècle*. (Vol. 4 of *Grundriss der romanischen Literaturen des Mittelalters*). Winter, 1978.

Jenkins, Elizabeth. *The Mystery of King Arthur*. Coward, McCann and Geoghegan, 1975.

Köhler, Erich. *Ideal und Wirklichkeit in der höfischen Epik*. Niemeyer, 1956.

Lacy, Norris J., et al., eds. *The New Arthurian Encyclopedia*. Garland, 1991.

———, and Geoffrey Ashe. *The Arthurian Handbook*. Garland, 1988.

Lagorio, Valerie M., and Mildred L. Day, eds. *King Arthur Through the Ages*. 2 vols. Garland, 1990.

Loomis, Roger Sherman. *The Development of Arthurian Romance*. Harper and Row, 1964.

———, ed. *Arthurian Literature in the Middle Ages*. Oxford University, 1959.

———, and Laura Hibbard Loomis. *Arthurian Legends in Medieval Art*. Oxford University, 1938.

Lot, Ferdinand. *Étude sur le Lancelot en prose*. Champion, 1918.

Luttrell, Claude. *The Creation of the First Arthurian Romance*. Northwestern University, 1974.

Morris, John. *The Age of Arthur*. Scribner, 1973.

Morris, Rosemary. *The Character of King Arthur in Medieval Literature*. Brewer, 1982 .

Owen, D.D.R., ed. *Arthurian Romance: Seven Essays*. Barnes and Noble, 1971.

Pickford, C.E., C.R. Barker, and R.W. Last, eds. *The Arthurian Bibliography*. 3 vols. Brewer, 1981, 1983, 1985.

Reiss, Edmund, Lousie Horner Reiss, and Beverly Taylor. *Arthurian Legend and Literature: An Annotated Bibliography*. Garland, 1984.

Schmolke-Hasselmann, Beate. *Der arthurische Versroman von Chrestien bis Froissart*. Niemeyer, 1980.

Tatlock, J.S.P. *The Legendary History of Britain*. University of California, 1950.

Treharne, R.F. *The Glastonbury Legends*. Cresset, 1967; rpt. Sphere, 1971.

Varty, Kenneth, ed. *An Arthurian Tapestry*. University of Glasgow, 1981.

Vinaver, Eugene. *The Rise of Romance*. Oxford University, 1971.

Weston, Jessie L. *From Ritual to Romance*. Cambridge University, 1920; rpt. Anchor, 1957.

Wilson, Anne. *Traditional Romance and Tale: How Stories Mean*. Brewer, 1976.

Index